D1587215

DE

30

Errata

1.   On p.xvii below last para: *insert*

Lastly, I am grateful to the Society of Authors as the Literary Representative of the Estate of John Masefield (*Conway*, 1891-94) for permission to quote the first stanza of the poem *Third Mate* in the dedication on p.vii.

2.   On p.5, line 7: *delete* short-sea

THE RIGHT KIND
OF BOY

By the same author:

The Fatal Flaw: Collision at Sea & the Failure of the Rules.

ii

Bernard Webb, apprentice, ship *Alcinous*, 1891.
(City & County of Swansea Museums Collection)

David Thomas

*

THE RIGHT KIND
OF BOY

A Portrait of
The British Sea Apprentice
1830-1980

Phaiacia

First published 2004 by
Phaiacia,
21, Heol Pen-y-Craig,
Ystradowen,
Carmarthenshire,
United Kingdom. SA9 2YP

ISBN 0-9541981-1-5

Printed & bound in Wales by
Pro-Print, Carmarthen.

For Janet

All the sheets are clacking, all the blocks are whining,
The sails are frozen stiff and the wetted decks are shining;
The reef's in the topsails, and it's coming on to blow,
And I think of the dear girl I left long ago.

John Masefield: *Third Mate.*

CONTENTS

Illustrations

ILLUSTRATIONS

ILLUSTRATIONS

***

Acknowledgments

W HERE to begin? It is, perhaps, invidious to single out certain people for mention from among the many who have helped me with my researches for this book. They range from private individuals to members of organisations including government departments, museums, professional institutions, historical societies, and shipping companies; yet if I were to mention them all in detail they would occupy at least a quarter again of the space taken up by the story itself. I must therefore offer my apologies to those who do not appear here by name: instead, they are listed as contributors (see p.397), and to them all, whether mentioned or not, I owe a debt of gratitude. I must, however, mention here several who not only offered material which turned out to be invaluable but who also encouraged me in my often lonely, and always solitary, pursuit of the apprentice through the ages. Their enthusiasm for and belief in what I had set out to do was a comfort and support, probably to a greater extent than they realised, and it was – and is – my abiding concern that I should not let them down. I hope they, and all the others involved (of whom, alas, several are now dead and so beyond the reach of mortal sentiment), feel after reading this book that their time and trouble has not been wasted. More than that, I hope they find in these pages, apart from a certain nostalgia, perhaps for a time they never knew, pleasure and interest and – dare I say it – a supplement to what they already know of this unique Britisher.

My thanks are due to, among others,

Mr Andrew Bell, sometime managing director of Curnow Shipping, whose unsolicited efforts on my behalf were thwarted by events beyond his control, but which, nevertheless, were a continuing encouragement;

Captain Willem Burger, my old friend, teacher and mentor, whose unshakable faith in my ability to get this project completed, and whose readiness to discuss its points objectively, constructively and disinterestedly, have been a continuing and much-needed buttress to my occasionally hard-pressed morale;

Mr James Cowden and other officers of the Liverpool Nautical Research Society, who directed my attention to several useful sources of information and provided much from the Society's own resources;

Captain Denis English, retired Shell Tankers master and superintendent, for his unflagging encouragement and convivial hospitality as well as for the useful material with which he provided me;

Captain Hugh Francis, friend, ex-colleague and critic, for allowing me to quote freely from his satirical piece *Recollections of Captain Bellwinch*, which appeared in *Nautical Magazine*, May 1992. The quotations head chapters 1-3 & 5-7;

Commodore Ian Gibb, retired P&O Cruises director, who very kindly, not to say trustingly, lent me his diaries and letters to do with as I wished, and gave me lunch to accompany his diverting reminiscences;

Mrs Elspeth Gregory, who, with her late husband, extended the hospitality of her home in addition to giving me *carte blanche* with the papers relating to the career of her late father, Commodore Alexander Mackay of the Royal Mail Steam Packet Company;

Mr C.S.M. Hamilton, Chief Examiner at the MCA, for going out of his way to unearth some obscure but vital items of official importance;

Captain Morgan John, sometime master of Shell's cadet-ship *Opalia*, for providing me with an enjoyable lunch, and a picture of the ship, not only in water-colours but also in reminiscence and a selection of printed information;

Mr Keith Jones, retired lecturer, for his graphic and very amusing recollections of his time as an engineer cadet under the Alternative Training Scheme;

Captain George King, sometime managing director of the BP Tanker Co., who gave me free rein with his autobiography, an evocative and nostalgic experience;

Captain Sandy Kinghorn, one-time Blue Star cadet, who gave me the freedom of his entertaining and vivid autobiography;

Captain Mike Peyton-Bruhl, who served his time with an archetypal South Wales tramp company and who took so much time and trouble to furnish me with an authentic picture of life in those hard-lying ships;

Mr Mike Spinks, retired Shell chief engineer, for his recollections of his time as an ATS cadet and for his views of the system at large;

Captain Barry Thompson, who went to considerable lengths to tell me about his time as a Pangbourne cadet and at sea, and who clarified many aspects of the story of the British Apprentice Club, New York;

ACKNOWLEDGMENTS

Captain R. Towner, at the MCA, for assisting my researches; and

Captain Dick Williams, also sometime master of the Shell cadet-ship *Opalia,* who furnished me with a lot of detailed information about the ship and about his own time as an apprentice in the company; and to his wife Joan, who was kind enough to give me a glimpse of the woman's view;

and all who so generously supplied me with papers, diaries, letters, photographs, conversation and other appropriate material from their private stocks of personal and family memorabilia.

"...although it may have its drawbacks,
the profession, as a whole, is not wanting
in attraction to the right kind of boy."

Frederick Stafford.
(*How to Go to Sea in the Merchant Service.* 1912.)

"...no-one has attempted to write the whole
story of the half-deck...Yet when we think of
the drama of the sea we are drawn rather to the
half-deck and its inhabitants than to the focsle,
the midship-house or the cabin."

Basil Lubbock.
(*The Last of the Windjammers*. Vol.1. 1927.)

INTRODUCTION

A N obvious question, perhaps, but it nevertheless deserves an attempt at a considered answer: why the apprentice, and not the master or another member of the ship's company, having, or fancying himself to have, by virtue of his professional standing, a greater claim on the reader's attention?

It seems to me that the apprentice was a combination of a number of things of particular and unique interest setting him apart from his brother seafarers in a way that lends his story a peculiar pointedness, not least among them the fact that he no longer exists. He represented – characterised – an era in the nation's history that, in these days of experiment, fashionable and questionable method, and superficiality, to say nothing of social degeneration and industrial metamorphosis, seems archaic to the point of quaintness; an era when values were satisfactorily defined and matters at issue simpler and more truthful in conception, less trammelled by the insidious effrontery of so-called political correctness. It was the apprentice's task to absorb the tenets of establishment as defined by the craft, trade or profession he had entered, and it is axiomatic that with the adulteration and corruption of those tenets as the decaying fabric of establishment the apprentice departed the scene. At sea, the trainee officer who has supplanted him is another creature altogether, and not yet fully-formed.

He constituted a peculiarly artless (to disregard his artful dodges in matters of work and victuals) and conspicuous bone of contention among the protagonists of the shipping *tableau vivant*, some supportive of the system that nurtured him, some emphatically – bitterly, even – opposed to it, for reasons that ranged from a perception of apprenticeship as an immoral exploitation of cheap (skilled) labour to one of its pernicious object of producing an "officer class", the stock inaccuracy aimed by spiteful levellers at any organisation's necessary officer, or management, corps; inaccurate in this case because for much of his existence the apprentice was defined not as an officer in embryo but as a trainee seaman, or deckhand. What he did with his opportunities after earning a place in the focsle was up to him, and it was the custom of the merchant service at large (to distinguish it from the Merchant Service of the Honourable East India Company) to select its officers not from some special or privileged group but from among the foremast hands, a process eventually narrowed down to the national system of professional certification the great virtue of which was its impartial accessibility: the examination for a certificate of competency was open to all, both apprentices and common sailors, able to prove a claim to having served the requisite sea time on deck. Whether for better or worse, the merchant navy has never been comfortably identified with those parts of its structure leaning towards the (rather more mythical than actual) naval style of an exclusive elite; professional excellence in the mercantile sphere rests upon different principles from those of its naval counterpart, though they have never been anything other than complementary in their roles as national bulwarks.

I have given the certification system fairly detailed scrutiny while taking care to avoid attempting a guide to the BOT examinations: their principles rather than content have been more apropos to the story, and any attempt to giver full details would be inimical to the spirit of this work – details which, incidentally, after the 1950s developed into a vastly complicated and constantly changing pattern that appeared to cause everyone concerned bewilderment and wonder, and a growing scepticism about its effectiveness. So I've resisted the temptation to go into cause and effect to any great depth, both with this topic and others where points of debate seem less than clearly defined, chiefly because to do so would be an indulgence taking me beyond my self-imposed brief, to say nothing of the limits of my competence. I hope, therefore, that the reader will be content with occasional sallies into the undergrowth that seldom stray far from the path we're supposed to be following.

An act of 1540 distinguished between *seaman* and *mariner*:

...the navy or multitude of ships of this realm in time past hath been and yet is very profitable, requisite, necessary and commodious...and a great defence and surety...in time of war...and also the maintenance of many masters, mariners and seaman, making them expert and canny in the art and science of shipping and sailing...[1]

– the mariner evidently somewhat more conversant with the art than the seaman *per se*, and on his way to mastering it. I've tried to clarify the distinctions between *apprentice, midshipman* and *cadet* at one level and between *seaman, mariner* and *officer* at another – not quite as distinguishable from one another as they might be – but it might be as well to mention here that the only instance of officer training during the age of sail occurred in the service of the elite trading houses which offered places in their ships for midshipmen, whose parents or guardians paid large premiums by the voyage and whose obligations to their commanders ended with the voyage; as, indeed, did the commanders' to them. The HEIC was the archetypal example, training both midshipmen and apprentices as officers and hands respectively, some elements of its practice continuing in the service of its successors, owners of first-class ships known collectively as the "Blackwall frigates". The term *midshipman* later became loosely used to denote either officer or seaman trainee, whether or not bound by indenture, and so falls within the compass of this book: precedent allows me equally loose use of terminology, free of the pricks of conscience beyond those requiring me to avoid ambiguity where it would damage the thread of the narrative or deflect the aim of the argument.

---

[1] 32 Henry VIII c.14 (Cunningham).

The apprentice was also a key figure in the affairs of the ship and the industry, though the part he played was given little enough credit by those among whom he worked, both as an equal and as a subordinate; not that being maligned as the lowest form of animal life did him any harm when he was made of the right stuff, which included a fair proportion of grit to alloy the often bitter irony of pride. Once the initial awkwardness had worn off he came, without ostentation, to know his own worth even if no-one else appeared to, and proved it when opportunity offered. Either that or he abandoned the life for a less demanding one, though it will be evident in the following pages that decline brought with it, in classic fashion, a considerable dilution of the spartan content of existence which had given him ample cause for retrospective pride of achievement, even if, as was sometimes the case, he deplored its worst aspects and welcomed the comparative ease of the new age.

Yet for all this he has been given barely a passing glance in the chronicles of the sea, his existence hardly acknowledged except by a few writers of boys' adventure stories. F.C. Hendry ("Shalimar") and David Bone drew pictures of life in the windjammer's half-deck[1] which, while fiction, made some success of portraying the real thing: the difficulty in handling the subject of windjammer life lay in its almost unavoidable colouring of romance; the more squalid and dangerous it was made to look the greater the aura of romance it seemed to possess, at least from a boy's point of view, which knows no logic. Writing for an adult reader, Conrad, for all his authenticity, made no attempt to play down the romantic – rather the contrary, in fact – and Lord Jim (a fictional product of the school-ship Conway[2]) blundered into unashamed transports of romance despite – or perhaps because of – the chill facts of life as they impinged upon his sea career, and one of the tale's subtleties exposes the pitfalls of the persistently romantic view of the life held together, paradoxically, by the harsh bonds of reality. Romance and imagination were, and are, distinct handicaps to the professional seaman – or mariner.

Perhaps the best modern account of the apprentice's life, portraying its tedium, dreariness, danger and limitations of outlook as well as its excitements, pleasures and diversions, is the true one forming part of the autobiography of Harold Owen[3]. Like his poet brother literate, perceptive and highly articulate, he described the life of a cargo-liner's apprentice as experienced, but not as closely observed, by the multitude in the days of brittle Edwardian caducity and mercantile supremacy immediately before the catastrophe of war stood western civilisation on its head. And post-WW2 Stanley Green directed the unforgiving beam of disillusion at the life in a humorous and sceptical account of his apprenticeship with a tramp company[4] that brought on his head sour opprobrium in reviews and comment by certain ancient mariners evidently

---

[1] Shalimar: *A Windjammer's Half-deck.*
  Bone: *The Brassbounder.*
[2] See Ch.3 *et seq.*
[3] *Journey from Obscurity.*
[4] *Whither O Ship?*

nervous of the truth as well as indifferent to good writing. Neither Owen nor Green made the sea their life's work, something of a comment in itself.

So much for the passing glance, a glance that was of its time, cast at a creature of his age rather than at one spanning the ages as a kind of Peter Pan, reflecting the distinguishing features of successive epochs while retaining his identity and stature virtually unscathed, until the end. I've tried to portray him in a series of scenes carrying him from the beginnings of industrial establishment through its rise to world pre-eminence into the time of eclipse, something not hitherto attempted and a task I've approached with some misgiving for the reasons which follow. I've also sketched an impression (and *only* an impression, not an analysis) of the mercantile marine's history with the aim of setting the stage, so that salient aspects and developments may be taken as read in the play itself. For a similar reason it has been necessary to touch upon the apprentice's beginnings, so a little space is devoted to the circumstances in which he came into being and through which he made his way towards the open reaches of mercantile consummation embraced by the bulk of the story.

Whatever his thoughts about it, he was aware to a greater or lesser extent of his peculiar burden, shared in varying degrees by the youth of other trades and professions, in being the repository of hope for, and trust in, the future, not only of an industry and a way of life but also of the identity of a nation, and that he has disappeared is only one of a number of indicators of the national condition. Also – and I believe this to be important – his story will enable the present-day cadet, his legitimate descendant, to fit some missing pieces to his own identity, which, as with everyone's, cannot be complete without a point of historical reference: knowing something of our origins and common past allows us to locate and better understand our present and give our conceptions of the future direction and balance. Without a knowledge of what has gone before we live in a vacuum, and insofar as I am at the mercy of whatever political bias has been imparted to my source material by the thinking and prejudices of its day I have attempted to sift the truth out of it with no other motive than loyalty to my subject.

In the matter of obvious questions, another must be: why this particular period?

Well, firstly, its end was determined for me: the last indentured apprentice completed his time during the early 1970s and the last vestiges of the system had been swept away by 1980. I had no difficulty in settling that point, further supported by the fact that no event or series of events becomes legitimate history until allowed to lie fallow for at least ten years, gathering about it some degree of perspective and proportion. I began to collect the evidence towards the end of the 1980s.

To decide a starting-point was less simple: whether at the very beginning, trawling the deeps of the Middle Ages, expending time and effort investigating obscure, far-distant details of little more than academic interest, or at some significant point of departure which would allow time for satisfying discussion without straining the covers of a manageable volume. I believe a hundred and fifty years, with a glance over the shoulder at tributary pre-history, will be acceptable to most. That century and a half, give or take a few years, commends itself as being the period during which the mercantile marine emerged, timorously and haphazardly, from the cocoon of protected monopoly into the acetylene glare of industrial revolution and commercial competition to be projected willy-nilly into a flurry of enterprise and development that made it the greatest organisation of its kind since the heyday of the Phoenicians. Early in the period it assumed a form that changed very little in essence and principle (perhaps a clue to its demise) until the end. Final eclipse (bar a scattering of short-sea operations to which the red duster remained loosely tacked) was one of several catastrophic, if least apparent, events marking the downfall of an equally great, and short-lived, world empire, an empire founded upon commercial aspiration and facility, not to say political design, a national adventure that appealed to personal ambition and integrity as much as, if not more than, the avarice and pliable morals attributed to it by present-day guilt mania, a mania as misleadingly erroneous as was the excessively sentimental and jingoistic view of Pax Britannica that characterised the high noon of Victoriana. It depended upon shipping for its establishment, maintenance and survival, and that same shipping depended in turn on empire for its own existence and *raison d'etre*. That it need not have done is neither here nor there: this isn't a discussion of business ethics and commercial policy. What matters now is that that was the way it was, and through their interdependence both empire and mercantile marine fell together, though Britishers still go to sea, if not in their own ships then in those of other nations which have displaced us on trade routes once the almost exclusive domain of the red duster. In this way they exemplify a curious trait of the British character, which seems, at various times, to have led it into subservience to foreigners rather than retain its destiny in its own hands. It was Elizabethan hubris that freed it from the coils of the Hanseatic trading empire, and the lassitude of a later Elizabethan (but quasi-democratic) age that seems to have led it back into a similar predicament.

I debated at some length the merits of historical chronology as the story's basis as against its division into topical chronology, and decided in favour of the former in the interests of cohesion and continuity while allowing some flexibility in occasional departures from historical sequence in order to improve the overall articulation and bind the fabric together as a whole. It will be noticed, I hope, that the chapters forming the chronology (1 to 3 and 5 to 7) conform to a pattern. Its components involved quite lengthy consideration in attempts to strike a balance between the relative merits of discussion of the apprentice's affairs in a purely social light and a discourse on the somewhat dull subject of his training. Accordingly, a good deal of entertaining material has had to be dropped, for training and education can't be ignored in this of all subjects. However, neither have they been allowed to claim the high ground, and in settling on the topical divisions of home background, school and pre-sea training, introductions to and conditions offered by employers including training at sea, general aspects of the life focusing chiefly on matters of accommodation, food and diet, daily employment and leisure, and the concluding process of examination and preparation for it, I've tried to make as wide a sweep of the life's elements as a single volume will permit. The process of elimination has meant that a lot of useful material has simply had to be abandoned along with the dross. There is, however, another risk: if a sense of *deja-vu* intrudes in places it will almost certainly be caused by the similarity of some facets of the life from age to age, and so from chapter to chapter, but closer inspection will reveal no exact parallels, there being changes in style where the principle has remained the same. An obvious example is the BOT exams which, once established in form, well before the end of the 19th century, changed very little except in content, and even that only, it seemed, with reluctance, giving rise to the popular sentiment that the BOT was permanently half a century behind the times.

Which could be the interpretation put on this story, for – once again after due consideration – a decision had to be made about a few relatively minor, but significant, items: units of money and measurement, and geographical place-names. I've made no move to update any, so such incidentals as prices and wages, spatial dimensions, weights and volumes, have been left as found, since this isn't a text-book on arithmetic and equivalents; neither is it a lesson in political geography, so place-names also conform to their respective chronological periods. I don't feel any sort of apology is required for this, since I imagine my reader to be knowledgeable enough to make his own conversions if and when he feels them to be necessary.

As a history, albeit a qualified one, facts are the work's mainstay, and here, too, difficulties have arisen, insurmountable in some instances unless manipulated and reformed, and I've allowed myself some licence where conclusive evidence has been lacking. Much of the raw material has been culled from old books and periodicals, supplemented by personal recollections and papers such as diaries and letters, and in taking assertions of fact from them I've been obliged to accept many at face value in the absence of official or authoritative verification. It is simply impracticable to check every statement by reference to its source, which in many cases has been lost, destroyed or passed on to some distant and obscure resting-place. Time has also played its negative part, precluding the kind of detailed investigation that would have extended the research phase of the work indefinitely without guarantee of a productive outcome. Consequently I've contented myself with the fruits of others' researches where my own have fallen short, but where disagreement has occurred between authorities I've taken pains to cross-reference supporting material, casting the deciding vote myself where impasse has arisen, and either indicating serious doubt where it remains or dropping the point altogether. The net risk is that in this way myth, legend and fallacy are perpetuated to a greater or lesser extent, impurities in the distillate of historical veracity, but without allowing them to corrupt the process, and having truth as my goal throughout, I've adopted the philosophy that their presence is a part of posterity's unavoidable, and not entirely undesirable, lot.

Another branch of factual reference is statistics, "the bane of good writing", figures which serve, as a rule, to lend an appearance of verity to general observation. Unfortunately the appearance is often – and sometimes intentionally – misleading, and such is the fragmentary and incomplete nature of the statistical evidence concerning the apprentice that I've been unable to compile anything having a safe claim to accuracy or proper coverage. The unsatisfactory result of the piecemeal arrangement of records over the years, with their differing terms of reference, has been exacerbated by arbitrary dispersal, loss or destruction, so I've contented myself – and, I hope, the reader – with random figures as and where they've come to hand. I can only apologise for this shortcoming, as it might be seen, while pleading honesty of intent.

Matters of accuracy apart, the picture is necessarily incomplete owing not to lack of material but to limitations of space and considerations of practicability, inclusive and comprehensive coverage amounting to the kind of indulgence that would fill several volumes the size of this modest and concise one. While a knowledge of anatomy is of equal importance to each, I've approached my subject more as a painter than a surgeon, seeking to produce a work of artistic aspiration rather than of academic analysis: in calling it a portrait instead of a history I hope to absolve it (and its author) from imputations of pretension and inadequacy, though it is as near to history as practical considerations have allowed.

There has also been a continual difficulty over the use of the telescope, as it were: in making use of anecdote – first-person observation – to such a marked extent there is an ever-present danger of the trees obscuring the prospect of the wood; close-ups of the apprentice himself, unless carefully chosen and placed, are always likely to reduce the field of view enough to cause us to lose our way. I have tried to prevent this happening while still keeping in close touch with the flesh and blood of the subject, something of a balancing act.

As manifestations of that flesh and blood quotations have presented their own problems. Their significance sometimes depends on who uttered them, sometimes on their aptness, and I decided on a general policy of anonymity in the interests of freedom and frankness: the voice is, with a few exceptions, that of the universal apprentice. The choice of exceptions to the rule is based on my evaluation of named individuals' respective importance to the story as well as in general affairs, while at all times I've respected the wishes of those contributors who preferred to remain anonymous or unquoted, though in the latter case the material they provided was no less useful in helping me to form an overall view and to examine particular facets of the story in more detail. Most of the quoted passages are self-explanatory and often continue the narrative flow rather than intercede merely to illustrate it.

And, as might be expected, woven into the story is the sea idiom, raising the question of usage. Terminology being a perennial focus of interest and debate the reader is sure to find items of controversy in my use of nautical colloquialisms, which I've employed as extensively as possible without excessive yo-hoing and shivering of timbers: no purpose is served by converting deckheads to ceilings (which in a ship would be to capsize its structure, a ceiling being a floor, though a floor in a ship is vertical and not horizontal, and so on...) or by digressing into a description of futtock shrouds or deep-tanks. It is dangerous, and invidious, to patronise the knowledgeable by explaining the obvious, so I can only suggest reference to other, purpose-written, works if the reader feels the need. As for long splices, I claim their usage in the usual way, though a list of abbreviations will be found after the appendices.

The term *master*, for example, with its extensive and varied historical application, has led to confusion even among those familiar with it, and I've taken care to avoid ambiguity wherever it would destroy crucial understanding. Otherwise I've left it to the reader's deduction, and often enough the difference of function between the ship's master and her owner as the master of the apprentice's indentures has no material significance: where it has I've pointed it out. In general I've chosen to use *master* as applied to the merchant ship in its ancient and proper place, rather than *captain* or *commander*, except where deferring to specific practice. For example, they were commanders in the BISN Co. and indeed until shortly before the beginning of WW2 wore not four but three or in some instances only two gold rings to denote their rank. Likewise I've referred to *the mate* rather than the chief officer (in sail *chief mate* was common), distinguishing him from his subordinates, the second and third mates, usage which continues in some services, aboard ship if not in official documentation and communication (a certain hapless cadet received a written ticking-off from the commander for referring to the ship's chief officer as *the mate* in his journal, to the cadet's discomfiture as well as baffled indignation). The officials who conduct the examinations for certificates of competency (which I call *tickets* while taking cognizance of the somewhat pompous insistence in some quarters that they are professional qualifications and not bus-passes, a fact which hasn't escaped my notice) as employees of the Maritime & Coastguard Agency (the BOT's present-day successor) are still titled Examiners of Masters and Mates, and for once I find myself, not without surprise, in full accord with officialdom.

In similar vein I've referred to the engineer as such, omitting the unnecessary and pretentious "officer" suffix as much in deference to custom as in the interests of rhythm and tone in the narrative structure. The reader may take it for granted that the merchant ship's engineer is an officer, and usually one who, in my experience at least, wasn't often given to standing on his dignity. As a characteristic (of, in general, the practical and phlegmatic older generation) it saved him from the genial contempt reserved by onlookers for those at sea prone to the very human (apparently) weakness of self-promotion, all the more wretched for the calling's essentially workmanlike ethos.

Another calculated risk comes of my use of the definite article applied to ships' names, deferring once again to the rhythm of the phrase rather than to any fancied correctness, except in the naval context, where *the* is never used, *HMS* being in all cases implied where not stated. The enormity (usually American but increasingly British as our estrangement from the sea intensifies) of calling a warship "the HMS" is, to be charitable, understandable, but I've used *the* where it seems appropriate to foreign – mainly US – warships. Similarly, the merchant ship sometimes has a name which sounds better so prefixed, sometimes not, *Canberra* sounding better unsupported, unlike *Malaga Factor*. An odd exception was the famous China clipper

8

The Tweed, a name which precluded use of the definite article while making it unavoidable. What John Willis, her owner, was trying to prove, if anything, is anyone's guess; perhaps he was taken with the French custom of prefixing names with *La* (as in *La Charlotte)*, and where they appear I've taken care not to fall into the American trap. Similarly the choice between being *on* or *in* a ship. *In* is standard naval usage, and the logical one: one lives in a ship as in a house, and not on it, so I've used this in preference to the customary merchant usage while allowing *on* to remain where quoted. Perhaps *on* stems from *on board*, but I won't pursue the point.

A point I have pursued, somewhat relentlessly, is the shipowner – the apprentice's master. Good and bad are variously perceived and defined, the latter being more conspicuous in the nature of things as well as being in the majority for much of the time. Nevertheless, where malpractice and neglect enter it the reader should keep the whole picture in view, not all of which lay in the shadow of parsimony and indifference. Neither was cupidity the owner's exclusive prerogative, for no small proportion of poor conditions aboard ship owed as much to the traits among masters and officers themselves. Many of the apprentice's woes were the result of the place he occupied in the eye of the officer, usually the mate where work and leisure were concerned, and the master as far as general domestic arrangements went. Ill-treatment, which was less widespread than simple hard driving, was often meted out by masters and mates who sheltered behind the owner's reputation, which in turn often came about through the behaviour of his proxies, a kind of vicious circle in which the apprentice was trapped for the duration. On the other hand I haven't entered into details of shipowning companies as matters of interest in their own right, but only where they have particular or passing relevance to the apprentice; that is to say that historical and commercial aspects of shipping companies have been left to other authors where they diverge from a direct bearing on the apprentice's activities. Likewise the ships, which I've dealt with only in outline wherever it hasn't been possible to set them aside altogether, their presence taken for granted. The reader interested in technicalities – the ship-lover, so-called – will have to turn to works specifically concerned with them, of which a few appear in the bibliography.

That said, it might be felt that I've placed undue emphasis on this or that ship or owner while ignoring others. To some extent true, it is less a matter of deliberate intent than one of expedient in the light of available space, once again, and those cited in any detail may be taken as evidence of a wider sphere in which, however, no two are alike in all respects. This isn't the least of the problems associated with an attempt to paint a broad picture on a narrow canvas, and failure to include all the possible examples doesn't mean that they have been overlooked.

Among them is an owner worth more than the passing glance he gets. He wasn't British, but in accepting all nationalities in the focsles of his famous blue-water windjammers he assisted numbers of British youths to further their aims, professional or personal, as apprentices of somewhat loose description. The late Captain Gustav Erikson operated his fleet from his Mariehamn base in the Aland Islands on austere principles that, far from discouraging the sea-minded, attracted them to the last stronghold of the commercial square-rigger until its dissolution with the death of its great exponent in 1947. To do it justice the story would require a book to itself.

As, indeed, would that of the cadet-ships operated by British owners, to which I've devoted a chapter, lifting references to them from their original places in the general chronology. To define their function clearly I've considered only those which were either adapted or purpose-built to train cadets (as their working complements were eventually termed, whether on indentures or ship's articles) for careers in the merchant navy, and not those vessels used as training ships for organisations not specifically concerned with professional requirements – such as the Outward Bound sea schools, Sea Cadets and other youth welfare and recreational bodies – though some receive incidental mention. Neither are the vessels and craft attached to schools and colleges included, except for the remnant of the Ocean Training Scheme as it petered out in connection with the Nautical College, Pangbourne. In any case, coverage is not exhaustive; many ships served only temporarily, and records have suffered a similar fate to others in the apprentice's milieu, evidence remaining mostly in a handful of fading memories, many too vague to be used with any validity. Where I have gone into details of the life, however, they can be taken as generally representative.

Few instances occurred of apprentices having the inclination, or finding the time, to keep a diary, an omission regretted in later years. Of original diaries, distinct from extracts published in biographies and autobiographies, only four have come to hand, on which I've drawn to varying degrees for both background and direct observation. One, though, stands out as an ideal example of its kind, far too well-written and significant to be chopped up and distributed piecemeal about the scene, so in Ch. 4 the reader will encounter the charismatic personality of Alexander Mackay, one-time master and commodore with the old Royal Mail Steam Packet Co. and here apprentice, first under Duncan, then Stevens, in the big 4-mast iron barque *Armadale* from 1899 to 1902. I've had to curb my enthusiasm for his graphic style, alas, and deal harshly with his efforts, reducing them to mere tokens in order to cover the span of his time from the beginning of his second voyage, when he began the diary. Doing this, and dropping dated entries in favour of a continuum of verbatim extracts, struck me as a better way of presenting his commentary than a selection of particular days and possible further adultery by *precis*; the effect achieved, of a more or less seamless running narrative, will, I hope, convey the picture with sufficient vividness, if not as finely detailed as it might be. Ch. 4 places it correctly in the general chronology, and shouldn't obstruct the broader flow of events.

Education, both general and professional, or vocational, constitutes a crucial element of the story, but where particular institutions are concerned I've had to be content with citing a few representative examples, owing partly to lack of usable information, partly to – yet again – lack of space, and partly to avoid replication. I've made no special effort to be complimentary about the educational establishment, either in its general, land-bound, form or in its specialist, maritime, guise, with the exception of most of the pre-sea schools, some afloat; they performed well for the most part, within their limited brief, their chief fault lying in an arguably over-romanticised introduction to a very mundane occupation as it became during their development, and a failure to transpose – or perhaps to promote – themselves into the latter half of the twentieth century without appearing impossibly archaic, relics of a departed age in the life-spans of their own progeny and a pointer not so much to their own outdated methods as to the degeneration of society about them. A few have survived, but only by embracing the new without reservation.

As for the general sector, as time passed it developed an inward-looking, self-interested stance in step with its own decline from the heights achieved in the austerity years immediately post-WW2, not least in the view of those who came to drink of its waters, a stance in which petty internal politics played a part as great as, or greater than, the interests of the pupil or student. It was (and is) a flawed stance vociferously and unconvincingly defended by its practitioners against outside criticism, including that of the students themselves, notably those most interested in furthering their (non-academic) careers in the real world. I've made no attempt to champion the cause of academe, whatever it is, but rather to indicate its shortcomings as seen by its theoretical beneficiary, the apprentice. In this respect I concede a certain bias, not without legitimate foundation, but where virtues appear (not necessarily defined as such by the establishment – for example firm discipline, the ideal of academic rigour and discrimination, and so on) I've attempted to give them due recognition. And I've drawn a distinction between *schooling* and *education* which I believe will be clearly spotted.

But here, as in other aspects of the story, I have to excuse myself from imputations of negligence, for not every school, college or training establishment has received mention, worthy of it though they might be. Some have escaped notice, some been noted without finding a place in the cramped accommodation of these pages, so, as with cadet-ships, owners and other groups, those given attention have to answer for all, at least in general principle.

Although far from comprehensive – concise would better describe it – the story would have lacked balance without inclusion of a somewhat shadowy figure, one I hadn't at first thought to include, but who, as research proceeded to reveal him in a significant light, demanded consideration. Rather less obviously an apprentice to the sea, the trainee engineer nevertheless deserves what mention I've been able to give him – more, indeed, but in this also I'd be venturing into a separate and extensive story in its own right. In some respects the engineer apprentice's claim to inclusion stems from a longer history than that of his deck counterpart, given a certain latitude of interpretation, which I've taken while steering clear of the shoals of prickly debate, or altercation, over the relationship between the two departments. I've attempted an impartial treatment of what amount to socially opposing forces, avoiding the acrimonious distinctions between deck and engine-room which have ever been the unprepossessing offspring of prejudice and selfishness in both camps. If "progress" has arrived at any point of genuine improvement in our condition instead of being nothing better than a set of improvisations just able to keep our way of life ticking over as a train of badly-meshing gears, it is in the gently-evolving merger of separate identities, though it would be an evasion of certain truths to ignore the fact, graphically demonstrated by the children of tradition who people these pages, that as the old specialisations cross into each other's domains, the old skills and attendant resourcefulness become transmuted and dulled. Technology, alas, robs the human hand (and mind) of its higher functions in the mass, whether on the bridge or down below, and it is a pity and an irony that as oil and water benefit from a formula for a miscible blend their great professional distinguishing features fall from them.

So I've included the engineer because, from 1952, he became as much a sea apprentice as his deck counterpart through the Alternative Training Scheme, which inducted prospective engineers direct into the seagoing role instead of drawing them from among those who had completed an apprenticeship ashore in one of the branches of the trade associated (preferably) with shipping. I've also risked condemnation, or at best derision, in drawing what I see as parallels between the latter-day engineer apprentice or cadet and the trade apprentice of olden time, who worked with his shipwright master in the building of the ship before accompanying him to sea as part of her complement, sometimes to take it up as his occupation, broadened with its content of seamanship and navigation. I have never been able to understand why the engineer has been confined to his specialisation and not brought into the overall operation of the ship, both to give him a better understanding and to widen his career interest. However, recent developments seem to indicate that one day the shipmaster, whatever his title, will have begun his career as both navigator and engineer, to whatever extent of expertise the technological despotism of the age allows.

Even so, where I've looked at the examinations for certificates of competency, I haven't dealt with engineering in as much detail as the deck department, since the engineer apprentice or cadet completed his time without facing the professional examinations, passing beyond apprenticeship to sail as a junior engineer during the interim. Here, too, however interesting it might be, I've decided not to pursue his onward progress, but to adhere strictly to my brief by excluding someone with his own story to tell.

Of greater interest than professional examinations, but unfortunately also amounting to subjects in themselves having only peripheral weight in this context, some other aspects of the life have had to be confined to only passing mention. The RNR's story, for example, would fill a book with ease, and presents a problem of extent – how much territory can it be granted without either loading it with overmuch attention or robbing it of its due while acknowledging that it represents naval rather than mercantile service? I've ducked the issue by leaving it out, bar mention in the appendices. Likewise the fishing industry, which certainly had its quota of apprentices with as much claim to a sea inheritance as their merchant service contemporaries: in 1549 an Act gave encouragement to the consumption of fish for the support of the fishing fleet, seen as a convenient, inexpensive and thorough school of seamanship, from which would come the seamen and mariners of the merchant and royal navies. Here, too, is enough material for a book, and far too little space to give it the attention it deserves, so I've omitted it, with some regret. There were also apprentices to the various pilotage services including Trinity House, but they, too, have been left out except for those who happened to be serving normal time as a condition of entry into the service of their choice.

Neither have I discussed unions, chiefly because the apprentice, by definition, wasn't eligible for membership except as a matter of form; also because digression into the quasi-political nature of union activities (a fact, despite their protestations to the contrary) would have added to the more tedious elements of the story, which I've striven to keep to a minimum. Apprentices did not go on strike – officially – or stand on questions of principle where they were to their own material advantage except in extreme instances and at risk of incurring contractual penalties, part of the cause of the unions' generally critical view of the system. It was a view usually expounded in the kind of plausible rhetoric that committed nobody to anything and failed to propose anything better by way of an alternative (though alternatives were proposed in idealistic profusion). Engineering in particular has felt the deleterious effects of an absence of a thorough and correctly-named apprenticeship, the term used at present to describe a travesty of training as it has appeared in a variety of *ad hoc* expedients.

War, of course, must be touched upon, which is all I've done with it. No overt heroics will be found here, only the observations of a handful who passed through it, like their shipmates, while attempting to continue their normal daily round – which, indeed, is what the merchant ship itself did. In any case war has been amply witnessed and documented in other, more specific, works. On the whole, the apprentice tended to look on it as a mixed blessing: if it meant more money, adventure and respite from some of the drudgery, it also meant extra duties and loss of sleep, and when it rose out of the sea or descended from the skies to touch him personally it was often more of an adventure than he'd bargained for. Like the men, boys died, too, but I haven't laboured the point.

And I'm afraid I've skirted another: for those prurient spirits to whom no window on life can be fully open without reference (preferably explicit to the point of irrelevance) to human weakness in its more lascivious and deviant guises, what follows will come as a sad disappointment. They are warned, therefore, that because such matters are as old and commonplace as the sea itself, like war already exhaustively explored, they exist here only between the lines. I've had neither the time nor the space – nor, indeed, the inclination – to indulge a non-existent taste for the lewd. Boys in the close and intimate company of men reacted as might be expected to the predicaments that occasionally confronted them, and as with most others at sea during the period covered by this story, learned to deal with them in their own ways, part of the process of growing to maturity. On the whole their reaction was – and usually is – rational and healthy, supported to a greater or lesser extent by the conventional moral codes that ordered shipboard life, and to a large extent still do. I don't condone homosexuality, which is a demoralising and sometimes dangerous human aberration, and see no point in expanding on it when it seems to have been worked to death by others for whom it seems to hold an inordinate fascination. As for the normal sexual appetites of young men in a male environment (but is the sea male – and are ships?) similar arguments apply; sufficient for my purposes to leave the reader to add whatever he wishes to my allusions and those of the apprentice himself. Any description we can offer of the sexual act can at best be only a variation on a hackneyed theme, at worst a banal repetition of a time-worn cameo of the reproductive process. But that said, living as he did in surroundings in which sexual relations formed a dominant topic of thought and debate, or at least of ribald and lightly-considered comment, amounting in some instances to a determined and ruinous obsession, it seems odd that in retrospect the ex-apprentice should be so diffident, almost prudish, on the subject. In this is more than a suggestion of false modesty, so to speak; the cause might be to do with conceptions of what constitutes literary propriety as a reaction to the excesses to which he was either a party or a witness in various locations round the world, some more notorious than others. We can look in vain among, for example, the classics of the sea for explicit reference to the intimate adventures of seamen ashore: Conrad's characters – Lord Jim, say – found it constitutionally beyond them to take part in the casual sensuality which has always been one of the life's staples. Similarly in modern popular fiction, based as most of it is on actuality. And in reminiscence old age appears to adopt a reticence over matters seen in a latter-day light drained of the sense of adventure and romance (however naive and unimaginative) imbued in them by the eyes of youth. The result is that, as readers of private and published records of a bygone social order, we receive an impression of action confined to aspects of man versus his environment, quite devoid of reference to the emotional side of his affairs: it appears not to have existed except in a very staid, orthodox and minor key, almost a cause for embarrassment in a juvenile, callow sense.

But the impression is a mistaken one, for in the apprentice's life women played a crucial, if meagrely documented, part, based to a greater or lesser extent on love in its variety of mood and quality, embodied in figures ranging from mothers to whores; indeed, they can hardly avoid doing so, since the entire story is of a love affair, between men and the sea, with women occupying a natural place along the shore.

Lying outside the story's pale, however, is the apprentice's subsequent career, not by any means confined to the sea. Wastage, to use the accepted, relative, term, accounted for the broad spectrum of occupations that followed, while of those that continued at sea only a small majority led to command – only a small minority of those that had begun with apprenticeship. Regrettably, I've been prevented by the usual restrictions from mentioning more than a handful of later careers, and those only very briefly, as part of the general narrative.

Which, whatever else it might be, isn't a guide on how to go to sea, nor a portrayal of what can be expected of it as a career. Times have changed since 1980, and with them conditions and prospects, but if a sea career is contemplated – and it should be given careful thought keeping in view its distinctive nature, not to be likened to other industrial occupations despite efforts made, often by people who should know better, to discount the sea's ineffable and unchanging character that will always set it apart from land-based callings – then here at least is an introduction. Furthermore, while I hope much will be learned from it (without any intention on my part of patronising the many mariners, ancient and less ancient, whose experience and knowledge are as galaxies to my basic solar system), it isn't a book of instruction: I set out to inform and entertain, nothing more, and perhaps direct the reader to more extensive investigation. My overriding concern is that as he reads he will come to see the apprentice not as a historical figure set in aspic – or pickled in brine if nothing stronger – but as a living personality who played a vital role in the growth and life of a nation. As a nation we owe him at least that recognition.

PROLOGUE

British Seascape: Rise & Fall of the Mercantile Marine.

DURING the disjointed peace that lasted from the end of Napoleon's career until August 1914 the British mercantile marine came of age. From a miscellaneous and disparate collection of shipping interests that had grown out of the decay of the old chartered trading companies it developed into an organised and regulated fleet that epitomised and represented the nation's mercantile and industrial supremacy; but it was a supremacy as transient as it was phenomenal. Brought about by a need to sustain both the country and its empire, changes in economic and political alliances which revealed a reluctance to continue in the role of world power (with its attendant responsibilities) saw its demise, one that went all but unnoticed by a people who have never, in the majority, known much about the existence and function of the mercantile marine. And if democracy produces government that expresses the comprehension and will of the governed, neither have they cared...

As the topography of industrial revolution and commercial opportunity emerged from the receding tide of war it was greeted with mixed feelings and – at sea at least – less than wholehearted enthusiasm. Yet for the first time British overseas trade, which had steadily improved in spite of desultory conflict, could be pursued without having to run the gauntlet: merchant ships no longer had to sail in convoy for mutual protection. Where wars did occur – and there were numerous scuffles as British influence spread – they provided shipowners with useful revenue from government contracts. The Crimea, Chinese intransigence, Raj and mutiny in India, the truculence of Zulu chiefs and the intractability of Boer farmers all came in the form of welcome bonuses for selected shipping. However, the flywheel of maritime commerce took time to gather momentum and the early decades of this period saw commercial progress hindered by entrenched reserve and almost supernatural conservatism. The country's rapidly-growing political and industrial prominence appeared to thrust upon the shipowner a standing that sometimes surprised or even bewildered him, and opportunities were lost by default. The beginnings of great enterprise were shaped with much fumbling, its consolidation with an element of discord and misdirected effort, and its decline and retrenchment handled in a spirit of recrimination and resentment.

One of the difficulties facing trade was the system of monopoly stemming from the chartered companies, and the fertile ground it provided for abuses of one kind and another. Free traders had been burrowing into its foundations, but it was not until Lord

Liverpool's 1813 Bill set a time-limit on the HEIC's charter that prospects began to brighten. Enactment of the bill opened the India routes to all, and in 1833 a further Act of Parliament did the same for the company's China operation. Of the company's shipping activity nothing then remained but a mail and passenger service between Bombay and Suez, and that, too, was destined for extinction through competition.

First tried, only to be prudently abandoned, by Richard II, protective navigation laws revived in Tudor times to be reinforced, augmented and recodified as time passed were now seen to be detrimental to the country's economic wellbeing, instrumental in maintaining prices of goods and shipping services at an artificial, inflated, level. Repeal, total and complete, was the goal of the new thinking, and in 1849 the body of the laws was removed from the statute book, to an accompaniment of dire prognostications from the losing side, composed chiefly of the landowning lobby, much of it with interests in shipping. In 1854 the remaining outpost, reservation of domestic coastal routes, was demolished.

But the prophets of doom were being disingenuous where they didn't lack perception, for Britain was in a commanding position at sea and had only to exploit it to retain the advantage. This would require, of course, renewed effort and determination, and for those who entertained visions of British ascendancy on the world stage shipping represented unbounded opportunity; competition from abroad would be not an overwhelming flood but a spur.

Examples there were in plenty, for those who troubled to take note rather than rail against perfidious Albion. Even before the warships had been placed in ordinary and Napoleon in exile the (ex-)colonists of New England had swaggered into the North Atlantic, trading to continental Europe in cocky indifference to British embargoes with two radical departures in ship-operation, demonstrating the superiority of new ideas in sail and hull design and the commercial soundness of running to a timetable instead of at the shipper's convenience. Crossing times were more or less consistent and dramatically reduced, to some 40 days westbound and half that eastbound, where before they had been little shorter than the 66 days of the *Mayflower*'s 1620 voyage. These American packets retained their primacy on the Western Ocean until overcome by the smoke of technology, while British sail totally failed to make anything of the growing emigrant trade to the New World.

The Americans were nothing if not commercial free-thinkers and it was from this quarter that the threat – or incentive – came, overshadowing challenges from other maritime powers including Holland. Enterprise was the name of the game, and little regard was paid to the tradition and custom that hobbled British efforts. No sooner had repeal opened the Far East to foreigners than a group of London merchants welcomed the arrival of the New York-owned full-rigger *Oriental*, 97 days out of Hong Kong with 1,600 tons of tea. They had chartered her for her capacity and speed, and while she lay in drydock at London a surveyor and designer took off her lines for appraisal: Bernard Waymouth, an officer of Lloyd's Register and later its principal surveyor and then secretary, eventually designed the aptly-named *Thermopylae*, but for the time being the problem lay in the serious deficiencies of British design. As Lubbock put it,

> *In model and design we had no ships that could compare with such vessels... Again, in the cut of their sails the Americans were first and the British, along with the rest of the world, nowhere.* [1]

Of the hull, Waymouth noted the marked change of form already evident in the Atlantic packets, one taken to extremes in the down-east flyers of MacKay and his contemporaries which stormed round the Horn to California with gold-fever in focsle and cabin. However, British minds were at work and the American penchant for rakishness and weight was more delicately interpreted, reaching its apogee in the China clipper, a type which combined sensitive sailing qualities with acceptable capacity. In its materials – variously hardwood, composite and iron – it had the advantage of the American model, the soft-wood construction of which predestined it to a limited life in the hands of the hard-nosed masters the trade attracted. But it proved all too vulnerable to the effects of head-on collision with steam and its heyday was as short-lived as it was glorious and supreme.

And herein lay the makings of a greater conflict, though its outcome held the key to British suzerainty over the oceans: if the American challenge had become a struggle for national predominance on established sailing routes, the more subtle threat, equally a promise, came from within, in direct response to the draconian legislation that had so dismayed the *ancien regime*. Civil war in 1861 effectively disqualified the States from further participation in either the sail battle or what might have become one in steam (attention became focused more on the development of trans-continental railways once the war had been resolved, while shipping took second place), at which point the line was already clear enough between the two camps under the red ensign alone. Sail braced itself for the coming struggle while steam, patient and inquiring, followed its rising star with dogged conviction.

Undeterred by logic the new breed of engineers added steadily to its stock of understanding and expertise; developments followed at an accelerating rate, and by 1825 some forty-five steamship companies were on the London register. Financially precarious and absurdly short-reached though their ventures were, it became obvious to any who cared to dwell on it that steam's claim to a place in the van of British shipping was irrefutable, and twenty-five years later the picture had broadened. Coastal services extended to near-continental points and the Mediterranean while more or less regular schedules governed transatlantic operations. For the most part, however, deep-sea enterprise was obliged to seek government aid, and to maintain the principle of free trade it came in the form of mail contracts once it was clear that the steamship possessed virtues unmatchable by the sailing packet. Yet the portents, if not the signs, weren't immediately clear: the advance of steam technology, bound up with

---

[1] *The China Clippers.* p.68.

improvements in the quality of materials and methods of construction as much as with propulsion, contributed greatly to sail's efficiency, and the result was a combined operation on routes which, on balance, complemented rather than countered one another, lending added strength to the fabric of the red ensign.

Having missed its chance in the transatlantic emigrant trade and looked on as the Californian boom embraced American shipping at large, British sail found the twenty years immediately preceding the opening of the Suez Canal kind to it in other spheres. The China trade fell largely into British hands, American pressure notwithstanding, while the discovery of gold in Australia transformed a desultory passenger service (suffering from an uncomfortably close association with convict transport) into a headlong scramble chronically short of cabin and hold space. With the supply of manufactures and materials hard on its heels, emigration to the antipodes suddenly became big business and for a while steam remained below the horizon. Then, in 1866, a barque-rigged steamer doubled the Cape and, bunkering at Mauritius (with coal brought out by sail) after a non-stop passage from Liverpool, pressed on to Shanghai where she loaded a cargo of tea for the return trip. Viewing this event (it was nothing less) with circumspection, proponents of sail might well have recalled steam's first successful attempt on the Atlantic crossing, when in 1834 the little *Royal William* had crossed from Quebec to the Isle of Wight in 17 days. *Savannah*'s crossing in 1819 was only steam-assisted, and barely so at that, so did not qualify.

Royal William's triumph was an earnest of steam's intentions, but although the names that followed hers into the wide span of the Atlantic's trade routes rapidly established themselves – Cunard, White Star, Dominion, Anchor, Royal Mail, P&O, Castle and others – they did so without directly threatening sail's arteries. But the 1866 voyage – the steamer was Alfred Holt's *Agamemnon* – represented a pointed challenge to sail in its *sanctum sanctorum*: this way had come the Portuguese, the Dutch, the French and the British themselves, and, in the dim long-ago, five hundred years before Christ, sailors despatched to the south with orders from an Egyptian king to find their way round a far cape and return via the Pillars of Hercules. Century upon century of wind-ships had held the line, now taken from them with almost perfunctory ease.

Agamemnon was also an example and demonstration of the engineer's achievement over the comparatively short period of 30-odd years: at 500 tons register *Royal William* had made a respectable 8 knots under the 200-hp impetus of her paddles. Holt's ship, 2,280nrt and able to lift 3,000 tons, had a high-pressure (about 60psi) compound engine driving a single screw, and her 10 knots was a speed described by her owner as "tolerable". It was also remarkably consistent, a virtue of far greater commercial impact than out-and-out speed and one that tipped the scales conclusively against sail and its erratic timekeeping.

Still, conflict between sail and steam apart, British maritime enterprise was beginning to enjoy the rosy prospect of dominion over the world's deep-sea routes, and a sense of exhilaration entered the minds and hearts of engineers and sailors alike, not to mention the men of commerce urging them on from behind, or leading them into the unknown with (often) a blind faith in benevolent destiny. Occasionally it faltered: trade depression in the late 60s affected sail and steam together, and struck a note of bitterness heightened in 1869 by the opening of the Suez Canal, giving steam a decisive advantage. From that point sail's strategy became one of consolidated withdrawal, and the first major casualty was, of course, the Far East route. The China clipper's day faded into a brief twilight while Merseysiders greeted the new epoch as the blue funnels of "the China company" came and went on the tide. As *Thermopylae* and *Cutty Sark* turned to tramping before ignominious departure for foreign flags the new and final age of sail concentrated on steady passage-making (a sharp revision of policy) and bulky low-value cargoes. Nitrates and guano, coal and coke, railway iron and building bricks became the staples under acres of storm canvas worked by smaller and in many ways tougher crews. The wooden ship might well have bred an iron man, but the great steel windjammer relied on one with muscles of whipcord and the constitution of a hyena. His contempt for the soft-living steam man was as forlorn as it was proud and defiant.

Steam's early ventures were born of a coupling of business sense that stood a chance of commercial success and engineering skill that did not. As the 60s passed the shipowning dynasties, as they became, began to fashion the British merchant fleet into a distinctive and intricate form that, in certain respects, was copied by its potential foreign rivals. As trade developed and extended hand in hand with improvements in the efficiency of the marine boiler and the reciprocating engine, so a pattern emerged that proved to be the connecting link between sail and steam. It was a pattern based on the same weft and woof that had supported commercial sail's operation, a principle upon which sail pinned its last hopes and which a growing sector of steam adapted to its own peculiar advantage: the steam tramp shared with sail the carriage of materials not requiring rapid transit but movement in large quantities; it accepted cargo for any destination and picked it up wherever offered, and the result was a paradoxical alliance of direct competition and involuntary cooperation, often, as in other spheres of shipping operation, under the same house-flag. From this sprang a trading system unique to British shipping and, as it turned out, vital to its own and the country's prosperity: if ever there was an invisible earner in the British economic spectrum it was the cross-trader, and the cross-trader was, typically, the tramp. Alongside it in that spectrum lay the country's dependence on trade for its livelihood, and not the kind of trade that catered solely and directly for creature comforts and needs: Britain had become the hub of world manufacture and her trade had evolved into a flow of raw materials inwards and finished goods out. Self-sufficiency and the agricultural base had been eclipsed by heavy industry.

By the turn of the century changes had been wrought not only in the pattern of legislative regulation of shipping but also in the principles of ownership: the division of interest in a ship into 64 shares (effected by an Act of 1823) held by people whose profit motive was leavened by virtually unlimited financial risk (protected to a greater or lesser extent by insurance) gave way to holdings by groups or individuals in a ship or ships governed by explicit and more attractive limited liability. Thus the shipping company directed by boards of shareholders rather than a ship financed by sixty-fourthers, many operated as family concerns, the family members retaining the controlling interest. Also, many concerns ran as managing owners operating several single-ship companies, a system under which profits were assured (assuming viable freight rates) and losses limited. A side-effect of this became evident as an impersonal attitude on the part of the shore organisation – the managing staff – towards the ships that would have been alien to the old sail owners and sixty-fourthers, and it signalled the common experience of austerity, if not outright wretchedness, in living and working conditions prevailing among the last wind-ships as they struggled to survive.

Nevertheless the picture in the opening decades of the 20th century was one of unparalleled supremacy. Still at work abreast of and in tandem with steam, sail comprised a small and shrinking proportion of some 12,440,000 tons of British-flag shipping just before the outbreak of world war in 1914, a figure which about 96 years previously had stood at only 2,426,969. It accounted for about 40% of world tonnage and about half the world's total trade. Prospects continued rosy, the free traders had been vindicated, and yet, looming war apart, clouds were gathering on the economic horizon, one of the biggest and blackest rising from the same location as the military threat. America's heavily-subsidised and somewhat inarticulate competition had evaporated with the disintegration of Collins's daunting but over-stressed Atlantic passenger steamship enterprise (the Collins of the great Dramatic Line of Western Ocean packets in the pre-Civil War heyday), and the abrupt collapse of Pierpont Morgan's bid to engulf the whole of transatlantic commerce in a single monolithic sea and rail combine. Britain's claim to dominance was *fait accompli*, but in Germany the ghost of the Hanses was abroad, its aim to challenge British prestige on British ground.

By this time British shipping had assumed a collective form that was distinctive and substantial and the legislative structure governing it a state of high efficiency, if well short of perfection. Weaknesses manifested themselves in more or less embarrassing ways and the spectre of *Titanic* lives on to emphasise the point, but nevertheless by 1914 a world-wide system of interlinked trading routes and official surveillance had come to represent British pre-eminence.

Pre-eminence, however, isn't self-sustaining, and unless vigorously and continuously cultivated evaporates. Opinion has it that at this point, had it not been for the deliberate accident of war, the process would have begun. War created a demand for tonnage as artificial and ephemeral as it was extreme, and even sail's extinction was postponed, or at least approached in a spirit of defiance rather than resignation. Emerging from the inconclusive fray much changed in its philosophy, structure and component units, the mercantile marine faced post-war trade with some ambivalence. To many it appeared that the earlier spirit of enterprise had leaked away to be replaced by a less pragmatic and somewhat defensive outlook. While in 1849 there had been no serious competition from foreign interests (the US excepted), in 1919 the situation was wholly altered: countries hitherto content to ship their goods by any carrier (usually British) had discovered, through necessity, the benefits of running their own fleets along channels well-greased with restrictive tariffs and selective subvention. This hit British free trade, as it was meant to, and those owners (of tramps, typically) who had made a good thing of government wartime requisition rates before selling up counted their blessings, among other rather more tangible assets. Surviving the total of 9 million tons sunk, the rest pressed on into a short boom, their ships manned by fresh blood in place of the 14,287 British seamen lost in the fracas.

Yet there was considerable confusion. While British shipping had been diverted into wartime service the foreign operations which had filled the gap now presented an all-too-substantial obstacle to the resumption of activity on the pre-war scale. Furthermore, having constructed a huge excess of tonnage, America set most of it to work under an umbrella of punitive tariffs, incontinent subsidy and exclusive cabotage. And with ponderous stupidity the Allies exacted retribution on a prostrate Germany by relieving her of all her merchant tonnage and dividing it between themselves. Virtually bankrupted by the war, the British government saw fit not to scrap its share, as others did, but to dole it out to shipowners as part-recompense for their war losses, supplemented by some 1.4 million d.w. tons of standard war shipping directly operated, as it had been, by government. For example Royal Mail, having lost more than a hundred ships, acquired 77 of these relics. In one fell swoop British shipping was rendered obsolescent while at the same time Germany geared up for rapid production of a brand-new fleet incorporating every possible technical advance while enjoying the financial and moral support of a national government benefiting from American aid.

The mirage of post-war revival seduced owners into a building programme which fuelled the fires of price inflation. The result was an appearance of resurgent prosperity, but just beneath the surface lay a sump of crippling mortgages, and no sooner had the immediate needs of the world been satisfied than stagnation set in the effects of which were aggravated by serious over-tonnaging. Loans went unredeemed and owners to the wall while shipping was laid up wholesale; what trade there was survived in a suffocating atmosphere of low freights and subsidised foreign competition in which tramp companies, characteristically operating with minimum capital reserves, fared badly. Liner companies resorted to attenuated services and protective conference arrangements while sustaining themselves on dwindling capital. On top of all this came the stirrings of another technological revolution in the shape of the diesel engine, quickly put to use by Germany but regarded with distrust and some contempt in Britain, while oil was beginning to make inroads on coal as a fuel for steam. It was a combination that soon proved a potent factor in the decay of British shipping activity. The spirit of innovation that had driven the industrial revolution in Britain seemed to have dispersed and seeded itself in distant places. In 1935 the government was moved to make a supportive gesture to tramp shipping caught in a mire of low freights by the introduction of its "scrap and build" scheme in the British Shipping (Assistance) Act, but it came with the admonition that owners were to make efforts to stand on their own feet. Indeed, for all their present troubles they weren't overly inclined to turn to government for help, preferring to operate free of the kind of bureaucratic meddling such recourse would entail.

Meanwhile the liner companies' predisposition for merger as a step beyond the conference produced a handful of giant conglomerates. Among them, P&O had been gathering together companies operating east of Suez, Ellerman those operating from the Mediterranean to East Africa round the Cape, including the Wilson Line, in its time the world's largest passenger-carrier; and Owen Philipps, better and more interestingly known as Lord Kylsant of Carmarthen, had transformed his Royal Mail Steam Packet Company into a huge combine spanning the Atlantic from Punta Arenas to the St Lawrence and through the Panama Canal into the Pacific. It had also taken the lead in the adoption of diesel propulsion. Most groups, if financially eroded, survived the prolonged depression but Kylsant, with grandiose designs, overreached himself, failed to redeem the government loans granted him under the Trades Facilities Act, in 1930 saw his empire fall in ruins, and ended his shipping career contemplating, from behind bars, the folly of issuing a fraudulent prospectus to cover falsified accounts. It was a tragedy, a *cause celebre* from which no-one gained except the lawyers.

Working in an altogether detached environment, the tanker was regarded as a pariah by British owners (and by British seamen), who remained remarkably impermeable to oil as both a fuel and a commodity to be transported, and so it was that the tanker charter market, flourishing on otherwise stony ground, drew its stock from other nurseries, notably Scandinavian. In the event most British-flag tanker tonnage was operated, right up to the end, by foreign oil majors, led by the Dutch and the Americans. The largest indiginous tanker fleet was born of an awareness on the part of government that if all other shipping markets could be allowed to find their own level with or without British participation, oil presented implications of an entirely different and infinitely more portentious complexion.

And all the while the dominions – Canada, South Africa and Australia, to say nothing of India and the energetic New Zealanders – were putting their own fleets together intent on maritime autonomy as the preliminary to greater things. Numerous hairline cracks were appearing in the body politic of empire.

Although still in the lead, by 1939 the British fleet had visibly diminished: after a post-war (1921) peak of 19.3 million tons it now stood at a still-shrinking 17.9 million. About a quarter of it lay in the hands of five major groups: P&O, Cunard, Ellerman, Furness Withy and, grown fat on the carcase of Kylsant's failure, Ocean, otherwise Holt's "China company" aforementioned. Most of the rest wore the house colours of the leaned-out tramp interests – Ropner, Runciman, Weir and, among a handful of South Wales operators, Reardon-Smith; and the Cardiff coal exchange was reflecting the changing times. As for sail, already hull-down on the horizon of retrospective sentimentality, *Garthpool*'s stranding at the Cape Verdes in 1929 saw the end of it on blue water, while the barquentine *Waterwitch*, of Fowey, made the last commercial coasting voyage in 1936[1]. In summary, at the outbreak, or resumption, of war the British fleet comprised 68 liner companies totalling 8,744,469 nrt and 129 tramp concerns at an additional 3,449,401. Together they formed a third of world deep-sea tonnage. At a glance the patient appeared reasonably healthy but the trend was ever downward: flying over about half the world's fleet in 1890 the red ensign now graced only a quarter of its units.

While hardly a welcome interlude – 29,000 merchant seamen lost their lives[2] – war applied a temporary brake to the progress of the disease. Mass production of utility ships countered an alarming loss through enemy action, but even so the net outcome was further decline with the fleet reduced by about 21% at war's end. Then, in the grey dawn of peacetime, the old bogeys returned: free trade on a sublimely one-sided footing remained government policy. Having got rid of the common foe (to the extent of succouring him with cash and technical assistance) erstwhile allies looked to their own interests while Britain resumed the commercial battle in a heightened atmosphere of political retrenchment. British shipping was coming to the realisation that it was in open confrontation with not only its like under foreign flags but also its own national administration.

Yet fresh opportunities existed. The British flag was in a good position to consolidate and then expand. What was required was nerve enough to raise fresh capital, but instead existing reserves were used to redeem long-term loans that could have been extended. The general idea seemed to be to reduce capital holdings and liabilities so as to keep losses to a minimum in the coming slump, which did not materialise. Far from it. In fact resurgence saw foreign interests poised to take full advantage, and between them they cut the British leading proportion of some 27% of world tonnage in 1945 to 18% by 1957, a situation which seemed to do little to ruffle the surface of the tranquil waters on which the shipowning fraternity drifted. In the absence of a spirit of aggressive enterprise shipowning was seen by many of its exponents as a congenial occupation: no risks need be taken, profits were reasonable, costs within the accountant's unimaginative tolerance. Complacency had become something of a fashion; fall we might, but there was still a long way to go, a fact not overlooked by the unions. Good conditions, they argued (and they had never had them so good), should lead to better...

Taken apparently in a spirit of contrition as much as in deference to fiscal necessity, government measures which produced a favourable exchange rate also attracted

---

[1] That is, of a square-rigged vessel; cargoes continued to be lifted by small fry including such classic types as the spritsail barge, familiar in east coast waters and particularly those in and about the Thames estuary.

[2] Coal-fuelled ships were a significant factor in the incidence of sinkings, the smoke they generated acting as a beacon for prowling U-boats and reconnaissance aircraft. British use of coal in preference to oil as a fuel was a fatal symptom of industrial inertia.

foreign interests to the British base, and as the 60s advanced the British-flag fleet expanded. However, much of the new growth's commercial loyalties remained with its roots, for all its readiness to employ British seafarers. And another development began to cause perceptible tremors: collapsing empire apart, a greater threat had appeared in the rapid expansion of fleets under the dubious auspices of flags of convenience, emblems of countries none too particular about the quality of the shipping that contributed to their national exchequers. Greek and American owners were only too glad of these havens, and Liberia elbowed Britain out of her leading position in 1970, morally supported by Panama. Meanwhile, more orthodox foreign-flag fleets continued to expand in their own right, having availed themselves of war-built American tonnage offered for sale at knock-down prices. As if all this wasn't enough yet another crack appeared in the dyke as the USSR embraced a policy of commercial invasion at any price in all quarters. Furthermore, the conference system found itself exposed to pressure from weasel-like competitors offering cut-rate services, and there seemed to be no alternative to the unsatisfactory solution of co-opting the invader, who then proceeded to break the conference agreements whenever circumstances suited.

By the mid-60s perceptions of the industry were that it was inefficient. Management was proving inadequate and clumsy, exhibiting a growing tendency to distance itself from the ship and her people. Always at a certain depth beneath the surface, cynicism that was in large part a product of two world wars found fresh currency and expression in the mutual abrasion of insensitive company administration and over-sensitive employee attitudes, and the result was a kind of internecine cancer that complemented the effects of outside erosion.

Closure of the Suez Canal in 1956 had altered the trend and direction of British commerce with the Orient: the passenger trade dissolved while the tramp's traditional function metamorphosed into increasing specialisation in bulk transport. Closely allied to each other, ro-ro tonnage began to make a serious bid for coastwise dominance while the container assumed a substantial authority in all spheres, though its effect was subtle and, from some angles, corrosive: the economics of scale played a key part in its establishment, and the international cooperation it demanded obscured national identity. The container-ship represented a capital outlay beyond the resources of a single company – even of a single group – and the need for pooled capital overshadowed the old conflicts of interest. As for the tanker, similar economic conceptions applied: the Suez Canal's closure both in 1956 and again in 1967 forced the pace and while the ship's capacity increased so the British-flag (not all British-owned, be it remembered) tanker fleet expanded. Between 1939 and 1960 its tonnage rose by 130%.

And so the 60s passed, marked by every appearance of prosperity. It was genuine enough in the sense that it was based on British registry and the employment of British sea and shore staff, but only as long as government incentives continued in force: for example, all comers had been induced through subvention to build in British yards with the proviso that the ships would be operated thereafter under British registry for a specified period, and in 1967 the Merchant Shipping (Load Line) Act allowed deeper loading, so increasing capacity without incurring extra cost. The red ensign became, in effect, a flag of convenience, and by 1975 foreign-owned tonnage amounted to more than half the British-flag total. At the same time world tonnage was growing while world trade was slackening, an ominous development exacerbated in 1973 by the OPEC oil-price shock; another price-ramp in 1978 wrought further havoc.

Around this time several occurrences brought about alarming changes. The mandatory registry period for foreign-owned tonnage lapsed, tanker owners faced increasingly-stringent regulations as well as diminishing freights, and oil-price increases reduced profits all round. The net consequence was a sudden exodus of the opportunist element from the British register: between the mid-70s and 1982 178 ships were removed, some 54% of them foreign-owned, and sold either for scrap or for further trading in direct competition with British operations. During about the same interval the UK-flag tanker fleet shrank by 50% and in 1984 BP turned its shipping operation over to the offshore register and dismissed all its seagoing staff. Meanwhile, back at the ways, British shipbuilding was entering a period of unmistakable terminal decline, its workforce in conflict not with its lax management (as it thought) but with far-eastern competitors evidently beyond its ken. In 1977 it contributed a mere 4% to the world total of new tonnage, and the figure continued to fall. The passenger trades alone seemed to be retaining some sort of grip on existence, but in the form of a relatively healthy, if modest, cruising operation in distant playgrounds.

By 1980 the Greek-owned (both home-flag and f.o.c.) fleet had become the world's largest, leading Britain by several places. Moreover, the British fleet was changing its character: in 1971 deep-sea tonnage comprised 59% of its total, a figure that by 1986 stood at some 28%. Giving as their reasons crew costs and the weight of petty regulation, ship-operators (it seemed by this time an anachronism to call them owners) were either moving to offshore or convenience registers, or diversifying into other spheres of commerce altogether. In 1982 British interests were operating 2% of f.o.c. tonnage and managing some 6% on behalf of owners whose distinguishing characteristic seemed to be discreet obscurity. Whatever fresh investment there was went into ferries, short-sea and middle-trade tonnage while the short-haul tanker made way for the pipeline. An offshore supply fleet nurtured on North Sea oil and gas from the late 60s was variously scrapped, sold off and moved to distant locations as activity in the fields changed from exploration to flow.

The prevailing state of the British register was thrown into relief in 1982 when the Falklands affair cast it in its role of support and supply. Fifty-four UK-operated ships were taken up from trade (to use the official term) for service in the war zone while outside it foreign tonnage had to be chartered to cover British deficiency at rates stipulated by owners and governments free to take advantage of the British predicament. The lessons of two world wars had gone unlearned by successive British governments, and the taxpayer, as usual, had to make good the omission. By 1983 the remnants of the foreign-owned sector had departed and government made it clear that no further incentives were contemplated, tacitly admitting patent uninterest in the merchant fleet's fortunes. The episode proved to be a watershed: it was the last time a British-registered and controlled fleet could have been regarded as adequate for defensive purposes (distinct from obligations towards NATO). Decline continued in a world-wide fog of debt and falling prices as far-eastern yards continued with an apparently suicidal building programme. The British fleet contracted almost month by month, carrying less and less of the country's foreign trade and bringing in less and less foreign exchange while its redundant workforce either swelled the ranks of the unemployed or turned instead to foreign flags or another occupation.

Four hundred years after the destruction of the Armada the UK fleet, having achieved world supremacy, had been allowed to crumble to less than 2% of world tonnage. As for the seafaring population, it continued to be what it always had been, an eccentric minor proportion of one composed mainly of shopkeepers. Napoleon might have added soldiers and (heavily-subsidised) farmers to his observation. The British mercantile marine had grown with and as an integral part of empire, and with empire's fall it died. As it was government policy to divest itself of its overseas responsibilities with undignified haste, if not with ignominy, so it chose to disregard an industry without which the nation (if such it remains) will return to parochial obscurity and financial dependence on foreign (and ill-disposed) whim, a state of affairs against which the earlier Elizabethans had set their faces and pledged their self-respect.

I

Origins and Forebears: Middle Ages to Industrial Revolution.

*

Captain Bellwinch hailed from an old seafaring family in Staines. His grandmother, Charlotte Dundas, always wore high-button boots and six fearnought petticoats when scandalising a crossjack. She had a tug named after her and was reputed to be able to box the compass with her bare hands[1].

*

A KEEN and reflective observer, one-time marine engineer and widely-read author, the late William McFee once remarked on our tendency to flatter ourselves that in our veins flows the blood of the old Vikings. He went on to say that no faculty seems more general among the world's peoples than that of going to sea:

The history of other nations upon the oceans we are apt easily enough to forget, and it is convenient to ignore that long period in English history when the Island Race was very insular indeed, and Englishmen were unknown in any waters save those close inshore at home. [2]

Not to put too fine a point on it, the British (to be more exact) seafarer has always been something of a misfit; restless, romantic to a degree, dissatisfied, curious, to say nothing of

wastrels and farmers, lazy clerks and penniless journeymen fond of the bottle, strong rogues and masterless men, as well as authentic adventurers for whom the native island was grown too small[3].

In calling us a nation of shopkeepers Napoleon exhibited characteristic shrewdness, though he apparently failed to note that it was the misfit sailor (and soldier) who engineered his fate.

Born in 1652, William Dampier was orphaned at sixteen and sent to sea in the care of a shipmaster trading to Newfoundland. Weather apart, the chances are that he was unfavourably impressed by conditions on board, typified in a description by a near-

---

[1] *Recollections of Captain Bellwinch.*
[2] *Sir Martin Frobisher,* p.2.
[3] ibid. p.4.

contemporary, Edward Barlow, drawing parallels between his accommodation and "some gentleman's dog-kennel", though it was a view perhaps soured by his being knocked into the hold and fracturing his skull as a form of introduction to the life that touched upon the traditional: apprentices and open hatches seemed to possess a peculiar mutual attraction. And the victuals were, also seemingly by (British) tradition, another focus of disgruntlement. In Barlow's words

We were now forced to go one quart of beverage to one man a day...of sour wine and stinking water, which was very hard with us; and the weather being very hot and always eating salt victuals, I could not get my belly full, which often made me repent of going to sea...[1]

Christmas was celebrated with

a little bit of Irish beef for four men, which had lain in pickle two or three years...with a little stinking oil or butter[2].

Whether or not Dampier similarly regretted his circumstances he continued at sea but soon transferred himself to the lesser rigours of the East India Company's Merchant Service. Then, on the outbreak of war with the Dutch (for the third time) in 1672, he moved to the navy and thence, through illness and partial recovery, into private ventures of questionable ethics linked with the discovery of Australia. Though attaining some standing as a navigator, hydrographer and biologist he personified the sinister side of seafaring: self-willed, recalcitrant and difficult in manner, he was a rebellious subordinate and a bad commander, as Alexander Selkirk had probably concluded when marooned on Juan Fernandez I.[3] Unpopular and incompetent, his honesty and courage not infrequently in doubt, he would have presented the conscientious apprentice with a model and example of how not to do it if the approval of his betters was to be earned, though a bent for high adventure would have been more than adequately satisfied; what was more, and not surprisingly among birds of a feather apt to slip into one another's company, it seems that Dampier's foibles were reflected at various times among his officers, whom he described variously as "rogues, rascals or sons of bitches"[4]. Quite possibly the more philosophical of them saw him as

---

[1] *Barlow's Journal.* Quoted in *The Merchant Navy,* p.16. (Hope, R.)

[2] ibid. Barlow was later apprenticed to the master's mate of the Commonwealth warship *Naseby,* in which conditions would have been generally more uncomfortable than in a merchant vessel. (See p.36)

[3] Sailing-master of the *Cinque Ports* galley on Dampier's 1703 expedition. Of his own choice abandoned by Dampier in 1704 he lived alone on the island until rescued by Woodes Rogers in 1709. Born in 1676 the son of a poor shoemaker, he had gone to sea in fishing craft as a boy, and after his rescue joined the navy. He died aboard HMS *Weymouth* in the rank of master's mate in 1721.

[4] *Dictionary of National Biography,* Vol.V, p.456.

a "character", neither the first nor the last, to be suffered with resignation and later fitted into a tap-room's voyaging.

His story is an object-lesson. The sea was more than mere water and weather, its unavoidable entourage comprising a bewildering agglomerate of disease, bad food, difficult companions, privation, isolation (but never precious solitude except in adversity), monotony, fear, uncertainty and other hardships unimaginable by the shorebound, and if time has softened the starker features and rounded the sharper edges, the crudeness is still there, veiled by the illusions of technology, hooded by the contrivances of language and social sophistry. But for all that there is a dexter, of course. Adventure need not have been entirely lawless, the making of a fortune not entirely unprincipled; integrity and courage had their places and (sometimes) their rewards, and with these as talismen the negative aspects of the life could be discounted, or at least borne with patience and optimism. Even so, something more was usually necessary and for much of the time – until decline set in – it was an acknowledged national trait: tenacity, to the point of pig-headedness, was an indispensable asset. Yet here lies a paradox, evidence of the fallacy of the nation's identity with the sea: wastage has been a problem from time immemorial, worsening as life ashore improves in material quality.

Where the urge to go to sea, whether or not the result of expedient, was varnished with grand illusion, it was frequently aimed at the mark of shipmaster. Or aspirations might run higher and a penniless youth contemplate his chances of becoming an owner – a rich one, naturally. Setting foot on the deck of his first ship the apprentice was distinguishable, if not conspicuous, by his upturned gaze (oblivious of the open hatch at his feet, metaphorical as well as actual), his mind fixed on one object, untroubled, at least for the first few hours, by any trace of doubt about his future course...

Britain emerged from the Middle Ages an agrarian society relying on wool as the staple and on shipping to provide access to markets on the Continent. The merchant became a man of consequence and took to forming gilds[1], fellowships of exclusive professional and vocational interests that regulated standards of practice and conduct, perpetuating them through the system of apprenticeship, which, from its beginnings in the 13th century until the mid-19th, was the only recognised form of industrial training. When wars on the Continent brought refugee craftsmen to these shores they too formed gilds, eventually gaining parity with, then superseding, the merchant gilds and incorporating the apprenticeship system. It remained in place more or less unchanged in principle and form for the next five centuries, vesting in the master (of the trade or craft) responsibility for training prospective gild members, obliging him to lodge, board, clothe, discipline and instruct the apprentice in the ethos and methods of the gild, which exercised overall supervision through its officers. By around 1450 this

---

[1] This spelling conforms to early usage.

was the accepted avenue into all skilled trades, with seven years the customary period beginning at age 14. An earlier start meant a correspondingly longer apprenticeship.

It was natural that with a system so widespread and so adaptable it should be set up in the sea's crafts. Like his longshore contemporary the sea apprentice was placed in the hands of a master (not necessarily the ship's master, though it was often enough the case at a time when owner-masters were common) and trained – or at least made to work – as a seaman, the direct equivalent of a journeyman ashore. In the Bristol gilds, for example, the mariners were classed on three levels – master, yeoman and servant, the last further divided into two classes, one those who had three years' sea-time behind them and were able to hand, reef and steer, the other those of no experience, raw hands. Then came the indentured apprentice, his particulars kept on record at the guildhall. His time served, he would be qualified to sail before the mast as yeoman, otherwise able-bodied seaman, there existing in the different trades more or less effective means of assessing his ability. From that point forward his rise to master (if he got that far) depended on circumstances, ranging from outright nepotism to opportunity, ability and the disposition of superiors – and, of course, on his own ambitions and intentions.

Some were articled under the auspices of Admiralty with the express purpose of fitting them to become officers, the appointed masters commanded to instruct them in navigation and seamanship as distinct from the method that often passed for instruction, a process of osmosis by which the boy absorbed whatever he could from involvement with the ship's work. In the mid-16th century the Muscovy Company, setting the tone for the chartered companies, required its masters to see that apprentices were taught navigation under proper supervision, and that records were kept of their work.

However, before then, by the mid-15th century, some five seamen's gilds were extant, taking apprentices on indenture in the ships commanded by their respective masters, but the boys' immediate antecedents had appeared in the craft gilds concerned with the ship's construction and operation. Although British seafaring before the outbreak of Elizabethan sea-fever was a timorous affair confined to the home coasts and short seas, overshadowed by the fleets of continental port-states, there was at least a complementary shipbuilding industry: the small yards, or hard-standings, which turned out clinker-built cogs and nefs and other vessels of wonderfully unhandy and unweatherly type employed shipwrights, carpenters, joiners, rope-makers and riggers, sailmakers and coopers and a small army of others. Most had their apprentices, who in some cases – the shipwright, for example – would find themselves at sea with their masters in the ships they had helped to build. And not only to continue in their chosen craft: often enough they would also be instructed (or would interest themselves) in the art of the seaman-navigator – the mariner – and turn to the sea as a trade, or profession, instead.

To some – to growing numbers as time passed – it was a heady prospect: authentic adventurers, perhaps, imaginations fired by second-hand experience of sun-drenched alternatives to the grey seas and lowering skies of their native patch. By the end of the 15th century the Portuguese had voyaged to the Orient, fingering the coast of Africa *en route*, and although British-flag venturing was negligible by comparison the yarns of sailormen at a time when crews were drawn impartially from any shore struck bright shafts through the smoky fug of waterside taverns. Officially denied the apprentice, they were clandestinely accessible, and the sea's entitlement to high adventure undeniable.

In 1634 John Maddocks was indentured for seven years to one Christopher Birkett (and the man's wife to boot) in the business of "shipwright and mariner". Twenty years later he was not only a master shipwright but also pilot, or navigator, of the *Robert* of Bristol, 90 tons burthen, on a voyage to Bordeaux[1], but which, alas, ended prematurely in capture by a Fleming. But by this time the seaman apprentice, bound to a specialist navigator through one of the gilds, was firmly established while Maddocks's kind of apprenticeship was dropping out of vogue. In 1572 Robert Harison,

Off thayge of xiiitine yeres, byndyth hym to be apprentice and servant to and with William Walker of this town of Liverpolle and his assignes, hym well and trulie to serve and obey in the art and science of navigacion...duryng all the whoolle terme of tenne yeres fullie to be expired completid and endyd...[2]

By this indenture Walker undertook to provide clothing, *meat, dryncke and ludgincke* and instruction, and at the end of the stipulated time to pay Harison 13/4d plus another outfit of clothes. The length of service on indenture was at the time governed by the Statute of Apprentices[3] of 1562, which decreed that it should not expire before age 24 and in any case be no shorter than seven years[4].

No changes were made to this until 1814, except for its extension and qualification by Act of Parliament in Anne's reign (1702-14): *For the Increase of Seamen & the Better Encouragement of Navigation[5]*. Under this, it was held, the navy would be assured of a supply of competent seamen when in need. In 1814 it was extensively amended by another Act, when compulsion was dropped, but re-invoked in 1823,

---

[1] Probably in the wine-trade, from which the measure *ton* evolved, the space occupied by a standard wine-tun in the hold. A measure of volume, not weight.

[2] Liverpool Town Books, Vol. 2. Appx. VI. (Twemlow)

[3] Also called the Statute of Labour or Labourers, of which it formed a part.

[4] Under the Poor Law of 1598 any poor workless child (*sic*) could be bound apprentice to ease the burden on the rates, and was often sent to sea in this capacity.

[5] By it pauper boys of the parish could be compulsorily bound to the sea aged 10, to be released at 21. Also, the master of any apprentice could pack him off to sea at will: the justices, mayors, aldermen, portreeves and other authorities whose consent was required for the purpose were mostly either directly or indirectly interested in the shipping business, and to them a supply of cheap labour was always welcome. The last thing they were likely to do was object to the intentions of the Guardians of the Poor or the masters of burdensome apprentices.

ostensibly to ensure sufficient manning for a growing merchant fleet but in the process providing the navy once again with a cost-free reserve.

Act of Parliament notwithstanding, however, it was possible to get command of something that floated well before the statutory age of release, and time on indenture was often honoured more in the breach than the observance, expiry or termination always subject to mutual agreement; moreover, the indenture was, and remained, transferable from master to master, both within a trade or profession and from one to another. At Walker's death four years after the document's signing, Harison's was altered to bind him for the rest of his time to Walker's widow, evidently a woman of parts.

Apprenticeship was not only a means of keeping up the numbers of seamen, but also, undoubtedly, a way of getting rid of refuse, the sea being a handy receptacle for it whether mineral, vegetable, animal or human, and boys, often occurring in over-abundance, were looked upon without much gladness. Sentimentality, however, has played its part in their emancipation (and ruin), Dickens's perhaps most prominently before modern times and muddle-headed social engineering, or tinkering, rose to favour:

The Board took counsel together on the expediency of shipping off Oliver Twist in some small trading vessel bound to a good unhealthy port; which suggested itself as the very best thing that could possibly be done with him: the probability being, that the skipper would flog him to death, in a playful mood, some day after dinner; or would knock his brains out with an iron bar; both pastimes being, as is pretty generally known, a very favourite and common recreation among gentlemen of that class.[1]

It was certainly a favourite and common recreation to portray them in that light and to read about them, and whatever the extent of Dickens's (or general) knowledge of shipboard discipline[2] his observations reflected something of the public's perception of the sea-captain as it had evolved from the outset. It wasn't without foundation in fact, though the experiences of James Knox were tilted towards the extreme, which, unfortunately, has a propensity for catching the eye at the expense of normal practice:

I got a berth as an apprentice aboard the Liverpool ship *Martha*, signing indentures for four years in November, 1819. She traded to Barbados and Demarara, where one of her owners had sugar and cotton plantations. The mate was a bully and a drunkard and was discharged without a character on our return. The second mate lacked experience though a good seaman, but the crowd were a mixed bag, scum and good men who knew their trade, hard cases and shirkers. They regarded apprentices as dogs to be kicked and ill-treated. One Sunday the captain had

---

[1] *The Adventures of Oliver Twist*, p.22.

[2] His father was an impecunious pay clerk. He (Charles) crossed to the USA twice, and to the Continent a number of times, during his literary career, in which he combined an over-developed sense of social justice with a gift for caricature that frequently descended into bathos.

words with the mate about the setting of sail, abusing him scurrilously and finally ordering him below. The mate not obeying instantly, the captain seized him by the collar and attempted to throw him down the after hatch, but failing, tore off the mate's waistcoat then jumped on him, after which he deprived him of his rank. The captain also quarrelled with the passengers, treating them like animals.[1]

As for the treatment meted out to the apprentices, Dickens might have spoken to Knox before writing *Oliver Twist*:

One of our number got hold of some liquor and was too drunk for duty. Johnston and myself were thereupon ordered to secure him to a gun and give him two dozen apiece. We refused, at which the mate laid into us with a rope's end. Johnston was hit in the left eye, which he very nearly lost. That day also, the cook was sentenced to be punished for spoiling the cabin dinner, and was lashed to the windlass. We took advantage of this to give him half a dozen each as thanks for his feeding, but again we were brought before the mate and given another rope's-ending for our act. The man who took his place at Liverpool was as bad, threatening on one occasion to brain us with a handspike. We in turn swore to do no work, and two of my fellows deserted. There was endless feuding in that ship. The cook was at the root of most of the unrest, or was blamed for it. The steward vowed to kill him, and one of our number [apprentices] aided him, trying to knock out the cook but instead occasioning his death[2].

What Dickens omitted to mention was that, however hard the conditions and treatment, the boys themselves were no angels, and quite as tough, if not tougher, than older men on board. Those who weren't usually slipped away. Nevertheless this sort of thing typified the popular view, which survived long after its uncertain authenticity, appealing more to the emotions than to the intellect and doing many good men an injustice in their perpetual conflict with a hostile environment and its bloody-minded creatures. As an apprentice of a later generation aptly put it, "...we didn't go to sea to be refined."[3]

Samuel Kelly served his time from 1778-82 in the Post Office packets on the West Indies run, finding somewhat better-regulated conditions than in ships like the *Martha*. He lived in the focsle with the hands but messed with the mates and, placed in the second mate's watch, was taught the use of the quadrant by the sailing-master and the use of his fists and small arms by the gunner. His station was in the maintop and his sail the main royal. He kept his turn at lookout on the fore crosstrees, where he found the exaggerated motion too much for his stomach at first. Sleeping on watch brought a flogging, and for being late heaving the log (every hour) a drenching with bucketfuls of sea-water.

In the islands he acted as salesman in the captain's private ventures, finding the best customers among the whores with whom he consorted, while at sea additional duties

---

[1] Reconstructed from the description in *Seamen All,* pp.70-86.

[2] ibid. pp.70-86.

[3] *Tramps and Ladies*, p.65.

included assisting the steward in attending the passengers. Almost at the end of his time his ship was captured by an American frigate but was shortly afterwards re-taken by HMS *Garland* and the voyage resumed. Arrived in London he was interviewed by the underwriters about the Americans' expropriation of some of the cargo, and seems to have been rewarded for his evidence, having enough money to drop into a brothel on his way back to the ship.

Offered a place as 4th mate in the HEIC he had to refuse because he could not afford it, and instead got a berth, through the offices of a crimp, as AB at £3 a month in a ship run only nominally by her master, the master's wife having the last word. In Kelly's case it was to the effect that no-one who hadn't served his time in east coast colliers could ship as AB, so he had to accept the rating of ordinary seaman while musing on the seaman's adage that women at sea are omens of bad luck.

The coastal trade that employed a major proportion of British seamen before the rise of the deep-sea fleet depended to a large extent on coal as the cargo, the greatest movement of it from the north-east of England to London with its beginnings in the carriage of "sea-cole" gathered from exposed seams before deep mining started. As did other trades, it produced its own type of vessel, and the collier brig with her way of life endured almost unchanged from Tudor times until the closing years of the 19th century, the apprentice integral to her operation. From him evolved the foremast hand, the cook, the mate and the master, in that order, a system which illustrates the apprentice's position as conceived and as it remained into the 20th century: he was an apprentice *seaman* and not an embryo officer *per se* (unless under Admiralty edict, and with one or two exceptions among shipowners in certain trades), though the officer is a seaman by definition. A certain sense of grievance was expressed by those who saw themselves as prospective officers when, instead of being taught the officer's duties, whatever they were understood to be, they received treatment similar to, and often worse than, that of the focsle hands, or "common sailors", who, of course, had served their time. In fact it wasn't until after the establishment of steamship companies that indentures moved generally towards a form of agreement on the master's part to instruct the apprentice in the officer's business. They were few, though, and restricted to the liner trades; most committed themselves to nothing more than the business of a seaman, which was taken to mean deckhand, until the end of the 1930s, though the apprentice's commitment to qualify as an officer was implicit in the agreement.

In the collier he was one of perhaps eight of his kind, living in the focsle, performing menial chores there and in the cabin. Often the son of a professional acquaintance of the master, even one of the master's own family, he served his time learning, more by example and experience than by formal tuition, about the coastal routes, the ships, the methods and peculiarities of the trade and the nature and handling of the cargoes. Navigation was rudimentary, rule of thumb its principle. At times of slack trade voyages were made to the Baltic and Mediterranean, and in winter, when ships were laid up, his place of work was among the servants of the master's household. *Servant*, whether at sea or ashore, was the customary alternative, or supplementary, title for the apprentice.

Boys fortunate enough to have parents concerned about their futures were sometimes found berths as supernumeraries so that a foretaste of the life could be sampled, a practice that occasionally misfired from either point of view: intended to put the boy off it stoked up his enthusiasm, and *vice versa*. In 1780 a certain William Richardson, aged 12, accompanying his father, master of the brig *Ravensworth*, completed three voyages in the comparative luxury of the cabin before taking up a formal apprenticeship to the master of the brig *Forester*, 350 tons. Completing his time he received a gratuity of £25 and the freedom of Newcastle-on-Tyne, *Forester*'s master being a freeman. He was also, evidently, a man of integrity, for he ensured that William attended Newcastle Trinity House School during the winter, where navigation was, so to speak, the core subject. When not at his books the boy was employed about his master's house as a general factotum. To a sailor housework was no indignity, since its principles and practice apply to the ship as a matter of course.

Detailed accounts of apprentices' lives during this period are rare, but among the colliers are a few of note. Vice Admiral Sir Samuel Cornish (d.1770) was indentured to a collier master, afterwards serving in HEIC ships before joining the navy as a seaman. A progression far from uncommon, it illustrates the reason behind compulsory carriage of apprentices (and the compulsory apprenticeship of all seamen), the merchant apprentice forming the raw material from which the naval man was fashioned, a process distinct from the custom of Admiralty-contracted apprenticeships[1]. Because of it he was in theory exempt from impressment, but it was a qualified privilege. Barlow was pressed the moment his indentures expired, to his surprise, since he was under the impression that exemption applied for some three years beyond his time. In fact he was the press's legitimate prey from the age of 18, time-expired or not, but only if he had signed indentures voluntarily (which he had), a regulation that excluded the pauper (parish) apprentice, who was accordingly liable to impressment from the outset, though the tendency was to leave him where he was until he had learned enough to be useful in a man-o'-war.

So the 18-year-old, whether pauper or eager hand, was the press's prime target, by that age being skilled in a sailor's work, his services at a premium in warships otherwise cursed with the sweepings of the gutter and the jails' detritus – even hospital cases. The navy took care to distinguish between the two, the ordinary man-o'-war's man never having seen any other kind of ship or service. Thus, except at the end of a long war, the navy had few men trained by its own hand, and in 1815, though many seamen had entered as boys and been raised in the service, it had been at the price of

---

[1] The Act of Queen Anne obliged masters to carry apprentices in numbers according to the ship's tonnage: from 30 to 50, one; for the next 50, one, and one for each 100 tons over that figure. For example, a ship of 300 tons was required to carry four, as was one of 350 tons, while one of 400 tons took five.

some twenty years of warfare; even so, they seldom formed more than a minority of a ship's crew. After 1815, though in theoretical existence, the press ceased its activities, at least in the traditional heavy-handed way for which it had become notorious.

Some pre-empted the inevitable, and one John Campbell, a Kirkcudbrightshire clergyman's son and collier apprentice, volunteered in place of the mate when the press paid his ship a business call in the 1730s. He sailed later as midshipman under Anson on his circumnavigation and became *Victory*'s first commander.

In later times one of the most conspicuous (and, in his own eyes at least, most distinguished) was Walter Runciman, owner of a tramp fleet of renown. However, forerunning him by a century, and of a different mould, was a name that stands alongside Drake and Nelson, if it doesn't dwarf them out of hand. James Cook, son of a farm labourer, was born at Marton-in-Cleveland in 1728. After absorbing the three R's at a dame school in Great Ayton he made a brief essay into farm work before apprenticeship, aged 17, to a grocer and haberdasher of Staithes, but almost immediately had his indentures transferred to one John Walker, a Quaker coal-merchant and shipowner of Whitby, who recognised exceptional abilities in his acolyte. As a result Cook found himself passing the winter months at home with the Walkers, not in the capacity of general dogsbody but under close supervision studying maths and navigation. Out of his time he signed on as a deckhand in the Baltic trade, later, in 1752, returning to Walker's service as mate. Three years after that Walker offered him a command, none too soon as those things were gauged, but Cook found collier life circumscribed and stultifying, and at the outbreak of war with France volunteered for the navy. The rest is history, though one of its less well-known facets was the loss to the Hydrographic Office of what would have been its greatest honour and distinction. After a good deal of spurious cogitation the Admiralty was prevailed upon by George III to appoint Cook as its first hydrographer, the decision arrived at during his absence on his third, fatal, voyage, an event that could have been prevented by earlier resolution. Instead, Alexander Dalrymple, hydrographer to the HEIC, was appointed; a capable man, but no Cook.

Until the 19th century no universal standard of accomplishment was required of the ship's officer: as in the colliers his fitness for the task was assessed within the respective trade, either through reports by the masters (of the ships) or by examination before a panel of qualified men, both proven hands and shipmasters. Some tests were more rigorous than others, of course, and owed something to local pride and jealousy. Blyth seamen, as Walter Runciman observed, always certified themselves the best in the world, and regarded Hartley (i.e. Hartlepool) men as inferior, putting it about that the Hartley men's recommendation of themselves amounted to

silvery, whining appeals to owners and captains, the former to give them a command, and the latter to take them on as able seaman, cook or mate.

Of the Blyth camp, Runciman continues:

It was (at the Dock House) that the most exacting examination of young men in seamanship, when they had honourably served out their time, was made, and a certificate of qualification was given them to sail on a union-manned[sic] vessel as able seaman. The committee of experts was not over-endowed with scholarship, but they were unequalled in their knowledge of their profession and showed no partiality against candidates who came before them.[1]

In some quarters the tests were not limited to technical skills. In the HEIC, for example, competence was of secondary importance to social and financial qualifications and only loosely regulated and assessed until, perversely, the approach of the organisation's demise. The Levant, or Turkey, Company, incorporated by charter in 1581, evolved by a roundabout but traceable route into the HEIC, incorporated by charter in 1600, to follow the Dutch round the Cape in a resumption of commercial interests blocked overland by the ill-disposed Ottoman Turks. And so, from the beginning of the 17th century, the apprentice began to assume the identity of midshipman, whose duties, however, originated on the lower deck, where, as a selected hand, he kept order. It wasn't until much later – the early 18th century – that he metamorphosed into a trainee officer whose outlook and prospects were vastly less restricted than, if not dizzily elevated above, the apprentice's. And yet, in contrast to the pragmatic complexion of collier practice, promotion, or outright appointment, to command depended less on ability than on social and commercial connections, plus financial standing that had to be firm enough to assure advancement in a similar way to the process of securing commissions in the army and navy. East Indiamen were too often commanded by professionally unfit men, whose lack of competence was balanced to some extent by some of the finest officers of the day. However, blissfully oblivious of all this, the latter-day HEIC midshipman was apt to indulge in visions of a future framed in gold, and had a realistic chance of achieving it. The chance improved when, in 1793, a proper system of compulsory examination was set up by the company alarmed at the consequences and implications of incompetence.

While the limelight, such as it was, played on the corporate ventures of the chartered companies, less spectacular, though no less valuable, enterprises were afoot on a steadily expanding scale, refuting the claims to maritime sovereignty made by the Spanish, the Portuguese, the Hanses and the Italians. In every arena of this activity could be found the apprentice, nondescript, of variable drive and ability, devoting himself as much to the avoidance of work as to carrying out his duties, performing his allotted function in a spirit of philosophical fatalism, prepared to make the best of his opportunities, not unduly dismayed by setbacks; the essence, in fact, of what was becoming the British maritime ethos, a hard core of sound, unspectacular commitment to a trade, or craft, that, as a way of life going beyond mere vocation, fringed upon the category of profession.

---

[1] *Collier Brigs and Their Sailors*, p.31.

Born in Kent in 1633, Edward Coxere recorded his experiences from the age of 14[1], when he was sent across the Channel to learn French. His father kept an inn at Dover, The Wheatsheaf, and, in the absence of any marked inclination in the boy to do anything in particular for a living, first apprenticed him to a cooper. The experiment lasted a week, after which, his mind not settling to a trade, as he put it, his lot fell to the sea. Coxere's problem was lack of motivation, not unusual in boys of his age but in contrast to the mood of another innkeeper's son, Robert Drury:

Notwithstanding all the education my father bestowed on me I could not be brought to think of any art, science, trade, business or profession of any kind whatsoever but going to sea...[2]

He entered the HEIC's Merchant Service, was shipwrecked on the coast of Madagascar and held captive by tribesmen for fifteen years, returning home in 1716. Then, after a slaving voyage to the scene of his adventure, perhaps in an uncomplicated spirit of retribution, he abandoned the sea in favour of a literary life, marked by publication of an account of his experiences.

More sceptic than enthusiast, Coxere was then sent to sea with James Moran, master/owner of the *Malaga Factor*, for a trial period to see if liked it. He didn't, and returned to his mother's welcome, and evidently less than that from his father, for after a while passed in idleness, the old tiresome tone sounded in my ears again: "What trade now?" which grew unpleasant for me.[3]

The upshot was a berth as a boy in HMS *St George*, second rate, inadvertently put out of commission by a fire before the cruise began, so returning Coxere yet again to the maternal bosom and, presumably, paternal exasperation. From this point his story unfolds with distinct undertones of *Treasure Island*, for next appeared at The Wheatsheaf an Irish sea-captain, resident of Amsterdam and occasional patron of the inn. Although he, Tilly, was no Billy Bones, nor was there a map of an island with buried treasure, parallels lay in Coxere's adoption by Tilly as his servant, followed by adventures of a piratical nature that earned Coxere treasure of a less prurient, though no less valuable, kind than pieces of eight. Captain Tilly brooked no nonsense, was a disciplinarian, and scrupulously fair: though he was severe he would not strike me nor suffer me to be struck.[4]

But the right note had been struck, for Coxere served Tilly through a whirl of trading and fighting ventures (the two were barely distinguishable from each other) for the next five months, so impressing his master that he was promised command by an early date. The boy was seventeen, and went on to sail under one of Tilly's captains (the Irishman's liberal conception of trade was sufficiently lucrative to finance ownership of several vessels) to the Barbary Coast flying Spanish colours of

[1] *Adventures by Sea of Edward Coxere.*
[2] *Dictionary of National Biography, Vol VI.*
[3] *Adventures by Sea etc.*, p.5.
[4] ibid., p.7.

convenience, or opportunity, in a prolonged action against his own countrymen that expressed something of Tilly's ambivalence in matters of national allegiance. Returning from the voyage the ship, at anchor in the Downs, was arrested on suspicion of succouring the enemy, and Coxere narrowly escaped an abrupt end to his career with the help of a Deal hoveller. Landing undetected, he made his way home in the guise of a Fleming, by this time fluent in Dutch as well as Spanish and French. The episode effectively ended his apprenticeship, for his next step was to sign on before the mast in a London ship at 41/- a month. He rose in due process to sail as master and acquired ownership of a small vessel before obscure and reasonably comfortable retirement.

To distinguish between one trade and another in terms of social or professional standing would be not only invidious but also misleading, and the collier and East Indiaman represent extremes of principle and practice that possessed equal validity and credit in their respective spheres. The wider middle ground, tenanted by the likes of Tilly, pursued its affairs for the most part screened from, or beyond the range of, the fitful glare of public attention, which is the merchant service's peculiar glory. Slate, for example, sustained its own obscure fleet of small vessels plying the coasts, while fishing supported a variegated and extensive fleet working at greater distances from home waters. A branch of it followed the whale.

If whaling strikes the onlooker as an occupation requiring nothing more intellectually taxing than brute force he has missed the point. The actual business of whale-catching was one thing, and demanded great skill, but the process of getting to the grounds, working them, and getting home again involved skills of navigation and seamanship of a high order, and whaling captains enjoyed considerable professional regard. Among them several names have echoed through the ages, Scoresby's probably loudest and longest. William the elder, born near Whitby in 1760, studied navigation and at 19 was apprenticed to the master of a Baltic trader. In 1785 he signed on as ordinary seaman in the whaler *Henrietta* and passed his entire career in the trade, retiring from command in 1823. His son William, whose brother Thomas became a doctor, was born in 1789. He found school, conducted in an atmosphere of pedagogic tyranny, a fraught affair, so his father took him on a voyage in the *Dundee* when he was ten. Whatever its purpose (perhaps to demonstrate the classroom's bearable pettiness when compared to the rigours of working life to come) he was returned to school until apprenticed to his father in 1803. Three years later he was sailing as mate, remaining in the trade until 1822, when he entered the clergy, later moving on to an academic life in which he distinguished himself. To him goes the credit for inventing the crow's nest and, in company with his father and another whaling captain named Jackson, the survey and charting of some 400 miles of Greenland's east coast.

Whaling was a hard school in an age of hard schools. From its beginnings in the North Atlantic it drifted into Arctic waters in the wake of the Dutch, then, in the late 1780s, rounded the Horn to meet its American counterpart in the South Seas.

Although obscure except in the autobiography left to posterity[1], Robert Eastwick painted as vivid a picture of the life as did Melville and Dana of theirs. Eastwick's father died a week before he was born, and his early years as an only child and his mother's indulgence produced a precocious brat impervious to discipline, at least to the insipid kind applied at home and school. His precocity was nourished and promoted by trips to London with his mother's stepfather, one Isaac English, a City man, when he was allowed, aged 8, to wander about the docks (Was old man English hoping for the worst, or simply trusting in the devil?), where he met seafaring men and, no doubt, plausible impostors who willingly stoked his imagination in exchange for treats in the public houses:

I did not then know the habit of exaggeration which is common to sailors, but believed implicitly everything that was told me.[2]

One cannot help wondering how much of that habit had rubbed off on the master mariner by the time he came to write his memoirs, conjuring up such an extraordinary scene. However...

Incipient leanings towards the sea crystallised at sight of *Resolution* and *Discovery* off Sheerness, ensigns at half-hoist and Cook's death recorded in their logs, exactly the kind of event guaranteed to confirm both faint-hearts and authentic adventurers in their respective convictions. Spoilt brat though he was, Eastwick was no faint-heart: he got himself embroiled in the Gordon Riots, ran away from a boarding-school that failed to curb his self-assertion and, at the end of his mother's long tether, passed into the hands of Dr Thomas Green at Merchant Taylors'. There he and corporal punishment collided regularly with no apparent damage to either and no beneficial effect whatsoever on his hardening resolve, which appeared to promise certain and substantial wealth and renown[3]. Further harm was done by the tales of two fellow-pupils, sons of a sea-captain, and with school running a poor second in a two-horse race Eastwick mounted a campaign of pointed agitation to end it. When he threatened to volunteer for the navy old English decided in favour of a quiet life and through his business connections arranged an apprenticeship with a well-known London firm, Enderby & Sons[4], operating several vessels in the "southern whale fishery". Eastwick observed that

it was the custom to article a lad for a period of four years to the seafaring profession, however respectable he might be [sic], and boys did not enter...life in the merchant service[5] as

---

[1] *A Master Mariner.*
[2] ibid., p.9.
[3] ibid. p.17.
[4] Mentioned by Melville in *Moby Dick.*
[5] Not to be confused with the HEIC's Merchant Service, in this instance the reference being to the general merchant fleet.

midshipmen, but as common apprentices, very dirty to look at, messing in the forecastle with the sailors, and being expected to perform all the most menial duties on board [1].

So much for social aspirations, and for the popular conception of "the seafaring profession". Eastwick was twelve when he joined the *Friendship*, a name loaded with sea irony.

In the mate he found the brutality of an animal and the vulgarity of a customs-house officer[2], a man who immediately set about making the new apprentice's "respectable birth and decent appearance" a burden to him. Mere sight of the boy moved him to volleys of oaths and vows to cut him down to size: a clean shirt was

a sure passport to being sent aloft, with a grease-bag around my neck. Each new article of apparel set him to discovering some filthy job to put me to.[3]

But perhaps the mate deserved a kinder press than he got from Eastwick. Faced with the task of managing a hard-bitten crew, not all prime seamen, and a ship commanded, as she was, by a kindly-disposed master (invariably seen as a weakness by certain elements in all crews), his work was cut out for him, and charitable instincts were the last sentiments to have been aroused by a twelve-year-old accustomed to seeing adults quail before his juvenile truculence. In fact Eastwick had the grace to acknowledge, if grudgingly, that the mate's methods hastened maturity, as they were meant to, an unabating round of impositions and indignities aimed at the boy's self-regard, a make-or-break process that was bound to succeed either way. In the event the *Friendship*'s mate was the first person in Eastwick's experience to treat him as a man and not a child, and the shock was shrewdly calculated. Its outcome lay in the lap of the gods, of course, and perhaps the balance was tipped by the advice of an elderly sailor in the ship, bleakly sympathetic:

There is no justice or injustice aboard ship, only Duty and Mutiny... Lads have to learn: discipline is good for them[4].

And for the community around them, for that matter...
Continuously at sea, the voyage lasted sixteen months, and during it Eastwick

gained a practical knowledge of many of a seaman's duties and...there was scarce any operation...in which I could not lend a hand...[5]

---

[1] *A Master Mariner*, p.21.
[2] ibid., p.21.
[3] ibid., p.22.
[4] ibid. p.25.
[5] ibid., p.25.

On his return home his mother failed to recognise him (one of the mate's vows realised, maybe...), with his childish petulance transformed into self-confidence and, even better, selfishness replaced by consideration for others. In short he was a classic advertisement for the value of a hard school as the remedy for the silly and sometimes dangerous arrogance of youth.

He sailed again in the *Friendship*, under a new master who took an active interest in his academic instruction, and added navigation to his stock. His last whaling voyage, under an American in another ship, saw him out of his time in 1790, before his eighteenth birthday, and certified "eligible for the duties of a first officer", that is, first mate. After this he went into other trades, retiring in 1824 when in command of the last of the ships he had owned.

With illiteracy common ashore, it was also prevalent among ships' officers and masters, allied, as the 19th century opened, with widespread incompetence. Commentators such as Coxere, Cook and Eastwick have to represent, albeit in a somewhat over-sanguine light, the multitude apprenticed to workaday masters, while at the opposite end of the scale was the boy with the connections and social position to enable him to enter the navy or – in some ways a better career – the HEIC as an officer under training. Towards the last days of the great company's existence, on the threshold of earth-shaking changes in the structure and function of the mercantile marine, Thomas Addison, aged 17, joined the *Marquis Wellesley* as a midshipman. The age requirement for new entrants was between 13 and 18. It was 1802, and the company's ships were fitted out to defend themselves, if necessary, though not very adequately, against thoroughgoing men-o'-war, and commonly and more effectively against pirates. They were also liable to co-option into naval service and their crews to impressment as the war with France, momentarily suspended by the Treaty of Amiens, smouldered its way towards Trafalgar and Waterloo.

One Matthew White, the India husband who accepted Addison, was a business acquaintance of Edmund Antrobus, a London banker and tea-importer on intimate terms with the Addisons, and he launched the boy on his career with a letter to his ship's chief mate which was presented after first calling on the company-approved tailor. This gentleman would discreetly have advised on changes to the list of outfit, more or less to his own advantage and the satisfaction of the new customer, also arranging to send the entire wardrobe, ranging from knee-breeches to telescope, buckle-shoes to sea-chest, oilskins to table napkins, aboard by carrier, the account to be settled when convenient. The HEIC officer's credit probably stood higher among such businessmen than that of his armed service contemporary, what with the company's trade monopoly and the custom of allowing ample scope for private ventures which usually yielded handsome returns, to say nothing of his prospects of staying alive long enough to pay his debts.

Next came Addison's introduction to the other midshipmen, housed not in the gunroom, as in the navy, but similarly in a mess presided over by one of the junior mates. The new hand was promptly despatched to the mizentop and ambush by a couple of sailors, to be triced to the rigging for an indefinite period of rest and reflection, but he had been tipped off (by whom he doesn't say, but items of germane information were often tendered by the outfitter as part of the service), and ransomed himself with the promise of a gallon of ale, a tactic that obliged him to treat his new messmates to five. The point of the exercise, apart from the proper need to impress upon the new chum the fact of his insignificance, was to introduce him to the midshipman's special domain and responsibility, the mizen-mast. As a custom it survived in sail to the last, not by any means universally but commonly enough to be recognised for what it was. Writing retrospectively in 1935 Captain Sir David Wilson-Barker, RNR, referred to it:

> ...in Green's...it was the rule that the midshipmen had to take charge of the mizen-mast and do all the work there under the charge of an experienced seaman.[1]

They were just as much under the eye of the officer of the watch at his post on the poop, quite possibly the reason for the practice in the first place. R&H Green was one of the well-found Blackwall-based successors to the HEIC, retaining many old traditions but running a much tauter operation and ultimately passing into the hands of the famous firm of Devitt & Moore, whose name became a byword in sea training under sail[2].

Marquis Wellesley sailed from the Thames in February, 1802, and reached Madras nearly five months later, a normal voyage on which Addison and another first-voyager were introduced to Neptune:

> ...we underwent the accustomed and awful ordeal of shaving by the hands of His Majesty's barber, thereby rendering us free mariners of the ocean.[3]

At Madras the peace was celebrated in the company of a squadron of French warships but later, on the homeward passage, preparations were made for an encounter with them in the resumed hostilities. Addison's action station was in the magazine as powder-monkey, but in the event the only disruption to the voyage took the shape of the Royal Navy, which helped itself to the best of the Indiaman's crew. Sailing on, they arrived at Deptford to learn of the disconcerting occurrence of the owner's bankruptcy and inability to pay their wages. The commander's salary at the time was £10 a month, the chief mate's £5, and so on, diminishing through the ranks to the £2.5s received by the midshipman, which made him about £2.5s better off than his contemporaries in other services and, in proportion to his responsibilities, rather better paid than the commander. That gentleman, as a matter of interest, would have been unconcerned by the owner's misfortune, since he usually cleared anything between

---

[1] Foreword: *Seamen in the Making*, p.vi.
[2] See Ch. 8.
[3] *The Old East Indiamen*, p.205.

£5,000 and £8,000 each voyage, sometimes more, through his private venture allowance of part of the ship's freight space and a portion (sometimes all) of the passenger fares. The space allowance was granted *pro rata* to all officers and petty officers. However, in this instance there was also open to the master and crew recourse to ancient custom, equivalent to law where not specifically embodied in it, whereby they held a lien on the ship and her cargo by way of unpaid wages; but Addison gives no indication of whether or not it was invoked.

On his next appointment, to the *Brunswick*, 1,200 tons charter, bound for Ceylon and China, he found himself senior of five midshipman and commander's coxswain, the other four on their first voyage, each accommodated in his own cabin attended by a steward. A one-time naval officer who had displayed rather more initiative than the navy had felt comfortable with, the commander turned out to be a martinet, though an impartial one and a keen observer of the social graces:

Two of us dined with him every day, and nothing could exceed his politeness and kindness at table[1].

Following standard practice they sailed in convoy, departing the Mother Bank in March 1804, falling into sea routine after clearing the Western Approaches:

On a Saturday (weather permitting) constantly exercised great guns, and small arms frequently, with powder blank cartridges. My station at quarters was aide-de-camp to the captain[2].

An improvement on powder-monkey.

Twenty-four days out their escort, the frigate *Lapwing*, parted company and with *Brunswick* as commodore the convoy pressed on free of the threat of naval interference, at least from the British. In the Mozambique Channel they fell in with a French brig, *La Charlotte*, four guns, and Addison witnessed both the wretched Frenchman's precipitate and unconditional surrender and an example of the cause of the navy's sour regard for his captain's methods. The HEIC's strict instructions were that its ships were only to be defended against attack, and it would have taken a dim view of this cavalier interpretation of an encounter with an obviously uninterested party, tricolour notwithstanding, which might, *in extremis*, have done the Indiaman, and her owner's pocket, some damage. As it turned out, *La Charlotte*'s entire cargo consisted of muskets, and she was handed back to her people after the hold's contents had been pitched overside in disgust.

If such diversions, whether complying with company standing orders or not, lacked enough pace and pepper a young man could apply for service in the HEIC's naval arm, a much more aggressive service operating as the Bombay Marine, forerunner of the

---

[1] *The Old East Indiamen*, p.208.

[2] ibid. p.210.

Royal Indian Navy and its republican descendants. Pirates constituted an intermittent nuisance which had to be suppressed in the company's trading interests, and Addison might well have heard tales, unnecessarily embellished, of the *Viper* incident during the closing years of the previous century. At anchor off Bushire the cruiser (as the company's warships were called) was assailed by local entrepreneurs in their dhows. In the absence of the captain, ashore with a couple of his officers on company business, the first lieutenant cut the cable and engaged the attackers, but received a shot in the head that killed him. Matters then fell into the hands of the remaining officer, a midshipman, who distinguished himself by continuing the action and variously sinking and driving off the pirates.

Even so, life in an Indiaman was anything but one of unfettered glory and gain, and confrontations with enemies weren't always attended by victory: if he survived, a midshipman could all too easily find himself reduced to a company pension (a scheme was in operation) and a pair of crutches. When the *Warren Hastings* was attacked by the frigate *Piemontaise* in June 1805 her shortcomings as a fighting unit quickly became apparent, in sharp counterpoint to the bravery of her officers and hands, who were finally overwhelmed by boarders evidently the worse for drink. Although they surrendered in order to avoid pointless bloodshed (they had their passengers to consider) they were brutally knocked about on the orders of the frigate's first lieutenant, for whose loutish behaviour the French captain later apologised; cold comfort for the Indiaman's commander and one of her midshipmen, both grievously wounded by knives and small-arms fire.

On *Brunswick*'s arrival at Trincomalee HMS *Centurion* courteously returned her 11-gun salute before sending over a party to select volunteers for the king's service, a compliment repeated by HMS *Wilhelmina* at Madras before she sailed as *Brunswick*'s escort on the passage to China, against a chance meeting with the French. Admiral Linois was somewhere about, smarting from an embarrassing meeting with a handful of Indiamen from which he had retreated in disarray under the impression, gained from their smart handling and naval-style formation, that they were warships. He was generally thought to be bent on recovering his dignity over and above fulfilling his obligations to liberty, equality and fraternity.

However, it wasn't until the following voyage, to China again after drydock in Bombay to cure a serious leak caused by a grounding in the Tiger River, that Nemesis caught up with them. Linois, in *Marengo*, accompanied by the frigate *Belle Poule*, gave the Indiaman's commander, with a crew by then almost entirely of lascars thanks to the navy's recruiting drive, no choice but to strike or be blown out of the water. Addison was taken aboard *Marengo* with the other officers and later landed at the Cape, from where he made his way home via St Helena, to sail on his next voyage as 5th mate of the *Marquis Wellesley*, under new ownership. As for the *Brunswick*, her voyage ended on the rocks of the African coast while in the hands of her French prize crew.

Addison here remarks on an amusing quirk of British merchant shipping practice which surfaced again in identifiable form in a later war:

According to the company's law[*sic*], having been captured by an enemy, or the ship wrecked or destroyed, the captain, officers and crew forfeit their pay and wages, consequently we have no claim upon the owners of the late *Brunswick* for at least twenty months' hard labour aboard of her[1].

The principle couldn't have been clearer; applying it, shoals and storms could be avoided and the enemy thwarted, so Addison and his shipmates had no-one but themselves to blame. Cessation of wages from the moment of a ship's loss through any cause was in fact enshrined in the Merchant Shipping Acts which wove their statutory fibres through the fabric of shipping administration as the 19th century sailed on. At least they weren't forfeit, but nevertheless during the 1914-18 war most shipowners applied the ruling to cases in which the ship was lost by enemy action, the implication being that master and crew had been lax to the point of negligence in allowing their ship to get in the way of a torpedo. The practice was resumed, but officially curtailed, during the Second World War.

In fairness to the HEIC it must be said that conditions shouldn't be judged by the standards and expectations of a later (and decadent) age. After all, service in the company's ships, and in less exalted trades including whaling, offered a chance of sudden riches, and on balance people like Addison were probably content to cut their losses and press on regardless. Moreover, it should be remembered that the ship's owner (the India husband) stood to lose all. Of course he was covered to a greater or lesser extent by the underwriters, but he couldn't afford, in such a service, a reputation for losing his ships, and so took a closer interest in them. It wasn't until much later, long after the HEIC had drifted into history, that comprehensive limitation of liability allowed him a full night's sleep and a less intimate relationship with the crude tools of profit.

So it was that Thomas Addison (who rose to the rank of 1st mate in the company's service) and Robert Eastwick lived on into an age of altered values and ideals in a world so different from the one in which they had joined their first ships that it might have been on another planet: travellers in time, they had journeyed from one universe to another of quite a different kind. Industrial revolution dragged in its wake social upheaval both ashore and at sea, and by the 1830s it had become clear that sail's centuries-old dominion was on the verge of irreversible eclipse. The ship's officer, steeped in the traditions of wood and canvas, was confronted with iron and steam and, to his disgust and bewilderment, the seagoing engineer. Not only that, but also, as time went by, official concern at the poor standards of competence among masters and mates, as well as their deplorable conduct, hardening into a decision to implement statutory measures aimed at improvement.

---

[1] *The Old East Indiamen*, pp.217-8.

As for the apprentice, he continued to thrive, forming the backbone of the "sea profession" and providing the merchant fleet with a supply of – within the limits of the system – competent and resolute officers. It was a supply all too often taken for granted, unforgivably by many owners, and in ignorance by a general populace that, when it thought about it at all, liked to see itself playing the part of seafaring nation.

II

Honourable Company, Sea Time and Tickets. 1830-1850.

*

The Court of Formal Investigation thought that the evidence tended to show that neither master nor steward knew anything about the dangers arising from letting a deck apprentice get at meat no longer fit for human consumption and said that since it is possible to envisage disasters in which a boy might run amok, it would seem proper that personnel be warned accordingly. The Court emphasised that careful thought must be given to the protection of masters and officers from being savaged by an apprentice, particularly in older vessels. Never trust a boy who barks.[1]

*

REFLECTION on the views of people who saw little merit in the apprenticeship system reveals a curious reluctance to admit that, while retaining essential principles, it made progress, albeit at an erratic pace, in the development of training and vocational education. Its detractors seemed to nurture to the end a Dickensian conception of a pauper boy, unloved and unwanted, with education and training combined "in the one simple process of picking oakum"[2]. For this reason, perhaps, and not a little in deference to social convention and prejudice, alternative titles were resorted to, improperly, when *cadet* and *midshipman* found popular currency. Nevertheless, apprentice he was, his life governed by the terms of his indenture, which, on the face of it, struck a nice balance of duty and responsibility between master and bondsman. In practice, though, particularly where the master's place was taken by a paid craftsman, as was frequently the case in the person of the ship's master, obligations tended to be one-sided, and before legislation took more than a cursory interest in him the apprentice was looked upon as a flunkey while his master's duties were interpreted in a loose and convenient fashion.

Parish apprentices (from which Dickens's near-caricature was derived), boys without parental support regarded as a burden on society, occupied the lower reaches of the scale; they were shipped out as soon as practicable, say at the age of ten, without much consideration of the prospective master's character and credentials. To all intents and purposes the boy's education was non-existent, and he found himself

---

[1] *Recollections of Captain Bellwinch.*
[2] *The Adventures of Oliver Twist*, p.10.

serving a man similarly endowed, the only difference between them being the master's professional accomplishments, varying in extent and depth but generally limited. Illiteracy combined with innumeracy at all levels, perpetuated by the system as it stood during the first half of the 19th century, the first move towards improvement occurring in the 1844 Factory Act, which sought to compel attendance at school until the age of 13 before beginning full-time employment. The governing classes (largely supported in their aims by the sentiments of the lower orders – the supposed beneficiaries – whose children would have been affected to the detriment of the family income) had it amended, however, and 10 remained the age at which school, run by church and charity, ended for most.

Deploring the situation, a Captain E. Blackmore wrote retrospectively:

Another and prevailing cause of the want of moral tone and intellectual cultivation in our seamen was doubtless the fact that lads went to sea at a very early age with little or no education or moral training, and few found the opportunity of acquiring them... There were good seamen in plenty but the deeper parts of the navigator's art, and thorough knowledge of the sciences upon which it is founded, as also general courtesy of behaviour and sobriety of conduct, are seldom attained without polite education and literary ability, the want of which...stamped the British sailor in the eyes of foreign nations with contempt.[1]

But there were exceptions, naturally: masters and officers of Post Office packets on government charter had been under instructions since 1793 to keep journals of events of public and commercial (to say nothing of political) interest in the countries they visited. The journals, examples of accomplished reportage and a source of foreign news of particular interest to merchants and businessmen, were placed on public view at the GPO.

At the upper end of the scale, enjoying benefits of a more decorous shade, was the midshipman, correctly named. Not bound by indenture, his terms of engagement were confined to the voyage, at the end of which he was free to either apply for re-engagement or try his hand at something else. Otherwise his contract was similar to the indenture in its balance of duties and responsibilities, and it was the arrangement favoured by the HEIC and its successors in their selection and grooming of officer material. Educated often to an advanced standard, the midshipman hailed from a family background well-heeled enough to afford a hefty premium, in the order of £50-£60 a voyage, out of which was paid the midshipman's wage, usually leaving the ship's owner with a balance by way of payment for his trouble.

And in between lay a wider expanse of seamen possessing an elementary schooling, one that at least enabled them to gather the gist of the contract before signing it. Cook was among them, his education at the dame school one that enjoyed more or less freedom from official regulation. It passed into the world children able to read and write with inconsistent and doubtful facility, attained in an atmosphere of mawkish

---

[1] *The British Mercantile Marine*, (1897). Quoted in *Seamen in the Making*, pp.88-9.

and maternalistic discipline which, as the foundation-stone of the English system, lasted well into the latter half of the century.[1]

As for home and family background, in the case of its own candidates closely scrutinised by the moguls of the HEIC, it followed no particular pattern. Finding conditions on board primitive to the point of brutishness, the parish boy would have entertained few regrets over his departure from the workhouse that had fed, clothed and sheltered him to the calculated limit of its cold-breasted pragmatism. The Indiaman's midshipman, on the other hand, left behind him a well-to-do nursery the only drawback of which was probably the unfortunate accident of his appearance at the scrag-end of parental aspiration. The younger, or youngest, son could seldom expect an inheritance, and his options were generally limited to those which would eventually, if not immediately, enable him to pay his way. In either case – parish orphan or failed scion – the sea's possibilities played a practical rather than a romantic part, and although boys heard its call with reactions varying from resignation to naive enthusiasm, the popular notion that the ghosts of seafaring ancestors influenced his choice of career (to use a modern expression) appears to have no foundation in fact. A seafaring father was as likely to be a deterrent as a farming one was to suggest the desirability of early embarkation, and most apprentices came from homes in which practicalities were the chief feature and money a focus of careful husbandry if not continuous anxiety.

Nevertheless the boy's own desires can't be summarily discounted; sea apprentices weren't all coerced and credit must be given to their own leanings and aptitudes freely developed. At a time when the country was becoming aware of the mercantile possibilities of a world no longer embroiled in large-scale conflict, adventure and the apparent chance of making a fortune while seeing foreign parts appealed to a certain spirit – to the boy who early became bored with school or who saw nothing better than a lifetime of drudgery in other trades or professions open to him. Often enough he pursued his goal despite every last particle of advice and persuasion against it.

Education seems to have been a matter for paranoia on the part of employers, who even as late as the 21st century reject applicants for posts on grounds of "over-qualification" (though the standards of qualifications might justifiably be in question). In fact, of course, the reason is that the better-qualified employee can with justification claim a higher wage than otherwise, but in doing so takes a calculated risk, for, as the Britisher discovered in later times, when he had attained a standard of expertise that arguably placed him at the top of an internationally-competitive occupation, the shipowner found it expedient to adopt foreign registry and pay less, whether for foreign or British crews. Insurance is a comfortingly acceptable substitute for competence, though as a policy, so to speak, it has its limitations.

Before repeal of the navigation acts the wealthy and the governing classes, shipowners among them, displayed this paranoia towards the idea of popular

---

[1] In Scotland rate-supported parochial elementary schools had been running since c.1700.

education, a state of mind owing much to perceptions of the causes of violent revolution in France, and because of it the development of education was in general retarded. Training of apprentices, for example, was never looked upon with enthusiasm by their masters except in a minority of cases, and had he not been forced into it the shipowner's support for the process would have been marginal or non-existent. In no instance, however, was it admitted that there was a need to educate or train above a certain minimum standard, the only voice arguing otherwise turning out to be, in time, that of the academic establishment, the motives of which were in turn open to speculation.

The school system was ragged in more ways than one[1]. While the offspring of the wealthy began their happiest years under the guidance of private tutors, the common ruck, where it received any tuition at all, attended the dame school. It was entirely privately-run by a middle-aged or elderly woman of no particular erudition whose "teaching", of a motley collection of up to thirty urchins ranging from infancy to working age, was rudimentary and steeply tilted towards the domestic. A small fee was charged. The alternative, or succeeding, choice was the common day-school, also charging for its services, run by an individual or group, the teacher usually unfit for other work, his product a somewhat crudely-finished article.

The children of the very poor received a perfunctory grounding at church-run charity schools, where the curriculum hinged about the Christian religion as interpreted by the clergy, extending to reading and sometimes simple arithmetic and writing. A notional effort at vocational instruction was occasionally made, mostly at an unskilled or semi-skilled level directed towards domestic service, farm labouring and the like. From this haphazard system evolved the monitorial arrangement, widely applied until abolished by the 1870 Education Act. In this a school of several classes, usually all in one room, or hall, was run by one master delegating teaching duties to senior pupils, or monitors. The first opened in 1803, a time at which, according to the MP Henry Brougham in an address to the Commons in 1820, Britain was the worst-educated country in Europe. *Plus ca change...*

In 1807 Samuel Whitbread's Parochial Schools Bill proposed elementary schooling for all, funded by the rates, a modest enough provision of two years' schooling altogether for children aged between 7 and 14. Even so, both church and paranoiacs opposed it, and it failed, unlike similar measures north of the border, where, pragmatic and essentially practical, education received a better general regard. The result was elementary schooling of varying quality remaining in the hands of church and secular bodies, prominent among which was the British & Foreign Schools Society, its establishments, popularly known as the "British" schools, serving their pupils until 1870.

---

[1] Formed in 1844, the Ragged School Union ran schools for the poor and destitute in the slum districts of the larger cities. Evidently euphemism counted for little in its practical eyes.

After the Reform Act of 1832 popular education assumed unprecedented importance, boosted by the secular organisations: formed in 1825, the Society for the Diffusion of Useful Knowledge produced cheap scientific and general text-books, including a species of school "reader" that earned the sinister homonimic "tenpenny nail", a term that survived until towards the end of the century and was apparently transferred, by association, to the teacher. One such was Hugh Davies the Nailer, a respected schoolmaster in the small rural community of Nefyn, on the Lleyn Peninsula, who, as well as diffusing useful knowledge among general pupils, taught elementary navigation to apprentices and others either about to embark upon or already following sea careers. How it came to be called a nail isn't clear: perhaps because the knowledge it contained had to be driven through the skull like a nail through seasoned oak.

Government tended to stand aloof from this hotch-potch of activity until an investigation of 1833 revealed that only one in ten children of school age was receiving a "satisfactory" education; the response was a government grant of £20,000 annually from 1833 to 1859 for the building of schoolhouses. They were supposed to have been placed in the poorer areas, but since the grant had to be supplemented by local subscription the schools actually appeared in the better-off districts, a miscalculation not entirely novel in political affairs but offset to some extent by the introduction of teacher training in 1840 which signalled the approaching end of the monitorial system.

So an elementary schooling was usually the best an apprentice could boast, though it was quite likely to have been a better one than his master had received, and good enough as a basis for the practical learning to follow. If he'd been fortunate he would have received the rudiments of a secondary (private, fee-paying) education or some sort of tuition in navigation, enabling him to apply to a shipowner of the better stamp, though this was by no means a natural progression, shipowners of whatever stamp tending to be unimpressed by boys likely to forget their places by virtue of a neat hand or a way with figures. Men like Walker of Whitby were growing fewer, and had never represented more than a scattered minority.

By contrast, Davies the Nailer exemplified a prolific section of the education system. Wales was sea-conscious to a marked degree, both in its coasting traffic and, as time went on, in the shipping it owned and manned trading farther afield, and it was natural that its schools should include navigation in their curricula even if they weren't in or near sea-ports or coastal communities. The Rev. W. Davies, PhD (no relation), was master of Froodvale Academy, near Llandovery, which prepared young men for entry to "Colleges, Universities and Mercantile pursuits"[1]. Its 1853 curriculum was stunning in its scope, or pretensions: English, Latin, Greek, Hebrew, Chaldaic, Syriac, French, German, arithmetic, geometry, algebra, conic sections, geography, land-surveying (the Empire was being mapped as fast as it expanded), civil engineering,

---

[1] *Maritime Memories of Cardiff*, p.59.

book-keeping, elements of philosophy, divinity, ecclesiastical history, logic and rhetoric, with navigation, astronomy and globes additionally. Pupils passed into the army, the church and the HEIC, though by this date the last was an anachronism at sea, replaced by the Blackwall firms that had taken over its routes bar the Bombay-Suez mail concession, which staggered along at a negligent pace for another thirty years or so despite the determined efforts of a youthful P&O to displace it. Chief among the newcomers were the family businesses of Money Wigram, Duncan Dunbar, and Richard & Henry Green, whose common practice was to accept midshipmen as trainee officers alongside apprentices making what they could of focsle life and a lower social stratum. Cadets entering the HEIC's service ashore – that is, in India in what became the Indian Civil Service but at this time was in effect a private government administering the company's Indian possessions and concessions – might have attended the Rev Davies's academy, but they would still have been required to pass through the company's own college, Haileybury[1].

Whatever the merits or shortcomings of his education, the Welsh boy, not necessarily from a poor family, had to contend with an additional handicap where his first language was his native one, for as soon as schools became accountable to education authorities English took precedence as the medium, causing widespread anguish. Welsh-only speakers were regarded as mentally deficient, though in most cases their reading ability, in Welsh, was far in advance of their English contemporaries, owing to the greater currency of the Bible in family life. A sea career, however, meant getting to grips with the alien tongue and the schools, with a commendable absence of sentimentality, made it their business to expedite the process. For example, Thomas Lloyd Evans of Maenygroes, near Newquay in Cardiganshire, ran a school for local children at his home, a modest, not to say squalid, thatched cottage. No fluent English-speaker himself, "Twmi", as he was known, insisted on its exclusive use while rigorously emphasising the maxim that it was "the language of success"[2], attested to by numbers of sea-captains who had benefited from his wisdom.

Although widespread, navigation instruction was piecemeal. One or two ancient foundations had been teaching it for generations, notably Christ's Hospital, which in 1673 had received £7,000 for the express purpose of teaching fifty poor boys mathematics and navigation preparatory to being bound apprentice to the sea at age 16 for a 7-year term. Pepys concerned himself with the school, making funds available, as did others at various times. Boys entered at about 11 years of age, with their parents' consent, the school undertaking to have them apprenticed within a month of completing the course. Leaving examinations were set by Trinity House every six months. The Charity Commissioners reported 50 boys at the school in 1837, and the TH exams continued until 1842 while navigation remained on the agenda until 1890.

---

[1] Founded in the early 19th century as the HEIC's administrative training college, it was closed in 1858 after the Mutiny and re-opened as a public school in 1862.

[2] *Maritime Memories of Cardiff*, p.63.

The philanthropic Sir Joseph Williamson, President of the Royal Society, bequeathed £5,000 in 1701

...to maintain a Free School at Rochester for the Instruction and Education of such youths there who were or shall be sons of Freemen towards the Mathematicks and all other things which may fitt and Encourage them for the Sea Service or Arts and callings leading or relating thereto.[1]

Navigation was taught until the late 19th century and in 1891 boys other than freemen's sons were admitted.

A free school was opened in 1712 by the master pilots and seamen of Newcastle Trinity House, offering navigation and mathematics. Its mainstay was made up of the Brethren's children but during the winter lay-up collier apprentices – for example William Richardson, he of the brig *Forester* – were also on the books. It closed in 1870, after which the headmaster, Mr W.H. Thorn, opened a school of navigation in North Shields.

In February, 1786, a famous navigation school was founded by the Board of Hull Trinity House, prompted by Jonas Hanway's[2] ideas for "naval free schools", though it had already ventured into the realms of pre-sea instruction when, in October 1729, it had arranged with a schoolteacher, one Mr Brown, for 12 children of the Brethren to be taught navigation, arithmetic, writing "and What etc". The Hull TH Marine School opened its doors in new purpose-built premises in Trinity House Lane with 36 pupils, nominated by Elder Brethren and Assistants, under the Rev T.O. Rogers, curate of Sculcoats Church, as headmaster. Appropriately, the boys paraded to church morning and afternoon on Sunday and attended chapel in the House on the first Wednesday of the month. The Sunday morning service in Holy Trinity Church and the chapel service (now weekly) still feature on the timetable.

On admission to the 3-year course, aged 10 or 11, the boy had to be able to read, and his parents or guardians, bound in the sum of £5, also stood surety against his misbehaviour or failure to complete the course, undertaking to provide him with clean clothing at all times. The uniform was uniquely and elaborately nautical: a white-lined blue cloth tail-coat with two rows of gilt buttons, stiff white cloth stand-up collar, gilt-buttoned blue cloth waistcoat, white duck (in summer) or blue cloth (in winter) trousers, white shirt, black stock and black boots or shoes, the ensemble topped off with a tall beaver, displaced in 1854 by a naval rating's pattern blue cloth cap and ribbon. In 1850, two years after the school had been divided into two sections, while the Lower School was supplied for the first time with the uniform, the Upper School exchanged the tail-coat for the short monkey-jacket (or "round jacket"), single-breasted and centre-fastened with a single button, decorated with two rows each of six (later seven) gilt buttons, with plain cuffs except for those worn by leading cadets and petty officers, which had cuffs with up to four slashes and buttons according to rank,

---

[1] *Seamen in the Making*, p.33.
[2] See p.56.

four denoting the Chief Cadet Captain, and a button with a gold flash on each side of the white stand-up collar above a short lapel. With a white waistcoat and white trousers, white or blue-striped white shirt and black tie, this became the traditional pattern for daily wear until the 1970s, with the blue naval cap exchanged for a peaked officer's cap with the Trinity House badge after WW2. When the school expanded in 1861 only fifty boys of the Lower School were supplied with the uniform, the remaining thirty with the blue-striped tunic previously only worn by those on probation (for their first 3 months). The tunic eventually gave way to the monkey jacket, and the next great change occurred in 1973, when merger with the Hull High School of Nautical Training (the Boulevard Nautical School) produced a first-year outfit of grey suit, blue shirt, school tie and black shoes, which would be usable elsewhere if the boy left during the first twelve months, the new probationary period. Staying on, he would change to the new nautical uniform of standard MN officer's square-rig with TH buttons. At that date the traditional uniform fell back into reserve, issued for wear only on special or customary ceremonial occasions. Remaining to the present day, the uniform has always been regarded, with no concession to the liberal trend of public opinion, as an essential element of the school's disciplinary system, upon which a large part of its excellent reputation stands.

From 1825 the boy leaving for sea was indentured at the TH Corporation's expense, the Board having first satisfied itself that he had achieved a satisfactory standard in his work and conduct and that the terms of his apprenticeship were likewise of an acceptable order; he departed with a Bible and prayer-book as a gift, talisman and admonition.

In 1834 the qualifications for admission were amended to provide exclusively for the sons of seamen and carpenters of Hull, a measure forced upon the Board by the increasing numbers applying for places as the port's trade grew with its berthing capacity. This was evidently allowed to lapse, for in 1867 the headmaster, Mr Zebedee Scaping, finding that a large proportion of the boys had no intention of going to sea but only to profit from the school's general quality, suggested giving the sons of seamen preference over those of landsmen in the allocation of places. Such was the school's reputation that in 1842 expansion was agreed upon and new accommodation together with a headmaster's house built adjoining the old building; then in 1848 a Lower School was established as a prep school for 40 boys aged 9 or 10 on admission.

Here, for two years before promotion to the Marine, or Upper, School, they were taught reading, writing and arithmetic, and required to reach a prescribed standard; failure meant an end to further progress and departure for other fields of endeavour. In the Upper School they learned "higher arithmetic", geography, astronomy, navigation and book-keeping before leaving for sea aged 13yrs 6mths to 14. Three times a year the Board advertised the numbers leaving, providing each with a certificate of proficiency.

By 1853 there were doubts among the Brethren about the standard of achievement, and about the adequacy of the financing, which was by voluntary subscription, and they accordingly approached the Dept of Science & Art. Subsequent inspection and discussion produced recommendations anent the methods and quality of teaching, organisation and scope of the school, including its extension to the provision of classes for masters, mates and apprentices, and in 1854 it passed into the control of a committee formed of the TH Board, responsible for operation and staffing, and representatives of the Dept of S&A responsible for the financing and upkeep of the buildings and the provision of books and equipment. In the Lower School the new curriculum comprised religious instruction, geography, history, reading, poetry recitation, spelling, copy-writing, dictation, slate and mental arithmetic, geometry, algebra (first 4 rules), English grammar and drawing. Instruction in the Upper School covered religious instruction, geography, history, reading, writing, dictation, English composition & letter-writing, slate and mental arithmetic, geometry, algebra, globes, navigation, nautical astronomy, chart-construction, steam engineering and magnetism.

In 1857 it was cited in an inspector's report as "the model school in every respect".

By contrast, a vague establishment opened in Bristol in 1733 under the auspices of the Bristol Guild of Merchant Venturers, at which, though tuition was free, attendance was chronically poor. It functioned only fitfully, outclassed by the Hull school and another in South Shields, the Marine School founded in 1837, which offered a few months' preparation for sea, also taking upon itself the duty of placing its output with reputable masters or owners.

Although not concerned exclusively with apprentices – not at all in the beginning – and failing to realise his notion of numbers of naval free schools, Jonas Hanway nevertheless directed his energies towards the formation of a body that assumed an important role in the scheme of things, its mode of operation continually adjusted to change, ensuring its survival into the 21st century. A public-spirited gentleman of progressive ideas, not to mention considerable personal resource and patriotic sentiment, he gathered about him a number of like-minded London figures, merchants and others, to consider ways and means of improving recruitment for and conditions in the navy, then with its attention on the Seven Years' War. The outcome, in 1756, was The Marine Society, its aim to recruit and outfit suitable men for the king's service as an alternative to the less discriminating methods of the press. At the request of a magistrate weary of consigning boys to the communal rubbish-heap or willy-nilly into the navy's lower deck, Hanway's compatriots extended their field of activity to include them and – though not as a perceived complement – the merchant service. In 1786 the society bought a merchant ship, the *Beatty*, fitted her out as a training-vessel, and renamed her *The Marine Society*, something of a prototype and model for later enterprises, all centred on non-seagoing permanently-moored ships in which the ideals of shipboard practice could be instilled in the trainees before release into the real world, though realism was the object of the exercise. It was one which possessed a somewhat greater measure of it when sail was still dominant than in later times when the wooden-wall had become an anachronism, if a novel one able to command the regard of a dwindling number of supporters valuing it as tangible evidence of order and discipline. The *Beatty* was replaced in 1799 by a ship lent by a favourably-disposed Admiralty, followed in turn by others as the demand grew and conditions altered.

The scheme began by apprenticing boys to the society for 2 years, to include 12 to 15 months in the ship before going to sea in the navy as boys, though some had their indentures transferred to shipowning masters under whom they served as regular apprentices. Vagrant or otherwise, they were carefully selected and vetted for character, or evident potential, all from poor backgrounds, their recruitment meant to benefit the service they joined in contrast to the effects of the inferior material finding its way in by a process of gravitation exacerbated by impressment.

Part of the process affected boys not of inferior material but who had little or no preparation beforehand. They had no clue of what lay beyond their own romantic imaginings or misgivings, conjured, perhaps, from hearsay or – rarely at this time – the contents of books and papers published variously by navigators, explorers and, with rather more prosaic motives, sensation-mongers and publicists of one kind and another. In any case school was something they wished themselves clear of at the earliest opportunity, in Scotland no less than elsewhere.

As the industrial revolution developed and shipbuilding extended into steam as well as iron and steel, Scotland came into its own. Not that seafaring itself had been neglected, or was a new departure; far from it, and Scots brought up in the Calvinistic atmosphere of the day went to sea without much heart-searching. There was a job to be done and a living to earn as much as any dream to be realised.

John Watson was born in the Fifeshire village of Largo in 1828 and schooled there until the age of 14. His father and paternal grandfather were weavers, and poor, a condition which didn't improve when, after his father died in 1832, his mother remarried. There was no question of extended education and he was apprenticed to the sea as the solution to the problem of his livelihood. While there was no sea tradition behind him the locality furnished one with which he became familiar at an early age, the substantial fishing fleet that supported Largo's economy. A famous native of the district also played a part: the story inspired by Alexander Selkirk's experiences at the hands of the hubristic Dampier was banned reading and therefore popular with Watson and his peers, whetting the appetite for adventure as much as it must have confirmed the stay-at-homes in their worst suspicions. Robinson Crusoe's narrative[1] is more than simply high adventure, though: it conveys an impression of the kind of man the region and the time produced, one given not to romantic self-delusion but to self-reliance, intelligent observation, practical facility and a sober religious faith, and as it appealed to them so the story must have reflected something of the character of the boys who read it.

At the other end of the country as well as the social scale, but also of a family of landsmen, James Killick was of Surrey yeoman stock. Born in the village of Cheam in

---

[1] Defoe's classic was first published in 1719.

1816, he enjoyed financial security with his father a City businessman and home a large manor set in spacious grounds well away from sight , sound and smell of the sea, but as the second of three sons he shared Watson's problem, and its solution. In common with others in similar circumstances his younger brother was "sent to America" to make his own way at minimum risk of embarrassment to his family, while Killick, through his father's business connections, was apprenticed to the sea. The whole affair was neatly and efficiently decided, arranged and settled by a man accustomed to deciding, arranging and settling, and Killick inherited his traits if not the family silver, pursuing his career from age 17 into its eventual form as a successful shipbroking and owning business.

If rigorous and down to earth, John Watson's schooling was limited while Killick's ran to higher levels. Both, however, started at sea in the same way, at the bottom of the scale of existence where differences of academic accomplishment were themselves merely academic, of little or no practical value to the ship. What counted was a combination of stamina and alertness together with the mental capacity to assimilate knowledge by experience, through observation, example and emulation sifted out of the daily round, mostly hard labour, a state of affairs that changed little after voluntary examination was introduced in 1845 with the object of assessing and attesting to the competence of ships' officers. The apprentice's hand was more accustomed to halyard and holystone than the sextant, if indeed it ever made the sextant's bare acquaintance, for the instrument was almost a total stranger to the grasp (mental as well as physical) of many shipmasters of the day.

The principles governing instruction, or training, at sea were well-established and not materially altered from their form at the beginning of the system four centuries before, embodied in their simplistic entirety in the terms of the indenture, and as far as the master and other interested parties on the same side of the agreement were concerned, that was sufficient. He agreed to inculcate the skills of the calling in the boy in return for the boy's willing to be bound servant and pupil: personal service in exchange for instruction, on the face of it an equitable arrangement. Practice, though, was apt to differ from the ideal, and a number of adverse factors marred a system through which the apprentice muddled his way as best he could. One of them was the absence of the master from the workplace: where he wasn't also the ship's master he wasn't in a position to personally fulfil his obligations, which passed by proxy to an employee: the shipmaster's interest, for all that it was incorporated in the indenture, was likely to be less conscientious – or, as the case might have been, more cursory. A valid but debatable point made by ships' officers was that they weren't employed as instructors, nor were the ships anything other than workplaces, their *raison d'etre* the mundane one of turning in a profit: let the *Marine Societies* of this world venture into the seas of altruism, all but clear of shipping at this stage.

It was often the case that behind the uninterested shipmaster stood an indifferent owner feeling that compliance with compulsory carriage of apprentices was evidence enough of public spiritedness without the added obligation of "training", a word in any case barely recognised, unearthly and undefined. The boy's presence was forced upon a master who wouldn't otherwise have troubled to engage him, and being compelled to do so in the interests of national security without recompense from the exchequer was cordially resented, more so when the "reservists", taken into naval service regardless of the master's manning problems, were returned unfit for further sea duty. No wonder the master looked on the system with a jaundiced eye, further inflamed when an act of 1844 confirmed and amplified the imposition.

Added to this was the fact that boys were viewed without much joy in most facets of life, being too many, with habits inclined to the rude and barbaric and requiring attention and interest largely seen as unmerited. For those at or beyond the social pale the difficulty could be overcome by sending them to sea, either in the navy's lower deck or indiscriminately into the merchant service, with a modicum of luck never to be seen again. Moreover, the antipathy felt towards the boy by society in general was readily assumed by the shipmaster, who voiced his sentiments in more or less conventional terms with the stock cliché that apprentices ate as much as seamen and did less work, a dictum that seemed to move its proponents to debunk it with every means at their disposal. But change was abroad, and with the disappearance of the navigation acts from the statute book went compulsion, with signal effect: numbers fell from 34,885 in 1848 to 17,411 in 1851.

An Act of 1835 introduced a seaman's register, with a separate record of apprentices. At first it indicated widespread evasion of compulsion, only 5,000 appearing on the books against what should have been several times that number, but as the system gained momentum numbers rose, reaching 40,000 in 1842. Nevertheless, whatever its achievement as a bureaucratic exercise compulsion was a failure from most practical angles: only a small proportion of the boys received the treatment and instruction that would have made it worthwhile, and wastage, aside from death and physical unfitness, cast a long shadow. Desertion, cancellation and transfer to other occupations were endemic, and writing in the 1880s Lord Brassey observed

> *It has been shown that when compulsory apprenticeship was in force apprentices constantly deserted. Then, as now, an apprentice of the same age as, and perhaps more skilful than, the ordinary seaman working by his side, was not unnaturally dissatisfied that his shipmate, with inferior qualifications, should earn £2 a month while his own earnings did not exceed 15s. Many boys, after serving three years at sea, are almost equal to able seamen; and if they see other men earning £3 a month while they are receiving perhaps 10s or 20s, they are naturally discontented and tempted to desert.*[1]

Rather laboured, but he makes his point. By compulsory apprenticeship was meant two things: most seamen had completed time on indenture before rating as AB, and shipowners were compelled to carry apprentices in their vessels according to tonnage,

---

[1] *The British Navy. Part V: British Seamen*, p.62.

as previously mentioned. Compulsory apprenticeship as the arbitrary practice of parochial authorities with respect to boys in their care was of no concern, and could not be. Following Lord Brassey's line of argument, the apprentice who deserted often sought, and found, a berth as AB, in which he received not only better pay but also better treatment, as far as it went. Nor did it mean that he had ruined his career, for records were neither meticulously nor comprehensively kept and his past could be reconstructed without risk of disclosure, if, indeed, anyone would bother to make inquiry. Neither was his path to command, if that was in mind, necessarily obstructed, since the system included the staging-post of able seaman. In fact, far from wrecking progress, desertion could shorten the process, roughly by the length of time outstanding on the indenture.

Summing up the discredited system of compulsion in a review, and referring more specifically to apprentices sent to sea by the authorities, the chairman of the Bristol Local Marine Board advised the Manning Committee thus:

...the system [of compulsion] has, instead of improving, greatly tended to the deterioration of the quality of moral character of the seamen themselves. Such apprentices were generally boys of no education or moral training and it was one of the great sources of annoyance to masters and owners that [the apprentices] never served out their time. At best they remained only until they had learned sufficient to get the wages of an ordinary seaman, and then deserted, in the majority of cases at the end of their second or third voyage. Those who remained were, whenever the ship was laid up, lounging about in idleness and contracting vicious habits whilst at the same time the expense of their support fell heavily upon the shipowner. In this way a great number of demoralised and unqualified men were introduced into our merchant service.[1]

Concurring, a prominent shipowner, Mr Lamport, declared that compulsory apprenticeship had been a "gigantic sham", adding to the sentiment expressed by Mr Richard Green (the Blackwall owner) to the effect that apprentices were considered very objectionable by shipowners generally.[2]

The ending of compulsion had another, and profound, effect, the first step towards a blurring of the distinction between midshipman and apprentice. The owner could henceforth please himself about taking on apprentices, and began to select them with an eye to their potential as officers, cognisant of the fact that the officers themselves had to be of a generally better character than hitherto. Competition (through "free trade"), it seemed, like the prospect of hanging, concentrated the mind, but care was taken to see that the indenture remained an agreement to instruct the boy only in the business of a seaman – a deckhand. If this tended towards marginal improvement in the boy's conditions of service (for which evidence is conspicuously sparse) it did nothing to improve the quality of focsle hands, already complained of, since the

---

[1] *The British Navy, Part V.*, p.61.

[2] ibid., p.60.

qualifying tests they had faced as apprentices were, trade by trade, dropped to be replaced by the examinations introduced in 1845 which, in effect, bypassed the focsle altogether. In theory the apprentice with time completed under indenture submitted himself to the examiners and passed direct to the afterguard.

Made compulsory by the MMA of 1850 (implemented in January, 1851) the examination and resulting "ticket" became, more or less by a process of auto-suggestion, the apprentice's motive for going to sea. It presented him with a clearly-defined path to the highest levels of a seaman's business while at the same time confronting him with a stumbling-block. In short, it injected a challenge into the system that was entirely novel and a positive attraction for many. Of course, after four years on indentures the apprentice could still choose to sign on as AB, and many did so – some because an officer's berth wasn't available – but it was now likely to be with the aim of making enough money to pay for tuition and examination. Likewise, the AB who had never served an apprenticeship was also eligible, as were the cook, steward, and others not signed on as deckhands though having lent a hand on deck whenever required: the only criterion set by the authorities was sea time.

With this development came a heightened awareness of the educational attainment of the boy applying for apprenticeship, and as a result the overall standard showed an improvement, an effect that confounded the pro-compulsion lobby, which battled on half-heartedly until firmly quashed under the 1854 MSA which, *inter alia*, ended compulsory apprenticeship for good.

As for the press and precipitate recruitment into the navy, an Act of 1853 brought continuous pensionable service to the lower deck, removing the cloud that had hung over the merchantman from time immemorial. Curiously, the act didn't abolish impressment itself, and while the Napoleonic wars saw the last of it in such robust form, it reappeared in later times, when the apprentice was again exempt, this time from the somewhat subtler but equally persuasive approach of the conscription order.

In its early form the certificate of competency distinguished between ships and trades, the apprentice seeking to qualify in first-, second- or third-class ships. Means of entry were distinguished accordingly, introductions to prospective masters variously the portentious function of parochial workhouse boards, through the good offices of a relative, family friend or business acquaintance, or acceptance, with pride or resignation, by uncle or father. In some trades, usually those of the first class, the only way in, whether as apprentice or midshipman, was by social and/or business association and recommendation; in other words, nepotism. In the second-class trades openings could be found by chance, through the dogged canvassing of shipmasters and owners; formality was either non-existent or perfunctory, and these were the days when a boy could still run away to sea and – as a rule – a rude awakening, without having to produce anything more authoritative than his own desires. If required, parental consent could be forged if not given freely, for ships were run by men content to accept a lad at face value, granted that the system of compulsion made chance engagement less than common, owing partly to the ship's already having her full complement of boys, partly to the owner's attitude towards the scheme and its creatures.

In some eyes a boy making his way to the sea was a romantic figure, but the reality was prosaic enough, and hazardous. On the other hand, householders in rural communities were disposed to offer hospitality to the footsore wayfarer passing their doors:

It was a frequent occurrence to see a poor boy-child passing through the village on his way from Scotland to Blyth or the Tyne, his feet covered with sores and carrying a small bundle containing a shirt, a pair of stockings and flannel pants, his entire outfit. My mother never...allowed...these poor wanderers to pass without bringing them home. They were...supplied with bread and milk while the tub was got ready...then...provided with night clothing and put to bed while she had their clothes washed, and mended if need be; they were then sent on their journey with many petitions to God for their safety and welfare. (1840s-1850s)[1]

Interview technique, to coin a phrase, varied. Even in its most elaborate form it was of a cursory nature from the boy's standpoint, most of the talking passing overhead between prospective master and parent or guardian, concerned less with the object in view than with such weighty matters as family fortunes, premiums and social connections. Thus the Greens' midshipman, successor to the HEIC's young gentlemen. Like other owners, Richard & Henry Green were obliged during compulsion to take apprentices (with what sentiments have already been mentioned), but it was the midshipman who was looked upon as the future commander. He signed a voyage agreement, while the premium his parent was required to pay was large enough to ensure that no riff-raff got into the act – no poor riff-raff, anyway. A notable feature of the arrangement was that more wards than sons joined the service, evidently seen by guardians as a welcome means of respite from onerous responsibility, lasting ten months or so at a stretch.

By contrast, the apprentice's engagement was an altogether humbler affair, a solitary confrontation on dockside or weather deck leading to the simple formality of signing the indenture in the presence of two witnesses. The document itself came in more or less standard form stocked by printers and stationers in all ports, one of them a certain William Stephenson at the *Eastern Counties Herald* office in Hull. Samuel Cole, master and owner of the 252-ton brig *Theodore*, of Sunderland, obtained the form from Stephenson after agreeing to take on Joseph Willoughby for six years in August 1845. Aged 14, from Sculcoats, Willoughby signed the indenture in duplicate, binding himself in the penal sum of £30 in return for a total wage of £35. No premium or surety was required by Cole, so neither parent nor guardian was involved, though how Willoughby was to find £30 if he decided to take his services elsewhere, or if they failed to satisfy Cole, isn't clear; a measure of trust was obviously understood.

---

[1] *Windjammers & Sea Tramps*, p.18.

The ceremony, or formality, of signing in the presence of two witnesses, one the local chief officer of customs or a deputy, completed, one copy was lodged at the custom house and the other handed to Willoughby, apprentice No.135,132 on the register as it stood at the time.

He had agreed to bind himself apprentice to Cole and Cole's executors, administrators and assigns (for example, a shipmaster in Cole's employ), to dwell and remain with them. He was to "well and faithfully serve" his master, keep his secrets, obey his lawful commands, do no hurt or damage, nor allow any to be done, to his master, and to warn him accordingly; was not to frequent taverns or alehouses except on his master's business; was not to play unlawful games; was not to embezzle, waste, lend or give away his master's goods without permission (as to the last two); was not to absent himself from service without permission, but was to demean and behave himself as a true and faithful apprentice. He was to render true accounts of all moneys in his charge, and was also to hand over to his master any wages, prize money or other sums paid him in the event of his entering Her Majesty's service. This meant that Willoughby's service in, say, the navy, had he volunteered (being exempt from impressment), wouldn't have returned him a better income than he received from Cole, who would continue to pay him in exchange for his naval pay. This would have made the boy think twice before abandoning Cole's by no means ungenerous employ for something that might have seemed more glamorous.

For his part, and on behalf of his various proxies, Cole gave the usual undertakings: to teach Willoughby the business of a mariner or seaman (in this instance the terms being apparently interchangeable, a looseness of expression that could well have served a deliberate purpose by clouding meaning and implication, though it was more likely to have been mere imprecision), to provide him with sufficient meat, drink, lodging, medical attention and washing (that is, laundry, and not personal) facilities, and to pay him the agreed sum in stated annual instalments. The boy was to provide his own bedding and clothing, and other personal items not provided by Cole, who, if he was called upon to provide them by the boy's default, was to deduct their cost from the wage – a suit of oilskins, for example. To judge by the indenture's general tone, Willoughby was from a modest home with probably an equally modest schooling behind him, one which, to gauge by the well-proportioned copperplate of his signature, had been sound enough in the basics.

He was one of at least two apprentices in a ship engaged in the east coast coal trade, a rough-and-ready training-ground not dissimilar in its elements to the North Atlantic run between Leith and Halifax, NS, on which John Watson found himself after signing a 4-year agreement to serve William Ovenstone, master and part-owner of the barque *Elizabeth*, 224 tons register. Broadly similar to those in Willoughby's indentures, the Scots terms struck a slightly less brusque note in requiring Ovenstone to teach Watson the art or business of a mariner(*sic*) or (quaintly unsyntactical) "seafaring business", as far as "the said apprentice is capable and willing to learn the same". This last phrase could have provided either party with a pretext for cancellation, but its accommodating tone was probably illusory. Both Watson and Willoughby found much of their learning a matter of personal initiative where it wasn't merely an incidental result of the officers' driving of ship and crew. Both the *Elizabeth* and the *Theodore* were ships of the second class.

The term *mariner* fell out of use, or was discreetly abandoned, at about this time, *seaman* remaining the definitive word until supplemented, where it wasn't replaced, by *officer*. The distinction is subtle enough. *Seaman* in this respect means the man before the mast, for all that the officer was a seaman; *mariner*, however, probably through introduction of the new examinations with their concomitant terminology, and possibly with reference to the Act of 1540 that implied a professional distinction between the two, was taken to imply a more extensive reach of professional ability, applicable to the navigator rather than the plain sailor, and in its ultimate application the shipmaster's particular distinction. Whatever his sentiments about the apprentice's professional destiny, the wise shipowner wasn't going to let himself in for contractual obligations likely to involve more expense than was necessary, and *seaman* kept whatever was necessary to a minimum.

Of Willoughby's previous existence nothing is known; of Watson's enough to conclude that he was no stranger to the way of a ship. It might be that Willoughby had already made a trial voyage or two, after the example of Edward Coxere and the younger Scoresby, at the usual risk of an unpredictable outcome. If he was determined, a tough regime was likely to harden the boy's decision, especially since the awkward element of pride entered the picture early on, making abandonment of a loudly-declared intention tantamount to defeat, publicly admitted. On the other hand a boy feeling himself coerced would not be swayed by the most liberal treatment, powerless as it was to offset the effects of, say, the weather.

So the apprentice's first ship wasn't necessarily his first experience of stark reality, though it took as many forms as there were ships. For those to whom it was the first, the close companionship of adults whose principal interest in him was as a workmate, and a none too handy or reliable one at that, came as a disconcertingly abrupt severance from boyhood. Yet the point of no return was a chimera, ever-receding before the advance of sea-time for all that the difficulties of breaking with a mistress (more demanding than any contractual master) whose thrall was a fatal weave of intimidation and fascination grew daily more numerous and complex, the relationship with the sea seen as terminal, a prospect one came to terms with for better or worse. To break with it required nerve, and most preferred to come to terms with slavery instead, while to a scattering of gifted individuals the prospect of cramped, dingy and verminous quarters, repulsively bad victuals, the filthiest and most menial work and the gruffness, if not active hostility, of the ship's officers, and often of the hands, came as a hail from a kindred spirit resurrected from some dim ancestral age: born seamen appear with as much surprise to themselves as to lesser beings looking on, while some labour for their entire careers under a misapprehension about their vocations that occasionally leads to tragedy.

Not that the officers and hands had time to spare (or the perception) to make anything of such nice distinctions: to them every first-voyager was a liability, at worst a source of worry and annoyance, at best a tyro requiring more or less supervision and inconvenience on the part of his shipmates. To senior denizens of the half-deck he was an object of similar sentiments, not to be left in ignorance of the fact whether through brotherly guidance or brotherly persecution.

James Killick joined the brig *Ganges* on 1st August 1833. Captain Bowlby not only commanded her and was part-owner, but had also built her, launching her in 1825 at Sunderland. Eight years wasn't old for a ship of her type, and conditions on board would have reflected less on age than on the limitations of the design. Accommodation for the apprentices and hands was dank, airless, almost lightless, damp and cramped, below the weather deck which was swept by green seas in bad weather, a portion of which got through the seams as the deck planking worked. Space was limited for all, cargo taking priority in a hull only 92ft long, 29ft 9ins wide and 16ft deep, weather deck to keel. She was registered at 262 tons. No record remains of her manning strength during the first half of Killick's time in her, but after a voyage ending in July 1836 the complement was master, mate, two apprentices (according to law), a cook and six hands. Killick joined in London and spent his first voyage in similar fashion to his last as an apprentice, on the run between there and Baltic ports, where they loaded mostly timber (deals) and timber products such as Stockholm tar, resin and turpentine.

In London, with the crew paid off, as was the case from July 5th to 28th, 1836, master, mate and apprentices would stay by the ship. In this instance Killick, the only apprentice, found himself performing the duties of servant, or steward, attending to the officers' creature comforts before his own. If carried, the only one aboard at a lower social remove was the cabin-boy, usually too poor or ill-schooled to secure an apprentice's berth – unless, of course, he was making a pre-apprenticeship voyage on approval, so to speak. He would be the dogsbody:

All hands having paid off excepting the mate and three apprentices the task of cooking fell upon the cabin-boy... As a rule he got along fairly well...[with] a plain meal, which usually consisted of soup and doboys, that is, small dumplings boiled in the soup... A double-decker sea-pie was...considered a luxury...and most sailor-boys could cook it. It was made in a large pan...of the following ingredients: a layer of potatoes, small pieces of beef and onions well seasoned with pepper and salt, and covered over with water; then a deck of paste with a hole in the middle to allow the water free access; then more potatoes, beef, onions and kidney, and then the final deck of paste and a suitable amount of water... It was a common thing while these exploits of cookery were going on for the skinflint skipper to stand over the boy and if he detected him taking too thick a skin from the potato he was lucky if he got off with a severe reprimand. It was usually an open-handed blow, intended to enforce economy.[1]

---

[1] *Windjammers & Sea Tramps*, pp.30-1.

And Robert Thomas, a Welsh-speaker from the village of Llandwrog, on the Lleyn Peninsula, found his skills called upon in circumstances for which any sailor has to be prepared:

We sailed in due time from Cardiff, and the cook losing his passage I had to take that berth, which was a pity, but an apprentice is nothing better than a slave, especially in this class of ship. That was a hard time for me on account of seasickness and ignorance of the work.[1]

Ignorance of the work, in the galley or elsewhere, was one thing; ignorance of the hazards that surrounded him from the moment he set foot on the gangway was likely to end the apprentice's career before it had begun, as Alfred Costello discovered. His experience was a first-voyage classic:

My first ship was the barque *Sir Charles Napier*, running across the Western Ocean. I did not sail, for keeping port-watch on deck one night missed my footing and fell into the empty hold, some twenty-four feet. After leaving hospital I was advised to give up the sea life, but after a spell ashore I became bored and found a berth in the barque *Elizabeth*, 355 tons, for the Far East.[2]

Perversity is a characteristic of the sea; boys looking for high adventure found drudgery and tedium while lovers of routine were too often (in their view) catapulted into mayhem and chaos. In written records the result is largely a blank page: high adventure in sail all too often ended in catastrophe and silence beyond the echoes of the *Lutine* bell, while tedium's heroes weren't inclined to recount their humdrum experiences. The consequent bias in surviving narratives lies towards the adventurous end of the spectrum, and tales of – remarkable by definition – narrow escape. Costello's inauspicious start might have made him an object of interest to the superstitious, ever on the *qui vive* for signs and portents, among them reincarnations of Jonah:

On my second voyage we ran into heavy weather in the Bay of Bengal and sprang a leak, then we struck upon a reef in the Duncan Passage, Andaman Is., and stuck fast. The captain went away in a boat with two sailors, leaving us in charge of the mate. We tried to launch the long-boat, but the seas stove her in, so we had to remain, resigned to our fate. I contrived to get a lamp fastened to the forestay in the hope that a passing ship might see it, but not until dawn did a sail appear, which, as it came closer, we saw to be the captain's boat. As the seas allowed, we jumped one by one into the water and were taken aboard, after which the wreck began to break up. Later we landed on Cowry I., finding there nothing to eat and little to drink and at night being overrun with rats. Next day we set off for Port Cornwallis, about 120 miles away, the captain warning us that if we fell into the hands of the natives it would be the end. We were nineteen in the boat, and very cramped.[3]

---

[1] *Shipmaster*, p.34.
[2] Reconstructed from *Seamen All*, pp.76-7.
[3] ibid., pp.77-9

There followed some 42 days of severe hardship – hunger, thirst and death – among the islands until finally Costello and six others made it to the coast of Burma. From there a naval frigate was despatched to rescue the handful who had remained behind on an uninhabited island. Ultimately, all except the captain and Costello died from the delayed effects of their privations.

So much for high adventure. Turning the coin, a good deal of the life's content of monotony was generated by the food, which, unlike high adventure, came in short supply and of distinctively poor quality in British ships, lacking both variety and nutritional content. Provisions were a matter of personal inclination on the part of the master or owner, victuals for hands and apprentices obtained as cheaply (and sometimes as dishonestly) as possible; condemned salt meat from Admiralty stores was a familiar item. Cabin stores, by contrast, were often surprisingly good and of wide variety, allowing for the usual problem of deterioration, but there were exceptions; masters were known to put economy before even their own wellbeing, content to ruin their stomach linings in the interests of those of their pockets.

In addressing itself to the matter, another Act of 1844 fell short of rectifying the problem, requiring the master merely to state in the articles of agreement what he intended issuing to the crew (and apprentices). The catchphrase was "sufficient without waste", a splendid piece of shuffling equivocation that set the tone for the nascent bureaucracy with which the ship gradually became overladen. Only biscuit, most durable item of sea diet, was prescribed, at the generous rate of 1lb per man per day. On it the British flag subsisted when all else had failed, as it frequently did, and with it the apprentice concocted some gut-wrenching dishes.

Scurvy was, of course, an ever-present occupational hazard, though it hung back in the wings most of the time, emerging only on long passages. Its cause wasn't understood except in a general sense – lack of fresh food – despite the findings of medical men over the ages, and its suppression was a matter of broad assumption. Among its various directives the 1844 MSA included a requirement for the daily issue of lime-juice ten days after the first meal of salt meat – beef and pork, reputedly, in cask – supplemented by the biscuit and, customarily, rice and dried vegetables such as peas and beans, eked out with the wizened or putrefying remains of potatoes, onions and whatever other perishable produce had been taken aboard. His sea diet tended to beget in the apprentice a certain picturesque asceticism; good, perhaps, for his soul.

As for medical attention, it was best avoided, and the Act also specified a scale of stores of suitably primitive variety, chosen by no less a personage than the Lord High Admiral, by proxy if not in person. It appears that a doctor, however lordly or high, was not to be trusted as the signatory authority.

Surviving his diet and whatever constituted medical attention, the apprentice followed an onward career that, until 1845, was unregulated by statute. As training, apprenticeship guaranteed nothing, and competence fluctuated wildly across the spectrum of ships' officers, from a trough of criminal ineptitude to a peak of professional expertise that, although sound in its respective sphere of operation, tended to be restricted to it. A competent East Indiaman's officer versed in the principles of ocean navigation and the management of large passenger-carrying ships inhabited a different world from the collier mate who, barely literate and ignorant of navigation beyond the essentials of coastal pilotage, and even that restricted to a familiar route, was equally competent in his own milieu. Both were required to pass a test before panels of their betters, and both were refused advancement on a poor showing, but there was practically no common ground between them apart from the obvious elements of seamanship without which the ship wouldn't move. As for the mass of miscellaneous shipping, an officer, or prospective officer, remained dependent on the good opinion and recommendation of his captain, his character being confirmed to a greater or lesser extent by an extemporised interview on engagement. As it turned out, this was inadequate, and the situation deteriorated to such an extent that government, alas, was moved to intervene in order to prevent the British flag from sinking in a sea of popular obloquy and self-induced dissolution.

Decline in professional accomplishment led to alarming increases in the incidence of wreck and other maritime misadventure. Among officers and men inexperience was rife, command falling to mere boys, or to owners who, not themselves seamen or navigators, relied on the mate or mates to run the ship. Not that youth was synonymous with inefficiency – far from it: boys of seventeen or so had proved themselves eminently capable of handling ships and their crews, and continued to do so where bureaucracy's intrusive tendrils were absent. Citing youth in command in connection with disaster was a *non sequitur* that made sense only to shorebound officialdom in its growing self-awareness. Nevertheless there was ample evidence of general moral decline that drew in its train a laxity and negligence that exacerbated the effects of one of the perceived causes of poor navigation, the convoy system developed during the Napoleonic wars.

A Royal Commission of 1836 was followed by other inquiries in 1839 and 1843, confirming the inadequacy of officers' educational and professional credentials, but acknowledging exceptions. For example, certain Sunderland owners and masters had set up a system of professional accreditation that met with conspicuous success, earning the approval and active support of other regions, London prominently. However, it was too limited in form and application to find national validity and finally, in 1845, an Order in Council empowered the BOT, as the executive authority answerable to Admiralty, to arrange and regulate voluntary examination and certification. In two grades, master and mate, each certificate was applicable to one of three classes of ship – foreign-going in general belonging to the first and second classes while the third embraced the miscellany of short-sea and coastal types above a certain tonnage, or capacity, and state of seaworthiness. Lacking the resources for central administration the BOT appointed local authorities as the examining bodies – in London the Corporation of Trinity House; at Gloucester, Milford, Plymouth, Portsmouth and Yarmouth the Sub-Commissioners of Pilots; at Hull the Hull Trinity

House; at Newcastle the Newcastle Trinity House; at Glasgow the Pilotage Board; at Dublin the Ballast Board and at Liverpool the Pilotage Commissioners.

Although the syllabus was specified the form of examination was left to the respective authorities, each devising its own with the general aim of testing knowledge of seamanship, cargo stowage, navigation and nautical astronomy. In some places it was entirely *viva voce*, in others partly written, while the standard in general proved to be over-optimistic, a challenge that many chose to decline, if not disdain, presumably in the interests of self-respect, all too vulnerable to searching inquiry. Some emphasised mathematics, some science, and some threw in a little extra: candidates coming before the Elder Brethren in London faced the ghost of the HEIC in a daunting test of their acquaintance with English Channel pilotage. How they viewed this can only be surmised; probably without unqualified enthusiasm, though the added cachet it must have given them could only have been useful, and quite possibly insisted on by the Blackwall owners. After all, the Channel was at the focus of the problem, littered as it was (and is) with the detritus of navigation through the ages.

Candidates for the mate's examination had to be aged 19, with either four years' attested sea-time in the case of non-indentured men, or satisfactory completion of at least four years' indentured service, otherwise a combination of the two amounting to the same total. Three-year indentures weren't uncommon, while some stretched to seven, but the effect of the new regulations was, over the years and without statutory dictat, to produce a standard form covering four years. Only an unblemished record of conduct was acceptable, as it remained, drunkenness assuming capital proportions amid trivia such as barratry and murder in the eyes of a BOT surrounded by a sea of inebriates and dipsomaniacs.

Chiefly owing to the standard set the voluntary principle wasn't a success, and the apprentice seemed, in the majority, to prefer making his way to the poop by the *ad hoc* path of old, so that by the end of 1846 the number of certificates issued in both grades (mate & master) amounted to the embarrassing total of only 200. As the overseeing body the Admiralty took a dim view and issued a directive to the effect that after 22nd March, 1847, no ship would be taken up from trade for Admiralty contracted service unless commanded and officered by duly-qualified men. The result was gratifying, if not surprising, reflecting not only the owners' anxiety to retain government charters but also the officers' keenness to keep their comparatively secure jobs, and by the end of 1850 some 3,000 certificates in both grades were at large.

Meanwhile reports from abroad still sketched a depressing profile of the British mercantile officer, lacking in both professional and social virtues apparently possessed by the foreign competition, notably and significantly the American, whose polish, if irritatingly (and deliberately) overdone, nevertheless cast his British counterpart's homely demeanour into a shadow bordering on the uncouth. To many the comparison was mortifying and frustrating, and whatever the final goad, whether overweening American presumption or sober pragmatism on the part of the Commons, the Mercantile Marine Act of 1850 making examination mandatory also brought its administration under the aegis of the BOT, relieving the motley array of local bodies of the task. The move emphasised and endorsed the positive aspects of abolition of compulsory carriage of apprentices: things were looking up, it seemed, and the apprentice found himself at the threshold of sobering change, as it were.

At this point the Admiralty ceased to figure in the system, passing all powers to the BOT, which established Mercantile Marine Offices in the principal ports with responsibility for supervising engagement and discharge of crews and all other matters to do with the manning of merchant ships, including the conduct of examinations and the issue of certificates, over which they held powers of suspension and cancellation. Behind them sat Local Marine Boards, composed of shipping people, which appointed the MMO's principal officers and staff.

The new certificate structure did away with the class of ship as originally devised, replacing it with one, foreign-going, and introducing another grade, 2nd mate, qualifying age 17, which joined the other two under the heading of "ordinary", with an optional Extra grade above master. The new 2nd mate's certificate's requirements were essentially the same as for the old, voluntary, mate's, which, together with the other voluntary certificates, remained valid as issued. Older officers not holding any and not likely to trouble themselves about doing so were accredited with their experience and ability variously attested to and issued with certificates of service in the appropriate grade.

The BOT now found itself in the unenviable position, having been handed them by the legislature, of having to keep several balls in the air at once in an attempt to accommodate a number of disparate standpoints. The standard of examination had to be equitable with what had gone before, and compulsory certification had to be seen as beneficial and not a discouragement, while officers eligible for certificates of service had to be demonstrably competent. In the seafaring fraternity there were exposed nerves in plenty, and inherent in the system a risk that serious cracks would develop, leading to breakdown, the stresses lying in the timing of the steps taken in changing the system, steps which, wrongly placed, conflicted with each other.

Briefly, while compulsory carriage of apprentices had been in force shipping had enjoyed the protection of navigation laws which made it appear an unnecessary inconvenience, circumstances in which voluntary examination had been seen as an idle conceit, of no practical value to either reluctant apprentices or owners untroubled by competition. Then when abolition of compulsion coincided with repeal of the navigation laws, throwing British shipping into open competition with foreign interests, voluntary qualification became insupportable while also casting a somewhat lurid light on the quality of the education system. While a corps of qualified officers should, and could, have been built up before repeal, through mandatory examination, the voluntary principle had proved a signal failure. Now, exposed to the depredations of foreign (largely subsidised) shipping, an urgent task faced a BOT made responsible for a viable merchant fleet, contemplating the sombre prospect of its possible paralysis owing to a shortfall of qualified officers as required by statute. The situation was distinctly uncomfortable, with the ludicrous undertones never completely absent from legislative affairs.

The difficulties boiled down to a problem as stark as it was simple, the need to reconcile the sudden demand for qualified men with the ability of the men to meet the qualifying requirements. To some extent the voluntary system had been free to set standards felt to be appropriate to the job, and in general they were high – hence, in part, the low numbers achieving them. As a general guide, all were expected to reach a level of ability comparable with the best that had gone before, such as the private arrangements of the HEIC, the natural additament of a selective recruitment policy that ensured (within the limits of certain social precedents) possession of a sound basic education – that is, a private one. Compulsory examination, however, could not afford to discriminate, and if it were to achieve its purpose – adequate manning levels – it would have to be pitched at a comparatively low level of educational accomplishment bordering on the mediocre, a fact of life the BOT was obliged to acknowledge while salving its dignity by reserving its right to raise standards "when convenient". The initial standard was at a level "as low as possible without prejudicing the value of the certificate", of which the following is an indicator in the 2nd mate's exam:

1. Express in figures, ten million, ten thousand and ten.
2. Add together 17,984 739 9 754 896 & 7,493.
3. In 97,864 cables, each 120 fathoms, how many inches?
4. Divide 8746887718592 by 9648.[1]

As a test of simple arithmetic (and, in Q.3, some simple professional knowledge) it was effective enough, as much a trial of the candidate's presence of mind as his knowledge of first rules. If the modern eye looks on this modest test with the patronising scorn its age is apt to adopt towards its forerunners, it might pause to glance at the modern examinee's unaided ability with simple figures. Progress is an elusive deity, given to dropping banana-skins in the path of its self-professed votaries.

The BOT was, of course, coming to terms with the paradox that faced it for the rest of its tenure of office, likewise its successors: the inescapable conflict between the interests of supply and demand. To some the government appeared to have made a noose for its own neck, given that a home-flag merchant fleet was a necessary adjunct to domestic and foreign policy which had embraced, with eccentric naivety, what amounted to unilateral free trade, a gift to the rest of the world's commerce.

As for preparation for the examination, virtually non-existent in its academic sense at sea, the cheap navigation schools recommended in the wake of the 1836 Royal Commission's report were envisaged as catering for the professional needs of the apprentice and officer, distinct from the schools offering tuition before going to sea, which had also offered courses of preparation for the examinations as they had existed before the 1850 Act. Personal, solitary, effort had also been an accepted method of

---

[1] *The Merchant Navy* (Course, A.G.), pp.212-3.

professional achievement, and books had been published with an eye to self-advancement from early times – for example *The Seaman's Secrets* as disclosed by John Davys or Davis, pilot to the HEIC on its first voyage east.

In the 18th century private schools had coached naval and HEIC midshipmen and officers for promotional examinations, and several principals, or proprietors, had published learned texts on navigation and mathematics in application to them. Notable among the sages was J.W. Norie with his *Epitome of Navigation*, who in 1800 was running his Naval Academy in Leadenhall St., offering courses approved by the Honourable Company. At a time when maths in the general (charity/church) education system was taught to only an elementary level HEIC officers were nearer in social and professional status to naval officers than to their brethren in lesser trades, and as well educated: in choosing the HEIC's Merchant Service in preference to the navy, sons of merchants and county families entered a service which offered a more secure and structured career than one in which officers were liable to spend a depressing proportion of their time on half-pay unless the country happened to be at war. Midshipmen sailed in this capacity for three years (say three voyages) before rising to 4th mate, aged not younger than 20, thence through the ranks to commander at the minimum age of 25. The company's training system had reached a finely-tuned pitch since the introduction of professional assessment: regulations of 1793 had required the 4th mate to serve at least one round voyage – say ten months – and be aged 19 (later raised) before presenting himself for examination for further promotion, each grade reached via progressively more searching examination of the officer's stock of navigation, seamanship and shipboard organisation. Not only that, but he also had to demonstrate a cultural facility – social poise and an informed mien were *de rigueur* – and pass exacting tests of physical and mental fitness including toleration of provocation, less to do with crew management than with passenger control, a much more ticklish business. Taken all round the HEIC midshipman's training, inherited in principle by his Blackwall descendants, was in many respects superior to the naval equivalent, gunnery included.

The company made arrangements with external bodies for examination of its officers, people like Norie and his contemporaries, one Thomas Lynn among them, who enjoyed the company's patronage for various reasons. In the late 18th century he had retired from the service complete with pension and the customary nest-egg to be appointed examiner of junior officers, an honorary post that brought with it little tokens of esteem and appreciation of a more or less negotiable kind. To help the candidates through their ordeal he opened his school a few doors away from Norie's, where the recommended navigation tables were further evidence of professional acumen. Competition was brisk: one John Hamilton Moore had set up a school at Tower Hill in 1772, later publishing his *New Practical Navigator* covering the syllabus for

that examination which every candidate for a Commission in the Royal Navy and officer in the Honourable East India Company's service must pass through prior to being appointed.[1]
 – much as he might have had to pass through a swamp.

A latecomer opened her Nautical Academy and Navigation Warehouse at 103 Minories in 1831, also basing the curriculum on naval and HEIC requirements, and keeping it up to date as the BOT stepped into the picture. Janet Taylor was another mathematician-cum-nautical astronomer and theoretical navigator, whose output went beyond mere tutoring of ships' officers. She produced her own stellar and lunar tables and a volume of *Luni-Solar & Horary Tables* as well as a popular manual, *Principles of Navigation Simplified*, of which she wrote excusing herself of the taint of presumption, rather disingenuously referring to the shortcomings of a woman's education (it could hardly have been worse than that of many of the men she taught), begging the reader's indulgence and acknowledging the assistance of one of her staff, Mr James Griffin, noted in an advertisement as "an enthusiastic lover of science" who guaranteed

a thorough and satisfactory knowledge of every branch of navigation and nautical astronomy, taught [and this was the clincher as far as the erstwhile apprentice and midshipman were concerned] in half the time usually required.[2]

Mrs Taylor's output didn't stop at books, for she also made navigational instruments, showing a sextant at the Great Exhibition of 1851, developed an artificial horizon, and a "Mariner's Calculator" for solving problems in spherical trigonometry. She also adjusted ships' compasses, sold them, and, it seems, made them under licence, as well as running a chart agency and dispensing the usual chart-room paraphernalia.

At school, as at sea, time was of the essence, linked as it was to financial outlay, and as well as Griffin's irresistible claims the Taylor method of lunars reputedly cut the length of the exercise (that is, ascertaining longitude) to a mere three minutes, vouched for and approved by the Admiralty, Trinity House, the HEIC and the King of Holland. The school offered two courses, fees payable in advance and followed at the student's convenience, the "Plane Navigation" course at 4 guineas and the "Nautical Astronomy" course at 2 guineas. Classes were held from 10am to 4pm and 7 to 9pm, with private accommodation available. Janet's husband George at first ran a navigation school in Fenchurch St., but closed it to join forces with his wife about 1845, presumably in view of the BOT examinations and the opportunities they seemed to promise.

Schools flourished and expired at other ports. Charlton's Navigation School opened in Whitby in the late 1700s, tutoring apprentices and mates in "Arithmetick, Algebra,

---

[1] *Seamen in the Making*, p.38.
[2] "Navigators in the Minories & Its Environs" in *Nautical Magazine* No 214, 1975.

Navigation, Gauging, use of globes and other mathematical instruments", while at South Shields the Marine School continued, under different titles, into the 1980s and beyond. From 1845, under the impetus of the voluntary exams, while existing schools adjusted their curricula to the syllabus, new schools appeared, many the limited but acceptably efficient (and affordable) enterprises of sundry sea-captains in premises that owed much to makeshift and expedient, from the back rooms of ship-chandlers to the parlours of their own homes and, in one or two instances, strategically-placed public houses.

Between them these schools and individuals, in harness with the BOT's empirical measures, developed the nucleus of what became a training system of world-wide repute and professional excellence, if not without its flaws; but it was an incomplete nucleus, for it failed to take into account an element already forming from the primeval mud of mechanical development and enterprise – the core of the industrial revolution, in fact. It was an element that in the end overshadowed its older complement: in the navy, dockyard schools for engineering instruction were inaugurated in 1843, though the Admiralty's conception of steam power was sceptical, not to say socially aloof, and the cause of the service's tardy exploitation of it while the merchantman's ran ahead by several lengths, albeit without the presence of the apprentice, whose domain remained, for the time being, in sail.

III

According to the Act. 1850-1894.

*

Then we would line up: Captain Bellwinch; Mr Spurnwater, the mate; Mr McBroon, the chief engineer; Ali, the donkeyman; Ali, the four-to-eight fireman; Ali, the twelve-to-four fireman; Doc, the cook; Doc, the second cook; and four of us apprentices, each equipped with fresh underpants, socks, soap and a towel. At a command from Captain Bellwinch we would all troop down to the stokehold for a bath in the hot-well. Once down below we would whoop and splash in wholesome high spirits and holystone the scurvy off each other until our skins glowed.[1]

*

THE Great Exhibition threw technology into significant relief, and with it the ramshackle state of education, still revolving with blithe inconsistency about the dame school and the monitorial system. In Scotland, however, George Birkbeck, a lecturer at Glasgow University, had initiated Mechanics' Institutes, part of their purpose the furtherance of technical knowledge through public lectures and reference libraries. From them, tardily in England and Wales, sprang a system of secondary technical schooling the benefits of which could not be fully embraced until, under the 1870 Education Act, school boards were set up under whose supervision elementary schooling to age 12 was made widely available, an Act of 1888 introducing, at last, a minimum leaving age of 10. With secondary education still in private hands (the great public schools having by sleight of hand assumed strictly private status) the board schools evolved an intermediate level above standard 6 carrying pupils with the ability to age 14 and in some instances 16, thereby making a better class of employment more generally accessible. Their abolition in 1902 led to the establishment of a proper secondary level following, separately, both grammar and technical disciplines.

In the process the academic accomplishment of boys taking up sea apprenticeship improved, and with it the standard of the BOT's professional examinations. Leaving school at about 14, the greater proportion of apprentices nevertheless lacked any kind of preparatory nautical instruction, a deficiency (as it was seen) the Department of Science & Art attempted to rectify by setting up navigation schools as part of the technical secondary system, supplementary to the fee-charging private schools already

---

[1] *Recollections of Captain Bellwinch.*

in existence. Their failure stemmed chiefly from the curious disparity between their curriculum and the BOT's essentially practical version, a gap bridged, where he could manage it, by the apprentice with his own efforts.

Noting this, perceptive elements of the shipping community took steps to establish a means of supplying the merchant service with a purpose-trained officer corps, hitherto confined, by common consent, to the midshipman, for all that the apprentice had made it his business to take the qualifying examination. On this premise, the first body to enter the field was Liverpool's MMSA[1], which negotiated the loan of a frigate from the Admiralty for use as a permanently-moored school-ship on the model of *The Marine Society*. Brought to a berth in the Sloyne, off Rock Ferry, *Conway* accepted her first cadets in August 1859 for a 2-year course recognised by the BOT as equivalent to a year at sea of the four required to become eligible for the 2nd mate's examination. The project's success led to replacement of the ship by a larger vessel, *Winchester*, in 1861 and again in 1876 by a still larger, the second-rate line-of-battle ship *Nile*, each in turn adopting the name of the first, but with the proviso in each case that the prefix HMS be part of the name, and not an indicator of status as applied to naval ships. The name accordingly became, oddly, and in particular because of the ships' mercantile role, *HMS Conway*, or, offically, the *HMS Conway*, and not, as some liked to give it, HMS *Conway*.

Looking on with interest, a similar group of individuals in London formed The Thames Marine Officers' Training Ship, obtaining from an indulgent (or overburdened) Admiralty the 50-gun frigate *Worcester*, together with a stricture anent her name similar to *Conway*'s. At her first anchorage off Blackwall she began her work in 1862, training cadets for eventual command of "the best ships afloat". As with her contemporary – and rival – *Worcester*'s training counted as 12 months' sea-time.

However, both required fees that, the question of accommodation apart, meant exclusion of a considerable proportion of raw material, and other ships appeared which, although not competing in officer training *per se*, gave boys a chance that would otherwise have been denied them. *Indefatigable* took in her first trainees in 1864, *Arethusa* in 1874, sending their progeny to sea for the most part on the lower decks of both navy and merchant service, but also a number into the half-deck. They were not to be confused with the "industrial" training-ships of which several entered service as youth reformatories, a nice point of irony from some angles. Their output was directed chiefly towards naval entry, that part of it passing into the merchant service regarded with a circumspect, not to say a jaundiced, eye by shipping people who, justifiably, objected to their businesses being used as a convenient repository for social refuse; they contained quite enough as it was.

In 1885, via the unorthodox diversion of liaison with a much younger woman and consequent public scandal, the merchant banker Charles Hoare retired from the social

---

[1] Mercantile Marine Service Association. Formed in 1857 of the port's shipmasters and owners, it became the shipmasters' representative body.

charivari and with his mistress established the training-ship *Mercury*, mooring her (the ship) off Binstead Hard on the Isle of Wight. Hoare had bought the barque *Illovo* and converted her at his own expense to offer places to "improved street arabs of 14 or 15"[1], giving them a rigorous preparation before passing them on to the navy, though here, too, some entered the merchant service as apprentices. In 1892 the ship was moved to her permanent berth in the Hamble, where extensive shore facilities were provided.

Meanwhile, thriving under the Department of Science & Art's scheme for nautical secondary schools[2], the Hull TH School's efficiency and consequent popularity had led to an intake of a large proportion of boys with no notions of taking up a seafaring career: in 1873 Mr Scaping was incensed to discover that half the boys taking the leaving exam had their sights set on shore occupations, and wrote indignantly to the committee to ask, quite reasonably, why the Trinity House should finance their education when board schools were open to them. As he put it, "The boys are trained for the sea service and they must go to sea when they leave the school."[3] As a remedy he suggested the merger of the Lower and Upper schools, eliminating the first stage during which the boy's options remained open. After some discussion of this, the outcome was an inclusive course in the newly-named Trinity House Navigation School (which included, from 1872, an Adult Section providing for candidates for the BOT exams including engineers, the newly-merged schools becoming the Cadets' Section) taking boys aged 11 for a 5-year course before their departure as apprentices, beginning in the autumn of 1873. It was calculated that the loss of the elementary school's grant would be balanced by an increase from the Department of S&A and fees from a new intake of paying pupils alongside the "foundation" boys.

Growing discernment on the part of owners in the selection, or acceptance, of boys as apprentices added to the difficulties of plans to run away to sea, and where it was still possible the opportunity lay at the meaner end of the market among owners whose concerns hinged in the main about the cost of a ha'porth of tar. One was a Mr H. Jones of Caernarfon, owner of the schooner *May*, whom Robert Thomas, aged 15, approached in the hope of something better than his £8 a year niche, or rut, as a country doctor's boots. Jones's going rate was threepence ha'penny a day all found except for bedding, clothing and other personal necessaries, and it didn't take Thomas long to spot the flaws in the deal, none of it in writing. Inquiries led him to another bulwark of Caernarfon's maritime community, Thomas Hobley, who offered a 3-year apprenticeship at the all-up wage of £30. It was as fair an offer as Thomas could expect, with his rudimentary education at the village school, ended in 1856 at 13, and equally spare grasp of "the language of success". And although it fell short of the

---

[1] *The Captain's Lady*, p.71.
[2] In the mid-19th century the Department recognised three in London and one each at Great Yarmouth, Hull, Liverpool, Newcastle, Sunderland, Aberdeen, Glasgow, Leith and Waterford.
[3] *History of Hull T.H. School*, p.49.

BOT's requirements, the indenture's three years would at least enable him to get a berth as a deckhand and earn enough to pay for the tuition and examination for his ticket.

Thomas was no romantic. He turned to the sea as the least of a number of evils and the only one affording some prospect of betterment in his quality of life, and of escape from the grinding poverty in which his father's death had left the family, never in any case having supported it at much above subsistence. There were thousands like him, honest boys determined to turn their fate to some advantage, whose relationship with the sea was one of wary pragmatism, and on the whole they experienced few disappointments. Others, like Henry Moffat, a citizen of Edinburgh, suffered from lively imaginations and, because of it, boredom with home and school and a dour, if not dire, Sunday routine of three kirk services interspersed with uplifting (or downcasting) readings from James's *Sermons Among the Tombs* and *Gleanings Among the Mountains*. School was a model of academic darkness and disciplinary simplicity:

Day after day I received a severe caning or a sounding blow on the side of the head...[1]

Expulsion preceded tutorage at home before starting work as a printer's devil, from which he was sacked, unjustly, over alleged sabotage. Meanwhile, always in the background of life in that city, the sea had assumed, for wayward spirits, an irresistible allure, so when HMS *Pembroke* anchored in Leith Roads Moffat saw the way forward and presented himself with a letter of introduction signed (without her knowledge) by his mother, to be taken on as a Boy, Second Class.

To the Captain of HMS Pembroke.
Sir,
Having a great desire to go to sea, and hearing that you are taking boys, I beg to offer myself. I was fourteen years old on my last birthday. I am strong and healthy, and have my mother's consent.
I am, Sir,
Your obedient servant,
Henry Young Moffat.
My mother's signature: (Signed: Margaret Moffat) [2]

At 12yrs 6mths (not 14) he could turn out an impressive letter, testimony, maybe, to the efficacy of daily canings and sounding blows to the head. In the event, however, his deception was discovered soon afterwards and he was returned ignominiously to the maternal bosom and a resumption of lessons, though not for long. A letter from one of his erstwhile boy shipmates, who had deserted to join a Geordie collier as an apprentice, was enough to revive the prodigal spirit, and he cleared out with a few

---

[1] *From Ship's Boy to Skipper*, p.10.
[2] ibid., p.24.

belongings to make his way to South Shields. There he stayed with the kindly family whose address he had been given to await the return from sea of his old comrade-in-arms, in the process finding a place in the brig *Premium*, her master offering, like Hobley of Caernarfon, a 3-year apprenticeship and £30:

> We went off at once to a lawyer, who drew up the agreement, and when all was settled I went aboard my new home, lying in the Howden Dock.[1]

And home it was, of course, rather than a mere workplace, one of the factors overlooked by the bureaucrats in their gathering (not always necessary or beneficial) presence as time went on.

The year was 1857, and the agreement followed the standard form of indenture, its terms not long overhauled by the 1850 MSA without radical change. Headed *Ordinary Apprentice's Indenture*, its difference from the earlier document lay in the absence of a clause about impressment and service in the navy, and the appearance of a new one requiring surety. But, as an agreement between consenting parties, alterations could be made on the spot and a surety, for example, struck out: as long as they met with the approval of a magistrate its terms and conditions were negotiable within the broad principles of its purpose. As before, it was signed (in the presence of two witnesses) in duplicate, the original lodged with the local customs or, if in London, with the Registry of Seamen, and a copy handed to the apprentice. After establishment of local MMOs the superintendent (the "Shipping Master") took charge of the original after endorsing it and the copy, and the master the copy, passing it to the apprentice on completion of his time or before then if he failed to stay the course, and endorsing it on the reverse.

This ponderous little exercise took place after the formality of introduction, which varied from owner (or master) to owner, but by this time impromptu methods were giving way to more formal ritual, frequently before senior managerial staff or directors. By 1861 James Killick, late of the brig *Ganges* and other ships, was in partnership with a James Henry Martin running a shipbroking and owning business, Killick occupying the post of ships' husband, or superintendent. In 1874 H. Clarkson Birch, as a prospective apprentice, came before him when he was one of a panel of four Dickensian characters, three partners and the head clerk, regarding the boy grimly across the boardroom table. In Killick, a tall fierce-looking man, there was a complete absence of geniality, ghost of the test of nerve employed by the HEIC's selection and examination boards:

> They all appeared to me hideously ugly... Whilst the other three looked at me as if I were a curious exhibit in a museum, Killick did the talking... He was a blunt, plain-spoken man, and

---

[1] *From Ship's Boy to Skipper*, p.44.

on that account was considered by my people to be what is known as a "rough diamond", and a man of sterling honesty.[1]

Clarkson Birch was a stranger to his interviewers, unlike the many who obtained a hearing through nepotism and whose backgrounds were known at least to the extent of their records at a pre-sea school or one of the training-ships, though paper virtue could hide a multitude of sins depending on circumstances. Albert Armitage's father was a physician of Scarborough, the prosperous head of a family of eight children. His son's interest in school was marginal, in the town's fishing fleet enthusiastic, and in 1878, aged 14, he started as a cadet in the *Worcester*, by this date at her permanent berth off Greenhithe. But far from leaving school behind, as he'd anticipated, he found it as vigorous as before with a slant towards the public school ethos including occasional tendencies in the cadets towards the neo-anarchy reminiscent of the schoolboy republics against which Arnold of Rugby had set his face.

A strict rule on board was "no smoking", extended to several rendezvous ashore including the cafes and tuck-shops patronised by the cadets but which in practice were safe houses. At least, they were until the Captain-Superintendent, Cdr. J. Henderson-Smith, RNR, made the mistake of carrying out a punitive raid on one of them, confiscating pipes and tobacco and calling forward the owners, a call to which they declined to respond. Moved by this to cancel all shore-leave the captain was booed off the deck by the assembled cadets, a performance repeated every day for the rest of the term. At its end, on their way to the station, they broke all the windows in the doctor's house to let him know their opinion of him as an informer, and on their return the following term resumed the war with a general strike. This produced a threat of mass expulsion, a serious tactical blunder on Henderson-Smith's part, since the cadets would have been delighted at the chance to call his bluff and face him with the hideous prospect of a derelict command; but fortunately for him, and the cadets, in the best tradition of schoolboy honour, if rather late in the day, one Shaw – "the most popular boy on board"[2] – stepped forward to claim his pipe and break the stalemate. His resulting increase in popularity among the cadets was balanced by summary disqualification of nomination for the Queen's Gold Medal, but again the cadets resorted to civil disobedience by refusing to vote for any of the other nominees, at which the beleaguered Henderson-Smith capitulated. He did so with remarkably good grace, all things considered, not only restoring Shaw to (official) favour but also recommending him for the Bengal Pilot Service, on which he had set his heart. The pipes and tobacco were returned and shore leave restored, at which the cadets gave the captain three cheers, and Shaw nine, and the matter was closed.

As for Armitage, he left at the end of 1879 with an extra pass in navigation and a first-class in seamanship to begin apprenticeship with a shipowning friend of his father. He went into sail, of course, but already steamship companies were, somewhat

---

[1] *An Old Sailor's Yarn*, p.13. Quoted in *The China Bird*, p.25.
[2] *Cadet to Commodore*, p.4.

gingerly, taking apprentices. They weren't, however, concerned about the training of engineers (even assuming they were about boys on deck), contenting themselves with the products of heavy engineering apprenticeships ashore, who were coming forward in sufficient numbers to obviate the need for any other form of recruitment.

One was James Robb, son of a merchant of Singapore, who, after schooling at an academy near Ayr followed by Harrow, started an engineering apprenticeship in 1881 with Hall, Russell of Aberdeen, who undertook to instruct him in the art and craft of engineers as carried on in their works. The term was six years, with pay at 4/- a week in the first, rising by 1/- a year. Joining a union without the master's permission was forbidden; he was to eschew gambling, night-walking, drunkenness and all other vice and immorality, as well as marriage, the last set apart only with an almost audible sniff. He entered a trade that had gathered about itself something of a monkish air; the marine engineer, as a variant of the species, was the creature of a nether world, in thrall to and enraptured with his massive pile of flying steel, communicating in a monosyllabic indecipherable tongue with arcane gesture and a profound and ineffable expression of eye. Engineering was a religion, and Robb's indenture gave the impression of barely restraining itself from saying so in black and white. The indulgence of worldly pleasures would bring upon the apprentice's head eternal damnation, the consuming heat of which was all around, the raging fires uncomfortably at hand. By comparison the humble sea apprentice dwelt in ethereal palaces of light and joy.

Absence from the place of worship was forbidden on pain of a fine of 2/6d a day; sickness had to be attested to by a doctor's note; he was to reside within half a mile of the gate, was to behave himself at all times and, importantly, was not to conceal his master's skaith, but to acquaint him therewith; that is, he was not to connive at his master's hurt or injury. The nominal working week was 60 hours, not including time at his books. He was to

> attend and take instruction in mechanical drawing, arithmetic, mathematics or kindred subjects, at an evening school in Aberdeen of good reputation for at least four months in each year.[1]

Whatever he made of it, Robb's apprenticeship looked a good deal better regulated and more purposeful than his seaborne counterpart's; he was in for some dirty work, but it was solemn stuff requiring puritanical application, its rewards abstract and mysterious, engendering a state of mind that, to the navigating officer, was baffling where it wasn't irritating and provoking. The oil and water syndrome was born of this early conflict of ideals and principle, perpetuated by segregation of the respective training grounds: exceptions apart, much of the abrasion between deck and engine-room stemmed from the incomprehension brought about by ignorance of each other's beginnings. Not only that, but whereas sail represented tradition and conservatism,

---

[1] "Story of a Scottish Engineer". Article in *Sea Breezes*, Vol 54/409. Jan.1980.

steam represented progress and innovation regarded almost with abhorrence by the deck man, who even resisted labour-saving mechanical devices invented by the more enlightened of his own kind. Between the two stretched a no-man's land of natural tension.

However, until the close of the century, deck apprenticeships in steam notwithstanding, sail remained the acknowledged training base although, by the nature of its work, organised instruction was all but precluded, the ship's day-to-day affairs considered instructive enough in their own right. The boy was still expected, never mind BOT exams, to learn by observation, inquiry and direct involvement, helped along in an *ad hoc* fashion by the disciplinary structure, variable and individualistic as it was. Official concern ended with sea time, the four years required of the candidate for 2nd mate becoming also, by the Merchant Seamen Act of 1880, the time required to qualify as AB, though no test or exam attached to the latter until half-way through the next century. The level of training required by the indenture was therefore not subject to a statutory standard, mere sea time remaining the training criterion for "the business of a seaman". The master made no declaration of intent to train the boy as an officer (with, by this date, one or two notable exceptions, most prominently the firm of Thomas & John Brocklebank, which specified "officer" unequivocally in its form of indenture), so his conscience was clear on that point at least. In the House, responding to a proposal by Lord Brassey for introduction of an examination for the rating of AB, a Mr Corry[1] stated, rather disingenuously, "We take apprentices really with the object of making our officers; it is not with the idea of making sailors; they are of too high a class for that."[2]

Exactly, but he was ducking the issue, which was to oblige him and his peers to adopt a policy of training made explicit under the terms of the indenture as they stood. He might have been one of the exceptions to the general approach to the matter, issuing an indenture with similar wording to the Brocklebank version, but if so it doesn't appear in any records of the time that remain. However, the worthy Lord Brassey had other strings to his bow, as was shortly to become evident.

Never at any time in the course of my four years' apprenticeship was I really *taught* anything. We never learned the slightest rudiments of navigation. The captain and officers treated us exactly the same as the focsle hands. The idea was to get as much work out of us as possible. (*The Tweed*, 1880s)[3]

... I had a brother stationed in India – Lieutenant in the 2nd Bn, 24th Regt of Foot... When I was in Calcutta, I wrote to him at Secunderabad describing my life, and the pictures I drew of poor little me in the bilges and up aloft during the hot season evidently touched him more than I knew. A fine soldier, a splendid athlete, and always turned out immaculately, he could not

---

[1] J.P. Corry owned the *Stars*, e.g. *Star of India*, all iron full-riggers, 1862-99.

[2] *The British Navy, Part.V*, p.273.

[3] *Yarns of an Old Shellback*, pp.5-6.

understand why a youngster who went to sea in order to learn his profession should be put to menial tasks such as cleaning out pigsties and round-houses, scrubbing out the mate's cabin and baling out the filth of the bilges. I had told him how the mate threw my navigation books overboard and refused to allow me to make any astronomical observations; confiscated my sheets and pillow-cases to his own use, and even made me wash his filthy clothing. This distressed him so much that he sent me a fiver and wrote to my father, imploring him to take me away from the sea. (Ship *Plassey*, 1884)[1]

An extreme example, perhaps, but not by any means exceptional, and a fair indicator of a deep malaise which continued to the end: people in authority of limited intelligence themselves resented any manifestation of it in others, particularly subordinates. What was more, owing to the depth and extent of changes in the structure of the "sea profession", senior officers found their rough and ready methods unequal to their mounting responsibilities, some adopting a defensive stance which included, apparently, consigning text-books to the deep. Tradition could be carried to grotesque lengths where it was perceived to be under threat; consequently, where there was less of it there was less extremism:

I told (the manager) I wanted to be an engineer, not a turner, and if I couldn't learn in his workshop I would go elsewhere. He told me to go back to my lathe and I saw him talking to old Taylor, the foreman, who came over and said "I don't know what boys are coming to. But you've been lucky this time; they need boys in the erecting shop. You'll start there on Monday." (1880s)[2]

Apart from employing officers of proven competence, better-class owners went further in issuing specific instructions concerning their apprentices and midshipmen, though there was considerable variation in their respective approaches. The Blackwall frigates were soundly run by the Greens, Wigrams, Smiths and Dunbar, but their boys received little training beyond practical seamanship and social deportment. Among those few who took a closer interest was the firm of Devitt & Moore, of which more anon, and the Brocklebanks, whose selection of potential officers gave preference to the sons of company servants, both afloat and ashore. At the end of the 50s they were taking in 35-45 boys annually, distributed round the fleet in batches of half a dozen or so, each boy required to equip himself with a sextant and Norie's *Epitome* or Maury's *Navigation*, while the ship's master was under standing instructions regarding the boys' training

Of the steamship operation, meanwhile, its continually expanding presence drew increasing numbers of qualified officers away from sail, usually for reasons of improved social conditions, the general trend being towards the liners, which, offering generally better standards of accommodation and victualling, followed regular voyage patterns and schedules. Conditions aboard tramp-steamers, on the other hand, were

---

[1] *Cadet to Commodore*, pp.22-3.
[2] *Adventures of an Obscure Victorian*, p.20.

often worse than in sail and attracted only a minority of sail men, not enough, as the fleets grew, to meet the demand. Accordingly, and with wastage an ever-present bugbear, owners began taking on apprentices in as large numbers as possible to give them, if nothing else, enough sea time to attempt the exam and return as junior officers. Poor as conditions were, they nevertheless bred a type which thrived on them, and tramp men, like the tanker men who evolved after them, took a peculiar pride in their acquired tastes. There was, too, a natural loyalty to employers, sometimes inexplicable, which the better ones recognised and nurtured, among them Walter Runciman, whose Moor Line of Sunderland-built tramps ("line" being a favourite misnomer of tramp operations) was one of the most successful and well-regarded – among tramp people – and he understood the value of a company ethos inculcated at an early age:

A lad who wishes to make the sea his profession should be apprenticed when 14 or 15 years old. For over thirty-six years[1] I have been taking four and six [sic] boys in each vessel at that age, and many became officers as soon as they got their certificates.[2]

Which suggests that some sailed as petty officers (e.g. bosun) while awaiting an officer's berth, while others didn't return to Runciman's employ.

One of the tramp's few advantages was comparatively early command, for the liner usually carried more officers (though in sail command came, on occasions, as quickly as the officers could get their tickets). Runciman claimed to be the first steamship owner to accommodate apprentices separately from the crew, to engage them as officer trainees (but like Corry without stating as much in their indentures), charge no premium (few would have paid for the privilege), and pay a wage (such as it was, and certainly nothing of an innovation where sail was concerned). But for all the possible and plausible quibbles about it the system was clear enough, and he persuaded other tramp owners to follow suit.

Discipline was an elemental part of whatever training was given, sometimes the only part, but while it was broadly defined by statute it varied in detail and interpretation from owner to owner and ship to ship. Fairly and rigorously administered its value was incalculable; interpreted with stupidity and brutishness it did deep and lasting damage, its worst manifestations leading to reform which eventually tipped the scales in the opposite direction to produce methods and practices as lax and dangerous (more so, in their official nature) as those which had brought about the change in the first place, going, as time proved, hand in hand with decline and fall.

While the master remained the ultimate authority on board, he was responsible to both his employer and the statutory authority at voyage end, and naval courts could be convened on demand to hear complaints against his conduct and take appropriate

---

[1] The Moor Line (The South Shields Shipping Co.) was founded in 1889.
[2] *Before the Mast – And After*, pp.101-2.

action. But the complaints had to be sound, and strongly substantiated, so the apprentice tended to suffer injustice (as he saw it) in silence, or at least with philosophical resignation, more so than the average deckhand by virtue of his implicit alignment with executive authority – indeed, explicit in the terms of his indenture. As a rule he displayed a high tolerance of imposition and inconvenience, confining his grumbles to the half-deck.

Discipline was harsh, punishment relentless, and I considered all sailors devoid of human feeling. The mate's favourite punishment was to sit us on a wet swab on the end of the spanker-boom. Another was to sit us on the royal yard in dirty weather or to grease the mast from top to bottom with slush. (1890s)[1]

... the hens had begun to lay and one morning I was sent to see if there were any eggs. There were three, which I slipped inside my shirt, telling the mate there were none, but as I stooped to wipe some dirt off my legs out dropped the eggs. As punishment I lost my afternoon watch below, sent up to red-lead the mizen-mast. (1879)[2]

It was all bearable, and discipline of that kind seldom killed anyone – on the contrary, death and injury usually occurred through lack of it. On the other hand the kind of bullying that sometimes took its place produced dire results, contributing to the problem of wastage, one of its components remaining desertion: apprentices who jumped ship were to be found in all the main ports of the world and quite a lot of the hinterland, particularly in the colonies. Under the 1850 MSA a master was entitled to give a deserter in charge, if he could catch him, or cancel his indentures if he couldn't, measures seldom actually resorted to if the boy's resolve evaporated in the face of unforeseen difficulties and he decided, as the better part of valour, to return to the ship. It took a particularly irredeemable and persistent (not to say unsuccessful) offender to move the master to drastic action, the almost invariable preference being to keep the apprentice on the strength with a warning and some form of non-terminal punishment, a situation which, running against everything the boy had planned, caused him much frustration in what his descendants would have recognised as a Catch-22 situation.

Robert Thomas found himself in one, though his discontent had less to do with overbearing discipline than with Thomas Hobley's business ethics, which had led him to purchase the barque in which the apprentice sailed on a voyage to Chile for a cargo of nitrate. The *Oberon* had been bought as an abandoned wreck, salved and patched up by Hobley before being despatched on what amounted to a suicidal – or rather, on Hobley's part, homicidal – venture all too apparent to the crew as the Atlantic put the ship to the test. They demanded that the master put into Montevideo for survey and repair, but it went no further than the caulking of a few seams above water, so they deserted, followed a day or two later by the apprentices, who felt they had no choice.

---

[1] *Fifty Thrilling Years at Sea*, p.18.
[2] *Spunyarn*, p.24.

Thomas and his companion tried to find work, fell in with a bad lot and were arrested, released, then lay low in a sailors' boarding-house until the ship had sailed with a fresh crew, never to be heard of again, while Hobley, no doubt, claimed on his insurers, if he had any. The other apprentice signed on before the mast in an Austrian ship and Thomas in an American, which crossed to Buenos Aires, where he signed off, having found the management methods on board too bucko. After a while he took a berth as an ordinary seaman in another American, bound for Boston, Mass. In this ship, though discipline was also robust in the Yankee tradition, he was decently treated and moved to remark, somewhat inconsistently, that "Americans are noted for good treatment to lads."[1] In some ships, anyway.

Another reason for desertion was unrelieved poverty:

We were much impressed with the glowing reports of fortunes being made in Australia at the gold-diggings, so we ran away in Singapore hoping to hide up-country then stow away in some vessel bound to Australia. But after wandering in the jungle for three days, narrowly escaping with our lives, we were glad to return, suffering agonies of fever and ague. (Barque *Archos*, 1883)[2]

The apprentice's conduct was reported on from ship to ship (if in fact he served in more than one during his time) and the verdict delivered on completion of service, satisfactory or better being the only acceptable standard. The midshipman, however, took with him a brief report made on his certificate of discharge: under the 1850 MSA a "paper discharge" or discharge note was issued on signing off and kept as part of a record of service and conduct to be presented when applying to take the examination. In 1900 it was re-issued in the form of a properly-bound booklet, a record of "continuous discharges", in the somewhat prophylactic idiom of the BOT; anyone else would have called it a continuous record, but the BOT wasn't anyone else and developed its own distinctive phraseology. Conduct was indicated by one of three cryptic notations – VG, G or DR. In practice anything other than VG – Very Good – damned the object of it out of hand while the master who had made it could rest easy in the knowledge that blame for the wretched incompetent's loss of livelihood couldn't be laid at his door. At worst he had simply declined to comment (DR – Decline to Report).

It was a curiously stultified system of reporting, one that over-praised the average on one hand and condemned it on the other. At best it weeded out the hopeless cases, at worst damned the deserving by faint praise – G was as good as a curse – and it remained in place until the MSA of 1970, enjoying the complacent endorsement, so to speak, of not only shoreside bureaucracy but also the master and the man. However, the 1970 Act, rather than replace it with a more truthful and precise form, deferred to the age of dissemblement and abrogation of personal responsibility with an unweildy

---

[1] *Ship Master*, p.48.
[2] *Seafaring*, p.94.

process of adverse reporting sheltering behind the equivocal facade of a "code of conduct" which was nothing more than another bureaucratic exercise providing no-one and nothing with anything of practical value, the word "discipline" having become discredited and corrupted through abuse. And by this date decline and fall had become a manifest development.

I knew one who sailed on one or two voyages with credit and then, because he was a member of an unruly mess, though himself having done nothing wrong, was given a "Good" discharge. That particular Blackwall service refused to take him again, and his guardians had to find him a berth with another service. The boy promised to do all he could to gain the approbation of his new commander but judge of his disgust when he was informed that his captain was not going to have Messrs So-and-So's leavings aboard his ship, expressing his intention of kicking him out at the first opportunity, and adding, "I suppose they'll want me to take the rakings of hell and Newgate next." (1860s)[1]

"Messrs So-and-So" was R&H Green, best-known of the Blackwall owners. Smartness was their hallmark, and the midshipman was expected to provide himself with a comprehensive outfit of uniform and other clothing, correct and neat dress a major part of the disciplinary ethos. By recommendation the outfitter was Silver's of Cornhill, who supplied everything necessary and quite a lot that wasn't, in the best tradition of the trade. The midshipman always joined and left his ship in the brass-bound uniform produced made-to-measure in a matter of two or three days,

... my uniform cap with its straight peak being the finishing touch. Placing it with its Green's badge on the back of my head, and carefully tucking the flaps of my waistcoat into my belt in order to show the buckle, I swaggered into Cornhill and, affecting a slight nautical roll, bumped somewhat forcibly up against a seedy-looking individual in blue serge much the worse for wear. The buttons on his coat were green with verdigris and on his head was a cap that I would not have picked out of the gutter. It was one of Green's midshipmen home from a voyage, and the language he treated me to turned the air blue. After extracting from me a humble apology he advised me to pawn my brassbinding and go home to my mother. (1880s)[2]

In London the New Zealand Shipping Co. ran a hostel for its apprentices, who were mostly New Zealanders, where they lived while their ships were in dock. It was overseen by a caretaker and staff, and although a measure of regulation prevailed the boys enjoyed considerable freedom and, in periodic confrontations, the belligerent disrespect of local youth. In Liverpool Legge's Apprentices' Home in Duke St. served a similar purpose though with no particular association with any company, where apprentices and midshipmen could put up while awaiting a ship or standing by:

Legge's was full of apprentices, and I listened with awe to their yarns, very much shocked at their language, but I soon got bravely over that. Next morning we repaired to the docks, landed

---

[1] *Reminiscences of a Blackwall Midshipman*, pp. 200-1.
[2] ibid., p.19.

on board, and I was standing gazing about with my hands in my pockets when a grimy individual came along and asked me if I was one of the bloody apprentices. On acknowledging this soft impeachment I was told to take my adjectival coat off and scrape out the pig-pen ready for its next occupant. The mate was cordially hated by all hands. (Ship *Ellerbank*; J&B Sprott, Liverpool. 1878)[1]

Cleaning the pig-pen was a common item on the training curriculum, which included any and all forms of labour, some pleasant enough, some disconcertingly obnoxious, all of it ready and waiting twenty-four hours a day.

We got very little time ashore in Sydney, only occasionally in the evenings and on Sundays. We were kept at work from six in the morning till six at night. We greatly envied other apprentices, who seemed to get plenty of leave, and added insult to injury by asking if ours was a reformatory ship. (*The Tweed*, 1880s)[2]

While at sea, in the barque *Glance:*

January 6th. 1880. Tuesday.
Taking down sails and putting up fresh ones, viz. bending fresh sails.

January 14th. 1880. Wednesday.
Fine weather, fresh breeze. My work now and for the next 3 days as "painter".
I have been painting the Lifeboats, Jolly Boat and Gig Boat. [3]

Except in one or two well-manned liner services the two-watch system, in both sail and steam, prevailed, involving all bar the idlers. The daily round at sea continued as before, a relentless alternation of 4-hour watches, the sequence broken only by the dog-watches which ensured that everyone sampled each watch in turn. By day the routine called for a helmsman beside the OOW, while the rest stood by to handle sail, occupied with various tasks about the deck; by night helm and lookout with the remainder standing by, able in fine weather to snatch a few winks of sleep. As manning in sail diminished, partly for economy, partly because fewer and fewer men were inclined to sign on when steam offered easier working, if not better living, conditions, the cry for all hands became more frequent, and it meant what it said: no-one was exempt; the ship came first at all times.

We turned to with holystones, went down on our marrow-bones and stayed there all through the watch, and whilst down we scrubbed – hard. Convicts do less work in a day than we did in an hour. Sand was flung carelessly down by the officer, and if it went in the scrubber's eyes,

---

[1] *Spunyarn*, pp.11-13.

[2] *Yarns of an Old Shellback*, p.34.

[3] Diary of William Powles, apprentice.

what odds? We scrubbed on, but took pride in making the planks whiter than our neighbour's, kept down to this performance while the AB's went aloft. (1870s)[1]

And at night:

Stuck on the focsle with the wind from the foresail shooting down your neck, straining your eyesight peering into the fog for ice – which you fancy every moment you can see but are not sure enough to hail the poop – all you can do is keep as calm as your nerves will allow and call yourself all sorts of a fool for ever leaving a comfortable home for this sort of thing. (1860s)[2]

Boatwork was generally looked upon as an enjoyable break from drudgery in port, particularly if the work included cargo-handling as in the WCSA ports – coal, coke, guano or nitrates, filthy and dangerous work as well as exhausting – but it didn't always constitute an alternative, nor was it invariably welcome. At Iquique, where the ship lay off in the roads under a dangerously fierce sun,

... the daily programme as far as we of the half-deck were concerned was: 4am: boat's crew turn out, clean boat, proceed ashore for tallymen, proceed back calling on the way at each ship from North America to secure a few edible biscuits[3]. 5.30am: land tally-clerks aboard ship, gulp down tepid tea or coffee. 6am: turn-to shovelling coal. 8am: sketchy breakfast. 8.30am: turn-to at coal, digging-down a purgatory. Four men and boys to each gang, one to hold the sack open, three to shovel, sailmaker and carpenter racing from gang to gang to act as sackholder and never a boy among them. 6pm: work officially ceased, but if a *lancha* was half-full we went on shovelling. We got into the habit of plunging overboard as we were, in singlet and trousers, for a swim as soon as the last lighter left. Then supper – biscuits, marmalade and tea – before taking the tally-clerks ashore. After that we were generally required to pull the captain ashore or to some other ship, which meant that we seldom saw our bunks before midnight. Then it was 4 o'clock again... (1870s)[4]

And if he was lucky enough to be in a crack clipper the apprentice would discover that boatwork was part of the key to her reputation:

Any other ship would have sailed through the Malacca Straits, but there wasn't enough hard work in that for *The Tweed*, and as there was no wind we spent two days kedging through. Called at 5.30 we started work at six, went on until dark, when the anchor watch was set, with half an hour for breakfast and an hour for dinner. Two boats were used with a kedge anchor in each. As soon as the ship had been hove up to one the rope of the other, which had been dropped ahead, was taken to the winch. It was killing work and we were glad to be clear of the straits and back at the ordinary work of sailing the ship. (1880s)[5]

---

[1] *Knocking Around*, pp.84-6.

[2] *Reminiscences of a Blackwall Midshipman*, pp.181-2.

[3] Acknowledged generous feeders, American ships carried good-quality stores, their biscuit a superior article to the Liverpool pantile.

[4] *Knocking Around*, p.113.

[5] *Yarns of an Old Shellback*, p.41.

Meanwhile, on the shop floor, the spirit of the new age was firmly in place:

Piece-work was unknown except for one particular job and it was a mark of the foreman's favour to be sent to do it, for it was possible to earn about 10/- a week extra by it. I'd thought of a plan to increase the output, but the three labourers who helped me were on a weekly wage and had no interest, so I said I would share whatever I made with them. Two were Glasgow toughs who agreed to have a go, and the third was a young Highlander, slow and stupid. When the Glaswegians saw the plan working they worked like tigers and kept the Highlander moving. Then one day I found the drive belt slipping and discovered that it was smeared with soft soap, so asked a man at a nearby machine who was in fits of laughter what he meant by it. He denied it and I said that if it happened again I'd rub his nose in it. We cleaned the belt but once again it slipped and the same man was doubled up with laughter, so I went over and hit him and down he went. The Highlander pulled me away, owning up to the deed, saying it wasn't right to work so hard because it would spoil the job for the next people. He was a real socialist and I told him that if any more soap got onto the belt I'd kill him. (1880s)[1]

Unfortunately for British shipbuilding and engineering soap continued to get onto the belt while overseas competition geared up for increased production, or at least punctual delivery of the goods; but the inevitable outcome – the job spoiled for all – took time to develop, as such things do.

Aboard the clippers racing home with the teas there was more than met the eye, kedging apart. While pay was poor there was every incentive to supplement it, and accommodation and other space was given over to "private ventures", at some inconvenience and not a little risk owing to instability and cluttered working areas. For all the underwriters knew this was the cause of some of their losses in the absence of evidence after the event. When the *Corea* (not one of the faster ships, and if this is typical of her operation it isn't surprising) loaded for home in the 60s she was stuffed to the gunwales with trading ventures. The cabin was jammed to the deckhead, the officers' cabin-separation bulkheads removed to allow passage past the blocked-up goods. Boxes of curios and bolts of silk were levered into corners, the cabin table piled high leaving space for only two to dine; the biscuit tanks brought on deck to allow tea and other goods to be packed into the lazarette; steward's stores reduced and stowed in his cabin so that he had to sleep on the pantry deck while his store-room did service as goods-space; coal went into the long-boat; salt provisions, ship's gear and deck stores into the crew's focsle; paint, oils and rope into the half-deck, and open decks and hatch-covers buried under cordage and spare spars. Boats were filled with vegetables; poultry, normally in coops, allowed to run free, and the gig the only boat clear for use – as a boat. Every nook and cranny below deck was full of trade goods, and apart from the unsightly shambles on deck the ship wasn't only overladen but also, through obstruction, difficult and dangerous to manage. In fact, what appeared to be the owner's generous sanction of this practice as an alternative to paying his

---

[1] *Adventures of an Obscure Victorian*, pp.16-17.

employees rather more than was absolutely necessary to hold body and soul together was very likely to separate them and put an end to the whole enterprise. Not that more pay would have deterred the ship's people from risking all for profit; it was regarded as a right, and even the apprentices managed to get involved, usually at the price of returning home decently clothed. Lacking hard cash, barter was their particular *forté*.

Practical safety being ignored – indeed, correctly seen as a hindrance to the efficient working of a sailing-ship in times when markets were volatile, steamships mounting ever more effective competition and crews becoming more difficult to find and keep – bureaucratic edict meant less than nothing, and the 1850 MSA's declaring the half-deck and other living-spaces prohibited for the stowage of cargo and stores was just so much empty print. In any case accommodation was cramped enough: the Act prescribed 9 superficial (i.e. square) feet per man, with a notional headroom of 6ft, so an area measuring 6ft x 1ft 6ins was the norm, coinciding with the bare minimum more or less by custom. An Act of 1867 increased it to 12 s/ft, adding that it was to be properly constructed, lit and ventilated, protected from the weather, and "as far as possible" (one of the many meaningless phrases beloved of the new bureaucracy) shut off from offensive odours from cargo or bilge. In other words, if it was not possible to keep out smells letting them in was perfectly lawful. Unfortunately there was excuse enough for corrective and prescriptive legislation: in a review of 1880 Lord Brassey remarked

> *In these days of close profits owners are sometimes tempted to cut everything in the shape of wages, food and accommodation to a minimum, and to treat the question of the health and comfort of their crews as a matter of altogether secondary importance.*[1]

Apprentices in trades employing smaller ships – brigs, schooners and the like, carrying slate, chalk, coal and so on – lived below deck forward with the hands in generally squalid conditions. In a 420-ton barque in the 60s, carrying ten hands and four apprentices, the senior boy lived with the carpenter and cooper in a makeshift space in the square of the after hatch also used for storage of tools and equipment. The seamen, cook and other apprentices lived in the raised focsle which, with about 5ft headroom, measured some 20ft fore and aft by about the same across at its widest, aftermost, part.

> *It was a foulsome and suffocating abode, and in bad weather the water and filth washed about the deck and among the casks creating the most intolerable and loathsome stench.*[2]

It was also infested with rats and other wildlife. The rules governing such spaces, not being retrospective, had no effect.

---

[1] *The British Navy, Part V.*, p.294.

[2] *History of Merchant Shipping & Ancient Commerce*, quoted in *A New History of British Shipping*, p.291.

In larger vessels fitted with deckhouses conditions were slightly less uncomfortable, and as a rule the apprentices' half-deck was set apart from the crew's focsle, either in a separate deckhouse or as a space under the raised poop contiguous to the officers' accommodation. But however situated, it was invariably cramped, prone to flooding, ventilated but seldom heated, and usually uncluttered with washing facilities.

... a damp, leaky hole called the apprentices' half-deck. There were no appointments whatsoever in this commodious apartment, 6ft x 12ft with running water laid on – rain and sea – from the roof. No bedding, not even a chair, and our messing utensils supplied by ourselves. Each in turn had to scrub out on hands and knees, and washing and mending was done in our own time. (Ship *Latimer.* 1890s)[1]

Cutty Sark had little space to spare, but she had an atmosphere of her own:

The accommodation for apprentices was in a small house at the fore side of the after hatch, and eight of us lived in a space about 15ft x 18ft. We were, however, very comfortable and happy except when the ship was taking water aboard. (1870s)[2]
– which was seldom, for she enjoyed a reputation as a dry ship, in that sense.

Midshipmen in the Blackwallers lived somewhat more grandly, as in Green's *Trafalgar*, where the mess, savouring more of the naval gun-room than the half-deck, was

... a fairly roomy sea-parlour made by knocking two or three of the state-rooms into one: a long table with a red and blue cloth was in the middle, while around it were the sea-chests of its occupants, serving as seats. A broad shelf ran round the sides, on it loaves of bread, sea-boots, onions, sextants, pickles, Norie's *Navigation(sic)*, etc etc. We slung our hammocks in the tween-decks outside with the exception of the third mate, whose swinging cot had its place over the table, during the day triced up to the beams. To minister to our wants a wretched individual shipped as midshipmen's devil. (1860s)[3]

As for victuals, it was in this department that tradition and British owners and masters excelled themselves, cheeseparing attaining the status of high art. Yankee ships were tough and hard-driving, but they pampered their crews' stomachs; Scawegians were clean, dull and well-fed; the French lived for their digestions; and the British practised a form of dietary asceticism embraced by all with a kind of perverse satisfaction – by the hands because they could grumble at it, likewise the apprentices; by the master because he could make something of it on the side; by the owner because enough was sufficient unto the day and waste akin to original sin. The cook, who was unqualified except perhaps by hit-and-miss experience, did what he

---

[1] *Fifty Thrilling Years at Sea*, p.18.
[2] *Yarns of an Old Shellback*, p.56.
[3] *Reminiscences of a Blackwall Midshipman*, pp.46-7.

could, either to ruin what was good or to work miracles with what was bad. And the apprentices were permanently hungry in any case.

This being my first Christmas away from home I find it very different in every shape and form. The victuals we get are <u>very different</u> to what we get on land, for instance, Sunday is our best day and for breakfast we have biscuits (full of insects called Weavels) and Butter worth about 3d a lb on land, and Tea – the dinner for Sunday is a kind of tinned meat made into soup and dough and it is known to sailors as Soup-de-Boulyon. For weekdays we have Biscuits, Butter and Tea for breakfast and Tea the same, for dinner one day we have boiled junk and Molasses and Rice next day Pork, next day Salt Fish, next day Pork and Peas Soup next day boiled junk & dough and the next day Saturday we have Salt Pork and Peas Soup. For our Christmas Day's dinner our Captain gave us something extra, viz – a glass of grog (rum) Plum Cake, Tinned Meat Dough and Potatoes. (Barque *Glance*, 1879)[1]

Taking this as an example of daily fare the continuing incidence of scurvy is hardly surprising, and the measures to counter it – Acts of Parliament concerned with the issue of the now famously ineffective lime-juice or a substitute[2] – of only indeterminate virtue. As for provisions, the BOT heroically resisted what pressure there was to prescribe a scale, salving its conscience by making "recommendations" as in a report of 1880 mentioning increases in quantities of fresh meat, fruit and vegetables but adding that it felt a mandatory scale was "not yet needed". By whom isn't clear, but certainly ships' people seemed to be in need of it – and if not yet, then when, and why later rather than sooner? The recommendations – most prominent of them the so-called "Liverpool Scale" of 1867[3] – were either received with amused scorn or, if adopted, taken not as the minimum but as the standard, going against the spirit of the measure which was, in fact, merely another completely spurious bureaucratic exercise lending an appearance of integrity to those who stood to gain by it.

We are now becalmed off the NE point of the island of Socotra, and I am just sent below because my hands...and my face are all covered with spots and very much swollen; it is what they call the prickly heat. I have written two or three letters already, but I shall not send them, as I will tell you all the news up to the present in this...   We left Gravesend on a Friday; on Saturday we passed Brighton...and at 12pm on Saturday night the pilot left us, taking ashore letters, one of which I hope you received...   I ate nothing for three days, as I could get nothing but salt junk and biscuit...but on Wednesday the steward...sent me in some soup, which I quickly demolished, and in the evening got some milk, so I felt pretty well all right. But I forgot to tell you on Monday it came on to blow rather fresh, and increased, till on Tuesday we had quite a gale, hove-to under close-reefed fore and main topsails. They were up nearly all night taking in the sails, pouring rain and something like wind. I was sent below because I was no good, being as weak as a child from sea-sickness. In our house all the chests were floating

---

[1] Diary of William Powles.

[2] See appendix 2.

[3] ibid.

about, and there was real confusion, but we got over it all right, excepting that we stove in one...of our boats and lost 900 gallons of water, which we are now feeling the want of. We are come to this island to see if we can't get some.

Nothing particular happened till Christmas Day, when we did no work and had a bottle of beer each. About three weeks after we left, the captain told Sails...to make hammocks for two of us, and so Wardroper and Foster...have not slept in the berth since.

At 12pm on the last day of 1863 we all got together with tin pots and one concertina and made a fearful row, marching round the decks until the captain and all the passengers had turned out. They gave us all some grog to let them go to sleep again, which we did after half an hour more at it.

On the 2nd of January we crossed the Line, when at 12.30pm we saw Neptune (I forgot to tell you he paid us a visit the night before and we sent him afloat again) in his car drawn by four men, dressed up to represent seadogs, on their hands and knees. He came along the decks, with the barber and the whole lot of them, and we (those that had not crossed the Line before, being all the passengers, three of us and two sailors who had been in the Hudson's Bay and Mediterranean service) were all duly brought up onto the platform, shaved with rusty pieces of iron with notches in them, and then very gently (as you may imagine) precipitated backwards into a sail full of water, where the seadogs ducked you...

(Blackwaller *Cospatrick*, March 29th. 1864: abstract of letter from a midshipman.[1])

Horror stories of bad victuals were endemic and repetitious; but in practice not all the food was bad, and much of its poor quality stemmed from long voyages and inefficient preservation. Where it occurred, starvation came about through incompetence as much as avarice and official inertia, and in spite of the rubbish he had to eat the apprentice seldom exhibited signs of malnutrition. Rather the reverse, in fact, and instances were rare enough to be remarked upon. Nevertheless, some part of his diet was the fruit of wit and cunning, and edible matter in any way accessible, whether cargo, ship's stores or legitimate fare, was permanently at risk.

I learned to broach cargo and pinch stores. I also learned to fight for the largest rootie on Thursday and Sunday. With a piece of sharp-pointed iron tied to a stick I waited an opportunity to harpoon dainties through the porthole of the cabin pantry. On one occasion two of us harpooned a chicken from the cabin table and the mates created more wind than a southerly buster when Harriet Lane was produced instead. (1890s)[2]

I was standing at the scuppers cleaning the tar off my hands when the port health officer boarded and expressed a wish to interview the European crew members. He looked me over and sternly said to the Old Man, "What have you done to this boy?" He measured my waist – 18 inches – then walked aft with the skipper. What he said I don't know, but I was berthed in the cuddy and fed up [*sic*] for a while. (1880s)[3]

---

[1] *Ship Alley*, pp.92-4.

[2] *Fifty Thrilling Years at Sea*, p.59.

[3] *Cadet to Commodore*, p.13.

A side effect, as it were, of the half-deck's customary fare was a tendency towards the habits of the gutter, a trait noticed by some owners and shipmasters with enough concern to take remedial action, as had been the case in earlier days among the more gracious commanders of East Indiamen. Captains continued to invite denizens of the half-deck to dine with them on a certain day or days in the week, the only time an apprentice received a foretaste of civilisation to come. The NZS Co's apprentices were patently officers under training (but again without explicit warrant) and Sunday dinner was an indicator of the fact:

We carefully washed our hands again in half a pint of water, vainly trying to remove tar and paint. Then we dressed with care. The saloon seemed luxurious after the dog-kennel of a cabin [i.e. half-deck]. Bird's-eye maple panelling, white deckhead picked out with gold, red-upholstered settees and revolving chairs, a soft red and grey carpet, well-filled sideboard backed with a mirror, cabinet, bookcase, brass lamp beneath the skylight, rack of muskets and boarding-pikes round the mizen-mast, a tiny fireplace and well-equipped table, snug and pleasing quarters for the master, mates and passengers. The snow-white cloth and napkins and the silver dishes and covers shone proudly while various good smells escaped. (Ship *Wairoa*, 1880s)[1]

And these from the same galley that produced a mess of salt junk and "dough" for the crowd – incentive enough to get on and pass for 2nd mate, though in fairness to the NZS Co it has to be said that the crews of colonial shipping fared rather better than their contemporaries in UK-based ships. Back aboard the *Glance* William Powles noted

December 27th. 1879.
A good breeze blowing SW. I quite forgot to put down that we have caught by harpoon lots of fish called "Bonitas" on an average 12lb each thus making a good feed for all hands.[2]

Surviving the diet, arrival in port presented not only an opportunity to freshen the menu but also hazards of a different kind and Sydney, for example, had in the 80s become a dangerous place for men, let alone boys, on a run ashore. This was, at a pinch, part of the reason for the captain's ensuring that the apprentices were kept at work from dawn to dusk, prevented from going ashore by day and by evening too tired to bother. As a counter to the temptations and concomitant risks of the city, the Missions to Seamen didn't appear there until 1896.

A number of such bodies featured in the apprentice's life, rising to prominence during the first half of the 20th century, but the archetype was "the Mission", the Anglican (in practice non-denominational) foundation that became the Flying Angel of world-wide renown, acting as much *in loco parentis* to the apprentice as for his

---

[1] *First Voyage in a Square-Rigged Ship*, pp.144-5.
[2] Diary of William Powles.

spiritual wellbeing. Whatever his religious sentiments he was probably its greatest beneficiary during the red ensign's heyday.

It originated in the work of a young clergyman, John Ashley, who, while visiting parishioners on the islands of Flat Holm and Steep Holm in the Bristol Channel, took to calling on the ships at anchor in the offing, anything up to 400 at any time in 1835, performing social services for their men as well as selling them Bibles and prayer-books and conducting religious services and studies. The work lapsed after his retirement in 1850 but revived during the Crimean War and, supported by interested parties including the National Church Society, soon began to spread, making the first move abroad in 1892 with a mission at Antwerp. Another followed, in Dunkirk in 1894, after which expansion moved east of Suez, south to the Cape and west to the Americas, and mission padres quickly established a tradition of integrity and untiring effort on behalf of their (often cordially profane and ungrateful) polyglot and nomadic flocks.

Nevertheless, a well-entrenched religious sense was characteristic of the age, Darwin's work notwithstanding[1], and seamen in general weren't averse to a good sermon and a few robust hymns. In any case they frequently found themselves forming a congregation by order, welcoming it where it also meant an hour or so beyond the call, or reach, of duty. The master – a Welshman as a rule, it seems – often took his relationship with his Maker as a solemn compact, and the bethel ship was a familiar feature of life in many ports, particularly where long periods were spent awaiting a cargo – ports where sail was still prevalent, that is, for steamships usually got quick despatch. Services were conducted by masters with a gift for oratory (or without it, as the case may have been) to which all were more than welcome, transport usually provided courtesy of the apprentices in the long-boat or gig. On the whole the practice was well-received, but in the wrong hands religion turned sour, and hypocrisy has been, as far as the Christian church is concerned, an abiding *bete noir*. Captain White, of *The Tweed* infamy, represented himself as a godly sort of chap, to the admiration of his shoreside acquaintances, although they were probably ignorant of the fresh meaning he gave to the term "holystone":

We hated Friday more than any other. At 6am we started to holystone the decks and kept at it all day and the following morning. Then the brasswork was cleaned and the ropes flumished[*sic*] down. At 4pm a crowd of the captain's Baptist friends came aboard for tea, saying that the ship was as clean as a man-o'-war and what a splendid man the captain was, at which we six apprentices had to retire to blow off our feelings. (Calcutta, 1880s)[2]

And of course they got none of the tea, unless the steward was either sympathetic or careless. Others were more fortunate:

---

[1] *Origin of Species* was published in 1859.
[2] *Yarns of an Old Shellback*, pp.46-7.

The Holy Terror possessed only two sorts of books, those on navigation, and the Bible –
which he called his sailing directions for the next world. Every Sunday afternoon in favourable
weather all hands mustered in the saloon, when he read the Bible, afterwards giving us a short
sermon, always to the point. He told us we had no chance of safe anchorage in the next world
unless we had faith in our Pilot and the "sailing directions". In port we boys had to go to
church with him, and Astoria was treated to a procession of four apprentices walking two by
two ahead of the Holy Terror with his grim determined face, then Jim Cargill with a pair of
revolvers flapping below his belt, followed by various members of the crew. Church was a
watertight means of evading worldly duties. (Barque *Invercargill*, c.1883)[1]

Between this sort of thing and the mate's deathless ingenuity, let alone the ship's
ever-present need of attention, spare time wasn't the problem it later became, and
when it occurred amusements were home-grown and hobbies mostly sailors'
handicrafts, with a light scatter of reading matter, stuff that had drifted aboard from a
variety of caches both religious and secular.

In the dog-watches we used to play draughts, cards, follow-my-leader. Jack Banks was the
leader, a Liverpool boy just out of his time. Nothing was too hot or too heavy for him. We
followed him or paid a forfeit, starting at the fore-tack, up the leaches of the foresail, topsail,
topgallant and royal, then across from mast to mast on a stay. The Captain, watching, enjoyed
it as much as we, but there were always four or five would not do it. Banks would tie a
handkerchief over a fellow's eyes and ask, "What will this man do?" One would have to kneel
and say the Lord's Prayer, another blacken his face with tar, and anyone not paying a forfeit
would be chased by all and beaten with belts and slippers. (1860s)[2]

Sickness continued tantamount to shirking, with no recourse to doctors' certificates
and best borne in silence unless definitely established as terminal. The invalid was a
pariah in the eyes of all; of the ship's people because it meant more work for them,
and of the owner in terms of cash loss:

Captain Hughes had left £100 of the freight money to pay my hospital expenses and passage
home. At London I presented myself at the offices of Messrs Fernie & Sons to be greeted by
"You are the most expensive apprentice we have ever had" and instructions to go away and
come back when the doctor had passed me fit. I did so, but my indentures had expired; they
were handed to me and so ended my apprenticeship, and as the Fernies seemed to think I was
no further use I had to look for employment elsewhere. Because of the illness I hadn't the
necessary four years at sea, so found a third mate's job in the *Falls of Afton*, a 4-masted full-
rigger owned by Wright, Breckenridge of Glasgow. The salary was £2.15s a month, an AB's
pay. (1884)[3]

---

[1] *Roaring Forties*, pp.75-6.
[2] *Rolling Home*, pp.48-9.
[3] *Hull Down*, pp.41-2.

In practice the third mate was still superfluous to the ship's officer requirement, and as far as his work went was indeed little more than equivalent to an AB, but the pay would have enabled him – in such instances as this – to save enough to try for his ticket sooner than if his indentures had been extended for the balance of the necessary sea-time. Not only that, but he might also have had better opportunity to prepare himself for the exam, though the ship remained devoid of study facilities, in both time available and the wherewithal to make use of it, for all that some people likened it to a place of higher education:

The focsle was my university and during the time I was an undergraduate, as the beautiful days went by, my life was always eventful. Trials and adversity came as they do to all of us but at the end of my apprenticeship I could make a square-rigged ship "do anything but speak" and had mastered the science of navigation well enough to take a vessel anywhere. (1865)[1]

A view coloured with retrospective sentimentality. In fact the sea's educational spectrum was narrow and its "graduate" unfitted for anything outside its peculiar demands except in a broad philosophical sense; its distinguishing feature was a kind of world-wide parochialism, antithesis of the university's ostensible intention and purpose, tending to channel the mind along vocational lines rather than open it to wider horizons. Moreover, the comparison, pretension apart, is unnecessary: an accomplished mariner, whether able to make his ship speak or not, had no need to draw irrelevant parallels when his calling was unique and honourable in its own right. The half-deck (or focsle) was in fact more of a nursery than a seat of learned discourse, and when nursery days came to an end the real business began, the practice of an occupation that came to be called, not a little self-consciously, the profession of the sea.

My apprenticeship having expired, I left for Liverpool in the Cunard ss *British Queen* and travelled with the emigrants for the sake of economy, arrived at Liverpool and received my indentures. In settling up Mr Edwards, a partner, asked me for a ha'penny to balance my account. I suppose this was strict business but it seemed to me sordid meanness considering the sum I had received for my four years' service. (1886)[2]

The 4-year requirement seemed a simple enough condition, but complication was setting in, steadily compounded over the years to come. First was the matter of remission of sea service in recognition of pre-sea training, anything up to 12 months, granted also in respect of the seagoing training-ships which entered the picture late in the century[3]. In the apprentice's case indentured time was sufficient if it had passed without interruption bar short intervals between voyages, the defining clause running:

---

[1] *Before the Mast – And After*, p.100.
[2] *Captain Fraser's Voyages*, p.54.
[3] See Ch.8.

Time for which Indentures of Apprenticeship are in force will be accepted as sea service, provided that the Apprentice has remained by the ship all the time, and the Indentures of the applicant are endorsed by the Owner or Master to whom he has been bound, to the effect that he has performed his service faithfully for the whole time agreed upon and provided also that the Local Marine Board are[sic] satisfied that no undue amount of service has been performed on shore. In the event of the Local Board being of opinion that the amount of service performed by the Candidate on shore has been excessive, they[sic] may determine how much further sea service shall be required of him before he may present himself for examination.[1]

So circumstances might arise to create a hiatus long enough to require extension of time, though it was seldom preferred to signing on before the mast, time which then had to be attested to by the ship's master as a standard entry on the paper discharge or in the later discharge book, with or without an accompanying note of testimony. In the midshipman's case (or, as he became known through the training-ships, cadet) and that of others with non-indentured sea service, the discharge papers had to show in sum the necessary time, which usually meant a total, including periods between ships off articles, appreciably exceeding the four years. This was the system as it remained, with minor variations, to the end. And in 1887 a compulsory sight test was introduced for navigating officers, a simple one in colour but with exacting standards, later extended to include a form test. Failure to identify the colour of any one of the pieces of knitting-wool used as the test medium disqualified the candidate from the examinations – and, as a natural consequence, from further seafaring unless before the mast.

Having settled all that, the next step was to attend school for long enough to gather a good idea of what was likely to come up in the exam. There was no question of gaining a broad grasp of the "profession" – the few pounds saved had to be eked out to cover the barest minimum of school time – only of reaching the standard of familiarity with it that would satisfy the examiner, who was himself distinguished by his preferences and habits, seldom concerned with comprehensive coverage of the subject because for him, too, time was limited.

Schools were present in all the major ports, most of them private, but, following the creation of the BOT's Marine Department, subsidy through the Department of S&A funded schools regulated by the BOT through the MMOs. They offered tuition at a nominal fee, but the private schools continued, partly because the demand exceeded the state schools' capacity, partly because of their reputation (as efficient crammers) and records of passes. Their ascendancy in this vital matter was owed chiefly to the curious discrepancy between the Department of S&A's curriculum and the examination syllabus, essentially a disparity between theory and practice.

By 1862 there were some 17 schools in 15 ports, while among the private establishments those which combined nautical tuition with their normal curriculum left the system one by one – the village school of Hugh Davies the Nailer, for

---

[1] *Ainsley's Extra Master's Guide*, p.3.

example, which taught exam candidates until the 1880s. Similarly, a Mrs Edwards ran a school in Caernarfon for a time. Of the new grant-aided schools Hull Trinity House was an example but a latecomer to the BOT exams; by the mid-60s schools offering preparatory tuition were located at Aberdeen, Leith (James Bolam's school, founded in 1855), Glasgow, Liverpool (founded in 1852 at the Sailors' Home), South Shields (the oldest, founded, as already mentioned, in 1837 to prepare collier apprentices for their appearance before the trade's examining panels), London (several variously located), Plymouth, Belfast, Dublin and a few other ports.

In 1855 a Mr Harry Riches, water bailiff and collector of Admiralty droits, was teaching candidates for the BOT exams in Cardiff, and by the end of the 80s there was a number of similar establishments, among them one run by Mr A. Munro in Bute St., handy to the docks and the MMO, where the exams were conducted, and another by Captain John Owen in Loudoun Square, not far away. In 1893 a school of navigation was set up in the Cardiff Proprietary School, later the Technical School, grant-assisted, but the following year attendance dwindled to nothing while Captain Owen and his contemporaries thrived on. The Marine School at the Guild of Merchant Venturers in Bristol started classes in the 60s but failed in the early 70s, leaving a gap until a new department in the Merchant Venturers' Technical College was established in 1898.

One of the successful schools under the BOT scheme opened in Plymouth in 1862 under the headship of a very able 28-year-old John Merrifield, a keen amateur meteorologist who persuaded Admiral Robert Fitzroy, the noted authority on tropical revolving storms, to supply a complete outfit of observing and recording instruments, and by the time of Merrifield's premature death in 1891 the school was the acknowledged leader in its field.

In London Janet Taylor's famous institution was taken over in 1870 by a Captain Broughton who renamed it, quite properly, Broughton's Nautical School; others were Potter's Academy at Tower Hill, Rugg's in the Commercial Road, and Baxter's in Leadenhall St. A Captain Chapman taught in Limehouse, joined in the early 90s by a Captain A.E. Nicholls to run the Chapman & Nicholls's Nautical Academy. Several names became well-known as authors of standard texts.

Strictly speaking, the engineer apprentice didn't figure in marine engineering schools, which offered courses for the BOT exams introduced by the 1862 MSA, for he went to sea not as an apprentice but as a junior engineer, with whom this story isn't concerned. However, a number of technical schools and colleges followed in the wake of the navigation schools to provide the necessary tuition for the BOT 2nd- and 1st-class certificates.

The engineer apprentice qualified as a journeyman at the end of his 5-year term, either through the schools at the naval dockyards or through classes at technical schools within reach of the works. The system was inconsistent until in 1877 the livery companies of London formed a committee with responsibility for preparing curricula for technical instruction, out of which evolved the City & Guilds of London Institute. In 1883 it was instrumental in founding the Finsbury Technical College, a model for others that followed, all concerned with institute qualifications for which the engineer apprentice was eligible before taking up a sea career.

Meanwhile, on deck, the 1854 MSA introduced home-trade certificates, in the grades of master and mate, four years' service on the new home-trade articles required to apply to take the mate's exam, while the foreign-going 2nd mate's exam could be attempted after 6 years' home-trade time, the certificate now classed as "Ordinary", i.e. square-rig, though valid in steamships. By the 1862 Act, however, an additional steamship certificate was introduced, the examination including all the ordinary syllabus with extra material pertaining to steamship practice, enough to render the function of an engine-room telegraph less of a black art than otherwise. So it still behoved the apprentice to serve his time in sail rather than in steam, whichever certificate he was aiming at: the new certificate was in effect an ordinary one with a steamship endorsement, indicating a holder not entirely ignorant of progress as popularly conceived. Few troubled to attempt the exam.

The new two-tier certificate structure – home-trade and foreign-going – profoundly affected the apprentice's status. Until its introduction he had served his time in any kind of trade, whether in home waters or distant, distinguished only by the old classification of ships; now, although home-trade service allowed him to take the foreign-going exam, he had to put in two more years than his contemporaries in blue-water ships, so home-trade apprenticeship went into steep decline, lingering only among those content to confine their futures to home waters, though they were better advised, in that case, to sign on before the mast. They were found chiefly in the collier brigs, where the BOT certificate buttered no parsnips with the indiginous examining panels, whose endorsement was required by owners offering berths. The panels went on examining boys as before, for a place in the focsle, BOT ticket or no BOT ticket.

As for the examiners themselves, who corrected the written part of the examination and conducted the *viva voce* part, reputations varied and personal idiosyncrasies assumed apocalyptic significance. Though appointed by the Local Marine Board they enjoyed considerable autonomy in their duties and in their views of what constituted competence, and in knowing them the schools' principals and staff were able to solve half the candidates' difficulties at the outset.

I went to old Martin in the Minories. Dear old Martin! He was as deaf as a post, but a good coach, and a gentleman. Some led him rather a dance, paid far more attention to the barmaid at the Three Nuns than to their work. I had only been at the school for a fortnight when he decided that I should go up. I passed, and got my blue paper. The day before, I got a letter from Green's appointing me midshipman in the *Melbourne* [1]. My father wanted me to go but I declined and eventually managed, through a bit of influence, to get an appointment in the P&O. (1870s)[2]

---

[1] See Ch.8.

[2] *Spunyarn*, p.39.

Following widespread practice Martin charged a flat fee for the course, no matter how long it took the student to get through it, so it was in his own interests to urge an attempt at the earliest feasible moment. The offer of a midshipman's berth in this instance is indicative of the promotion prospects in a company that, once representative of the new age in displacing the old HEIC, was now itself on the wane while clearly retaining its seagoing staff without difficulty. As it happened, P&O was, to all intents and purposes, its replacement in turn.

Perhaps because of the confines of the examination room, as oppressive to them as to the candidates, examiners were often brusque and sometimes impatient, disconcerting for the hapless candidate; no bad thing, though, since a table set with little models and a sextant resting safely on a shelf were worlds away from conditions in practice, and an ability to keep one's head in trying circumstances was an essential quality of the officer, as the HEIC had so fully appreciated after painful experience. The best chance of ensuring examination by a genial old salt rather than an irritable tyrant was to know your stuff – and his:

The examiners were Professor Towson, author of *Towson's Tables, Great Circle Sailing* and other practical works, and for seamanship Captain McLord; both nice gentlemen, the latter noted for his shrewd, searching questions. (Liverpool, 1869)[1]

Different marine boards, different kinds of examiners: Professor Towson was a mathematician who conducted part of the navigation exam as a *viva*; other boards selected only shipmasters-turned-surveyors, sometimes to conduct the exam as a group, sometimes single-handed. In London, Steele was encountered in isolated terror:

After a fortnight's swotting I hoped I was ready for the ordeal. The navigation was comparatively simple, but on my way to the orals room a fellow emerged, very crestfallen: "That swine's sent me back to sea for six months because I was wearing a buttonhole. God help you." I knocked at the door. A thunderous bellow. I put my face round the door. "She's all aback forrard!" he roared. Ah! We'd been put wise to that little trick, and I gave the answer before crossing the threshold... I was presently sweating as if I'd run a mile under a tropical sun. His object was to bewilder and rattle me. He asked me details of the duties I should expect to perform as second mate of a windjammer. "God help the ship that gets you for a second mate! Your cargo's afire in the after hold. Duty?" I brought her head to wind, battened down my hatches and carved holes in the deck for hoses. Then I clawed off a lee shore and dealt with a range of impossible emergencies at the same time... "That'll do!" he snarled, but he didn't kick me out. Instead he turned to the window, filling his pipe, then seated himself. "Here you are," he growled, and handed me the coveted blue slip. "Too dandified for a windjammer!" (1890s)[2]

---

[1] *Captain Fraser's Voyages*, p.55.
[2] *Knocking Around*, pp.150-3.

MMOs (they were soon known colloquially as Shipping Offices) were also opened in major colonial ports where examinations were conducted as at home. In some quarters a belief existed that the standard in these far-flung outposts was lower than at home ports, but it was, of course, a fallacy insofar as standards varied from port to port anyway.

The first question he put to me was "What age are you?" I told him seventeen that same day. "Oh! What time were you born?" I noticed the clock on the wall standing at two minutes to ten, and told him 10 o'clock. "Then sit down for two minutes," he ordered. In the course of the examination he handed me a sextant to read. Nervously I told him 74 degrees, 14 minutes and 45 seconds. "You are wrong," he said, and visions of being put back for six months floated across my mind when there was a knock at the door which the old gent answered, talking with his back to me. Hurriedly picking up the sextant again I saw that the reading was 74 degrees, 4 minutes and 14 seconds, unclamped the vernier and moved the tangent screw until the instrument showed the reading I'd given the old boy, and replaced it. Closing the door, he asked me to repeat my answer. "You are wrong," he said again, sharply, then took another look at the sextant. "Why, you've shifted it, you young rascal!" I felt confused, and confessed, but he was an old sport, actually smiled, and agreed that I'd proved I could read the instrument, so I secured my certificate. (Hong Kong, 1880s)[1]

The blue slip was the examiner's token, exchanged for the certificate when it had been prepared, until the close of the century elaborately enscripted on vellum. With this the ex-apprentice set off to begin the real business of his career.

I went back to my old lodgings and attended a navigation school for three weeks before going to Greenock for my examination. I got through all right and went to spend Christmas and New Year with my married sister. As soon as that was over I returned to the ship to see if Captain Dick had an opening for me but found he had given up command to Captain John Scott, late of the *City of Dublin*. However, I met Captain Dick on board and he took me below to meet the new captain. "Look here, John, here is a young man I can recommend to you as bos'n. You won't find a better man." I was pleased when Captain Scott agreed to take me, and I was pleased to go. (1868)[2]

At this date sail was still comparatively well-manned, and trade depression added to the scarcity of berths, particularly among reputable companies like Smith's City Line, where a bosun's job with a 2nd mate's ticket was as good as any other.

---

[1] *Seafaring*, pp.135-7.
[2] *From Ship's Boy to Skipper*, p.298.

IV

The Diary of Alexander Mackay, 1899-1902. (Abstract)

*

Ship Armadale.
Hull, July 16th. 1902.

THIS certifies that Mr A.S. Mackay on the expiry of his indenture in Jany. last at Melbourne, was rated 3rd Mate of this ship, under my command, thence to this port, to date. During the time in port – and of course at sea, he was reliably sober always, and attentive and intelligent in performance of his duties. He leaves now at his own request – for exam purposes.

John H. Stevens.
Master.

*

THERE was no seafaring tradition in Alexander Stuart Mackay's family. His mother, a native of Banffshire, was one of seven daughters of a civil engineer, his father a house-painter and journeyman, though conflicting documentation also describes him as an artist. He might well have been both, but in any case he followed his trade in Edinburgh, where Alexander was born, at Lawmarket, in June 1880, one of eight children all of whom except he and a sister died in a diphtheria epidemic. She was Margaret (Maggie), Alexander's senior by six years and part of the diary's inspiration; it was written partly for her benefit, though there was also a steady exchange of correspondence, witness to a close and affectionate relationship.

His father died when Alexander was six, after which the boy's upbringing was heavily influenced by his aunts, whose opposition to his early desire to go to sea sprang from an understandable concern about Mrs Mackay's being left without a man in the house. As a result, after attending Dr Bell's Academy in Dean Village, he was apprenticed to a chemist, not without reluctance and an unalloyed wish and hope for a change, about which he constantly agitated, finding an ally in his sister. Eventually the aunts and his mother bowed to the inevitable (likewise the hapless chemist) and on January 10th, 1898 – rather late at eighteen, but still in time – he signed a 4-year indenture with J&A Roxburgh of Glasgow and joined the *Armadale* to sail for Australia.

No personal record was made of the voyage, which began at Liverpool on 14th January with calls at Melbourne, Sydney, Shanghai and Tchio (New Caledonia) and ended at Glasgow on 4th April, 1899. During it Mrs Mackay died, probably another part of the reason for the diary's beginning on the following voyage, assuming a symbolic significance. It was kept, with one or two intermissions, until 1904.

The firm of Roxburgh agreed to pay Mackay a total of £30 - £4 the first year, £6 the second, £8 the third and £12 the last, plus 12/- a year in lieu of washing. No premium was demanded, only a surety of £20 agreed to, payable by either side on default. The indenture conformed to standard with the usual undertaking on the part of the master (Roxburgh) to instruct the apprentice in the business of a seaman.

The company's fleet was substantial, in later years comprised entirely of steamships. Begun in 1872 with the launch of *Ettrickdale* at Barclay, Curle's yard on the Clyde, it was characterised by 4-mast iron and steel barques, the *Tweedsdale* of 1875 first of the type ever built, representing the new – and concluding – age of the heavy carrier that followed in the wake of the clipper. The 1914-18 war put an end to all but one of the steamers and the ensuing depression did the same for the firm, which, as the Helmsdale S.S. Co., wound up its affairs in 1922. By that time Alexander Mackay was sailing as an officer with the Royal Mail Steam Packet Co. on his way to command.

He served his entire apprenticeship in the *Armadale*. At 2,015 tons gross register she was a 4-mast iron barque (not a full-rigged ship, somewhat misleadingly suggested by Captain Stevens's letter of testimony), sister of *Braccadale*, launched at the Linthouse yard of Alexander Stephen in 1887 to be followed in 1889 and 1890 by the steel 4-masters *Carradale* and *Fascadale*. They were built for the Australia trade and that was where Mackay found himself at more or less regular intervals, but by the turn of the century steam had all but ousted sail on the route and Roxburgh's sailers turned to tramping before sale to foreign owners, bar the *Clydesdale*, lost by fire in 1903. Last of the sailing fleet, *Torrisdale* [1] was built in 1892 by Henderson and sold to other British owners in 1910, to be wrecked two years later. Mackay sailed as her 2nd mate after getting his ticket in 1902.

By any standards *Armadale* was big, and something of a handful for her crew, though she sailed well enough without particular distinction, making average passages of around 91 days between Europe and Australia, a comment on changed times and priorities when compared to the voyages earlier made by James Baines's American-built wooden flyers[2], rushing out to Melbourne from Liverpool with emigrants, aiming at 60-day non-stop runs. She measured 225.2ft x 40.5ft x 23.8ft with a 30ft topgallant focsle and 37ft raised poop, setting conventional canvas – double topsails, single topgallants and royals on fore, main and mizen. Accommodation was located beneath

---

[1] Mis-spelt *Torresdale* in some references.

[2] The famous Black Ball Line of Liverpool, not to be confused with the equally famous New York-owned line of Western Ocean packets of the same name.

the poop (master and officers) and in two deckhouses, the hands' focsle immediately abaft the foremast, the apprentices' house abaft the mizen, both exposed to boarding seas in traditional fashion. In total her complement numbered around 27, though she was certified to carry 43; she allowed nobody, officers and apprentices included, much time for idling.

In command of the barque for her first 14 years, Captain William Duncan had joined Roxburgh at the start in 1872 and in 1901 retired to settle in Scotland, handing over to Captain Stevens, under whom Mackay served on his last voyage before going up for his ticket. Duncan was a sound shipmaster, but he had his moments, as they all did, and do, and Mackay's observations reveal something of the strain under which the master of a windjammer continually laboured, faced with not only the task of handling the ship and variably-competent crew but also commercial pressures that by this time were massed against the sailing-ship. Under Stevens the problems were, if anything, heightened, and before wireless the master's responsibility was total while his authority was being defined, limited and channelled by legislation strengthened and consolidated through the great Merchant Shipping Act and bureaucratic *tour de force* of 1894.

On Mackay's first voyage *Armadale* loaded a cargo of nickel ore at New Caledonia, where she was in company with Law's 1,549gt *Sutherlandshire* , an iron full-rigger. *Armadale* completed first to sail on November 24th., *Sutherlandshire* on the 29th., though they kept in company as far as the North Cape of New Zealand. Thereafter no sighting was made until *Armadale* anchored off the Tail of the Bank the day after her erstwhile companion's arrival. The voyage was considered a race, but it is unlikely that any formal arrangement had been made, and whether "racing" or not the masters were bound to make the best passages they could. There was always a spirit of rivalry between ships anyway, and bets were frequently placed by their people, whose anticipation of the outcome went some way towards promoting enthusiasm in working the ship. Among apprentices, however she might be privately regarded, pride in the ship was a natural sentiment, to be justified and vindicated at every opportunity.

After a month at home Mackay rejoined in May, 1899, finding Joseph Stevenson aboard, one of the previous voyage's apprentices and a direct contemporary: he had signed indentures on 13th January, 1898, and was two years Mackay's junior. The other two were new faces, Rupert Stuttard, aged 15, and Henry ("Tim") Jones. Duncan was the master, J. Mahoney mate, F. Richmond 2nd mate and Peter Waddel 3rd; petty officers were carpenter, sailmaker and lamp-trimmer, with thirteen deckhands, steward and cook. At various times during the voyage the crowd included Scots, Irish, Swedes, Dutch, Germans, Norwegians, Belgians, Japanese and an American, about par for the red duster at the time. They sailed in ballast for Baltimore on 10th May, Mackay with mixed feelings, the captain with his wife and baby...

May 10th. Wednesday.   ...I won't be sorry when we're outside; although I don't know anyone in Greenock it was a wrench. I'm very glad that there was none of my friends seeing me off;

there would have been a scene. Discovered four stowaways, who will go back by tug. The Old Man would have taken them if we had not been going to the States. I am in the second mate's watch with Stuttard. Our first watch on deck 8-12. Port watch below.

May 11th.　Set sail for Baltimore, light breeze springing up. No shanteymen this time. Lashed the spars and nursed the baby. Felt very low-spirited. I hope nothing is wrong at Edinburgh.

Here was a new departure in the training of apprentices, and perhaps unique, the ticklish business of playing nursemaid. The duty was shared among the boys in rotation and not looked upon with gladness, but whatever his feelings about it Mackay seemed to keep most of them to himself.

May 12th.　Fine breeze, slipping along, took in royals and t'gallants. Big steamboat passed homeward bound at 2am. She looked fine, a blaze of light. NB[1] till 11.30 then shovelled ballast in No.3 hatch.

May 13th.　Sighted a barque carrying main t'gallants at 4.30am. All hands shorten sail at 10.20pm and got below at 11.20 – lost an hour of my watch below. Took in main and crossjack and fore upper topsail. NB. Clear sky although it blows and heavy squalls.

May 14th. Sunday.　Had a sailor's pleasure, turned out my chest. Stuttard better today. Apple pie for dinner. At 5 o'clock 560 west and 30 miles south of the Fastnet. Had a fine sing-song of hymns.

And so the voyage proceeded...

16/5　Light variable wind. Rain squalls. Clearing the tween-deck and NB. Sighted a barquentine, too far to signal.

17/5　Tomorrow is the Queen's birthday. At home they will be looking forward to the picnic. I wonder what's the matter with this pen, there's too strong a flow of ink.

18/5　The rovings of the main upper topsail blew adrift and we went up and replaced them, a nasty job with her rolling so much. We're standing by at present; Stuttard is sick again. 4pm I loosed the mainsail and mizzen upper topsail. On the main I had the nearest scrape of going overboard I have ever had. The sail blew into a balloon and knocked me away from the yard. I thought I was gone. Jam for tea. Got it from Jones. He's a nice fellow I think. The picnic will be over now. I hope they enjoyed themselves.

20/5　Must be somewhere off the banks as it is so cold. Made a bread pudding for all in the house. Splendid. We cleared out the spare bunk and put the rubbish in a box, put a mast in it and used Stevenson's old clothes-bag for a sail and dumped it. The Old Man spotted it and wants to know what it was, but hasn't found out yet.

---

[1] Nursed baby.

Duncan's troubles were beginning, by the look of it, the unthinking skylarking of the half-deck distorted and magnified by the grave lens of responsibility...

21/5   It seems an age since I was in Edinburgh. I can hardly believe it is only a fortnight. I wonder how long it will be before I am there again. The mark underneath was made by the baby, young William, with a handful of hash. It isn't the first mess he's made here. High living today; for breakfast ham and eggs, dinner plum pudding, goosenargh[*sic*] cakes and vanilla jelly. Tea bloater paste and queen's cake, with ship's food thrown in. We live high for sailors, don't you think?

Yes, but not unusually at this stage of the voyage, the effect of the contents of hampers brought away with them being to wean them onto ship's fare as gently as self-restraint allowed. And the question – as well as the whole mood of this entry – betrays something of what, or who, was in mind while making it.

26/5   Calm. Over the side scrubbing. Signalled the *Lucania*. Sighted another steamer at 7pm, an oil-tank[*sic*] with engines right aft.

28/5 Sun.   Fire Island at 4.45am having taken about three times as long as we should. The 2nd mate got his left leg foul of the crossjack brace as we were putting about. He can hardly walk now. Had a shave – mark well what I do say. Had a fine sing-song tonight.

30/5   Spliced a new tail on the main t'gallant, bent gaskets and NB forenoon. Land on the lee(stbd) bow. It is Long Island. No more bread as the flour is finished.

31/5   Made a dandyfunk today, it was A1.

1/6   Sighted Sandy Hook. Got a piece of wire from 2nd mate to learn splicing on. Repaired the door curtain, others shining the brasswork in the house. Furled t'gallants and put about 8pm.

2/6   Sighted Barnegat light 11pm; two schooners at 4.30. I was making the main royal fast at the time by myself. NB.
N.B. NB does me out of some good jobs.

5/6   Our towboat, the *Chicago*, came out about 9. Towed right up to Baltimore and made fast alongside to discharge ballast. Five hands cleared away with the boarding-house runners. Turned to after dinner and unbent every sail and stowed them; a good record, and short-handed, too. Awfully tired when we finished, too tired to eat. Washed, lay down, and fell asleep.

At Baltimore. 5th June – 8th July, 1899:

...Spread the poop awning and washed down. Jones entered upon his duties as nurse for the day. A fine job.

...Stevenson went ashore for grass for the goat. Went ashore tonight to the Seamen's Mission. Jones & Joe [Stevenson] there also.

...I think the letters must have had the addresses wrong as we have not had any yet.

...Two more hands cleared, leaving four. Went ashore tonight with Jones to the Maryland Institute and saw an exhibition of drawings, paintings and clay modelling by pupils.

...Cleaning stringers and sweeping hold. Shifted ship to Sparrow's Pound (steel town) about 10 miles below Baltimore.

...Went round the iron-works this afternoon. A great many people on board but very few girls. Went to the Methodist church this evening and enjoyed it.

...Laying strong battens in the hold. Sold my blue counterpane to the cook for $2. Today is my 19th Birthday. I wish my time was over and I had my ticket.

...Tarred new tarpaulins. My hands are in an awful mess. No letters yet. I hope everything is all right at home.

...Called at 6, breakfast at 7, dinner 12 to 1. Swept the hold and laid the other floor[1]. Went aboard the steamboat, had a look round, spoke to the 3rd engineer.

...Sawing dunnage. Two apprentices off the steamboat came aboard, decent fellows.

...Had a letter from Campbell; everything's all right at home.

...Knocked off at 6am. Never had a spell all night. Went up to the store with Jones and had an ice-cream. Left my razor to get set, 23c., rather stiff.

...First letter from Maggie, with a piece of hawthorn. Two of us must stay aboard, orders from headquarters[2].

...Getting ready for bending sail. The Old Man and Mrs Duncan took Jones and the baby to Point Breeze tonight, so Joe and I went and left two aboard. We enjoyed ourselves A1. Switchback, merry-go-round and all kinds of amusements. Plenty of girls, they look all right being dressed in white.

...Bent sails. Mizen royal must have been bewitched because everything seemed to go wrong with it. The Old Man sat on us about going for a swim. Between that and the mizzen royal I've

---

[1] Correctly, *ceiling*. In ships of this design the hold was open-floored (i.e. undecked framing) and it was necessary to lay a deck, or ceiling, of strong planks (battens) across the floors to support the cargo clear of the bottom-plating. A later development was the logical one of fitting a permanent watertight iron or steel ceiling to form a double bottom.
[2] Captain Duncan.

done more swearing today than I have ever done since coming aboard. Miss Gantz from The Grove came aboard tonight. A fantastic girl. We showed her round.

...In the punt with the painter painting the ports. Jones was up in the city with Mr[*sic*] and Mrs Duncan and the baby. The Old Man signed the crowd on.

Armadale's painted ports, like some other Roxburgh ships' colour schemes, were upside-down for a period in her career, for no discoverable reason.

...There is a dispute about the cargo. The Old Man won't take any more and the M.S. Company say we are not loaded.

Here was a delicate state of affairs. By this date the load-line was a statutory requirement, its placement a matter of calculation according to strict rules; in theory the ship could neither be overloaded nor need be left light, and as far as a deadweight cargo such as the one in question – steel rails – was concerned she should have been at her marks before the hold was full; in other words, fully-laden without being filled to capacity. However, Captain Duncan might well have had reservations about the distribution of the weight, concentrated, as it had perforce to be, in the bottom of the hold and in the tween-deck, deciding that undue and uneven stress would be imposed on the ship's fabric if a full load were taken. He would have had in mind the coming passage round the Cape and across the stormy Southern Ocean, during which, in fact, his fears were realised, as Mackay presently described. Meanwhile, the apprentices were preoccupied with less apocalyptic matters...

...Miss Gantz came aboard and invited us to tea. We could not all go so Joe and I went and Jones came up in the evening. Enjoyed ourselves splendidly. Went for a walk to the lighthouse through The Grove. Joe gave his photograph to Miss Gantz and got one in return.

...Filling spaces between cargo with dunnage. The mate is a weed.

...A bailiff came aboard and placed the ship under arrest.

...Got all ready for hauling out into the stream. Bailiff still aboard. The Old Man has gone up to town.

Where he evidently managed to settle the dispute, probably with the aid of an actuary and at some expense, which would be frowned on by the owners. The worry of this sort of thing, part of the shipmaster's daily round, was quite undetectable to the rest of the ship's people except perhaps for the mate with command in prospect. To the apprentices it meant almost nothing other than the possibility of an extended stay in port.

...Towboat *Chicago* came alongside bringing the Old Man and the pilot. They took the bailiff back to the Point while we hove short. Took us in tow shortly after 3pm. Picked the new hands into watches. The Jap is ours.

Baltimore – Cape Town. July 9th – August 28th, 1899.

...Caught aback three times. Got my oilskins ready for oiling. Painter pumice-stoning the poop. He can do it all himself for all I care. Carpenter chocking the cargo off.

...Took a sea over the poop. The cabin ports being open she filled the cabin. Result, Old Man chasing round.

...Heavy weather with the fore royal blown away. 1500 miles from Baltimore in 7 days.

...Mrs Duncan playing the piano which creates a longing in me to hear the same well-played at home.

...Got part of a water-melon from his noble highness.

...Several sailoring jobs, among them my first long-splices. We have all had ourselves measured so that we may tally at the end of the voyage. Height 5ft 10.1/2ins., chest 39.7/8ins., stomach 31ins.

...Had a shave, Jones ditto, Sqab [Stuttard] nil. Very homesick.

...At the wheel 10.30-12.00pm. Did a day's work and got it wrong. With Chips in the morning, then NB the best part of the afternoon.

...Did a day's work and got it right.

...Broached Mrs Ingham's toffee. Pie from Harriet Lane and part of our extra ration.

...At the wheel from 6 to 8am. Finished *Sandy Scott's Bible Class* and loaned it to Chips. I have had toothache since yesterday.

...Carpenter sawed the f.t. gallant (yard) up for toms to shore the tween-deck beams from the lower hold.

They weren't fairly out into the South Atlantic yet, but already the cargo's effects were becoming apparent with the tween-deck requiring this makeshift strengthening. What was more, the crankiness induced by the loading – top-heavy with the weight of rails relatively high up, in the tween-deck – had made the normally sea-kindly ship prone to swamping, particularly dangerous, of course, when it occurred over the poop. Not yet alert to the situation's implications, however, Mackay's thoughts were on food, home, his studies, his reading and toothache, while Captain Duncan, all too well aware of them, would certainly have been pondering the problem of making a safe passage – or even making one at all...

...The cat had six kittens in the third mate's bunk. Kept two and dumped the rest. Toothache a nuisance.

...Shifted mainsail and miz. lower tops'l. I never saw such a mess before. If the Old Man would stay away it would be much better.

...Made an average of 11 knots an hour [*sic*] for the last 24 hours, sometimes she was going 8 and then romping along every bit of 14.

...Joe nearly set the house on fire trying to boil some water for cocoa. I got the deuce of a scare waking and finding the house full of smoke and flames. The house filled with water at 3.30am, got it dried up. I have been reading R.L. Stevenson's *Katriona*, a rattler and makes me wish I was back in Auld Reekie.

The conflagration preceding the flood was caused by a stove Joe Stevenson had put together from tins, fuelled with colza oil, slush or whatever came to hand. It was highly illegal to have anything of the kind in the half-deck.

...Chips says the tween-deck beams are sinking.

...She is rolling heavy. The decks are always awash.

...Carpenter, some hands and the captain down below in the tween-deck wedging and shoring the cargo, which began to shift during the first watch. I was sent down with the others to relieve them, to put up the shores and toms that had fallen. The Jap was scared. I wasn't much behind him as the rails rushed from side to side when she rolled heavy. The rails in the fore tween-deck have broken 14 thick iron stanchions[1]. The after part of the cargo in the tween-deck and lower hold took charge, and still the Old Man thinks of going on. To what? God only knows. Turned in after watch but could not sleep because of the noise of the rails and the rolling.

...The rails in the fore tween-deck took charge and the watch took to their heels, Old Man and all. All hands called so turned out feeling in better spirits than for a few days. We put her on

---

[1] The solid (2-4ins thick) iron pillars standing between decks in the hold, the lower tier between the floors and the tween-deck beams, the upper between the tween-deck and the beams of the weather deck above. Their spacing was usually at alternate beams. They served to strengthen the decks, passing the weight they carried to the floors and (in the tween-deck) to the deck above, acting as an integral part of the ship's structural strength. The effect of damage to them would depend on how the damaged pillars were grouped, but in general it would have been to weaken the decks and hence the ship's resistance to stresses. Damage to pillars in the lower hold would result in sagging of the heavily-laden deck above, and in turn of the weather deck above that.

the port tack and she is steadier now. We are bound to Cape Town. I did not like the idea of running the easting down with the cargo as it was. By Mercator sailing I find that we are 480 miles from Cape Town.

...They have lashed the toms to one another and the whole to the stringers. Forward they have filled up the spaces with spare battens and deck planks and all odd pieces use everything up and lashed with chains fore and aft. The carpenter deserves great credit. Everything is done that can be done. I wonder what Maggie and everyone else is doing at home. They will be surprised when they see our arrival reported.

...Marmalade tart and curry & rice for dinner. Broached the shortbread, splendid, but not enough of it. I was in the hold with the Old Man during the middle watch. Everything seems all right. I hope it holds. Today has not seemed like a Sunday because we have worked all day.

At Cape Town. August 28th – September 28th, 1899.

...A great many ships in the dock and a few in the bay, amongst others the *Heathfield* that was in Shanghai with us. There are square-rig 4-masters besides liners &c. The towboat *J.E. Fuller* met us and towed us to an anchorage outside the dock. The Old Man went ashore and came back with fresh meat, veg &c. He brought us an orange each. Delicious. We ought to be very thankful for our escape for it has been a great danger. We have a slight starboard list, riding to stbd anchor. Cape Town looks fine lit up. I have the 10-12 watch.

...The surveyors were aboard. The *Corbrook Castle* left for home with the mate.

We aren't told why the mate left. Possibly because of the cargo trouble. Assuming that standard practice had been followed its stowage was the mate's responsibility and Duncan would have been within his rights to dismiss his chief officer for being at fault. However, the point is purely conjectural, and if he had been dismissed the mate could have looked for another berth among the ships in port. Mackay certainly didn't grieve over his departure, having already delivered himself of judgment on the wretched man. Meanwhile, life in the half-deck followed its appointed path while England issued Kruger with an ultimatum, the ship moved alongside near a coaling berth, and gangs of stevedores arrived to begin unloading the cargo preparatory to re-stowing it more securely. Here was yet more expense for the owners.

...ashore with Jones to Cape Town cathedral, but did not care for the service.

...Had to give Sqab a thrashing for cheek at dinner-time. It has done him good. Jones's turn to nurse the baby this week.

...Jones and Joe ashore to the Mission. A mission fellow came down last night and asked the Old Man to let us stay at the Mission after 10pm. Very good of him I consider.

...Went aboard the *Norham Castle*. One would think they lived in a hotel. A double t'gallant yard barque came in, the *Indian Empire*.

This was one of Duncan's (no relation) famous Empire Line and among the newest, built by John Reid on the Clyde in 1896, a 3-mast steel barque of 1,164gt., rather small for her day but nevertheless rigged for easier handling without royals and having split t'gallants, making up in spread what was lacking in height. When seen here she had completed a passage from Penarth with coal and was taking stone ballast for a run to Australia and a chance of finding either grain or coal for a paying freight, a situation typifying the way sailers were having to make their livings. In command was David Watson, son of the John Watson of Largo introduced earlier, and who had served his time with his father in Duncan's *Onward*. He went on to sail as 3rd mate of the *Persian Empire*, also under John Watson, was promoted 2nd mate at eighteen, and mate of the ship at twenty-one. He passed for master in 1874 and in 1875 was transferred as mate to the *Indian Empire* (I) at the request of her master, who was ill and burdened with an incompetent man. This was at Calcutta, and on the homeward passage the captain died to leave David Watson in command aged 23. George Duncan confirmed him in the post on arrival home, and he remained *Indian Empire*'s master for the next 19 years, leaving her for the *Celestial Empire* and moving on to take delivery of the new *Indian Empire*. In 1902 he was given command of the new 4-mast steel barque *Colonial Empire*, leaving her in 1904 to take up the post of the company's marine superintendent, from which he retired in 1916 aged sixty-five. Last of the fleet, *Colonial Empire* went ashore near Belle Isle *en route* from St Nazaire to Port Talbot in November 1915. The negotiation of her sale as a repairable proposition was the last task David Watson performed for his employer.

Norham Castle was a small steamer, one of Currie's Castle Line, at the time in competition with Anderson's Union Line on the UK – South Africa run. Built in 1883 at 4,241nrt, Kipling had said of her, in an effusive letter to Sir Donald Currie, how "splendidly comfortable" he and his family had been and how "thoroughly looked after...including their three children". He had felt that they had "tested the resources of the line most thoroughly" and that the voyage they had made in the ship had been "wholly delightful", ending by asking, somewhat disingenuously, how the company built "boats" that did not complain in a seaway.[1]

Boats! This piece of lax terminology seems to have been a mark of the steam age, for nowhere will *boat* be found applied to wind-ships, particularly among such knowledgeable people as Kipling. Mackay himself refers to "steamboats", not without perceptible disparagement, perversely emphasised by his observations about living conditions aboard them. Pride in the spartan existence of the sailer's half-deck was mixed with implicit admission of envy of standards in the better class of steamer, and Mackay at last openly admitted an intention to make the change at the earliest

---

[1] *Union-Castle Chronicle*, p.321.

opportunity. His impatience with poor Captain Duncan was a symptom of the disease, as also of the simplistic, uncluttered and intolerant idealism of youth.

...Asked the Old Man about a picnic. Yes, we can go, but Jones is unwell. Got to the Institute[1] at 7am and met a party of 14 from the ships. Walked through the town to the foot of the mountain through scrub and large boulders. I was looking after Jumbo off the *East African*. He was played out. At last he took a bad pain in his leg, he said. We voted to stop and as Miss Billis was very tired, too, we sat down. The others were a long way ahead. I tried to find a way up but toothache started and I sat on the grass and nursed my jaw. The others sighted us from above and came back. After a while we set out for the Institute arriving about 7pm. Had tea, a wash, met Jones and then spent a fitting evening to a most enjoyable day. There must be a lot of Scotch people here to judge by the names of the houses.

...In the hold fixing cargo with Chips. Painter got drunk and had a scrap with the mate.

...Lost my job in the hold through nearly chopping my thumb off. Asked the Old Man to let Tim and I go to the Institute for a social evening. He let us go after giving me a talking about going ashore. Stevenson swears he will run away here because of the cargo. I want to go also, but don't want to lose the time I have in. If my turn comes, well, it can't be helped.

...We still have a stbd list. It's the cargo in the lower hold that causes that. Some of the hands wish they'd never shipped with us.

Cape Town – Melbourne. September 29th – November 8th, 1899.

...The toms in the wings are all slack[2].

...Sighted a steamboat at 4.30pm, the *Devonshire* from New York to Melbourne, one of the company's steamers, a proper tank. I'd rather be on her than where I am from here to Melbourne. Course SSE, light wind, rolling a great deal.

...An awful job getting the crossjack up, a new sail. It was no joke on that yard being battered with wind and rain and the sail like iron. When we got back on deck found Sqab missing. Everyone looking for him but could not find him. Came to the conclusion that he'd gone overboard when he walked out from under the focsle-head where he'd been sleeping.

...Got my seaboots on again and dry socks, a comfort to have dry feet. Old Man, Carpenter and Sails down in the hold all forenoon. Everything is all right they say. We are in 32°S the mate told me. I think the Old Man is very foolish coming so far south. Finished mother's jelly.

...Lime-juice today. Saw a moon rainbow.

---

[1] Alternative (colloquial) term for the Seamen's Mission.
[2] Indicating further sagging of the tween-deck.

...With the Old Man filling his soda-water locker. He opened a cask of bottled stout. Every bottle was empty, blown the corks out. Oh, dear. Well, well, well. Two hands on the other watch laid up leaving five men and two boys, a big watch for a 2,000-ton ship.

...Abreast of Albany. Old Man is chopping and sawing wood in the fore tween-deck with the aid of Professor Sereno alias J. Stevenson.

...Washed my bunk out and aired my bed. The others scrubbed the paintwork and Joe broke the lamp glass. Sheer carelessness.

...I think we have seen the last of the *Macquarie*. She seems to be off round Tasmania.

This was on 27th October, when *Armadale* was some 365 miles from Port Phillip Heads. *Macquarie* had come up with her 6 days previously and overhauled her, at this time manned by some 30 midshipmen, 16 apprentices and 14 ABs, a startling comparison with *Armadale's* sketchy complement. Built in 1875 by R&H Green for their Australia service, she had been bought by Devitt & Moore in 1887 and ten years later had taken the place of *Harbinger* in the Ocean Training Scheme. On this voyage she was bound for Sydney, taking the safer (and often quicker) route south of Tasmania rather than through the Bass Strait. Since Mackay makes no mention of it, it's possible that neither he nor anyone else aboard *Armadale* knew anything of the OTS and *Macquarie's* part in it.[1]

...Put about at 7.30pm owing to a light on the weather bow. Old Man brought her up in the wind before the clews were up. The yards came round with a rush, main yards went back again. It's a wonder no-one was hurt.

...Sighted Cape Nelson.

...2nd mate gave us the shanty *Poor Old Man* on the main t.g. halyards. The Old Man was out doing his bit. Sqab's left thumb is badly poisoned. Shackled the cables to the anchors.

...Spent the middle watch between the fore upper tops'l yard and the poop. Pilot schooner *Mavis* came along and we got the pilot aboard at 8 bells. Passed through and signalled the Heads at 1.30pm. Heard from the pilot that the *Shamrock* had lost[2]. Hard lines. Chips has won the sweep. Anchored after all the usual manoeuvring up the bay. We are to discharge at the old railway pier at Williamstown tomorrow. I would rather have gone to P. Melbourne as it will cost too much to go up to the city often. The boatman brought the letters aboard. My small portion was 10. Up til after 1am reading them.

At Melbourne. November 9th, 1899 – January 20th, 1900.

---

[1] See Ch.8.

[2] *America's* Cup, of course. This was *Shamrock I*, Sir Thomas Lipton's challenger, which lost all three races of this year to Pierpont Morgan's *Columbia*.

This was familiar territory from the ship's previous voyage, when Mackay had experienced the hospitality for which Australian ports were already famous among sailors the world over. The most casual of (perfectly innocent) meetings were apt to blossom into warm friendship within days, if not hours, and for apprentices the phenomenon was a boon and a blessing, providing virtually a home from home which negated the difficulties associated with their state of chronic impoverishment. Australians had a knack for giving the impression that it was they, and not the visitor, who benefited from the contact, creating a welcoming atmosphere that frequently led to an apprentice's decision to clear out and try his luck in a land apparently awash with opportunity and goodwill. It might indeed have been, but it was also hard and uncompromising in its demands on the would-be settler, raw and crude in its methods once beyond the superficial and slightly gauche sophistication of the cities.

Even if the British were a seafaring nation, Australians, to a far greater degree and chiefly through an acute awareness of hereditary and familial ties with the "home" country, were sea-minded: ships figured in their everyday affairs as they did not in the parochial existence of most Britons, and voyages were prominently reported in the press:

The Argus.
Melbourne, 10th November. 1899.

The trim four-masted barque Armadale, Captain W. Duncan, arrived late on Wednesday night from Baltimore, USA, with a cargo of steel rails consigned to the Railway Department. The voyage was an eventful one, as a tremendous gale encountered on August 25th did so much damage and shifted the rails that the vessel put into Cape Town to execute repairs and trim the cargo. This work occupied 33 days. The voyage began at Greenock, which port was left on May 9th. She arrived at Baltimore on June 5th, loading an entire cargo of rails, and sailed for Melbourne on July 8th... Moderate SW winds were experienced until falling in with the NE trades. These winds were lost in 11°N, 29°W. She crossed the equator on August 11th. Fresh to moderate S trades were met with and dropped in 24°S 27°W. When in 29°S 12°E the Armadale encountered a fierce gale, which increased to hurricane force, causing a furious high sea to run. The cargo shifted and broke away 14 stanchions in the 'tween decks. The vessel was put up for Cape Town to effect repairs. She arrived at Table Bay on August 28th. Portion of the cargo was discharged from the 'tween decks and all the rails in the division of the hold were re-stowed. Part of the cargo in the lower hold was re-stowed, and necessary repairs to the vessel were made. Cape Town was left on September 29th, moderate northerly and westerly winds prevailing to the Leeuwin, which was passed on October 28th. Thence to Cape Northumberland fair winds from the north and thence from SE were met with. She sighted the Cape on November 2nd where a strong easterly gale came on and continued till the 6th. This culminated in a severe thunderstorm, followed by moderate light winds and constant rain, with dense fog to Cape Otway. Captain Duncan reports having spoken the Macquarie, ship, London to Sydney, 40° 42′S, 110° 48′E on October 22nd. This ship was in company from October 18th to 30th inclusive. The Armadale was berthed yesterday morning at the Williamstown railway pier.

Somewhat lacking in constructive inspiration and clarity, but notably better-informed than the present-day British press's grasp of maritime matters, and factual enough bar the earlier sighting of *Macquarie* than recorded by Mackay, which was on the morning of October 21st.

...Spent a very enjoyable evening. Everyone pleased to see me. Got aboard 12.30am. We are only to go ashore in turns, watch and watch. That's the old mate's doing. He's an old weed.

...The mate was ashore and the 2nd and 3rd went ashore and got drunk leaving no officers on board. Ashore with Forbes[1] after dinner met the Old Man so turned back and shook up 3rd mate and got him aboard before the Old Man arrived, a good thing. Some girls came aboard whom Joe knew. They knew me, but I never set eyes on them before.

And far from diminishing, Captain Duncan's woes were changing shape and multiplying:

...The Old Man called Chips, Painter and steward loafers and everything else he could think of. He accused the steward of being drunk because he had forgotten the flour for bread which everyone can do without.

...Woken up this morning by Chips cursing frightfully and offering to smash the Old Man and the mate. The mate sneaked ashore and got a policeman to stay with him all night. It's him that's the cause of all this trouble, carrying tales to the Old Man. Steward paid off today and we are all very sorry because he is a nice fellow. Jones is acting steward now.

...The Old Man gave us our share this morning, Joe especially for going ashore last night out of turn. Told him he would cancel his indentures and that he had contaminated all of us in the house, and that I am the leader of the whole blooming lot. He wound up by saying that if we all did an honest day's work we would be only too glad to turn in instead of going ashore. Whoever heard such rot? I've had two rows with the mate. If he troubles me much more I'll lay him on his back. He is at the bottom of this, the old weed. Letter from Maggie and a pile of papers.

...Jones and Joe went on the hunt for totties. Not difficult to find them in Williamstown.

...Over the side chipping and painting. Three girls came aboard to see Joe and Jones. Jones swore he never saw them before, and he's walked one of them out.

...Finished the chipping, only the painting to do. Sqab is up at the Grindlays[2], and was there all

---

[1] Forbes Morrison. Met on the previous voyage, the Morrisons lived in the suburb of Hawthorn.

[2] Captain Duncan's in-laws.

day yesterday. A steamboat lying each side[*sic*] of us loading hay and wheat for the Cape[1].

...Boat alongside for the wood for the Grindlays. The third mate, Peter Waddel, and I were sent in her so we hoisted sail and set out on a pleasure trip. Alongside a wharf, after we had flung it all up on the quay Grindlay, who appeared with Captain Neversweat (Sqab) gave Waddel a shilling for 4 drinks. Getting out of the boat the two sixpences dropped out of his pocket. One went overboard, the other I managed to save. The boatman made it up so in we went to the Customs Hotel. I had a ginger ale. I was very thirsty.

...Saw the first turret steamboat I've ever seen, the *Orange Branch*, an ugly tank.

...Asked the Old Man for a pair of boots. I was surprised when he told me to go up to the shops, choose them, and he would pay.

...Mate called me about 1am to do watchman as Stewart [deckhand] was drunk. Went ashore and met Brady's old girl Emily Hornby and her sister, both very nice, but we did not get his message delivered.

...Went to the Presbyterian with Tim and heard a splendid service. Met the Hornbys just outside, accidentally, of course, and went for a stroll down Back Beach.

...Finished cargo in No.3 hatch. Cleared away the flooring[*sic*], swept out, and they started loading at 3.30. I have the tallying job, which is all right.

...Gave Sqab a pasting for cheek.

...To a concert at the Sailors' Rest given by Miss Katie Grindlay, Mrs Duncan's younger sister, a noted singer. Shore people had to pay, sailors free.

It was the custom to hold rowing regattas on the Yarra for ships' boats, and there was great rivalry for a cup or other trophy bought with contributions from the ships taking part. Crews were picked from among the stronger men and apprentices, who naturally looked forward to the event and took every opportunity to practise for it, whenever possible during working hours. For this reason the mate was apt to look on the affair without enthusiasm, and *Armadale*'s man was no exception, making a point of permitting the choice of boat's crew first from the focsle, although in this instance there seems to have been an absence of keenness among the hands, and he would have been better advised to have given the apprentices first refusal, as Mackay darkly hinted. In deliberately (and probably vindictively) crushing the natural expression of loyalty for the ship characteristic of the half-deck despite rough usage (though *Armadale*'s was benignly treated), the mate exemplified the outlook of a certain kind of sea officer whose inability to exploit the positive, even when he possessed the insight to identify it, led to so much unnecessary discord and, indeed, disenchantment

---

[1] Outbreak of the Boer War, to 1902. Supplies for Buller's army.

with the life. Recreation of this kind could only be beneficial for all concerned, including the ship herself, and whatever small proportion of ship's work was delayed or shelved because of it would be more than balanced by the freshening of morale: for all the mate knew, work would be tackled with renewed vigour as a result; but such a notion was evidently beyond the reach of his imagination.

The ship carried two lifeboats in davits, one either side of the quarterdeck just forward of the poop, and a gig, probably stowed in chocks on the roof of the after deckhouse. Mackay's mention of its being slung in davits could mean that it was manhandled into place while the lifeboat it displaced was either temporarily stowed on deck or moored alongside clear of the davits.

...The boat slung in davits today. I was picked as one of the crew but that old weed the mate objected, I think because he does not like me. I consider myself as good, if not better, than some of those forward. I hope the crew is all Britishers.

...Boat's crew refused to go in the boat and practise. So much for the mate's choice. Waddel refused duty owing to the mate hunting him round.

...Out with Ethel for a walk down Back Beach. Got aboard after 10. If anyone at home sees this diary they will say I am a flirt.

...Joe brought two girls aboard after 11pm last night just as I was about to turn in. They are nothing more or less than prostitutes. It's a wonder Joe doesn't think shame of himself for keeping such company. Could not sleep because of the row the drunks were making coming aboard.

...Shifted ship to Victoria Dock astern of the *Star of Victoria*. Knocked off about 5.30 and went aboard. Saw John Binnie, went ashore with him. Met Forbes and Billy Mac. Met Sqab outside the Eastern Market. Got aboard after the usual accostings at 10.30. In the city I met Tricky Wilson, Taylor's old girl.

...Up till 1am finishing the quoits for Forbes. I am going up there to stay until Monday. We're going to work on Boxing Day, though it's a general holiday here. The Old Man gave me 10s today. Out of my pay, of course.

...Have been at Forbes's since Sat evening. Could not wish to enjoy myself better. Had a fine time Sat night. To the Presbyterian church on Sunday; preacher was pretty good but not enough life in him. Visited the zoological gardens. Christmas Day was very warm. Spent the day with Forbes's aunt at Camberwell. I got several Christmas presents. One would think I was one of their own family, the way they have treated me. I have enjoyed myself immensely and will always look back on the last few days as some of the happiest of my life. Started letter-writing but did not manage anything owing to some of the fellows off the *Star* coming aboard.

...Coming aboard I met Tim and Joe and we all saw the New Year in. Kept our bell going until the mate came out. He gave Sqab his New Year present, a clout on the ear.

...On the dock road I was warned by a coloured chap to look out as gang with knives was waiting to stick anyone up. Got round a bend and saw a fight in progress. Someone shouted my name so I went over and found Anderson and Larsen [deckhands] in the row and tried to square matters up, a hard job but I managed eventually. A chap belonging to the *Surrey* was hurt. A mixed-up story but it began by giving one of the stick-up gang a hiding. When I got aboard who should I see but the Old Man in his pyjamas. He wanted to know why I'd been ashore as it was not my turn. He told me he would speak to Mr Morrison [Forbes's father] about encouraging me up to the house. It was my evening aboard, true, but I was on board all day and it was New Year's Day. If he sat on me he ought to say something to Jones and Joe, but of course Joe is his favourite.

...400 bales of wool, 266 ingots of spelter loaded. Two years tonight I joined the ship in Salthouse Dock. I hope the next two speeds[*sic*] by. I hope to let everyone see then that I love my sister and have not forgotten my mother. By God's help and if he is willing I will make a name for myself and gain the top ladder[*sic*] of my profession[1]

...Out to Preheran to say goodbye to Ethel. Her mother was ill so only saw her for 10 minutes. She wants me to write to her. She is a very nice sensible girl that any chap might be proud of. If I get to know a girl anything well they want me to write to them; I will, but I don't see much use in it. We will finish loading by Tuesday. The log we had is now shaped into a t.g. mast and painted. The new steward arrived. I don't think I like him.

...Had tea in a restaurant in Burke St., as much tea, bread and butter as we could eat for 6d along with steak and potatoes. Set out to Armadale[the suburb] to say goodbye, something I don't like. Had a parcel from Mrs Morrison containing a dozen tins of jam and books for me. They treat me as if I was a relation. Oiled my oilskins and washed some clothes.

...To Hawthorn. The Old Man put in an appearance and tried to pump me about matters aboard and then commenced to talk shop before the others, a bit off. I was scared he would go aboard and find the mate sprung and the others in the house ashore.

...400 bales from lighter and wharf, 400 more to come, then heave-ho! and we're bound for London Town. I will be just as sorry to leave this place as I am to leave home. Everyone has been so kind to me.

...Towed out into the bay and anchored off Williamstown. At 10pm the mate told us to go ashore for the Old Man. Took a jar of whisky on the q.t. to Grindlays. All the way back the

---

[1] 1908 passed for Extra Master, Dundee. 1914-18 Lt RNR: mentioned in despatches after Jutland. Captain, RMSP Co. 1927 Elected Elder Brother of Trinity House.
1939-45 Commodore of convoys. 1942 mentioned in despatches.
Founder member of the Hon Company of Master Mariners, later Warden; founder member of The Anchorites; committee member of the Missions to Seamen; board member of Port of London Authority and Southampton Harbour Board; member of the Sail Training Association – *inter alia.*

boat leaked badly and the third mate had to bale all the time. The Old Man was scared. Mrs Duncan has a baby girl.

Melbourne – London. January 20th – May 22nd, 1900.

...We have started our homeward journey and everyone in the house is affected by the dumps. Joe can talk about nothing but Nellie. One is as bad as the other, and I Chris and Ethel.

...Passed through the Heads at 10.15. Washed down. Spent the dog-watch cleaning drawers, putting shore clothes away. No more using then for 3 months.

...Furled the royals. It was so dark we could not see the gear and might as well have had our eyes shut. Called 3 o'clock to furl courses and t.g. sails. A good beginning losing our watch below already. Abreast Flinders I. 2pm. That's the last we shall see of Australia for some months.

...I wonder if the other one is thinking about me as I am about her. Girls are occupying the thoughts of the half-deck. Course ESE.

...Knotting rope-yarns for spunyarn. Thank goodness there is not a full cargo of rails to be anxious about, so let her roll. Very little water coming aboard.

...Fixed up the spinning jenny for spunyarn. By Mercator's I make it 4,069 miles to Diego Ramirez.

...Two Wednesdays this week as we crossed the 180th meridian this morning.

...Made a splendid bread pudding. Position 52°45'S, 165°54'W. I want to make a long passage that I may get a good bit of my time in. Duff twice a week now.

...Wind fell light then took off altogether, tumbling about all day. A hen flew overboard, plenty of excitement, all the watch over the side in bowlines trying to catch it. The Old Man was bossing the job, but lost the hen. The whack day is changed to Thursday.

...The Old Man has been poulticing Sqab's jaw. It has burst. Thanks to Mr Morrison we enjoy our tea every night.

...Making sennit. Duff today, enough to give one an appetite for more.

...Inner jib-sheet carried away at 10pm. Set everything during the forenoon. The Old Man doing his bit (of shouting). Wind NW.

...Slipping along. The girls are on the towrope.

This was a common metaphor: the towrope stretched all the way to the destination, usually when it was a home port, or home-from-home port like Melbourne. Sometimes the girls left behind were referred to, sadly (as the apprentices liked to think) paying out another rope as the ship sped away; but the chances were that they were busy hauling on one attached to another inward-bounder...

...Made an arrangement about the duff. One watch Sunday, other watch Thursday, much better as it gives us a decent piece. We had ours today. <u>Behold in me a sailor bold who ploughs the stormy main, but I would rather plough my way through a duff, be it rich or plain.</u> How's that for poetry? A sudden inspiration as I was running along the deck.

...Set the topsails. Had the shanty *Away to Rio* sung by Smith while heaving up the main topsail. Inner jib halyards carried away, which kept us busy till 7 bells. The Old Man is on the warpath trying to find out who is marking the poop with their boots.

Shanty titles were as variable as those of any folk songs, likewise the wording though the theme was usually consistent. Some alternatives in this instance were *Away for Rio, Bound for the Rio Grande,* and simply *Rio Grande.* By tradition it was an outward-bounder for capstan or windlass, but here was used to cheer the work of sweating down the halyards, adaptation and improvisation the shanty-man's privilege and grace. In any case tradition was at this time faltering and the seaman's stock of songs dwindling as steam rendered them redundant except as entertainment. The river was not the famous Rio Grande forming the border between Mexico and Texas, but Rio Grande do Sul, an insignificant stream entering the Atlantic on the Brazilian coast just north of the border with Uruguay, at its mouth the minor port of Rio Grande.

...I am deeply interested in *Joan of the Sword* running through *The Windsor* [1], the best yarn I've read for some time.

...We ought to be having strong westerly winds instead of easterly. We'll be 110 days this passage I think.

...With Stewart in the foretop splicing the inner jib halyard block to the pennant.

...Put the patent log out. Misty. Heading about E. Fresh pork today. It wasn't up to much, what we got. Sighted a ship at 6.16pm, too thick to ascertain her name. Old Man says she is probably a Yank by her build.

...Draughts is the game now. Everyone is draughts crazy.

Sunday, 11th March, 1900.
...Old Man gave orders to furl royals. Had to take in t'gallants also. It's enough to make a saint swear. 12.40 before we got below. Sighted Diego Ram, at 5am. Abeam just before 6 o'clock, about 10 miles away. Heavy rain and snow squalls. Horn abeam at 1.30pm. Sighted an outward-bounder during the forenoon and a ship coming along the same direction as ourselves.

---

[1] Among magazines received in Cape Town.

Began to signalize[*sic*] her when we sighted another outward-bound barque snugged down on the weather bow. The ship is the *Thessalus*, 35 days out of Wellington, the barque is the *Admiral Peterhoff* of Hamburg, Stettin for Coquimbo.

...Staten I. abeam at noon. 5 ships in sight.

...On the Falklands Banks. Thick fog at 2.30pm. I had the 12-2 wheel. Salt fish for dinner. They speak for themselves.

...Joe told me an awful tale and had me proper, about hearing from one of the ships that Mafeking and Ladysmith had been taken and that Russia and France had declared war against England. I could not sleep for thinking about it. I am jolly glad it is not true because we have lost enough lives in the Transvaal already. Did a 2nd mate's navigation paper and got it right – everything!

...Hove-to all night. Tremendous sea from NE.

...My wheel this morning. I get it every second day, and lookout the same evening. Glass still low.

...Last night at 12 it was blowing heavy with squalls and raining and high seas. The watch was on the poop. She was full nearly all the time. Pooped three seas. Some got through the skylight and wet Jones's bunk. It is a mercy we have a full cargo in, or I don't know what it would be like. I am scared to picture it. At 11.45 she took some heavy seas. Course NE. Anything to windward of that and you can swim round the deck. After dinner the Old Man got the oil bags out but the worst of it was over, the sun was shining. Swabbed the house out and caulked the washboard. Had a game of draughts with Joe and got licked. A lifeline stretched along the decks. About time, too.

...Started to shift sail. The Old Man was about rushing things. He himself bent the gantline on the fore upper topsail. All hands hoisted away. The hitch slipped and the sail went overboard and sunk almost at once. It was only an old one, but if it had been one of the hands who had bent it I'd pity him. A good job it wasn't.

They were getting into lower latitudes now, and finer weather, where the usual practice was to change the canvas, setting fair-weather sails – the older, worn ones – in place of the heavier, newer stuff set to cope with the gales and storms of high latitudes. Though not all the canvas was always changed – to save time and labour it was sometimes confined to the square-sails and everyday fore-and-aft ones – there was plenty of hard work for all. As a 4-mast barque, though no sail plan is extant for her, *Armadale*'s full suit would have totalled something like 14 fore-and-aft sails (staysails, jibs, spanker) and 15 square sails (course, upper & lower topsails, topgallant and royal on fore, main and mizen). By comparison with the old China clippers it was a basic outfit, lacking such exotic items as bonnets, studding-sails, water-sails, Jimmy Greens and high-altitude stuff like skysails and moonrakers, none of which would in any case have added anything to the barque's performance: not only would such a profusion of canvas have been beyond the crew's capacity to handle efficiently, but it would also have caused the ship to labour instead of fly, with her flat-bottomed bluff lines. As it was, *Armadale*'s canvas was ample for her needs without being generous enough to allow the loss overside of one or two sails to go unremarked. Duncan's slippery hitch occasioned a lot of disrespectful amusement.

...A year ago today Mother died. By chance the part of my Bible I read for today was read by Rev. J. Kirk, our minister, at the burial. But that is not the strangest part. I read the same piece (1 Corinthians 15; 35 to end of chapter) last year on the day she was buried unknown to me as we were at sea off the Western Isles[1].

...Shifted fore-and-aft sails, main royal and miz. royal, t.g. sails and topsails. Such a cursing up aloft in the miz I have not heard for some time. It is strange how some people get excited over trifles[2].

...Tarring down in the miz. Others up the fore. Joe helped the painter in his watch below to grain the forward house. He'll get no thanks for it.

...Put about at 1.30pm. Had a wash in the rain and catching rain water. 78 days out and we have not yet got the trades.

...The Old Man has come to the conclusion that the port watch are the Jonahs. He says he will retire as he has had enough.

...Put the wheel awning up. Fine day, occasional light showers.

...Sharks swimming about but did not catch any. I wish we would, then we would get a shark breeze.

Sharks were responsible for a multitude of ills and misfortunes, mostly imagined; as a result catching them was less a matter of sport or an addition to the diet (they were considered inedible) than of ritual exorcism of accumulated and threatened calamity, such as a succession of foul winds. The creature was usually done to death with gleeful savagery and its mangled remains returned to the sea after removal of the jaws (for decoration) and the spine (for a walking-stick nobody ever used) and the tail or a fin, which would be nailed to the bowsprit to invoke a fair wind.

...We have the trades now.

...Almost forgot the entry for today – that is, we're on hard-tack again. Better than I expected but still they smell strongly and taste of rotten stockfish.

---

[1] The Azores, not to be confused with the Scottish islands.
[2] The mizen was the apprentices' mast. Certain half-deck personalities are being mocked.

126

1. *Armadale's* apprentices, 1901. L-R: Tim Jones, Alexander Mackay, "Phos" Forster, Joe Stevenson. (Mrs E. Gregory)

2. Ship's company, *Armadale*. Brooklyn, 1902. Apprentices, standing L-R: Joe Stevenson, (steward), Alex Mackay, (bosun, 2nd mate) "Phos"Forster, (carpenter), Geordie Rangdale, (-,-,-, cook). Seated, centre, Capt. J.A. Stevens - "A top-notcher". (Mrs E. Gregory)

PLATE 1

3. Hands & (seated, front) apprentices, *Vanduara*. Swansea, late C19th.
(City & County of Swansea: Swansea Museums Collection)

PLATE 2

4. Cadet of the BISN Co., c.1906.
(Author's collection)

PLATE 3

6. Apprentices (in caps) & acting 3rd mate, ss *Winkleigh*, 1931. (S. Squirrell)

5. Apprentice S. Squirrell, ss *Monkleigh*, 1928. (S. Squirrell)

PLATE 4

7. Straight left & guard. Apprentices, ss *City of Bath*, 1927.
   (A.Niblock)

8. Shore rig. Apprentices, ss Pareora, 1931.
   (E.J.White)

PLATE 5

10. Scrub round. Apprentices, ss *Pareora*, 1931.
(E.J.White)

9. Apprentices & friends. Dunedin, NZ. c.1929.
(E.J.White)

PLATE 6

11. Apprentices on stage, 1931.
    (E.J.White)

12. Before the first trip. Apprentice Hubert Thomas
    (aged 14), ss *Pentraeth*, Swansea 1928.
    (Author's collection)

PLATE 7

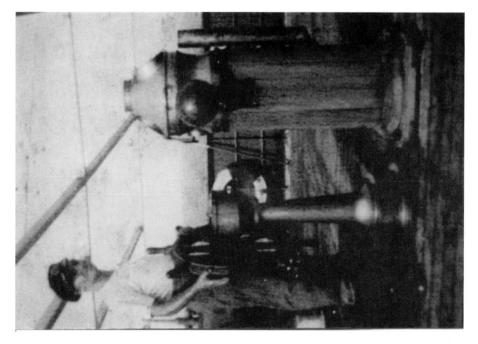

14. The trick, ss *Vera Radcliffe*, 1934.
(Capt W.B. Thomas)

13. Smoke-oh during boiler-clean, ss *Vera Radcliffe*,
Sunderland, 1934.
(Capt W.B. Thomas)

PLATE 8

15. On the bridge, mv *Sambre*, 1935.
   (J.D.E. Lewis)

16. Dog watch, mv *Sambre*, 1935.
   (J.D.E. Lewis)

17. Needlework, mv *Sambre*, 1935.
   (J.D.E. Lewis)

18. Attending memorial service for King George V.
   mv *Siris*, 1936.
   (J.D.E. Lewis)

PLATE 9

20. Up the flue, or as clean as a whistle. ss *Llanover*, 1934.
(Capt M. Peyton-Bruhl)

19. Shooting the sun, ss *Llanover*, 1934.
(Capt M. Peyton-Bruhl)

PLATE 10

21. Commander (2 rings), officers & cadets, ss *Devon*, Sydney NSW, 1934. (Capt I.E. Thomas)

PLATE 11

22. Captain, officers & 4 cadets (seated), ss *Silversandal*, Manila, 1938. (J.A. Gunn)

PLATE 12

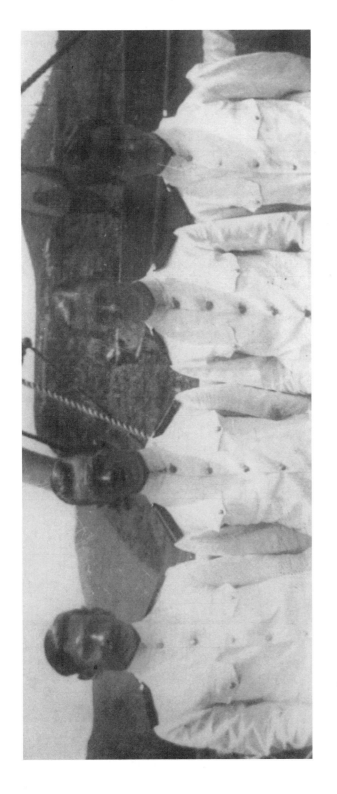

23. Changed for lunch after a morning on the winches. Cadets, ss *Silverteak*, St Helena, 1941.
(J.A. Gunn)

PLATE 13

24. L-R: Sparks, 2 DEMS gunners & apprentice, ss *Baron Renfrew*, 1941.
   (Capt G. Gunn)

25. Four apprentices, 2 in gunners' hats. 4.7-in gun, ss *Baron Renfrew*, 1941.
   (Capt G. Gunn)

PLATE 14

27. Vintage cap, vintage (4-in) gun, MAC *Adula*, 1944.
(Dr F. Evans)

26. New cadet, new cap. Southampton Sch. of Navigation, 1943.
(Dr F. Evans)

PLATE 15

28. "Apprentices are not to attempt take-off." Swordfish, MAC *Adula*, 1944.
    (Dr F. Evans)

29. A bird in the hand...   Liverpool, 1944.
    (Dr F.Evans)

PLATE 16

...Made a dandyfunk and started to cross-point my chest lashing. Joe had the 6-8 wheel tonight.

...The Old Man hit Joe on the nose and made it bleed badly this afternoon. Naturally there is ructions. Joe had said he would log the Old Man, and it had come to the Old Man's ears. What does not? He came across after tea and went for Joe while he and I were having a game of draughts. He called him everything. Then after I came off the lookout he called Joe up on the poop and gave him another blowing-up, the mate standing by. That old beggar ought to be dumped. He must have started the Old Man a second time. I don't know what he said to Joe.

Evidently the strain was telling on Duncan, as it also seemed to be on others, and common sense, let alone discipline, suffered accordingly. Why Joe had taken it into his head to take, or threaten to take, action against the captain Mackay doesn't say; perhaps it was an instance of familiarity breeding contempt, Joe's being, as Mackay mentioned, Duncan's favourite. Be that as it may, it looks as if first Joe, then the Old Man, and then Mackay, allowed hubris to get the better of them.

...While I was in the paint locker getting oil to oil the poop-deck the Old Man came along and began to talk to Chips about the working man, loud enough for me to hear. I guessed what was coming next. Not all of it, though. Then he started to find fault with the apprentices. Said they were no good. Said he had had lots of other boys like the ones he had now. They would not do what they were told and went ashore every night until 12 o'clock and they were not able for their work next day. That put my back up. I told him that if he included me amongst those who went ashore every night he had made a jolly big mistake, as I had been ashore once out of my turn without leave, and that was New Year's night. He groused about a bit, getting his wool off, and I was wild. He said we did not think anything of telling lies to shield ourselves. I told him I never told a lie to shield myself from anything I did wrong. I had not been brought up that way. I would own up to it. He told me he would like to get one who never told lies and he would put him in a glass case. I told him I was sorry I could not apply for the honour as I was not guiltless; I had told them on occasions when really required. He said he had been told I went ashore every night. I told him he believed too much and he went away shortly after. I could almost swear the mate is partly to blame; if anyone else I'd like to know. When I came aft on the poop he said to me, "So you keep a book with everything in it." I had told him that I could show him in black and white that I had never been ashore out of my turn without leave. He asked me if I put everything down. He evidently thought I kept it for the purpose of proving anything against him, because he said, "God help the captain sailors get in their power." I wonder if it worries him having given Joe the grip of him. Burgoo this morning and a bit of duff for dinner. Rats in the house. One crawled over me last night.

...Dandyfunk and crackerhash is the order of the day.

...Stuck my sheath knife under the nail of my middle finger left hand while picking maggots and weevils out of the biscuits. First time I've done so, as previously we've indulged in the fresh meat. A year ago today we sailed from Greenock.

...Soft tack today. Cook made a tart. He makes one nearly every Sunday for us. Very good of him.

...Had a rat-hunt in the house. Caught it and gave it to Tom Cat. The Old Man nabbed Sqab pinching ship's apples, then found some in my bunk. Sqab had put them there. He seemed quite pleased he had caught him, said he must be sharp to bluff him. If only he knew. Kitten caught a rat in the house.

The crisis passed. As the ship drew closer to home the petty upsets of the voyage began to assume their true proportion, not without some shamefaced regrets and, on Duncan's part, a rather touching attempt to make it up to the half-deck, where evidently, and fortunately, a spirit of contrition prevailed:

...3 vessels in sight at daybreak but all stood to the N. Had the Old Man in showing us his discharges[*sic*] and yarning, also giving good advice.

...130 miles from Ushant at noon. Put the anchor over and bent the cable. Did 2 azimuths.

...Sighted a red light at 11pm. Got quite a scare. Called all hands. Got her off and shortened down to topsails.

Arrival London. May 23rd, 1900.

...St Catherine's light abeam at 3am. Beachy Head at 8am. Signalled to B. Head. Dungeness abeam at 12 o'clock. Signalled. Hove to and took the pilot. Towboat *Conqueror* alongside about 8.30. Skipper gave the Old Man a present and he gave them a chunk of salt horse. Had dinner, furled courses and set royals. Dover abeam at 3.30pm. Passed through the Dover Strait, saw a great many little coasters and a sunken steamer, only funnel and masts above water. Towboat skipper and Old Man bargaining about the towage, settled for £45. Clewed up, made fast the royals, t'gallant sails and u. topsails. Gave the towboat our hawser and went below for our tea. The Old Man is logging all those who were absent from their work in Melbourne. Mean old weed. Washed dungarees and had a shave. Worked nearly all the middle watch getting braces put away. Gravesend at 6.15 pm, river pilot aboard and tug ahead, the *Mosquito*. Nearly ran a barge down. The river is crowded with them going down broadside-on with the tide. Saw all sorts of ships and steamers. What a traffic on the river. No wonder Britain is such a powerful maritime power. All those splendid vessels. Got up to the London Dock, got in, and made fast and cleared up by 3.30. A letter from Forbes and 2 from Maggie. Tim went home as soon as we had knocked off. Hoop shillarity! Going home when the focsle is painted. All's well at home and I thank God for that.

After a fortnight or so at home Mackay rejoined in London on 19th June, 1900. He and Jones were the seniors as before, the half-deck's complement remaining unchanged. Captain Duncan, for all his voiced intentions to leave the ship, was still in command – indeed, other reasons apart, he wasn't likely to have left just yet since his wife, young son and baby daughter had stayed behind in Melbourne. But he was growing weary of the life.

Armadale sailed in ballast on the 28th for Larvik, a small port at the entrance to Oslo Fjord, where she loaded timber during a stay from July 2nd to 31st, enough time for the crew to go adrift and the apprentices to make friends ashore. Girls brought flowers on board to brighten up the half-deck. She sailed for Melbourne, stopping briefly off Margate for mail and a few odds and ends of stores, arriving at Port Phillip on 3rd November after an uneventful voyage – uneventful, that is, outside the alarms and excursions that were a normal part of a windjammer's passage. As before, the route lay to the eastward round the Cape, this time without having to call at Cape Town.

Mackay was by this time thoroughly at home in the ship, and his diary entries show an easy familiarity with her people and the work. He called the apprentices the "Too Soon Gang". But, like most sailors, he suffered pangs of homesickness before settling down to the voyage:

...Wind hauled fair to NW. Under way [from Margate roads] by 11am. Foul anchor, had a good deal of trouble clearing it. Set everything. Signalled Dungeness. My left hand so badly skinned by the chain jib-sheet that I can hardly use it. The Old Man said I ought to know better. A pleasure steamer, the *Britannia*, came right under our stern and gave us three cheers and we replied. Felt homesick and seeing all those people has made me worse. Plenty of steamboats going up and down.

As usual, food became the dominating aspect of life, and it showed no improvement on what had gone before:

...A beastly hungry day. No extra bread, no potatoes, a few beans and that horrible Harriet Lane. I asked the Old Man for more. He said we are getting the same amount of flour, etc as last voyage. It ended by him telling the steward to give us some biscuits and afterwards the mean old beggar asked how many he had given us. Lime juice today.

...The Old Man sent for me this morning and showed our bread weight on the scales. He said I will get no more. If I can't find enough to eat he'll lose by it, not me. He said if only we were as smart at working as at eating our bread we would do well. I should like to put him on the whack. I'd reduce his fat for him.

...Shifted the storm for the big jigger. If hunger is felt aft here it reigns supreme at the other end of the ship. The men have music instead of food for tea.

...What food for Sunday – heartburn from that beastly Harriet Lane all day and evening. Made a jelly but it was a failure. Abreast of Teneriffe.

...Had a good dinner, beans and curried fowl (skeleton) and roly-poly. I have named this day the day of plenty. Position 40°S, 14°30′E.

...1400 miles from Port Phillip Heads. Old Man says we are getting too much beans and flour. Accuses the steward of giving us over our allowance, says he never had such a gluttonous crowd and he hopes the hoodlums (the Norwegians) will clear. Getting cargo gear up from lazarette and forepeak.

...2nd mate doused Sqab with a bucket of water when he was asleep during his watch on deck.

...Blowing strong, heavy squalls with rain. Clewing up the main the lazy tack carried away the chain tack and surged it right off the bollards[*sic*], narrowly missed the 2nd mate, swept along to where all the hands were standing at weather gear and hurt one or two. The rest bunked but we managed to clew it up again. Furled crossjack, main, mizen and mizen u. tops'l, fores'l and inner jib and wasting time hanging around. Blowing heavy when we left the deck. Old McQueen[1] was on the lookout for over 5 hours. Poor old fellow I am sorry for him. My wheel 6-8. I had Sqab's woollen helmet on but my nose caught it from the hail. Cook washed out twice so it was biscuits for breakfast, only a very few beans for dinner, half-cooked. McQueen was washed about and is laid up. Rolling heavily taking a deal of water aboard. It requires some skill to eat your food and look after the dishes. Set the fores'l at 6pm and were kept on deck frigging about with the mizen u. tops'l. No water served out.

...We have a good job picking the stalks from raisins in the cabin. Old Man superintending.

...Lost my job raisin-picking, I suppose because I ate three.

There was, of course, no compulsion to study, and no time allowed during working hours unless time spent standing by while watch on deck could be made use of. Not that the apprentices were unduly concerned, low as it was on their list of priorities. Yet there were occasions when the master or an officer might be moved to impart something of the wisdom of his calling, and the quirky Duncan was no exception, though even in this sphere his generosity was less than munificent:

...Old Man explained the barometer and aneroid to me also an instrument I never heard of before, the symsometer[2]. Cut Tim's hair. Painter put a new fret in my banjo.

...Have a beastly cold in the head. Reported land at 10 o'clock. I could have sworn it was land. The Old Man took me into the cabin and showed me where land was. We shall be up to C. Otway at 8am tomorrow if the breeze holds.

The voyage ended as most do, with the sudden abandonment of routine, the slightly bewildering plunge into the bustle of shore life and a return to contact with the inhabitants of another world:

---

[1] One of the ABs, old and worn out, who had declared his age in the 50s but was probably in his 70s, facing homelessness and dereliction unless he could get a berth in a ship.
[2] ?

At Melbourne. November 2nd, 1900 – January 14th, 1901.

...C. Otway abeam at 7.30am. Signalled. All hands had tea together. Working all 2nd dog-watch and were lucky to have our watch below. All hands at 1 o'clock. Dropped anchor off W'town at 10 past 2. Furled all sail and finished by 3.15. Had a feed of biscuits and turned in. Turned out at 6.30am for doctor's inspection. Mrs Duncan and the Junior Captain came off first thing in the customs launch. Old Man went away with them before breakfast. Had a wash and shave and a look at the latest papers. 2 letters from Maggie and a photo of Mother. Everything is well at home. Sausage for breakfast, soup and apple tart for dinner. I shall turn in early tonight as we have a hard day's graft before us.

Which included the tedious but crucial task of tallying cargo. It fell to everyone, even the Old Man, and Duncan took his turn with the others. Berthed first at Williamstown, the ship had to be moved to Port Melbourne; there was maintenance work to be done on hull and gear, quarters to be turned out and cleaned, errands to be run...

...Watched the crowded river steamers and wagonloads of people going along the road. Made us quite sorry that we were tied down to this confounded job.

It didn't occur to Mackay – or, apparently, anyone else on board – that among the throng ashore envious glances might have been cast in their direction, the ship, quiet alongside, seeming to represent a freedom denied the man on his way to office or factory – to some confounded job. In a few weeks, or days, she and her crew would be flying towards distant shores while the same wagon would be taking the same people along the same road past yet another bird of passage briefly pausing. It wasn't so much a dissatisfaction with his lot that distracted the sailor's attention as a natural restlessness that denied him the sense of place – to say nothing of complacency – which the landsman took for granted. If Mackay had been free to go ashore the time would have come when his eyes would have turned seawards and the same disquiet touch him knowingly on the shoulder. It was a disease, the cure for which was quite likely to be worse than the complaint.

...Saw Dud Finlay on the wharf, 3rd on the *Ismailia*. Went aboard. A fine vessel, everything of the latest. Introduced to chief officer and 2nd engineer.

...Joe and I went out to Hawthorn. We were sitting on the verandah when who should pop into the garden but the Old Man, Mrs D and the son & hair. I did a bunk; Joe did not know what to do. I kept out of the way.

...Ashore with Joe, got outside a whacking great pie.

...Stevedores refused work today when our fellows started slinging the cargo on the wharf. Mr & Mrs Morrison were down last night. The Old Man was drunk and had quite a yarn with Tim.

...Mrs Morrison told me the Old Man would not let me away, but would let me go Christmas Day. How kind of the old fraud.

...Joe and I got ashore in time to see our boat[1] returning after winning the heat. Saw the final which was a close finish, our gig coming out on top. Good old *Armadale,*

And old McQueen had run his course. He had proved little better than a liability, and in those days of reduced – if not inadequate – manning sentimentality, his only hope, had no place, if indeed it ever had. The romance of sail lay in the eye of the beholder, not in the focsle or aloft on a windswept yard, and the sea was (and is) a demanding mistress, and heartless. McQueen was past satisfying her and so was cast up on the beach amongst the other flotsam. The term "beggar" held more meaning than mere idiom:

...McQueen was paid off today, poor old beggar. I wonder what he will do now. Ericson is trying to sell his [Ericson's] clothes to get booze.

Only slightly less tragic was the fate of younger men who, sometimes too late, realised their incompatibility with the life. At least they still had time in which to strike up a working acquaintance with something better suited to them: some succeeded, some drifted into obscurity, and some went to pieces among the wrecks (McQueen one of them) that haunted the quays and sailors' homes. Many took their chances with the opportunity that Australia seemed to promise and were never seen again: Sqab Stuttard had never quite come to terms with life in the house, and as time passed the possibility evaporated entirely. Mackay had been exasperated by him, likewise the officers and Captain Duncan, and his reluctant compliance with the demands of the ship had never been more than intermittent, ever apt to dissolve into recalcitrance which must have veiled a deep-seated misery. In the end the friendships he formed ashore in Melbourne must have tempted him into desperate expedient, and perhaps ensuing confusion exacerbated by indecision born of remorse:

...A letter from the Forbeses[2] asking for us off. Stevenson and Jones could go but I had to stay and tally cargo, but later Old Man told me I could go. Tim, Joe, Harry and I set out at 9.30. Sqab stayed aboard.

...Old Man went for Sqab again last night and told him that if he went ashore again without permission he would give him a thrashing and take the consequences.

...Sqab turned out to wash the cabin dishes.

---

[1] The crew comprised Johnson, Christensen and Flid (all sailors), the 2nd mate, and Tim Jones as cox, presumably chosen for his relatively light weight. There were seven boats altogether.
[2] Morrisons.

...Sqab cleared out last night. He is a silly young beggar to go here. It would have been better to have waited until we got home then left the ship. He never said goodbye to any of us. He left his chest, so I'll collar that for what he owes me. Also it's a better chest than mine. I expect he's gone to the *Hespa*, a Yankee barque that laid alongside us in the swinging basin.

Which was unsubstantiated conjecture, though a possibility, in which case the deserter had jumped out of the frying-pan: Mackay had met the *Hespa*'s mate and concluded that he ran a "hot ship". In any case, that was the last of poor Sqab.

But it was in the sea's perverse nature that for every disillusioned absconder there was a newcomer eager to immolate himself in the flames of fancied passion, and H.L. Forster – "Phos" – put in an appearance, to Mackay's evident approval.

...Had a fellow down today who served his time as a chemist and intends to take up ploughing the stormy main as a profession. He is to join the *Armadale* and of course will stay in the house. He seems a nice fellow and I think we will get along all right.

...I gave the new chap a list of things he would require as it is better than going to an outfitter's and getting a lot of useless stuff.

...Joe and I went up to Forster's, and the new chap, for dinner. They were a very nice family and I think Mr Forster is a very nice gentleman. We were introduced to some of Forster's chums, spent a jolly evening and got aboard by 11.30. Finished a letter to Maggie and enclosed a piece of seaweed from Sandringham beach.

...Forster came down tonight. His chest came down yesterday. Showed him where to stow his gear. Squared up the house. The Old Man showed some friends round and of course must needs show them the house where it is dirty. Forster starts on Monday.

And very nearly ended his sea career before it had begun, though not by the time-honoured open-hatch method. His near-demise at least had the merit of being thoroughly seamanlike, with none of the absurdity attaching to clumsiness about the deck. Her cargo completed, *Armadale* had gone to anchor off Williamstown while Duncan saw to the final details of the ship's business without having to worry about his crew making a last-minute bid for freedom. While there, the apprentices acted as gig's crew, running errands and ferrying people to and fro:

...Landed Mrs D on the Gem Pier. She got the *Gem* across to Williamstown. We were lying on the weather side of the pier and made three attempts to get off. We were successful at last but what a struggle. Several times I thought we would be driven ashore. Got over to the other pier and lay there to wait for the Old Man. Raining and blowing very heavy. The *General Gordon* went on the St Kilda Bank during a heavy squall. The Old Man and 2 friends put in an appearance at 4.15. He was going across in the *Queen*. He told us to get under the piles and get a tow from the *Queen*. We tried to get under the pier. Got through all right but could not get away from the wharf without running a very great risk of going ashore. Decided to put back and told the Old Man. He said I should try the *Gem*. Went across to the other pier and lay astern of the *Gem*'s berth. It being the weather side I had a very hard job to keep her from being stove in against the wharf. The *Gem* came alongside. I got aboard and told him I wanted a tow. He told me he would not tow me as it was too risky with such a sea running. But then I told him what ship we were from and what the Old Man had said. He told me he only did it as a favour for Duncan and with the condition that only 2 stayed in the boat. He gave us a line but it was very short and that was the cause of the trouble. Sent Joe and Tim aboard the *Gem* and kept Forster in the boat with me. The *Gem* began to come astern trying to keep clear of the snags and sea and wind caught her and blew her broadside-on. The painter being short shoved us in towards the piles and *Gem*'s stern gave us a pinch. I told Forster to look out for himself which he did like lightning. She gave us a second squeeze and swamped us and I got into the water and made for the piles. Forster was on top. How he got there I don't know, neither does he, lying on his stomach with his hands stretched out to me. I got hold of his fingers, that was enough. I got my legs from between the boat and piles just as she gave the final crush. Then started salvage operations. We got all the gear belonging to the boat except the backboard and rudder and my knife, sheath and belt, which I lost. As there were plenty of people on the wharf I got them to give us a hand with the boat onto the wharf, then Tim and I went across in the *Gem*. Bummed our passage to Williamstown to tell the Old Man while I left Joe and Phos to look after the boat. Told the Old Man. He took it much quieter than I thought he would. I was soaking and the wind cutting through me like a knife. The Grindlays kindly gave us tea, the first since 7.30am and it was after 7 by then.

Later the damaged gig was got back aboard complete with crew, but no wonder Duncan was subdued. His apprentices had coped with a situation partly wrought by the captain, an error of judgment that could well have been construed as negligence in the inquiry that would have followed any fatalities. The *Gem*'s skipper had showed more sense but seemed to have lacked the courage of his convictions, deferring to a deep-sea man's wishes. Mackay's surprise at Duncan's reception of his news betrays a certain naivety and a wonderful unconsciousness of the incident's implications, which would, of course, have ruined what would otherwise have been a stay as enjoyable as any before, with social life revolving about the hospitality of the families whose affairs had become so intimately bound up with the ship's. Naturally enough, it had reached a climax over Christmas, which Mackay had spent with the Morrisons:

...Joe stayed on board as the Old Man would not allow him to find a substitute from among the men. Hard lines on Joe, jolly hard lines. We arrived at Hawthorn and stayed there until 1pm. Then we all set off together to Camberwell. Tim got a splendid book entitled *How We Kept the Flag Flying*, about Ladysmith. Joe and I got a spiffing pipe each. Like a mug I said I didn't smoke. Ought to have said I did. Tim took charge of Joe's. We enjoyed ourselves immensely, left about 11. Tim went down to the ship and I went up to Hawthorn, stayed all night, turned out about 8. Went to the Royal at night. *With Flying Colours*, a splendid piece. Got the last train. Turned in about 1. Was woken up by an alarm-clock playing *Absent-Minded Beggar* and *Soldiers of the Queen* alternatively[*sic*]. I had to roll it in a blanket to keep it from waking the others. It played for 20 minutes. Got down to the ship by 7am. I have had a splendid time.

...Went down the bay to the *Ozone*. The vessel was crowded, over a thousand aboard, I should say. Landed at Sorrento, went to Queenscliff first. The boat went on to Dromana and called back at Sorrento later. Only 2 hours at Sorrento, rather short. I was with Chrissie.

...Ended the Old Year and began the New. Had a few words with the Old Man, fell asleep about 11. Tim woke me to wish me a Happy New Year. Same to everyone. Turned in again about 12.30. Turned out by the sailmaker we had on my first voyage at 4am to wish me the complements[*sic*] of the season. He is on the coast here.

The Sydney consignment had been unloaded together with the cargo for Melbourne, so with a full load consisting of baled wool, copper ore, spelter ingots and bagged wheat, with the incident of the crushed gig still fresh in mind, they sailed for London. This time Mrs Duncan, with the baby and young son, accompanied her husband, who planned to retire at the end of the voyage.

Melbourne – London. January 14th – May 6th, 1901.

It was wet and cold as far as the Horn, Mackay suspecting the stowage of cargo as the cause of the ship's tendency to fill her decks:

...At about 6 o'clock Tim was carried in. He had been knocked down by a sea when going for coffee. He had a swollen jaw and bleeding lip, sopping wet but no bones broken, unconscious when picked up. We undressed him and did what we could. He did not know anything about where he was or what was the matter. It was wonderful he got off so easily. Turned out after 7 bells. No bread, but we had a little left from yesterday. Shipping heavy water all afternoon. Blowing heavy with squalls from NNW. Galley flooded out, washed our rooties away. Focsle washed out at same time. Playing water-rat with Chips as some of the ports were coming adrift. House is not very wet but we have plenty wet clothes.

This was the kind of situation produced by the weather that pursued them out of the Southern Ocean into the South Atlantic after rounding the Horn on 18th February. And, as the passage dragged on, the customary irritations sprouted in the house:

...Joe has begun to make himself disagreeable. It is the beginning. Well, I hope he succeeds.

...I wish this passage was over or that I was in the starboard watch.

But there were compensations, chiefly in the shape of an improvement in the quantity and quality of the food, Mackay attributing Duncan's apparent change of heart to the presence of his wife:

...Fleas are pretty bad. They must have come from the cargo. I wish Mrs D. had always come with us. The ship is altogether different.

...Joe and Jones had another fierce argument. Result, additional dislike for Bluenose (Joe). The two blackguards are together now, since changing watches. Never mind. Everything has an ending.

Including the voyage, which lasted 112 days, an unremarkable time either way. Tim Jones had been badly shaken by his accident, and on arrival left the ship facing the possibility of having to give up the sea. The others stood by the ship and went home on leave in turn, or, in Forster's case, to stay with friends. Mackay resumed his diary on June 6th as the ship was re-floated after a brief drydocking. She sailed the same day for New York with a ballast of chalk, Tim Jones's place in the house taken by a first-tripper, Geordie Rangdale. And Captain Duncan's place was occupied by Captain John Stevens, something of a contrast.

London – New York. June 6th – July 12th, 1901.

...I had my socks drying on the bridge manrope[1] this morning. I was aloft when it began to rain so bemoaned the fact that my socks would get wet. When I came down they were gone. The steward brought them across after dinner and told me the Old Man took them in. He had rolled them up in pairs. If Duncan had done that I should have expected the sky to fall in. What a difference between them. I wish I had served all my time with Stevens.

A sentiment later revised in the light of closer acquaintance. For one thing, the ship seemed to be less responsive to Stevens's hand than she had to Duncan's temperamental facility, and the passage to New York was embarrassingly prolonged, though not entirely because of the captain's assumed failings. They ran into a frustrating sequence of alternate calm clear weather and windy foggy conditions, able neither to make way with all sail set nor to set all sail in favourable winds for fear of collision.

...I don't mind this weather but I am sorry for the Old Man. The owners won't be pleased at his making such a long passage, but we have not had a chance since clearing the channel.

The stay at New York was hectic, a whirligig of oppressive heat, the working out of the chalk and the loading of resin, shifting berth, constant attack by swarms of mosquitoes, visits to other ships, places of interest and amusement ashore, Coney Island the great attraction, and calls at the Mission, housed afloat at Brooklyn and presided over by the popular Dr Hayes, renowned for his lavish teas as much as his sermons. And Tim Jones rejoined them after a passage out in the *Minneapolis*, making a crowded five in the house. They sailed for Melbourne with general cargo – resin, wire, steel sheet, steel rails, paper rolls, sawn pine, sawn walnut, machinery, barrels of oil, lime juice, bicarbonate of soda, glucose, soda ash, nails slates, plaster, grease,

---

[1] The manrope running along the flying bridge linking poop and apprentice's house, on which was fitted the standard compass.

organs, desks, tin-tacks, sandpaper, wooden pails, clothes-pegs, mousetraps, pins and "all Yankee notions". It was rounded off with cased turpentine and gasoline on deck, altogether a valuable cargo, particularly for a sailing-ship in times when the usual load was low-value bulky stuff like coal, nitrates, guano and so on.

New York – Melbourne. September 4th, 1901 – January 4th, 1902.

Once again the route lay past the Cape, and once again Captain Stevens was cursed with fluky winds and bad weather. By this time Mackay was an apprentice only by contract, approaching the end of his time, and, what was more significant, of youthful naivety, approaching what Conrad called "the shadow-line" between youth and manhood. Evidence of it appeared in heightened self-confidence.

...Had a row with the second mate over striking one of the hands. The man was in the right. The 2nd took advantage of him and struck him when he was not looking and I intervened. For that I shall once more be on the black list.

...By a Mercator's sailing I find we are 7,866 miles from Melbourne which means an average of 9 knots right through to arrive on Dec 24th. So unless we get a breeze soon and a strong one, too, we will have the pleasure of spending Xmas and perhaps New Year at sea. This head wind must tell on the old man a great deal but he does not seem to worry or fret very much. I would like to see him hang on a bit better and longer, but of course he knows best.

And there was always study to occupy the time, its importance rather more obvious by this time:

...Finished a Newton's paper yesterday and got it right.

He doesn't expand on this, but it would be fair to surmise that he was following a course set by Newton's Navigation School in London, a forerunner of the correspondence courses that gained widespread, and later universal, currency from the 1930s on. Whether or not Roxburgh paid for it isn't known, but it wasn't likely, while there is every reason to suppose that apprentices of Mackay's calibre and sentiment availed themselves of the facility at their own expense – or their parents'. In any case Mackay's efforts seemed to meet with Stevens's approval.

...Had another visit from the old man this afternoon, he asked me if there was anything I wanted explaining I was to come to him.

...Finished the "Rule of the Road" yesterday. Thank goodness, too. I hope I won't forget it. Did two charts today, one of which has puzzled me for some time. I find them much easier now. There only remains the logarithms to grind up again and that is navigation complete.

Mackay's prognosis was correct: they failed to keep a 9-knot average although Stevens's course had followed the 40th parallel (he didn't appear to consider the stormier great circle course) and Christmas found them still at sea:

...Wednesday 25th. Christmas Day.
Last night was our 8 hours in. Spent the middle watch at the braces, the breeze being very unsteady with occasional light showers of rain. A glorious day with a light W'ly wind. Had salt fish for breakfast which was not up to much. Played draughts, crib and read during the forenoon, and occasional jig at the brace. Wind hauling to N. We all had dinner together, consisting of pea soup with vegetables (preserved) which was excellent, brawn and preserved potatoes (the latter were fair) then followed the duff, made by the steward and removed very quickly by us. The whole meal was supplemented by a lemon jelly made by Tim which gave an excellent finish to our Christmas dinner. Later on we had tea, so we cannot complain [of] being empty today. Rather the reverse. Played Ludo, draughts, etc. My 4 to 6 wheel. Tim took it for me while I served out the water. For tea we had a cake made by the steward for us. It was very nice but would have been better if it had been a few days old. It was exceedingly kind of him. Had a constitutional during the dog-watch to wear off the bad effects of stuffing. Glorious evening, full moon, fine N'ly wind, slipping along during the puffs. Course E ½ N. Posn 40°44'S, 117°1'E. I hope they had as fine weather in Melb. today as we had. I would not have objected if we had spent today where we spent last Xmas day but I must not complain. I wonder what they are doing at home now, it is 2pm with them so I suppose they are having dinner. No grog served out to the hands whereat some of them are very much displeased and give vent to their feelings in uncomplimentary language.

A modest enough Christmas dinner, but sumptuous by comparison with what had gone before, when there would have been no remarking on the freshness of the cake, nor, perhaps, alternative uses for soft bread:

...Fine day. Worked all day to finish the poop just before 8 bells. Scrubbed the house floor with sand and canvas. Our bread being very doughy today, Tim spent the evening modelling men[*sic*] and women's heads of it. We have quite a collection stuck along the beam.

And they were still at sea at the end of the year:

...Had a great old middle watch this morning. Bouted ship. Hauled mainsail and foresail up, furled m. and miz. t.gan.sails. Set foresail. Squared the yards to a SW'ly breeze before we left the deck. Painted around the decks and stoning poop gratings. 249 miles from C. Otway at noon. Set m.t.gan.sail at 11.30am. Miz. and f. during afternoon. M. royal during dog-watch. Set mainsail about 10.30pm. I think we might have had sail on her much sooner. We lose a great many fine chances. This is the last day of 1901. I remember four years ago I was looking forward to joining this hooker and now, well, I am looking forward to leaving her. Not that I don't like her. I wonder where I will be four years from now. "I wonder, I wonder." Ring out the old, Ring in the new. Ring happy bells across the (snow) sea. The year is dying. Let it go. Ring out the false. Ring in the true. Here endeth the year 1901.

...Several days ago I thought I should have my letters tonight. "Blessed is he (or she) who expecteth nothing for he shall not be disappointed." That is a good proverb. I was having breakfast this morning when it struck me that it would be just on the stroke "o' twal" at home. It was 5 to 9 with us. My thoughts went back with a rush and I could picture myself the various scenes being enacted and remember Hogmanay 4 years ago and wish that everyone was alive who was then. But God's Will will be done. We may not see today the silvery lining, which by and by to edge the cloud will steal, but let this thought hush every vain repining, God sendeth all and his will is our weal.

Slowly, they beat eastward, frustrated not only by the wind but also by progress itself:

...Wind set to E dead against us. Put about at 12 last night. "All hands". Put about again at 3.30am. On star. tack scrubbing the rail, pin rail and t.gall. rail. Signalled a steamer bound W this forenoon. Adelaide Steamship Line. She did not understand our signal, she was using the old code[1].

At Melbourne: January 4th – March 6th, 1902.

The Argus.
Melbourne. 6th January, 1902.

The barque Armadale, from New York, arrived in the bay on Sunday morning. She has changed her captain since her previous trip to the port. Captain Duncan, who commanded her on that occasion, having retired from the sea and settled down in Scotland [2]. His successor is Captain J.H. Stevens, formerly of the Nithsdale. The Armadale, which left New York on September 4th, crossed the line on October 29th, and had a very tedious passage till the westerly winds were picked up, this accounting for the fact that she was 122 days out. Nothing eventful occurred to break the monotony of the voyage, and the vessel, laden with general cargo, has arrived in good order.

The passage should have taken around 90 days: 122 was something of a record. Poor Captain Stevens, for he wasn't unlucky only in the weather but also, in Melbourne, with the crew, among whom, no doubt owing to the long passage, friction had reached a point of bitter antagonism. A sailor served the bosun with a summons for assault, and that and other court cases involving the exploits ashore of drunken hands occupied an inordinate amount of Stevens's time. Mackay was sympathetic:

...The old man (poor old chap) had to pay several other visits to the Police Court in connection with the hands getting drunk, creating a disturbance, and getting run in.

While on board matters took a serious turn:

---

[1] The International Code of Signals was revised c.1900.
[2] Later returning in command of Roxburgh's *Torrisdale*.

...A great to-do forward among the hands. A fight resulted in Bourne getting his arm sliced open and the police coming on board and taking 4 of them to lock-up. The focsle reeked of foul air, drink, heat and blood. There was blood forward and right aft to the cabin door.

...To the end of our stay in Melbourne the hands, sailmaker, carpenter and cook were going ashore on the bust and getting run in. The fact of the matter was the old man was too good to them and much too lenient. Such conduct would not have suited me had I been in his place. I felt very sorry for him.

But leniency was becoming fashionable; in the end it would make its contribution not merely to the downfall of the ships' circumscribed society but also to that of a much wider sphere. Good order and balance has to be continually worked at and rigorously upheld in the face of sustained pressure from the forces of chaos, and at 21 Mackay was well aware of the fact. A shipmaster – the representative of good order – serves his ship badly by being kindly to one and all, for he does so at the expense of those who depend upon and look for even-handed discipline and civilised standards. Crews of sailing-ships at this period included a large element of low-grade humanity that lacked natural morale and saw leniency as a weakness – which, in effect, it is.

And among the apprentices time was working its interminable passage. Tim Jones's health had been unsteady since his return, with no tendency to improvement, and his indentures had expired before arrival. In better circumstances he could have expected to work his passage home as either AB or uncertificated 3rd or 4th mate, but Stevens made it plain that he wanted no potential invalid on the articles; accordingly, friends ashore stepped in with an introduction to a Mildura fruit farmer, and Tim left to go fruit-picking. It was better than nothing, and possibly beneficial for his health.

Likewise, both Mackay and Stevenson ran out of their time:

...We were both paid off in the shipping office the same day, Saturday, 11th January. Joe shipped for the run round to Newcastle in the *Albyn*. £4 for the run and 10/- extra if he joined in the morning and bent sails. I called him early, he took what gear he had left in a parcel and said goodbye and went. His chest and bag had gone previously. Exit Joe from the *Armadale*. I felt quite lumpified about the throat when I said goodbye to him. No wonder, we were put through the mill with a vengeance our first voyage. The fellows now have a good time compared with our first 15 months. Well good luck go with him. He has all my best wishes for his future but my own private opinion is unless he takes a tumble to himself and mends his ways he won't be much of a success if he has to carve his own way out.

Joe wrote from Sydney to say he was hoping for a berth in a ketch due to make a voyage to New Guinea, and that was the last word from him. As for the diarist himself, his intention had been to go ashore to take his ticket in Melbourne. However...

...After making inquiries about the school fees etc and reckoning what money I had (about £7) I found that I might manage it. The fees were £4.4s (rather more than I expected £3.5s I was prepared for) £1 for exam fee. That left just £1 or slightly over for expenses. Now came the rub. The *Armadale* was to load for Hull. I reckoned the middle of March before she got away and four months home. That meant July before I got home. Now that did not suit me so I decided for a steamer home. Another reason for passing at home was the RNR. I heard that I should have to pass again at home[1]. I told the old man the decision I had arrived at. He gave me a quite fatherly talking to and asked me if I had thought well over [it] and offered me 3rd mate's job[2]. He said he would fetch me back 2nd next voyage but could not guarantee [it] until he saw them at the office. Then as a further inducement he told me the agent reckoned to get us away by Feb. 20th. He told me to think it over. Well, I did, and thought I might as well do so.

So he sailed as 3rd mate of the *Armadale* at £4 a month. In the apprentices' house were Geordie Rangdale, Phos Forster and two new chums who would, as Forster had done, sign their indentures on arrival in the UK. After signing on, Stevens told Mackay to muster the hands...

...I thought to myself "now here's a lecture for some of them as several had been on the drink." My feelings can better be imagined than described when he started to speak to the effect that <u>Mr</u> Mackay had been promoted to 3rd officer and was to be treated and addressed as became his position. I wished the deck to open and swallow me, but no such thing occurring I had to put on a bold front and face it out.

He allowed the diary to lapse while in Melbourne, resuming it at sea, but because of more demands on his time, partly owing to bad weather on the run to the Horn, confined entries to one a week. The ship settled down well as soon as the disruptive effects of the shore had worn off, and in the house the atmosphere was evidently a happy one. They sailed on March 6th, rounded the Horn on April 27th in wintry weather – gales with snow and sleet, too far south to sight it with Stevens determined to find all the wind he could in latitude 57°S. The favouring winds followed them into the Atlantic. Sickness struck a number of the crew and officers, from colds and flu to neuralgia and liver trouble, and the steward went down with Java fever which killed him. Several hands sustained injuries, weakening the watches, and the ship made only fair time to pick up the trades on 25th May. They crossed the line on June 1st in longitude 5°W, and passed the Western Is. on the 27th, by which time the old steward had succumbed and been buried at sea. From then on progress was slow in light variable winds and, later, fog, clearing intermittently to enable them, on July 7th, to sight Land's End, and Portland Bill on the 8th. Off the Goodwins foul winds set them over towards the Texel, from which they laboured back to be met by a tug some 35 miles off the Spurn on the 15th. They docked at Hull next day, 132 days out, another poor run.

---

[1] Not so.

[2] The ship had not carried one after Mackay's second voyage.

...September 29th, 1902.

Got home at 4.30am July 17th. Went to school next day. Found the seamanship master was away for 4 weeks. He came back about 4 after I had been away. Then Bolam[1] went. As bad as ever. Went up on August 27th and got ploughed on Day's Work which was ridiculously easy. However, went up a fortnight later, no nerves this time. Romped through. Went up to London Sept. 11th. to see Mr Bidmead. He had gone on his holidays. Saw manager. Stayed in London a few days then heighed me home again. Opened correspondence with Mr Bidmead which resulted in me getting several letters of introduction to Glasgow shipowners.

Did not accept the Clan Line offer. P. Henderson promised me an appointment on the new boat when she was finished. Missed the *Loch Torridon* for which I was sorry. Saw Roxburgh, they wanted a 2nd for the *Torresdale*[sic] to join on Tues. 30th. Clinched with the offer as I am tired of sitting at home and I have got the salt water wind-bag fever in my marrows again and long to be a-Rolling a-Rolling upon the deep blue sea. Join her in Cardiff bound for Algoa Bay. "Black diamonds" I suppose. Then fair[sic] ye well my bonny young maid, for we are bound to Rio Grand[sic]. And away to Rio etc.

A.S. Mackay.

2nd Officer.

---

[1] This would have been James Bolam, the Leith school's principal.

V

Harriet Lane & Dandyfunk. 1894-1914.

*

It was on those occasions that Captain Bellwinch took time off to deliver a homily to us apprentices on the evils of drink and women, and enlarge on the risks to our growth should we stoop to unseamanlike conduct like pleading for more food or begging for more than two hours' sleep at a stretch or demanding pay and shore leave and suchlike extravagances.[1]

*

THE BOT's indifference to the academic proficiency of boys taking up apprenticeship was one of the system's great strengths; whether on the parish or a well-heeled black sheep, with concomitant levels of schooling behind them, from the official point of view there were no distinctions between them. If democracy can be so described, the BOT had stumbled onto a Good Thing, more or less fortuitously.

Abolition of the school boards under the 1902 Education Act saw them replaced by the local authorities, and the state system henceforth offered low-cost elementary and secondary schooling to age 16, though the minimum leaving age remained 10. Outside the state system private and "public" schools, both preparatory and secondary, continued, grant-aided where they met the new Board of Education's criteria. Among them were the pre-sea school-ships *Conway* and *Worcester*, while *Mercury* continued to demand only nominal fees or, in deserving cases, none. Ashore, the pre-sea schools set up under the Dept. of Science & Art were merged with the technical secondary schools, and in 1913 special regulations concerning standards and curricula were instituted for nautical schools.

For those proposing to enter a craft or trade schooling was available to the requisite age of 15, while sea apprenticeship was generally begun at 14, with or without pre-sea training, which could begin as young as 11. In 1909 advice about employment was for the first time at the disposal of school-leavers through the labour exchange, then in 1910 LEAs were given the resources to offer advice and assistance. It might well have included the merchant service's openings, but in 1901 the Shipping Federation had set up an advisory and recruitment department aimed at a seaman intake, acting on behalf of owners not themselves having a suitable mechanism. Meeting with little success it

---

[1] *Recollections of Captain Bellwinch.*

shifted its sights to recruitment of apprentices (still in the accepted deceit of their being apprentice seamen while tacitly acknowledged as prospective officers) and the scheme flourished, the boys' careers followed, in theory, by the Federation through to completion of their time.

By this time boys embarking on engineering careers were passing through at least two years' secondary technical schooling beforehand, while the deck apprentice (as the seaman apprentice was coming to be known, colloquially), cadet or midshipman was required to have either the same or an equivalent in the non-technical (county secondary or private) sector. Otherwise he attended a pre-sea course lasting variously from a month to two years, earning remission of sea-time of up to 12 months. Insofar as it was seen as a form of safeguard against employment of square pegs, the leaving, or "passing-out", certificate of the pre-sea system was coming to be the only means of passage through the hallowed portals of the better steamship liner companies, which continued to demand apprenticeship in sail wherever practicable. For its own part the dwindling sail tonnage accepted all comers, granted that pre-sea trained boys, either as a condition of future careers in steam or because they wished to serve in sail before its final disappearance (now clearly inevitable even in the most romantically-misted eyes), got first refusal.

The significance of advancing technology wasn't lost on the training-ships, which through one incentive and another overhauled their curricula, *Worcester* discontinuing its RN entry in 1907 when the Admiralty gave notice that midshipmen were to be made familiar with basic marine engineering, having introduced instead a W/T course in 1902, though it wasn't sufficiently intensive for the specific purpose of full operation of the apparatus. Presumably it was felt that the future deck officer should be on at least nodding terms with the arcane processes of Signor Marconi's invention, to what end isn't clear[1] but possibly so that he should remain in overall comprehension as well as (eventual) command. On the other hand, for similar reasons differently viewed, *Conway* introduced engineering knowledge into its programme. Each was allocated a number of places as midshipman, RNR, offered to suitable cadets on leaving, while a gracious Admiralty was also pleased to grant temporary status as cadets, RNR, to all while in the ships, a reflection on the trend of disciplinary ethics. The RNR was seen as something of a social and professional distinction, not without justification, but not all shipowners agreed on the point: P&O liked its officers to be in the reserve (and its ships to wear the blue ensign), echoing its earlier policy of recruiting them exclusively from the navy itself, while Alfred Holt was conspicuous in frowning on the whole idea, not merely because of the inconvenience of periodic loss of the officer to the navy but also, perhaps, owing to an atavistic disapproval of a resemblance to the old compulsory carriage of apprentices with its naval connotations. The Blue Funnel Line was, quite consciously, the quintessential merchant liner

---

[1] A W/T watchkeeping certificate was eventually produced to enable apprentices to keep a listening watch in ships carrying only one radio operator.

company, with decided ideas about the conflicting merits of naval and mercantile practices, and its colloquial sobriquet of "the Birkenhead Navy" owed much to an ironic comparison of its methods with those of the Senior Service. However, like P&O but unlike Runciman, Watts and other tramp concerns, it did not yet take apprentices.

As something of a counter to the lapse of naval entry, P&O joined with *Worcester* in a scheme of sponsored apprenticeship, paying half the fees of boys provisionally accepted as junior officers and giving assistance with the cost of obtaining the 2nd mate's certificate after serving the requisite time with an approved sailing-ship firm. Parents were under bond to guarantee their sons' remaining with P&O for at least three years after appointment.

A Bluecoat boy[1] joined *Worcester* in 1903:

I was suddenly projected from the Elizabethan age into the Nelsonic age. Instead of the frowsty odours of cloister and classroom were the sea breezes of the Thames estuary. Instead of being under the eye of the dame I was handed over to the not-so-mild charge of warrant and petty officers and found myself, with other newly-joined cadets, encouraged to become a hard case, a tough nut, 'a brash seaman, a man of the world, to issue orders, and obey them instanter![2]

Although no longer including navigation in its curriculum, Christ's Hospital evidently retained a vestige of its ancient connection with the sea while directing its best efforts towards Oxbridge, seen as the reward of hard work and ability, rigorously encouraged by the headmaster, the Rev Richard Lee:

We trembled in his presence. Most boys avoided him in sheer funk. He was in charge of a peculiar institution the conduct of which had been laid down three centuries earlier, classical rather than modern. But like many other boys, in my silly ignorance and innocence, I failed to exploit its manifold boons, blessings and opportunities.[3]

And so to sea. *Worcester*, however, after the way of her kind, evoked a more positive response, chiefly through the advantages possessed over ordinary schools, what with the uniform and other nautical paraphernalia as well as the novel surroundings and a teaching staff inclined towards an easier relationship with their charges, to some extent owing to the source of discipline's being vested in the officers and petty officers. Richard Buck was the headmaster, "a true pedagogue, benign and courtly", assisted by eight others,

all good chaps and very efficient at their task of packing our immature minds with specialised knowledge; friendly, sympathetic and anxious to cultivate us.[4]

---

[1] Pupil of Christ's Hospital.

[2] *Sea Prelude*, p.25

[3] ibid. p.16

[4] ibid. p.16

– for the sea, presumably, and not for whatever favours the cadets might have had in their gift. At the head of the impartial and vigorous executive department was Commander David Wilson-Barker, RD, RNR, captain-superintendent from 1892 to 1919, looking the part, with an air of authority no headmaster could achieve. Unexpectedly, his wife was French, "full of vivacity and wit, and most of the older cadets were in love with her", and she graced the table at breakfast, which it was the captain's custom to share with the (cadet) officer – or mate, so termed – of the day:

The silver, glass and flowers, the bright sunlight through the skylight, *The Times*, the porridge and cream, the two eggs and rashers, the hot scones, the toast and marmalade, the hot coffee and the late appearance of the captain's wife in a *decollete* of startling charm...[1]

Eight years later breakfast had become lunch and the captain less affable, something of a sombre ritual in the conspicuous absence of the *decollete*'s vivacious exponent, reason unknown.

Tradition and custom upheld the privileges of seniority, promoted manliness and engendered a spirit of community. Boxing, swimming, boat-pulling and sailing featured prominently, with an intermittent annual 12-oar cutter race against *Conway*; the cadets slept in hammocks, "slewed" round the upper deck arm in arm during leisure moments, manned the ship's boats to maintain contact with the shore (seniors first in and first out) and chanted war songs and incantations. Responsibility came in the form of promotion to petty officer (cadet captain) with duties as OOW, the overseeing of divisions and parts of the ship, care of the boats, and discipline. When sick they were marooned in the hospital, a hulk moored nearby attended by matron. Prize day at the end of term was marked by sextants, telescopes, binoculars, atlases and globes, star-charts and leather-bound volumes, and Lord Brassey presenting a five-guinea cheque. A leaving certificate on vellum attested to its holder's proficiency and entitlement to remission of sea time, with which talisman the ex-Bluecoat boy went off to join a barque owned by George Milne & Co of Aberdeen – or any other reputable concern.

Meanwhile the *Mercury*, from 1908 under the superintendence of the all-round sportsman, athlete and scholar C.B. Fry, following his marriage to Charles Hoare's erstwhile mistress, came under the inspectorate of the Admiralty and the Board of Education, offering a secondary technical course to boys of good character between 12 and 15½ on entry. As a consequence of Hoare's financial embarrassment arising from his social misdemeanours fees of £30 p.a. were charged from 1898, while the training was becoming increasingly dominated by the formidable presence of the new Mrs Fry, taking as her model old Sparta in fitting the boys for the life to come.

And as an improved alternative to the so-called industrial training-ships and their identification with "the criminal classes" several nautical training schools appeared

---

[1] *Sea Prelude*, pp.38,39.

drawing their following from the poor and the destitute. The first, accepting boys aged 14 to 15½ untainted with reformatory or criminal records, was the Lancashire Navy League and National Sea Training Homes for Boys, opening its doors in 1903 shortly before occupying permanent premises in Birkenhead. The boys were indentured for 3 years to the school itself, which, like *Mercury*, came under the Board of Education and Admiralty inspection. Another was the Watts Naval Training School at Elmham in Norfolk, which boys entered aged 11, preference given to the orphaned and destitute rescued by Dr Barnardo's. These and other schools gave their trainees enough academic and practical instruction not only to enable them to pass into the lower decks of both navy and merchant service but also the more adept a chance to embark on apprenticeship with shipping concerns of the less discriminating sort.

So much for the boy fortunate enough to have had at least some guidance in his approach to the sea. Many set out in complete ignorance after a schooling distinguished for nothing save confirmation of its pupils in a future utterly lacking in prospects or hope. Harold Owen, younger brother of the poet Wilfred, while conceding his father's best efforts and intentions in favour of the older son's literary propensities, suffered the worst that the state and church school system could offer. A railway official, his father had very little money, the family lived variously in the poorer districts of Shrewsbury and Birkenhead, and a talent for drawing and painting was defeated by the need of practical means of earning a living. Born in 1897, Owen attended free schools which perpetuated the worst traits of Dotheboys Hall, with incompetent, apathetic masters possessing neither hope nor vocation and pupils from slum homes, ragged, dirty, lousy, ulcerated and snotty-faced:

...nothing mattered... We were all cold and hungry and...the general physical condition of the school was so low that energy was absorbed[*sic* – dissipated?] by merely sitting and vacantly staring.[1]

Between that and the no-man's land of the neighbourhood through which Owen had to pass to and from school, learning in the process to defend himself while detesting the squalid ignorance all about, he made no progress and earned a reputation for violent behaviour; unfairly, because he kept clear of fights unless goaded, when he would wreak havoc. His artistic flair proved to be the means of escape from this quagmire, and by dint of the kindliness and vision of the principal of a technical college's art department he became a full-time, conspicuously under-age, student with the prospect of a tutorship before the age of 17. It was dashed, however, by the Board of Education's issuing a decree that 21 should be the minimum age for such posts, and the impracticability of continuing as a student without paying fees. The principal had done all he could, and Owen senior hadn't the money. He was adamant: his son must get a job and support himself, and having already, in a peculiarly diffident and oblique way, introduced him to ships and their men during walks round the docks at Liverpool

---

[1] *Journey from Obscurity*, p.22

and Birkenhead, the inference was obvious. Owen accepted his fate with mixed feelings.

But it would be misleading to suggest, by these examples, that boys were going to sea because they had failed in other directions, or because they lacked a positive urge towards something else. As ever, preventing them from following a fancied nautical star was often a problem, and determined attempts in the face of parental obstruction usually succeeded through *fait accompli*: it was still possible to run away to sea, but without the dubious advantage of an apprenticeship. Leslie Morton, for example, the same age as Owen but more fortunate in being a boarder at Dulwich, absconded while travelling by train back to school at the end of the summer holidays in 1910, and found a ship in Liverpool aboard which he sailed as a deck-boy on a voyage to the WCSA.

During holidays with his grandmother in Wallasey ships had caught his imagination as they were catching imaginations in shoals: the phenomenal increase in cheaply-produced printed matter, from newspapers and magazines to books, the market for which had exploded with the spread of basic education (with all its faults), meant that boys' adventure yarns were widely available, and eagerly devoured. Naturally, the sea featured prominently and ruinously, the British part of it highly-coloured and romanticised. Jim Hawkins had appeared in serial form and later – 1910 – in the book, Stevenson's great classic joining distinguished company from the pens of a wider spectrum including R.M. Ballantyne, Fenimore Cooper, Jack London and Dana, to name only a few. Also well into his stride was Conrad, whose *Lord Jim*, *Youth* and *The Nigger of the Narcissus*, while attracting critical attention as adult works, appealed no less to schoolboys free at last from the improving animadversions of *Sermons Among the Tombs*. In 1908 Frank Bullen's *A Son of the Sea* appeared, typical of its kind at the more sentimental end of the scale, a tale of a cabin-boy's rise from rags to riches and an ideal target for parental censure. Ballantyne, on the other hand, wasn't merely entertaining but – according to *The Atheneaum* – also instructive:

> There is no more practical way of communicating information than that which has been adopted in this series. When we see such information as a man of fair education should possess about icebergs, northern lights, Esquimaux, musk-oxen, bears, walruses, etc., we must admit that a good work has been done...[1]

This somewhat exotic "fair education" revolved about such titles as *Fighting the Whales, or, Doings and Dangers on a Fishing Cruise* and *Sunk at Sea, or, Adventures of Wandering Will in the Pacific*, but worried parents could try countering their subversive effects with the Rev Jackson Wray's *Geoffrey Hallam, or, the Clerk of the Parish*, a title not likely to fire the imagination so much as drive it to desperation relieved only by something like Jack London's classics, *The Call of the Wild* (1903) and *The Sea Wolf* (1904).

---

[1] Advertisement in *A Son of the Sea*, appx. p.4.

However any of these might have affected his education, James Bisset had exhausted school's possibilities by the time he had reached standard 7 in 1897, so his father placed him as a clerk, not of the parish but in the Liverpool office of the London & Provincial Marine Insurance Company at 4/- a week. As a way of purging him of symptoms of sea fever it was a spectacular miscalculation, for there before him on the desk was spread an entire seascape of catastrophe that left Wandering Will's adventures in the doldrums of the village pond: fire, stranding, dismasting, mutiny, collision, damaged cargo, storm and calm, the sort of thing that turned men's hair white overnight and gave the sea its irresistible appeal to boys with a dread of the commonplace, besides which Liverpool was approaching the zenith of its fame as a port despite the gloomy prognostications of those who had opposed the opening of the Manchester Ship Canal in 1894. In the stream flowed a constant kaleidoscope of shipping, while the docks were a seething medley of multifarious cargoes and visions of distant parts, so Bisset's attempt to stow away was hardly to be wondered at. He failed, received a leathering from his father to underline an order to stay away from ships for the rest of his life – the classic incitement to do the opposite – and was moved to another clerking job, this time with the Anglo-American Oil Co., where he came face to face with supermen, masters of the firm's tankers. It was too much, of course, and the upshot was another altercation with his father after abortive attempts to find a berth among the city's shipping businesses, followed by examination by the family doctor at Bisset senior's request, to confirm the hopeful theory that his son lacked the constitution for the sea. But when the doctor demurred, saying it would make a man of the boy, he capitulated with good grace.

The ensuing interview with one William Thomas, shipowner, of Water St. shows some interesting comparisons with the situation fifty years before. Somewhat more formal than Robert Thomas's encounter with Thomas Hobley of Caernarfon, it was equally unedifying (Bisset's father seemed to have a gift for making the wrong moves), sharing the streak of meanness that characterised the scruffier elements of the British shipping operation. Father and son were ushered into the presence of Thomas himself, whose seedy turnout was an indicator of how he had made his reputed million. Another was the premium demanded, twenty gold sovereigns, returnable on satisfactory completion of the apprenticeship as per the *Ordinary Apprentice's Indenture*, which, after the 1894 MSA, included a clause by which the master could, if he chose, teach the apprentice navigation. It was a tentative move towards acknowledgment of the contract's implicit purpose that nevertheless steered clear of an open declaration of intent, though some forms contained an optional undertaking to teach the boy the "business of an officer", but in any case Thomas chose not to make it while also striking out the provision of an annual payment of 10/- in lieu of washing: the sea would be all round, free of charge. And whereas Hobley and his contemporaries had offered some £30 for a 3-year term, Thomas (and many of *his* contemporaries) offered, without a hint of a blush, £3, £4, £5 and £8 for the successive years while implying that after the boy had got his ticket he would be under some sort of moral obligation to apply for re-engagement under the Thomas colours rather than to offer the fruits of his training to some other employer. There was, of course, no question of Thomas's paying school and exam fees – seamen as such did not, after all, take the BOT examinations – but the premium would be returned, which would surely cover it. Naturally, it would accrue no interest over the four years – not, that is, as far as Mr Bisset was concerned. However, the practice of demanding a premium was by no means universal, and in some instances it was paid back as wages (which, to give him his due, cast Thomas in a less grasping mould than some), in others constituted only an article of good faith in its token sum.

By the turn of the century the writing, which had been on the wall for some time, was becoming clearer to owners like Thomas with their handfuls of barques and full-riggers hard-pressed in the freight market by the steamship; yet the steamship owners at their worst were worse than their counterparts in sail. In 1913 Harold Owen's father – inexplicably for a man apparently familiar with ships who had made a voyage to India before the mast – arranged for him to join some wretched concern that not only didn't bother about an interview but also took indifference into the realms of crassness by instructing him to make his way to Algiers to await the arrival of a ship which had lost one of her boys overboard. Owen senior seemed quite ignorant of ways and means, apart from lacking the funds for a course of pre-sea training, and although having Liverpool on his doorstep was evidently unaware of the Shipping Federation's scheme. Incredibly, he was fully prepared to send his son off into the blue, a situation from which the boy was saved at the eleventh hour by an uncle, a tinplate broker of the port who used his contacts to place Owen with a steamship company of a less casual stripe. He also lent him the money for uniform and other requisites, amounting to £17.10s.

In some respects Owen was lucky. School had given him nothing in the way of academic equipment, let alone formal qualifications, and apart from his art and reading his accomplishments amounted to nothing except a certain self-confidence and a will to learn, assets which, he discovered, were in many respects more valuable than scholastic attributes in a following that his elder brother scornfully and crushingly (though ambiguously) described as "the last resort of the unintelligent"[1].

At the same time others were getting off to a start as promising as the new age could offer: as sail retreated before steam's inexorable advance P&O's conditions of engagement underwent appropriate adjustment, and *Worcester* cadets no longer had to serve their time in sail beforehand. Instead they were appointed direct on interview, signing 3-year indentures. And the interview was a more decorous affair altogether than the demeaning and furtive assignations favoured by the lower orders; what was patently officer material was made aware of the fact at the outset, less a matter of privilege than one of obligation and responsibility which would receive its carefully-gauged rewards.

---

[1] *Journey from Obscurity*, p.65.

Timorously, I entered the portals of 122, Leadenhall St for an interview with Mr Acton, head of the Officers' Department. (He) had come ashore as a chief officer on account of a serious foot injury... he treated junior officers with exactly the same amount of polite attention as he would extend to a captain; and he informed me in quiet, measured tones with that air of old-world courtesy that he had a very nice Australian ship in mind for me, the *Pera*...in his consideration very suitable... My indentures were duly signed, in the presence of Mr Acton, by one of the Directors, Mr Ritchie, a tall imposing man...in a frock coat, who hurried (in)...signed without reading a word of the document – neither had I – shook hands, and wished me good luck in a kindly if preoccupied manner... By means of it, I was apprenticed for three years, without pay, to the great P&O Company. (1913)[1]

Without pay! William Thomas of Liverpool was looking more philanthropic by the day; but then, conditions aboard a P&O liner were rather more civilised than in a tramping windjammer, and parents able to afford *Worcester*'s fees, even subsidised by the P&O scheme, could probably stretch to an allowance for their prodigal. There was, after all, considerable social and professional mileage to be gained from being spoken of in the same breath as the self-proclaimed successor to the HEIC. And yet... No doubt it was good for the boy's soul, but the defining streak of meanness running through the body politic of the shipowning fraternity, however tenuous and however cloaked in decorum, left a peculiar after-taste of contempt on the palate, which, at small cost, need never have developed. In later years the price of its assuagement became prohibitive through the activities of those who knew how to exploit it, and it played a significant part in the collapse of the home-flag fleet.

And while all this was in train the engineer apprentice continued his sober progress, starting at 15 and qualifying after five years of workshop and technical school training. John Lamb, son of a widow whose farm in Northumberland offered him neither prospects nor interest, left school at 14 too young to start in his intended trade, and since idleness was out of the question his mother found him a job as a glass-blower's assistant at the Northern Glassworks in Gateshead, helping to make light-bulbs, entirely by hand. It was a dead-end job, not to be compared with an engineering apprenticeship with its prospects of great things via the chief's cabin and its professional kudos. Lamb kept faith with himself and in 1905, just after his 15th birthday, began as an apprentice fitter with Clarke, Chapman & Co., iron founders and manufacturers of ships' auxiliary machinery.

As it assumed greater importance, training at sea was subjected to the strain of mutually-opposing forces: on one hand a growing body of administrative and academic opinion claiming to recognise a need for a proper system in place of one where, in the main, haphazard prevailed, and on the other an establishment, while acknowledging the need for competent officers, baulking at suggestion of a competence exceeding a practical minimum, largely because of the cost, which it

---

[1] *A Sea Affair*. p.26

would be required to meet, or at least to subvent. The spread of pre-sea training-ships and schools balanced by an expanding system of professional schooling for the BOT exam tended in some quarters to induce a complacent indifference towards the apprentice's instruction and training at sea, which, in sail, had not the detrimental effect it had in steam. By its nature, sail at least imbued a seaman's skills (which included mental and physical alertness) in the boy by involving him intimately with its everyday occasions, while steam substituted mere drudgery unless deliberately shaped and tuned to the purpose. Rugged conditions apart, sail at its worst was a better training medium than steam at its worst, and the fact remained that with a few exceptions the apprentice was still only a seaman – a deckhand – in embryo, neither cadet nor midshipman being, in practice, any better off. Nevertheless, the picture was showing a perceptible improvement and an apprentice determined to get on was able to draw on a richer well-spring of assistance than had the preceding generation, including the expertise of people and organisations beyond the confines of the ship, brought within reach by the widening field of activities of the very factor that detracted so much from the traditional aspects of sea-training, steam.

Running expanding mail services that by the turn of the century were for all practical purposes world-wide, the steamship not only brought home within a few weeks of the half-deck's correspondents but also enabled schools to run courses of guided study that could be followed almost regardless of the abilities and interest of the ship's officers. Established in 1910, the School of Navigation at Glasgow's Royal Technical College was first in the field with one devised by its principal, Captain C.H. Brown, his example soon emulated by the King Edward VII Nautical School in London, which in 1904 had taken over the pre-sea training course first set up by the Poplar School of Engineering and Navigation. Others followed suit.

Tardy as it was, the idea of training towards a defined end in a properly-arranged pattern had taken firm root, and the days of an apprentice's being left to his own devices were drawing to a close; not a moment too soon, either, for foreign-flag competition was making itself felt, particularly from the direction of the ancient Hanseatic trading bases, where ideas and training methods were evolving along characteristically thorough lines illuminated by the view that money so spent constituted a national investment of predictable security. Even so, training as a point at issue failed to sway statutory sentiment as expressed in the 1894 MSA, which left it as found, couched succinctly enough in the undertakings of the indenture, still substantially the same as in Tudor times: an apprentice in a cog or a nef, galley or carrack, could have exchanged his document with one signed by a boy in one of Runciman's Black Sea tramps without experiencing any material improvement and quite possibly some deterioration; for example, the subtle distinction between the seaman and the mariner, with the Elizabethan having the advantage. The only change in this respect, other than the occasional alternative, or option, of instruction in an officer's business, was that the apprentice was to learn the business of a seaman *in steamships*, quite another proposition from his business in sail.

No ordinary seamen were carried; why carry ordinary seamen when there were apprentices to do their work and at nominal pay for which the owners were already largely reimbursed by the premium? (Barque *Springbank*, 1904)[1]

This was common, and while the motives of owners (such as Andrew Weir in this instance) were open to question the apprentice himself was expected to show an interest. If it met with no response that was his misfortune, but usually someone on board would offer advice and instruction, if only in passing and at his own convenience. A few masters made a point of seeing to it that the boys received and absorbed instruction, while others were specifically directed to do so by the owners. W. Montgomery & Co were among the last in sail, operating a few biggish full-riggers including the famous *Grace Harwar* (1,877grt). Captain Faeron commanded their *Fitzjames* (1,951grt), and at the start of her maiden voyage in 1902 found this among his orders:

We wish you to make the apprentices your especial care. You are starting with six, all green, although four have served two years in training ships. Be very particular as to their conduct, especially when in foreign ports. Do all you can to inculcate a system of thorough and steady discipline; give them every opportunity and all the assistance you can in the study of their profession, whenever you perceive a willingness to learn. Try and turn them out smart and efficient young officers by the time they are due to pass their examinations, so that if we are able to continue to employ them we may find them of real use to us and a credit to their captain and themselves. Advance as little as possible to your sailors and apprentices that they may have less inducement to leave the ship...[2]

It appears from this that the boys were destined to serve their entire time in the ship under Faeron; and the implication of the closing instruction exemplifies a universal practice, based on the principle that the more pay an apprentice had in credit the less likely he was to clear out, leaving it behind. Logical enough in principle, the idea was laughable at the rate of pay offered, and certainly the last thing to deter a boy contemplating desertion.

As for the "thorough and steady discipline", it wasn't particularly oppressive but it was applied with more or less rigour, especially in sail, where the safety of the ship and her people was crucially dependent upon prompt obedience to orders, orders having several tiers of authority and responsibility behind them. In practice all responsibility rested on the master's shoulders, of course, and his authority stemmed from that fact, embodying the decree of both statute and owner. Captain Faeron's instructions were an instance of the latter's while of statute's the indenture was a broad declaration as were, for cadets and midshipmen, the ship's articles of agreement, in which chapter and verse left no doubts about crime and punishment. Embezzlement,

---

[1] *Crackerhash*, p.10.
[2] Quoted in *The Way of a Ship*, p. 275.

damage to master's property, absence without leave, unlawful games and taverns were the classic prohibitions[1], entailing cancellation, as did failure of the master to meet his obligations. Under the MSA other offences included damage to ship and equipment, wilful injury to her people, refusal to obey lawful commands, desertion, combining with crew to impede the voyage, damage to stores or cargo, and smuggling, all of which incurred a range of punishments from fines to imprisonment with or without hard labour.

Lawful commands embraced all orders from abandon ship to daily routine and the tasks set by the mate, all contributing to the definition of "training" no matter how dreary and repetitious.

The two-watch system (four hours about broken by the dog-watches) still prevailed in sail, extended by progressive association to steam, with scattered exceptions in liner operations, and the apprentice worked accordingly, except that "daywork", hitherto the province of the idlers, was creeping into vogue in the steamship. Zealous mates devised a fiendish combination of daywork and night watches that gave the apprentice next to no time to dwell on the injustices of life, while in port, following time-honoured custom, there was no shortage of extra duties:

Barque Dunard.
Santos. Wed. 16th October 1895.
My Dear Mother,
We have arrived at last 55 days out from Cardiff one day more than last time neither of them very smart passages. I have not seen Santos yet we are only laying at the bar so I cant tell you if it has altered any. This will not be a long letter dear because there is such a lot of work going on it has been a pretty fair passage nothing remarkable has happened. I am very comfortable here dear my outfit is in splendid order as yet I cannot thank you enough for what you done for me when I was at home I am sorry I was in the sulks the day you wanted the Photogroup taken but to tell you the truth dear I was wanting to get on the move again not that I was tired of you all but I was of leytonstone[sic]. I could not write much from Cardiff the coal dust was 1 inch thick all over the show & I did not unpack for a week used to sleep on my chest the cake and biscuits lasted two days Percy brought some tinned meat milk & mustard so we had enough to last a passage & I have got some left. Well I am expecting to get called now so I must bring it to a close give my love to everybody at home dear including my new brother sisters etc.
I remain your loving son Viv.
PS The mates are not bad the Chief Mate is a bit of a prig & the Second Mate is a jolly nice fellow up to any devilment is very young and only just out of his time.

---

[1] While some early indentures, and later ones in other trades, such as engineering, forbade marriage and fornication, there is no evidence of a clause popularly supposed to have existed forbidding entry to "houses of ill repute" – presumably brothels, not all of which were ill-reputed. Perhaps some unusually far-sighted element of establishment felt that, while the term *fornication* covered them, prohibiting entry would be to deprive the boy of an essential component of his education...

And later:

My Dear Mother,

This is my last but one letter before we leave so dont look for any more dear. We had a Pamperio[sic] to-day and dragged our anchors (two out) & went ashore I dont know if anything has gone wrong but shall find out tomorrow. Last night I had to take the boat alongside an American Barque to fetch the Captain & the River police chased us and caught us he wanted to see our permit but the Captain gave them some grog & made it all right I dont have to row the boat now I'm Coxwain & only steer & look after it & we always wear our uniforms She is a fine gig boat and painted white with varnished teak gunnals & two raised (The companies) Flags on her bows she looks quite flash. Well I must close now so with very best love to all.
I remain etc. [1]

At the guano ports boatwork included using the ship's boats to lift the cargo and, as ever, the customary round of duty as crew of the captain's gig. At sea the steamship routine was well into its stride, an eternal grind of chipping, red-leading and painting relieved by soogeeing paintwork, which made the prospect of study attractive and help of the kind anticipated by Captain Faeron's instructions gratefully welcome – to some:

I was working hard in my spare time to master the rudiments of navigation. It was mostly a case of finding out for oneself but occasionally an officer would go out of his way to proffer instruction, but with or without [it] we were expected to become competent navigators. [As we did so] the more inclined were the officers to hand over watchkeeping duties and gradually ease their own minor duties onto [our shoulders], sorting the interested [from] the uninterested. [Some] cadets thought this a way of "putting on them" and resented it. (PSNC, 1913)[2]

No small part of training was recognition of and cheerful acquiescence to seniority, in its extended form manifested in the officer ranks from 3rd mate to master. In the half-deck it was a matter of custom, to some extent adjusted to fit the circumstances, but broadly based on sea-time served. Captain Faeron's apprentices, all first-voyagers, would have worked out a pecking order by any feasible method from the toss of a coin to force of personality, if not of arm, and the pre-sea trained boys were likely to have asserted their theoretical sea-time; unresolved dispute would usually be settled out of hand by the mate. A boy in the final months of his time, whatever his earlier circumstances (for example, being possessed of 12 months' remission and so never advancing beyond the third year of actual time at sea), was usually conceded to, though he often enough found himself removed from the debate by actual or honorary promotion, to 3rd mate or AB as a rule, anything more senior, such as 2nd mate or bosun, occurring only in emergency. If it appears to be unwontedly laboured,

---

[1] Contributor's private papers.
[2] *Journey from Obscurity*, pp.168-9.

seniority's importance in the interests of peace and harmony could never be overestimated; a fundamental element of the disciplinary code, it placed responsibility on young shoulders by measured degrees and pre-empted the outcome of potentially demoralising dispute. But there was seldom much privilege attached to it, and customarily greater inconvenience: at best the seniors had the pick of the berths and the choice, where it existed, of tasks comprising the day's work. Otherwise it was share and share alike in a bond of adversity, as it was seen.

The mate said, "I'm going to tell him I want you third mate." And off he went, and soon came back. "All right," he said, "you're third mate. The Old Man says you're the only apprentice he never heard answer an officer back." For over three years I'd served the ship, and now I was to act third mate and, drawing no pay, still live in the half-deck. The third mate of a sailing-ship was pretty much of a nobody. (Barque *Silberhorn*, 1899)[1]

While at sea "training" was loosely and widely interpreted in circumstances that were dynamic, expedient and indeterminate, ashore the engineer apprentice's environment was static, methodical and limited, and by the turn of the century an easily-discernible and effective system – in theory at least – was in place, divided between practical example and classroom tuition, the 5- or 6-year term reducible by up to 12 months by attendance at an approved technical school. There was no shortage of training venues in an industry leading the world in shipbuilding – marine engine works, auxiliary and special-purpose machinery works, shipbuilders and repairers, while openings existed in naval dockyards which had their own schools, equivalent to the technical schools approved by the BOT. Apprentices went into either the navy as artificers or the merchant service as junior engineers. Both civilian and naval apprentices were drawn, ideally, from among applicants with three or four years of secondary schooling behind them, either technical or with a technical content. There was no question of the parish pauper or Barnardo's destitute getting into the system, nor those with dubious backgrounds or deficient schooling: the sea was the place for that kind of flotsam.

I wished to know something of the theory behind the machines, and signed on for two nights a week at night school. Soon I wanted to study more than maths and machine drawing, so I enrolled as a mechanical engineering student with the ICS, at the rate of 10/- a month. The course continued all year round so I was well ahead of the other boys. To find the 10/- I bought newspapers from the local depot at three a penny and sold them at a ha'penny each. In this way I was able also to buy a text-book now and again in Newcastle Big Market. For 6d one could expect all the pages and at least one cover. My knowledge accumulated until I was looked on as one of the leading apprentices. (1900)[2]

---

[1] *Ships and Memories*, pp. 200-1 & 205.
[2] *Backward Thinking*, pp.17-20.

Impressive but strikingly dull, indicative of the lack of imagination, if not enterprise, that was such an integral part of the engineer's peculiar ethos; where the sea apprentice suffered to a greater or lesser extent from romantic delusion his engineering contemporary tended towards the stolid in his outlook.

Balancing the weight of restriction it contained as a bureaucratic fiat, the 1894 MSA made a number of provisions for the apprentice's wellbeing, some already in place by previous Acts, others newly-devised, all devolving onto the shipmaster's shoulders, dealing with such matters as repatriation, hospital abroad, accommodation and means of lodging complaint, of which, as before, the apprentice seldom, if ever, availed himself. And ashore, where the proprietors of boarding- or lodging-houses had been free to charge what they wished, overcharging an apprentice would incur a fine of 10/- though what was understood as a fair charge in the absence of an official scale seems to have been a matter for individual and arbitrary settlement; but it satisfied the bureaucrats if no-one else, as did the appointment, in 1892, of an Inspector of Provisions lacking the power to enter suppliers' premises and therefore any point to his existence.

As for the victuals on board, while the Act required the master to declare the proposed scale in the articles there was still no mandatory specification and the so-called Liverpool scale[1] continued as the model in company with one recommended the same year by the Shipping Federation. The theme that replaced "sufficient without waste" was now "full and plenty", and this was a sample in 1897:

Breakfast: Irish stew, bread, butter, coffee.
Dinner: Soup, beef, potatoes, bread.
Tea: Cold meat, bread, butter, tea.
Supper: Bread & cheese.[2]

Bread was, in fact, biscuit, though soft bread was baked twice a week in most ships, insufficient to accompany every meal. Beef was salt junk, tea and coffee milkless. Potatoes lasted about a fortnight and the butter and cheese were rancid within a week or less. The quality of both victuals and cooking varied, of course, as it always had done, and at best satisfied – just – a basic need; at worst the apprentice ate substances that a farmer would have hesitated to accept as pig-swill, and the state of affairs became serious enough to engage political attention in the person of the President of the BOT, the Liberal MP David Lloyd-George, who, among a number of radical reforms in divers spheres, introduced the first mandatory dietary scale in 1906. Intended as a minimum, like those (non-mandatory) that had gone before it was seized upon as the standard and, taking advantage of permitted substitutes, the bill of fare generally fell back on the salt meat, biscuit and dried peas of old acquaintance. The issue of lime-juice remained compulsory, with a safeguard against the practice

---

[1] See appendix 2.
[2] *The Shipping Federation*, p.58.

suspected of being the cause of the increased incidence of scurvy in the 70s and 80s, issuing the cordial not as a supplement to but instead of fresh provisions, which continued to be the main bastion against the affliction rather than the lime-juice itself. The Lloyd-George Scale, as it was called, remained in force more or less unchanged (though honoured more in the observance than hitherto) until 1939.

Improved victualling was marked by sail's disappearance – not that steamship owners invariably fed their crews any more excitingly – taking with it the improvised recipes concocted by generations of apprentices in attempts to simulate variety; these and a species of tinned mutton made only rare appearances after 1918 and by the 30s had slipped into unregretted oblivion:

After we had been at sea for ten days the fresh meat and vegetables were finished or had gone bad. For the rest of the voyage we lived on hard tack with salt beef and pork, tinned mutton, coffee and tea. A restricted amount of water was drawn by pump each day. The mutton came in 7lb cans, the label bearing the words *Harriet Lane*, which might have been the distributor's Melbourne address. It gave rise to the myth all sailors including myself believed[1]. A lady of that name, working at the canning factory, had fallen unnoticed into one of the vats; her remains were served up on Saturdays. (Barque *County of Pembroke*, 1896)[2]

And so it was called. Corned beef replaced it, though it (corned beef) had been on the scene for some time in accordance with the master's preferences and domestic economics. From it the cook produced a soup graced with the title *bouillon* – the "Soup de Boulyon" served aboard the barque *Glance* back in 1879 – from which, through the corruption of *bouilli*, seems to have evolved the term *bully*.

Not as sophisticated as Harriet Lane were the home-produced dishes of much older vintage, their origins lost among the first attempts at preserving meat and manufacture of a durable form of bread, resorted to in efforts to extend the limits of the menu by illusion. Dandyfunk was a hash of ground biscuit (pulverised in a canvas bag using a fid or mallet), jam or marmalade (or both), meat-fat or galley slush, and water, baked uncovered to emerge in a slab of granitic consistency and enigmatic flavour; but as with all folklore there was no set formula, and it varied according to individual interpretation, ingenuity and available ingredients.

We procured a pie-dish...filled it half-full [*sic*] with ground biscuits well-mixed with pieces of fat salt beef or pork. Then a layer of salt meat was spread on top of the biscuits. More ground biscuits and salt fat were added until the dish was full. Finally, molasses were[*sic*] spread all over, half an inch thick, and...the whole concoction was given to [the cook] to be baked. Sunday dinner was indeed a luxury. Soup and dandy-funk were the inevitable *plats du jour*. (Ship *Denbigh Castle*, c.1910)[3]

---

[1] Hardly, unless this is a confession of juvenile gullibility. Cannibalism wasn't among the sailor's proclivites except *in extremis*; but he enjoyed grisly legend for its own sake.
[2] *Sail Ho!*, p.51.
[3] *Windjammer to Westminster*, pp.8-9.

Its complementary creation was cracker-hash, ground biscuit mixed with dregs of pea or bean soup and scraps of fat salt meat together with anything else that suggested itself; also baked, it, too, was of durable consistency and elusive flavour. A midshipman's muffin was a much simpler affair and rather less challenging to the palate, merely a biscuit soaked in water and then baked in an effort to lighten its consistency, the result a more or less soggy and flaccid slab of dough on which could be spread whatever came to hand. A kind of porridge, dogsbody came into the "instant snack" category, produced by adding ground biscuit to one's ration of soup until the desired degree of inspissation was achieved, then eaten without further refinement. A predilection for these dishes brought on outbreaks of facial wens and boils, while the diet's overall deficiency had the effect, over time, of conditioning the stomach to austerity:

Here it was, the food that we had talked about for months...the food that, in our dreams, we had eaten time and time again, only to awaken to the inevitable biscuit. We sat...over our plates, and then...the dreadful truth dawned...I could not eat it. I forced a little meat down, swallowing with difficulty, and then felt that I would be sick if I took another scrap. Looking round at my companions, I saw that they were in the same state... Disconsolately we admitted defeat. (Ship *Denbigh Castle*)[1]

As well as victualling the 1906 Act addressed itself to the other most prominent item on the half-deck's agenda of existence, accommodation, but in the curious way of official edict contented itself with adjustment of current regulation rather than take account of matters from a fresh standpoint. The result was an all-but-undetectable increase in elbow-room per man from 12 to 15 superficial feet to include messroom and ablutions, with sleeping space taking up not more than the previous 12 s/ft. Plumbing wasn't specified, nor were sanitary arrangements, although in 1906 the lavatory hadn't entered architectural thinking either afloat or ashore except as a facility best kept in the background, which in the ship was the sea. Access to it varied on a theme of crude makeshift. Otherwise there were the usual strictures about "proper" ventilation and lighting, prohibition of use for stores and cargo, and so on, with existing tonnage under no obligation to undergo modification. It meant that sail, practically obsolete and no longer being augmented to any appreciable extent with new tonnage, retained its primitive distinction, while in steam the arrangements ranged from bare conformity with statute to comparative and sometimes *ad hoc* luxury (modified passenger accommodation) to meet the needs of an increasing complement of apprentices to whom sail was becoming the object of detached romantic interest alone, fabulous and unattainable.

Some of the incentives for improvement stemmed from the changing complexion of the manning question: for the first time firms were placing advertisements for

---

[1] *Kicking Canvas*, p.102.

apprentices, a sign that the sea was beginning to lose its appeal for a boy not only better schooled than his predecessors but also finding his imagination captured by thrilling new developments and their possibilities. The Wright brothers made their point in 1903 with a 12-second flight in which was concentrated more excitement and potential than in a 12-month voyage in a short-handed barque or plodding steam-tramp. And in July 1909 the boy aloft struggling with the gaskets of a bloody-minded fore-royal as the Dungeness pilot approached looked up to see a Frenchman chug by overhead in a machine that took sails into the realm of practicable fantasy. There was something of a mood of resignation in the words of the *Worcester*'s secretary written in 1912, a year in which the brash presumptions of progress (as well as the lamentably inadequate measures of the bureaucratic machine) were brutally refuted amidst the ice of the North Atlantic:

...the sea, as a career, cannot be said to offer any great inducement to the town-bred boy. He is brought up amongst pleasures and (picture) palaces[1] cheap literature, and a hundred and one easily-obtainable and pleasurable excitements which must tend to his selection of a shore berth rather than risk the discomforts of a sea life. Again, with the disappearance of the sailing-ship, most of the romance from a boy's point of view has gone. A dirty-looking[sic] steam-tramp stealing down one of our great waterways does not suggest a picture at all coincident with the yarns with which all boys are familiar. And yet there is no calling that offers more adventure and romance than the sea[2]. For those ardent young spirits that must have as an accompaniment to their imagination of things nautical a shipwreck, with a little piracy and hidden treasure thrown in, there are still great possibilities[3].

What's this? Adventure and romance with an increasing burden of red tape? Pirates and hidden treasure in the dawn of the air age? Shipwreck bringing in its train courts of inquiry and professional ruin? To some minds there might have been a flavour of romance in the picture of a captain going down with his ship (though staying afloat with it was the aim of the exercise), but behind such apparent heroics lay a grim choice between decent suicide and shameful survival, the consequences of hubristic carelessness of which the *Titanic*'s fate was, so to speak, the tip of the iceberg. In her wake followed – with considerably greater care – similar ships faced with another hazard, the gradual but irresistible rise of competition from the air, and the ardent young spirit, whether town or country bred, was henceforth torn between the attractions of two opposing forces. And in the conflict to come (from which the air threat benefited in rapid design development) the kind of boy who in an earlier age would have kept his station in the din of attack by a vengeful Admiral Linois, plotted the downfall of another ship's boat's-crew in a Blackwaller's mess, or applied himself with determination to his books in what spare time the mate allowed, would be found

---

[1] *Mid pleasures and palaces though we may roam...* – old song.
[2] The Wright brothers and their contemporaries would have disagreed.
[3] *How to go to Sea in the Merchant Service*, p.6.

instead in the skies above the trenches where romance withered in a less prosaic fashion than among the dessicated little ports of the WCSA, where, in the last of the big sailers and in the coastal and deep-sea steamers of the PSNC and its like, the apprentice found precious little time for sightseeing and treasure-hunting. If, that is, his romantic naivety hadn't been dealt a blow at the outset:

Indentured and brassbound, I joined her one wintry January afternoon in the East India Docks. My first impression was one of complete surprise. Gaunt spars towering into the grey sky above the cranes, decks littered with rubbish, and the grime of London over all. My new home was a bare box-like apartment about ten feet square with iron walls and wooden bunks round three sides. It was half-filled with coal, firewood, odds and ends of rope and assorted rubbish, inexpressibly cheerless. The captain called me aft and asked me a few questions, winding up by inquiring whether I wanted to go to sea and advising me that I should do better to buy a rope and hang myself. The interview left me rather crushed. (Barque *Arethusa*, 1904.)[1]

Adventures ashore were limited by the depth of the pocket, a fact that didn't escape the notice of the mission padres, by this time running an institution taken for granted by boys whose religious awareness varied from zealous to mercenary, and a port unable to boast a mission was unlikely to appeal to the penniless half-deck. By 1913 the Flying Angel had premises in San Francisco (the first outside Europe, in a city that was the haunt of every vice in the book, where apprentices vanished at an alarming rate, a state of affairs that was to some extent moderated by the great earthquake and fire of 1906 with their purgative effects), Callao, Valparaiso, BA and Bahia Blanca, and in other major ports in the Orient, South Africa, Australia and New Zealand.

After we had received pratique...the first launch to come alongside was the Flying Angels Mission [*sic*] with the familiar figure of Mr Newman sitting in the stern sheets. He...had...a phenomenal memory for names...because after paying his courtesies to the Captain he came along to the half-deck and greeted myself and Joe Elliott, Billy Williams and Hough by our correct names and gave us an urgent and ardent invitation to come up to the Mission...holding out the tempting bait of a bunfight after service on the Sunday. (Callao, 1911.)[2]

This is an awful hole. I thought Antofagasta was pretty bad but this is the last place God made and he forgot to finish it...one short, narrow street and a few houses... A cable car, which brings the saltpetre down to the ships, runs up the side of the mountain. The full car...pulls the empty one up. To get ashore, you row alongside a little pier and swing yourself onto it from the boat with a rope... All hope of coming home is gone. The skipper has given us the Cape Town address... It is hard luck! (Letter home, barque *Aristomene*, Caleta Buena, 1904.)[3]

---

[1] *A Gypsy of the Horn*, p.13.

[2] *The Long Wake*, p.57.

[3] *In Sail and Steam*, p.92.

Newman was typical of the best of his kind, his methods based on fair exchange rather than guile. The mission chaplains were a recognisable breed and an extraordinary credit to the church amongst a largely profane and reluctant flock: aboard ship on a voyage the clergyman was regarded as an omen of ill-fortune, but he was welcome enough in port. The mission was seen in essence as a feature of leisure time, what there was of it, and its presence wasn't missed at sea in a system that kept leisure to a bare minimum. The combination of the two-watch routine and day-work left little enough time to attend to personal matters – dhobi, make and mend, perhaps study – let alone idling. In sail the diminishing size of crews meant plenty of disruption to the watch below, whilst in steam the faster pace of life and an apparent inner urge to compensate for the absence of sail's natural demands led the mate to ensure that the apprentices never lacked for occupation, in or out of hours. In consequence there was little in the way of ready-made entertainment, and when not sleeping or occupied in some necessitous way the ship's company turned to more or less homespun and traditional pastimes – gathering to yarn and sing (dying out with sail), model-making with materials to hand, fancy ropework with a practical application, perhaps boxing when someone was keen and knowledgeable enough, cards, dice and the first proprietary board-games, along with a miscellany of reading-matter gleaned by chance from ashore and other ships.

The men had a foo-foo band; the drum was made from a flour-barrel with oiled canvas stretched over each end, three marlin-spikes formed the triangle, a tin whistle, a concertina and paper-covered combs. We generally concluded the evening marching round the decks headed by the band, the music and laughter echoing eerily across the lonely seas. (Ship *Latimer*, 1890s.)[1]

In port, cargo-work and Flying Angel apart, boat-racing died with sail, while on regular runs friendships among the local populace characteristic of Australia and New Zealand and to some extent South Africa was noticeably absent in other outposts of Empire, particularly India and the Far East, where the British, whatever might have been their social background in the mother country, occupied a plane of existence to which the merchant seaman and officer were as a rule denied access, had they been tempted to achieve it. And they in their turn looked down on the indiginous citizenry, bar a few independent and inquiring souls aiming to benefit more than most from their travels. Otherwise the appeal of more prurient attractions depended on funds and personal taste, as they always have done:

The older apprentices took us ashore to the dives in Market Street, in cellars beneath the shops. There was a stage, and drink available night and day; they were human cesspools,

---

[1] *Fifty Thrilling Years at Sea*, p.61.

beastly entertainments staged for the benefit of simple sailormen[1], and I left in a hurry but was persuaded to enter another reputed to be decent. A troup of girls was dancing the can-can, mother-naked, but hardly had they started than two men began blazing away at each other with revolvers, which emptied the place in seconds. I didn't have enough money to try the gambling dens. (San Francisco, c.1898.)[2]

There was a general reluctance among apprentices, at least in retrospect, to admit to enjoyment of this sort of thing, yet they did, certainly in the closing stages of their time, even if only to demonstrate a conception of manliness, equally a means of relieving the accumulated stresses and frustrations of months, or at least weeks, at sea. Perhaps honesty conceded something to modesty, if not an oddly incongruous prudishness, when placed before public attention, and only a very few declared their interest with candidness and perception:

...the cafes were open all day and night and along the waterfronts there were the sailors' dives and hideouts...always mysterious with dim lights and tortuous secret-looking passage entrances. From them would come crude music from accordion, mouth-organ or banjo, as half-drunken sailors beat out a dance tune. Inside a motley of seamen and girls stamped their feet in time to the rough music, swaying crazily in drunken efforts to dance between the jigging tables. Over everything hung a heavy pall from the fumes of cheap red wine and strong black coffee. Broken glasses lay everywhere and empty wine bottles danced among themselves as they bounced and cavorted to the jump and sway of the trembling floor. The table-tops swished with red and black pools, which, cascading now and again to the floor, took with them their load of cigar and cigarette ends to be pounded and squelched by the thumping feet. I liked wandering in and out of these places; my insatiable curiosity and determination to find out everything for myself recognized no bounds and this led me on to treacherous and always dangerous ground...reckless in my eagerness to visit the shanties, wine-shops and dance-cafes and to seek out for visitation all the lowest and roughest waterside haunts and vice-dens where sailors foregathered; but I was actuated by the romance of these places, the smoky semi-darkness, the rattle of the cheap pianos and the general atmosphere of men, the sea, and ships. (PSNC, WCSA, 1913.)[3]

The words of a town-bred boy. It was a romance that just outweighed the squalid and sordid, saved by the contrasting connection with the sea's guileless desolation, an atmosphere – an illusion – swept away by the cataclysmic effects of the impending war, whirled back in time never to be recovered in quite that way again. So much for hidden treasure.

And home leave, like shoregoing, was granted only at the master's discretion:

---

[1] Not quite. Their benefit was the last consideration, quite distinct from their exploitation and robbery.

[2] *Fifty Thrilling Years at Sea*, p.53.

[3] *Journey from Obscurity*, p.173.

I dared not go home before dark, having sold most of my kit. My suit consisted mainly of patches, and when the maid opened the door she hissed at me to go away or she'd call the police. Mother gave a cry before hugging me while brothers and sisters gathered round. After a great feed I had to relive that terrible voyage for the benefit of all but that night Mother came to my room and implored me to give up the sea; in the morning Father offered to have my indentures cancelled. Within a few days I was a hero among the girls round about, but the moment I mentioned abandoning my odyssey the gleam died in their eyes; I told Father I'd decided to carry on. (1890s.)[1]

At least, that is, until the time came to face the BOT and prove that four years of cracker-hash, daywork, night-work, sea watches, superficial feet, customs old and new, missions, dives, desultory instruction and perhaps promotion to AB for the last couple of months or so had amounted to a sufficiently thorough introduction to the sea.

There was still no requirement to attend school before the exam, but although there was a definite slant towards a recognisable means of instruction and training it behoved the apprentice with serious intentions to attend a course, either at one of the private schools still flourishing or at a college offering approved courses at minimal charge, for example:

School of Navigation, Robert Gordon's Colleges, Aberdeen
School of Navigation, Royal Technical College, Glasgow
The Nautical College, Leith
Nautical College Dept., Central Technical School, Liverpool
LCC School of Engineering and Navigation, Poplar
King Edward VII College, Commercial Rd., Limehouse
Navigation School, Plymouth
Marine School, South Shields
Trinity House School (Adult Section), Hull

Chapman & Nicholls's Academy was taken over by the British Sailors' Society in 1903 with fees subsidised by the society's funds, changing its name to the King Edward VII Nautical College, where the society had its headquarters. Other private schools in London continued, most prominent among them Rugg's, Baxter's and Broughton's, some run in conjunction with a business such as a nautical optician's or chandlery.

James Bolam, continuing to run his academy in Leith, was not a mariner but "a fine mathematician and theoretical navigator". He agitated for support for nautical schools from the Scottish education authorities although well aware that such a move would put an end to the independent private establishments. In 1902 the Scottish Education Board asked him for a report, with the result that in the following year his academy

---

[1] *Fifty Thrilling Years at Sea*, p.68.

became a department of Leith Technical College. Meanwhile, lagging in Scotland's wake as usual, the LEAs in England and Wales began a similar process in 1908 which continued in fits and starts until after WW2. Among them were schools in Cardiff, by this time at the hub of the coal export trade, one of which was the resoundingly-named Neptune Nautical Academy, opened in 1910 by Captain W.C. Aubrey-Rees, author of a definitive text on shipmaster's business later in his career. Another was the Cambrian Nautical Academy, opened in 1906 by Captain J.R. Williams but closed in 1912 after the ephemeral fashion of many.

The tuition method that had come into general use took the form of a series of lectures and tutorials running through the examination syllabus in an endless round, so that prospective candidates could begin at any time and continue either until they had arrived at the starting-point or until they felt they had absorbed enough to make an attempt on the first, lowest, but in many ways the most difficult, of the summits confronting them. The private schools charged fees either according to time spent on the course or at a flat rate covering the complete course, sometimes extended to cover whatever extra time a student required, while the state-approved and aided schools charged only a nominal fee or none at all.

When time began to hang a little heavily on my hands I decided to...attend a private nautical school in Liverpool, run by one Captain Coghill. This was similar to many such establishments...being conducted...by retired sea-captains. Fees...were very low and I did not have to work too hard. Captain Coghill was a pleasant if somewhat eccentric gentleman, and I thoroughly enjoyed my days at his rather odd little house of learning. His methods were very effective, despite the easy-going nature of the place, and I picked up a great deal of knowledge. (1903)[1]

I enrolled at the MMSA school, conducted by Captain d'Arcy Morton. There were about seven in the class, which ran for six hours a day, covering elementary maths, navigation, chartwork and seamanship. Captain Morton recommended our joining a gymnasium to learn the art of boxing, not in the BOT syllabus but a useful accomplishment in the practical business that confronted the ship's officer from time to time. I also played football on Saturday afternoons, working up a thirst for the evenings, spent touring Liverpool on the trail of Cain's ales. The pubs closed at eleven, by which time we were usually suffering from Cain's foot and mouth disease. (1903)[2]

The minimum age at which one could hold a 2nd mate's ticket was 17 (from the date of compulsory certification, the earliest mate's certificate in its time requiring a qualifying age of 19) and it now came in three versions. The "ordinary" or *Foreign-Going Ship* required at least twelve months' service in square-rigged sailing-ships (as distinct from square-rigged auxiliary-sail steamships); the "fore-and-aft rigged vessels only" version, which allowed the holder to serve in steamships, as did the ordinary

---

[1] *Windjammer 'Prentice*, p.83.
[2] *Sail Ho!*, pp.235-6.

ticket, but not in square-rigged sailing-ships, and the *Foreign-Going Steamship* version, which neither required nor allowed service in square-rigged sail. The so-called ordinary certificate had been modified in its requirements by force of circumstances, fewer apprentices finding it possible to complete four full years in square rig as fleets either diminished or evaporated under their feet, and the genuine square-rig certificate followed suit. The situation led to a certain amount of exaggeration in claims to seamanlike qualities, and justifiable irritation and scorn on the part of those who had put in the full time in blue-water sail; but they were a dying breed.

As for the examination's form, it had now settled into one it retained with only detail adjustments for the next seventy years, a number of written papers followed by a *viva-voce* test which, as well as assessing the candidate's grasp of seamanship in its various aspects also brought up weaknesses detected in the foregoing written part. Flag signalling was also tested, both semaphore and in the International Code. And it paid to appear neatly turned out, good manners being as important as anything else, particularly where the examiner's temperament was inclined to the testy. His reputation was an integral element of the test, bureaucracy in one of its few human guises and all the more awe-inspiring. The exam itself was still being conducted under the aegis of the Local Marine Board, however, so that standards and content varied from port to port. Examiners were free agents in what they chose to ask, as likely to drift beyond the limits of the syllabus as stick within them, presenting baffled second mates with masters' problems and disconcerted masters with probings into the dim recesses of memory. There was nothing wrong with this in principle, but to men whose time and funds were strictly limited a syllabus was a syllabus and not a base camp for wider exploration, and they finally voiced their dissatisfaction with irregularities which included the appointment of examiners not actually in possession of the certificates for which they were examining. It was a classic instance of the route by which bureaucracy extends its hold on affairs, largely through the consequences of default or incompetence involving some degree of culpability, and the upshot of this particular affront to the norm was the BOT's taking direct control of the machinery of examination in 1914, including appointment of examiners.

I went up after six weeks at school. It was in two parts, written and oral, the oral conducted by Captains Sargent and Keating. They gave me a hard time of it, but I knew most of the answers. One of Keating's questions was about the procedure to follow if the vessel ran short of provisions. Having experienced it during my last voyage I gave the correct answer including the signal, NV, and he said I obviously knew all about it, and that was that. A few days later I collected my certificate on parchment. (Liverpool, 1903.)[1]

---

[1] *Sail Ho!*, pp.236-7.

VI

Ping-pong at the Chelsea Hotel. 1914-1945.

*

Life moved in the ordinary routine of the deep-sea tramp. At the end of the morning watch a bell sounded in the fore part of the vessel followed by a gong aft to reassure Captain Bellwinch that the ship was still in one continuous piece. Then the Swedish fog-horn blew for breakfast. At one bell in the forenoon watch a whistle sounded for prayers. At seven bells the house-flag was run up at half-mast for lunch, at one bell in the afternoon a gun was fired for tea and at three bells in the last dog a rocket was sent up to indicate that dinner was ready.[1]

*

WRITING in the 1880s Lord Brassey had deplored "a regrettable ignorance of modern languages and commercial affairs" among merchant service officers. By the commencement of the Great War the situation wasn't much improved, and while boys were signing indentures at 14 or 15 with barely a couple of years' classroom inculcation of a foreign language at their disposal, if they'd benefited from a secondary school place at all, there was no official incentive to pursue it. The 2nd mate's exam demanded no more than a basic facility in English, while abroad most local people with whom the apprentice and officer came into contact could speak English well enough to satisfy the ship's needs. The fact was that the requirements of a sound schooling and a sea apprenticeship conflicted, the first compelling attendance to age 16 for the School Certificate (introduced in 1917) while the second usually commenced a year or two earlier. However, the raising of the minimum age of eligibility for the BOT exam, to 18 in 1918 then to 20 in 1930, brought the School Certificate into the system's ambit and shipping companies began to specify it as a condition of engagement where applicants had not attended a pre-sea course issuing its own qualification. Brassey's criticism had been aimed at the system rather than at the schools, and after the 1914-18 war, when the leaving age was raised to 14, and in some areas 15[2], boys were leaving the county grammar schools with at least an introduction to another tongue, dead languages apart. *Conway, Worcester* and the

---

[1] *Recollections of Captain Bellwinch.*
[2] Fisher Act, 1918.

167

Nautical College, Pangbourne, offered French, the NCP also Spanish, to which *Conway* changed.

After the elementary stage state schooling continued at secondary level in three separate categories – grammar, modern and technical. The modern curriculum was geared to commerce and industrial trades, while the technical varied according to local industrial requirements and opportunities. Government grant and LEA funding covered elementary schooling, while the private and public schools continued as before. *Worcester*, *Conway* and the NCP took their cue from the private sector, to which they had belonged in their own distinctive way from the beginning.

After the minimum age requirement for 2nd mate rose to 20 indentures were frequently signed at 16, though 15 and sometimes 14 remained common in some quarters, typically the miscellany of tramp operators with whom apprenticeship was still the preliminary to becoming an AB, the usual outcome and a convenient and theoretically profitable way of passing the time between completion of indentures and coming of age, as it were: the inter-war depression ensured that berths as uncertificated officers (say 4th mate) were virtually non-existent. It wasn't until the 1944 Education Act, making school compulsory to age 15, that it became the lowest age for taking up an apprenticeship, at which point secondary schooling was begun at 11 or 12; accordingly, the apprentice or cadet (one or two owners perpetuated the term *midshipman*, improperly) had in theory a minimum of four years' secondary schooling to his credit with the chance of the School Certificate as evidence. In Scotland, meanwhile, an education act of 1918 took primary schooling to age 12 followed by an intermediate level to 15, though the statutory leaving age remained 14 until 1947. A comprehensive secondary level carried the able to 17 and the Scottish Leaving Certificate.

1939 was the date set for extending compulsory schooling to age 15 in England, Wales and Northern Ireland, but the war intervened, compelling evacuation[1] and consequent disruption, exacerbated by the absence of teachers called up for military service, though some schools were back on home ground within weeks, there to remain. The overall effect was serious debilitation of the system evidenced by, among other things, an increase of illiteracy not quite compensated for by a broadening of social outlook. *Worcester*'s people had to relinquish the ship, required by Admiralty for emergency training purposes, and move to other premises for the duration, finally taking up the offer of Foot's Cray Place, whose owner handed over the keys of the country seat near Sidcup free of charge. A nearby flooded quarry provided token boating facilities while *Cutty Sark*, doing duty as an equipment store at the Greenhithe berth, was visited several times a week. Meanwhile, after one or two uncomfortable brushes with modern warfare, *Conway* was obliged to abandon her Rock Ferry berth in 1941, shifting under tow to another off Bangor pier, not long previously occupied by the reformatory ship *Clio*. With her white gun-deck strakes blacked out *Conway*'s

---

[1] Operation Pied Piper, September 1st. Designated regions.

appearance led local citizens to assume the worst in phlegmatic spirit: when the duty cutter's crew, in working rig, landed at the pier to pick up stores, they were confronted by two old ladies who asked what they were "in" for and their bafflement deepened when the ladies expanded the question by asking what offences they had committed.[1]

By the outbreak of WW2 the pre-sea system of shore-based schools and (more or less) permanently-moored ships was firmly rooted, despite a few anxious moments during the depression years, when, for example, *Conway* experienced a particularly lean time of it, rescued from possible closure by one of its keenest patrons, Lawrence Holt. Blue Funnel and its associate, Elder Dempster, added their own residential training schools to the picture after the war, but apart from that the pre-sea sector reached a state of maximum activity at the end of the 30s with the establishment of three prominent institutions. Among them, the NCP offered

> *... a carefully-balanced curriculum which includes an adequate proportion of general school subjects to the standard of the School Leaving Certificate.* (Prospectus, 1936. p.8.)

The college was the immediate successor to Devitt & Moore's Ocean Training Ships Ltd., originally conceived as an integral element of a combined shore-based and seagoing training arrangement using the cadet-ship *Medway*[2]. After two years at the college cadets would spend a year at sea in the ship, then another in the navy as cadets or midshipmen, RNR, at the end of which, with 3 years' sea-time (a year's remission for the college course) behind them, the last year would be spent in "cargo steamers" before attempting the BOT exam. The plan was nothing if not ambitious, to the point, as it turned out, of impracticability, a grand strategy that foundered on the incomprehensible requisitioning by the bureaucratic establishment of the *Medway* in 1918 and failure to replace her with anything suitable[3]. The net result was a two- or three-year shore-based pre-sea course approved by the BOT and Admiralty, similar to *Worcester*'s and *Conway*'s. Somewhat incongruously, the college occupied a gracious property near the village of Pangbourne, a country house set in spacious grounds, and nearby premises enjoying limited river frontage, purchased by Sir Thomas Devitt with the proceeds of sale of the cadet-ship *Port Jackson* in 1916. The first cadets joined in September, 1917, after heroic preparations had been made in quick time by Captain Montanaro, RN (Rtd), late captain of The Marine Society's training-ship *Warspite* and governor of the Royal Merchant Seamen's Orphanage at Snaresbrook. To everyone's profound dismay he died in the Spanish 'flu epidemic that swept in on the heels of war, to be succeeded by a figure of less commanding stature. Nevertheless the college sailed on in landlocked distinction to survive serious financial problems training cadets chiefly for merchant navy (as it was officially titled in 1922) entry, with limited

---

[1] *The Conway*, pp.181-2.
[2] See Ch.8.
[3] ibid.

numbers for the navy and RNR nomination. As were *Conway* and *Worcester* cadets, they were designated cadets, RNR, while at the college[1].

The NCP was distinguishable from its older contemporaries by its academic policy, formed with two principal considerations in view: the ever-present chance of a cadet's changing his mind while at the college or soon afterwards, and the need to attract an intake by means of a less confined outlook than was general among pre-sea schools. It was a realistic approach: boys of 13 or 14 were often mistaken in their aspirations, and with an awareness of what was to come as opposed to what had been romantically anticipated they were given an opportunity to continue with "normal" education; moreover, in some parents' eyes the merchant navy didn't amount to an attractive career prospect, not only for social reasons but also, as the trade depression deepened, for those of security of employment. By way of reassurance the college was recognised as efficient by the Board of Education in 1925, and from 1926 offered the School Certificate as well as its own passing-out qualification. With its higher fees justified by a distinct public-school ethos it was able to survive competition with *Conway* and *Worcester* in spite of its late beginnings, albeit with a sound claim to a maritime pedigree in many ways more authentic and fitting than those of its waterborne rivals[2].

Some 200 cadets followed a rigorous schedule from 6.45am to 9pm (9.30 in summer) divided between school, manual work and training, games and sport, social organisation and hobbies, church services, inspections and parades, with limited "shore" leave. In the mid-30s the curriculum included navigation, nautical astronomy, seamanship (with boatwork on the river), signalling and engineering, with English, history, geography, and science "giving a general view of physics and chemistry". French and Spanish rounded it off, either of which could be taken for the School Certificate, which, while optional, was vigorously promoted, perhaps less for its value to shipowners as employers than to the school's reputation, for shipowners were content with the college's certificate as it stood. Supply in any case exceeded demand during the interregnum, and when the conflict was resumed in 1939 cadets – apprentices – were accepted with any level of academic achievement, with or without pre-sea training, though indentured apprenticeship declined in favour of cadets on articles, more easily shifted from owner to owner according to the fortune of war.

The consequences of financial depression brought the cost-effectiveness of pre-sea training under closer scrutiny. While the traditional element was represented by such as *Conway*, *Worcester* and Hull Trinity House School, a reformed approach characterised most of the shore establishments, the NCP at the expensive end of a broadly technical spectrum embracing institutions like the Royal Technical College in Glasgow, King Edward VII School in London, and in Cardiff the new Smith Junior Nautical School, set up in 1921 with a fund raised by the local shipowner Sir William

---

[1] Admiralty approval for all three granted in 1917.
[2] See Ch.8.

Reardon Smith. It offered a 3-year course divided into a 2-year preparatory course and a 12-month cadet course, by which the BOT approved 6 months' remission of the sea service required for the 2nd mate's exam. Numbers were such that boys could join the cadet course direct from outside secondary schools. Although barely more substantial than the *Flying Dutchman* after the 1914-18 war, sail still affected training's state of mind, while counter to it ran a growing sense of the new order, the different methods and priorities of the steamship operation, and the picture was, as a result, neither fully nor satisfactorily defined. Although the academic world began to take a broader and weightier interest in pre-sea training it appeared to suffer a degree of confusion about the ideal approach, while the practising mariner took his own view for granted, bogged down as it was in method and principle lagging behind current developments. Unlike the engineer, content with his almost purely technical identity, the navigator had become less sure of his ground, an emulsion rather than a blend of the technical and the quasi-technical.

In perceiving a need to change towards the technical, some schools appeared to veer too far away from the abstract elements of the officer's function – his general demeanour, marking him as a leader prepared not only to perform executive duties but also to shoulder the accompanying responsibility, a responsibility changing in nature and in many respects becoming heavier. In short, an ideal balance of the technical and classical (grammar) to run in tandem with a regime of character development, and this was where views differed.

The dilemma became clouded and complicated in the mid-30s by a third dimension, uncomfortably ignored by the public and studiously refuted by a prevaricating political establishment: the prospect of another major war with Germany. Viewing this with a sceptical and radical eye the director of the School of Navigation attached to the University of Southampton succeeded in his efforts to establish a pre-sea course embracing all the current conceptions in a system attuned to the contemporary scene, including a semi-military content in line with the schools' OTC's, by this time widespread in both private and state sectors at secondary level. The most significant departure was the course length, 9 months (extended to 12 post-war), aiming at a less immature intake than the training ships and the NCP. G.W. Wakeford saw value in the martial ethos for the development of character, and in a shorter course for an older age-group impatient to get to sea. The school's first intake joined in 1937 to mingle with older men "up for their tickets", an influence regarded in many quarters with ambivalence but which possessed the great virtue of tempering romance with a shrewd smack of reality – unless, for the sanguine, enhancing it. It wasn't by any means a unique arrangement, but the disciplinary structure was, impressing itself more or less unexpectedly on the school's adult community.

I was sixteen when I joined. The course counted as six months of the three years required for a temporary 2nd mate's certificate, combining academic and practical instruction with a heavy dose of pure naval barrack routine. The quality of instruction was high. We learned navigation by sun and stars, chartwork, ship construction and stability, cargo stowage, compass work and practical seamanship. It was interesting and we longed to get to sea and put it all into practice. Sometimes we caught sight of heroic characters fresh from the U-boat war, who strolled along in duffel coats and salt-stained caps. How we admired them, tried to imitate their style, their carriage, their free and easy ways. Unlike them we were not free. We lived under an iron discipline imposed from above but executed by cadet upon cadet in an hierarchy ranging from Junior Cadet to Cadet Captain, five grades through which selected individuals could pass, all in nine months. We paraded with rifles and gaiters, drilled endlessly, marched past our officers and were as smart as marines. Punishment, freely given, took two forms, "overtime" and drill squad. Overtime – unpaid – involved joining a working-party to sweep, chop, carry, wash down or dig. Drill squad, in full kit with rifle and bayonet, was awarded in half-hour units up to two hours on any one indictment. The practice of carrying six bricks in the pack was happily discontinued in my time. Both giver and received of the punishment could find themselves sweating shoulder to shoulder, the senior cadet sentenced by a more senior one: the punishment combined suffering and absurdity in equal measure. On enrolment we became members of the Home Guard, the normal minimum age for which was 17, but we were not normal: at 17 we went to sea. We mounted guard. A cadet stood at the gate, rifled and bayoneted, a clip of five live rounds safely in his greatcoat pocket, challenging masters and mates as they wandered back from the pub. The guard commander, a Junior Leading cadet, was required to patrol the grounds. I would steal from shadow to shadow, Sten-gun at the ready and twenty rounds stuffed down my gaiter. The Sten was a HG weapon, a thoroughly unreliable machine-pistol on a stick. We made contact with larger guns during a week's course at HMS *Excellent*, part of the navy's mythology of terror. Everybody below the rank of commander moved at the double, and the roads between the buildings were filled with running men. Under the tutelage of navy chiefies we learned 6-inch gun drill (but the MN only had 4-inch) and fired Lewis guns, Thompson sub-machine guns and .45 pistols, and with a dummy Oerlikon shot at moving pictures of aircraft Otherwise we were addressed as "gentlemen" by the officers, allowed to smoke and frequent selected hotels though under age. Instead we broke the rules and drank in local pubs where the beer was cheaper and a seaman's uniform was served regardless of age. I learned a distaste for military discipline and an admiration for well-executed foot-drill, deep detestation of authoritarian organisation and an abiding interest in nautical astronomy, and an inner need to keep my shoes well-polished. We went to sea well-prepared. Convoy lookout came easily and the heavy machine-gun on the bridge-wing had a certain familiarity; but we had quickly to learn humility in the hope that by deference to experience and conscientious application to duty we might achieve the dizzy altitudes of the salt-stained heroes who came ashore for their tickets. (1942)[1]

And in 1943 the school acquired, as a practical gesture towards inculcation of sail's ineffable values, the ketch *Moyana*, used for short coastal cruises.

Thirdly came a new kind of training altogether, in which Wakeford took an active interest. In 1941 the first Outward Bound Sea School was set up, the brainchild of Kurt Hahn, who had imported the idea of rugged adventure-type instruction when he established Gordonstoun School in Morayshire. It had to be evacuated, and was re-sited for the duration at Aberdovey, a particularly happy choice which continued in

---

[1] Contributors' private papers.

being after Gordonstoun returned to normal after the war. The enterprise also attracted the interest of Lawrence Holt, with his midshipmen in mind, and, as he had saved *Conway* from financial embarrassment not long before, so he supported Hahn's scheme, also sending prospective midshipmen on the course and seconding officers from the Blue Funnel fleet as instructors, involving them in the rigours of the programme as deeply as the boys.

...its regime was no less spartan despite its move south. The muster consisted of Gordonstoun boys, *Conway* cadets, a mixed bag of young men from factories and offices, and half a dozen or so Blue Funnel midshipmen. Part of the Code of Honour was to pledge that we would not smoke... We were also not to be afraid of reporting back-sliders, loyalty to the code being thought nobler than misplaced loyalty to our fellow-criminals... The Warden, Hogan, was a social worker from the Midlands and our relationship with him was cool. The academic staff were schoolteachers with a bent for the outdoors. The nautical staff, who supervised the schooner *Prince Louis* and the ketch *Garibaldi*, were Blue Funnel officers. (There were) expeditions over Cader Idris pacing ourselves against Marine Commandos under training, athletics every day, sailing and pulling heavy naval cutters, orienteering, cold showers each morning and a mile run the rain. (1941)[1]

Social workers weren't viewed with much gladness by youths whose robust and positive outlook placed them in another sphere altogether from that occupied by some of the people with whom such figures normally attempted to deal, and they were inclined to let their sentiments show in various unmistakable ways; sneaking on one's fellows was in any case a piece of social manipulation to which they took natural exception. The course lasted four weeks, at the end of which a report was sent to employer or sponsor couched in blunt terms referring to qualities of leadership, self-reliance, physical and mental stamina and social accomplishments of a basic, rugged kind. The run in the rain formed part of a progressively tougher test ending with a 32-mile cross-country hike involving stated objectives and trials of initiative.

If the Outward Bound idea hinged about traditional conceptions of rugged self-reliance combined with team spirit its methods were forward-looking and beyond reproach. The general effect on mind and body was one of exhilaration taken to the limits of tolerance – in occasional instances beyond – in a process of self-discovery that was on the whole beneficial and even enjoyable, in the knowledge that its duration was finite. By contrast, the system that evolved in the *Mercury* took ruggedness into the realm of bitter fantasy as the disciplinary regime became ever more paranoiac in the hands of Beatrice Fry, who, for all CB's vaunted attributes as a man of parts both physical and intellectual, had assumed the stature of a colossus in the shadow of which cadets discovered in themselves reserves of stoicism for which, by the evidence, they were later grateful. A few, of course, did not, and weren't.

---

[1] *A Love of Ships*, p.121-2.

In a towel, with bare feet, we crossed the gravel drive to the showers in a converted garage, where we received a dollop of soft soap on our shaved heads. In the tepid water we scrubbed ourselves with the floor scrubbers provided and cleaned our teeth under the eye of a uniformed PO, to whom we had to present our reddened bodies for inspection. The drill was to make a jumping turn with the handle of the toothbrush pressed against the teeth, the *Mercury* bathroom salute, then wait while he satisfied himself that our sins were washed away and we were fit to attend a High Church of England service in the chapel. I never understood why the priests[*sic*] did nothing about Ma Fry's unchristian behaviour, and the smell of the incense she burned at the altar sickened me. I pitied her "fouls", the ones whose sins had found them out; like 2037, made to scrub himself until he almost bled, then pass all his spare time standing at attention outside her study, and the public thrashing given 2442 Woodgate. He got it for coming last in the 1-mile run Ma Fry sent a group of us on for cheering 2037 when he ran well in the (segregated) fouls' race on the annual sports day, attended by some admiral. She was enraged when 2037 came in first with most of the ship cheering him on, the boy whose spirit she tried to break, and sent us round the course promising disciplinary action for whoever came last. I'd agreed with Woodgate that it was unfair to threaten us for supporting a fellow *Mercury*, and we determined to give her a piece of our mind. Since 442 was leaving for the navy that week he deliberately dropped back to come last, and must have let her know how he felt when summoned to her study, because next day we were all called to witness punishment. We were lined up before a vaulting horse and 2442 was brought in under escort. He stood erect and defiant, looking over the ranks of disciplined *Mercury* boys whose hearts he knew were with him, then Ma Fry had him strapped to the to the horse and flogged. He never made a sound, and his silent contempt gave me joy. Afterwards we were marched off to the incense-filled church to pray, and I wanted nothing more than to spit at the chaplain as he passed. But we were disciplined. The place gave us a sense of community, and one of accomplishment. I'm grateful for my *Mercury* experience. (1931)[1]

Which was evidently more subtle than it appeared. Meanwhile, far below these flights of innovation and evolution obscure institutions were still doing what they could for boys lacking any kind of family or financial support, to say nothing of employment prospects:

I was schooled at an orphanage in Swanley which took the children of servicemen killed in the war. We were taught navigation in the top class and sent to sea willy-nilly. I got a place with Ropner's. (1935)[2]

The Great War left its mark in a variety of forms. Set up during hostilities, the schools' OTC's were organised chiefly in the private sector and army-orientated until, in the later war, air-mindedness produced an equivalent ATC supported by the air force as an economical means of giving youths a basic introductory training. Neither did the sea feature until war had resumed, when the Navy League, unaided by the Senior Service (notoriously shy of involvement with sea training enterprises outside

---

[1] Contributors' private papers.
[2] ibid.

its own immediate milieu) started the Sea Cadet Corps which, by war's end, was firmly established in cities and towns throughout the country, giving boys from the surrounding districts a light training modelled on the navy's lower deck, much of which came in more or less handy later on.

I joined the Ilford Sea Cadets in 1942. The officers were mostly retired MN or RN petty officers. About seven of us went to sea as apprentices in tramps or tankers. During summer holidays my friend Dennis King and I spent a lot of time on the Woolwich ferry. If you didn't get off you only paid for one crossing. After some searching I learnt about deck apprenticeships and arranged a transfer from the South-East Technical College to the King Edward VII College and a pre-sea cadet course.[1]

Halted at the outbreak of war in 1939, the education system's development resumed with the far-reaching measures of the 1944 Education Act, acclaimed by *The Times* as "the greatest and grandest educational advance since 1870". *Inter alia*, it confirmed selection by ability at age 11 and reaffirmed the leaving age of 15, by which time grammar school leavers had taken the School Certificate, though the act did not come into full effect until 1947. Now nation-wide, state education offered primary, secondary and further levels, divided and streamed in most areas according to pupils' examination performances. As for the sea, boys were still taking to it with the minimum possible schooling behind them, depending on the conditions set out by the shipping companies.

I owned a dinghy at seven and was a good oarsman and fisherman. We lived fifty yards from the sea on a fine sandy bay named after my mother's family (Ferris). To get to the grammar school (Larne) I had to take the ferry across half a mile of tide-swept estuary, and took an oar to help the ferryman when needed. My father was a master with the Lord Line of Belfast, commanded the *Lord Templeton* [2] at 28. My mother's family was the oldest on the island (Islandmagee), dating from their landing from Scotland in 1582. I'm at least the fourth generation of seamen.

My favourite reading was *Sea Breezes* and *Lloyd's Register*[3] from which I obtained the addresses of shipowners, and I wrote to most of the leading companies without any luck. When my father saw that I wasn't to be turned back by lurid stories of his early days he contacted the managing director of Workman, Clark and the result was an offer of a place[*sic*] with Ellerman Hall, Port Line and Blue Funnel. I shied away from Blue Funnel as they wouldn't offer further employment until an officer had his master's ticket. I chose Hall Line. (1924)[4]

This last curious proviso of employment with Blue Funnel is an elusive one. A number of individuals have attested to its existence, but it would have conflicted with the company's earlier policy of accepting applicants with square-rig 2nd mate's

---

[1] Contributors' private papers.

[2] Probably the 3-mast barque *Lord Templetown*, owners T. Dixon & Sons (the Lord Line).

[3] More likely *Lloyd's List*.

[4] Contributors' private papers.

certificates. However, times were hard and places few, and as the BISN Co set out conditions of acceptance for people with a Higher School Certificate, who would not normally have considered the sea as a career, so Blue Funnel's policy shifted to require a master's ticket in each watch. This measure apparently accorded with the company's practice of underwriting its own risks (as well as building ships of well above normal strength requirements, while navigating them along courses inked-in on the chart), but it seemed a perverse idiosyncrasy to take pains to train the midshipman only to pass him on to the benefit, in effect, of lesser companies, and to employ instead people who might have been total strangers to Blue Funnel's methods. And it was, of course, a policy that could be implemented only in the conditions obtaining at a time of trade depression, with master's tickets queuing up in their dozens for every vacant berth.

I left school at 13, a place at Saxmundham where my father had a garage business. My education was nil. We were never taught to write, only print. I used to sit there looking up at the map of the world on the wall. My brother joined my father, and I wanted to go to sea. I had a grandfather at sea; they said he was a purser. We never knew when he died. He was the only one apart from my uncle, who was with Tatem's. The schoolmaster said "Why not go to a sea school?" and the training school at Wallasey[1] was the only one that would accept me apart from *Ganges* – the navy. The local parson got me a place there, but people didn't know much about it. I went to the Wallasey school before I knew much about my uncle. It was full of young offenders, Dr Barnardo's and that, and nearly got closed down once or twice. I was there for twelve months. The food was horrible. We each had an aluminium bowl. Meals were weak cocoa, two rounds of bread and a it of margarine. I did a bit of business, got a pot of jam and sold it at a ha'penny a scrape. Saturday we'd go down to the ferry pier at Wallasey to a little baker's shop where they sold all the stale cakes and cream buns at a ha'penny a bag. We ate as many as we could and took the rest back. (1926)[2]

I was the first and probably the last of my family that had anything to do with the sea. We lived in Benfleet. My father was away wandering and no-one knew anything about the sea or ships. I was at a little prep boarding school in Malden. I don't know who paid the fees – an uncle, or it may have been the officers' association. When I was fifteen I came home on holiday and Mother told me I'd have to get a job; there was no more money for school. What did I want to do? Right out of the blue I said I'd like to go to sea. I didn't know why, just suddenly thought of it. I had no school qualifications, absolutely nothing. (1933)[3]

I came from a seafaring family in Dundee. My father was a chief engineer in the Allen Line. Mother's father loved the sea; his family owned fishing-boats and after studying to become a doctor at Aberdeen University the sea won. He commanded a sailing-ship and was lost at sea. When Mother's first husband died leaving her with a small son, she obtained a job through connections with the Allen Line as a stewardess, to provide for her son. There she met my

---

[1] Lancashire Navy League & National Sea Training Homes.

[2] Contributors' private papers.

[3] ibid.

father and when, on one occasion, both their ships were in Boston, they were married at the Seamen's Mission.

Father left the sea when his father died to run the family business, building ship's engines and boilers, but it didn't survive the depression. They had six children, and our half-brother. Of the seven six went to sea, three on deck, two engineers, and for a time after the Second World War my sister was a stylist-hairdresser with Cunard. Father was against us going to sea, and sent three of us on a fishing trip in a trawler with one of his friends. We fished near Bell Rock and I've never been so sick in my life; the stink of the acetylene and the fish was enough, without the pitching and rolling, and I just lay on a coil of rope hoping the trawler would sink. I was never sick again. When I told my father I still wanted to go to sea he said, "You'll go and bloody-well stay there." I was eleven. When I was fourteen he died, not long after the business collapsed, leaving Mother in very strained[*sic*] circumstances, and I decided to get a job to help. Two of my brothers were serving engineering apprenticeships by then.

I was educated at Dundee High School, a grammar school; the school song was in Latin. After the business collapsed I went to Morgan Academy, which only cost £4 a year, for books. After I got a job I went to night-school until going to sea at seventeen. It was very difficult to get a place. (1933)[1]

My home was on the south shore of the Firth of Forth with a view over the whole expanse with its passing ships. Fishing craft put out from Musselburgh and units of the Atlantic fleet sailed up to Rosyth from time to time. At night the light on Inchkeith flashed across to us. Together with a literary diet of Bartimeus[2], Taffrail[3] and others all this led to a bid at the age of twelve to go to Dartmouth[4], firmly turned down by my mother, my only parent after the death of my father and his business, a shoe manufactory. She said it was too early to think of such a career, unconventional in the family and unaffordable, but there was enough to send me to Herriot's, a day school in Edinburgh, where there was no encouragement towards the sea, so I forgot about it until several friends departed, one to Dartmouth, three to *HMS Conway* and one to sea direct as an apprentice. One of the Conways was a close friend, and I determined to get there, though discussion at home was aimed at putting me off the sea at a time of depression. However, the fees could be met, and to the *Conway* I went.

The shipping scene from the *Conway* was a continuing source of interest and encouragement – ships of the Harrison, Ellerman, Blue Funnel, Furness Withy, Henderson and many other lines entered and left Liverpool and Birkenhead docks and passed up and down to Bromborough or the ship canal; coasters, tugs and lighters, the Irish and IOM packets, passenger liners of the Cunard and White Star, and now and again a relic of olden times, once a 4-masted barque, a thrilling sight.

We wore RNR uniform, very proudly, and handled our boats under oars, power and sail and talked as nautically as we knew how. It was a good education for the job we would have to do, if in some respects old-fashioned[5]. Why learn to box the compass in quarter-points when ships'

---

[1] Contributors' private papers.

[2] Paymaster-Commander Lewis da Costa Ricci, RN.

[3] Captain H. Taprell-Dorling, RN.

[4] Age of entry to the BRNC as a cadet at the time was 13½.

[5] At this time *Conway*'s fortunes were on the ebb, partly for this reason, partly because of the depression.

compasses were marked in degrees? Why the intimate details of sailing-ships' rigging?[1] Scholastically the standard was modest but the training developed our sense of responsibility. Sport was encouraged; sailing was half-sport, half-instruction. It was an enjoyable time, good for us to be thrown together and to learn to take orders from our peers; there was a purpose to it. There was much discussion about which shipping company to join, and Old Boys would visit, in between ships. We learned that BI had a cadet-ship. I chose Alfred Holt, but much depended on the captain's recommendation; he was on Old Conway who had served his time in sail and transferred to the navy as one of the Hungry Hundred[2]. Each term two cadets were offered appointments as probationary midshipmen, RNR. I was one, but determined to say nothing to Blue Funnel until a later date. (1934)[3]

I was supposed to have gone to the Royal College of Music, but changed my mind; thought I'd rather go to sea. When I went I took my guitar with me. (1936)[4]

My mother's father was brought up on the sailing-ship owned by his father. He was a Dane. After a time as a purser he set up as a chandler and shipping agent in Southampton; he was a court interpreter (spoke nine languages) and vice-consul for several Baltic countries. His business was very prosperous but overwork killed him in his mid-40s and he left his family penniless. My mother had to leave her posh finishing school and take a job with a family friend, managing his bookshop near the main dock gates in Southampton, where she met my father. He was Dumfries farming stock but became a marine engineer, chief with RMSP[sic] in 1941. He supervised new construction from 1919 and went back as chief of the *Alcantara* from 1935 to 37, retired in 1944. We moved around a lot. I started school in Belfast then went to a prep school in Ilford, followed by a public[5] school, Campbell College, which directed its pupils towards the professions[6]. I was quite good at chemistry and maths but useless at most other things, so the professions weren't for me. It was either farming or the sea, and salt water won. Father had no objection, but said I was to go on deck; he felt that engineering didn't receive due recognition. So I left school at 16 and had a spell at the Southampton School of Navigation, which had just opened. (1937)[7]

---

[1] Why indeed?!

[2] Cdr F.A. Richardson, DSC, RN. In 1895 100 RNR officers were offered permanent regular commissions as lieutenants, in which rank numbers were short, with the proviso (characteristic of the Senior Service at the time) that there would be no promotion above that rank unless through war service. They were so called because of the nature of the career in the merchant service, essentially casual employment.

[3] Contributors' private papers.

[4] ibid.

[5] People are apt to confuse private with public schools; the latter are, of course, the descendants of ancient foundations intended to provide schooling for deserving sections of the community, and are comparatively few in number as well as having altered in their principles to become more private than public.

[6] The sea not being defined as such, of course.

[7] Contributors' private papers.

One of my father's brothers was an engineer with the RMSP, eventually chief of the *Reina del Pacifico*, quadruple screw. Three younger brothers also went to sea as engineers. My grandfather established a credit drapery business in the Gorbals, married, had a family of five daughters and three sons, moved to a house in a good suburb, then to the Clyde coast. My father and his brother were taken into the business, and after surviving shrapnel wounds in the war he carried on in it, married in 1920, raised a family, played golf and ran two motor-cars. When Grandfather died in the early 30s neither my father nor his brother could keep the business going and it folded within two years, so I was brought up in a rented house on the south side of Glasgow while Father worked as a clerk on £3 or £4 a week. I had an enjoyable boyhood; passed the 11-plus[1] and went to a good grammar school where you could get intermediate and higher certificates (Scottish) if you could stick the pace; but when the business failed I had to get a job. I found one as an errand-boy with an optical shop at 12/- a week, and learned about cameras and such things so that I was offered a job behind the counter at 15/-. It wasn't for me, though. I was more interested in the way the gadgets worked and talking with the optical repair men, who advised me to do something about my education. One of my engineer uncles had started with Weir's at Cathcart, and suggested applying to them for an apprenticeship, but entry was by written exam and I hadn't looked at my books for a year. So it was back to my school books and the library. (1938)[2]

My School Leaving certificate, Central Welsh Board, showed credits in maths, geography, French and German; passes in English would have gained me matric, elevation to the 6th and possibly entry to the RAF; I was already in the ATC. I got a job as a temporary male clerk in the Army Audit Office at Chichester, but the utter boredom drove me to find something more satisfying, and I chose the sea without an inkling of what it would entail. (1941)[3]

Father was manager of ICI's Australia-New Zealand department. I was born in Brixton Hill, oldest of three brothers and a sister. When I was five we moved to Guildford where I attended a prep school until I was 15, then we moved to West Horsley where I took the examination for an apprenticeship at the RAE and failed. When I was asked what I wanted to do instead I announced that I'd go to sea, and after Father had calmed down I was enrolled at the Sir John Cass Technical Institute in Aldgate, registered for an apprenticeship with either Prince Line or Ben Line. The pre-sea class numbered about twenty. Most stayed only a few months, but a few over a year. We received a very good grounding – maths, English composition (reports), technical drawing and nautical subjects with practical work, lifesaving and fire-fighting, and boatwork in St Catherine's Dock. In the blitz I didn't miss a day of school, travelling to and from Surrey, sometimes held up by blocked streets. We had lunch in the Seamark Club, near Tower Hill, within walking distance of the school. (1941)[4]

Eton's programme was strictly classical, and didn't suit me at all; whatever I learned I've forgotten. My inclinations were towards a different kind of life from anything that would follow that sort of education, and I thought I'd like to join the merchant navy. I had a long and sensible discussion with Father, and he agreed with my point of view, with one proviso – I

---

[1] Correct term "scholarship". The term "11-plus" followed the 1944 Education Act.
[2] Contributors' private papers.
[3] ibid.
[4] ibid.

would go to the *Conway* first. I wasn't much of a hand with maths and there was an entrance exam so I had to have coaching, and passed easily. Never considered joining the navy; didn't have the brains.(1941)[1]

The only family connection with the sea was an uncle, killed in a fall from aloft in HMS *Ganges*. My father had been a labourer at the Pontypridd coke ovens, and seized an opportunity to train for a teaching certificate. He was teaching at a primary school in Croydon when he married my mother, who had been qualified as a teacher before the war. I was born in a two-up, two-down terrace they'd bought, and my interests in ships probably started when accompanying my father with parties of schoolchildren on trips to the Continent and Scandinavia.

During the depression members of the family in South Wales came to stay, and an aunt looked after me while Mother was supply teaching; marriage barred her from full-time posts. I suffered no deprivation, but want was only a familiar rail journey away. We took long family holidays, and in Cowes I bought a book entitled *Sailing for Beginners*. I won a scholarship to Whitgift and joined its Nautical Society, which wasn't very active, and my parents gave passive approval to my wish to go to sea. Once Father took me to London where we watched a tramp passing through the locks; he hailed a shabby-uniformed third mate and asked where they were bound. The ship represented romance itself; I had no desire to go into the navy.

Whitgift wasn't evacuated but Selhurst, the municipal grammar school, took those who wished to Hove and then Brighton GS, which we attended in the afternoon while the home school had the morning. When France fell Selhurst moved to Bideford, which was a delight. Ships discharged into lorries on the quays and with friends I boarded them to chat with the crews. I learned to sail in an 18-foot lugger, a line-fisher, hired at 2/6d an hour with its owner.

For school cert I took the three separate sciences instead of Latin, and general science and maths. I was approaching my sixteenth birthday, and went on to the School of Navigation at Southampton. (1942)[2]

I was accepted for apprenticeship but not until I'd reached sixteen, so I went to the Cass school for a year. Others there were waiting for their first ships, already placed with companies, and didn't take the full course. We were taught maths, English composition including report writing, technical drawing, signalling, chartwork, compass-work and ship-construction, practical seamanship, lifesaving and fire-fighting. (1942)[3]

ss Badarpur.[4]
25th February. 1943.

- I am afraid Ian's career will be fixed by the time you get this. I most sincerely hope it is not the Merchant Navy. A boy like Ian, fond of games, sailing, etc would find it like a prison. During my time I was out in a lifeboat once and that's all the sailing I got and as much as the majority get. Ships work day and night in most places, and that was in peacetime. This

---

[1] Contributors' private papers.

[2] ibid.

[3] ibid.

[4] Burmah Oil Co., Rangoon. No address given because of wartime security precautions.

company's ships never stop except for a fortnight's drydocking each year when the officers work longer hours than when running normally. We do our two four-hour watches on the bridge at sea plus one or two hours' other work and in port from six to six am or pm, and on sailing days you may have been on all night then you carry on with your watches next day to say nothing of messing about for hours mooring and unmooring. I have no doubt he will say he likes it just as I did, but the day will come when he wants to get married and then he will think differently. If he doesn't get into one of the half-dozen better companies goodness knows what kind of people he may get with. The pay as you know is not good compared with jobs requiring as much skill ashore and on the basis of pence per hour a farm labourer is better paid. In the MN you're a sort of jack of all trades. I think a lot of this wanting to go to sea business is not so much wanting to go to sea as abroad. You can go abroad in all sorts of jobs. I think I would like to have been a geologist if I'd thought about it in time and had had the brains you see plenty of the world that way... [1]

Which echoed the sentiments of many whose decisions in haste had given them, if not the leisure, plenty of cause to regret it. Two more disparate scenes of operation than the *Conway*'s and the likes of ss *Badarpur* didn't exist (the letter's writer was an Old Conway). Apart from which it was one of the life's natural components to become world-weary and cynical by the time one took on the peculiar responsibilities of the 2nd mate: promotion seemed to have creaked to a halt and the hours were long and inconvenient, providing, among other things, opportunity for morbid introspection. As for Ian, the lesson he drew from his uncle's letter was that tankers should be avoided like the plague. *They* weren't what the sea was all about, and although his father added the observation that the MN didn't amount to a respectable career, he applied to Blue Funnel after failing the medical and interview board for BRNC, Dartmouth [2].

Nepotism continued as crucial as ever to getting an introduction to a company, more so during the depression. Noticeably after WW1 supply began to outweigh demand, not only because more boys were coming forward, for their various reasons, but also owing to the diminishing size of the operational fleet once the post-war boom had passed. Naturally, cadets from the pre-sea schools enjoyed first pickings, though a few owners were known to favour entrants innocent of the preconceptions (and misconceptions) such places instilled in their offspring. Blue Funnel was one, while British India's rather ambitiously (indicating one of the typical effects of an imbalance of supply and demand) putting it about that matric holders (those who had passed the higher School Certificate exam for university entry) would receive priority cut out the pre-sea system at a stroke, though with what degree of success remains unknown; probably negligible. The net result was a recruitment system that conformed to statute, accepted as distinct from written except for random enlightening references:

---

[1] Contributors' private papers.

[2] The new Britannia Royal Naval College opened in 1903, while *Britannia* herself was kept at her moorings as a store until broken up in 1916.

Those who intend to adopt direct entry should make application to the offices of the various shipping companies selected, though they should be warned that competition is very severe and that personal recommendation is almost essential for successful application. (1935)[1]

"Personal recommendation" certainly lends nepotism an aura of integrity and respectability, even elegance, essential not only to successful application but also to the liner company's corporate image.

A friend of Father's happened to be the engineer superintendent of the City Line, so I was lucky. It was very difficult to get a place. (1933)[2]

Uncle Walter, who'd sailed as an engineer with Alfred Holt, arranged an interview through his friends among the office personnel. (1942)[3]

...my father wrote to a Col Lawrie with whom he had served in the Territorials and who was an executive somewhere in the Alfred Holt group [and] some time in November I had in front of me at last the application form... It was duly completed and despatched and, shortly before Christmas, I received a letter instructing me to report to Liverpool early in January for interview and a medical examination. (1941)[4]

One of my father's brother officers in the RE happened to be the son of Sir William Reardon Smith, hence my rapid enrolment. (1944)[5]

While such as the BISN Co saw the situation as an opportunity to improve on the educational standard of their intake, others, typically in the tramp sector, availed themselves of the increased supply of good-quality crew supplements or substitutes at no extra cost, relying as much on the layman's ignorance of the system as on early school-leavers:

Those of us who went into tramps had generally not had pre-sea training – you know, as long as you could walk into the owner's office you were on. I was eighteen and had a Higher School Certificate but all I was told was that I was bit old to be taken on. (Sun Shipping, 1936)[6]

We were five children; two brothers, three sisters. John wanted to go into the navy, but it needed private means, so the merchant navy seemed the next best thing. I don't think he knew what he was letting himself in for. Father was in the Indian Army, 31st Lancers, and retired to live with us in Laugharne. I barely knew him; we lived in the nursery, only brought out on state

---

[1] *Seamen in the Making*, p.168.
[2] Contributors' private papers.
[3] Contributors' private papers.
[4] *A Love of Ships*, pp.53-4.
[5] Contributors' private papers.
[6] ibid.

occasions, and when Father died he left Mother to manage on a pension of £72 a year from a grateful Indian Army; otherwise I expect we'd have ended up in the workhouse or something. John went to prep school, then Trent College in Nottingham; he didn't bother with Higher Cambridge because the chance came to go to sea. He was always playing around the boats at home, going out with the fishermen, to Mother's horror. She was convinced they'd dump him overboard; they were such a lot of gangsters. The sea was what he wanted, but Mother didn't know how to go about it, and there was no-one to help. Quite how she got John a place with Foster Hain[1] I don't know. I expect she wrote letters on someone's advice. (1929)[2]

The move towards advertising for applicants before 1914 was halted by circumstances, and while the result was a dearth of career information the industry saw no need to promote itself. Consequently many who found their way through the maze of obfuscation landed in situations to which they were unsuited, which drove away from the sea those who, with proper guidance and an informed approach, would have found places better attuned to their inclinations and temperaments. In the event shipping was the net loser.

The Shipping Federation continued with its apprenticeship scheme in conjunction with some forty companies, most in the tramp sector and profoundly obscure; among the better-known were the British Molasses Co., the Cairn Line, Chapman & Sons, Constantine's, Houlder Bros., the King Line, Prince Line, Turnbull Scott, and a handful of Cardiff-based concerns enjoying more or less notoriety in certain quarters – Chellew, Claymore Shipping, Morel, and the Pentwyn Shipping Co. among others. The SF appointed its recruits as required by the contracting owners, to follow their progress in a detached and pragmatic fashion; no premium was charged, and wages of £10, £12, £18 and £20 were paid for the successive years, with a £5 bonus on satisfactory completion.

I'd never heard of the Shipping Federation, but at its office in Leadenhall St I had an interview with Captain Trigg and his assistant, Mr Tite, and an introduction to Kaye, Son & Co. I say "introduction", but in fact I never saw a soul from the company, nor entered its offices in Fenchurch St, and I've no idea what my parents thought of this offhand procedure; not even an interview with my employer. (1935)[3]

At least the boy wasn't expected to make his way to Algiers to await the unscheduled arrival of an alleged ship, so in this particular instance at least the system could be said to have improved, albeit to some extent less than in leaps and bounds.

When war broke out again to precipitate shipping into a dramatic reversal of peacetime *ennui*, the SF worked with the MOWT to operate a "pool" whereby apprentices could be appointed to ships as required, irrespective of owner. Nevertheless, places were still difficult to come by, owing to extensive tonnage losses

---

[1] Better known as the Hain S.S. Co. Ltd.

[2] Contributors' private papers.

[3] ibid.

combined with a flood of applications from youth fired by a variety of urges from patriotism to an aversion to military service and the spectre of conscription into Bevin's labour corps. Even a tanker laden with aviation spirit seemed – from the shore – a more attractive prospect than the 1,000-foot level of a Kent coal-mine.

One or two boys from the locality had gone to sea, one in the exotic rank of bell-boy, so my pal Ernie and I solicited the help of a man whose son had gone to sea, and he drafted a letter of application to the Anglo-Saxon Petroleum Co., which, he said, was second only to the Blue Funnel Line. Mine was the only letter despatched – parental veto! To apply to a tanker company in the middle of war showed my utter ignorance. Anglo-Saxon had already lost eighteen ships. (1941)[1]

I wrote to nearly thirty companies, and seven put me on their waiting-lists – the Anglo-Iranian Oil Co., Blue Funnel, Reardon-Smith, Anchor, Ellerman City, Andrew Weir and Crawford's of Glasgow. Clan Line requested me to attend their office in Hope St., Glasgow. (1944)[2]

Interview technique – where there was one – retained much of its traditional brevity and chill, leaving the interviewee little the wiser, and often more mystified, than before the encounter. Commonly it took the form of a handful of questions with little or no indication of how the answers had been received until the final (usually delayed) pronouncement; there was seldom an opportunity for discussion of points of interest to the victim. The single most prominent change of practice was the disappearance of the *ad hoc* confrontation with the captain on board; ships' husbands, superintendents and chief clerks or directors became the usual inquisitors, ensconced in the oppressive surroundings of the company's head office. If he was lucky the successful applicant would be told on the spot, but more often had to endure a period of suspense awaiting the verdict by letter; similarly the wretched reject. For the successful, the next step was the signing of indentures, unless the company employed cadets on ship's articles. Union-Castle did this, setting up its own recruitment scheme in 1917 with a preference for Conways, Worcesters and boys from the NCP. Also, paying due respect to its close ties with South Africa, the company provided places for boys from the new training-ship *General Botha*, opened in 1922 at Simonstown, where she lay at her permanent moorings. Union-Castle's were true cadets, not apprentices, on articles as members of the ship's company and recognised as officer trainees – at least, on paper, for beyond that they shared a common identity with the apprentice and the so-called midshipman.

It wouldn't be unjust to say that the name accorded us – "midshipmen" – was our only dignity, for there was no doubt that we were cheap labour, instructive though the work was. By

---

[1] Contributors' private papers.
[2] ibid.

the time we'd served a couple of years most of us were as capable and reliable as the average quartermaster or AB, though paid a fraction of their modest wages. (Blue Funnel, 1936)[1]

And there was nothing offhand about Blue Funnel's selection procedure:

In due course I received an application form, then an interview appointment, with a second-class railway ticket. I'd never been away from home before and the interview was an intimidating experience, made more difficult by the strange English accents. I'd already had an eyesight test, and after a medical I was told my application would receive consideration, taking into account the results of the school leaving exam. (1936)[2]

While a few years later the process was augmented to ensure that the first-voyager wouldn't be quite as raw as his predecessors, also giving him, perhaps, a slightly improved chance of survival under the severe stress likely to be encountered in the U-boat campaign:

With the School Cert under my belt I told Blue Funnel I was at their service, and they suggested[sic] a course at the Outward Bound Sea School at Aberdovey, where the month passed quickly. On contacting the company once again I was told to enrol for a pre-sea course at the Liverpool Nautical College and kit myself out as per enclosed list. After learning about dead reckoning, shove ha'penny and the life to come from candidates up for 2nd mate I was instructed to report to the company's Birkenhead office, in uniform, with my dungarees. After an unhappy interview during which I was roundly criticised for my performance at Aberdovey I presented myself to Captain Waite at the Gladstone Dock, where I was kept busy as his assistant seeing to ships' lifeboat stores and equipment. After ten weeks I was handed my indentures for signing and later instructed to report aboard the *Glenapp* in the Canada Basin. (1942)[3]

Shell – the Anglo-Saxon Petroleum Co – took a leaf from P&O's book by sponsoring apprentices as a recruitment ploy, arranging for their training with Wakeford's draconian enterprise at Southampton:

My father and I journeyed to St Helen's Court for a mid-morning appointment but were kept waiting until mid-afternoon, told that the delay was because the interview panel were lunching with one of the captains, who had just sunk a U-boat. The interview was an indeterminate affair, and in spite of not knowing the capital of Australia I was sent for further appraisal to G.W. Wakeford. I was set a written examination beforehand consisting of general knowledge and "intelligence" questions, and on an outline map of the Mediterranean had to plot as many ports as I could. When interviewing me Wakeford said that when he was seventeen he had been acting bosun with a crew straight from jail, and that he was 3rd mate at eighteen. I formed

---

[1] Contributors' private papers.

[2] ibid.

[3] ibid.

the opinion that he was a braggart, and on subsequent acquaintance that he was a bully. I was accepted for a course at South Stoneham House. (1942)[1]

And elsewhere, the hurdle of the officious nobody:

I was directed to the Marine Department, where a gruff individual asked me my business and told me to wait while he consulted with the marine superintendent – "A very busy man, you know." After a delay I was directed to Captain McKinley's presence and an interview lasting about twenty minutes. He told me there was a waiting list of at least thirty, and the company had lost a number of ships; also that it was the company's practice to select its cadets from training-ships like the *Conway* and *Worcester*. There was no hope of getting into any of them and the 3-month course at the Royal Technical College in Glasgow was booked up for the next twelve months. McKinley suggested applying to the pool as a boy seaman[2]. Out on the pavement again I called on Hungry Hogarth's, not afraid of a few years' hard labour, but was informed that there were "hundreds" of applicants and no berths. Eventually I got one as a cabin-boy on an explosives tender, where I found plenty of encouragement from the highlanders on board and at least got myself a discharge book. I wrote to tell McKinley what I'd done, and coming home on leave found a letter offering me an appointment. (Clan, 1945)[3]

– possibly by McKinley's shifting him along the waiting-list past boys of less obvious keenness. The company was another employing cadets, not apprentices, maintaining them as far as possible on ship's articles for the full span of their time. By comparison apprentices were at some disadvantage, thrown into relief during WW1 when ships on government charter for the duration were occasionally held on standby reserve, out of foreign-going service, sometimes long enough to affect the validity of their apprentices' sea-time. A ruling was accordingly brought in to allow such idle time, so to speak, to amount to no more than 1/5th of the indentured time before ceasing to count as part of that time, the deficiency to be made up by service on f-g articles in some suitable capacity, unless the indenture time itself were extended. The rule remained in force thereafter causing problems made more acute during the depression years, which not only saw ships laid up with apprentices forming all or part of their caretaker crews but also, as a result, led to a scarcity of seagoing berths, so that many never completed their time.

Contingencies apart, however, the standard 4-year requirement remained in force with remission of up to 12 months for pre-sea training, the pattern accepted throughout the industry with, it appears, one exception. During the 30s and the opening years of WW2 the conspicuously prudent Blue Funnel, to the chagrin of aspiring officers backed by the credentials of such as *Conway*, brushed aside the BOT's recognition of

---

[1] Contributors' private papers..

[2] Though, of course, he could have done so as a prospective apprentice. Perhaps McKinley wasn't aware of this; perhaps he was concerned to keep a potential cadet in the offing rather than lose him to another employer.

[3] Contributors' private papers.

equivalent sea time (not so much a regulation as a courtesy that no owner was obliged to observe: employers were free to specify whatever length of indentured service they wished, though it would obviously have been futile to have required longer than the statutory 4 years) and presented indentures conceding only 6 months' remission, possibly another manifestation of the effects of supply and demand. The applicant could like it or lump it, for behind him were others either unaffected by the matter or prepared to shrug it off as a minor irritant. Furthermore, notwithstanding an over-supply of applicants, the company could well have considered three years too brief a period for the proper indoctrination of its constitution, unless, in its characteristically considered fashion, it aimed to keep its midshipmen employed for a little longer than otherwise in face of an uncertain post-certification future.

The indenture arrived for signing and it was upsetting to find that it was for a term of 3½ years instead of the three to which my *Conway* Extra Certificate entitled me. So I had a problem – accept the condition or look for another company, which would delay my going to sea. Holt's would certainly not change their rule for me, so I signed. (1934)[1]

At all events, the practice was quietly dropped during WW2. To offset it, though a permanent feature from the outset, the midshipman – or his parents – could take slightly chill comfort from another little quirk of the Birkenhead Navy: it required neither premium nor surety, the agreement binding on both parties "in honour", the implication being that to break one's word would incur penalties beyond the power of mere money to atone for, a guilt that would nag the conscience for the rest of one's mortal span. It meant that the wages were at least wages and not the returned parental outlay, as was the case with, for example, Port Line (also calling its novices "midshipmen"). The first year of service was in any case probationary, while the "honourable undertaking" of the apprentice to give the company first call on his services after passing for 2nd mate was a comment on the popular belief that only holders of master's tickets were acceptable. It arose, possibly, from the company's following widespread practice in a time of over-supply by which the outsider with the master's ticket would get the 3rd mate's berth before the outsider with the 2nd mate's ticket. If so, both could have taken second place to the ex-midshipman returning to his *alma mater* with his new certificate still wet from the printers, but steeped in company lore.

Although, naturally enough, differing from company to company, the wage remained generally low by custom and tradition. Blue Star paid some £40 for 4 years in 1919, Tatem of Cardiff £60 in the mid-20s, British Tankers (the Anglo-Iranian Oil Co) £60 in the mid-30s and Royal Mail £90, Ellerman Hall £96 in the 40s and in 1945 Hain paid £60 while Port Line paid nothing, only returning the surety as pocket-money, the balance forfeit if the indentured time wasn't completed - £30 for a 3-year term, for instance. Otherwise the lowest figure appears to have been £40 (e.g. Evan

---

[1] Contributors' private papers.

Thomas & Radcliffe, 1934) and the highest £96 (E/Hall, 1940). The comparison with Robert Thomas's pay a hundred years earlier is interesting, considering the effects of inflation: in the late 30s a good-quality lounge suit cost £5 (say 6 months' wages in ETR's service) and 100 Player's cost 5/-. Thomas could buy a suit for a few shillings, and the equivalent of the Player's for mere pence.

I was to be taught the business of a seaman in steamships, and if bedding, clothing or other necessaries were provided by the company their value was to be deducted from my pay, which was £10, £12, £18 and £20 for successive years, plus 2/- a year in lieu of laundry, and a £5 bonus on satisfactory completion. (Kaye, Son & Co., 1935)[1]

They didn't ask for a premium. We were paid 5/- a week for the first and second years, 7/6d for the third and 10/- for the fourth. We supplied uniform and other clothing, sextant, text and exercise books. (Royal Mail, 1936)[2]

T&J Harrison employed cadets on articles. Promotion to 4th officer during the final year depended on ability and conduct, and the company would "endeavour" to place them as junior officers after passing for 2nd mate. Even with few such openings during the depression at least the thought was there, in black and white. The wage was paid monthly "as far as possible", amounting to £9.15s., £13, £16.5s. and £22.5s for the successive years, which included a "small bonus" at the end of each year.

Echoing the methods of the HEIC of Robert Eastwick's day, during the 1914-18 war wages of those on articles were stopped from the time their ships were lost from any cause including enemy action; however apprentices, for what it was worth to them, remained on pay and were simply appointed to another ship, or, if necessary, transferred to another owner's employ – for example, when the last windjammer of the first owner was torpedoed, together with his business. When the next war broke out the same arrangements would have been resumed but for protests from seamen's and officers' organisations, by this time firmly rooted and effectively articulated, supported by some owners. The result was a ruling in 1942 that extended pay to a fortnight after arrival home following wreck or sinking, with compensation for loss of effects, pay supplemented from the opening of hostilities by a war-risk bonus. The Pool – the SF/MOWT administration – ensured that appointment to another ship would be made without delay (after survivor's leave), facilitated by the move towards engagement of cadets rather than apprentices, and the system worked smoothly throughout the war.

The war-risk bonus effected a revolution in the apprentice's standard of living. Varying slightly from company to company – some paid a little more than the official figure, and there was a "tanker differential" – the system came into operation in September, 1939. The apprentice/cadet/midshipman was treated to £5 while aged

---

[1] Contributors' private papers.
[2] ibid.

under 18 and £10 thereafter – *per month* – riches beyond his wildest dreams, at least as they were at this stage of his career, rendering his actual pay (the figure stated in the indenture, which remained unchanged) ludicrously meagre. Some received a little more than the £5, some the full £10 regardless of age, some the lower figure for the first two years of their time, based on a starting age of 16. Whatever the permutations, however, it meant that in return for serving as the target for surface raiders, U-boats and dive-bombers the apprentice could afford food, clothes and presents without having to pawn his sextant or barter his shirt. The only anomaly was the official division of the bonus into two age-groups, since the enemy certainly gave no indication of similarly dividing his attentions, but as with "free trade" the British Government wasn't to be moved by consideration of how the competition viewed matters.

In 1944, for example, Runciman was paying apprentices £10, £12, £18 and £20 through their time with a £5 bonus on completion, to which was added war-risk bonus of £5 p.m. for the first two years and £10 p.m. for the second two. There was also, as in peacetime, a soap allowance of 1/- a month (the 12/- a year in lieu of washing, as it was phrased) and overtime payment (hours of normal time not stated, at master's discretion) of 1/3d an hour for the first two years and 2/6d thereafter. Among others, Prince Line retained the war bonus to hand it over in a lump sum at the end of the apprenticeship, a practice variously denounced and lauded by its beneficiaries, among whom were, presumably, those who received the interest on the accumulating capital – not the apprentice, apparently.

My pay was £10, £12, £18 and £20 for the four years with £5 bonus at the end. I also got a war bonus of £6 p.m. for the first two years and £12 p.m. for the last two, which included the tanker differential. (Shell. 1942)[1]

However, with the rate of pay and other preliminaries settled, the way to the first ship lay open. The process of joining her, popularly supposed to be more clearly recalled than later appointments, was for many the age-old whirl of bewilderment and incomprehension, a torrent of half-formed impressions the significance of which became apparent only some time afterwards. The most striking were, as ever, to do with the alien appearance of the accommodation, the furnishing, the food and the general demeanour of one's new companions, exacerbated by a heightened sense of one's wretchedness and awkwardness, pre-sea preparation notwithstanding. First encounters with disillusion could be dampening:

From the moment...I first met Poole I suspected...that my mental image of the sea life was far different to reality; if the process of discovery was gradual, the facts at last became crystal clear. Nor was there any other way for me to have learned the truth. But although I realised that

---

[1] Contributors' private papers.

going to sea was not the romantic affair of my dreams I was reluctant to admit even to myself that I might be mistaken in the choice of a career.

I flinched inwardly at the prospect of having to acknowledge to friends at home that they were right and I was wrong. I reflected that it would not always be wartime, and tried to imagine what things would be like at sea normally.

Poole did not like working with the sailors. He detested the sea, and was always urging me to profit by his advice, to go home at the end of the voyage and return to school. Why stay at sea, I asked him, if he hated it so? His reply was that it was too late to back out now, and in any case for him it was either this or the trenches. (PSNC. 1918)[1]

Just as it had always been, here it was still, the curse of pride and the horror of admitting to a miscalculation after making a more or less public declaration of intent...

The old mate, Mr Thomas, kept me off the deck until the weather eased, when I appeared with my new gear on. The oilskins rubbed my elbows and wrists raw, and I must have been a pathetic sight, because he said, "Swallow your pride, lad – swallow your pride. Get out of this. It's a dog's life, a bloody dog's life. Just swallow your pride and tell 'em you want to come home. (ETR, 1934)[2]

And, of course, tradition was evident, especially where it kept expenditure on the owner's part to a minimum – some owners, anyway:

She was laying[sic] alongside at Sunderland, T on the funnel and none on the table. Oh, I thought she was a giant. Joined December 4th, aged 14 years 1 month. I thought there'd be mattresses on the bunks, but no, so I had to go ashore to some ship-chandler and get a donkey's breakfast for 2/6d, a week's pay in my first year. We went out to Bahia Blanca in ballast. Freights were hard to get. (ss *Monkleigh*. Tatem, 1927)[3]

Like its contemporaries – the others in the tramp sector – Tatem suffered during the depression from shortage of capital and from the effects of the liner companies' incursions into the charter market to bolster dwindling revenues from regular operations. One was the Federal S.N. Co., which ran a "branch line" for a number of years[4], a handful of general cargo carriers originally German and handed over as war reparations:

My first ship was the *Pakipaki*, ex-*Trewellard* of St Ive's, ex-*Ammon* of Hamburg. I joined – appropriately – on April 1st. She was bunkering at Swansea, covered in coal dust. I was the only apprentice; the others were on leave. I had a nice uniform with brass buttons which I wore

---

[1] *Pilot Aboard*, pp.41 & 46-7.
[2] Contributors' private papers.
[3] ibid.
[4] See Ch.8.

under my dungarees on my first job, cleaning the growth out of the bilges, mark of the previous trip's grain cargo. (1928)[1]

By this time uniform was almost universal, if not universally worn, among officers as well as apprentices, so that the ancient epithet "brassbounder" could no longer be applied to distinguish the apprentice from his superiors. It was either the standard MN pattern with its distinctive buttons, facings and cap-badge or one of similar cut with the company's own design of attachments. The MN uniform emerged from wartime circumstances and the German inclination to treat merchant service officers without the courtesy (such as it was) accorded officers in the armed services, going to the extreme of executing a ship's master as a civilian engaged in criminal activity after he had sunk a U-boat by ramming. An Order in Council of 1918 prescribed a uniform, revoked and re-drafted by another of 1921 which included a cadet's or apprentice's distinctive mark in the form of a gilt cord and small button on each lapel of the "square rig" (blue) uniform and on the epaulettes worn with tropical rig. Again, company patterns differed, some having no facings at all, others favouring three cuff-buttons after the fashion of naval midshipmen, while caps sported badges in designs varying from the simple house-flag in a wreath of laurel-type leaves (though the official MN leaves are oak) to more elaborate confections topped with either the MN (Plantagenet) crown, or the king's crown by special dispensation. The title *Merchant Navy* was granted by royal decree in recognition of its function during WW1 as the country's fourth arm of defence.

Serving one's time was a pleasant process since the company regarded us as an investment. Not more than two sailed together, and none in the small steamers. A real effort was made to train us, we dined in the saloon, and full uniform was worn except when doing chores about the bridge and officers' deck. We kept the middle and morning watches and in port helped to supervise cargo work. The food was excellent, although there was a rumour that the fish had already done a round trip in a mail-boat. My first voyage was UK – Bermuda – Jamaica – Colombia – Panama – Acapulco – Los Angeles – San Francisco – Vancouver – Panama Canal – UK. (Royal Mail, 1934)[2]

Mr Lamont actually walked with me from the Shipping Federation office to the company's office in Broad St., EC2, and accompanied me to the director's office. It was rather like dealing in slaves; he had to have it known that the SF was doing its job. Anyhow, I was taken on, then he came all the way with me through Houndsditch to Dock St where we got to the business of the gear. A funny old boy named Bushell was in charge of the stores and a kind of shop in the Sailors' Home & Red Ensign Club. He dished out Nicholls's *Guide* and *Seamanship* and *Norie's Tables* then measured me for my outfit. I had to have a suitcase and sea-bag with lock and bar, and they arranged to have most of the stuff sent to the ship, leaving me with the uniform and one or two items. My father accompanied me to Paddington, and there was Mr

---

[1] Contributors' private papers.
[2] ibid.

Lamont, who always saw apprentices off in person, to be met at the other end, conducted to the ship, and delivered into the arms of the master. They had to be careful about it because magistrates were sending boys to sea who were likely to abscond *en route* [1].

On the ship was this enormous quantity of gear which on the whole wasn't very suitable. I never wore some of it. Long-handled pants, as I called them, and the Federation boots, a humorous idea, clumsy things with wooden pegs in the soles. They'd have been handier on a farm, really; working boots, with laces. You'd sort of clump round in these things. There were four of us. We had to go up to the Cardiff shipping office to be seen. We didn't sign on; just had to be seen by the shipping master to make sure we existed, in the presence of the ship's master. We clumped up wearing these great boots. Some AB's were standing around, and there were cries of "Here they come, the poor buggers!"

The *Cape St Andrew* had been out for seven years. In that time her apprentices had served out their time and their reliefs had done the same; they were off so fast we never saw them. We were all first-trippers, not put to work with the lascar crew but given our own jobs. One lad had done two years in a torpedo factory, another a bit of time on his father's baker's van and the other was a poor lad from South Wales who had absolutely no guts whatsoever, and no brain, either. Hopeless. We lived in two-berth cabins opening onto the weather deck with heavy weatherproof doors with mosquito-netting inner doors. There were no bunk-rails or boards, so sleeping could be precarious. The furniture consisted of "wardrobes", half-length cupboards one above the other, a collapsible table fixed to the bulkhead and a collapsible canvas stool. In one cabin the previous occupants had made a chest of drawers and a small settee from bastard teak, very well done. The cabins measured 12ft x 6ft. The washbasin emptied into a tin can and above was a rack for a water carafe and glasses. Lighting was by a central deckhead fitting replaced at 9pm by an oil-lamp. There was no running water in the bathroom but instead a bucket on a wooden rack across the bath with a tobacco-tin to bale the water over one's head. The lavatory, shared with the junior engineers, had a leaky service pipe which distributed a fine spray over the sitter, who required oilskins. (Sun Shipping, 1936)[2]

My first month "at sea" was spent at Greenock, when I attended a one-day course learning the arcane secrets[*sic*] of the Hotchkiss and Lewis machine-guns, then we shifted ship to Glasgow to load – mainly whisky – for America. Until we sailed there was only one other apprentice on board, at the end of his time; the other three had been sent home on leave. It was then that I learned my first lesson in respect for one's seniors. We were issued weekly with a bar of Lifebuoy to wash ourselves and one of Sunlight to wash our gear, and one evening the other apprentice blamed me for losing the Lifebuoy, grumbling that he'd have to shower with Sunlight. Fed up with the performance, I said he could shower in moonlight for all I cared, and went round with a tender jaw for a week afterwards. (Prince Line, 1942)[3]

There were five midshipmen including me. The senior, in his last year, was a South African, Thompson, a *General Botha* boy, who controlled us forcibly by means of his size. Farquahar

---

[1] Seldom, if ever, as apprentices, though; the custom had quietly expired with compulsion. They were, however, still sending them off as deck and galley boys, giving them a chance to help themselves out of trouble.

[2] Contributors' private papers.

[3] ibid.

had been torpedoed in the *Medon* and spent twenty-three days on a raft before a Portuguese ship picked him up; two days later it was also torpedoed and he spent ten days in a boat, from which experience his report led to the company's equipping its ships' boats with fishing-lines. Briddon had been in the *Deucalion* when she was sunk in Operation Pedestal[1], after which he had supplemented the hard-pressed crew of the *Ohio*[2]. I regarded these two as heroes. The word was that we were to sail to New York as convoy commodore. My smart white tropicals were going to be an embarrassment, and my pith helmet was an object of ridicule. As long as one had a uniform suit for wear at mealtimes and dungarees for all other occasions nothing else was required. (Blue Funnel, 1942)[3]

Which last observation carries more weight than it appears to, indicating one of war's subtler contributions to the erosion of social order, expedient acting against the customs of peacetime which included, among such prestige companies as Alfred Holt, dress regulations made to seem trivial and superfluous in the face of cataclysmic events. Return to pre-war standards in the ensuing peace, so-called, was never entire, and deference to authority never as positive as before; so decline, in fits and starts, almost unnoticed, gathered momentum...

Appreciation of customs and standards was axiomatic in the training process, things not taught so much as assimilated in a perception of it (training) that continued in an ambivalent light as the earlier war gave sail its quietus for all practical purposes. But much of sail's attitude in its worst aspects remained, and steamship owners, chiefly of tramps, took little or no interest in formal training arrangements, content to leave the matter to chance and the theory that the apprentice was bound to absorb the elements of his calling through mere juxtaposition and self-motivation. The part played by the master and officers depended, as ever, upon individual inclination, the mate's, characteristically, being to issue generous helpings of work from an inexhaustible stock of dreary and limited variety. At the other extreme the apprentice was expected to be as unobtrusive as possible and when unavoidably conspicuous to conduct himself in a civilised manner. As for the formal contract between him and his master, the phrasing of the indentures persisted in conveying the impression that whatever his daily occasions they were designed to transform him into either a seaman or a deck officer, if not a happy fusion of the two.

The different versions of the document were published respectively by the BOT, the Shipping Federation and a number of shipping companies, and, beginning as before with the master's undertaking to use "all proper means" to teach the apprentice the business of a seaman, by the end of WW2 the agreement was to instruct him in the duties of a deck (or ship's, or navigating) officer, some retaining the reference to a

---

[1] The relief of Malta, August 1942. Damaged by bomb near-misses, *Deucalion* dropped out of the convoy escorted by the destroyer *Bramham* but shortly afterwards was attacked again and set on fire, and sank after an explosion. (*Malta Convoy*.)

[2] Texas Oil Co. "*Ohio*, famous, fabulous, never to be forgotten" – Admiral of the Fleet Sir Phillip Vian, KCB, KBE, DSO. Quoted in *Malta Convoy*.

[3] Contributors' private papers.

seaman's business (i.e. soogeeing, chipping rust, bilge-diving, brass-polishing, painting, looking out, steering, knotting and splicing, etc.) as a kind of precautionary reservation and save-all. Some examples for the period include the BOT's *Ordinary Apprentice's Indenture* (*the business of a seaman* [1919] and *navigation, seamanship, the business of a seaman and of a ship's officer as customary on steamships* [1940]); Alfred Holt & Co's *Apprentice's Indenture* (*the business of a seaman* [1924] and *the business of a seaman and, so long as he applies himself diligently thereto, of a ship's officer* [1943]); the Shipping Federation's *Ordinary Apprentice's Indenture* (*the business of a seaman as practised in steamships* [1927] and *the duties of a deck officer* [1942]); and Royal Mail Lines' *Cadet's Indenture* [1] in the 30s (*business of a seaman and ship's officer as practised in steamships*). The BOT form appears to have been the first to provide the *option* – deletable – of the apprentice's being taught an officer's business, defined as instruction in navigation, after the 1894 MSA, but few employers took it up until it became part of the text proper. The phrase in the Hain S.S. Co's *Apprentice's Indenture* of 1945 ran: *taught navigation, seamanship and the business of a seaman and of a ship's officer*, drawing a nice distinction, like some others, between the officer and the hand.

The significance of all this is that for the first time since the abolition of compulsory carriage of apprentices, before which time indentures sometimes included the word *mariner* (with its implications) either with or instead of *seaman*, the apprentice was officially recognised as an aspiring officer rather than AB, and measures were taken to confirm and support the point. Among them were the proliferating correspondence courses that followed Captain Brown's example: at first the choice and personal expense of the apprentice, after WW1 shipowners began to adopt them as part of their training programmes, making guided study a condition of engagement, or offering to subsidise the cost while recommending the wisdom of the apprentice's taking advantage of his opportunity.

The only time I learned anything was from the 2nd mate on the *Basil* when I was AB after my time. He used to bring me the sights to work through. It was never done in Tatem's. (Booth S.S. Co., c.1930)[2]

The BTC had a correspondence course for apprentices. On the *British Princess* the 2nd mate, a Welshman named Davies, tutored us and there was a well-stocked library which I greatly appreciated. At sea we took bridge watches at night, myself the 8-12 with the 3rd mate and the senior apprentice the 4-8, and during the day worked under the bosun. I took morning and noon sights and azimuths, and fixed the position by cross-bearings when on the coast. The senior had the afternoon off and took star sights on his watch. (1932)[3]

---

[1] Introducing the *indentured cadet*, another variation on the theme.

[2] Contributors' private papers.

[3] ibid.

We were supposed to do a correspondence course, but never had study time. The 2nd officer told us we had ample time on bridge standby, but we were always half asleep then. (Ellerman City, 1933)[1]

The company provided a correspondence course from the Southampton School of Navigation and on daywork we were expected to study after tea. On two of my ships we had an hour after lunch. On watch we took sun and star sights, compass errors and deviations, took bearings and wrote up the log. When with the 2nd officer I also corrected charts and wound the chronometer. (Royal Mail, 1936-40)[2]

Captain Thornton was a bit of a forward thinker in apprentice training, and at sea the three seniors were on bridge watches. I stayed on day-work. We had field days when the watch below had to turn-to on deck and I worked Saturday and Sunday afternoons on the bridge learning to steer, signal and keep a lookout.(Prince, 1941)[3]

Academic training was almost non-existent. The captain once asked me if I knew how to construct stereographic projections and eventually showed me. Later there were annual written examinations, but they made little impact. My professional knowledge came through pre-sea training, rough experience at sea and a few weeks' instruction at school before taking my ticket. (Shell, 1942)[4]

The chief officer's dictum was that we studied in our time, not his. He was a fair man, but a bit of a taskmaster. I met him a few years later when I was 5th officer of the *Empress of France*. "Well," he said, "you got a good training with me, didn't you?" (Clan, 1945)[5]

In keeping with its characteristic thoroughness, Alfred Holt started early on with a training system managed by the midshipmen's department, set up in 1916 barely twelve months after the company had first taken on apprentices; it was responsible for their selection, engagement, appointment and instruction, keeping them under the close scrutiny enjoyed by the average laboratory specimen. Progress at sea was monitored, and continuity between voyages maintained by instruction while boarding at the midshipmen's hostel in Riversdale Road, unless sent home on leave. The return to sea was with the next instalment of the course of study devised by the department, to be completed by voyage end. It was a great advantage to be in ships following a regular schedule of liner services beginning and ending in home waters, and to sail with officers as involved in the training programme as the midshipmen themselves[6]. The arrangement continued, with refinements and minor adjustments, into the 50s.

---

[1] Contributors' private papers..

[2] ibid.

[3] ibid.

[4] ibid.

[5] ibid.

[6] See appendix 3: Letter to masters, c.1916. (Alfred Holt & Co.)

Near the bottom [of Riversdale Rd.] the company owned a large semi-detached house ...known as the Midshipmen's Hostel... Two widowed sisters of uncertain years administered the house efficiently, looked after us well but stood no nonsense... Brian Heathcote of the dark brown voice lived next-door... the spartan bedrooms were furnished as dormitories [and] lights-out was at 2230. [The interval between reporting to the company and appointment to a ship was spent in] classrooms at the Birkenhead office re-learning the navigation forgotten while on leave, or in the company's rigging-loft at Vittoria Dock being instructed, in an atmosphere pungent with the odours of manila rope and Stockholm tar, in rather advanced rope and wire splicing...[Classroom instruction came under a one-time 2nd officer]: Danny Pierce...had served at sea as a Blue Funnel officer until his eyesight failed... Legend had it that...he had been supervising the discharge of some live pigs...the animals being hoisted ashore one at a time in net slings. As Danny looked up at one lift...the pig urinated catching him in the eye, blinding him temporarily and changing the whole direction of his subsequent career. (1941)[1]

Four boys are usually berthed together, supernumerary to the crew, and mess with the officers. In the first year the midshipman does most of the menial work for his shipmates and spends a lot of time cleaning paintwork, scraping and painting and cleaning bilges and holds. In port he watches cargo and helps to work it with the crew. Later he is attached to a petty officer to learn the work they have to do and it is only towards the end of his time that he becomes acquainted with the technicalities of an officer's work. His studies are directed from the Liverpool office. In his watch below he is required to do a certain amount of study with papers on seamanship, navigation, ship construction, chartwork, cargo work, etc. He must not only read certain books but must [also] study the ship and her work. He keeps a daily log of his doings and observations. He has a Morse lamp for signalling practice and there are sailing- and motor-boats for his instruction. While ashore he attends school at head office, where his previous voyage's work is overhauled and preparation made for his next voyage' studies. He also attends the Signalling School and the rigging loft for further instruction. He is required to provide himself with Norie's Tables, Nicholls's Concise Guide, *Fletcher's* Seamanship *and Borch & Perrot's* New Trigonometry, *and sextant and binoculars.* (Information Publication, Alfred Holt & Co.,1935)[2]

There was no standard guide to the shape and content of study courses other than the syllabus for the 2nd mate's exam, until, following establishment of the National Maritime Board in 1917 (reconstituted in 1919) as a panel of owners', seafarers', and government's representatives, instituted by the SF in cooperation with the Ministry of Shipping, the Central Board for the Training of Officers was formed in 1935. It was one of the fruits of a petition signed by some 23,000 merchant navy officers and officials presented to Parliament in 1933 calling attention to the haphazard means of entry to and training in the merchant navy, pointing to poor-quality raw material and the exploitative methods typical of the seedier (and, indeed, the not-so-seedy) exemplars of the industry. The board's principal function was to devise and administer

---

[1] *A Love of Ships*, pp.61-4.
[2] Quoted in *Seamen in the Making*, pp. 171-2.

a uniform system of training and study for apprentices and encourage employers to adopt it. The scheme's mainstay consisted of a series of annual examinations which had the effect of channelling the content and progression of the study courses available. The board's moderate and variable success was given a boost by the onset of war with its mounting pressure to speed up and intensify the training process, and in 1942 its name was changed to the Merchant Navy Training Board, on which sat representatives of owners, navigating officers' associations, the Board of Education, the Scottish Education Department and, in its wartime attire as the MOWT, the BOT. Together they settled on these tenets:

1. A standard training and instruction syllabus.
2. Periodic progress reports from the ship's master.
3. Annual examinations on board.

The nautical schools variously adjusted their courses to suit and offered new ones, no longer paid for by the apprentice but by the owner supplemented by grants from the SF and the Board of Education. However, owners weren't compelled to take part, and those who did took care to advertise the fact, while the scholastic standard of new entrants remained as erratic as the quality of employment, given an overall improvement on what had gone before.

Some sort of note came from the owners saying that I was to buy a sextant, possibly something to do with the Award of Merit [received] from the SF, but the Old Man said not above £5. A new one would have cost £15. I got used to the old thing. The mates had sail experience, very practical men, wise in seamanship and that sort of thing, but they did navigation by rote. They had this funny system of adding up the haversines and dividing [the result] by two, without any idea of how it worked. I tried it but there was no virtue in it. Now and again there'd be a bit of a panic and we'd be told to do some study before being set one of these training board exams. It wasn't a bad system so far as it went, and then of course there was Ronald Hope's outfit, the College of the Sea. We had quite a lot of old books, and being bookish I bought a lot. In fine weather the 3rd mate would be told to give us some instruction, and we worked through Nicholls's *Guide* and *Seamanship*, with Norie's Tables.

At other times we worked cleaning bilges and all those time-honoured things. All right, perhaps, for a short spell, just to see what it was like and understand what people were doing, but after that it was a waste of time. The system was rather brutalising in some respects. I didn't go to sea expecting an intellectual profession – I had this romantic image, wanted it the way it was – but at the same time it seemed to me that we were frightful dogsbodies. Once I refused to clean vomit out of the chief engineer's bath after he'd deposited it there. I just said I wouldn't do it, and they couldn't do much, really. I was inclined to give the chief officer direct replies. I felt that if the job depended on that sort of thing it wasn't worth having. (Mitchell Cotts, 1936)[1]

---

[1] Contributors' private papers.

"Ronald Hope's outfit", a charitable foundation, had become a prominent feature of the apprentice's life by the time he – Dr Hope – took control in 1947 following service at sea during the war and election as a Fellow of Brasenose, Oxford. The outfit was the Seafarers' Education Service, set up in 1919 by Dr Albert Mansbridge with the moral and financial help of the philanthropic and visionary (and almost, it seems, omnipotent) Lawrence Holt. Founder of the Workers' Educational Association, Mansbridge sought to include seafarers of all ranks in his plans, initially through the supply of circulating libraries to ships. The first was put aboard Blue Funnel's *Aeneas* in 1920.

On the SES's governing body were representatives of the UK Chamber of Shipping, the SF, officers' and seaman's organisations, the Library Association, adult education interests and the Missions to Seamen, the last already supplying books to ships *en passant*. Mansbridge later observed

It [the SES] exists, above all, in the interests of Youth at Sea. To my colleagues and myself nothing has been more hopeful in recent years than the steady advance of interest in the training of boys at sea. It is fully appreciated that in modern times those who are to be officers must have every advantage in technical and cultural education, and the Service hopes to play its part in this most valuable work.[1]

By 1935 some 442 foreign-going British-flag ships possessed libraries of 50 to 100 volumes, some of which, mostly technical works specified by the MNTB, were on permanent loan. The range of titles included every kind of good-quality material from popular novels to the classics, biography and history to travel, drama and poetry, all given an appreciative reception when reading constituted the chief pastime, for both pleasure and self-education. In the 30s an apprentice borrowed

Agatha Christie	*Murder on the Calais Coach*
Jeffery Farnol	*Peregrine's Progress*
Denis Mackail	*Bill the Bachelor*
T. Plivier	*The Kaiser's Coolies*
Frank Richards	*Old Soldiers Never Die*
L.C.N. Stone	*German Family*
H.G. Wells	*The Sea Lady*
G.B. Shaw	*Caesar and Cleopatra*
BOT	*Regulations Relating to the Examination of Masters & Mates*, 1930.[2]

So much for *Gleanings Among the Mountains* and the doings of Wandering Will.

---

[1] *A Challenge from the Sea*, p.19.
[2] Listed in *A Challenge from the Sea*, p.37.

Nevertheless, reading on its own wasn't enough, and English composition was encouraged, the Thomas Wall Trust funding the prizes for essay competitions open to apprentices and ships' boys. Prize material or not, their efforts received in return critical appraisal and the best examples – of essays, short stories and other items – appeared in the quarterly *The Seafarer*, first published in 1934 and circulated with the libraries as well as being on sale by subscription to a general readership, and still in production, ever on the lookout for suitable contributions from serving and retired seafarers, though evincing towards them a faintly patronising and pedagogic air.

Then in 1938 the SES's governing body set up the College of the Sea with a brief to assist any seafarer in the study of almost any recognised subject, whether remedial or to advance existing accomplishments, including hobbies and preparatory study for public exams. Tuition took the form of correspondence courses conducted by volunteer tutors of the highest calibre.

And, rather late in the day perhaps, but facilitated by the changing nature of the sea's employ whereby ships' people were establishing more frequent and regular contact with the shore, the Company of Master Mariners was founded in 1926, distinguished as "Honourable" in 1928 when the Prince of Wales became its first Master, granting a royal charter in 1930. In 1932 it was admitted to the London gilds (or guilds) with an approved livery, 200 members eligible as Freemen and Liverymen of the City. Among its aims and objects were the education, training and qualification of young seamen, cadets and apprentices, to which end boys were apprenticed to liverymen of the company, required to submit annual essays and keep a log, and given the opportunity to become freemen in due course.

However, whether an apprentice of the Honourable Company or one of the great mass of the unwashed, much of this background activity lay beyond his ken, arresting his interest only when it devolved onto the cares and fleeting pleasures of the half-deck's segment of the daily round, broadly divisible into the eternal categories of work, sleep, leisure and the menu, in a constant permutation of priority according to circumstances. Perhaps work tended to sink to the lower levels and food rise to a more or less permanent high, continuing to vary widely in quality and quantity between companies and ships while maintaining, in places, a precarious identity with the stipulations of the 1906 Act and the romantic days of sail. Some improvements were made in 1940 without re-drafting the scale, not tackled until 1957, by which date no shipowner was known to restrict the victualling to the BOT's somewhat lacklustre list of groceries, for all that certain chief stewards enjoyed popularly-bestowed opprobrium in recognition of their efforts. Lime-juice – or, as the 1894 Act recognised, lemon or other – kept its time-honoured place, still playing a useful role in the absence of refrigeration. Ice-boxes became a familiar component of the ship's *equipage*, either the portable variety lashed on deck something like a modern container or as an insulated ice-room, neither of which kept cool for more than a fortnight. With its abrupt introduction of modern, if utilitarian, tonnage, WW2 saw the last ice-boxes replaced by a proper domestic refrigeration plant.

The meat in the ice-box went bad in less than a week, then we were on salt horse. The veg lockers were inadequately stocked and ran out at the same time, so it was tinned and (mostly) dried vegetables thereafter. We were strictly on Lady Astor's pound and pint, told that she lived on the victualling scale for three months to test it before it became law. Well, maybe, but if so she wasn't expending her energy as we were – she certainly didn't keep watch and watch.[1] (NZS Co., 1925)[2]

Before Kylsant got full control[3] you could have a good feed on what was on the cadets' table before the steward brought anything from the pantry, but by the time I left you'd be hard pushed to make a square meal from everything in sight. (RMSP, 1926)[4]

On the night watches we had to make cocoa for the officer. He often complained how weak it was. We were always hungry, the apprentices. (Tatem, 1927)[5]

We helped the ice-box thaw because the meat in it was rotten anyway; we pulled out the drain-plug. The chief steward used to wash the meat in Condy's fluid to get rid of the maggots and the potatoes came aboard in bags marked "Pigs Only". (ETR, 1932)[6]

Each week we went to the chief steward to get what was left of our whack after some portion of it had been held back for cooking – such as ½lb of sugar instead of 1¼lb – but the rice pudding still came unsweetened. There was always a squabble with him over the lime-juice; he maintained that its issue was supposed to start ten days after the fresh meat ran out. (ETR, 1934)[7]

We dined in the saloon. The food was usually good and our main grumble was poor preparation. In the *Araby* we dined in the engineers' mess, but the food wasn't much good, maybe owing to economies but also to poor preparation and serving. In the *Ruler*[8] the feeding was outstanding because we were supplied by either the Americans or the Australians. (Royal Mail, 1936-40)[9]

On the *Malayan Prince* we were served by a sneering, haughty steward in the saloon. On the *Sicilian Prince*, [where we were] regarded as low life, we ate in our own mess, collecting the

---

[1] Nancy, Lady Astor. First woman MP, Unionist member for her Plymouth constituency from 1919 to 1945. She pressed for improvements and extensions to various BOT-related Acts.
[2] *Way for a Sailor*, p.47.
[3] Kylsant took over the ailing RMSP Co in 1911 and effected a change in its fortunes, evidently partly by means of housekeeping economies among other, questionable (as they turned out), measures.
[4] Contributors' private papers.
[5] ibid.
[6] ibid.
[7] ibid.
[8] A wartime MAC-ship.
[9] Contributors' private papers.

food from the galley. It was a separate menu from the saloon and the crew, tasty and plentiful but rather monotonous, a round of mince, stew, shepherd's pie, sea pie and curry. (Prince, 1942-45)[1]

The *City of Cape Town* had proper domestic refrigeration. I always found the food good, but in that ship it was superb. (Ellerman Hall, 1944)[2]

Sustained by shepherd's pie or maggoty meat and animal feed – separate bills of fare for saloon and focsle or half-deck stand out as one of the most stupid and ineffective attempts at economy exercised by British shipowners, the few paltry pounds saved (if they were) more than offset by the degree of discontent and actual subversion resulting – the apprentice always found his day replete with work, now dignified by the title "training" no matter how closely it resembled the laborious drudgery of the dark ages, as it still did here and there.

We were put to work on anything from splicing moorings, erecting shifting boards, steering, painting from the truck down, shovelling coal, tarring down, oiling decks – you name it, we did it. The first-year man got the dirtiest jobs, but no matter how you looked at it we were cheap labour and nothing else. Not paid overtime, we did any job outside the sailors' normal hours. Many a time I found myself hauling on ropes, shifting ship on a Sunday with the crew in their leisure gear looking on and jeering. (ETR, 1934)[3]

Trimmer. I nearly killed myself on that job. There was a door in the bulkhead between the empty cross-bunker and No.3 hold with a two-foot sill and a ramp on either side. I had to fill my barrow in the hold, wheel it up the ramp into the bunker and through into the stoke-hold, dump the coal at the furnace door, then go back for more. After four hours I could hardly stand, until I got used to it after about a week. Just fell out of my gear, poured some water over myself, climbed into my bunk and passed out. But in the morning I'd find my dungarees and singlet washed and dried by someone. They were good shipmates. The ship used four tons of coal a watch, and I had the job when a fireman went sick and a trimmer took his place. No way could I do a fireman's job; you had to know what you were doing, handling a slice and that. (ETR, 1934)[4]

We chipped rust and did other dirty jobs; tallied cargo in port. Sometimes it was day-work, sometimes watches, 4 on and 4 off at sea – 2 hours on the wheel, 1 on lookout, 1 on standby. We weren't paid overtime. On the outward voyage in ballast coal stowed in the hold had to be transferred to the bunkers at the rate of 40 tons a day. We did that. (Ropner, 1935)[5]

Using apprentices to perform the trimmer's task was a frequent practice in white-crew ships until officially stopped in the late 30s, but one or two companies – Blue

---

[1] Contributors' private papers.
[2] ibid.
[3] ibid.
[4] ibid.
[5] ibid.

Funnel, for example – made a point of prohibiting it from the outset. Apart from its patent iniquity there was an ever-present risk of serious, if not fatal, consequences. In many cases, though, the practice was purely the initiative of the ship's master – via the mate – and even where they suspected its presence in their ships owners denied it. Not a few genuinely knew nothing of it, as they knew nothing of other characteristic eccentricities of British sea-lore, steam having tended to place ship-management at a remove from its object that would have elicited the scornful contempt of sail owners in their heyday, for all their faults.

Most of the absurd efforts at economy weren't so much due to the owners as to the masters and officers. In those depression years they were so keen on this idea of saving every penny, to be good boys. We used to do ridiculous things like trying to straighten railings using cotton waste soaked in paraffin wrapped round them and set alight. Once a beam fell through the tank-top, and they had us down there; lit a fire in the tank and tried hammering the hole closed. We were choked, you know – nearly asphyxiated – and they hauled us out. Things like that, all to save a bit of money. The officers, particularly those who'd been in sail, had a rather old-womanish attitude. (Mitchell Cotts, 1936)[1]

But of course it wasn't all work, and not all work was cheap labour. Now that the ship no longer had to be worked on its way leisure time played a larger part in the life, and the two-watch system was abolished in 1936. On the other hand the steamer worked more ports in a voyage than the sailer had done, and although the allure of foreign parts constituted one of the career's attractions it tended to dissolve in the event, for more than ever was there a need to despatch the ship with a haste that in sail would have seemed almost lunatic. As the mate made clear in one way or another, shore leave was a privilege and not one of the job's perks by right; time off usually meant the interval between one spell of duty and the next, so it came to a choice between excursion and sleep.

At the Mission there'd be tea and buns after the service. That was the main thing; you went there to get your tea and buns. Sunday nights there'd be inter-ship boxing. We went in for it to get the half-crown for losing. If you won you got five bob, but we never won; we were all sprats, little ones. When I joined the ship the captain looked at me and said, "Puir wee bugger!" Those cadets off the Royal Mail and Blue Star boats, they fed a lot better than us. Oh, yes, it made a difference. (Tatem, 1927)[2]

The senior apprentice was about a year older than me, with about a year's sea-time in. The word "macho" wasn't current at the time, but he essayed to be it, with an attitude rather than a physique that partook of the masculine. There was a right way to do everything; certain practices were essentially male, and the cardinal sin was to appear in any way soft. An essentially male practice was to go ashore when in funds and drink a gallon of beer at a sitting,

---

[1] Contributors' private papers.
[2] ibid.

so he did it, and expected me to follow suit. Native wit kept me fairly sober, aided by periodic retreats to the loo to be sick, a secret and dignified process as a consequence of which I frequently brought him, gait unsteady (his), back to the ship. Sailors preferred Birkenhead pubs because an awesome Liverpool chief constable had stamped on all music, even spontaneous singing, unless licensed, which virtually none were. Our joy was to drink and sing and chat up the girls, but in our sort of pub there were only women of a certain age commiserating in groups over their absent husbands. (Shell, 1942)[1]

During WW2 a greater than usual movement of crews between ships produced a surge of seamen of all kinds adrift on the periphery of society, enough of them to attract the notice of the community and even of Parliament, as a result of which moves were set afoot to improve their vaguely derelict (as landsmen saw it) condition, particularly since they were, *pro tem*, national heroes. Representatives of government, owners, officers and ratings accordingly formed the Seamen's Welfare Board in 1940, its brief to provide economical and good-quality board and lodging, on a non-profit-making basis, in British ports. While he was entitled to its benefits the apprentice didn't, as a rule, have need of them since he usually went home between ships, but the occasional instance arose when ships were delayed or lost.

I got to know the twelve-hour journey from London to Glasgow very well and took a spare jersey and slacks to change for a sleep *en route*. I spent nights in MN hostels in such places as Glasgow and Newcastle waiting for ships, slept in the Sailors' Home in Greenock (1/-) and made my way with trunk and kit-bag to outlandish places like Whistlefield, on a deserted Scottish loch, the nearest railhead to some remote tanker berth. (Shell, 1943)[2]

The new hostels – later hotels – supplemented existing facilities organised by charitable and religious bodies in both home and overseas ports (the familiar Sailors' Homes, for example) which had appeared as evidence of efforts to counter the more prurient enterprises of the likes of Paddy Doyle and Shanghai Brown (who, according to legend, was paid with some of his own style of service by the apprentices of the barque *Springburn* in the 1890s, finding himself at sea before the mast bound round the Horn with a sick headache and a bucko mate for company), and they were more or less taken for granted without necessarily generating a sense of benefaction. The seaman was accustomed to view efforts made for his wellbeing, when he encountered them, with a tolerant and world-weary eye, expecting nothing more than he got and neither surprised nor dismayed at its eventual disappearance, an outlook that contributed much to the moderate stance of his union leaders, comparatively speaking. Some of his philosophy rubbed off on the apprentice, naturally enough.

At Liverpool entertainment was always to be had at Atlantic House, with dances at the Apostleship of the Sea, the Flying Angel and the Gordon Smith Institute for Seamen. A cadet

---

[1] Contributors' private papers.
[2] ibid.

had to remain on board for night duty, so between the three of us we had two nights off and one on, when we cooked bacon and eggs around 2am for the duty officer's and cadet's supper, usually shared by the stevedore foreman. (Clan, 1945)[1]

From the apprentice's point of view the inter-war years probably constituted the heyday of the Flying Angel and its contemporaries. Youth was still prepared to accept, or at least tolerate, ecclesiastical overtures when leavened with social activities which the padre was – had to be – adept at organising, from picnics to football matches, dances to boxing tournaments. But shortly after WW1 another contender for the apprentice's favours arose, its exclusive aim his best – secular – interests when ashore in a strange and hazardous port. New York could be depressingly expensive and lonely, and in the piping days of prohibition casually dangerous. During the next war some sections of its populace went out of their way to extend a welcome to the battle-jaded ally, an *entente* boosted by the unexpected visit paid by the Japanese to Pearl Harbor, but anticipated, for the apprentice, by some twenty years in the shape of the British Apprentice Club.

In its prospectus of 1936 the NCP assured parents that their sons' welfare in foreign ports would be the concern of several agencies – "arrangements" had been made with the Missions to Seamen and the Overseas League, the latter a "patriotic society" membership of which would cost cadets £1:

> *Cadets can be put in touch with their fellow members wherever they go and thus never lack opportunity for friendly social intercourse with compatriots in whatever part of the world they may find themselves.*

How many took advantage of this is a matter for conjecture, but the apprentices' outlook seldom extended beyond the field of maritime affairs, and "compatriots" in this instance seemed to assume that he identified himself with shorebound expatriates, which wasn't the case. Unlike them, he hadn't emigrated, or taken up service in a colonial possession, and seldom played a part in overseas society except as a bird of passage, a contact with the home country rather than another of its prodigals. However, like the Missions to Seamen supplied with the NCP's magazine *The Log*, was the British Apprentice Club:

> *...all ex-Pangbourne cadets are cordially welcomed there and entertained while in port.* (NCP Prospectus, 1936.)

A number of colourful and discordant accounts of its beginnings were – still are, for that matter – current, one of the more prosaic putting it down to the rescue of a millionaire's son and heir from the icy waters of the Hudson by a couple of apprentices, and the millionaire's grateful response.

---

[1] Contributors' private papers.

I was a member 1922-3, when apprentice on the *City of Evansville*. We used to lie at Lilly's Wharf for three weeks or so loading for the Far East. The club was run by two very charming ladies. We were asked always to wear uniform when visiting. It was started in memory of a famous WW1 American, Admiral King[1].

The truth is somewhat less ingenuous. In one of those quirks of sentimentality woven into the patchy fabric of the US-British relationship, two wealthy doyennes of New York society, the Misses Moyca Newell and Katherine Mayo[2], hit on a way of expressing the appreciation of people in America ("the people of America") for the hospitality extended to American servicemen stationed in Britain during the war. And further, gratitude for "the sleepless[*sic*] gallantry and sacrifice of British merchant sailors", of whom, they said very appositely, 47,000 were killed and wounded in the process of transporting American soldiers to the theatre of war and supplying them while there. It seems a trifle eccentric to express gratitude for the conveyance of one's nearest and dearest to the gates of hell, but although the 47,000 didn't sacrifice themselves exclusively to that end, the sentiment was genuine, a contrast to the indifference of the British – the "maritime nation" – towards their seamen once the emergency was over: after it they begged in the streets as their forebears had done in the wake of the Armada.

But there was yet more, still in a spirit of inverted logic though none the less welcome: Miss Newell and Miss Mayo approached Mrs Page, widow of Walter Hynes Page, US Ambassador to the Court of St James from 1913 to 1918 and "friend of Britain in her sorest need"(he was instrumental in moving Congress to approve American intervention in the war as Britain's ally), to ask permission to dedicate the club to her late husband's memory, seen, as it was, to be carrying on a tradition with the apprentice as his country's envoy. Mrs Page gave her consent, and no doubt something more substantial to augment the contributions freely made by the Newell-Mayo circle, taking her place on the club's governing board, succeeded by several descendants as its story unfolded.

The club opened its doors in December, 1921, taking the "opportunity to renew the pledge of gratitude to those who gave us the Utmost[*sic*] Gift, an opportunity to show the real America through the outstretched hands of welcome to the young sons and brothers now standing in their stead"[3], and the young sons and brothers, perhaps at first a little bemused by the real America, took what was on offer at face value and

---

[1] Contributors' private papers. (Admiral E. King, USN. Not around at the time: he featured in the later war as an Anglophobic participant in the running of the Battle of the Atlantic.)

[2] (1868-1940): Journalist and author of several controversial and searching studies of social conditions about the world including, most famously, *Mother India*, a detailed exposé of native customs including child marriage, caste and politics under the British Raj, which produced indignation and anger among Hindus.

[3] *BAC Review*, Vol.1, No.4, p.2.

were duly grateful in their turn, if later plaudits are anything to go by. The club occupied a suite of rooms in the Hotel Chelsea on West 23rd St., a New York landmark still extant, and remained there until changing times saw fewer British apprentices in the port, in rather less straitened circumstances than hitherto and inclined to spend what time and money they had in a more free-ranging fashion.

Unlike the Flying Angel and its peers, the club possessed the great attraction of a secular, not to say anarchic, policy. Penance wasn't sought in return for innocent pleasures and the place was, so to speak, conscience-free:

The Club being run by Apprentices of the British Merchant Marine, there are no rules except those enforced by the majority...present on any given occasion...[1]

– the majority gently influenced by the presence at all times of Miss Newell, Miss Mayo or someone of their team of capable assistants, prominent among them the indomitable Mrs Hollon C. Spaulding[2], who, with Miss Newell, received the OBE in 1947 for her work. The purpose of this intrepid band of American matronhood was

...to establish a Fireside Corner and provide hospitality for the cadet officers of the British Merchant Marine visiting New York, where they are free to do the things they enjoy [sic] – ping-pong, billiards, dancing, reading or just sitting around the tea table talking, making the Club as much like home as possible...[3]

Notes, 1922.
March 26.
Dame Clara Butt, giving a recital at the Hippodrome, sent the BAC a present of 20 tickets, with her greeting. At the close of the concert the cadets, all in uniform, gave her three cheers, whereupon Dame Clara sang specially for them Land of Hope and Glory *and* Annie Laurie.

October 31.
On the invitation of Miss Margaret Stevenson Mrs Spaulding and cadets Bernard, Newcomb, Bolton, Ralph, Bell, Verney, Thomas, Horne, Harris, Vizer, Rigby, Barker, Chambers, Hall, Spriggs, Bowyer, Graville, Lidiard, Ewer, Rogers, Russell and Crisp attended the Hallowe'en dance given by the probationary nurses of the Presbyterian Hospital.[4]

By the end of 1922 1,292 apprentices had become members[5] – some, of course, never to return, which was in the nature of the life they had chosen.

My last trip was on the *Ixion*... The lady looking after the club was a Mrs Spaulding, a very friendly and fine person indeed; she was responsible for picking out the girls who

---

[1] *BAC Review*, Vol.1, No.4, p.1. (1924)
[2] Lucile B. Spaulding.
[3] *BAC Review*, 1952.
[4] *BAC Review*, 1922.
[5] Beginning on the first visit membership continued thereafter until one's time was out.

attended the club evenings. There were dance nights and on Sundays we had games and a sing-song. Arrangements were made for sight-seeing tours, ski trips, etc and on one occasion we were taken to see a musical comedy on Broadway; on another about thirty of us, including the girls, went to a dance at the Pennsylvania Hotel. (Blue Funnel, 1924)[1]

Jim and I were looking forward to the prospect of free suppers at the Mission and the Apprentices[*sic*] Club, cakes and buns, chocolate-coated dates, figs, ginger-beer and ice-cream. But the 3rd mate and his cohorts decided to smarten us up and sheared our scalps then applied hair tonic – kerosene – before threatening to give us a singe as well. Luckily the 2nd mate, Mr Thomas, appeared and asked them if they hadn't something better to do, and that was that. In the evening we, visited the Club. Removing our caps not only revealed our convict-style haircuts but also released a pungent odour which kept everyone at arm's length. (Reardon Smith, 1928)[2]

There were police patrols in the Lower Brooklyn area, motor-cycle and sidecar with mounted machine-gun. In the club refreshments were always available – coffee, soft drinks, biscuits and fig rolls with something more substantial on dance nights. There were usually one or two volunteer ladies to supervise and a sprinkling of refined young ladies to help, and shake a leg, quite a few partners on hand for the Sunday evening hops to gramophone music. The club's secretary was a gently-persuaded volunteer from among the senior apprentices likely to be in port for more than a week, whose function was to keep a log of happenings and take action when the fig rolls were running low. Sometimes small groups were entertained at Miss Mayo's house in Bedford Hills, and I organised a trip to an original Australian convict transport[3] moored in the Hudson. On another occasion I went with a party to a college in lower NY State where we endeavoured to instruct those about to visit schools in England in the art of cricket. (Federal, 1928)[4]

Needless to say, the girls and refined young ladies had impeccable credentials, and neither the estimable Mrs Spaulding nor the other ladies were remotely connected with what might have been read between some unfortunately-phrased lines.

I was one of eight apprentices on the *City of Bagdad*, and we visited the club together. Mrs Spaulding was a lovely lady who took a motherly interest in us and ran the club like a ship. The log had to be kept daily and signed by all, and some City Line apprentices had presented a ship's bell they'd acquired. I used to visit the Radio City theatre one night a week and the club the rest of the time. There was a waffle night, when girls turned up to make them, with sandwiches and coffee on other nights; as we were on a good feeder we left the sandwiches for

---

[1] Contributors' private papers.
[2] *Let Go Fore & Aft*, p.10.
[3] The barquentine *Success*, which carried not convicts but emigrants, after which she did service as a prison hulk in Melbourne before going on show as a "convict" ship in Sydney and later in England. She crossed to the States in 1912 for the same purpose, was converted to a cargo motor-ship in WW1, sunk in collision with ice, raised, and returned to her alias as a convict transport, shown from place to place including the Chicago World Fair of 1933.
[4] Contributors' private papers.

the lads from the tramps – but not the waffles. Mrs Spaulding told me never to wear gloves when going up and down ladders; she said bare hands gave a surer grip. (1933)[1]

Apart from the friendly atmosphere, lounge and other amenities, the fridge was always full of sandwiches and fresh milk. There were at least forty of us at any one time and cleaned it out every evening. Being young and fairly stupid we couldn't resist the Oasis Tavern next-door to the hotel, but the sandwiches kept us fairly sober and everyone was well-behaved on club premises. (NZS, 1944)[2]

What an exciting time, seeing Betty Grable, Tommy Dorsey and Benny Goodman with my American friends. A juke-box in the corner operated without money but this was known only to a few, who urged newcomers to feed it and later collected the booty to fund visits to the bar downstairs. (Reardon Smith, 1944)[3]

It was our misfortune that at the time we were in port most of the big Cunarders were also, and their cadets more or less took over the club while their officers did the same at the Officers' Club near Times Square. (*Baron Forbes*, 1944)

I joined the club as a survivor from the *Yorkwood*. A principal patron was Madelaine Carroll whose husband Sterling Hayden was a master in the American merchant marine. She supplied tickets for shows and events at Madison Square Gardens and more suitable clothes for the winter when she saw the lightweight suits we'd been given on landing at Florida. Mrs Spaulding used her connections to get us repatriated sooner than otherwise; I visited the club over the next two years and her hospitality never waned, supported by local families. Her dedication was truly remarkable. (Constantine Shipping, 1943)[4]

Repatriation meaning, of course, a return to the war after a spell of survivor's leave, two weeks, before appointment to another ship, either of the company to which the apprentice was indentured or the first available under the SF/MOWT pool arrangement.

Experiences in both wars were similar: boredom, extra duties, extreme conditions (and some improvements), tension, bemusement, incomprehension and a daily expectation of the unthinkable. Occasionally, war exploded all round, but for most of the time the battle was, as ever, with the sea.

The convoy numbered over 80 ships. We spent our time on the bridge watching for signals with a telescope and repeating them to our next astern. At night signal lamps replaced flags. We also kept the log, made tea and generally made ourselves useful. Usually there were only three watchkeepers – officer, helmsman and cadet. The night watches seemed endless, the dim blue stern-light of the ship ahead and the vague shadows of nearby ships the only things to be seen. A storm blew up and we were ordered to scatter and re-form when it had passed, and for

[1] Contributors' private papers.
[2] ibid.
[3] ibid.
[4] ibid.

three days we rode it out, swept by heavy seas and a polar wind, sleet, snow and frozen spray. On the open bridge we sheltered behind a canvas dodger. The extra bunker coal on deck blocked the freeing ports and the well-deck filled, causing a serious list, and for some time, as we rode with wind and sea on the quarter the mate and his men waded about waist-deep clearing the ports. After two days of unbroken labour the ship was righted and we rejoined the convoy, a pitiful sight with gaps everywhere and the ships well battered. (PSNC, 1917)[1]

I kept the 12-4 with the 2nd mate, the senior apprentice the 4-8 with the mate. We knew of ships where the apprentices were keeping watch about, perhaps the last British deep-sea sailors to do so. We had no regulation hours, and worked on deck in the forenoon watch as well, mostly maintaining boats, always swung out in readiness. Otherwise it was chipping, painting and general sailorising. On the bridge we handled the signal flags, in constant use in convoy. There was quiet competition between ships for the quickest repeat of the commodore's signals, and occasionally it was possible to see through the telescope the commodore's signalman making up the hoist, and your response would go up almost at the same time. With practice we could name the flag at sight of the first couple of inches to appear. By day a lot of signalling was by Aldis (*Keep closed up* was the commonest order), but night signalling was severely restricted and radio silence kept at all times. Frequent speed alterations were necessary to keep station, and it was our job to phone the directions to the engine-room: *Down four, please* or *Up two* (or *Up you*, which passed unremarked by a deafened engineer below). In fog we streamed a marker astern which scooped up a fountain of water for the benefit of the next ship in line. We were also responsible for the patent log, reading and managing it, and in pilotage we worked the engine telegraph and kept the movement log; often one of us took the wheel, better able to understand the pilot's orders: the crew were Chinese, good sailors. The old quartermaster coming to the wheel at midnight addressed us with perfect propriety: to the 2nd mate "Good morning, sir" and to me "Good morning, boy".

Apart from the 4-inch gun at the stern, which served no purpose in convoy, our armament consisted of two twin-Browning Colt 0.5-inch HMG's on the bridge wings. The other apprentice had the port gun, I the starboard, and from somewhere we found a couple of tin hats which we painted with MSS[2] and felt very smart. We did a little practice firing from time to time. The captain insisted that in action whatever I did I was to "fire that gun", which I did in fine style, never sure of what I was firing at; a convoy was a dangerous place. (Shell, 1942)[3]

The *Glaucus* was slow, and the Atlantic convoys were terrible, making only 3½ to 4½ knots, sometimes bare steerage way. Some of the old coal-burners were real cripples, restricted to particular times for boiler-cleaning[4]. We sheered about all over the place in bad weather. Half-way across it was the custom to have gunnery exercise, when the four of us were sent to the engine-room, not to learn about engines but to prevent our being injured during the practice. It didn't matter so much about men and officers because they were wage-earners, but the Old Man was responsible to the company for us, and the company to our parents, so he didn't wilfully put us at risk. The gunnery didn't seem to be so much a threat to the enemy as a

---

[1] *Pilot Aboard*, p.61.

[2] Matt Surface, Side. The other was MSD – Matt Surface, Deck: both grey.

[3] Contributors' private papers.

[4] That is, blowing tubes to clear the soot.

danger to ourselves; it tended to be a bit indiscriminate. Shrapnel flew about. (Blue Funnel, 1944)[1]

So it went on, and if you were particularly unlucky your ship stopped a torpedo...

It was a clear moonlit night with a slight sea and swell, and I was on lookout on the port wing, my sector from dead ahead to dead astern; the 3rd mate was on the starboard wing and an AB on the wheel. When the standby man came up before calling the next watch I asked him the time, and just as he told me – 2325 – there was an almighty bang and a blast that knocked us flying. When I got up and gathered my wits we were dead in the water with a starboard list and smoke shrouding everything. I wasn't hurt, so grabbed my lifejacket as the Old Man rushed out and ordered abandon ship. The boats on the port side had been blown inboard and everyone was running for the starboard boats, where the deck was almost awash; so I followed, with my grab-bag, an old gas-mask case containing my ID card, Mars bar, extra pair of socks and my camera, and some personal papers. My boat was already launched, so I jumped for the falls and lowered myself to it. There were fifteen aboard, and we had to bail like mad; she was clinker-built and hadn't touched the water for two years at least, but in spite of our efforts she settled to the gunwales, then the people from the other boat, which had capsized, tried to board us, and over we went as well. I lost my grab-bag.

Meanwhile the ship had settled by the head, and I made for a life-raft astern of her, where seven others joined me. The second cook was hanging onto the propeller, and we managed to save him before the ship went down. You could hear things breaking adrift inside as she slowly sank, and as we watched a shell hit the funnel followed by a regular stream, about sixty, obviously from the deck-gun of the U-boat that had torpedoed us, though we couldn't see him. At about 1.30am the ship, well on fire, went down and the U-boat materialised, no light showing. A voice hailed us in English, asking for the Old Man. None of us knew where he was, and if we had we'd have been tempted to point him out; he was a miserable old devil who'd given the four of us a difficult time one way and another. Instead we told the voice our port of departure and what we'd been carrying – nothing, only water ballast – and he slid off leaving us alone again.

But not for long, and when he reappeared I saw, to my amazement, my mate Hancock on the casing, and the 2nd mate said, "What the hell's he doing there?" When the voice told us someone should help Hancock to get to the raft because he couldn't swim, he dived in and towed poor Hancock over. The U-boat had kept at a distance to avoid damaging the raft, because a chop had got up.

Hancock was a bit of a hero. After fighting for possession of an oar with a DEMS gunner he'd floated about on his own before the U-boat loomed up and he'd got a grip at a ballast intake or something; it was only doing a couple of knots. Some sailors pulled him aboard and the commander questioned him, to no useful end, since none of us knew anything of importance, and the session ended with the German telling him that when he got home he wasn't to return to sea or it would be the worse for him if he got caught, but the four of us were back three months later. The German had startled Hancock by revealing that he knew the apprentice's home town as well as he did. His English was certainly immaculate, and before

---

[1] Contributors' private papers.

leaving he gave us our position – 485 miles NW of Puerto Rico – and wished us good luck, ignoring a fireman's request for a tow to the nearest island.

At dawn we sighted the boats, one in charge of the Old Man, and left the raft after finding the biscuit tanks empty – momento of Suez – and transferring the water tank. The galley-boy and DEMS gunner, both 18, were missing. Then we set off for the West Indies, linked by a gantline.

I thought it a bit of an adventure, but some of the older men were downcast. Our ration was an ounce of water three times a day, a spoonful of pemmican, as it was called, two Horlicks tablets and a spoonful of condensed milk. We collected rain in the sail. Though the nights were comfortable the days were terribly hot, and all I had on was a singlet and trousers, but others were worse off. Hot oil had scalded the 4th engineer over about two-thirds of his body and on the seventh day he died. His brother, the third, was in the boat, and removed the fourth's gold ring before the body was put overside, and after that things got very bad. None too soon, on the morning of the ninth day, HMS *Saxifrage* picked us up and landed us at San Juan, Puerto Rico, where we were kitted out in donated gear, mine a pair of white-striped green pants and a pink shirt. I was more worried by what they'd think when I got home than by what had happened in the boat, but later, after an overnight earthquake, we were given suits and a passage on a United Fruit ship to Norfolk, Va., from where we went on to New York and a glorious three weeks being feted and entertained.

The voyage home was a let-down, three of us on the *Empire Allonzo* – me, another apprentice, and the Old Man. But I won't dwell on that. (ss *Putney Hill*, Counties Ship Management, 1943[1])[2]

And then, come war or peace, came school, exams and examiners. As ever, sea-time was the crucial factor rather than what had been learned, and whether the closing months had been spent in the half-deck, or as an uncertificated officer or a rating, no-one looked upon extra time with favour unless it meant necessary funding for what was to come. Blue Funnel's idiosyncratic devaluation of *Conway*'s credentials meant midshipmen serving more than the BOT requirement, time wasted that could otherwise have counted towards the mate's ticket and which, in fact, later did so; but at least one Conway called the company's bluff:

By the time I was appointed to the *Glenogle* I was feeling restless, partly owing to the routine nature of the work and partly because I had enough time in for my ticket; also, I was 21. So I wrote asking to be released from my indentures, saying I'd completed the three years normal for a *Conway* boy, and that another few months wouldn't be of any benefit to me. On arrival home I was summoned to the marine superintendent, not noted for affability towards junior officers, and in a chilly interview gained my release, with the implication that I'd stepped out of court. I was made no offer of future employment, from which I supposed that

---

[1] The submarine was U-203, Kapitanleutnant Hermann Kottmann; lost, presumed sunk, 25th April, 1943.
[2] Contributors' private papers.

my RNR appointment and early release hadn't appealed. Still, the indenture was endorsed to the effect that I'd served to the company's entire satisfaction. (1937)[1]

For many the end of a personal era was significant in ways not anticipated at the outset, and, the need to earn a living apart, considerations of the future embraced more than straightforward progression to command and whatever might lie beyond.

During the last two years I had a think; I liked the sea and liked to be near it, but the captain said, "Look, boys – you're going to finish now, and if I find you at sea again I'll kick your bloody arses. I've been thirty-five years at it, and only two of them at home. (1916)[2]

Thinking of the stupid bantering chaff and the repetitive inanities of double-meaning that passed for conversation in our shipboard life I felt despondent and wondered whether, perhaps, I was just being priggish in wishing to discover deeper and more subtle meanings in things; but in my heart I knew that what I sought was right and true. And, as always when thinking this way, I became hot in my hatred of the board schools that had so ill-prepared me, half-realising with bitterness the demarcation between the instructed and the uninstructed, knowing that I was on the wrong side of the fence. Unhappily I wondered if, in the turmoil of ships and the sea, foreign ports and whore-shanties and the troublesome business of being a tough young hard-case mate[3], with my love of exploration up every tortuous path, I was not already lost. This life at sea, in spite of its crudities and hardships, was much better than being an office-boy in some obscure Midland town. Anyway, I had no choice; I would get my tickets. (PSNC, 1915)[4]

Which, with time served with the Pacific Steam Navigation Company, would be for *Steamship, Foreign-Going*, while the square-rig ticket from this date forward rapidly assumed the interesting but ambivalently-regarded status of anachronism.

[I went to] the Nautical College, Liverpool...[and] after endless study and swotting...entered my papers...with my application to sit for my [ticket]. On the Monday morning, in a new suit from Gieves, clean shirt and hair well-combed, I presented myself along with twenty or thirty other applicants for the examination, [held]in a large room [overlooked] by the Almighty in the person of the dreaded Captain Sargent...at his high desk...Quite a large [proportion] were taking square-rig tickets...[For the seamanship exam I confronted Sargent at a table littered with] models of windjammers, masts, yards, coastlines, miniature tackles and [other familiar objects]...He said, "I see your last ship was *Naiad*...She was my last command in sail. Tell me something about her." [I did so and he appeared quite interested. Then he asked me about the *Lusitania* [5]] and by the time I'd finished...nearly two hours [had passed]; the others outside had decided that I must be having a very rough time...Sargent finished...by

---

[1] Contributors' private papers.

[2] ibid.

[3] In a general sense, that is: 3rd mate, to be exact, and uncertificated.

[4] *Journey from Obscurity*, p.101.

[5] The writer left his windjammer in New York on completion of his time and worked his passage home in the liner. He was at the wheel when he saw two torpedoes strike the ship forward, bringing about the ensuing tragedy.

asking me to me to tack…and wear ship, [then if I intended taking a master's ticket in sail, adding, on my affirmation, that I'd require to know a lot more seamanship]…

I was appointed 3rd officer of the…*Tyria* and…found a world of difference…between life in a windjammer and [in]…a steamer[1]. (1918)[2]

Then, in 1930, the so-called square-rig certificate was discontinued, not least because too few examiners were qualified to conduct the exam. As for the examining authority, the Act of 1914 (the Merchant Shipping (Certificates) Act) which had placed control of the conduct and arrangement of the examinations in the hands of the BOT direct, didn't succeed in entirely eradicating the examinations' regional distinguishing marks, which persisted in the *viva* while myth and fable continued to surround the individuals in whose power lay the candidates' professional life and death; perfectly ordinary men continued to acquire, or inherit, sometimes to their own bafflement, a Brobdingnagian stature:

I discovered that a new subject had been included: trigonometry, plain and oblique-angled [*sic*]. Having left school at…thirteen and a half, I knew nothing of this subject, nor of algebra and geometry…   However, I attended Captain Tate's School of Navigation in Oswald St., [Liverpool] and at the end of two weeks handed in my papers…   Monday, Tuesday and Wednesday were…allotted to the written papers, which included navigation, nautical astronomy, trigonometry, chartwork, tides and reduction to soundings, and a free essay. As my topic I chose *Joining my First Ship* and in my innocence told the truth, describing the drunken crew supervised by officers themselves "three sheets in the wind". I was called before the examiner, who was not amused, and was told that all he required were the names of the…officers, whose certificates he would deal with. Then he handed my paper back with the suggestion that I choose another subject. I chose *Tides and the Augmentation of the Moons' Semi-Diameter*. This time I must have struck an acceptable note…   Each morning the names of those who had failed in their previous day's work were read out, and they left the room…No wonder we listened in fear and trembling for our names…   Thursday and Friday…was mostly devoted to oral work and signalling. The few who were left by Friday afternoon faced the greatest ordeal of all, Oral Seamanship and Rule of the Road at Sea. Failure meant a sentence of three to six months' sea service before sitting again! Even the…charm of a pretty receptionist was denied us. Instead, a grumpy old male clerk called out our names…   I entered the hallowed room, and stood before the old captain, who…had sent his own son to sea for six months[3] - but his ship was lost and he was never seen again. He was sitting behind a table loaded with models of ships…   His white torpedo beard and ruddy face made his pale blue eyes look doubly cold…[and] at one point I stumbled…   "Feeling nervous, Lindsay?…If you're nervous before a bloody table – what will you be like at sea?" [After] my last question [he]…pulled a small blue pad from [a] drawer…signed one of the…forms…and handed it to me…   All I wanted to do now was to get to the door…   Success is always sweet, even if it has

---

[1] No further sea-time in sail was required for higher-grades of square-rig certificate; 12 months sufficed, and by this time was about the most that could be had.

[2] *The Long Wake*, pp.127-131.

[3] Presumably *back* to sea, for failing to come up with the right answers.

been achieved more by luck than by knowledge... This lack of knowledge and application was brought home to me the hard way a few weeks later, when I was alone on the bridge and in charge of the...watch on a Geordie tramp steamer. (1919)[1]

Preparatory tuition varied from port to port but within the bounds of a family likeness, some schools forming departments of technical colleges, others perpetuating the *laisser-faire* of earlier days in the enterprises of individuals, some of them mathematicians and theorists without sea service, others sea captains come ashore for one reason or another. Typifying the scene's general perspective was the pattern in South Wales, a region passing through its high-water mark of coal export, metal-working and tramp ownership. In 1914 Mr D.E. Manson began teaching BOT candidates at his school in Newport, Mon., shifting to the hub of commercial activity in 1918 and premises above a café in Queen St., Cardiff, next-door to the Alexandra Hotel, where Captain Beavan gave seamanship lectures in the saloon. Beavan had set up a school with Captain Jutsum in 1902 and kept it going when Jutsum returned to sea in 1914, later joining forces with Manson. They moved to better premises in 1920 and again in 1923, when Beavan went back to sea for his health, his place taken by Captain Vickery who shortly afterwards departed for a post at Sir John Cass, to be replaced by Captain F.G. Merrifield. Merrifield worked with Manson until the latter retired in 1930, when he was joined by another sea captain, Gibbs, for a few months, in his turn replaced by Captain T.G. Jones. At that point (1931) Captain W.C. Aubrey-Rees closed his Neptune Nautical Academy, passing his students to Merrifield before following Vickery to Sir John Cass. Merrifield and Jones continued together until in 1936 Merrifield accepted a post at Cardiff Technical College in place of a lecturer who had joined the BOT as a surveyor/examiner, Captain T.E. Lewis. Jones pressed on alone until, a few months later, he and his activities were absorbed by the Technical College's navigation department, where he worked until moving to a teaching post in Bristol in 1945.

The Technical College's navigation department accordingly captured the entire tuition market in South Wales, catering for all grades of certificate, after its beginnings in 1919 with an intake of 15 candidates. In 1925 the BOT recognised the course of 3 months, regular attendance earning equal sea-time. An apprentice could therefore enrol after completing 3 years 9 months at sea, though of course he remained on indentures and pay, such as it was, for the full 4 years. The concession applied equally to shorter indentured service, to the accepted minimum of 3 years, so that those who had already earned remission of sea-time from a pre-sea training course of the kind offered by *Conway* and her contemporaries could attempt the exam after only 2 years 9 months at sea, cadets having to show their time on articles, of course.

In London the distillation process resulted in two schools, King Edward VII, which dealt only with the 2nd mate's exam, and the Sir John Cass Institute. During WW1 two shipmasters, Thornton and Wood, taken prisoner when their ships were sunk by

---

[1] *Sailor in Steam*, p.28.

the raider *Moewe*, conducted navigation classes in the POW camp, and after repatriation set up the Thornwood Nautical School in the city, absorbing three others including Broughton's, then in its turn being taken over by the Cass Institute in the 20s, an event marking the end of private tuition in London as well as Board of Education approval and grant aid for the institute, prompting an observer to remark, sourly, that cramming would henceforth be funded by public money.

Depression in the 20s nearly forced the closure of the School of Navigation in Plymouth, avoided by support from a number of influential figures, but the further slump in the 30s brought about merger with the Plymouth and Devonport Technical College in 1933. When a Mr Keast took over a year later, innocent of both navigation and seamanship, the deficiency was made good by sundry naval officers *en passant*, and while numbers remained low the pass record was maintained in spite of the premises being reduced to a single room for all purposes at the outbreak of war. When Keast retired in 1944 a Captain F.W. Johnson took over to begin a resurgence that carried the school into the post-war era on an optimistic note.

Because of the drift away from the sea during the 20s and 30s, war and the abrupt increase in demand for tonnage produced a dearth of officers that had not happened in the earlier conflict, and adjustments were made by the BOT (as the MOWT) in the shape of MOWT (Ministry of Shipping) Notice No. 197[1], which provided, *inter alia*, for time served beyond the normal requirement (3-4 years) for 2nd mate to count towards qualifying time for 1st mate. By it, an apprentice at sea when his indentures expired could count the remainder of the voyage as valid sea-time up to the total required for the 1st mate's exam without first having passed for 2nd mate, provided he had accumulated enough watchkeeping experience. Few went for it, those who did mostly RNR people who had completed their time in the navy, unable to get ashore for long enough to study for and sit the exam for 2nd mate. The other change was a reduction of qualifying sea-time for 2nd mate from 4 to 3 years, with a corresponding drop of the minimum age to 19. The certificate issued was designated *Temporary*, exchangeable for a full ticket on completion of normal sea service. In practice the temporary document was usually kept until exchanged for a 1st mate's ticket, since it had the validity of a full ticket in application. The measure remained in force until the former peacetime arrangements were reinstituted in 1948.

As for sea-time itself at this period, there was little delay in its accumulation, with leave almost non-existent and the pool arrangement in force, with its higher incidence of cadets on articles than apprentices on indentures.

My time ended in 1939 – 3 years 8 months. Conditions had suddenly improved. Wages shot up[2] with various increments, and proper paid leave came in. When I started, you went on leave

---

[1] See appx 4.

[2] Not exactly. Wages didn't rise until the war-risk bonus scheme ended, when they rose to incorporate it.

and that was that, so you didn't, unless it was a day or two at the master's discretion[1]. (Sun Shipping)[2]

An examination for EDH was introduced in 1936, required for promotion from ordinary seaman to AB and regarded as ancillary to the 2nd mate's certificate though not mandatory; candidates were, however, required to possess a lifeboatman's certificate, while the MN Defence Course, begun in 1937, was obligatory from 1939, divided into the categories of Ordinary and Gunnery.

The difficulty of finding a berth during the depression deterred many from attempting the examination, while voices were heard condemning a system which continued to hold examinations and issue certificates as if nothing untoward were happening. A school of opinion had it that the exam should be strictly competitive with passes awarded according to demand, but the obvious objection was that this would introduce vagaries in place of a consistent standard which was desirable as much in fairness to the candidates as in the interests of overall competence. In any case bureaucracy jibbed at such a radical proposal, departing from a norm that had been hewn with so much solemn confabulation from the resistant stuff of establishment conservatism.

When I paid off the *Prince Rupert City* the future looked bleak. Ships were laid up everywhere and qualified men on the scrap-heap, willing to take anything on offer to keep their families. I decided there was nothing worth attending school for, but I had to get a job, so found one in London as a vacuum-cleaner salesman, commission only, and lost money. Then one as a ticket-taker at the Leicester Square Theatre, 30/- for a 6-day week. There was a racket in tickets and I played along for a while, but in the end told the others I'd had enough. As it happened I was moved to the dress circle as usher, and soon afterwards Scotland Yard broke the thing up and people were dismissed. I was never questioned. (Reardon-Smith, 1931)[3]

In fact WW2 enforced a kind of adjustment of standards through the reduction of sea-time unofficially augmented by a less rigorous assessment of the candidate's fitness for the job – being sent back to sea for fumbled answers in the *viva* was unknown, for example. Also, the increase in demand brought many back to the fold from the hinterland – the Leicester Square Theatre, meat-portering at Smithfield, debt-collecting for an advertising agency, general factotum in a department store, and deckhand in foreign-flag ships among its landmarks. Those who had found berths in the focsles of British-flag ships were among the lucky ones.

I signed on as AB in Union Steam's *Awatea* and found that the free and easy atmosphere was due to the seamen's union and its blackmailing practices[4]; all the crowd thought of was the

---

[1] This applied to officers on articles.

[2] Contributors' private papers.

[3] *Let Go Fore & Aft*, p.46.

[4] This was the New Zealand organisation, whose euphemism for blackmail was, as elsewhere, "free collective bargaining".

next strike and the next booze-up, but I stuck at it and eventually made bosun. Then in late 1941 a new 3rd mate joined, an old pal from apprentice days, he with his ticket and me only the bosun. It made me think, and I decided to go up for my ticket, nine years late. But I'd had a good grounding at the sea-school and my fiancée helped with stuff like the [Collision-Prevention] Rules, and I passed with flying colours at Auckland in 1942, when we got married, and after a short honeymoon I resigned from the NZ seamen's union and joined the Officers' Guild. My first job was 2nd mate of the chemical carrier *Piri*, owned by ICI.[1]

I didn't go up for my ticket because of the slump. Things were very hard, masters sailing as AB's. It didn't seem worth it, so I went with my father, in the garage. (1931)[2]

He'd got as far as his 2nd mate's ticket when the bottom dropped out of shipping, so he took anything – peddling silk stockings, whatever; temporary jobs, in London. Then Mother spoke to a man in the village who had connections with an aeroplane factory – Boulton Paul – and he thought he might get John something. So John went to Dumbarton and had a magnificent job, following the nuts and bolts round the production-line, a Shop's Progress man. From there he would have progressed, presumably, but the war came and he joined the navy. It was what he'd always wanted. (1931-39)[3]

But for the ones who decided to continue in the certainty of a berth or in hopes that something would turn up, either in time to save them from the uncharted wastes of shore prospects or in the shape of an acceptable change of course away from the sea, the schools at least offered a way of killing time.

The Cass Nautical College was in Jewry St., off Aldgate. The instructors were quite good, under Captain Thornton, their personalities reflected in the degrees of student attention. On Thursday afternoon was an inspiring session on cargo-handling, ship's business and the like, so the drill was to sign on at Mansell St labour exchange soon after midday and draw the 14/- dole, pop into Dirty Dick's for a half of mild and bitter and a cheese roll, then bus to the Elephant & Castle and the 6d matinee, something like Quentin MacLean at the Wurlitzer and a couple of films.

In the exams the *bete noir* was Captain Baker, a renowned killer on seamanship and Rule of the Road, but I breezed through. It must have been his annual Good Day. On the other hand I made a pig's ear of my chartwork, but they let me take it again the following week and gave me a ticket. We got the lifeboat ticket for good attendance, a day's boating in the docks. The first-aid ticket was a travesty. Six 1-hour talks in school then a five-minute visit to a surgery in Southwark Bridge Rd to tell someone how to fold a triangular bandage and find two pressure-points. While waiting about for a ship I played rugby for Vauxhall Motors, which led me into a new line of business and I settled for a shore job. (1934)[4]

---

[1] *Let Go Fore & Aft*, p.103.

[2] Contributors' private papers.

[3] ibid.

[4] ibid.

I got my ticket at the worst of times. Most companies had waiting lists as long as your arm, and what made it worse was that cadets whose abilities had left something to be desired were mysteriously being signed on. I had no connections and found it impossible to place my application before a responsible person, constantly running into some clerk at the door with the power to refuse or grant an audience with the proper authority. After two years I was still waiting. (1934)[1]

I stayed for a time at Jack's Palace, the Sailors' Home in Dock St., Limehouse, next-door to the shipping office and exam rooms. The food was abominable, chiefly coarse rice, and in the "cabins" bare feet picked up splinters. Before I got my ticket the Crystal Palace burned down and King Edward VIII abdicated. (1936)[2]

Navigation was a failing paper and a friend of mine could only answer three questions, so he knew he was out. I stayed with him at his parents' house in Kensington, and went along with him when he went on the town to celebrate his demise. We ended up at a bottle party somewhere at three in the morning, and when we finally got to bed as dawn was breaking I'd decided not to go on. But I woke as usual, staggered down to Dock St., and a week later learned that I'd passed. My friend slept on, and was carpeted by the chief examiner, who sent him back to sea for three months, and I never saw him again.

Trade was picking up and personnel were suddenly in short supply, particularly company people. RML had invested in us, unlike some who chucked their apprentices out at the end of their time suggesting it would be a good idea if they had their master's tickets next time they looked in[3]. One of RM's chief competitors was Vestey's Blue Star Line, where RM-trained officers were welcome, but I was seduced by promises of cruising, and went off in the *Atlantis* as 5th officer having the time of my life. (1936)[4]

I signed on at Leith Nautical College to get the feel of the exam, held every four weeks at Glasgow. I gave myself six weeks, which the others said was pushing my luck, and anyway why not enjoy more leisure on the dole? Most hadn't had a *Conway* training, and most companies didn't give the sort of training I'd had with Blue Funnel, even if the practical side had been overdone; in our last year we could have had more bridge experience and greater involvement with planning cargo stowage and ship-management. Instruction at Leith was very good. One of my *Conway* term sat the exam with me and we sailed through. (1938)[5]

I stayed at the Seamark Junior Officers' Club at Tower Hill. It was started by Tubby Clayton, the Toc-H man. Fellow in charge was a South African, also a reverend, and the matron was a Miss Parsons, called "Aunty" by everyone. It was quite a nice place. The school was very good, some good masters. Aubrey-Rees wrote *Shipmaster's Business*, L.P. Taylor a book about cargo stowage, and another chap, Murray, did met. and Rule of the Road. Aubrey-Rees did navigation, chartwork, stuff like that; Taylor did the stability, seamanship and so on. Cameron, the principal, was a very good chap, though some said King Ted's had a better,

---

[1] *Ahoy!*, p.114.
[2] Contributors' private papers.
[3] Among which Blue Funnel was not numbered.
[4] Contributors' private papers.
[5] ibid.

Captain Chase. Everyone called him Charlie Chase, after the comic actor, but there was nothing comic about him; strict disciplinarian and a very clever fellow. But Cass's was good. I studied for all my tickets there.

Aubrey-Rees was a bit of a pedant, always on about the Rule of the Road. Someone called it contradictory, which fired him up. He said, "Let me tell you something – those articles were drafted by lawyers", and this chap said that was obvious. A-R glared at him and said they weren't in any way contradictory, could only be read one way; lawyers had consulted him for technical details and between them they'd done a good job[1]. He got really steamed up about it. He was a funny old boy. Murray, though – when he lectured everyone sat up. He took exactly three months to go through the syllabus and knew exactly what was coming up in the next exam. He'd ask "What is time?" and we'd offer one or two novel ideas. "No!" he'd say. "*Time is the chronological means of registering the passing of events and phenomena!*" All these little angles. He could make an obtuse subject sound easy. Cameron was the same. (1938)[2]

Captain James Boyd ran a school in a single room, spartan accommodation and well-worn instruments, but he was a brilliant instructor, always achieving good results. All grades were accommodated in the room, home-trade mate to master foreign-going. Seating was by seniority, master f-g nearest the tiny gas-fire. We did signals every morning, 9 to 10, and one afternoon a week was given to seamanship, Rule of the Road with ship-handling, rigging jury rudders, running kedge anchors and headings of square-riggers in fog. A few of the examiners had square-rig tickets and were given to such questions. Boyd took a 6-month fee, which allowed a couple of attempts, exams held once a month in Belfast. Brown, Son & Ferguson published a book called *Self-Examiner for Masters and Mates*, and we worked through it, with Boyd on hand. The exam consisted of three days of writtens – principles of navigation, practical navigation, chartwork, met., seamanship and an essay, leaving seamanship orals and signals, all over by Friday. Particularly dense candidates were sent back to sea, but it never happened in my time. The general perception was that you had to have a fatal accident or create a chain-reaction of collisions to qualify. (1940)[3]

Most apprentices stayed at the Seamark Club if attending the Cass school. I was there during the fire-bombing. One night the place next-door was set on fire and we all went to fight it. It turned out to be a champagne warehouse. Most of us slept under the tables. Studying was difficult. Others stayed at Jack's Palace, convenient to the King Edward VII school. (1940)[4]

---

[1] Of what, though, isn't clear, for collisions still occur under rules which are essentially the same as when first drafted, on an *ad hoc* basis, in 1862. Changes based on sound logical principles are still heroically resisted by the establishment, with no good reason. In this respect at least Aubrey-Rees was an exemplar of the official attitude (and indeed of the compliant attitude of most watchkeeping officers), regarded by many, including this author, as pig-headed. The collision-prevention rules, so-called, provide nothing of more practical use than a retrospective yard-stick for apportioning blame and liability after the event. That they don't prevent collision is self-evident, and in fact can be shown to contribute to its cause. (See *The Fatal Flaw*.)

[2] Contributors' private papers.

[3] ibid.

[4] ibid.

Classes were held in the lower hold, as it were – as near to and below street level as possible. Instruction was in a series of lectures in a never-ending repetition, so you could turn up at any time and pick up the threads as best you could, like going to a continuous film-show. It was accompanied by intensive tutorial work.

I first lodged at the Seamark Club, and met Tubby Clayton once. It was supervised by a loquacious lady called "Aunty", assisted by various failed or hadn't-tried 2nd mates. In the blitz we slept in the cellars and every morning had to clamber over piles of rubble to get to college. Eventually I moved to the sailors' home in Dock St., an experience no apprentice should have missed. Ratings and officers were segregated, the officers in a large hall like a prison. Doors banged and feet pounded night and day and at the main entrance a ship's bell was struck at regular intervals to remind us that we were still sailors. The rooms were called "cabins", windows so filthy nothing could be seen through them, and Dock St. was pervaded by scents from the spice warehouses at St Katherine's Dock.

The MMO and exam centre was a few yards along, past a church. The exam was held in a large hall, the examiner and his clerk at a table with a phone which rang continuously and was loudly answered. The air-raids complicated matters: we'd be sent to the cellars on our honour not to discuss the exam. Hopwood reigned. What a miserable man; created the impression that by coming for examination you were admitting to being a criminal. He lost patience with me when I told him he was putting me in a false position, something about a vessel at anchor, and sent me out to think things over. Then there was the ritual reading of the barometer and hydrometer. The hydrometer stood on the mantelpiece in a jar with directly below on the floor a water-stain, as if people had knocked it over in their terror. You corrected the barometer reading by means of little formulae mugged up beforehand, and if you were lucky you applied them the right way. The exam ran something like Knowledge of Principles (3 hrs); Practical Nav 1 – tides, DR, compass (3 hrs); Prac Nav 2 – astro, chartwork (2 hrs); Cargo work and Ship-construction (3 hrs); English (1½ hrs), then orals (How long, O Lord?) and signals. Some bought Walton's *Know Your Own Ship*, also little handbooks on seamanship and so on in the belief that their chances of survival were increased thereby, but most of us got along with Nicholls's *Guide* and tables, and the famous *Nicholls's Seamanship & Nautical Knowledge*. The books had to go back to the beginning with everything, possibly a reflection of the general standard of education; knowledge of maths in particular tended to be slender, even arithmetic. The lecturers were mainly of non-military age, though some weren't in good health. Murray taught met., a funny little bird-like man always nipping in and out. He was fond of drawing a map of the world on the board with all the currents and winds in one go, quite a feat, if monotonous after the first half-dozen demonstrations. He was a nice man but not very forceful; more of an academic. Aubrey-Rees was rather fierce, full of satire and biting wit and so forth. He conducted seamanship oral lessons, used to announce the number of times he'd done so on each occasion, something like "This is the 430th time..." in a very grave tone.

Taylor took cargo-work and ship-construction, co-author of the Taylor & Trimm book, perhaps the youngest of the bunch, an academic sort of chap but with a habit of saying things that didn't quite hang together, somehow. I noticed it in his book. It used to fascinate me so much that I paid little attention to what he was actually talking about. I daresay he was very bright. Trimm seemed to suffer from chronic bronchitis and a runny nose, a little hunchbacked man. Others were shadowy figures, all good at their job, which was to push us through our tickets. We were encouraged to bring back notes of the contents of the exam, which they'd seize on to work out the odds on a certain question appearing in the next exam. The pass rate was quite good. People had to attend classes to claim the pay for studying, and it wasn't done to skulk off in those hard days.

The people at the Red Ensign Club were a rather sad bunch, some of them. Of course there were always the ones working hard for their tickets for about three months then getting away, but there was a sort of sub-stratum of old chaps suffering with their stomachs, rheumatism, that sort of thing, who just lurked about in a state of semi-consciousness. You wondered what they were waiting for. They seemed too poor in health to go to sea. (1940)[1]

Shell gave me 3/- a day, and staying at Jack's Palace cost 2/- a night, so I had a bob to live on. Also stayed at the Seamark Club, run by a little spinstery woman we used to tease mercilessly, but she always took our side against our critics. During the blitz the place went on fire – roof on fire and flames all round – and we had to get her out. Poor Aunty was rushing round gathering up the last bloody hat-pin – "Aunty, for the love of Christ, the building's coming down!" – "I'll come when I'm ready," she said. After I went back to sea I heard that she'd died, poor old dear.

I hadn't carried any books with me at sea, so I had to start from scratch at King Edward VII. Rule of the Road had to be learned as though it were still peacetime, but in the convoys we'd never seen proper lights, only the dimmed ones to follow. Captain Chase was a good teacher – knowledge of principles, and I enjoyed spherical trig. I'd never had an oral exam before, and found it uncomfortable. The examiner asked me about the height of clouds and I hadn't a clue, so he said something about the height a Spitfire flies, with a sort of smile. Rule of the Road and so on. Absolutely fair and searching, and possibly a bit more affable than in peacetime. I knew most of the answers and got by on bullshit with the rest. (1941)[2]

I lived only half an hour away from the college, across the Mersey, but many had to find accommodation in the city, which was difficult. We lunched at the Flying Angel, cheap and often better than what could be had elsewhere, because of the rationing. For the exam we had to go to Southport because the Liverpool MMO had been bombed. I passed after re-sitting signals and went back with the Hall Line, relieving on the *Consuelo*. (1943)[3]

I found that many other companies paid their cadets while studying, while Union-Castle didn't, and wouldn't. This rather upset me, and after an altercation with them I joined Prince Line. (1944)[4]

The very name of Keating struck terror into every heart, but my inquisitor was benign and I got my ticket, a temporary one automatically becoming permanent on expiry of indentures. My plan was to chum up with someone and work together but my partner proved a non-starter, his love-life taking precedence, and when I went back for mate's he was still trying for 2nd mate. (1945)[5]

---

[1] Contributors' private papers.

[2] ibid.

[3] ibid.

[4] ibid.

[5] ibid.

My indentures continued in force while I was at the Cass college, making up the 2½ years' sea-time sufficient for a temporary ticket, which eventually came into my hands. But fearing a Far East posting for a year or more and separation from family and girl I left Shell, which had treated me generally very well, and looked elsewhere. (1945)[1]

[1] Contributors' private papers.

VII

Every Islander's Heritage? 1945-1980.

*

Captain Bellwinch was a mariner cast in a certain mould. Many's the time he would punch me playfully in the neck with a fist the size of a York ham then catch me as I spun, poleaxed, to the deck. "Well, boy!" he would boom. "Do you know your articles?"

"Not all of them, sir," I would say, doing my best to boom back. This pertness tickled him and, in a trice, I would be picked up like a rag doll, throttled resolutely for some minutes then set down again. Then he would chuckle, "Boy, I like your spirit! Tell the mate I said to stop your pay for a week!"[1]

*

THE 1944 Education Act wasn't merely an Act of Parliament; it was also an act of faith in the country's future at a time when the outcome of the war could be assumed with certainty, victory which would present the nation with a challenge to its powers of recovery, among which schools and industrial training schemes would play a crucial part. Preferably free and for all, schooling, interpreted as education, would be the mark and staff of Utopian fulfilment.

Broadly, the Act defined a schools system divided into private and public (state) sectors, these in turn into primary and secondary levels graded towards employment openings shaded laterally between the extremes of technical and classical orientation and vertically between those of unskilled service and the professions. Much of the private sector was geared to a classical form, but in the state sector in England and Wales arrangements favoured a tripartite system of secondary schooling succeeding a comprehensive primary level, its branches designated grammar, modern and technical. Despite a rising clamour of disapprobation by groups more given to sentimentality and class prejudice than to pragmatic appraisal, the system quickly attained a position of respect, not only among those who benefited directly, among them children from poor homes who by it stood a realistic chance of escape from their circumscribed roots, but also among those looking for appropriate standards of educational achievement in prospective employees. Whatever its weaknesses, the system worked to the satisfaction of those to whom its strengths mattered most, the employers in whose

---

[1] *Recollections of Captain Bellwinch.*

hands lay the means of the nation's economic recovery. Prominent among them were, of course, shipowners.

In 1951 the School Certificate was replaced by the GCE, the main difference between them being the GCE's division into separately-examinable subjects, graded at Ordinary ("O") and Advanced ("A") levels, the first taken at age 15 when departure from (grammar) school was officially permitted, while the A level, taken at 17 or 18, opened the door to higher education or some professional vocational following. As a result shipowners began to specify passes (not grades: the system had not yet got round to evading responsibility for a pupil's proper advice anent his strengths and weaknesses and the consequences of failure and seeking instead to protect him from the very thought of such a traumatic prospect) at O level as a condition of acceptance, with or without pre-sea qualifications or training. The usual, modest, requirement was three subjects including maths and English language, the third preferably a science, preferably physics; some companies specified four, some were prepared to consider only one or two. Foreign languages, though, continued to occupy *terra incognita*.

Political idealism flying the banner of "equality", rooted in the social effects of two world wars, in turn nurtured by vested interests, brought about the dismemberment of the tripartite system in the 60s to replace it with a comprehensive one in which the meaning of excellence – a striving towards high quality, by definition a process of selective distinction as well as adherence to high expectations on the part of both pupil and teacher – was degraded and vociferously disparaged as "elitism". The bright were not to be cultivated at the expense of the dim, if the dim were to be accommodated at the expense of the bright, and the process degenerated into one of indiscriminate mediocrity. The dim grew no brighter, the bright less distinct, and to lend the Augean system (avoided wherever possible, on behalf of their offspring, by those in high places who had been instrumental in creating it) a simulacrum of efficiency the examinations were tinkered with: in 1964 the CSE was introduced, purporting to give the holder a currency in prospective employers' eyes. In the event it achieved nothing, the employers no more impressed by it than they had been by the Dunce's Certificate of a hundred years before. Further tinkering produced a compromise, the GCSE, with which employers had to be content, if not happy, while the A level was retained in a more or less attenuated form.

Whatever the GCSE's educational value, it possessed one characteristic that set it apart from the GCE in this respect, claimed by its proponents as an "advance" (towards what?). The GCE had set a standard below which the examinee failed, clearly and categorically, disqualified from any claim to facility in the subject, but not from further attempts having, as at the beginning, a definite objective. The GCSE, however, like the infamous CSE before it, dissembled, awarding a "grade" by which no candidate was declared a failure. Through it the educational establishment, bending the knee to the anti-"elitist" element in its midst, passed on its responsibility to industry – to the real world as distinct from the looking-glass world, as it had become, of teaching – the onus of judgment shifted to the employer's shoulders so that failure remained alive and well, lurking in the undergrowth of the interview or between the covers of the application form, from where it disclosed itself with considerable cruelty. Shipowners weren't disposed to adopt the schools' liberal, not to say dishonest, view of the principle of grading, and anything below a C was regarded as a failure, a verdict often coming too late for the hapless applicant to rectify. The schools spared themselves the embarrassment and discomfort of dealing with failure, actual or potential, and continued into complacent decline, dismissing or indignantly repudiating accusations of incompetence and distinctly uncomplimentary comparisons with the standards prevailing in the systems of the country's industrial competitors – its "partners", politically-speaking, in Europe.

In 1972 the leaving age was raised to 16, but the 70s witnessed a loss of confidence and sureness of aim in education reflected in industry, shipping in particular being confronted with formidable foreign competition, a large sector the shipbuilding and heavy engineering that had offered the apprentice engineer so much opportunity. The higher leaving age also had its effect on recruitment to the sea service, traditionally dependent not merely upon a basic scholastic standard but also upon induction at an age when the life's peculiar discipline was more easily assimilated. While educational quality had not substantially improved – rather, had in many ways deteriorated – the schools' disciplinary ethos had decayed to such an extent that the sea's appeal was considerably diminished. The difficulties of recruiting suitable raw material were, however, balanced to some extent by the decline of the home-flag fleet, and boys setting off on the adventure of a working life bathed, in the immediate post-war years, in the effulgence of renewal and optimism, at a later date were caught not in the glory of a new dawn but in the sad wonder of a pale sunset.

My father met my mother on the *Almeda Star*. He was 2nd mate, she a shop assistant relieving her sister for one voyage for her to get married. I was born November, 1930 and from 1 year old to about 2½ lived aboard the *Celtic Star* in Rothesay Bay. She was laid up due to the slump, my father on half-pay as a sort of shipmaster/watchman. In 1936 he took command of the *Viking Star* but came ashore because of ill-health and became a marine superintendent. He died in 1951. I went to school at Romford and Brentwood until 16½ then joined Blue Star as a cadet. (1947)[1]

I had two cousins in the navy but my immediate family were mining stock, my paternal grandfather the last. He was a foreman coal-trimmer, coaled Scott's *Terra Nova* for the last Antarctic voyage. My maternal grandfather was a compositor for the *Evening Post*; he often took me to the docks when I was small, and perhaps that impressed me, though I wanted to join the air force; my father was in it. But my stepmother was against the idea so I said I'd go to sea, like Uncle Tony – not an uncle but a friend of my father – a marine engineer.

I left Swansea Grammar School without the School Certificate to become a fitter and turner, then go to sea as an engineer. I wanted to get away from home, anyway. The headmaster

---

[1] Contributors' private papers.

wanted me to stay on. If I'd wished to take an engineering course at a college it would have been happily received, but what I wanted to do was frowned on. (1947)[1]

The seafarers were on my father's side, starting in the 1500s. Several reached flag rank and the family fortune came from privateering, though profligacy had all but wiped it out by the turn of the century. Father retired in 1948 and died the same year after reaching flag rank, unusual for an engineer. He was only 48. I attended Gresham's, at Holt, both junior and senior schools, evacuated to Cornwall for the war. There were two headmasters in my time. The first, Newall, went into the Admiralty; the second was a cousin of the late Lord Olivier, Martin John Olivier. The "i" had been added to Oliver. He left under a cloud in the 50s, and though I don't know the official reason sadism isn't beyond the bounds of possibility. My family had been at the school since the late 1700s, but this cut no iced with MJO, who voiced his disapproval of a pupil's joining the merchant service. It wore not a uniform, he said, but a livery. I had some good times there despite attempts to poison a generation with the dreadful food.

I was accepted as a "sixteen entry" to BRNC but at that point Father died leaving us without enough money to finance a naval career, so I applied for a place at Warsash.(1950)[2]

I considered no other career than seafaring while at Merchant Taylors. The school song had lines about ships leaving port for the world and the school tower was a prominent mark visible from the Crosby Channel; but it was rare for a pupil to adopt the sea, and then it was usually Grey Funnel. Oxbridge was the favoured destination but Dartmouth would pass at a pinch, so in my first year in the sixth I began a process of naval induction, successful at local level but disrupted before the Dartmouth interview by my breaking a leg playing rugby. Although the navy offered assistance to get to the interview I let it go.

To remain another 18 months at school trying to catch up on missed work was unthinkable, and my parents supported my plan to go to sea, though my mother preferred the navy for its social cachet while my father warned me that I'd have to stick at it at least until I'd got a master's ticket. He worked for Elders & Fyffes at Garston Dock and often took me and my brother to see the ship he was preparing for cargo work. An uncle was at sea with Elder Dempster and a frequent visitor, while holidays with relatives in Hereford yielded salty tales from old Bill, who'd served his time in sail before going through both wars with Harrison's of Liverpool. There was also the overhead railway to and from school, with its shipping scene between the Pier Head and Seaforth.

My father was keen for me to serve my time with a company where I'd get my hands dirty, firmly believing in the dictum of telling others to do only what one had done oneself, and decided on NZS because of the cadet-ship – no soft options like Elders & Fyffes, but happily he didn't go to the other extreme. I couldn't wait to finish with school, and although the headmaster clearly thought I was on the road to perdition he wished me well. My parents must have wondered if all the sacrifice in pusuance of a good education had been worth it. (1958)[3]

My father was a fitter with Mather & Platt. His father had been a butcher. My mother was a railwayman's daughter. Our first house was a back-to-back terrace in Offerton. My first school was Kale Green, then, at Offerton, Bank Lane Primary, where I failed the 11-plus miserably

---

[1] Contributors' private papers.

[2] ibid.

[3] ibid.

and went to Dialtone Secondary Modern. A good school within its limits, about a thousand pupils. The head was very strict, very correct, always wore a pin-stripe with a carnation. He was a dab hand with a cane; everyone went in fear of it. The academic standard wasn't very high, but thorough as far as it went; no GCE or anything like that, only school reports. Most of the boys took up engineering apprenticeships, otherwise became unskilled or semi-skilled artisan types.

When I was fifteen I started to wake up and think ahead; used to look at Dad when he came home stinking of mystic[1]. He said whatever I did I should stay off the shop floor. Well, I always had an interest in ships; used to cycle thirty miles to watch them in the Manchester Ship Canal. Sometimes I'd get a ride on one to Manchester and cycle home from there. Only on the small ships, though. When I said I wanted to go to sea Mother wasn't very keen, but Dad was happy enough, and my decision stuck. I got a scholarship about that time, to Stockport College of FE, where I did GCE work with a group from which three went to sea, one as an engineer cadet, one into the navy, and me. I joined Blue Funnel. (1960)[2]

But, contrary to popular opinion as fashioned by political interests, not all secondary moderns were dead-ends:

I didn't pass the 11-plus so went to the local secondary modern – Weston Grange County Modern. The general standard was excellent and I left with enough GCE O-levels to get an apprenticeship at sea. A lot of the lads and lasses there went back to grammar school to do A-levels and go on to university. (1966)[3]

And engineers of the new generation were no slouches:

My grandfather was a sailmaker by trade; worked on the river all his life. The school was founded in 1701 by Sir Joseph Williamson to teach maths for RN intake, but it was just a boys' grammar school when I was there. Left at sixteen with eight O-levels. How I got them I don't know, because my mind was on other things, some sort of an idea about running away to sea. So I went for this alternative training scheme because I wanted to get away as quickly as possible, not wait until I was 21. (1966)[4]

After the war pre-sea training was accepted as more or less *de rigueur* but by no means compulsory; some companies went as far as insisting upon it, others only to express a somewhat equivocal preference. Remission of sea time for attendance at schools and training-ships, of which numbers reached a peak during the late 50s, varied from nothing to 12 months, with a tentative 15 granted for pre-sea training incorporating both O- and A-level passes, though A-level entry remained the exception, the certificate marking a kind of bifurcation at which the horizon of career possibility extended beyond the confines of a life at sea, at least in the merchant navy.

---

[1] Emulsion used to lubricate lathe work.

[2] Contributors' private papers.

[3] ibid.

[4] ibid.

The navy offered something more challenging in some respects, with a wider social ambit if one rather over-prescribed by convention, and ever at the mercy of the winds of political expedient.

My mother's family included Grimsby trawler owners; her cousin married a chief engineer in Anglo-Saxon and their son went to sea with P&O, commanding *Canberra* in her early days. My parents loved the sea, and yachting, though Father, an engineer, leaned towards motor-cruisers rather than sail. I was determined to join the navy, and finally got their consent, though I failed the Dartmouth entrance exam and went to Pangbourne instead on the strength of the result[1], thinking I'd go into the navy by that route. In time I realised that I didn't have the academic ability and turned instead to the merchant navy. By the end of my time at Pangbourne I was 17 and anxious to get away, but the war was still on and a Pangbourne cadet was lost on his first voyage at the time. My parents weren't happy about it and Father suggested staying on for a term to improve on my poor exam results, but it didn't appeal to me. There'd been some unhappy moments and on one occasion I'd run away, so I hit on the idea of an Outward Bound course, and Father sent me to Aberdovey in 1945. I did all right there, was a watch-captain, and we won most of the inter-watch competitions, which gave me confidence and showed there was hope for me after all. [2]

From an Outward Bound log, August-September, 1960:

...a very informative first-aid lecture with a series of ghastly slides. Three chaps fainted and some thought the slides were a bit off but I think such things are a good warning.

...three or four porpoises appeared and a cry of "Shark!" We just laughed until a black dorsal fin streaked towards us. We were out of the water so fast that the instructor admitted we could move when we wanted to.

...To the pictures to see Saturday Night & Sunday Morning.

...The fire service here is pretty disgusting and the drill was pointless as the pump motor doesn't work. Apart from that the fire officer did not know what he was doing.

...a lecture by a local fire officer and his intrepid assistant. They gave us a few demonstrations of how fires can be easily started but unfortunately nothing went wrong.

...Exped to Afan Fawddwy, 3,000 feet. A long and hard trek, terrific scenery, and we were first to gain the summit. The third party had not appeared by the time we were ready to carry on at about 12.45pm, so we left the message and started for home. The route was extremely hard going but as we neared the old cottage we realised that we were first again and had to do all the chores. Mr Kemp got there as were preparing tea and later the second party, but when the third party had not arrived by 9.30pm we were worried and took the Tilley lamp outside so they would see it, also blew a whistle at two-minute intervals. At 10pm Mr Kemp organised a

---

[1] Dartmouth entry was competitive, so the standard varied.
[2] Contributors' private papers.

search and sent two of us off to telephone the school. Soon the lost party was found having mistaken their route and found their way back to the quarry valley, and the search was thankfully ended. The Land-Rover came roaring up full of instructors who went home mumbling about their futile journey. We came home by the mountain route climbing Trengelly[sic] and other lesser peaks. I thought I wasn't going to make it at the pace Mr Kemp set and I don't think I'd have gone much further, all the same I was glad I kept up with the first party. We got back about 6.30pm and after a meal and a bath I was amazed to find myself sprinting to town to the pictures.

...One of the instructors who is training to be a clergyman told us that we are provided with all we really need. I did not fully agree with him.

...took a packed lunch and stayed out in the dinghies all day. I helped to crew a Rover dinghy without an instructor. While on the beach doing some work on one of the GP's a wave swamped the Rover and she turned over. The breakers on the bar were very fierce and the lifeboat went to her aid, pulled them out and towed the dinghy within our reach. We went into the breakers to right it and had a very rough time. We continued sailing after lunch and another dinghy capsized, but as it was a GP with an instructor it was soon righted and baled out. We had a very exciting and interesting day and enjoyed every minute...[1]

However, after an interval of static recovery and renascence pre-sea training picked up the torch of progress and change in a slowly-strengthening economy, making adjustments in an *ad hoc* and piecemeal fashion that in the early 60s took up an entirely new course following a perceived change of principle in the career, one which strove towards a flexible pattern that would, in theory, increase opportunities of shore employment post-sea service. The old ways lingered, but finally petered out later in the decade, a process foreshadowed, inadvertently and symbolically, by the loss of the *Conway* in 1953, when she parted her tow *en route* to a long-awaited refit to strand on the foreshore of the Menai Strait and break her back as the tide ebbed. She was succeeded by a hastily-expanded shore base at her last anchorage off Plas Newydd, seat of the Marquess of Anglesey.

Meanwhile the School of Navigation at Southampton had taken up new quarters at Warsash, on the Hamble[2], from where *Moyana* made her coastal and short-sea forays with crews of cadets under officer-instructors, the extended course of 12 months earning 9 months' remission. And in Plymouth the nautical school expanded its brief in 1947 to include a 12-month pre-sea cadet course, approved in 1951 by the MOT and Ministry of Education as equivalent to 6 months at sea. They represented the new age and a growing sector of shore-based state-controlled schools and shorter courses begun at a later stage of the educational process.

---

[1] Contributors' private papers.
[2] 1946.

I was educated at King Edward VII School at Lytham St Anne's until starting at the School of Navigation, Southampton. Father thought it was the best place after looking at *Worcester* and *Conway*, impressed by the way Wakeford ran it. Father had served his time with Ellerman Hall, my grandfather was a chief engineer and his father had also been at sea. Uncle George was with Clan Line and Uncle Herbert with the United Africa Company[1]. Uncle John started as a cadet with Eagle Oil in 1919 and became commodore. Both sides of the family were at sea for as far back as can be traced, and the only question was whether I'd go on deck or in the engine-room. In fact Father wanted me to go into the Foreign Office but didn't stop me in my intentions. His father had advised *him* not to go to sea... (1953)[2]

Warsash.
18th January. 1953.
Dear Mother,
   This is the first opportunity I've had to write and the first time I've sat down in the three days I've been here. On Waterloo station I met a cadet with the same fears as myself. At the school we were immediately given tea. After this we were set tasks such as cleaning, polishing and tucking in bunks. I didn't sleep that night. Next morning at 6.30 went for the run. After brushing seniors' and intermediates' clothes we made their bunks and scrubbed the deck. After breakfast the staff instructor drilled us for about three hours. In the afternoon he had us again for more. We get inspected twice daily. After dressing we again had drill, this time a practice for church. The service was ordinary. I doubt many listened. I've only had two washes since I arrived. They say you get a few more after about three weeks. I've had to sacrifice shore leave so that letters may be written. I very much doubt whether I'll be able to do much swotting for GCE. I've got some work waiting as I write, two battle-dresses and a bugle to be cleaned...I'm dead tired but don't worry on my account. I'll be alright, I think.
   Love to Jean and yourself,
   Ian.[3]

From which a mother would conclude that her part in her son's life had abruptly changed, and diminished:

   ...due to tomfoolery on "quarters", Harris, an SLC, was held responsible for something he hadn't done, or at least not held[sic] an active part in, and was demoted. McNish who was a supernumary[sic] JLC was promoted in Harris's stead. It certainly has been a change for the better.

   ...went sailing for the first time in my life with Noyon, who, living in Guernsey, knows quite a lot about it.

   ...I am lucky to be going on the first cruise of the term in the Moyana.

---

[1] Later the Palm Line.
[2] Contributors' private papers.
[3] ibid.

...There's certainly advantages to being a JLC as now we have our own washplace and plenty of time to wash.

...To start with I was second-in-command. Overnight a fresh gale blew up and the forecast wasn't good, which decided that we should stay in Weymouth all next day. The engineer taught us, as if we didn't already know, how to tie a bowline and do a backsplice. Then Captain Stewart gave us instruction in rowing and Lt-Cdr Price some hints on chartwork. Next morning the wind went down. We practiced[sic] man overboard, the time taken to pick him up was three minutes but conditions were nearly ideal. (Moyana)

...Last Tuesday I was duty SLC which means that I took a record of all the happenings throughout the day and made a note of them in the log. Then I had to superintend "sunset" and lastly go the rounds with the officer of the week after lights out.[1]

In 1961 the BP Tanker Co was among the better-found concerns specifying O-levels for applicants who might also have been required to have attended, or to attend after provisional acceptance, a pre-sea course. Likewise the NZS Co which, accepting boys direct from school, appointed them to its cadet-ship[2]. In fact pre-sea training didn't become obligatory until drastic overhaul and revision of the entire system in 1965, and while new entrants continued to follow the traditional path of apprenticeship, others chose – or were obliged – to embark on the new ONC/D system, a sandwich-type training which drew upon itself somewhat ambivalent comment as neither fish nor fowl: for what little could be learned in such a fleeting attempt at introductory preparation – a matter of a few weeks – it might as well have been left out of the system altogether[3]. Subsequent intervals ashore during cadetship were planned as instalments culminating in the examination for – as it eventually evolved – the certificate that displaced the 2nd mate's ticket, the so-called Class III (Deck) qualification.

A publicity project in 1961, an element of the Commonwealth Technical Training Week, sought to portray seafaring as a worthwhile career option through displays and exhibitions. At the time over 1,000 deck officer entrants were needed annually to maintain manning levels, and while engineers continued to come forward in preference to doing National Service[4], a significant drop in numbers marked its end despite introduction of the ATS in 1952[5]. The nature of change of pre-sea training had been signalled by the Southampton School of Navigation's approach, the shorter course for an intake of school leavers which rendered the *Conway/Worcester* pattern, as an alternative to conventional secondary schooling, anachronistic. In 1968

---

[1] Contributors' private papers.

[2] See Ch.8.

[3] By 1980 Warsash was running a 6-week course. All courses, however, included a survival at sea course and a 1-day fire-fighting course.

[4] See appx. 5.

[5] Alternative Training Scheme (ibid.)

Worcester's operation moved ashore and the ship went to the breakers while *Conway*'s hitherto naval style was scrapped with the captain-superintendent's retirement to give place to that of a "normal" secondary school under a headmaster and LEA control. In that year *Mercury* closed[1] while the NCP changed its style and name in closer alignment with the public school system it had courted almost from the start, becoming Pangbourne College but retaining a distinctive disciplinary structure based on the RNR uniform and its corresponding ethics. Its curriculum aimed at access to higher education while also providing for a diminishing minority intent on the sea, both naval and mercantile. Intentionally or not, it was an illustration of the disparity between improved education and the status of the sea career, which had been steadily losing the battle with shore occupations.

The Shipping Federation specified pre-sea training as a condition of engagement by the firms it represented, and it was prevalent among applicants in general, only 1 in 4 joining ships straight from school in the early 60s to serve the full 4 years. The system gradually shrank out of existence as the ONC/D entry increased until, in the early 70s, indentured service along traditional lines came to an end, all trainees henceforth signing articles as cadets with contracts of employment incorporating obligations to conduct and follow the MNTB scheme of sandwich courses. The apprentice had at last, after some six centuries of traceable antecedents, reached the end of his career. The event went unremarked beyond a few trite observations to do with the march of progress and development and murmurs of welcome towards the new age that, closely scrutinised, lacked something of conviction and owed not a little to fashionable appearance. Something had certainly been lost, but whether or not its replacement was in all respects an improvement wasn't, outside the purely political argument, at all clear, and there followed a steadily increasing trend towards a process of continual reappraisal and adjustment that took on some of the hallmarks of confusion of purpose and uncertainty of principle.

With the apprentice went the training-ships which, grimly retaining their customs and traditions in an era of social upheaval, had found themselves on the threshold of the unthinkable, perpetuating an oddly detached quality of life which, for all its virtues – and they were many and profound – bore little resemblance to what was evolving at sea, and in this respect they had signally failed: the whole point of the training-ship as originally conceived was that its values and principles would be transferred to the ship at sea as its offspring took up their careers. This was so as far as it went, but it was on far too small a scale to have any influence on the direction of affairs overwhelmingly governed by forces of economics and commerce having nothing to do with the ethics inculcated by a system based on the shining simplicity of noble ideals. The result was that they were seen to nurture a compelling sense of suspended reality which their broods found either addictive or baffling and distasteful. Few passed through without experiencing cardinal effects on their outlooks and personalities. *Conway*, for

---

[1] See appx. 6: letter from captain-superintendent to cadets.

example, allowing for the accident of being shore-based, was in all other respects a ship, in which the executive department overshadowed the academic, as had always been the case, though the accent was now on gaining enough GCE O-levels to meet the shipping companies' requirements. Up to eight were offered, supplemented by the *Conway* Passing-Out Certificate, while the "special studies" class continued beyond the normal course of two or three years, preparing a handful of cadets for A-level and either naval entry or other, non-seafaring, paths. The largest proportion of the intake followed the 2-year course:

Jan. 4th. 1960.
Arrived Conway *1500. Issued with rest of kit 1930. Duffle coat missing. Must see about this on Sat. Am enjoying it here very much. Felt a bit homesick for a while*

March 2nd.
Went on gig's crew. Forgot to put my blind up, so McCowan made me do it 30 times. Film was very good – The Glen[*sic*] Miller Story.

March 14th.
*Seamanship all morning – Rule of the Road with Slob. Two house cadets broke into the Marquis's[*sic*] bedroom to have a smoke and got caught. Letter from Mum. Scouse for dinner. Muck.*

March 20th.
Watched gig race between Hold and Focsle. We lost. Had a fight with G———. A good sermon today by a chap from Vancouver.

March 28th.
On power-boat's crew this morning but didn't get off the knots test. Was engineer. Quite good fun actually. Went to PD for Greasy and the papers.

March 30th.
Bloody cooks on Mess 3. They need a trough to eat out of. H—— wrote his name in butter on the table and they threw milk and porridge at each other.

March 31st.
Cooks on Mess 3 again but one of them was punished for bad manners so he will be doing cooks for dinner. End of term routine pinned up. Hooray.

And a year later:

Jan. 20th. 1961.
Reveille 0715. To Port Main to get No.2's tools from Marlow then to early breakfast. To the dock with Moynet, Dock CC, and found No.2 dried out with a hell of a list. Tide had only just turned so we hung around while No.1's crew went to PD to collect Mr Rhys Edwards. Eventually got No.2 afloat and fuelled up and after a bit of mucking around got her started. Had to go over to the Vaynol foreshore to pick up a couple of anchors and warps from the

moorings. A very messy business. Afterwards over to the cutters and gigs to bale them out. I was cox, so dropped Puckett in the first cutter, Rawlinson in the next, Seabrooke in the first gig, then carried on on my own to the next gig and tried to board her but forgot about the eddy and No.2 nearly left me stranded in the red gig! Anyway, I picked the others up and went back to the dock where we scrubbed the boat, and that was that for the morning...

...Out in the yellow cutter and raced House cutter's crew. What a mess – most of them New Chums.

...There is some sort of rumour going round that we will be having TOAST for breakfast from now on. If I see toast on the mess I'll have another eye test.

...Dinner. Some soup or other, boiled ham and peas and spuds, then spotted dog and custard. The diet is slowly improving.

...Got going on the extra work for the March GCE (maths). It looks most discouraging. Went to sleep in physics. Geography last period. At ten to six we left in the bus for Caernarvon GS to see their performance of Twelfth Night. *A terrific show. The girls were marvellous. I'm going to write to one of them.*

...To the canteen with Edwards and on the way we saw that cadet who ran away being carted down to sick-bay on a stretcher. He was picked up on the road by a motorist, unconscious.

...Writing this in the rec-room. The only place where I can sit and think. I long for solitude, peace and quiet, but there are always people about, and from one end of the term to the other I'm never alone, though I suppose I'll have to get used to having people around all the time when I get to sea. I'm counting the months to go now. All ten of them. It seems to stretch infinitely into the future, but it's only a drop in the ocean of life, really. When I think of what I'll be doing this time next year it makes the two years here seem awfully short.

...The chaps on the mess found out that it's my birthday – we're all 4th termers. Morland-Green started singing "Happy Birthday" and all the rest of the messes joined in. I don't feel any older. 17 now.

March 7th.
Great news. During break Eric told me that BI have returned my birth certificate and eyesight test form and have accepted me provisionally! I have to apply again next term for interview during the summer leave. Eric told me they said I am "just the right kind of boy"! Pretty good.

April 6th.
Eric told me I've been nominated to represent Conway *at a meeting of cadets from all the training establishments in the British Commonwealth.[1]*

April 8th.
Eric in a good mood. Called me the glamour boy of HMS Conway...

---

[1] Commonwealth Technical Training Week, 1961.

...Well, I finally did it – a junior rate. I could hardly believe my ears when Eric read out my name, and when I went up to shake hands I couldn't see anybody else.

...A meeting in the Camp gun-room of all CC's and Eric gave us a talk about how important our rates are, and that we should enforce the rules conscientiously and so on.

...After school went fishing in one of the cutters with Edwards and Hall. All we caught was a starfish, but it passed the afternoon pleasantly, sitting in the boat (at her mooring) talking sex and other such matters.

...Well, that's the last day of summer leave over, and no more Conway *leave. What a queer thought. It once seemed that the last term would never come. But I don't feel like leaving old* Conway *now, in spite of the fact that I haven't been at any school for much longer – must be the traditions and her fame. Anyway – 8.55am from Cardiff tomorrow and sausage and mash at the end of it. Ugh!*

...Slob gave me a talk about being a senior PO and warned me against being pally. I must realise, he said, that I have to cut myself off to a certain extent.

...I don't know if I'm doing the right thing with this division – some are moaning that I change my mind too much, and the chums in the starboard hut say it's an unhappy one, though I think most of them disagree with that.

...God this damned division is worrying me. I don't know if I'm doing the right thing or not. P——— says a lot of things behind my back and I can't do anything about it. I can imagine what Kimber felt like, and Smith and the rest, but I'd like to cut ———'s throat for ballsing things up last term. Someone else should have got the damn rate. And I think someone else should have got this one as well.

...Only 7 weeks left. It's going too quickly.

...Finished the essay Greasy made us write about a love affair, and he read it this afternoon. He said he'd put a line through any pornography, but I was just clear of the mark.

...Had a good game of rugger this afternoon, and would have scored a try if McGill hadn't tackled me cleanly. Watched the First XV against a team from the Otaio. *We beat them 35-nil.*

...Should have played a team from Holyhead County School this afternoon but out of 1,000 pupils they couldn't rake up a team. Pretty useless.

...Dance at St Winifred's. It started about 6pm and we had to bash on until nine before we had anything to drink. Had to dance with the 6th form only – introduced to them and had to grab a partner for the evening. Mine was a girl from Thailand with an unpronounceable name, but her nickname was Zoom or something. Had a drink in the pub before the bus left, Green (CPO) threw us out.

...A cadet in Mizzentop's been accused of stealing a couple of quid from a master's pocket during PT. Mr Greenland had left his trousers in the master's changing-room. After a lot of lying the cadet broke down and admitted it, and the Skipper has informed the committee of management. He'll probably be expelled. He's done similar things before. A terrible business.

And of course there was the ship's dance:

...Just realised that I should have sent invitations to the nurses as well, but since old Fanny didn't tell me anything I'm not taking the blame for any dithers. I'm just about sick of this term. Went to see the galley manager about waiters, but he wasn't there.

...None of the girls were much good; in fact, horrible. I had to dance with Miss Taylor, St Winnie's head, and Mrs Howard-Davies because Eric told me to spread my favours more evenly. The dance began at 7, supper at 8.30, finished at 10.45. After rounds we all went to Tak's cabin for drinks – Green, me, Wog, Tak, Arab. We split a bottle of Dubonnet, a half of gin, and one of Vodka, and I had a stout. Drank the stuff neat with a dash of lime now and again. Got to bed at 2.30, absolutely done, and felt a bit sick. But I've got 12 months' remission.

...At evening quarters Eric said we are too familiar with the galley staff – damned if I am. He went on about what it would be like at sea if we ordered people of greater experience around, or got familiar with them, etc if they were junior to us, and on about being an officer and a gentleman not seeming to apply these days. Flogged my plastic cap and badge for 9/6d. I'm coxing the QB's gig tomorrow.

...What an absolutely rotten day. I've finished with Conway *now. QB's shook hands with the staff and Eric then we got on the first bus and the 8.05 train. A bar on it, so we crammed in and started drinking in misery, then split up at Chester. Some blokes were crying, and I felt lousy. Everywhere is foggy. I felt lost, somehow, and sorry to have left all those great blokes. Still, life's like that, I suppose I'll be seeing them again, somewhere...*[1]

As time passed heavier emphasis was placed on the academic in the training pattern, in particular where it bore on the increasing sophistication of technology as it displaced the traditional conceptions of seamanship and navigation. Discipline was watered down to accommodate fashionable ideas of what constituted "maturity", a precocity which, as generally interpreted and indulged, implied a slacker attitude in general and a breakdown of formal order greeted by many as indicative of "progress", but by others, of a less sanguine frame of mind, as further evidence of decline and fall, certainly evident in the state of shipping under the red ensign. The Outward Bound schools continued, but in a way that would have had the late Kurt Hahn reaching for the axe. "Self-discipline" was the comfortable, or complacent, catch-phrase, and although the outdoor life was still the ethical focus its pursuit was a distinctly *laisser-aller* affair by comparison with the original idea. Shipping companies dropped the

---

[1] Contributors' private papers.

practice of sending cadets on courses, and Aberdovey abandoned the training-ketch in favour of small craft and canoes. For whatever the reason – possibly partly of cost – the change was symbolic of the subtle transition of moral perception from self-reliance to self-interest, a change which proved inimical to the essentially cooperative nature of shipboard life, further eroding the attractive qualities needed to balance its negative aspects; they, in turn, seemed to be multiplying, accounting to an increasing degree for the lack of interest in the sea as a career.

Viewed in a comparative light, in terms of pre-sea training the traditional engineer apprentice with his 4½- or 5-year spell in an engineering works ashore underwent the most comprehensive change, granted that the system wasn't a preparation for the sea so much as for an engineering career regardless of environment. However, an appreciable decrease in numbers coming forward from this system caused the shipping industry some concern, and while National Service went some way towards a check on the trend owners foresaw a time when, conscription abolished, it would border on crisis. Not only that, but there was also an increasing need for people possessed of a better academic, technical, grounding to cope with the mounting sophistication of ships' machinery: under the ATS the engine-room itself played a major role in its prospective overseer's training. The system would, it was felt, not only enable the shipowner to recruit straight from school, freeing him from the vagaries of the union-plagued shore industry, but also improve the engineer's identification of himself with the ship rather than only with its engines, so promoting a better working and social relationship with other departments, particularly the deck. Furthermore, it was hoped that the scheme's openings in the direction of an engineering degree would enhance the occupation's image and attraction. Nevertheless, while the new system can be assessed only hypothetically as offsetting the effects of conscription's termination, numbers again fell thereafter to render the shortfall of qualified and (more importantly) committed engineers a chronic problem.

The scheme took the form of a phased programme of training divided between college, ship and engineering works, the last, owing to the virtual disappearance of heavy industry, later supplanted by time in college receiving as much practical instruction as possible. The first phase was 2 years at technical college before going to sea with the employing company as an engineer cadet. The course was full-time, with practical instruction during the summer vacation in a yard or works, leading to either OND or HND as the first step towards the BOT/MOT 2nd-class certificate.

Anglo-Saxon, or Shell, was the scheme's prime mover, all too aware of the fact that the peculiar conditions of the tanker trade were the least attractive despite what was undoubtedly a promising career outlook, on average better than in general dry cargo and passenger trades. The company looked for GCE O-levels in maths, physics and English language, but as time passed the breadth of selection had to be widened to meet the demand, lesser qualifications being accommodated through entrance exams and streaming according to ability, provided for by introduction of the MET grade for those below the O/HND ability band. The grammar-school intake, never large enough, took up cadetships immediately on leaving at 16, while the secondary modern entrants, aged 15 on leaving, were usually sent to yards or works as general dogsbodies for the 12-month interim.

In 1958 the NZS Co came up with a variation, replacing the opening college-based phase with two years in the cadet-ship *Otaio*. Cadets signed 4½-year indentures at a £50 premium, returnable as pay in a similar arrangement to that for deck cadets. The system worked, regardless of the not entirely pragmatic forecasts of the traditionalist lobby, and in a paper presented to the Tanker Operation Group in 1960 Captain D.A.S. English of Shell summed it up by stating, *inter alia*:

Originally there was opposition to and suspicion of this scheme, felt by some likely to produce good theoretical but poor practical engineers. These fears were not without some justification and care has been taken to see that the practical aspects received due attention. Several years' experience of the scheme has resulted in the conversion of most, if not all, of the deepest dyed-in-the-wool traditionally-trained engineers. We ourselves feel more than satisfied that our "Alternatively"-trained officers will meet the challenge of the future, but they have yet to pass that critical 25-30 age range...

At which, of course, marriage or its imminence assumed a prominent and peculiarly subversive footing in the officer's calculations, subversive chiefly through the change in women's attitudes, increasingly assertive and less stoic than those of earlier generations.

By the end of the 70s the traditional engineering apprenticeship was extinct, the signing of indentures a feature of history. A 4-year engineering training had to include full-time education between 16 and 17 and a year's training in the use of tools and general engineering practice "at an industrial training centre" approved by the Engineering Industry Training Board with ATS cadets in mind, both "certificate" and "diploma" groups aiming at the TEC/SCOTEC diploma at the end of Phase 1. Certificate cadets were accepted with four CSE "passes" – at Grade 1 in maths and physics and Grade 3 in English[1], while the diploma entrant had to present at least four GCE/CSE passes at O level including maths, physics and English. There was also a special entry for 18-year-olds on a course leading to HND/BSc Mar Eng., for which they needed an A-level GCE in maths or physics, having studied both, or H-level CSE in both. To be eligible for the BSc two A-levels or three H-grades were necessary. The HND (later the Higher TEC Diploma in Mechanics/Engineering(Marine)) and BSc led to qualification as chartered engineer.

The problem underlying this fantastically convoluted selection and option arrangement remained the hoary one of retention of qualified personnel at sea. The old system had failed to impart an adequate grasp of technological advance, but in

---

[1] Setting linguistic, or "communication", skills at a low priority reflected general ability, which became apparent in the texts of individuals' journals as time passed.

equipping the new engineer for his task the new schemes simultaneously did likewise for shore posts of acceptable status, and wastage remained a persistent bane.

Outside the pale of school and pre-sea training, and not specifically orientated towards service in the merchant navy, the Sea Cadet Corps continued its efforts to nurture a spirit of national identity and service preparatory to a possible naval career. As an extra-mural institution and youth organisation its appeal only gradually diminished in post-war years. It was also established in the dominions and colonies, even those without a seaboard: in Rhodesia[1] boys were required to join either the schools' ACF's or the Sea Cadets at the age of 15, though the SCC accepted entrants at 14:

> The Sea Cadets were looked upon with some derision by most at school. We tended to be individualists to whom the rigid order of the ACF was distasteful. In the Sea Cadets we found a greater variety of instruction and less bull, taught things like semaphore and Morse signalling, ship recognition and practical boatwork with elementary navigation. TS *Mashona* had a fine converted ship's lifeboat on Lake MacIlwaine, a few miles out of Salisbury, attended by a couple of pulling-boats and a few sailing-dinghies, where we spent Saturday mornings cleaning and maintaining them and putting out in them. There was an annual camp and sometimes exercises resembling the exploits of wartime naval divisions, attacking defended *kopjes*[2] and stumbling about in the bush toting Lee-Enfields and Brens, firing blanks with indiscriminate ruthlessness. The army cadets called us Seaweeds, an epithet we adopted as our standard, carried into rather more bloody encounters than the training exercises whenever we came into close contact with them; a combined ACF and Sea Cadet camp was an experiment never repeated, as far as I know.
>
> They didn't have a very clear idea of MN ways, but among the officers, and particularly in Sub-Lt Tam Graham, I found plenty of goodwill and encouragement. Mr Graham was keen to see me get a place at *Conway*, in contrast to most of the masters at school, whose indifference to my future was patent and rather crushing, if understandable: I was a late-comer from abroad (Australia) and not among the brightest. Only the art master showed an interest, attempting to move me in the direction of commercial art. But I was sick of school, though proud enough of being at one with a reputation for excellence on a par with the best English public schools (Churchill School, run with an iron grip by its famous and feared head, Hougaard), and not very happy at home, and the sea held out the prospect of escape. So I left. The Sea Cadets made the last couple of years bearable. (1959)[3]

The war-risk bonus scheme ended in October, 1947, when wages would, logically enough, have reverted to pre-war levels. But of course prices had risen, and through pressure from officers' and ratings' organisations and subsequent agreement on the NMB the bonus was added to the basic figure to settle on a rate of £75, £90, £105 and

---

[1] Never actually a colony, Southern Rhodesia had been granted semi-dominion status and self-government in 1923, later illegally rescinded by the British government, with disastrous consequences.

[2] Afrikaans: isolated hills in otherwise flat surroundings.

[3] Contributors' private papers.

£120 for the successive years. By the mid-50s companies were vying with each other for new recruits as their fleets expanded, offering incentives of one kind and another from better wages to bonuses. Shell, for example, anxious to offset the tanker's natural drawbacks, offered a £30 bonus on satisfactory completion of time, while expiry of indentures at sea brought a change of status to cadet, on AB's rate of pay. Paid leave of 36 days a year at the rate of pay current on indentures was introduced, with a subsistence allowance of 5/4d a day additionally in the UK, while pay rose to £105, £140, £155 & £323 with up to 3 months study leave paid at the final rate, and voyage leave of a month for every five served plus a day, or pay in lieu, for each Sunday at sea.

As for the engineer cadet, the terms of his agreement were on a par with the deck apprentice's, his pay in the mid-60s in the order of £150, £180, £210, £240 & £275 for the successive years, with lodging/subsistence allowance when appropriate – for example, during Phase 1 in college. Operating its seagoing alternative to college in the *Otaio*, the NZS Co returned £44 of the £50 premium in annual instalments (the odd £6 unaccounted for...) and paid both deck and engineer cadets at the rate of £9.15s, £13.10s, £14.15s, £16.15s & £19.10s a month over the five-year period, deck apprentices receiving the first four years' rates, starting at the second if entitled to 12 months' remission.

It was difficult to obtain an apprenticeship because of additional wartime manning by DEMS people and loss of tonnage, but after many letters of application I received an interview with Watts Watts. The only question that made an impression on me, put by an elderly marine superintendent, was, "Do you stutter?" Stutter or not, I wasn't offered a place, but eventually found one with Athel. (1946)[1]

My cousin Walter encouraged me to apply to P&O but they turned me down, so I looked to alternatives. My father had an indirect connection with Cunard, and I think there was a bit of string-pulling because the result was an apprenticeship with Port Line. (1946)[2]

As ever, the balance of supply and demand affected the significance of incidentals like speech impediments and strings for the pulling, and as the recruitment drive gathered momentum in step with the fleet's expansion they became spurious. Once the immediate post-war confusion had made way for the dog-days of the late 50s, the 60s and early 70s, career prospects took on a breadth and accessibility largely unknown in earlier times, owing in no small measure to the near-disappearance of nepotism. Boys – and girls – with a basic secondary schooling behind them found not only a wide choice of employment (though differences were being steadily eroded by regulatory measures bearing upon working conditions) but one also actively soliciting their interest. With a handful of GCE O-levels and evidence of the right temperament

---

[1] Contributors' private papers.
[2] ibid.

(liberally interpreted, not always accurately) the sea-minded school-leaver was free to choose what appeared to be the ideal service, or trade. As for parental influence, it remained much as before in its perception of the sea as a suitable calling but lost much of its weight in the social metathesis of the 60s, which, releasing youth from the trammels of adult guidance, also cut it off from a good deal of adult interest, and youth organisations suffered accordingly, though at sea the process was somewhat retarded by the filter of inbred conservatism and tradition, which seemed in some instances to have retained an echo of the methods of naval impressment:

My brother was a deck cadet with Shell, home on leave. When he saw that the company was putting on some sort of exhibition promoting apprenticeship – the Alternative Training Scheme – he went along and got chatting to people without letting on that he was already with them. They gave him all sorts of flannel, and he told them that he had a brother interested in going to sea, and they said, "Oh, give us his name and address and we'll get in touch." So within days I had an *express letter* – "Come up to St Helen's Court for an interview." I was just approaching my O-levels, almost 16. So I went up to London. There was a group of us. They gave us aptitude tests and medicals and all that, interviewed us, and sent us on our way, then a few days later came another letter: "We are pleased to say that you have been accepted by the Anglo-Saxon Petroleum Company" – and I was in the bloody merchant navy. I hadn't done a thing myself. I got my O-levels – maths, physics and English – and suddenly I was an engineer cadet. (1952)[1]

First the company doctor had to be faced, but apart from a specimen of urine my state of health seemed to be taken for granted. Next the interview, conducted by the chairman of the board himself, John Mills, aided and abetted by the man in charge of cadets, James Fowler, and a marine super, Captain "Nelson" Rice. It was a cursory affair. I was asked, among other forgettable things, the height of the building we were in, and whether I had noticed the flagstaff on the roof. I wasn't invited to ask anything about what I could expect from the company. The whole proceeding was an example of how not to do it. Anyway, at the end of a week I was notified of acceptance and later came a list of gear. (NZS, 1952)[2]

The school's careers service had a book about the MN, so I wrote to several companies. Most wanted pre-sea training, but Blue Funnel took only *Conway* boys or boys straight from school, like me. I had to go to Liverpool – India Buildings – expenses paid. It was a magnificent place. The ground floor was all shops and a restaurant and a huge branch of Lloyd's Bank with company offices on the floor above. The cadets' department was on the 7th floor. Commissionaires were running about all over the place, very grand. I was interviewed by R.E. Hutson, who was in charge of midshipmen, as the cadets[3] were called. He asked what Father did, what school qualifications I was hoping for, why I wanted to go to sea, and what I thought my career progression would be; my hobbies; why I wanted to join Blue Funnel. Questions like that.

---

[1] Contributors' private papers.
[2] ibid.
[3] Apprentices!

Well, they accepted me, but there was a gap of a few months before the Outward Bound course, so I took a job doing chemical analysis of foundry samples. I got well into it and was offered a special apprenticeship to train as a metallurgist. It was a good offer, but I decided to stick to the sea.

I got my gear from the Liverpool Sailors' Home. Mr Bird was the man there, a gloomy chap. It was good stuff – sea-boots, collar-detached shirts, duffel-coat and so on. It lasted well, came to about £60 altogether. Father paid. (1961)[1]

After WW2 the National Institute for Industrial Psychology produced a so-called Seven-Point Plan for interviews, and with this as a guide Blue Funnel's format followed a coherent pattern, described by R.E. Hutson:

For such a plan to work in shipping there had first to be a definition of the ideal ship's officer in terms of his ability, character and personality. From this a list of relevant headings could be used by an interviewer to choose those young people who came closest to the ideal. On this basis the fleet was manned for another thirty years.[2]

The headings were:

1. Physical.
Assessment of eyesight and general fitness by the fleet medical officer.

2. Academic.
Passes in the appropriate school exams with strengths in maths, physics and English.

3. Achievements.
"Success" in anything attempted was looked for – sport, youth activities and so on – on the assumption that a similar outcome could be expected in service with the company.

4. Interests.
The occupation of spare time in the limitations imposed by the ship was important, so recreational pursuits would lean towards arts and crafts and away from such pleasures as the theatre and spectator sports. The accent would be on a constructive use of leisure.

5. Personality.
It was hoped that the interview would filter out the undesirables – the "difficult, argumentative, noisy, selfish" – and turn them away from shipboard life. [Alas for such tender leaves of hope in the harsh climate of experience!]

---

[1] Contributors' private papers.
[2] "Blue Funnel Training". Article in *The Nestorian* (no date). J. of the Blue Funnel Assn.

And as Hutson went on to observe:

Matching applicants to the job by objective interviewing was not always understood [and there were] those who still preferred to exercise favouritism or subjective assessment based on qualities unrelated to job requirements. This was well illustrated when two young men who had been accepted as promising juniors on the office staff applied for transfer to the fleet. They were unsuccessful. Great was the consternation to discover that boys who were good enough for the office were not acceptable in the ships. In fact it was never a matter of being "not good enough" but of being unsuitable. The requirements at sea are rarely the same as ashore. [1]

BP had its own training division, headed by Captain "Ronnie" Marsh; he had superintendent status and conducted my interview at Britannic House. One of his favourite lines was that only last week he had turned away a lad with a phenomenal number of O-levels. Later, you learned the truth. (1964)[2]

Mum was forever making suggestions about ways of making a living other than going to sea. The idea of working for the council or a department store nearly drove me mad, hardly less so the attempts she made to tie me up with the daughters of friends, all as alluring as a robber's dog. Not for me, chum! So I deliberately went against her wishes. I joined the Air Cadets because the Sea Cadets were too far away, then came visits from shipping companies and reps from the services, and the careers teacher gave me a book about the MN. I made all the arrangements while my parents were away on holiday.

At the interview I was asked what my father did for a living. Mine had left British Steel for a job with ICI as what they called an inspector on the terylene-spinning section, making sure that the bobbins of terylene and nylon and other fibres were flaw-free. The others gave their fathers' occupations as doctor, master mariner, manager of this or that, farmer... I don't like to think I was ashamed, but when I was asked about mine I explained all about inspecting the bobbins. He just smiled and said, "What you mean is that he's a process worker. Don't worry, we're not interested in social status. This isn't the Royal Navy. We just like to know our cadets' backgrounds. You've nothing to be ashamed of. My father was a fisherman." (BP. 1968)[3]

Not that such a mundane fact had anything to do with his son's being a remarkably elephantine social blunderer.

And by 1980 a novel element was more or less firmly in place, though the companies who had taken on girls as cadets along with the new political ideology were getting wise to what was involved, already anticipated with mixed feelings by all except, apparently, management, politicians, minority pressure-groups and the girls themselves, who were not, as many imagined, pioneering a new age but perpetuating an old aberration. Women at sea (in an executive capacity) were an age-old

---

[1] "Blue Funnel Training", op. cit.

[2] Contributors' private papers.

[3] ibid.

phenomenon, and although there had never been an official bar on them the 1970s saw them as the minority they always had been. Moreover, they tended to be selective as the male was not, steering clear (or being steered clear) of the less gentlemanly areas of the industry. BP's advice to its young women was to avoid confrontation with the men (that is, the hands) and to BEHAVE THEMSELVES, which to at least one new entrant came as the first intimation of what she had let herself in for. It was equally an earnest of what the company saw it had let itself in for, apart from whatever problems attended the training of cadets in general. The cost of exchanging common sense for political conformity (for they seldom, if ever, agree) was, and is, a phenomenon in its own right. R.E. Hutson was responsible for Blue Funnel's adopting the politically-correct line (indeed, he was in no position to repudiate it), and recruited some 20 during his time in office, not without fear of the consequences:

After several years' experience I concluded that unsuitable girls, like unsuitable boys, would fail, but that the difference in sex was not a main factor. Of course one had to take the obvious precautions, especially when the girls were going ashore or when they were in the holds with the dockers. The only girl I knew to have been raped (not in this company) was in a ship on the South American coast, by dockers when she was watching cargo. It was essential for the girls to take taxis while passing through the docks on their way to or from the ship. In most ships the masters and other older men would have a fatherly concern for them and there were few difficulties. However, great care had to be taken with the initial selection: they had to show the necessary degree of determination to hold their own in such a masculine and closed society...[1]

One of the most conspicuous consequences was the wastage factor, not surprisingly, and only a very small fraction of those who began sea careers reached the upper levels. The net loss meant a lot of fruitless expenditure for the employer in what was essentially a political rather than a practical exercise.

As a term, *training* had been one of largely careless usage at sea, representing little better than a process of killing time while picking up the rudiments of the trade where they fell to hand. Post-war, however, the more positive elements of the system gained weight and, although still leaving something to be desired in both theory and practice, training assumed a hitherto underplayed significance. No small part of its importance sprang from an accelerating development of technology in its application to navigation, cargo-handling and ship-control, paralleled by advances in engine design and efficiency, engine-room automation and control, and – revolutionary in its effect – the exclusive use of oil fuel, after a passing experiment with nuclear energy[2]. With some exceptions – Americans were conspicuous in their adherence to the steam-turbine – the diesel engine assumed a universal predominance during the 80s, older

---

[1] Private papers.

[2] The term *nuclear-powered* is incorrect, lending itself to media sensation and public misconception. The power lies in the steam generated by nuclear-fuelled boilers, and the ship is no more nuclear-powered than she was coal- or oil-powered.

steam tonnage with a viable life-expectancy being re-engined in the interests of economy.

Nevertheless the accent was on operation and function rather than on component and systems design, and as far as the seagoing deck or engineer officer was concerned training tended towards the superficial, the methods of operating, and using the information from, equipment and plant rather than in depth of understanding of its conceptual and theoretical principles. As before, the level of training remained as low as possible consonant with current perceptions of safe practice, influenced, as they always had been, by considerations of cost. Noticeably, the academic element gained ground, if not entirely at the expense of the practical, and the correspondence course quickly became *de rigueur*, followed with more or less diligence according to the balance between personal motivation and the employer's interest. "Study time" took on the ritualistic guise of a "right" which, once granted, was variously interpreted by its beneficiaries, as also by those responsible for its observance:

Study time was a problem, and eventually we decided to assert our constitutional rights as per company regulations. The senior man was elected to serve the ultimatum, albeit a timorous one in face of the mate's trenchant personality, which earned us a kind of wondering respect among our contemporaries in other ships. A kind of frayed pride came of surviving the trials of his autocratic rule, and besides, there was something likeable about him, granted even in moments of our blackest hatred. It was shameful to have to admit that we wouldn't willingly have let him down.

Robbie was away for some time while the atmosphere grew taut with foreboding, and when he returned, blank-faced, I broke an oppressive silence with a defeated "Well?"

Wearily, he dropped onto a bunk. "The bastard," he said flatly. "The sly, low-down, unprincipled rat-bag." (We'd been on the Aussie coast for some time.) Fritz started to say something but his voice cracked on a squeak and he subsided with a shrug, then Robbie went on, "He's given us an hour a day" and I brightened, asking him what was so bad about that. "Seven hours a week," he continued bitterly, "to be equalled by seven in our own time."

"Goodbye Saturday afternoon," bleated Fritz, "and that only makes three before bridge watch, anyway. Have I missed out somewhere?" He paused, then added with perverse inconsistency, "I s'pose we can kiss goodbye to free Sundays – "

As the implications dawned on me Robbie explained: our usual turn-to time was 0700, but the mate had just decided (by coincidence at the moment Robbie had presented himself) to amend it to 0600 owing to press of outstanding tasks ("Those frigging cranes," moaned Fritz). However, since our studies were such a concern to us – he was pleased to hear – we needn't turn-to on deck but instead get down to our books for an hour before reporting to him at 6 bells with the evidence, when he would allocate the day's work as usual. We avoided each others' eyes, and after an interval Robbie said, "Whose bright idea was it, anyway?" (B.I. *Bombala*, 1963)[1]

By this date the MNTB had instituted a form of continuous record of progress, not universally adopted but in common use. Reconstituted in 1942 from the old Central

---

[1] Contributors' private papers.

Board for the Training of Officers, composed of representatives of the BOT, LEA's, shipowners, officers' and ratings' organisations, nautical schools and colleges, the board was responsible for the general arrangement of training and study including the setting and marking of annual exams. The curriculum served as the basis for all correspondence courses and schemes of shipboard training, variably efficient as they were, embracing practical seamanship, maths, navigation, general science, ship construction & stability, engineering knowledge and "application of English" – that is, report-writing, which demanded a basic clarity of exposition without undue regard for the niceties of expression and style. As a rule stylists drew upon themselves suspicion and condemnation as a mark of the system's "progress".

Among the companies which had early set up training schemes independently of the MNTB or its predecessor was the BP Tanker Co (earlier the British Tanker Co), its training division providing a correspondence course, setting exams and awarding proficiency prizes, equipping each ship with the necessary text-books. No small part of the training was disciplinary:

Apprentices are expected at all times to obey willingly the orders of senior officers, to be well-mannered, courteous, and tidy in appearance and to make every effort to secure a high standard of attainment in the examinations set by the Company.[1]

Study time included 2 hours of "ship's time" on each of 3 days a week, balanced by at least as much in the apprentice's free time. The programme followed a pattern of daywork in the first year, a combination of that and bridge watchkeeping in the second and third years, and bridge watchkeeping exclusively in the final year. Cargo-work was a prime element throughout, with practical navigation "encouraged" and stress placed on signalling, so much so that the BP fleet enjoyed something of a reputation for its facility with the Aldis:

The 12 to 4 was ideal for practice, and the apprentice entered into the spirit of the thing with, at first, more enthusiasm than skill, leaning heavily on the capacity of people in passing ships for concealing their bewilderment. The effect of his most famous gaffe could only be guessed at, because the other watchkeeper acknowledged all he sent without apparent wonder. His opening gambit was the unconventional *What shit?*, which elicited the other's name, port of departure and destination while the apprentice cursed under his breath before compounding the felony by giving our name as *British Bacon*, acknowledged without query. At the end of the proceedings, looking crestfallen, the Aldis jockey asked me how he'd done. "Shit hot," I said. (*British Beacon*, 1967.)[2]

Anglo-Saxon provided similar facilities, but through the King Edward VII Nautical School, and among the examinations set were those leading to supplementary certificates, for example in proficiency as a lifeboatman, as helmsman, as an Efficient

---

[1] Prospectus, navigating apprenticeship, BP Tanker Co. 1961.
[2] Contributors' private papers.

Deckhand and – instituted finally in 1952 – Able Seaman. Blue Funnel continued its practice of closely monitoring the progress of its midshipmen, both during and between voyages, accommodating them between ships at the midshipmen's hostel, Holm Lea, next-door to which lived the head of the midshipmen's department, Brian Heathcote, who passed control to his successor, Richard Hutson, in 1953, and it was Hutson who saw the old order metamorphose into the purpose-designed residential training facility *Aulis*, opened in September, 1963.

However, as the 50s passed there was a general perception of shortcomings in the system, and the beginnings of a move to improve on both the training and the "image" of the career. As the British fleet expanded so the problems which had dogged it all along increased, wastage compounding the initial difficulty of recruitment. As the most rapidly-expanding sector of the industry at the time, the tanker operators felt the effects most acutely, and in his address to the Tanker Operation Group Captain English also remarked

In my company our aim is first to select the right type of youths for our future masters and chief engineers, secondly to train them, and thirdly to keep them in our service throughout their working lives. To do this it is necessary to offer the well-educated boy leaving school a clearly-defined, well-paid and progressive career, having satisfied ourselves he has the capacity and temperament to learn and fit into our trade. In this endeavour we are, of course, in competition with a host of shore employers looking for precisely the same kind of material.

Are the right numbers of boys of the right type still prepared to make the sea their career? The answer can only be a cautious yes. Britain has always been fortunate in respect of potential deck officers but there has in recent years been a fall-off in numbers of applicants and the effects of this were acutely felt recently in a shortage of junior deck officers. The position is slightly easier today, but it may well be due to the reduction in numbers of ships in service. There is no doubt, however, that whatever the cause – and theories abound – the sea service is losing some of its long-held appeal for adventurous-minded youngsters.

Today the tanker-owner cannot be entirely satisfied with a training system that rests with the indenturing of a youth, leaving him to find his own way with such help as he can get from all-too-frequently disinterested[sic] senior officers. True, the majority of MN officers have made the grade by themselves, but many technical developments have occurred in the post-war marine world [which] call for the learning of new approaches to old problems. Additionally, the tempo of operations has increased greatly, and in no trade more than in the transportation of oil ...

Which, at the sharp end, looked like this:

Wednesday, 9th March. 1957.
Mena al Ahmadi.
0340 called for bridge duty. Rather chilly, wind NxW force 2. Just before 0500 the pilot boarded and assisted by two tugs we proceeded alongside No.10 South Jetty. 0521 in position and commenced discharge of ballast. I stood down at 0530 and assisted in hoisting flags and attending to lights. Following this I assisted on deck till 0930 with a break for breakfast 0715-0735. 0850 the loading commenced. Cargo: Kuwait crude 35,350 tons.

1400-1645 assisted with loading operation. On deck again at 1930 for completion, battening down and preparing for sea. Completed cargo 2230, ship ready for sea, awaiting papers, pilot, etc.
(Apprentice's journal, Shell ss *Zenatia*)

There was nothing wrong with the indenture system, only in the way it was implemented by individuals; training depended on people's goodwill. The mate saw Archer and me as nothing better than skivvies. Academically I did quite well, though after I'd won the Thomas Gray Memorial Prize I got fed up with study and let it slide. (Shell, 1948)[1]

Standing by the ship at Cammell Laird's we were on weekly wages, receiving one penny, all that was left after deductions. Three of us took it in good part but Roger, the most dedicated, the only one who bothered to study at sea, trained on C.B. Fry's famous training ship, wasn't amused. I think it was the start of his disenchantment with the sea career. (Athel, 1949)[2]

I was sent to keep a lookout on the bridge wing when we ran into heavy driving rain crossing the Bight, from midnight to 0400. I couldn't see any ships, or the point. (Blue Star, 1949)[3]

The mate decided that the nightwatchman shouldn't spend his time lounging about so provided me with a turk's-head paint-brush, black paint and orders to paint the hatch-coamings by torchlight. When the captain saw the state I was in when I gave him his early morning call he wanted to know why, so I told him. He said that even thirty years before apprentices weren't treated as badly, and he must have given the mate a rollocking because my night-time labour was abruptly curtailed, with very bad grace. (Hain, 1949)[4]

And in P&O's *Iberia:*

...Did a lot of corr co maths. Strathmore *in with us – big party in 1/O's cabin.*

...Settled down to the month's essay, A Voyage of Discovery, *about Matthew Flinders. This took most of the afternoon, then did a general science paper on Radar. The lunchtime (rubber & ruler) test series has terminated but the mile walk has taken its place (22 times round the bridge).*

...Did the C/O's indent and several CC questions. Only a few to do now. At 9pm a terrific WSW swell caused the closing of all deadlights.

...Did CC from 3 til 6 when eyes got very tired so stopped. Exam results – av. 91.6% which may get me a prize. Reading B.I. Centenary.

---

[1] Contributors' private papers.
[2] ibid.
[3] ibid.
[4] ibid.

...Instructed in the art of wire-splicing by "Shady" Lane. I managed a not too hot one. Then back to CC. Filched 1lb of ice-cream from the fridge and scoffed the lot.

..."Woman overboard" alarm at 2.05. Found in laundry after search position had been sent out. This delayed work on CC but finished practically another two books. Only 8½ questions left.

...Completed all correspondence course. Hurrah! Handed it in. (Cadet's diary, 1957)

As Captain English was addressing the Tanker Operation Group his company was already involved in what became a radical departure from not only the system of training as it had evolved but also with the notion of apprenticeship *per se*, though it had still a few years to run. In collaboration with the navigation school at Plymouth, the MOT (the BOT's current alias), the Ministry of Education and other shipping interests including Blue Funnel, Shell sent a batch of apprentices to the school in September 1960 to attend the first Mid-Apprenticeship Release course, its purpose the general overhaul and refreshment, to say nothing of filling in the blanks, of the apprentice's accumulation of professional wisdom. The course was residential, lasting 6 months, and was soon emulated by other schools, drawing their raw material from nearly all shipping companies employing apprentices and cadets. Characteristically, Blue Funnel instituted its own course, based at the midshipmen's hostel and later *Aulis*, after Richard Hutson had conferred with the authorities over the question of remission of sea-time for the periods spent at the shore base between voyages. From this had sprung the idea of MAR, when *Conway*, asked to play a part with its residential facilities, declined, so missing, it would seem, an opportunity that might well have changed its subsequent fortunes. Shell consulted with Hutson, approached Wakeford at Warsash, who declined to become involved at that stage, and so took its custom to the more amenable atmosphere of Plymouth.

Elder Dempster, as a partner of Blue Funnel in the Ocean Group, commented on the new arrangement in dry and prolix fashion:

In past years there have been some who have lacked the self-discipline needed to apply themselves to their studies. It has become more and more apparent that the shipping industry is appreciating the value of Mid-apprenticeship residential[sic] courses of 6 months at an approved nautical college to encourage a midshipman to keep up to date with his theoretical work... The MAR course is now recognised by the MOT and in future all company midshipmen will spend six months of the apprenticeship attending a residential course at the Liverpool Technical College. This 6-month period will count as full sea-time.[1]

Which was to say that it counted in full as part of the sea-time required for 2nd mate. The technical college's resources were combined with what the company offered, facilities greatly expanded when the company's residential facility, River

---

[1] "Training for Service in our Fleet". Article in *E.D. Fleet History, 1852-1986.* p.494.

House, opened in October 1962, where the course was divided into two 3-month sessions, the first after 18 months at sea, the second a year later. The company was categorical about the course's purpose, which was to

> ...*supplement and expand the academic training which in the past was based mainly on the correspondence courses; develop all aspects of officer-like qualities; open up new spheres of interest, activities, hobbies and team sports, including boat-building, sailing and expeditions; broaden the views of cadets and cultivate their interest in all aspects of the shipping industry; and to give them an opportunity to study French to enable them to converse more freely with African officials at ports in some of the independent countries of West Africa.*[1]

They were also encouraged to give their attention to such vocational subjects as meteorology, oceanography and astronomy, which, although relevant to the ship's work, lay outside the syllabus for 2nd mate – as, indeed, did much of the course's content, for all its virtues, thereby incurring the old problem of retaining the cadet's interest. His abiding vice was to wilfully confine his attention to the narrow path of the examination curriculum and to resist, passively or actively, efforts to divert his attention from it, however improving they happened to be. It wasn't so much the fact that he resented these diversions as that he regarded them in a somewhat casual light, transient fripperies the sole virtue of which lay in their unimportance. Far from being a period of intent application to professional matters, the course was looked upon as a welcome break from the serious business of shipboard routine.

Aulis was quite new. Len Holder was in charge, a second mate with the company. They'd built an extension to the old middies' hostel at Riversdale, where we lived in dormitories. There was a lot of drinking, and sometimes complaints from local residents about cadets making a noise coming back from the pub. I was blamed for not stopping it once, as the senior man present, but it hadn't been us, only some engineer cadets in another group. I was hauled up to account for it, and told them I was back in my bunk, reading. Len Holder had paid me a visit and confirmed my story, so I wasn't punished. Seniority was important. (1963)[2]

I heard about the MCR course[3] but no-one was able to tell me much about it beyond the fact that it was running and that it wasn't important. My inquiries came to nothing, so after a while I let it go, with my time cut out trying to keep up with the correspondence course. Later, I met one or two who'd been on it, and thought maybe I'd missed out on a bit of a laugh. (BI, 1964)[4]

I presented myself with some forty others at the Empire Memorial Club, known as the "Stack of Bricks", on the Commercial Road, for a college course half-way through my time; it was supposed to fill in the gaps to date, but its value was limited. For one thing there was too little emphasis on 2nd mate's work while we dabbled with master's stuff. Sport was

---

[1] "Gateway to the Sea". Article in ED house journal *Sea*, 1962. p.14.

[2] Contributors' private papers.

[3] Alternative title: *Mid-Cadetship Release*.

[4] Contributors' private papers.

encouraged, which proved how unfit we were, social life depended on the weight of our wallets and contact with the Fursedown Ladies' Teacher Training College in Tooting, and local hostelries were popular, especially the one right opposite, the Coopers' Arms. Then there was the Prospect of Whitby and, on the Isle of Dogs, the City Arms. The BP people threw in £3 apiece to buy a clapped-out Bedford Dormobile and as a shareholder I travelled free; others were charged, risking summary eviction at 30mph for refusal or default. We struck up friendships, of course. My buddy was George Downer. He perished on the *British Crown* off Umm Said[1] about three months later. (King Edward VII Nautical School/BP Tankers, 1966)[2]

Hailed as a success by the establishment, if not by all who drank of its waters, the course led, for this reason among others, to the further development of the ONC/D sandwich scheme, offering openings to a new degree in nautical studies, or science, as a form of alternative to the extra master's certificate, which began to die on its feet, not unmourned. The scheme was viewed in a somewhat ambivalent light by all except, apparently, the schools and colleges and those who entered it as students, drawn mainly by its underlying motive, which was to establish a parallel between shore-based and sea qualifications, though to exactly what end was never entirely clear; thinking was muddled between the conflicting arguments of "updating" the sea qualification structure and giving it a greater validity in shore applications, something shipowners, notwithstanding the noises of approval some of them felt obliged to make, looked upon without active enthusiasm. It was also hoped, rather vaguely, that through it the sea career would appear more attractive to school leavers.

Unfortunately certification arrangements have little effect on the overriding consideration in the matter, which is the quality of life. Where once upon a time the affairs of the ship as both workplace and home had engendered qualities of communal life with shared interests, shorter voyages (cited, paradoxically, as an example of improved conditions at sea but which tended to diminish commitment to ship and shipmates with inevitable and obvious consequences) and altered trading standards and methods brought about a deterioration of enough moment to tarnish the attraction of the life in the eyes of boys of initiative and ability – "adventurous-minded youngsters" – whose imaginations were in any case being exercised along other avenues of opportunity. And, conversely, as the industry found itself obliged to accept school qualifications that in many respects fell short of the ideal, so the new training structure was seen, in its liberal nature, to be less demanding than the old certificate system with its rigorous, if narrow, standards.

Be that as it may, the changes went ahead, supplanting the old system entirely, training becoming more academic and the certificate sequence extending to additional lower grades in order to accommodate calls for personnel with at least some sort of bridge watchkeeping accreditation. Under the 1970 MSA the Class III (Deck)

---

[1] Caught fire after an explosion in the cargo tanks and declared a c.t.l., November 1966.

[2] Contributors' private papers.

Certificate was superior to a new Class IV, introduced as the basic bridge watchkeeping licence, and a Class V for home-trade waters.

By 1980, with much British-owned tonnage under FOC, British officers were seen as comparatively expensive to employ, not least owing to the training to which they were entitled by statute; the FOC operation's commitment to training was either non-existent or of a much lower order than under the red ensign. Third-world officers not only cost less to employ but also less to train, financed as most of their training was by their respective governments. While not necessarily less than that of their British counterparts (though opinions varied on the point), their expertise was perceived by most operators to be adequate, giving, if nothing more positive, a viable chance of the ship's getting safely from A to B. With the underwriters behind them that was all the owners required in the new age of expedient and short-term business, hardly distinguishable, on the surface, from the age of a century before...

The ONC/D system began with several variations on the theme but settled into a typical format commencing with the 2-week induction course at college. It was followed by 6 to 9 months of sea service and "guided study", the exciting new term for the correspondence course, a further 18 weeks back in college, another 12 months at sea, and a final college session of 18 weeks preparing for the ONC in nautical science and the 2nd mate's exam, from parts of which the ONC counted as exemption. The total period of training amounted to 3½ years, followed by 6 months at sea as junior OOW before full watchkeeping status was attained. The OND scheme, requiring as its ideal two A-level passes, ran along similar lines with more exemptions from 2nd mate and some from the 1st mate's exam, leading ultimately to a BSc in nautical science or maritime studies.

Adjustments had effected slight changes by 1980, the 2-week induction course prefacing Phase 2 (10-12 months at sea); Phase 3 (38 weeks in college, passing for EDH and lifeboatman's certificates, R/T restricted certificate, first-aid certificate and the TEC diploma which exempted holders from parts of the Class III exam); Phase 4 (12 months at sea); Phase 5 (14 weeks in college leading to the Radar Observer certificate and the Class IV) and Phase 6, 4-6 months at sea to complete time for the Class III certificate.

The training officer was a difficult, sarcastic man. The only certificate I took was lifeboat. Sandy Yates and I had to teach a dozen young Indian ratings all about it, then we all took the test together in the Royal Albert Dock and passed. We had the blue-eyed boy of chief mates whose idea of training was straight out of *Two Years Before the Mast* – no set hours of work except 24 a day, and as for training – "You'll get all you need at school when you go up for your ticket, laddie!" Training! I have to laugh. On the *Queda* we were allowed on the bridge only on Sundays to present journals and do the day's run. And on the *Kenya*, homeward bound, 310 passengers, sudden fog passing Gib: cadet ordered to the bridge, captain mans radar with the C/O, and cadet on the RAS plotter. Never seen it before in my life and now I'm supposed to know how to use it. Too late to learn now, though, and as thick as a hedge. All those lives depending on the plot being correct. I was terrified for the next 6 hours. (BI, 1964)[1]

The company took a lively interest in our progress and falling behind brought a sharp rebuke, with a summons to the citadel if you didn't pull your socks up. The ultimate sanction was, of course, the order of the boot. Nothing like that happened with us, but two Scots lads, engineer cadets with P&O, got drunk in the Westoe at lunchtime and came back to tell one of the lecturers his fortune; they were on their way north within 24 hours, *sans* job. Conversely, if you did well you got a letter of congratulation.   (S. Shields/BP Tankers, OND(Deck), 1968)[2]

Two little lads with raindrop suits and brothel-creepers came up to my cabin and reported, saying they were deck cadets. I thought, deck cadets! Well – all right. Then along came two young men in greatcoats, in uniform. Smart, assured young men. Engineer cadets. Of course Shell went all out for the ATS with the express purpose of getting a better type of engineer, while the deck side didn't seem so important; standards weren't stressed there as much as for engineers, and the company seemed satisfied with what it was getting. (1950s)[3]

Better type of engineer or not, down below the ATS shared the watch with tradition in more or less wary concord, neither on its own sufficient to meet demand, particularly after the ending of conscription.[4] Uncertificated engineers and those sailing under dispensation continued to play a prominent part in the manning of the engine-room.

Beginning with the 2-year opening phase at technical college, the scheme continued with 18 months at sea as an engineer cadet (though some companies specified indentured service as distinct from an employment contract) and a third, shore-based, phase at a suitable works or shipyard to bring the total time to 4½ years, with further sea-time necessary as a junior engineer, a minimum of 15 months, to qualify for an attempt at the 2nd-Class Certificate, the OND exempting a candidate from Part A and Section 1 of Part B.

By 1973 the course had been shortened to 4 years by reduction of Phase 2 to 12 months (later split into two 6-month periods following phases 1 and 3 respectively), by which date the new grade of MET, lower than the OND, had been introduced for much the same reason as had been the Class IV(Deck) certificate. The Advanced MET exempted holders from those parts of the 2nd-Class exam hitherto accorded the OND, while the OND earned exemption from them and from Part 1 of the 1st-Class exam. The HND was a 3½-year course carrying the same exemptions as the OND while also leading to the exam for Chartered Engineer, enjoying degree status.

The almost constant state of flux in both deck and engineering training structures reflected something of the indecision over ways to deal with the recruitment difficulty,

---

[1] Contributors' private papers.
[2] ibid.
[3] ibid.
[4] Last draft demobbed November, 1962. See Appx.5.

which possessed two distinct facets, one the ever-decreasing interest in the sea, the other the educational standards of what interest there was, both falling worryingly short of what was ideally required. No small part of the changes, and the level of training, amounted to compromise in order to maintain the supply of new entrants even though the fleet as a whole was, by the 80s, in apparently irreversible decline. Not only that, but also the colleges, threatened with extinction, were anxious to keep classrooms occupied rather more than they were interested in the quality of instruction and student achievement. The two are, of course, mutually inimical: the higher the standard the fewer the numbers, a fact of life studiously repressed by the politics of the system.

One of the greatest and most valuable innovations of the ONC/D and ATS schemes for deck and engine-room respectively was the contiguous locations of the departments while ashore, engineer and deck cadets sharing not only the college's facilities but also the accommodation; for example, at South Shields and at the Blue Funnel/Elder Dempster hostel arrangements in Liverpool. Foreseen and hoped for, the result was an improvement in relations between the two departments from which the ship herself should, all other things being equal, have benefited.

In coll we passed the summer vac in drydock. They weren't instructed to look after us, weren't paying either, so we were cheap – or free – labour. At one stage I worked on the foreman's Ford Pop, otherwise making tea for the lathe operator. I did some work on the *British Sportsman*, but the rest of it was rubbish. Then I did my final year at Cammell Laird's. Sounds very grand, but as long as you were inside the gate they didn't give a damn what you were doing. I'd failed my OND at Stage 1 so at C-L they sent me to Riversdale one day a week to get ONC. It got me back on the straight and narrow. I'd been very cavalier about my studies in those first two years. (Shell/ATS, 1953)[1]

Then they put us on watches. Horrendous, being yanked out of bed at four in the morning. I was on the Second's watch, but more importantly, on with the Second's junior, this fellow Bert, a right bloody conniver. Traditional man[2], his first trip to sea and me a rookie cadet. First thing every bloody morning and afternoon was carboning the boilers – bashing the carbon off the burners. I didn't actually do much of it, but I was there. It was bloody stinking hot; I'd never come across such temperatures before, and the first half-hour of the watch was a bloody purgatory. There I was in this red-hot place, where I didn't want to be, doing a job I didn't want to do. Afterwards we'd have a cup of tea, then there'd be the job of analysing boiler-water, simple for us because we'd done it in college. Also simple were the bilges – "Ah, the pump's not pulling; suction must be blocked." That was for us, every time. (Shell *Tracurus*, 1954)[3]

We always wore uniform, of course. If we weren't in boiler-suits we were in uniform. I was quite surprised at ships where there was no uniform; staggered, in fact. It just didn't look right.

---

[1] Contributors' private papers.

[2] Product of the shore-based apprenticeship scheme.

[3] Contributors' private papers.

30. At the sign of the Flying Angel. Durban, 1946.
    (Capt J.C. Moffat)

31. Sunday morning ritual: Bonzo, Chicko, Tom, Gerry. ss *Marsdale*, 1946.
    (G.L. Frost)

PLATE 17

33. Counting feet, ss *Gatineau Park*, Sydney NSW. 1947.
(G.L. Frost)

32. Cleaning holds after a coal cargo: 2 apprentices, ss *Marsdale*.
Vila Constitucion, Argentina, 1947.
(G.L. Frost)

PLATE 18

34. Paint your ship, sir? ss *Clan Macrae*, 1946.
(Capt J.C. Moffat)

PLATE 19

35&36.   Variations on working rig. Shell, 1946.
(Capt R.J. Williams)

PLATE 20

38. First-class passenger "Taormina" with minder.
ss *Empire Talisman*, 1947.
(Capt A.H. Osgood)

37. ...two in the bush. On leave, Liverpool, 1947.
(Capt A.H. Osgood)

PLATE 21

40. Time off, Alexandria. Shell, 1946.
(Capt R.J. Williams)

39. Passing ships: two brothers meet, ss *Empire Star.*
Adelaide, 1950.
(Capt A.H. Osgood)

PLATE 22

41. The tea trade. Apprentices, Palmer's Drydock Co., Swansea, 1948.
    (H.S. Llewelyn)

42. Alternative training scheme: engineer cadets. Shell, 1955.
    (D.M. Jones)

PLATE 23

43. Practical seamanship class. Plymouth Sch of Nav. 1957.
     (W.B. Gibson)

44. "Ample time is set aside for study." 1961.
     (BP Tanker Co.)

PLATE 24

46. *Practical navigation, forenoon watch, mv Landaura*, 1963.
(Author's collection)

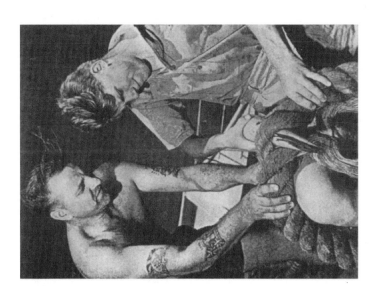

45. Learning the ropes: bosun & apprentice, 1961.
(BP Tanker Co.)

PLATE 25

48. Study in black & white. mv *Chantala*, 1962.
(Capt M.L. Bechley)

47. Full away: the developed apprentice. ss *Ottawa Valley*, 1953.
(H.S. Llewelyn)

PLATE 26

49. In the swim, mv *Chantala*, 1962.
(Capt M.L. Bechley)

50. Two of the seven Ages of Man: cadet and chief officer, mv *Chantala*, 1962.
(Capt M.L. Bechley)

PLATE 27

51. Crossing the Line, mv *Chantala*, 1962.
(Capt M.L. Bechley)

52. Alternative training. Missions to Seamen, Hull, 1967.
(I. Squires)

PLATE 28

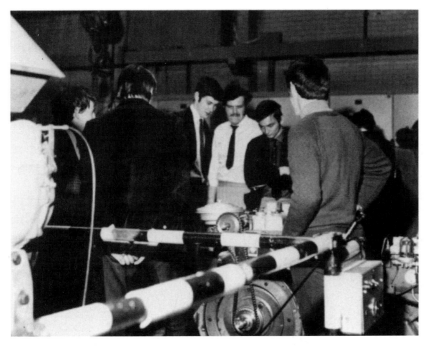

53. Alternative training, workshop visit, Dursley, 1971.
    (I. Squires)

54. *HMS Conway*. Quarter-boys, Christmas term, 1961.
    (Author's collection)

PLATE 29

55. Classic cadet-ship: ss *Devon*, BISN Co., 1934.
(Capt I.E. Thomas)

56. Classic cadet-ship: ss *Durham*, Federal S.N. Co., 1930s.
(Author's collection)

PLATE 30

57. tv *St Briavels*, South American Saint Line, 1947.
    (SASL Newsletter)

58. *Opalia*. From the water-colour by Cadet P.H. Green, 1970.
    (Capt M.T. John)

PLATE 31

THE FOUR-MASTED BARQUE "PAMIR."

59. *Pamir* under Union S.S. Co's management, 1947.
   (The Trident)

PLATE 32

We had laundrymen, but cadets did their own. It was part of the training. We had to clean our cabin; it had to be immaculate, the toilet immaculate. Captain's rounds on Saturday morning. Stewards served us at table but you could tell they weren't happy about it; Guinness-soaked wrecks. (P&O/ATS, 1970)[1]

When I joined there were 29 of us ATS cadets, and by the time I joined *Canberra* for Phase 3 there were only six of us left. Some went as soon as they finished their time – didn't even try to get their tickets, to get something out of it. (P&O, 1971)[2]

I joined this 150,000-ton OBO as extra 2nd. Single-handed watches. At 5 o'clock one afternoon things started to go wrong and only one man there – me. I happened to go into the workshop and found an engineer cadet fixing a pin in his glasses or something. I thought – Ah, just the boy! and told him to go and deal with some minor problem or other while I saw to the catastrophes, then I pissed off in a hurry. When I got to the control-room eventually there was this cadet with his thumb up his bum. "Excuse me," he says, as if he's talking to a moron, "I don't think you quite understand. I was just down here fixing my glasses. I'm not on watch or anything like that." Well – Jesus! When I'd got over the shock I kicked his arse and told him to get out there and just *do* what he'd been told. (P&O, 1974)[3]

Training apart, conditions on board showed a general and steady improvement, given that the appreciable differences between companies and ships during the early post-war period became blurred through both the design of new tonnage and the wider span of accordance with agreements arrived at between employers and unions (if not the employees themselves). The outcome was that the best tended to lose their distinction while the more rugged lost their perverse appeal for the wilder spirits. However, the yardsticks by which quality of accommodation and victualling were assessed followed an obvious tendency, and not all so-called improvements earned universal approval. Partly owing to proximity to machinery including main (diesel) engines and partly to mechanical ventilation (air-conditioning) systems, noise levels became problematic, while the placing of accommodation at the after end of the ship added a see-saw effect to the often perceptible flexing. Many were of the opinion that, on balance, the older designs had been more comfortable. Furthermore, weighing comfort against considerations of safety that took on a flush of paranoia in bureaucratic circles produced a marked tilt towards the latter with a fine disregard for, or blindness to, the subtler value to a ship's efficiency (and therefore safety) of pleasantly-appointed living-space. Safety, so-called (much of which was mere window-dressing), lent a tone of clinical austerity to the accommodation that played its part in what came to be identified as "stress".

On one point, however, there was no serious dissent – the vital one of diet and victualling, which received the attention it had, by custom, been denied from time

---

[1] Contributors' private papers.

[2] ibid.

[3] ibid.

immemorial, and in fits and starts, at differing rates, the food on board improved in quality, variety and preparation, its presentation all the while evolving into the economically logical one of the cafeteria, though saloon service complete with resentful (white) stewards remained in passenger ships and some others. Not least because of its prominence in the minds of the public at large, which, after wartime stringency and the peacetime rationing that followed, gained an unprecedented significance, diet was seen as a positive incentive to recruitment, and no foreign-going shipping company could afford a reputation for poor feeding, generally defined as occupying the fringes of the BOT scale, for all its marked improvement. For example, biscuit and salt provisions were dropped in 1957, and with them centuries of hard-case tradition lamented only by those to whom an atrocious excuse for food had drifted into the rosy sunset of nostalgic retrospection. Even the worst feeders sought to advertise an appreciably better standard than the statutory basic.

However, a tradition loth to quit the scene was the system's manipulation by those responsible for its proper stewardship, and ships' pantry stores continued as a lucrative source of illicit perquisites attaching to the catering department, often enough with the active connivance of the ship's master. Gradually, with an almost audible tearing sound, it slipped out of vogue, as did time-honoured methods by which the half-deck supplemented its meals. In terms of quantity at least, the daily allowance was adequate to the point of shameful waste, and into the wake's pother went galley slops that would have made the pre-war apprentice – let alone his wind-ship predecessors – weep with chagrin.

Our accommodation, on the main deck beneath the bridge on the starboard side, had been for passengers before the war, when twelve had been carried. Our cabin – we didn't use the term half-deck – was quite comfortable, though without running water. There was a thing called a compactum for washing in, but nearby was a shower with hot & cold, and a toilet. (*Port Adelaide*, 1945)[1]

...a cabin marked *Midshipmen*. For two cadets it was very small: two bunks with a desk between, a porthole looking forward towards the bridge, a compactum, a chair, a small wardrobe, all in polished mahogany set off with brass fittings and porthole rim. (*Clan MacNeil*, 1948)[2]

We had a main cabin with three bunks, settee and chest of drawers. The study was just big enough for a small table, a settee and three small wardrobes. Bathroom and toilet were across the alleyway. (Hain *Trelawny*, 1949)[3]

...Gell and I are in a very small cabin with another cadet who doesn't arrive until Thursday, called Carradine. He has already done a trip. We have to share wardrobes, etc. As the saloon

---

[1] Contributors' private papers.
[2] ibid.
[3] ibid.

is being painted we have our food in our cabin, brought along by our "boy". It is in the following position. X marks the spot. It is about 8ft wide and 15ft long [See p.238]. From sitting on the bunks, which are Dunlopillo, the sleeping shouldn't be too difficult. We each have a light over our bunks to read by.

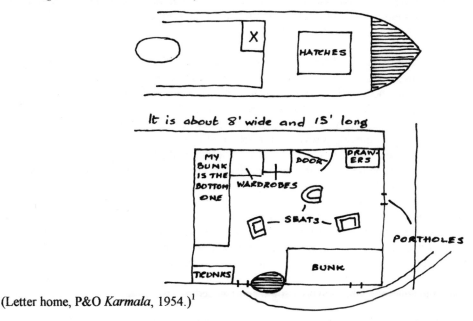

(Letter home, P&O *Karmala*, 1954.)[1]

Everything was very spartan, painted metal, but when the apprentices came along extra accommodation had to be put in, and being British the bunks were wood. Two to a cabin, three cabins – six engineer apprentices and some deck apprentices, a lot when there were only thirty-odd people on board. We were on a milk-run, Thameshaven to Mena, which exploded the myth about seeing the world; but then, if you want to see the world you don't do engineering. (Shell *Caprinus* (T2), 1955)[2]

Nor, for that matter, do you opt for tankers, though in fact engineers had as good – or bad – a chance of seeing the world as anyone else on board.

...At 9.30am we boarded the BR ferry Duke of York *at Harwich, and the three of us shared a cabin. At Bremen we were met by a tall Gentleman wearing sunglasses and tanned by tropical suns, who introduced himself as the captain before taking us to lunch. By 5pm we had arrived at the dockyard[sic] and noticed our ship with a buff funnel and red Shell. "My home," I thought, "for the next few months." Our first duty was to report to the Chief Officer who showed us our cabin. It was about 20ft x 30ft. On each side was a wide bunk and wardrobe. We had a table on which we would do our studying and writing. Although the shower was next-door we also had a hand-bowl with hot & cold water. The floor[sic] was covered by a deep red*

[1] Contributors' private papers.
[2] ibid.

carpet. There was curtains on the port, at the door and in front of the bunks. It all looked very homely and comfortable. (Essay: *Joining My First Ship*, 1957)[1]

There was an inspection every Sunday morning; we had to do all our own cleaning and washing and the rest of it. We had a strip of carpet in the cabin. Used to tie a rope to it and throw it over the stern to stew for a few hours. Polishing the floors[*sic*] and portholes. The deck cadets laquered the brass. (ATS, Shell, 1955)[2]

On the *Kampala* two of us shared a cabin – two bunks one above the other, a settee or day-bed, chest of drawers, saloon chair, washbasin, single wardrobe (but big enough), two windows looking out on the boat-deck, starboard side. On the deck a fitted carpet; curtains and upholstery in matching floral cotton fabric. A jalousie inner door and similar window shutters, a bulkhead fan and the usual Punkah-Louvre fresh-air blowers. We shared the officers' showers and lavatory. I thought it was comfortable until I joined the *Bombala*, where two of us occupied a double cabin and the senior a separate single. The double one was palatial, bunks at opposite sides behind curtains, double desk with two chairs, two ports looking out over the raised quarter-deck and No.4 hatch, fitted carpet, shower and lavatory *en suite*. Drawers in the desk and beneath the bunks, with two wardrobes, provided ample space for our gear, and the ship was equipped with a full-scale laundry complete with dhobi-wallahs, so our whites were unusually clean and smart. The single cabin was a hutch by comparison, but it afforded a privacy I coveted. The accommodation was air-conditioned, and there was no way of escape through the ports, which opened only at the top third, so the atmosphere, if cool in the tropics, was a bit claustrophobic. One bulkhead of the double cabin was part of the engine-room casing, and the noise and vibration took some getting used to. (BI, 1962)[3]

Accommodation on the *Botany Bay* was brilliant; double cabin with single beds, not bunks. We had our own accommodation – study, day-room, the cabin, and ate in the officers' saloon. (ATS/P&O, 1970s)[4]

The food was awful, liver and dried egg for breakfast, things like that. Duff at weekends, but it was terrible. We ate with the officers, though, a paradox: there we were, minding our table manners and the food barely edible. Then the stewards contracted syphilis or something and we had to serve as assistant stewards. We also had to do the master's and chief engineer's washing, for which we got nothing, no time off or anything. (Shell, 1945)[5]

Samgara sported hot & cold running water to the washbasin in the half-deck, and we forged a key to the steward's store. On top of that we were put in charge of the military food store in No.3 tween-deck, and I wondered if there was some sort of catch. The drawback with filching

---

[1] Contributors' private papers.
[2] ibid.
[3] ibid.
[4] ibid.
[5] ibid.

from there was that the booty had to be eaten on the spot, and a 7lb tin of peaches with condensed milk between two was a severe test. (Blue Funnel, 1946)[1]

The catering staff were Goanese, with a British chief steward, a superior type who dressed like a purser; he'd once been a steward with Imperial Airways. The food was all right, better than in the white-crew ships, where I found British cooking at its worst. We never went hungry; there was always bread and cheese, though never fresh milk. The bread was weevily, though, and eggs stale. Sundays were marked by chicken and BOT duff. Often there were tab-nabs, usually fruit cake said to be darkened with gravy-browning, with afternoon tea. My first meal consisted of kippers followed by pork chops. I hadn't seen white bread since the outbreak of war. (Athel *Empire Paladin*, 1946)[2]

We were grudgingly allowed into the saloon for meals, but some ships had an apprentices' mess. For breakfast we got corn-flakes or porridge, bacon & egg or dry hash and egg, or kipper, with bread and marmalade; light cooked lunch or perhaps cold; and for dinner soup, a stew or hot-pot, and a pudding of the weighty steamed variety. We also saw tinned tomatoes, sausages, salt fish, curry & rice, corned beef, Spam, salads, prunes and ice-cream. (Hain, 1950)[3]

...Food has been good all along, but excellent lately. Sunday it was Turkey and Christmas pudding, today Roast Pork, and Fish and "French Fried Potatoes". Once a week we have pancakes – two, three and sometimes four each. Peach Melba was on last night, and ice-cream, and we often get trifle. Of course there is the inevitable cold meat and salad and Curry & Rice, the latter being shunned by practically everyone. I have an egg every day. (Letter home; P&O *Karmala*, 1954.)[4]

The shunning of curry & rice was an indicator of the expectations of the times, but P&O people weren't the connoisseurs of it to be found in the saloons of the BI fleet:

The first impression was visual as the steward brought the side dishes – colours a bit lurid but perfectly in keeping. Then the saffron rice, light grainy stuff piled up until you cried enough; after that the curry, from a choice of perhaps three on offer in a repertoire that seemed endless – meat, fish and vegetarian kinds, all works of art. There were no limits. I stuffed myself with chilli patties, poppodums, Bombay duck, chuppaties and every sort of salad vegetable, some I'd never before come across, gorged on the curry and drank great draughts of iced *pani*, to no effect. Sunday dinner was a *tour de force*; no-one bothered with things like roasts, also on the menu; curry was king. There were five galleys altogether, catering for passengers, crew and officers and the various dietary customs of India. We'd drop in on them in the course of our work round the decks, and the *bhandaries* always gave us something to try, delighted at our approval, which wasn't particularly discerning. Eating was a sensation, an entertainment, and a good curry seemed to promote waves of mutual goodwill and wellbeing,

---

[1] Contributors' private papers.

[2] ibid.

[3] ibid.

[4] ibid.

helped, in some quarters, by large scotch-and-sodas. After *Conway*'s stuff it was a revelation. (BI *Kampala*, 1962)[1]

We met the cadets from the Union Steam ship, parked across the way at Wooloomooloo, and invited them over. They were amazed at our accommodation, and even more amazed to learn that we ate in the saloon waited on by our steward, amazing us in turn by confessing that they had to get their meals from the galley and eat in their cabin. (BI *Bombala*, 1963.)[2]

Having a cook who wasn't a piss-head made a hell of a difference. If the ship was a good feeder you didn't mind the bullshit, but if the food was bad you'd get thoroughly demoralised. On the *Bombardier* we hit really heavy weather and the cook took to his bunk with a couple of bottles. We got some bread from the second steward and for the best part of a week lived on piccalilli sandwiches. The cook was blotto. We tried to sober the old bugger up. He was good when he was sober. (BP Tankers, 1968)[3]

On the *Pando Strait* we ate in the saloon at our own table. On the *Canberra*, if one of the cargo ships was in they'd come over to visit us and we'd lay it on thick, show them our menus. We'd be poncing round, immaculate in white boiler-suits, white shoes – white gloves, even. A complete and utter load of shit, of course, but in a way they seemed to expect it of us. (P&O, 1970s.)[4]

But to one facet of the life, the effect of which was fundamental and far-reaching, all other considerations took second place, and that was length of voyage. Here, also differing widely between company and company into the 60s, not least owing to the nature of the respective trade, time spent away from home became an overriding, not to say emotive, issue, the answer to which seemed obvious, and the obvious was taken as the ideal: shorter spells of service, if not voyages, also featured among the recruiting attractions. As with accommodation, it was a measure which ignored the voice of dissent emanating from the group to which long voyages were either of no concern or positively attractive, a distinct but eccentric minority upon which, at one time, the ship's efficiency had depended.

We did an 8-month trip, then back at Rotterdam most of the engine-room crowd paid off and were replaced, all by Geordies. Then away for 3 months before drydock in the Tyne, where all the blokes who'd joined in Rotterdam were relieved – off you go, lads! Meanwhile me and this other chap from Liverpool, and the chief, stood by. Then comes sailing-time, another crowd joins, and off we go again for another 3 months. This means, now, that I've been on this bloody ship for 13 months, during which I've had 2 days at home, so I sat down and thought

---

[1] Contributors' private papers.

[2] ibid.

[3] ibid.

[4] ibid.

things through and – well, this is no bloody good. The grub's rotten, the conditions are rotten, every bloody thing's rotten. So I wrote to Joe Shell – *Dear Sir, Bye-bye*. (ATS, 1956.)[1]

In general, improved conditions were attributed to the NMB's work combined with the unions' activities, which, uniquely among the breed, and not without the owners' willingness to compromise, maintained a record for moderation broken only by one major strike, in the 60s, and an occasional wildcat embarrassment, none of which involved officers and apprentices except as affecting their ships' operation.

As for health, it assumed greater importance than ever, over and above the fitness requirements for new entrants and serving personnel: international immunisation certificates were required against listed communicable diseases, while on board medical facilities had to meet stringent regulation, with expert medical advice available through radio contact with national and international advisory centres. Ships carrying 100 persons or more were required, as hitherto, to carry a doctor, but many carried one anyway for as long as economic considerations allowed.

We heard a rumour the one of the cadets on a cadet-ship had gone down with peritonitis and been operated on at sea, unsuccessfully. He was buried at Aden. I was never able to substantiate the story, but it was the kind of thing that might well have happened. (BI, 1962)[2]

In the absence of a qualified doctor – or surgeon, as he was still officially titled – *The Ship Captain's Medical Guide* had to act as the advisor at the master's side, and not a few regarded themselves as competent knife-men, ever ready to prove the point, sometimes with success. Cadet-ships, however, carried properly-qualified medical men.

Whether it was supported by Dunlopillo or a donkey's breakfast, the apprentice's capacity for sleep sought legendary expression as a way of passing leisure time, which was itself a problem. In sail there had never been enough, similarly in the two-watch system in steam when fully-exploited by the mate, but once the post-war order had established itself the question became one of too much idle time and its constructive occupation once such prosaic pursuits as study palled. In reality there was never a shortage of something to do connected with the ship herself, but an active mind and body needed variety.

Do not spend most of your leisure time sleeping at sea or in cafes and cinemas when you are in port.
(BI *Cadets' Manual*, 1950s)

Already well established, the SES and the College of the Sea continued to develop their activities and influence, offering between them a remarkably high-quality library service and a variety of study courses by correspondence from academic subjects to

---

[1] Contributors' private papers.
[2] ibid.

hobbies, with annual competitions and several bursary-type awards, as well as outside degree courses in cooperation with Ruskin College and the Open University among others. Books of all kinds were available for sale or on loan by request, and from time to time tutors went to sea to hold regular classes in spare-time pursuits. Films and, eventually, video-tapes supplemented the conventional library, which was changed at frequent intervals and kept up to date. By the mid-60s over 3 million books a year were being supplied to some 1,800 ships. On top of all that the private firm of Walport contracted to supply feature films and projection equipment, kept up to date in circulating boxed selections. They were very well-received, and apprentices found themselves employed (unpaid) as projectionists. The film-show became a popular and valuable feature of the ship's social life, promoting the spirit of community as the privately-viewed video film did not: video players and TV appeared in cabins in the 70s as an essentially detrimental social development.

Recreation? Very little. I was just grateful for the time off. It was wonderful to be able to just sit down and read a book without being called upon to do something, but it was very rarely that I could. We carried an SES library. (Shell, 1945-8)[1]

During time off we spent most of it in our bunks, reading, anything and everything. Corn in Egypt was the SES library and old magazines donated by the seamen's missions, like *The Saturday Evening Post*, and even women's magazines had a readership. (Athel, 1946-9)[2]

...I've developed, or rather increased, my reading. We have a relatively good library on board. I've read A Duel of Wits *by Captain Peter Churchill, and* The Sea Shall Not Have Them *by John Harris. I can recommend them to you.* (Letter home, P&O *Karmala*, 1954)[3]

...On a few ships Crossing the Line is a big occasion with full dress-up but we did it on a small scale. Up midships there was two of us. A 5th engineer, Bell, from Greenock, and myself. It was all quiet and peaceful that evening and Bell and I had no idea what was stirring up! We soon found out when we were invited to the 3rd engineer's cabin for a drink. We were grabbed and given the works and afterwards a certificate. (Apprentice's diary "Travelogue". Shell *Flammulina*, 1957)[4]

And it was in tankers, where the isolation and remoteness of the trade weighed heavily on the mind, that entertainment found its most original expression in an age becoming increasingly reliant on the ready-made:

THE VERENA *BROADCASTING CORPORATION.*
The idea was jointly mine and apprentice Galloway's, using the ship's PA system, the 5th engineer's record player and a mike made from a spare telephone. My cabin, directly beneath

---

[1] Contributors' private papers.
[2] ibid.
[3] ibid.
[4] ibid.

the radio room, was the studio. The success of the project was largely owing to the efforts of the apprentice, Angus McTartan on the air, but all of them – six deck and four engineering – played their parts with enthusiasm and talent. The VBC went on air after the bond issue on Wednesdays and Saturdays from 1800 to 2030, adjusted to include some BBC Overseas Service programmes

Colonel Bogey *started the proceedings, followed by a programme parade.* Listeners' Choice and Forces' Favourites *came from the BBC,* Melody on the Line *from us. There was a quiz with a can of beer as a prize, and* Smash Hits *was an idea from Radio Luxembourg. A hated record was played, then smashed (sound effects dept.), and "using the hammer" became a family joke. Galloway wrote a serial play,* Incident off Yemen – *pirates and the apprentice's heroic exploits with the navy to the rescue.* Verena Magazine *included anything going, and* Skiffle Club *was a live show. About half the ship's complement listened in. People hurried to hand over the watch to be in time for their favourite programme.* (Shell, 1958)[1]

And the resourceful Galloway went on to produce a ship's magazine in the *Hindsia*, aided and abetted by one of his compatriots:

Yes! We made it! Magazine Number Two; and we trust that you will once more enjoy our efforts. We must admit, however, that we could do with a little more support from you. Any article, no matter how small, will be of great help. Magazine No.1 was read by just over 94% of the ship's company – and enjoyed! Let us take this oportunity[sic] of thanking all subscribers and those who have made this issue possible.[2]

We ambled to and fro between the Gulf and China at eight knots, and with plenty of time to get things done they were usually left until the last moment. We passed the time playing crib, reading, listening to music on the Japanese tape-recorders that were all the rage, cheap in Hong Kong, and plunging into a mania for chess: endless tournaments, and heated discussion of strategy and tactics. (BI *Landaura*, 1964)[3]

The films were generally very good, well-chosen, full-length, so that you had to take care about showing times; a 3-reeler would run into the change of watch. Not very often we'd get a box of rubbish, but there was never any porno stuff, and it was before all that inarticulate junk like *Terminator*. A lot of war and westerns; those spaghetti westerns with Clint Eastwood were popular. Blood and snot everywhere.

We could always study in our spare time, but we kept that to a minimum. There was the library, from the Marine Society, and magazines and books from the Flying Angel – the Flying Tab-Nab, we called it. And the occasional semi-naughty – cunt yarns – that came aboard in places like Hamburg and Antwerp. There were card-schools and drinking-schools, horse-racing and board games like Monopoly and draughts. Cribbage was popular. Towards the end of my time video machines were appearing. (BP Tankers, 1968-70)[4]

---

[1] From *Marconi Mariner*, Nov/Dec, 1958.

[2] Contributors' private papers.

[3] ibid.

[4] ibid.

The Flying Tab-Nab continued to feature in shoregoing, but as time passed and the pocket's contents increased it lost the prominence it had enjoyed in sail days and pre-war. And, affluence apart, interest in matters spiritual steadily lost ground against the temporal side of existence, while the number of missions, with the Missions to Seamen and the Roman Catholic Stella Maris as the leaders, diminished.

The padre at the Durban Missions to Seamen was a tremendously enthusiastic individual who took a great interest in apprentices. He understood the situation, youngsters away from home for the first time, and in my case, as was his custom, he wrote to my parents to say he'd met me and that I was in good health. (Port Line, 1946)[1]

In some part, though, the decline in popularity arose from circumstances outside the apprentice's control – changes in port working patterns and cargo-handling systems together with the pressures from which they evolved made for quicker turn-rounds and consequently less time for shoregoing. Not only the Flying Angel but also the café and cinema of official censure felt the pinch, as did that archetypal manifestation of Anglo-American rapport which itself was evidence of something – some quality of innocence and trust – seen as old-fashioned and slightly naïve, the British Apprentice Club. After playing its valuable part in WW2 it soldiered on into the lean times of the late 40s (when the estimable Mrs Spaulding received the OBE in recognition of her efforts), and 50s before closing its doors for the last time in 1961, following a move to the Seamen's Church Institute in August, 1960, while the Chelsea Hotel developed the faintly seedy patina of dislocated longevity.

Of course it had no connection with the sea other than its fortuitous accommodation of the BAC, while in the United Kingdom, sailors' homes and some missions apart, there was a similar absence of hotel accommodation for seafarers at reasonable (modest) prices until brought into existence by the exigencies of war. Started as the Seamen's Welfare Board in 1940, charged with the provision of seamen's hostels in British ports, the MN Welfare Board, as it became in 1948, expanded its operation to provide hotels of varying standards (though in general they conformed to a prescribed formula) offering board and residence for all merchant seafarers and their families. In their clientele they reflected changing times, slipping into decline as the 70s advanced and finally retracting to the main hotel and HQ at Lancaster Gate.

I stayed at the MN Hotel for a while when up for my ticket. It was okay. The cook had his off days, just like at sea, and the rooms were clean, if a bit on the gloomy side. The place was a sort of rendezvous for the seafaring community, a part of which comprised shambling characters of no fixed abode beyond the approaches to the bar and, by the look of them, no fixed employment either. They seemed to be on the brink of some sort of moral abyss, tolerated but generally avoided. No-one knew quite what they did to keep body and soul together apart from draw the dole. Sometimes we joked about them, as seamen will about what others see as

---

[1] Contributors' private papers.

tragedy, but there was always an uncomfortable feeling that they were a warning to us. (Cardiff, 1964.)[1]

Another connection between sea and shore ran into difficulties that were a product of the times, but after judicious adjustment survived in an attenuated form. Begun in 1936 by Viscount Sandon, a member of the LCC's Education Committee, and Edmund Watts of tramp-owning fame, the British Ship Adoption Society had been forging links between ships and schools without a break and with gratifying success for the first thirty years of its existence, seeing imitators appearing in parts of the Empire and in foreign countries. But alas, by the 70s problems had developed stemming from social, educational and commercial changes which saw a breakdown in the school/ship relationship and a faltering of the society's progress; accordingly, it changed its policy to one based on personal contact, following the fortunes of the adopted seafarer instead of an adopted ship to achieve mixed results while further difficulties arose over the question of funding and the fees required of schools taking part. This might have finished the scheme had not the SES stepped in to take over the society's affairs, itself in turn absorbed by the Marine Society, and ship adoption, as it was still called, continued on a reduced scale but with enthusiasm among its youthful supporters, in whom it was hoped would grow an awareness of the sea which, among the population at large, was conspicuous by its absence. The individual involved at sea was usually an officer, originally the ship's master as the representative of a wider shipboard effort which inevitably included the apprentice, who tended to regard his role with some ambivalence, possibly owing to an uncomfortable awareness of his as yet not far distant remove from the happiest days of his life.

The captain laid a big file on the table and explained that it contained letters from a school in London. Soon my mate and I were up to our ears in them, all from Sir William Collins School for boys in Euston. The letters asked about voyages and ports of call, etc., and it was our job to write back. I thought it was going to be quite interesting. (Shell, 1957)[2]

The 3rd mate came in and said, "Guess who's going to be giving our school a talk next week", and my heart sank, but he reassured me. It was his official pigeon, and he was interested in one of the teachers. He hadn't come to tell me to take the job on, only to brag about his (hoped-for) further amorous adventuring. He spent a lot of time writing letters, answering what we considered to be hilariously daft questions from the children ("How round is your funnel?"). He was very good with them, actually, but we had an uncharitable suspicion that most of his avuncular enthusiasm was a display for the teacher's – and ultimately his own – benefit. (BI *Bombala*, 1963)[3]

---

[1] Contributors' private papers.

[2] ibid.

[3] ibid.

Not least as a recruitment attraction, paid leave was introduced post-war[1], though an apprentice could still find himself borne away on a 2- or even 3-year voyage – the Bank Line's style was world-wide tramping with no guarantees – until, during the 60s, the aeroplane entered the picture and "flying leave", as it was called in the BI, became first a privilege and then a standard condition of employment, with stints away from home reduced, by stages, to 3- or 4-month spells unless, as was the case with cadets on the ONC/D scheme and the ATS, the shore-based phases intervened. For example, paid leave was granted at the rate of about 6 days per month served in the early 60s, about twice the rate of ten years before. In some trades, ten years later, leave amounted to double that again, and the openly-stated aim of the officers' associations was a one-for-one agreement, no doubt some part of the reason for British owners' deciding to either flag out or turn to some other business.

Relationships with school friends altered, of course, though my best friends didn't change. I grew away from them, mostly; thought they were a bit immature because I'd seen so much, though all I'd seen was the ship. But I laid it on pretty thick, just to impress; one of the perks of the job, and they sensed it. They seemed little lads compared to me. (Shell, 1946)[2]

I was at home after my first trip – 12 months – and my girl said, "You're not going to stay at sea, are you?" She couldn't believe it was something you did as a career, sort of opting out by going to sea. (RFA, 1951)[3]

...John and I went ashore to Chowringhee. It has completely turned my stomach, and it will be some time before I go ashore here again. The squalor round the docks was unbelievable; millions of filthy, emaciated and deformed human shapes littered the streets begging for money from us two "burra malim sahibs". John was carefully removing money from one pocket to the other, for a persistent little wretch was hanging onto him, and discovered there was a hole in the other pocket by seeing the "wretch" running off with about ½d cash. (Letter home, P&O *Karmala*, Calcutta, 1954.)[4]

The first time we went ashore was Haifa. Ended up in this bar with birds all round, you know, plying us with drink, and after we'd been in this place for half an hour we were paralytic. Stoned. When our money ran out that was it, we were chucked out. It was courtesy of some engineers that we got back to the ship at all, because we were in a hell of a state, just lay in the bottom of the liberty-boat. The chief got to hear of it and said, "This isn't fucking good enough, you know, blah, blah, blah – " Anyway, we were confined to barracks, but at La Plata the chief's wife interceded. "Let them go ashore," she said. "It's an interesting place." So we got a train to BA and the first bar we came to, straight in, drinking Martini at about 9d a glass. Big glasses. We got paralytic there as well. Eventually found our way back to the station and staggered onto this train, and who should be sitting there but the chief. So that was us barred

---

[1] Paid study-leave in 1950.

[2] Contributors' private papers.

[3] ibid.

[4] ibid.

again. It became the pattern – go ashore, get pissed, get barred, and eventually go ashore again. (Shell/ATS, 1955.)[1]

...We played football against a local side in Port Swettenham. The heat was rather too much. Iced orange squash afterwards at the Marine Club and got back to a dinner of salmon mayonnaise, cold turkey and chippolatas, fruit salad and ice-cream. The second engineer said he is finished with football.

The chief officer gave us an afternoon off here and Doug treated us to the Marine Club[2], opened three months ago. It has a palatial, cool hall, dining-room, library, officers' lounge, Billiard room and beautiful swimming-bath. We swam for an hour then sat in the bar drinking iced orange squash, then Doug and Sid played billiards while I read the paper in the lounge. The outing cost only $5, including taxi there and back, the only method of travelling for a European. Very pukka. (Letter home, P&O *Shillong*. Singapore, 1955.)[3]

Most of the people were very poor. I'd heard of people begging for food at the ships, and when I went ashore for a walk the children soon gathered round, asking for bread, shoes, shirts, etc. One little fellow came along with his little brother begging for something to eat. Seeing the gold stripe on my epilet[sic] he remarked, "You good chief, you get something to eat for us." (Apprentice's diary "Travelogue", Shell *Flammulina*, Punta Delgada, Azores. 1957.)[4]

ss Hinnites.
Colombo, 17th November. 1961.
Hi Bren,

It's a good thing that I have your letters to reply to 'cos there isn't much to talk about. I have just seen an English murder film on deck, also a Laurel & Hardy comedy.

As you will see from this and the picture-postcards, Capetown and Table Mountain made a fabulous picture to just lean on the rail and stare at. The disappointment was that we couldn't get ashore 'cos we were only in for a few hours. I would have loved to have gone up Table Mountain in one of the cable cars.

America is fine, but in films you only see the good parts and not the wooden houses with brick paper stuck on the outside. I just can't get over it...

Well, now you can look at the pictures on the other side because I have finished and I hope you all have a very Merry Christmas and a Happy New Year. We will have 3½ days of parties as the apprentices get Christmas and boxing day off.

Love, John.
(Letter home. Shell/ATS)[5]

mv Atreus.
Voy. 28. Liverpool-Manila-Liverpool.

---

[1] Contributors' private papers.
[2] Connell House, since demolished.
[3] Contributors' private papers.
[4] ibid.
[5] ibid.

...Norbury and I requested shore leave and although the mate was somewhat dubious about our not being accompanied by a senior midshipman, it was granted. I liked Rotterdam because it was so modern and open, but my friend was not impressed; he said it had no character.

...Visited the middies on the Demodocus*. I'd have enjoyed seeing more, but contented myself with gaining a rough idea of where the places of interest lay with a view to visiting them homeward-bound.*

(Singapore)

...All hatches being worked. Went ashore for a swim in the excellent open-air pool at the Mariners' Club where I met the Doc and the chief Sparks. (Bangkok)

...Did not think much of Manila. It seemed very shabby and badly planned. Everything was very expensive and there was little variety. We spent a pleasant evening at the cinema.

...Found my way to the Peak. The view was marvellous.(Hong Kong)

(Midshipman's journal, Blue Funnel. 1961-2.)[1]

I was about 8 months at sea before setting foot on foreign soil. The lucky place treated to the contents of my wallet? Marcus Hook. Yes, that was my question as well. Three months passed after that before I saw Suez and realised that it wouldn't bother me if I never saw it again. And you'd think the Isle of Grain would have been a second home, but not so. There was a song, *Take me back to Abadan, for I'm a British Tanker man*, but I never saw the place. What I did see a lot of, though, was Bandar Mashur. Somebody said that if the world had piles they'd be somewhere up the Khor Musa, and I wouldn't dispute it. (BP Tankers, 1964-6.)[2]

What a place. We got alongside about 1000 and the Third, the alcoholic professional[3], went ashore straight away with the electrician, an ex-passenger-ship man, or perhaps animal would better describe him, and with 35s (EA) each they got pissed as rats, bagged off, and brought back a couple of souvenirs – gifts, that is – before going on watch at noon.. There I was, wondering, and thinking, "What *is* this place Mombasa?" Well, I found out. It was the Sunshine Day & Night Bar, about 100s for an all-night session, but I chickened out at about 0300 and somehow got back to the ship and safety. (ATS/P&O *Somali*. 1968.)[4]

My first run ashore was at Mombasa, with a warning from the chief officer about watching my step. I was with the senior cadet, so felt safe enough. After a very staid beer at the sports club watching the end of a game of cricket in the gathering dusk we hit the town. First stop was this dump called the Rainbow Bar – neon lighting, layers of tobacco-smoke, zinc-topped tables running with spilled drinks, a crowd of sailors – Scawegians, Italians, Germans, Dutch, what-have-you – and lots of girls, Africans, young and over-made-up. The barman and waiters were Africans got up to look cool – but which looked ridiculous – in sunglasses, T-shirts and chewing-gum, dodging round with glasses and bottles among the tables. Presley's *Jailhouse Rock* was pounding out from the garish Wurlitzer and conversation was a mixture of shouting and sign-language. With the drinks came two girls. They sat in our laps uninvited. Mine put a surprisingly soft arm round my neck, brushed my ear with her tongue and bawled "Buy me a

---

[1] Contributors' private papers.

[2] ibid.

[3] Colloq. – "Professional Third", i.e. uncertificated and not aspiring to higher rank & responsibility.

[4] Contributors' private papers.

drink, hey, Johnnie?", half deafening me. I didn't realise that I had heard the sea's oldest phrase, and as I signalled a waiter the other cadet grinned at me round the steep headland of his girl's upholstery and the record changed to a 500-decibel issue of *Blue Suede Shoes*. I hadn't read about any of this in *Hornblower* or even *The Cruel Sea*, and assumed it was what the chief officer had warned me about. (BI *Kampala*. 1962.)[1]

If shoregoing presented hazards and potential disaster as necessary adjuncts to excitement and diversion, it was only the other side of the same coin, and the ship herself, while at sea, possessed potential of at least equal degree, if different in nature:

I was working with two quartermasters on the starboard accommodation ladder, which had been turned out and lay at deck level. I was painting it, working towards the end, and reached the landing platform; as soon as my weight came onto it it tipped and pitched me into the sea.

We were doing about 14 knots, and there I was in the ocean, on a fine day, with the ship rapidly disappearing. However, I had the comfort of knowing I'd been seen, I was wearing only shoes and shorts, which I discarded to make swimming easier. There was a wind, about Force 4, and a bit of a swell, and I trod water trying to conserve my energy, though after about half an hour I started to get cramp and remembered that the 4th mate had seen a shark the previous day; but I was past worrying about it. Then I had this strange sensation of feeling very foolish; I thought of my cabin, the clothes I'd hung up and various other things in it, personal articles and furniture: there was my cabin, tranquil and calm, and here was I in this ridiculous situation.

The ship came back, but instead of slowing down it went straight past, to my dismay. Then it turned again, and this time I was seen. But the drama wasn't over, because as they lowered a boat the mate – incredibly – fell out of it, and they picked him up first and got him back aboard. All the time the ship was getting closer, so I was able to swim to the ladder hanging down the side and climb to the deck, where I was met by the doctor and whipped into sick-bay. He found absolutely nothing wrong with me except a bit of cramp.

The mate and master didn't seem unduly concerned and I didn't get a rocket; I think they were too relieved to do anything drastic, but after lunch the mate gave me a job varnishing the bridge-wing cabs. He thought it best for me to have some work to do to get my mind off the incident, like getting back on a horse after a fall. Anyway, I suffered no ill-effects. (*Port Fremantle*, Panama-Auckland. 1947.)[2]

Whatever its other virtues, the incident was an instructive exercise in relative values, the mate of more use to the ship than the apprentice, who, if he survived, sometimes found himself setting foot on the bottom rung of another kind of ladder, promotion to uncertificated junior officer; and the engineer cadet, returning to sea for a final 6-month spell to complete his time, might be promoted to junior engineer, which in any case would follow expiry of his time. In the deck apprentice's case watchkeeping, either with a certificated officer or under the eye of the master, would replace the round of day-work and perhaps offer a chance of catching up on book-

---

[1] Contributors' private papers.
[2] ibid.

work before the fraught business of school and examination began, either for the last phase of the ONC/D scheme or for 2nd mate *en bloc*.

My last voyage, on the *Homer City*, lasted 13 months, 4 beyond the end of my indentures – I had to wait for the ship to return to the UK to pay off. I signed on as u/c 3rd officer for the voyage, and had to spend my first month's pay – £29.10s – on a sextant. (Reardon Smith, 1950.)[1]

After leaving the *Rakaia* I joined the *Surrey* as u/c 4th mate, a simple matter of shifting cabins without much change in my duties, since there were no cadets, but I had the 8-12 solo except in coastal waters. My pay went up to £28 a month. With a ticket I'd have got £32. (NZS/Federal. 1954.)[2]

...Arrived off the [Sydney] Heads with Bendigo, Cretic *and* Orsova *but taken in first. Captain told me I was[sic] Cadet Officer (£34 a month) as from 20th December. Spent afternoon in Jo's cabin then over to* Bendigo *for dinner.*
   ...Got changed and stood on gangway to meet Captain's guests. Dodged C/O in afternoon and polished my sextant box. Gangway stations for girl-spotting at 9.30.
   ...Went round the hatches measuring up with the surveyor.
   ...Cargo work til 12. 3/O took both launches away for testing so did me out of a job. Took party of 40 scouts round the bridge. (Diary, P&O *Iberia*, 1957.)[3]

The term *cadet officer* was favoured by one or two companies including, in later times, Blue Funnel, signifying a senior cadet or apprentice still doing his time but deemed responsible enough for more elevated duties than hitherto, not always symbolised by a rise in pay.

...Molle and I joined Clytonius, *myself as senior. I took the 12-4 for the first half of the trip, Molle the 8-12.*
   ...Passed Minicoy on the evening of the 24th. Work included checking lifeboat stores and colouring the cargo plan. Did a couple of exam papers but it was too stifling to attempt much.
   ...Worked on Notices to Mariners received in Singapore.
   ...Arrived Taku Bar 23rd. Working cargo the gangs seemed to do the opposite to whatever they were asked. We were very glad to get away, and Molle and I swapped watches.
   ...They worked it so that half the gang knock off while the other half works, so that you have only half the men who should be working actually doing anything. It's a throwback to 24-hour shifts when everyone sympathised with them. Now they're getting their own back by working only 4 hours a day.
(Port Swettenham.)
   ...Loaded tea. Molle and I did the nights between us, tallying it from a concealed position on deck. The reason for the James Bond routine was that the agent suspected certain tally clerks

---

[1] Contributors' private papers.

[2] ibid.

[3] ibid.

of manipulating the figures. Put in a lot of swimming. Captain Liptrot kindly allowed us to take the motor-lifeboat to the beach. (Trincomalee.)
(Midshipman's journal, Blue Funnel. Birkenhead-Manila-Liverpool. 1964.)[1]

The ships were overmanned, really, down by the head with extra certificated mates, so our chances of promotion before time were nil. The only time I got to keep a bridge watch was for a short period when the officers had all gone down with dysentery or something after scoffing a chicken curry brought aboard at Chittagong. We hadn't been invited to join them so were the only ones on our feet apart from the Old Man. (BI *Nuddea.* 1964.)[2]

In ratifying the changes of structure and nomenclature of the certificates of competency the 1970 MSA included the engineering department in the introduction of a universal classification distinguished by department as shown in brackets. Thus, equivalent to the first four deck classes were four engineering classes, the new Class II equivalent to the old Second-Class certificate. As the prime mover behind the appearance of the lower classes of certificate, expedient was well garnished with plausible and euphemistic justification, but the Act wasn't fully implemented until 1981. The last 2nd mate's ticket was dated October, 1978, by which time the apprentice as an indentured servant was extinct.

As was sail, finally, from the professional point of view[3]. In 1949, when a Martin Lee presented himself for examination after serving his time in Erikson's square-riggers, he was refused and told to put in 12 months in steam/motor ships, neatly reversing the ruling on the last ordinary, or square-rig, tickets. Erikson had died in 1947 and his son disposed of the remains of the great fleet of windjammers, a handful that was all the evidence left of the old sailing man's dream of a commercially-viable wind-ship operation. The fleet's disposal left open the question that would never be answered: perhaps the new age, swaddled in safety measures that stifled the reasonable assessment of acceptable risk, would never have tolerated Erikson's aspirations; perhaps he simply didn't live long enough. Lee's certificate, uniquely for its day, bore witness to his proficiency in both steam and square-rig.

The wartime reduction of sea-time and age of eligibility for the 2nd mate's ticket reverted in 1947 to the pre-war regulation, and eventually a large proportion of the time was gained as equivalent time at school, on both pre-sea and pre-examination courses, including the MAR/MCR, altogether a maximum of 21 months which counted towards the 4/5ths of indentured time required on foreign-going service. The ONC/D scheme followed similar lines and by 1980 had displaced the 4-year sea-time

---

[1] Contributors' private papers.

[2] ibid.

[3] That is, until revived in the form of square-rig endorsements developed by the Nautical Institute in application to the various square-rigged training/recreational/historical-replica vessels that appeared on the scene as time passed.

system in a balance of some 2½ years at sea against about 14 months in college, falling short of the 4 years by some 4 months:

Phase 1: 2 weeks' induction including short fire-fighting course;
Phase 2: 10-12 months at sea; guided study;
Phase 3: 38 weeks at college: EDH, lifeboatman cert., restricted R/T cert., first-aid cert., TEC Diploma & exemptions from maths, science and principles of navigation in Class III.
Phase 4: 12 months at sea; guided study;
Phase 5: 14 weeks at college; Radar Observer cert & DOT Class IV cert.;
Phase 6: 4-6 months at sea to complete time for Class III.

Those with the TEC/SCOTEC Dip and Class IV received the Class III at the end of Phase 6 without further examination, while A-level entrants bypassed the diploma and Class IV exams to take the Class III exam direct, with certain exemptions. The Radar Observer course was introduced in 1948, a 3-week separately-conducted introduction to the principles of radar operation which, to conclude from a mounting toll of accidents, were grossly misunderstood by watchkeeping officers. Its essence was the mystery of relative motion and the triangle of forces, or velocities, which led to some classic near-misses and collisions before the secret was mastered by the majority. To some, though, it remained stubbornly obscure, shrouded in the toils of black art finally rendered superfluous by replacement of the operator's skill with computerised plotting systems and their push-button answer to human frailty, to say nothing of a cheaper alternative to thorough training.

The schools themselves entered a time of plenty in the 50s, proliferating in all the major and some minor ports, both at home and in British possessions abroad. Paid study leave began with an agreement on 8 weeks through the NMB in 1950, later extended to 12, which metamorphosed, as the ONC/D scheme gained momentum, into continuous pay throughout the training period both at sea and ashore. Like everything else in an increasingly-bureaucratic system, the schools steadily shed their individuality and in the mid-50s the last of the privately-run institutions went out of business, Nellist's probably the most famous of its time.

The Nellist brothers ran their academy on Tyneside, a relic of earlier days founded by their sea-captain father at the turn of the century. Mathematicians and theoretical navigators, the brothers were trained teachers who had never been to sea, conducting their modest establishment in Summerhill Terrace, and later Winchester Terrace, Newcastle, charging fees *pro rata* of 10/- a week at its close, with an enrolment fee of £1. The brothers shunned pretension (which cost money) and their school was a traditional crammer, as distinct from the new-age crammers under the LEA's, claiming a pass-rate of 90% at the first attempt and losing nothing of its prestige in the face of state-aided competition (the fiercely-independent Nellists responded to the LEA's advances in 1945 with a contemptuous dismissal of "socialist money"), typified in the South Shields school which charged a flat rate for the course, on which the student could remain for as long as it took him to pass the exam, within reason. In the early 50s it was a 9-week continuous programme of lectures and tutorials which could be picked up at any stage and followed through to completion of the cycle. The course lengthened as time passed until, in the 60s, changing to one of academic terms and a programme that had to be followed from its start. It was increasingly geared towards the ONC/D scheme and away from the traditional 2nd mate's requirements, more convenient for the teaching staff than for the seaman-student.

The school was in Summerhill Terrace overlooking a private park which, like the houses, had seen better days. The gardens' iron railings and those around the park had been sent for scrap back in 1940, since when dogs and children had roamed freely. A tarnished brass plate alongside the open front door announced that this was indeed Nellist's Nautical School.

A shabby green door opening off an uncarpeted hall bore a card inscribed *Office*. I knocked and a rasping voice bade me enter. Threadbare carpet partly covered dusty floorboards while bulging bookcases lined the walls of a high, square room. Near the window sat an ancient lady hunched over what was surely Mr Remington's original typewriter. A high, black fireplace held just enough flickering coals to constitute a fire – even in July the house felt cold – and standing with his back to the hearth was a tall, severe-looking man, thumbs firmly hooked in the waistcoat of his navy-blue suit. Beneath wavy grey hair and beetling brows, belligerence stared. I rightly took him to be Mr Billy Nellist, the principal...

Jacky, the other...brother, was much less fearsome: a mustard sports-jacket and dark trousers gave him an almost casual air, and his gleaming bald pate seemed to accentuate the intelligence shining behind the spectacles.

They were a quaint pair, who ran their school magnificently, knowing all the answers and all the short cuts. They could make the Traverse Tables seem beautiful, knew the *Nautical Almanac* backwards, made the ABC Tables as simple as their name, and even knew logarithms to five decimal places by heart...

A retired shipmaster taught us the finer points of practical seamanship; how to rig a jury rudder, or a heavy derrick. A retired Royal Navy yeoman of signals came weekly to explain and teach morse code, semaphore, and the International Code of Signals. For an extra half-crown each he would turn out on Saturday mornings to give us Extra Signals, as he called it...

As Jacky...the more patient of the two, explained, our examinations were not a test of what we knew so much as of our ability to think, to come to grips with the problems and solve them. The oral examination, he said, was mainly to detect an agility of mind, to see what was required and do it, the essence of good seamanship. The man who could learn a set of rules and apply them, he argued, could easily pick up another, and, eventually, devise his own...

Once a week a group of us would have Private Discussion in the snug. The tanker men...would detail the precautions needed when loading crude oil, and the mysteries of tank-washing and gas-freeing were revealed. Chaps from Baron Line and Runciman's would explain how to carry coal and how to prepare the bilges before switching to bulk wheat or barley. Aristocratic types from the BI would describe the loading of jute, tea and deck passengers on the Indian coast, and a rugged Yorkshireman from Ropner's gave an excellent description of the way to carry Australian iron ore. Those of us...from Blue Star, Royal Mail and Port Line were able to clear up a few matters about refrigerated (reefer) cargoes, the subtle differences between carrying apples, lamb, chilled beef and oranges. The examiner was likely to ask the tanker men how frozen lamb should be carried and an iron-ore man about a cargo of crude oil or sugar, so these sessions were vital to our education.[1]

Of the "socialist money" schools King Edward VII in London – "King Ted's" – was among the best-known:

...Arrived 8.50. Met Mike Hughes, Gathercole, Munday, Tipper, King, Hooker, Dabbs and Parson. Pep talk by Captain Myerscough then joined Class 2. Lecture on seamanship. After lunch assessment test put me at advance level in maths. Maths all afternoon. After tea studied maths and articles.

...Maths tutorial first, then GSK. Good lunch with John and Mike. Signals, tutorial, then Principles lecture. Studying most of evening.

...Paid fee for course £6. Letter from Allan who is on radar course and coming back to finish chartwork.

...Dale sits next to me. Very nice chap from BTC.. We help each other. Did just over an hour on "How is she heading?"

...Sextant practice on roof at 2.30. Bought Munro's Primer.

...Started charts. All signals correct.

...Chartwork, Instruments, Rule of the Road and Maths. Spherical trig and Nav 6.45 til 10.

...First aid lecture. Very comical.

...Passed both lantern and letter test[2] with only a little trouble. Lunched with the boys.

...Seamanship, signals and knowledge of principles.

...Just beginning to realise how much I don't know.

...In First Aid class poor old Dick passed out. Stuffy atmosphere.

...Got form for benefit at Labour Exchange. Received £80 from Company for my last year.

...For a fee of £1.10s and a farsical[sic] exam I passed St John's First Aid.

...Due to harder maths paper Capt. McLaren is turning part of the tutorials over to it

...Studied for a couple of hours this evening listening to gram records at same time.

...Went along to Ensign St and put in papers.

...Still finding I only know a smattering. Tired and rather dispirited.

...Dozens of articles I don't know. Identities by the hundred. Did more rules and watched TV.

...Last day at school (I hope). Muller failed special eyesight test but has been granted permission to sit for his ticket. To Silver's, fitted for uniforms. Did no work at all in evening. Watched TV.

...Letter from Mother wishing me luck (which I'll need). Studied all day.

...Still a lot to learn. Very sore throat.

...Good luck card this morning from Jean, Mother and Dad. Attendance cert to P&O. Arrived Ensign St 8.45 with Thompson, Dick, Hunt, etc and was agreeably surprised at the papers, GSK and chartwork. Finished at 2.10 and had chartwork orals with Capt Wallace. Studied in evening. Dad phoned to ask how I was getting on.

...Prac nav and maths today. In latter made a silly mistake.

---

[1] *Before the Box-Boats*, pp.39-45.

[2] BOT eyesight test.

...In signals Thompson couldn't write fast enough, so the result is in the air. Writtens I feel relatively happy about. English – essay My Next Leave.

...Feeling very tired.

...Up at 8.30. To Dock St Capt Wallis[sic] my examiner and I shook all over. What a shocking time – I wouldn't like to go through that again. I was lucky on articles – 2, 4 and 16. Sent me out for an hour to learn about tacking. He then handed me the certificate – passed orals. What a relief. Watched Under Milk Wood. *Ridiculous.*

...Passed writtens. To Head Office to tell them. Put in application for signals on Wednesday. Lunched with the boys and had extra signals.

...Now a 4/O in P&O. Very easy signals orals from Capt. Thompson. Went along to P&O where signed on as 4/O. Mr Copeland is giving me as much holiday as I want!! Met Dad for lunch in Oxford St. Letter from Co. enclosing last month's study leave pay.

...Signed on for a radar course on Sir John Cass[1]*.Very boring morning. Thank goodness for the tea-break. Lunch in a pub.*

...Played on the Decca 45 and Marconi Mk IV.

...Last lecture. The penny has just dropped [2].

...Orally examined on the Marconi IV.

...Written exam finished 12.10. Received [Radar Observer] certificate. By bus to 122 where Copeland told me I am to do coastal on Socotra.

(Diary, 1957.)[3]

Horror stories of the examination were customarily endemic, not least because of the examiners' generally fearsome reputations. However, as changes were wrought in the system, and in society at large, a softer approach was adopted, whether for better or worse a matter of opinion, granted that softer (i.e. more liberal) ways are one of decline's classic symptoms, and that is what had set in by the mid-80s. It was accompanied by a diminution of the incidence of terror in the exam, and a fading of colour and texture typical of an age in which forthright opinion and attitudes were becoming *declassé* for reasons mostly of sham political consideration. Complaints about the overbearing ways of examiners, savouring of whining petulance, were nothing more than a sign of the general malaise evidenced, as it always has been, by an increasing tendency to litigation and the doctor's surgery. Examiners risked offending candidates (at one time, of course, the risk lay with the candidate, whose recurrent nightmare was an examiner offended by inept answers, an entirely proper and healthy state of affairs) by testing them too rigorously, and their (the candidates') side of the issue is therefore hardly worth attention. But here, too, the apprentice had already quitted the scene, playing no part in the strange assortment of values that had gained currency.

---

[1] The Cass school ran a large motor-launch, *Sir John Cass*, equipped with radar for practical instruction in the lower reaches of the Thames.

[2] Relative motion???

[3] Contributors' private papers.

Some examiners appeared to be in an extremity of misery, which rubbed off. Maybe it was the boredom of listening day after day to people reciting the Articles, and the need to think up questions on the spot for answers to which proper credit had to be given. They had to think rather quickly themselves, keep things on the move, give the syllabus coverage. The seamanship exam took time to shake itself free of the silly things asked in days gone by, like rigging a jury rudder, shifting the spare prop, things that would be impossible in a modern ship. Better to radio for a tug. It meant that both examiner and candidate were talking about things boned up from text-books. (1950s.)[1]

The written exam occupied the first three days, six papers altogether, followed on Thursday or Friday (depending on one's place on the alphabetical list) by the oral and signals exams. The results were made known early the following week, writtens and orals separately but which had to be attained together within a 6-month period, along with signals and other incidentals such as the radar observer certificate, the fire-fighting course and first aid. After the war what had been the gunnery and DEMS courses became the MN Defence Course, a 2-day affair run by naval people covering basic convoy work and self-defence measures, discontinued at the end of the 60s. Most looked upon it as a piece of mild entertainment as well as a useful supplement to personal funds – the navy made a small payment for attendance...

The 2nd mate's examination took this form:

Monday: am: GSK 3 hrs. pm: Chartwork 2 hrs; chartwork oral.
Tuesday: am: Prac Nav 3 hrs. pm: Maths 2 hrs.
Wednesday: am: Principles of Nav 2 hrs. pm: English 1½ hrs.
Thursday/Fri: Orals & signals.

GSK (General ship knowledge) embraced ship-construction, stability, equipment and operation; chartwork a basic knowledge of coastal and estuarine navigation; practical navigation, so-called, elementary astro-nav including reduction of sights; principles of navigation the understanding of formulae, time, projections, solar and stellar systems, sailings, etc; maths a basic grounding in algebra, logs, mensuration, geometry, plane and spherical trig, and English a simple test of ability with attention paid to spelling, legibility and neatness – the exercise a choice of essay, précis or report. The ONC/D exemptions left the candidate with navigation, chartwork, signals, English and orals.

Captain Wallace's sending a candidate out of the room to learn about tacking was a curious incident when sail was officially defunct and Martin Lee had been sent back to sea to learn about steamship seamanship; but possibly Wallace's question concerned a lifeboat under sail, though sailing a ship's boat any distance was becoming, if it wasn't already, an anachronism. In any case the Wallaces of the time were only human, and

---

[1] Contributors' private papers.

particularly inept answers as likely to play on their nerves as their questions on the candidates'.

I studied pretty hard but couldn't believe my eyes when I saw the papers. I might have set them myself, and I got through them in record time. For orals at Dock St I had Captain Wallace, a gentleman of the old school reputed to hold a square-rig ticket, and for being noisy. Not a sound came from the room as he dealt with the fellow ahead of me, an Aussie who, when he emerged, told me he'd been thrown out. When I went in Wallace told me I'd done very well in my writtens and asked me about BI. Then he began. The usual things – read the barometer, tie a few knots, demonstrate acquaintance with the sextant and so on. Rule of the Road was merely an extension of the writtens and I knew them inside-out. How is she heading I'd played in my sleep. Wallace was evidently impressed, and I found time to reflect on how elegant I'd look with a gold stripe on my sleeve, and that maybe the girl in my life would say yes at last to a spot of naughties. But...

I'd spent nearly all my time as the only cadet or as acting 3rd mate, and never got my hands dirty learning my trade. I was a whizz at navigation, knew all about met., could handle my cutlery with panache and knew a thing or two about dazzling lady passengers. But seamanship had been noted from afar, done by apprentices in Hungry Hogarth's or Harrison's instead of swimming out at Breach Candy[1]. Wallace put me on the focsle on the way up Garden Reach[2] and asked me how I'd hang off the anchor ready to pick up the buoy. Easy, I thought, we'd done it often. I told him I'd put a *kalassi* over the side in a bosun's chair to take out the pin, and the crew under the *serang* hangs off the anchor. Job done.

With that everything changed. Wallace exploded, and we spent the next hour going through every detail of the task. Somehow, in an appalling display of trial and error, I passed, with a warning, and I left the room with the chit as Wallace went out of my life forever. (1954.)[3]

Captain MacAree was held in awe. I got off to a good start with a bollocking for my chartwork, which had failed me in the writtens; then he barked that he'd noticed I was a *Conway* boy, and as I admitted it hopefully he went on to say that I'd better be hot stuff because he was one also. Then he got going on me. The experience was one of sheer terror from start to finish, reaching its nadir when I put a ship aground in a buoyed channel. I passed, just, and went round in a state of shock for hours. (Cardiff, 1964.)[4]

I was among the first to go through the OND. Had to take orals seamanship, chartwork and navigation, and an English essay. Agar examined me for orals, an aquiline nose and triangular sort of face, with hair swept straight back, like Dracula, and a little pointy beard. He'd fix you with hawk-like eyes as he asked the questions. I didn't dare look at the clock, but all the time I was thinking, Please God let this end soon; I don't care if I fail, just get me out of here. I couldn't answer this question about lights. I racked my brain, tried every combination that occurred to me. Eventually I dried. Total blank. I said, "I'm sorry, I just can't remember." I felt

---

[1] A popular seaside resort at Bombay.

[2] A stretch of the Hooghly below the bund and the docks at Calcutta, where ships lay to buoys awaiting berths alongside.

[3] Contributors' private papers.

[4] Contributors' private papers.

like crying, and he said something, asked me could it be to do with fishing-boats. So I gabbled something or other. "Yes," he said. "I'll let this one pass. Just don't make another mistake." So I got through. I was lucky. (S. Shields, 1970.)[1]

Meanwhile, after a spell at sea as a junior with a Class IV certificate (after the 1970 MSA), the engineer cadet was having similar experiences with the 2nd Class exam (or the exam for a Class II (Engine) certificate). As the 60s ended his return to sea after Phase 3 in college (the "approved engineering training centre" that had taken the place of a works or yard) was for some 6 months as a cadet before eligibility for promotion to junior engineer and completion of his time.

Cadetship is for 4 years and includes 2 at college on theory and workshop training, one year at sea and a final year in college. The TEC Diploma is taken at the end of the first two years and the Higher Diploma in the final year. The DOT Class 4 examination is taken on completion of the 4-year course at which time those who gain a full Higher Diploma will be granted exemption from parts of the Class 2 examination. Some cadets with A-level passes in maths and or physics may be accepted for courses for the Higher TEC Diploma in Mechanics or Engineering (Marine), or for a degree in marine engineering.[2]

We only had to do Section 2 of Part B – EK and orals. In college was this chap H.S.W. Jones, head serang in the engineering department, doing stuff largely about steam recip engines! Not a bit of bloody good to me because I'd been weaned on turbines, but they were still asking questions on it, the BOT. I mean, we had to do the *feathering paddle-wheel*, for Christ's sake! The argument was that there were still paddlers out of Cardiff, so we had to know the geography of the feathering bloody paddle-wheel.

We had all these exemptions, which was the argument put forward when they cut our study leave to 8 weeks. Already got Part A, you see. But there was this bloke up for orals, asked something about the tail-end, rudder or something, which of course we'd done. But this clown turns round and says, "You can't ask me that – I'm exempt naval arch." Well, he failed. (ATS, 1956.)[3]

And then, quite suddenly, it was over. Either boning up for another attempt or looking for a berth to put in more time on examiner's orders, failures were left behind as the career picked up speed and meaning, with appointment to a ship as – usually – 3rd mate, exceptions occurring where companies were retracting services through run-down of business, merger or flagging-out, in which case something less exalted might have to do. For some, the sea had exhausted its appeal, or unexpected eventualities dictated a change of course:

Just as I was about to collect my ticket I noticed that my eyesight test certificate was out of date, and taking the test again I failed. National Service was in force, and the government kept

---

[1] ibid.
[2] *Full Ahead*, pp.47-8.
[3] Contributors' private papers.

tabs on us through the dole, so while the company's offer of a purser's job didn't appeal, the alternative was the army, in spite of my having done the RNR subbies' course. So with the help of friends I secured a passage to Australia on the *Iberia* and left the UK for good. (NZS, 1954.)[1]

Captain Smith was in charge of cadets. He said that as I had nearly 3 months' voyage leave due he wouldn't pay study leave although the contract[*sic*] said otherwise. Needless to say, I didn't darken the portals of One Aldgate again, and found a good berth with Blue Star. (BI, 1964.)[2]

After picking up my ticket I informed BP that pastures new beckoned, a decision I've never regretted, and after a written dialogue with Safmarine I joined Canadian Pacific. My first appointment was 5th officer of the *Empress of England*, my first task duty boots on the night watch. (1967.)[3]

---

[1] Contributors' private papers.

[2] ibid.

[3] ibid.

VIII

Bloody Schemers & Reluctant Opalians.
Cadet-ships, 1890-1980

*

Way back in the mists of antiquity when the first Cadet Ship was on her maiden voyage, there were on board two cadets, normal intelligent youths who gave promise of becoming equally normal intelligent officers; but unfortunately they never did. Nothing they could do was right.

And nowadays they are still hard at it, applying their ghostly ineptitude to every job. If a lubberly lashing is seen, if a pot of stone-colour is spilt, if fifteen chipping-hammers are lost overside in a day, if the mate detects rust under new red-lead, it is always the same story – "Somebody Else did it" or "I Dunno Who". "Find him," orders the voice of authority, but of course that is impossible. Poor pathetic couple! By now they must have mangy whiskers. The peaks hang half off their bedraggled caps. They are continually shivering as the wind blows through their threadbare jerseys. Their bony knees protrude through the holes in their Miller Rayner[1] bib-and-brace dungarees. They are forever trying to stick dismal little patches on their useless seaboots, or tying the flapping soles up with rope yarns. They are always trying but never succeeding, doomed forever to haunt cadet ships.[2]

*

Part 1. Sail.

WHETHER or not the event triggered the thinking of a number of philanthropic individuals is now pure conjecture, but during 1888-9 an extraordinary voyage took place that, distinguished by its air of the bizarre, was arguably the first essay into seagoing cadet-training *en bloc*. It came about as the result, apparently, of a whim, unless of something less ingenuous and distinctly sinister, and although completed without undue mishap was never repeated. Among other contenders, disaster was given a chance to demonstrate its talent but – miraculously – missed it.

---

[1] Miller, Rayner & Haysom. The BISN Co's officially-appointed tailors/outfitters.
[2] From "Alas, Poor Ghosts" (Anon.) ss *Devon* Cadets' Magazine No.3, April 1935.

The ship was the *Mercury*, and the voyage only one of several facets of the eccentric that had become her stock-in-trade. Comfortably settled at her supposedly permanent berth off Binstead Hard she was readied for sea on the orders of Charles Hoare, careful not to disclose his plan to the boys beforehand: their first intimation of what was afoot came when they were turned-to for weighing anchor. As the ship got under way Hoare wished them farewell, adding a note of bathos by distributing a handful of marbles each "to play with at Gibraltar". Neither he nor his mistress, Beatie Sumner, sailed on the voyage, which commenced on 19th October, an unpropitious time of year to entrust 132 inexperienced cadets, with their slightly rusty officers and 20 paid hands, to the elements in a ship that had been gently rotting for three years. Not only that, but she had also been modified to represent – complete with open gratings in place of hatch covers – a warship of vaguely Nelsonian extraction. Had it existed at the time, the "safety" industry would have had an attack of the vapours, a feminine trait to which Beatie Sumner, later the Ma Fry of grim recollection, was conspicuously immune.

Before they had cleared the Needles a leaking sea-valve obliged them to put back to Portsmouth, where yet further delay was occasioned by discovery of a rudder defect. They eventually sailed on December 1st, straight into the teeth of a westerly gale which forced them to heave-to off the Isle of Wight, circumstances that set the tone for the rest of the passage, during much of which the boys had to be kept below for their own safety. Storms escorted them to Gibraltar, where they spent Christmas, the boys presumably finding their marbles useful for passing the time if not as trade goods for more prurient commodities and interests, and New Year's Day found them storm-tossed in the Bay of Lions, crew lashed to the masts and boys battened down below again as seas swept the decks. Surviving this – the old ship was a vindication of her builders' skills as well as those of her current masters – a 2-month stay at Villefranche gave everyone time to recover and brace themselves for the return, finally accomplished on Easter Sunday, 1889.

Why the voyage was undertaken remains a mystery, beyond a suggestion that Hoare felt an urge to demonstrate that his brainchild was no mere egotistic decoration. But there was something unnerving in his behaviour, not only in his choosing to remain safe ashore but also in his parting words to the boys, in which he "pardoned" them for their past misdeeds as though administering the last rites. One can't help wondering whether he stood to lose more than his social reputation (already in tatters) or make a fortune out of the ship's not unlikely disappearance. Since most of the boys were orphans, or at best lacked familial ties, loss of life would have been of little consequence, an Act of God, so-called, accepted as the sea's prerogative. However, the ship resumed her duties none the worse for her adventure and probably somewhat better off, certainly raised in the esteem of her progeny, who must themselves have basked in a ray or two of glory.

Some 10 years earlier Sprott's full-rigger *Ellerbank* had carried 16 apprentices, but she was in no other sense a cadet-ship, her owner's sole concern that of substituting as many boys for paid hands as possible. Indeed, the only surprising thing about the practice is that numbers of ships weren't crewed entirely by boys for perfectly sound reasons. As it was, the few that came close to it were manned in this way for a more altruistic purpose altogether, stemming from an awareness that unless training of suitable material were placed on a footing of proper order with a clearly-defined objective the already alarming wastage would increase while the surviving remnant would be seriously deficient in the necessary skills. Needless to say, the awareness lay not with government – the ever-aloof BOT – but with private concerns and individuals taking sail to be the natural medium for the task.

There was – still is – a lot to be said for that view, not from the technological standpoint, obviously (which seems to have seduced and channelled mankind's imagination), but from one of a need to train mind and body to a desired pitch of alertness and agility as well as to nurture a spirit of community and mutual regard without which life at sea – and ashore, for that matter – degenerates into mere brutishness. Symbol of the enigmatic progress of civilisation, the steamship had not the wherewithal for forging character possessed in sometimes over-abundance by sail. Moreover, steamship owners in general felt no obligation to carry apprentices at all, among the few exceptions being Elder Dempster – two "midshipmen" had signed on the ss *Charity* in 1853, for example – and Runciman's Moor Line, which took apprentices almost as soon as it began trading in 1889, though the training varied widely in conception and application. Steam came to mean not training so much as utilisation – exploitation in some eyes – the example taken from sail and aggravated by the apprentice's exclusion from the processes of the voyage's execution: at the very worst in sail he could at least see himself taking a hand in helping the ship on her way, while in steam only drudgery filled his days, with lookout and helm to relieve it, each representing formalised boredom.

Long before the war I advocated that firms large enough would purchase or build one or two 3-masted square-rigged schooners[sic] each of 450 to 500 tons deadweight. The idea did not appeal to any steamship firms I know of, but this did not prevent me from getting estimates in this country and Denmark, where the finest of these vessels are built and owned. Only the war prevented the scheme's full realisation.[1]

Writing this in 1924, Walter Runciman had no doubt attempted to set up a cadet training-ship scheme, though no record remains except of a gesture post-war when he had taken a few apprentices on cruises in his yacht *Sunbeam*[2]. Large sailers, he asserted, were no good, for their very mention gave underwriters acute insomnia, a line of thinking characteristic of a certain kind of shipowner and, in the event, inimical

---

[1] *Before the Mast – And After*, p.10.
[2] Originally Lord Brassey's. She was presented to the NCP in 1918 after war service as a hospital ship, but proved unsuitable for training cadets.

to the precepts of cadet training, in which the risks and liabilities automatically cut out the more comfortable elements of insurance. Large sailers were, in fact, the only logical choice.

However, the committed sailing-ship owners Devitt & Moore, who had burnt their fingers, so to speak, with steam, were conspicuous among the minority aware of and concerned by the training problem, their policy anent apprentices an enlightened one brought into sharp focus in cooperation with Sir Thomas Brassey[1]. In 1890 they launched the Ocean Training Scheme, Brassey undertaking to fund it through a majority shareholding while D&M brought their experience and expertise to bear, mainly through the enthusiasm and energy of the company's co-founder's son, Thomas Lane Devitt. A founder partner of the Orient Line, he obtained from it the scheme's first two ships, the fast passenger-liners *Hesperus* and *Harbinger*, putting them on D&M's traditional UK-Australia route, particularly suited to the project. The ships were run as normal commercial ventures with the explicit proviso that profits accruing would be ploughed back into the scheme: neither Brassey nor Devitt saw it as anything other than a non-profit-making arrangement from which British shipping at large would benefit. As it happened costs swamped income from freights, fares and cadets' premiums, the deficit offset by Brassey's own financial interest combined with dividends from outside investments and the substantive support of a few steamship owners. Runciman wasn't among them, and indeed on his own admission they weren't known to him: he seemed remarkably unacquainted with household names.

In the prospectus issued shortly after the scheme's inception D&M took pleasure in announcing, somewhat euphuistically, that

...the improved plan of professional education of sons of gentlemen for Officers of the Mercantile Marine...with the view to meet the wishes of parents anxious to send their boys to sea under proper care and discipline, has proved a success.[2]

It explained that each ship accommodated midshipmen in a deckhouse fitted out with cabins and a messroom, attended by a surgeon and taught, by a "naval instructor", navigation, nautical astronomy and "the higher branches of the profession" including theoretical and practical seamanship. Here the system made a classic slip, for the midshipman was supposed to learn not the higher but the lower branches. It became a point of contention that over-emphasis was placed on subject-matter not the apprentice's concern: to say, as some later did, that they knew enough to pass for master, or at least had been dosed with it, was to miss the point, knowledge enough to pass for 2nd mate giving the apprentice quite enough to grapple with.

Be that as it may, five voyages were reckoned sufficient to meet the sea-time requirement, four in the case of Conways and Worcesters with full remission, and any shortfall had to be covered by signing on somewhere – possibly with D&M – as either

---

[1] See appx. 7.
[2] Quoted in *Painted Ports*, p.127.

AB or u/c officer. Paid in advance of each voyage, premiums started at £70 (£60 with 12 months' remission) to diminish by £10 a voyage, with additional charges for laundry and school stationery. Raper's *Epitome* and the requisite drawing instruments were available at cost on board. The boy provided his own bedding, but eating utensils accompanied a dietary "equal to that of the officers", which isn't to say the same as, but it was probably better than in most ships, if never enough.

Testimony of good conduct from the last school had to be produced on application, made in person at the company's Fenchurch St office, where the "candidate" was "inspected"; physical fitness and sound eyesight were prerequisites. Integral to the disciplinary structure, seniority was designated by voyage, as were the classes of instruction, conducted in alternate watches morning and afternoon – 1st, 2nd, 3rd and 4th/5th – and the BOT agreed to remission of time with a minimum on articles of 38 months 12 days, *pro rata* for Conways and Worcesters, a neat little piece of bureaucratic pedantry possibly based on a calculation of the balance between length of voyage and time off articles between one and the next.

An iron-built (by Steele of Greenock in 1876) full-rigger of 1585gt, 253.5ft in length, *Harbinger* was a noted passage-maker originally fitted out to carry 200 passengers in 1st to emigrant classes. Her midshipmen (up to 40) lived below and in six 4-berth cabins in the deckhouse, leaving enough accommodation for 30 saloon passengers and space for cargo, usually wool on the return passage. In the focsle lived the normal complement of paid hands.

Popular with all, Melbourne was the terminus. Unlike most UK ports it offered recreational activity on site, as it were – in the river and out in Port Philip Bay, where ships' boats took part in competitive events, some exclusively for them, at a time when sailing-ships were sometimes spending lengthy periods awaiting cargoes, although D&M had made arrangements for quick despatch assisted by preference from UK wool merchants sympathetic to the cause. A gig-race in the Yarra in 1894 was memorable for its extension to a finish off Dover, beginning with a tie between *Harbinger*'s and *Parthenope*'s[1] entrants; in the ensuing tie-breaker *Harbinger*'s stroke sprang his oar just short of the finish with the boats again neck and neck, and although the winning crew generously shared the prize, whatever it was, the bets that had been placed weren't settled to anyone's satisfaction so the race was transferred to the ships, both loading for London. It resumed with the bending of sail, yet another tie and excuse for an evening of celebration before sailing, when the ships parted company. They sighted each other at the Horn and again in the NE trades, meeting finally in the Western Approaches and pacing each other to Dungeness where, at long last, *Harbinger* brought the contest to an end by picking up a tug first to pass Dover ahead of her rival. No record exists of the time taken, but *Parthenope*'s recorded passages were remarkably consistent, suggesting that this example took some 80-85 days, a fine run. *Harbinger* was sold to Finns in 1898.

---

[1] Full-rigger, 1563gt. The Australasian Shipping Co. (Gracie, Beazley & Co.) (Lubbock).

Also an iron full-rigger built by Steele, but 3 years before *Harbinger*, *Hesperus* was slightly larger at 1859gt on a length of 262.2ft., though as a cadet-ship she accommodated only 18 saloon passengers.

Harvey and I went to London, and he spoke to the mate about me. I was promised a berth as AB, which was more than I expected, for the *Hesperus* was a grand ship. Most of her focsle hands were Italians and there were about forty midshipmen aft. (c.1895.)[1]

"Aft" being figurative; like their brethren in the sister-ship the midshipmen lived below and in the deckhouse in comparative ease with two stewards to keep the quarters clean, get meals and wash up, and like their brethren were soon described by their officers and others in authority as "schemers", shortly afterwards amended to "bloody schemers". An instance of their claim to distinction occurred in Sydney, where they pawned their sextants and heavy-weather gear for more spending-money after the £12 voyage allowance had run out. Then they learned that the homeward passage would be east-about and not, as expected, via the Cape, and to their consternation the captain refused them an advance to recover their possessions, so to comfort themselves they lifted the pawnbroker's sign and the ship sailed in April 1892 for a winter's crossing of the Southern Ocean with thinly-clad midshipmen and at her jib-boom three golden balls.

Quickly established, training-ship tradition rested heavily on key figures, "characters" whose habits and foibles outlived them in a continuing folklore, typified by those of *Hesperus*'s bosun, Old MacGregor, for whom a shipload of schemers held no terrors. It was his custom to rouse them from their bunks with a rope-end after a nod to social decorum, a sardonic, *sotto voce* request of the young gentlemen to be good enough to turn out.

The owners were well-served by him, an excellent seaman of the old school and most careful in expending ship's stores. We were running the easting down, holystoning the decks, when a big sea came aboard and washed everyone along the deck. I brought up with my arms round a small capstan, half-drowned, when I heard MacGregor shout, "Hang onto them holystones, m'lads!"[2]

She carried only 29 midshipmen and 10 passengers on her last voyage in 1898. Under Captain Maitland were 5 mates, nautical instructor, surgeon, chief steward with 2nd and 3rd stewards and an assistant steward, 2 cooks, baker, butcher, bosun and mate, carpenter and 14 AB's. The passage to Melbourne took 87 days, a good one without the ship's being pressed. Mainstay of the entertainment was a series of concerts staged by passengers, midshipmen and crew, with a special performance, by

---

[1] *A Modern Sinbad*, pp.89-90.
[2] Midshipman R.C. Bickley, *Illawarra* 1899-1900; quoted in *Painted Ports*, p.143.

popular request and seniority fiat, put on by the first-voyagers. And there were the usual diversions:

An old lady among the passengers seemed to think we were there for her special convenience. She brought a pet cat and some potted ferns with her, which we were supposed to put on deck whenever it rained, while the cat was a pest. One day a few of us got hold of it and made a length of twine fast to its tail, similarly the potted ferns, and working the strings like puppeteers from the break of the poop had them performing a sort of gavotte, the cat on its forepaws. The audience was loud in its mirth, which attracted the old lady, and we made ourselves scarce, but there was a devil of a row afterwards.[1]

Bought as the *Melbourne* from R&H Green in 1887, *Macquarie* was an iron ship of 1965gt, fitted for her role as successor to *Harbinger* by accommodating her midshipmen in the 2nd- and 3rd-class passenger cabins and dividing the tween-deck emigrant space into classrooms. Saloon passengers were still carried, and by custom associated freely with the ship's company except for the exclusion of women from the midshipmen's sing-songs, which wouldn't have been the same in their presence. A feature of life was the weekly newspaper, *The Skyscraper*, in which a series of gently satirical articles appeared as extracts from a (fictitious) passenger's diary:

The thing which has charmed me is the behaviour of the midshipmen, never grumbling, always cheerful, it is a treat to listen to their innocent prattle, and to catch snatches of their sweet songs as they work...[2]

None of which, alas, have survived, but whatever the quality of the boys' sweetness and innocence, passengers saw only their lighter side. In Melbourne and Sydney gangs of larrikins loitered about the waterfronts preying on unwary (i.e. inebriated) sailors and apprentices, who from time to time disappeared without trace. Accordingly the midshipmen went ashore in gangs themselves, dispensing with fists in favour of boots, stones slung in kerchiefs, lengths of piping, and buckle-belts. Sons of gentlemen some of them might have been, but the nursery was a long way behind them and the schoolroom a dangerous, if exhilarating, one.

Next to go was *Hesperus*, sold to Russians in 1899, her place taken by *Illawarra*, another iron ship, measuring 1963gt, built in 1881 for D&M by Dobie of Glasgow. Like the others, she retained limited passenger accommodation, housing her midshipmen similarly. She kept *Macquarie* company until the latter's sale in 1904, when she continued alone until joined in 1906 by *Port Jackson* from lay-up in the Thames. At about this time the midshipmen exchanged their title for cadet, but schemer none the less. The newcomer was a 4-mast iron barque, 2213gt, built in 1882 for Duthie of Aberdeen, and proved a great success with D&M, beginning with a special charter to the Marine Society carrying 100 boys from the moored training-ship

---

[1] Reconstructed from *Painted Ports*, p.142.

[2] Quoted in *Painted Ports*, p.121.

Arethusa. On her next voyage she carried 22 OTS cadets and 50 *Arethusa* boys, a carefully-gauged highly-explosive mixture, most of the cadets transferred from *Illawarra*, sold to the Norwegians in 1907. After that *Port Jackson* carried on in solitary splendour until joined by the famous but ill-fated *Medway* in 1910, carrying boys from the Marine Society's training-ship *Warspite* on selected voyages until the outbreak of war.

All hands were standing by to shorten sail, already reduced, and at about 2pm we hove to with fore and main upper topsails split. The decks were full to the rails and the door of our deckhouse was in splinters, like the dinghy on the roof, and the poop skylight glass had been smashed. While we were furling the remnants of the main upper tops'l midshipman[*sic*] Parry-Jones fell to the deck, about seventy feet, but within a month was up and about. He said the rigging had broken his fall. (1909.)[1]

We'd been furling sail in heavy weather, and on our way down Bezelgette disappeared, last seen on the lee shrouds, which was a mistake, for [there] the wind blows you outboard, off the shrouds. It was impossible to lower a boat or round-to without endangering others, so we carried on. (1911.)[2]

Bezelgette's loss is the only one mentioned in connection with the OTS, evidence enough, even if there were others, of the thoroughness of the training and sound seamanlike practice displaced over the ages by the artifices of the safety industry in its bureaucratic mission to protect us against our own ineptitude and carelessness, to say nothing of the savour of life in the face of its natural risks. *Port Jackson* was sold in 1916 to a Hartlepool owner who put her into Admiralty service training RNR midshipmen, work cut short the following year by a torpedo.

The archetypal sail-training ship, *Medway* was the culmination of experience and development that should have led the way to greater things. As it was, war intervened to end her career, together with the concept she represented, on a note of unnecessary wretchedness that is one of the hallmarks of the bureaucratic system. Built by MacMillan of Dumbarton in 1902 for Spanish owners, it was significant that Britain's ancient sea rival had gone as far as commissioning a purpose-designed cadet-training ship. Registered as the *Ama Beganakoa* at Montevideo, her owners' registered office was at Bilbao. She was a 4-mast steel barque of 2516gt on a length of 300ft with accommodation for 30 cadets and their instructors with a full standard complement including 16 AB's. She carried no passengers but some 4000dwt of cargo, partly in two deep-tanks also used for water-ballast.

Not surprisingly, she was an instant success with the OTS, training not only her own cadets but also outsiders, apprentices and cadets on the books of steamship companies holding the balance of shares in the enterprise, which, in 1909, became

---

[1] Reconstructed from *Painted Ports*, p.127.

[2] ibid., p.156.

Devitt & Moore's Ocean Training Ships Ltd. For example, six cadets (actually apprentices) from the NZS Co's *Rimutaka* joined her in Hobart for a passage home in 1915, wartime risks notwithstanding.

The loss of *Port Jackson* left her the only sailing cadet-ship under the red ensign, when, rather late in the day, prompted perhaps by Germany's declaration of "total submarine war", discretion was adopted as the better part of valour in confining her to a run between the WCSA and South Africa. During this period most of the berths were reserved by the Admiralty for RNR midshipmen, similarly to *Port Jackson*'s arrangement, and in the event all cadets were, willy-nilly, made temporary midshipmen, RNR, to be whisked off to the fleet after 12 months in the ship. The press appeared to be alive and well, if using kid-type gloves instead of bludgeons.

Her first master was Robert Jackson, late chief officer of *Port Jackson*. He died in 1914 to be succeeded by a phlegmatic Welshman, David Williams, who remained until she was requisitioned. Never slack in the matter of discipline, he was a genial personality, cool and unflappable. In 1916, on a run from Bordeaux to Barry with pit-props while the cadets were on leave, the ship was becalmed for several days off the Lizard, a sitting duck. To relieve the tedium – and perhaps the tension – Williams and his ship's company, which included a crowd of runners, went swimming overside for an hour or so in broad daylight, a sight which might well have baffled any stalking U-boat commander into suspecting a trap of the Q-ship variety. At all events, the passage was safely completed.

The one that followed exemplified the system as it had evolved. Mr Philip Devitt inspected the ship at Barry before she sailed on September 12th, a custom in sail that lingered on into steam in a half-hearted way for a while before becoming too much of a chore for a softer-living generation. On the articles were chief and first, second and third mates, surgeon, instructor, bosun with 16 AB's and 2 OS's, carpenter and sailmaker, 2 cooks and 2 stewards. And cadets, 26 of them. The cargo consisted of 202 tons of general, 1906 tons of cement and 1543 of coal. The cadets were, of course, in their late teens. By comparison the ages of the rest of the ship's company were an apt mixture – Williams was 40, his chief mate 42, but the three other mates were respectively 23, 19 and 17, and the instructor in his 20s. The bosun was 34, balanced in not untypical fashion by the carpenter at 71 and sailmaker, 57. It was a nicely-gauged blend that worked well where a mob of spirited youths needed more than a disciplinary ukase imposed from on high. If sail was being superseded by steam there was nothing out of date about *Medway*'s hierarchy, representative of the majority of sail's dwindling corps of practitioners, in which shellbacks weren't as prevalent as a later age is given to suppose, but constituted a solid nucleus of experience and skill. It was a young man's life, exacting every shred of vigour and enthusiasm from material that either toughened with age or disintegrated at varying rates.

First port of call was St Vincent, in the Grenadines, where the time passed pleasantly:

Oct 8th. Sunday.	*2pm: three divisions of cadets ashore.*
Oct 11th.	*Port watch cadets entertained by friends on shore. Commander and 2nd officer in attendance.*
Oct 12th.	*10.30am: cadets left ship for picnic.*
Oct 14th.	*am: cadets' boat exercises, school ashore, and deck duties. pm: cadets boating and bathing on the beach.*
Oct 15th. Sunday.	*10.15am: cadets mustered and inspected.*
	2.15pm: cadets' leave party.
	Returned 5.30pm.
Oct 16th.	*All cadets left ship for picnic. Returned 6pm.*

(Log abstract)[1]

From which it appears that while U-boats couldn't rattle Captain Williams, Friday 13th found a weak spot...

From St Vincent they continued to Santos, then round to Tocopilla, arriving on January 30th, 1917. There, apart from school work and ship's duties, sailing and cricket against a local eleven occupied the time. Ever the prudent seaman, Williams saw to maintenance, particularly important after the rough work off the Horn. Rigging was inspected and overhauled, the sprung mizen royal yard condemned and the fore royal yard repaired. All the while cargo was being worked, 3,700 tons of bagged nitrate loaded after discharge of the outward consignment. They made a 42-day passage to Cape Town, encountering icebergs on the way, and returned going east, a classic 62-day circling of the Southern Ocean – and not, as often claimed in such instances by impressionable romanticists, of the world.

She remained on this route until, in 1918, disaster overtook her, not in the shape of the overt enemy but in that of a more treacherous one within, bureaucratic edict, as pointless and uncompromising as ever. In spite of remonstration substantiated by all the evidence of her value to the nation in her training role, she was requisitioned for conversion to an oil-tanker, an act of criminal stupidity made ludicrous by its futile outcome. Even the voice of an indignant Admiralty was of no avail, and the ship was ordered to Cape Town where her midshipmen were dispersed and a crew of runners signed on to sail her to Hong Kong. There she was cut down and, because the war came to an end at that moment, making her effectively redundant before she could be used as intended, lay idle as an oil-storage barge until taken up by Anglo-Saxon in 1921. Thereafter she ran occasionally as the *Myr Shell* until broken up in 1933. What made the affair such a wasteful exercise in official pig-headedness was the fact that Anglo-Saxon had earlier reached an accommodation with D&M to continue the ship's training role while in service as a auxiliary sailing tanker. Wanton vandalism would have been avoided, but the faceless ones stuck valiantly to their paper guns, and thus the ignominious finale.

---

[1] *Last of the Windjammers, Vol. II.*, p.187.

By this date, using the proceeds of *Port Jackson*'s sale, the new college had been established at Pangbourne and a search begun for a suitable square-rigger in which the cadets, up to 100 at a time as it was hoped, would spend 12 months as part of the college course. *Sunbeam*'s value in this respect was very limited and she was finally rejected in favour of an auxiliary 3-mast topsail schooner[1] bought from the Admiralty in 1919. Originally a private yacht of 871 tons Thames measurement, *St George* was fitted out to carry 40 cadets and 5 hands. She was commanded by Lt-Cdr J.H. Blair, RNR, an energetic disciplinarian with a wartime record of submarine service and earlier polar exploration and experience, for which he held the Polar Medal and was distinguished by the sobriquet "Polar" Blair. He had served his time in the Glasgow-registered *Lochs* of Aitken, Lilburn & Co.

St George was selected rather than a commercial square-rigger after consideration of the trading situation: notwithstanding the brief post-war boom freights for sail were so low that, set against operating costs, nothing but a prohibitive deficit would have resulted. The only alternative seemed to be a smaller ship which, although carrying no payload, would at least cost less than otherwise to run. Or so it was hoped.

The plan was doomed, however. It began in 1920 with a cruise to Teneriffe, starting in mid-January and running head-on into heavy weather which made a mockery of instruction among 30 prostrated boys, for whom the experience was, Blair averred, good training even if it seemed unduly hard. The cruise ended in April to be followed by another with 60 boys, when the upshot of prolonged calms was a shortage of water and victuals, trying conditions that might have appalled parents but which, in Blair's acerbic eye, amounted to yet more rugged training.

The routine on board revolved about a two-watch arrangement, port and starboard alternating morning and afternoon in the classroom and on deck, echoing the old OTS system. Blair shared the task of instruction with one or two members of the college teaching staff, taking classes in Rule of the Road and seamanship while forming the private opinion that some of his charges were "hopeless and a waste of time". Never seeking popularity, he didn't find it, but earned a wary respect from the boys, vastly more useful in the circumstances. The ship trained about 100 cadets on five cruises altogether before the college governors reluctantly concluded that she was an overpriced indulgence at a time when the college itself was struggling to stay afloat, and in May 1921 sea training was dropped from the curriculum. The ship was sold the following year and no further attempt made to revive the idea.

So ended sail training for the professional under the red ensign. It had not, however, been entirely in the hands of D&M, nor exactly under the red ensign: in 1908 White Star (the Oceanic Steam Navigation Co.) bought the *Mersey* from James Nourse for service as a cargo-carrying cadet-training ship. She was a 3-mast full-rigger of 1829gt, fitted to take 60 cadets with a regular crew of 6 to 8 AB's depending on cadet

---

[1] Wrongly described as a barquentine: she carried only square topsails and topgallant on the fore, above a fore-and-aft foresail.

numbers, bosun, carpenter and lamp-trimmer. Under Captain F.W. Corner (late captain of *Macquarie*) the officers included three mates, a schoolmaster and two assistants, and a surgeon. Catering was in the hands of two officers' stewards, a cadets' steward and a cook: food was generally adequate, though the cadets grumbled at it and lost no time in impressing on their parents the need of a hamper to tide them over the worst of their trials, which was replenished at the Australian terminal ports before the homeward passage. With the officers and instructors aft and the hands forward under the raised focsle the cadets occupied a tween-deck flat between the main and mizen masts, attending school and chapel in the deckhouse above, called the "general room", also serving as a recreation space. They were grouped in three watches (to enable them, as the prospectus put it, to get the requisite amount of sleep), each under a cadet PO answering to a cadet CPO, one watch attending school in the morning, the other two in the afternoon, and in heavy weather and other times of need re-grouped in two watches. Many were Conways and Worcesters, among them RNR midshipmen, so between that and the senior instructor's (or headmaster's) rank – Lt-Cdr F.C. Cross, RNR, was a White Star officer – the ship was entitled to wear the blue ensign. Training was flavoured accordingly, though Captain Corner's unadorned presence ensured a proper sense of proportion and served as a reminder that the ship's service was mercantile and not naval, geared as it was to the requirements of the shipping group to which White Star belonged, Associated Steamship Lines, part of Pierpont Morgan's colossal International Mercantile Marine Company.

Aged 14 to 17 (18 if from *Conway* or *Worcester*), applicants had to produce the usual evidence of health and character on interview, and were indentured to Ismay, Imrie & Co., managers of White Star, who obtained a concession from the BOT allowing ex-Merseys to take the 1st mate's exam after serving 2 years (with a 2nd mate's ticket) as junior OOW in ships of the group, the normal requirement being service as the only, or senior, watch officer. Similar dispensation was granted in respect of the master's exam, which, on the strength of time in the *Mersey* without any further time in sail, was for a square-rig, or ordinary, certificate, a practice frowned upon as an impertinent presumption by a dwindling coterie of pure sail men. As with D&M, premiums were stiff - £70 or £60 for the first year (4- or 3-year indentures respectively) dropping to £40 and £30 respectively for the remaining years. While there was no requirement, implicit or otherwise, for the ex-cadet to offer his services to the company as a certificated officer, a £10 bonus was paid to those who did and were accepted.

Instruction covered English grammar and composition, history, geography, arithmetic, algebra, plane and spherical trigonometry, navigation and nautical astronomy, compass-work, meteorology, marine surveying, technical drawing, chartwork, ship-construction, French or German, and "ambulance work" including first aid; in addition were more specialised subjects – ropework, rigging, tackles, cargo-handling and stowage, log and lead, boat-work, signalling, anchor-work, Rule of the Road and basic engineering: a small oil engine generated power for lighting.

Quarterly exams and the cadets' work-books were open to inspection by the BOT, and parents received regular reports. They were also kept advised of the ship's whereabouts and progress by means of post-cards sent from the Liverpool office whenever the information came to hand: in 1914 the ship was fitted with wireless, which improved on the system of reporting via Lloyd's signal stations and meetings with homeward-bound ships.

The ship traded chiefly with Australia on the established White Star route, out via the Cape and home round the Horn, but occasionally she diverted and made short voyages to fill in time awaiting cargo for the UK.

There were over eighty square-rigged ships flying the Red Ensign, quite a sight. The full-rigged ship *Mersey*, the White Star training ship which had always traded to Australia, came in. She carried 80 or 90 [*sic*] cadets, a big crew, and was a very well found and fine looking ship. One evening we saw the boat pull off from her, Navy fashion, with four oars out each side, and they were going round all the British ships, hailing them...a very cultured voice hailed us. One of our people said, "What do you want?" and the voice said, "Have you any *Conway* boys aboard?"...this rather crude sailor said, "No; everybody's parents in this ship were[*sic*] married!" (Barque *Beeswing*. Valparaiso, 1911.)[1]

Thus the power of suggestion, in this case the blue ensign's, the ship's appearance and the company's reputation, which polished accents in the ears of all with a sense of social irrelevance. In this instance *Mersey* had brought a coal cargo from Newcastle, NSW.

Life on board was, naturally, active and demanding, boredom excluded by order, and when the demands of the ship herself were few, as in fine weather, PT was substituted for work aloft, and a canvas swimming-pool rigged; when becalmed for lengthy periods cadets were allowed to take a plunge overside. A library offered more sedentary pleasures, and the presence of the captain's wife – it was Mrs Corner's custom to accompany her husband – effected a civilising influence with cadets being invited to tea and co-opted into the production of entertainments such as the Saturday evening concerts which enabled the "Mersey Minstrels" to limber up for a wider audience at the Sydney Missions to Seamen, where they were apparently a popular act. And among such a virile and vigorous ship's company the surgeon was kept busy attending to a more or less constant stream of minor injuries though few illnesses. On one voyage an ever-present likelihood caused a stir when a cadet went down with acute appendicitis in heavy weather off the Horn, and the operation that followed – the surgeon assisted by Captain Corner, Lt-Cdr Cross and a cadet holding the instruments (who fainted and dropped them) – was a success.

Discipline was taut, as in other cadet-ships then and later, based on a system of rigorous work rather than draconian punishment, which kept the pressure down in what would otherwise have been a hard-pressed container. Nevertheless, shoregoing

---

[1] *The Long Wake*, p.23.

meant a welcome release from sustained strain, when cadets, no paragons of virtue, got into scrapes. Drunkenness was an ever-present problem, particularly in Australian ports, and not only among cadets, who took their examples from the sailors and occasionally the officers, some of whom drank excessively and obviously. On one occasion an assistant schoolmaster went adrift for ten days or so to reappear under storm canvas in heavy weather of his own making, to be sent home on the next available White Star liner, a convenient service which also bore homeward a cadet who had overstepped the bounds of propriety by writing a love-letter to Mrs Corner.

But roistering apart, in her inimitable way Australia offered the cadets ample wholesome diversion in the shape of generous and indiscriminate hospitality on the part of local families, picnics and sightseeing trips organised by various benevolent bodies including the Flying Angel with its encouragement to attend Sunday services, regattas, and sports fixtures with other ships and local teams, all of which balanced the hard work in the holds unloading and preparing for cargo.

Altogether some 132 cadets passed successfully through the ship, the balance of a figure which included some 15% lost by cancellation and desertion, on the whole a good record. Then, in late 1914, it was decided that war posed too great a threat to the scheme, not only as an obvious hazard but also in its requiring the RNR people for service in the fleet, so the ship was sold, passing to Norwegian owners. Meanwhile Pierpont Morgan's empire had run into financial storms and was taken into the hands of the receivers that year, and White Star's problems precluded all further interest in sail-training.

Elsewhere under the red ensign – in the dominions and colonies – one or two ventures embarked briefly, none of any note except for a determined effort by New Zealand owners, the Union Steamship Co., which ran the *Dartford* as a cadet-ship from 1908 to 1912, an iron-built ship of 1327gt bought at a time when the company was experiencing a shortage of qualified officers. She began with only 12 cadets, but success prompted expansion and when she was finally taken out of service she was carrying 44, of whom the first dozen had completed their time. Curtailment of her career seems to have owed much to the old bugbear of cost and commercial viability.

Leaving government out of the argument, there appears to have been no shortage of will to set up sail-training schemes, but certainly a shortage of coordination and, apparently, of communication between those who variously professed and acted upon plans. The Brassey/D&M scheme and its White Star counterpart were successful without at any time evincing an inclination to combine resources, while Runciman's alleged efforts seem to have been conducted in limbo during the same period, at all events coming to nothing; and after the war, when perhaps the three together would have been able to launch a fresh training initiative, only D&M made the effort while others lay low as recession concentrated their minds on the mundane prospect of the balance-sheet.

Others, that is, with two exceptions, but who ran true to British form in being out of step with each other and all others. One seemed at first oddly reticent about his ideas, confining them to his immediate (and unimpressed) business associates, while the other failed to arouse the interest of possible backers, and here again was evidence of this inexplicable inability or disinclination to combine resources, assuming that anything was known of one by the other.

Ever a supporter of rigour as an ingredient in the embryo officer's training recipe, Lawrence Holt attempted a revival of sail-training along the lines of the Ocean Training Scheme (a title that would have sat well with one of the several Alfred Holt aliases, Ocean Steam) by obtaining a quote of £29,000 for an auxiliary full-rigger from Thompson of Sunderland in 1932 but failing to persuade others including Richard Holt, his elder brother and senior partner, of the virtue of the idea. The ship was planned as a bald-header (no royals) 220ft long, 38ft beam, with two cargo hatches and hand-operated winches, windlass and pump, her 52 cadets accommodated in the forward tween-deck with, in a single deck-house, showers, lavatories, an office or study (in Blue Funnel study was called "office-work") and a library. Officers and other personnel were to have been the master and three mates, chief and 2nd engineers, radio officer, doctor, instructor, sailmaker, carpenter, bosun and 16 hands, 2 cooks and a steward. Shelved though it was, Holt continued to nurse the idea to bring it forward again in the late 40s when his late brother was no longer an obstacle, this time as a 3-mast barque 205ft long with three hatches and electric winches but no auxiliary, to take about 24 cadets and a dozen hands. He managed to interest the navy, P&O and the British & Commonwealth Group, proposing to run the ship as a commercial operation under Alfred Holt management, drawing cadets from all four parties to the scheme, but on mature consideration the other three decided that sail was after all an expensive anachronism and withdrew, leaving Holt the visionary with no choice but to reluctantly abandon his brainchild which, in other countries – Britain's trading rivals – would in all likelihood have met with support. To console himself he could at least look with some satisfaction upon his firm's new cadet-ship *Calchas*, for she seemed to be making a success of things in a thoroughly modern fashion.

For whatever the reason, Lawrence Holt gave no indication of awareness of the other sail enthusiast, who declared himself too late in the day for any possible conjunction of effort with either D&M or Runciman but apparently neither loudly enough nor in the right quarter to catch the Holt ear. Sir William Garthwaite was what might be called an owner of opportunity, collecting a fleet of big windjammers as they emerged from the brief post-war boom at knock-down prices, to keep the red duster flying under sail for a short and ill-starred interval that amounted to its death-throes. Of the fleet of six only *Garthsnaid* went to the breakers in one piece, after surviving two dismastings (the sort of accident that, as the journalist/sailor Alan Villiers pointed out, was an indicator of the lack of expertise among masters with the latter-day version of square-rig tickets). *Garthforce* was hulked at Durban after collision with an iceberg in 1921, *Garthgarry* broken up at Barrow in 1924 after getting there jury-rigged, *Garthneill* laid up then hulked in 1926, *Garthwray* stranded and lost in 1924, and *Garthpool*, last commercial square-rigger in service under the British flag (though registered in Canada where Garthwaite traded under the rather prosaic style of the Marine Navigation Co.), put ashore and lost at the Cape Verdes to bring the operation to an end. It is tempting to speculate on the risks attaching to the practice of renaming a ship, as Garthwaite did: as he gathered his famous fleet of sailers in a similar manner during the 20s Captain Gustav Erikson made a point of either retaining or restoring the original names, and even the disaster of WW2 failed to snuff out his enterprise. But Erikson was a hard-nosed professional with no illusions and a lifetime's experience of sea trade and seamanlike practice, compared with whom Garthwaite amounted to a rank amateur. Hardened businessman as he was, Erikson nevertheless paid due respect to at least one of the sea's ancient superstitions, by which he certainly lost nothing.

Garthpool's loss was an isolated incident barely noticed by the preoccupied world, having no readily-apparent bearing on the sail-training question, by that date virtually a dead letter as far as the British were concerned, but shortly afterwards this appeared in *The Times* of December 12th, 1929:

Sir,

May I crave the hospitality of your columns to make an appeal to those who are interested in the movement to supply the Empire with a steady flow of officers trained in sailing ships?

Since Messrs Devitt & Moore and the late Sir Thomas Devitt gave up their training ships, the Port Jackson *and the* Medway, *some ten years ago, the training of young officers in sailing ships afloat has been neglected. Messrs John Stewart & Co carried cadets until the sale of their last ship, the* William Mitchell, *some two years ago, and I have always carried about ten cadets in the ships of my fleet, but now, with the loss of my four-masted barque* Garthpool *on Boavista Island on November 11th last the British Empire is at the present time unpossessed of any deep-sea sailing ship in which to train our future officers[1].*

My object in writing this letter is to suggest that the time has arrived when a square-rigged sailing-ship for training purposes should be constructed. This ship would be equipped specially for carrying a large number of cadet officers and it should also be arranged to carry cargo in order to cover part of her expenses. According to estimates received recently, such a ship would cost about £40-50,000, and from my experience in running the Garthpool *I imagine such a ship would cost somewhere about £2,500-£3,000 a year to run. It would, therefore, be necessary to give the ship an endowment to produce this amount per annum, which could be done by an annuity insurance.*

Will those to whom this matter appeals kindly get in touch with me at the address below, and, according to the responses received, I will endeavour to form a committee to take up the question in more detail?

Yours faithfully,

W. Garthwaite.

Whatever the response no further correspondence appeared in *The Times* and nothing more was heard of a movement to supply the Empire with sail-trained officers – if indeed any such movement existed. Nothing, that is, except for a forlorn attempt

---

[1] Presumably ten cadets were carried in *each* ship of the fleet, though the point is by no means clear.

by the Australian Alan Villiers, which, alas, ran true to form in being well out of step with the others, some five years after Garthwaite's letter and coinciding with the official renunciation of sail as a training medium under the British flag – though numbers of British boys filled all available berths in the Erikson fleet as apprentices of somewhat loose description.

A native of Melbourne, Villiers served his time in sail, partly in British, partly in foreign-flag – Scandinavian – ships, but instead of trying for his ticket turned to journalism. Perhaps this lack of proper qualification had something to do with the difficulties he experienced in putting his plan into effect, a single-handed revival of sail-training using his little full-rigger *Joseph Conrad*, bought from the Danes with the proceeds from a book. As the *Georg Stage* she had trained boys on cruises in the Baltic and North Sea since 1882, and although still sound was heading for the breakers when Villiers discovered her in 1934. She was of iron, measuring only 212 tons on a length of 100ft.

Unable to get her onto the British register as either a training- or an ordinary cargo-carrying merchant-ship, he eventually succeeded in classing her as a yacht through the good offices of the Royal Harwich Y.C. Villiers's well-known aversion to bureaucracy is wholly understandable, though the BOT surveyor who inspected his ship in Harwich failed to ask for sight of his (non-existent) certificate when checking the officers' qualifications, taking his possession of one for granted. If Villiers had been able to register the ship as a merchant/training vessel he would have had to produce his credentials as master, short of employing someone in that capacity, so as matters turned out official obstruction played into his hands. At his own expense he fitted the ship out to accommodate 16 cadets, advertising places in her for a long training cruise. He had some trouble filling them, and after several changes during the voyage only six of the boys were English when they rounded the Horn on passage from Tahiti to New York and the end of the affair. Only two of those were resolved to make the sea their occupation.

> *I have heard it said that I charged large premiums, that the boy who will most benefit from sea experience could not afford to pay. Well, the* Joseph Conrad *was entirely a private venture. I was left to get on with it as best I could. She cost me something like £100 a week to run. But I had no intention ever of making her pay, as a school ship. Education cannot be made to pay*[1].

Not, in this form, as it would be recognised by an accountant, anyway. But that was the point, of course, and on it sail-training foundered. So much, too, for Garthwaite's estimate of operating costs: as the *Georg Stage* the ship had soaked up £3-4,000 a year not counting depreciation, maintenance, survey and repair costs. In fact not only sail but also the great age of philanthropy had passed, swept away by the winds of commercial expedient, to put it kindly.

---

[1] Article "The Joseph Conrad" in *The Trident*, May 1947.

Villiers charged £150 a head, and in a couple of cases – deserving, not "deprived", boys – nothing, which even with a full complement meant barely enough to fund a two-year cruise free of incident. As it happened, incidents in plenty marked its progress, beginning with weather damage in the North Atlantic, followed by collision and stranding in the safety of New York harbour, exacerbated by a chronic problem in the matter of suitable officers, among whom none could be trusted as a lieutenant, or first mate, able to share with Villiers a little of his heavy responsibility. Nevertheless, he completed a 57,800-mile circumnavigation that began at Harwich, touched at Funchal for repairs, and took in Nassau, New York, Rio (after landing a party while standing off the Brazilian coast north of Pernambuco), Tristan (hove-to for an hour or so while islanders came looking for handouts), Cape Town, Bali, Singapore, Sydney via the Sulu Sea and a few of its islands, the Bismarck Archipelago, the Trobriands, Solomons, Guadalcanal and Owa Raha. From Sydney they sailed to Melbourne where funds ran out threatening an end to the voyage before Villiers met some picturesque – or shady – characters whose "exploration" company (in search of gold) financed necessary repairs in return for a passage to New Guinea via Auckland. Near Samarai the ship touched on a coral reef, saved by some desperate work with the boats and anchors, before sailing on to call at Lord Howe Island and Papeete, where they rested before setting off on the final leg to New York. Starting on October 22nd, 1934, the voyage lasted 2 years 19 days, at the end of which Villiers was obliged to sell up. It had cost him some £15,000 and at its end he was saddled with some £3,000 of liabilities, mostly to cover the expense of repatriating everyone, raised by sale of the ship to an American. In that year – 1936 – the British authorities officially disqualified sail as an acceptable medium for sea time (which is to say that no-one was qualified to examine candidates for square-rig tickets, and sail alone wasn't regarded as sufficient grounding for steamship certificates) after the Shipping Federation's dismissal of it in a report of 1934.

Villiers's was a noble effort, and the fact remains that if he hadn't been so stubborn (and sentimental) about the red ensign he might have received support – in America, for instance, where the ship went on to train young people for a few more years. He might also have tried his luck in South Africa, Australia or New Zealand while keeping faith with the cloth, where sea-mindedness in the general public was conspicuously keener than in Britain. There was, after all, no need from the point of view of the ship's people to make a show of the much-vaunted but by this time suspect British sea-fever, for they were a truly international group – Danes, Finns, Germans, a South African, Australians, Americans, New Zealanders, English.

And, noble effort that it was, it also shed a harsh light on something about British shipping – about British national integrity, in fact – already apparent to those few in the country's business world able to see beyond their noses: that British maritime interests were in terminal decline, many of the reasons for which were beyond the country's control, but their effect exacerbated by a malaise best described as political and social indifference to the sea. A hole had already been dug in the ground in an attempt to bypass the footling (but, to a "seafaring" nation, daunting) sea crossing to Europe, but behind its ostensible purpose it provided a convenient means by which an island nation could bury its head in the sand, a tendency that was becoming a national trait. The outcome was inevitable, if avoidable had the will been there, and only the circumstances of another world conflict delayed its onset. Villiers with his brave little ship couldn't hope to be anything more effective or significant than a straw in the wind – and he had, after all, changed the ship's name...

In some ways the *Conrad* was a bridge between the true mercantile sail-training ship that had preceded her and the so-called youth-training – or recreational – sailers that followed after WW2, unconcerned with professional matters except incidentally. By then that duty had been shouldered by the cadet-ships owned and operated by steamship companies once wholly reliant on the supply of sail-trained officers but which had decided that running costs had perforce to be met by the ship's earning power, something sail couldn't achieve and which even a modern steamship would be hard-pressed to realise. In a time of trade depression shipowners weren't disposed to be either philanthropic or altruistic, particularly under a political administration that acceded readily to their disinclination to avail themselves of subvention when it would mean, inevitably, a tighter bureaucratic grip on their affairs. It was this as much as any apparent discord between the relative merits of steam and sail as the training medium that dictated the trend, so the steamship took over where the *Medway* had left off. Had sail been a practicable commercial proposition the story would almost certainly have been different.

And it bears a sad footnote in the shape of the German 4-masted steel barque *Pamir*. Under the Finnish flag (as one of the Erikson fleet) she was arrested in Wellington in 1941 on the rather shaky pretext, on the part of the New Zealand government, of war with Finland. Then, in 1943, fitted with an auxiliary engine and accommodation for some 80 cadets, she was placed in the hands of the Union Steamship Co. as managers to run between New Zealand and the WCSA as a trading cadet-training ship. She traded profitably at wartime rates but post-war, carrying cargoes between New Zealand/Australia and the UK, ran up heavy losses, and in 1949 the New Zealand government decided against her further operation, not only on grounds of cost but also because her training capacity was far greater than was required by the New Zealand merchant fleet. After a final voyage to the UK she was laid up at Penarth with her sister, *Passat*, and in 1951 sold to Belgian breakers. However, she made one more voyage, with British cadets, to South America, before passing into other hands and further lay-up in Hamburg. From there, refitted as a German cadet-ship in 1954, she made further training voyages, brought to a tragic end in a storm in the South Atlantic in 1956, in which she was lost with all hands including some 50 cadets. As far as British cadet-ship training was concerned, the episode drew a conclusive line under the sail/steam controversy, for all the wrong reasons.

Part 2. The Modern Era.

When the *Dartford* was taken out of service cadets still short of sea-time were transferred to a steamer, the company's *Aparima*, specially fitted out just as her predecessor had been, and her cadets became the first of a new breed over which debate ebbed and flowed in more or less emotive mood between two camps, one affecting to scorn sail as self-evidently out of date, the other to disparage the steamship as a moulder of character. The idealistic wing of the controversy was peopled mainly by seafaring men, inveighing against the respective opposition in speeches, articles and books, none of which amounted to anything cogent in respect of the real issue, which was the natural focus of attention on the part of those responsible for meeting costs – shareholders, owners, management and other vested interests: it was the bald fact that sail training was no longer affordable on a scale that would make it a viable introductory base for the sea service.

Yet the arguments were never very consistent on either side, and the question remained open: had the British MN retained its world lead in numbers and tonnage the trend of thinking on the subject might have led to its reintroduction supported by shipowners in their own commercial interests. As it was, decline and fall ensured that the matter never resurfaced, with the exceptions of Lawrence Holt's abortive proposition after sail had been officially discredited, and the later *Pamir* misadventure.

Exemplifying the somewhat woolly thinking involved (as mentioned, post-WW2 time in sail was accepted, but only in part, for the purposes of the BOT exams), the Shipping Federation expressed, in its report, the opinion that a boy trained in sail wouldn't necessarily(*sic*) acquire the qualities that make a good officer in a steamship, any more than would a boy trained in the steamship itself. It went on to declare, rather vaguely, that in sail there would be no opportunity for initiative and the assumption of responsibility; that beyond a monkey-like agility aloft the boy wouldn't develop any characteristics that he couldn't develop equally well in a steamship, and it was obvious that the actual work required in a steamship would be best learned in that type of ship. However that may be, and the argument is startlingly simplistic, it completely missed an important consideration given little or no attention elsewhere: that what a steamship *did* offer was an earlier acquaintance between deck and engine-room that smoothed some of the roughness inherent in their relations, stemming largely from the mutual misunderstanding born of totally separate training-grounds. The extent to which the ship suffered from the effects of this social discord seemed to escape the notice of the pundits until the more enlightened – for example, Lawrence Holt – brought the disaffected factions forcibly together both in shore establishments and afloat. It might, in passing, have been interesting to observe the effects of sending prospective engineers to sea for a time in sail, but the point is now purely academic.

Actually, none of the SF's observations departed from rhetoric, with opinion set forth as established fact, insofar as it went, which fell short of confronting the core of the matter, namely the demands made on the boy's physical, mental and moral capacity through the elemental processes of self-preservation. Sail was by its nature vulnerable to the caprices of its element to a degree that steam was not, and depended absolutely on the quality of its manpower, power not merely of muscle but also of mind and morale. The apprentice in sail was engaged in the business of survival as deeply as any of his shipmates, and his responses to the challenge, conditioned and educated by direct experience, formed the foundation on which sail training placed its values. In the same report special emphasis was laid on the value of boat-work as a means of developing self-reliance and initiative, the boat under sail, of course, in nice contradiction of the argument against it: if a small boat under sail possessed the desired qualities, essentially action in the struggle for survival, how was the windjammer devoid of them? In fact each shared the same qualities, the difference only a matter of degree with the balance inclined towards full-size blue-water sail.

Moreover, in the matter of initiative and responsibility, even a cursory examination of the methods employed by the sail-training ships would have shown these to be the two primary elements in the system's aim, which was first to mould the man, and secondly to produce the navigator. On the whole, responsibility was placed upon the boy's shoulders to the limit of his capacity as perceived by his officers.

But of course the debate was hypothetical, and the SF returned to *terra firma* on a note of relief by pointing out that there were in any case no sailing-ships available, qualifying the statement with the somewhat defensive assertion that even if sail were the proper training medium there was no possibility of funding enough sailing-ships to make the process the universal one it should be, the implication being, quite correctly, that the MN wasn't the place for cultivating an elite within its pale; to have any validity sail-training would have to provide for all. The conclusion was, therefore, that sail-training schemes would not be recognised, and this was the general complexion of the reception Villiers got when he turned up with his ship and the naïve (in the circumstances) trust in British officialdom's perception and enterprise. He was not the first to discover that this branch of the national character acted in direct opposition to enterprise of any kind except where it concerned support for foreign competition.

In the absence of sail companies adopted one or both of two approaches to apprenticeship (discounting a third, which was to eschew it and its parallels altogether). One, already in place, was to carry apprentices (by whatever their title) in general service vessels as in sail, on average something between two and eight to a ship; and the other was to carry them in droves aboard one or two cadet-ships, the progeny of which were intended to be officers in the company's fleet. The cadet-ship's contingent was usually balanced by numbers dispersed among the rest of the ships in the company's service, in some cases not being appointed to a cadet-ship at any time, in others spending some specified time in one, and in yet other instances being transferred in either direction at random or as circumstances demanded.

At the outbreak of war in 1914 the British India S.N. Co was operating the largest single fleet in the world, over and above its numerous ancillary units and local services. It numbered 126 ships totalling 570,243gt. At war's end 25 had been lost to leave a still substantial holding which, however, was hard-pressed to maintain the network of services developed since the 1860s. Not only that, but also in the management's mind was expansion, and between this and the customary turnover and retirement figures the company looked to its apprenticeship programme (begun in 1906) and the sources of officer replenishment, deciding to increase the training capacity by operating two ships along lines established by the *Berbera*, a general service vessel adapted in 1916 for training 25 indentured cadets. As a measure in anticipation of shortages its obvious advantages were outweighed by the apparently less obvious risks, thrown into tragic relief by the attentions of U-boats in carrying out Germany's policy of total submarine war: in 1917, suffering the same fate as *Port Jackson* and *Aparima* that year, she was torpedoed and sunk, three of her cadets losing their lives. It seems that, apart from White Star, only Lord Brassey and D&M, in sending the *Medway* beyond the U-boat's range, had any conception of the hazards of modern warfare and the possibility of losing numbers of young men at a stroke. Perhaps wholesale slaughter in the trenches had dulled the senses of people in responsible positions even outside the purlieus of Whitehall, but at all events BI pursued its training policy undeterred, fitting out *Waipara* and *Carpentaria* to take 32 and 28 cadets respectively from 1917.

In common with other cadet-ship operators, the NZS Co and its close associate, the Federal S.N. Co., BI hoped that by virtue of a better-organised and orientated training programme well-ballasted with company ethos, wastage could be contained, if not reduced, but in the event there was no conclusive evidence either way. Many, however, expressed their dislike of the system, chiefly in what was seen as its over-solicitous approach to the supervision of young men who considered that such impositions had been left behind with school and boyhood. The apprentice preferred to see himself as an adult in an adult world – more specifically, a man in a man's world – and only a "proper" ship would answer; but choice of ship in BI, as in the service of other companies, fell outside the conditions of engagement:

Your appointment to various vessels within the Company's fleet are subject to some thought and consideration...aimed at providing you with the best training available and to give you as wide an experience as possible of the Company's service. Your own preferences are of secondary importance... If your first appointment is to one of the Company's two Cadet Training Ships you will discover that the cadets must of necessity carry out all duties which would normally be done by a Deck Crew. The academic and theoretical part of your training will be learned by means of organised classes and study... In Cadet Ships it is possible to organise and make special provision for your recreation in a variety of ways...

This was the blunt introduction to the company's *Cadet's Manual*, c.1960, based on the original drafted by Captain J.V. Reilly, who commanded three of the cadet-ships between 1919 and 1934 – *Carpentaria*, *Woodarra* and *Nardana* – units of a series in service until the company's demise under the P&O banner during 1971-75.

Captain Reilly's manual began with "hints" of the kind best received as orders, such as punctuality, the "surest sign of good order". The cadet not punctual on all occasions could expect rebuke in no mean terms, which he was to accept in the right spirit, making every endeavour to avoid a repeat performance. In the company's service "strict discipline [was] essential", and imposed with more or less rigour from above, the conceit of "self-discipline" not yet having emerged from the process of social evolution, or degeneration. Organisation on board was typical of cadet-ships generally and applied to BI's, with a few concessions to the spirit of the age, post-war. The cadets were allocated to two watches, port and starboard, each supervised by a cadet PO in turn answerable to the cadet CPO.

The cadets' lives revolved about a routine of duties none of which were particularly arduous but strictly observed. Watchkeepers, helmsmen and lookouts were rotated from alternate watches, parts of the ship made the responsibility of respective watches while at sea, in port and when arriving and departing, while those not on watch followed the daily timetable in the manual, a fairly intensive agenda filling the time between 5.30am and 9pm, with short intervals to gather breath and wits and take in nourishment.

There was no study on Saturday afternoon, but whether this meant time off for the watch concerned or time at work about the decks with the other watch isn't clear. Sunday, however, was free after normal routine concluded with divisions at 10.30am and an "address" by the captain. Cadets had to keep a journal and navigation work-book, open to inspection, the journal a record of employment while "all navigation" was entered (neatly) in the work-book using the "BOT method", guaranteed to be the most laborious one in practice.

Four hours on and eight off, bridge watchkeeping was a mixture of tedium and mild responsibility, keeping a lookout (on the lee wing) and, with permission, acquaintance with the navigation in progress; the cadet was to read the night order book, scrutinise the chart (careful not to soil or deface it, a capital offence) and note salient details, familiarise himself with the heavens, calculate compass error and the DR position, write up the bridge log (under the OOW's guidance using stock BOT phraseology), familiarise himself with the use of the hand-lead, and when entering and leaving port was to tend the telephones and "take note" of what was happening about him when anchoring, docking, and carrying out other evolutions. Meanwhile the watch on deck would be employed in some way "profitable to their training", in such tasks as heaving (not swinging) the lead, making knots, bends, hitches, sennit and matting for use about the ship, splicing rope and wire, canvas-work and maintenance of covers and awnings, inspection and lubrication of steering-gear and deck machinery, maintenance of boats and gear, derricks, cargo-handling equipment and wires, and the steel and wood decks, and – the apprentice's eternal and inexhaustible *bete noir* – the scaling of steelwork and the mixing and application of paint.

In port the day usually lasted longer although cargo-work seldom went on through the night: only the gangway and moorings required watching round the clock; the routine was varied as much as possible by semi-recreational pursuits with the boats and by social interchange with the shore and other ships which often included team sports, the general mood of thinking behind it all being to keep youthful energies at maximum stretch with minimum opportunity for introspection (that is, thought) and random experiment.

Very little was left to chance. Between cargo-watching in port and watchkeeping and "various employment" while at sea, the cadets had little time to sit about and grumble, or even occupy themselves constructively. Recreation was fortified and furnished by the ship's recreation fund, to which cadets were expected to contribute. Private gramophones weren't prohibited but chiefly owing to limited space were discouraged. The CPO kept the fund's accounts, doing "all in his power towards maintaining all articles in as efficient a condition as possible".

If gramophones were frowned on, other means of making a noise could be devised or found, and among the rec fund's articles in at least one ship were musical instruments:

A liner with 34 cadets arrived...on Sunday morning. Notified from Sydney of her coming, the chaplain was early on board. As a result twenty cadets and the chief officer came to the evening service. Next day there was a football match and in the evening a special social at which the ship's jazz band played. (Adelaide, 1930.)[1]

As for the academic work, someone had been giving ambition some realistic treatment, and the curriculum stuck to its correctly-defined objective, the comparatively elementary one of the 2nd mate's exam. Among the few standard works the cadet needed were

Newton's or *Nicholls's Guide*
Fletcher's *Modern Steam Seamanship*
Nicholls's Seamanship
Saul's *Figure Drawing*
Norie's Nautical Tables

Towards the end of each voyage examinations were held in navigation, seamanship and English composition, and reports sent to the company's head office on the cadets' conduct and general ability together with exam marks and overall performance in everyday seamanship, navigation and signalling.

Both on board and ashore dress was a matter of close attention, offering opportunity for privilege according to seniority. Cadets with less than three years behind them had to wear uniform ashore while the more seasoned could please themselves within defined limits which stopped short of extreme fashion: Oxford bags could usually be guaranteed to bring the duty officer to the boil, but on the whole cadets weren't

---

[1] *At the Sign of the Flying Angel*, p.188.

particularly dress-conscious beyond the emotions aroused one way or another by the niceties of uniform.

I went ashore to see a new Charlie Chaplin film. The cinema was stuffy, made worse by having to wear uniform, and in the darkness I removed my boots to relieve my swollen feet. Placing them under my seat I sat back and enjoyed the film, but when the lights went up I discovered my boots – gone. My return to the ship was an embarrassed detour through the side-streets, resplendent in uniform minus footwear. (*Waipara*, 1919.)[1]

Which could have made the difference between life and death:

The Domain in Sydney was a dangerous place, and on one occasion I was chased by a razor gang, owing my escape to youth and fitness. (*Waipara*, 1919.)[2]

After a year you were a pretty good sailor. On deck we did everything – quartermaster, Chippy's mate, bosun's mate, winchman. The winchman had to look after the winches – scraping, chipping, painting them; they were in a hell of a condition [when we joined]. Then we had to know how to work them. Lamp-trimmer was another job – you had to get the clusters ready for night cargo-work and so on. On watch we steered, hour on, hour off; and scrubbed the deck, cleaned the brass, polished the windows. We were employed *all* the time. On standby during the day I'd be told off to check the lifeboat gear and things like that. No sitting about. The day began at 6am, wash down and scrub through using half coconut-husks and sand[3]. PT for an hour at 8, shorts and vests in all weathers, even 45°S in winter. Some put on the gloves for a bit of sparring. A favourite stunt was the order *Ten feet off the deck – GET!* and there'd be a mad scramble for derricks and rigging, with a wallop for the last one away. Then it was dress for school or deckwork before breakfast and turn-to again at 10 til 1 o'clock. Lunch til 2 then back to it til 5. Dinner at 6 – we had to wash and change for that. Then we were free til bed-time, but in the night we'd be turned out for lookout. The worst spell was the last one, 5 til 6, so you stood down to join the work of the day. It was pretty hectic. In port we had to handle all the hatches, all the plugs[4], 90 in each hold. Everything was done by us. We had to learn...

We always had a wonderful time in Brisbane. The English-Speaking Union[5] organised hockey matches and cricket matches and so on, and we turned out respectable teams. Usually played against the Brisbane ladies. Carly Hanson was their skipper; she was pretty good. We put up two teams, then the thirds, then the junglies. And we had pulling races on the river over a 1-mile course, port v. starboard; then there'd be a dance in the evening at the Brisbane Yacht Club, usually a fancy-dress do. Brisbane was my favourite port...

---

[1] *Voyages & Fragments*, pp.17-18.

[2] ibid., p.21.

[3] A practice in Indian-crewed ships, taking the place of holy-stone. BI's general service crews were lascars.

[4] Insulated hatch-covers.

[5] Founded in 1920 to foster friendship & understanding between the peoples of the USA and the British Commonwealth. Local groups in prominent towns & cities. HQ in New York City.

A day out of Fremantle we found a stowaway. The *Nardana* was coming the other way and the captains agreed to transfer him. The SW monsoon was blowing. I was in the boat with the 2nd officer in charge and we got away nicely rowing downwind to get in the *Nardana*'s lee. When we got there the 2nd officer told me to follow the stowaway up the ladder, and when I got to the deck I met some old pals – "How're you doing, how're you doing?" We yapped and chattered until suddenly a voice shouted from the bridge, "Not a bloody social occasion – get off!!" So I scrambled down again PDQ. We rowed back under our ship's lee and got hold of the guest-warp. She was going about 3 knots, and we dropped back, dropped back, then hooked on, both together, fore and aft, and up we went. That was the training. In another ship the fellow would have been landed in Colombo and left there. But not with us – no fear!

I was PO of the deck, port watch, and the job was to unship the jumbo derrick. It was one of those built-up jobs, all angle-iron, a 30-tonner. We had to lift it, lay it on deck, scale, chip and paint it, put it back. At sea, with the ship rolling...

We were coming down from Manchester, all the masts down. Harris was the CPO, and had everything geared up, four men to a mast – winchman, two on the trees, one at the fid. Well, we passed under this bridge and Harris blew his whistle and up went all four masts together. Superb timing. Then came this yell from the bridge – *Lower away!* Just ahead were these power lines crossing over. Lift, fid out, lower away – just in time! Then up again, all together, all at the same time. Pretty good! We could do it...

Getting the holds ready for cargo the Old Man wouldn't employ shore carpenters, so we were doing the battening-out. This second-tripper, Bunting, came trundling into No.3 shelter-deck – the bridge-deck space. Came in from the foredeck, from the bright sunshine. We were all working in there, boarding up the trimming hatches, putting up stanchions and boarding them and pasting paper over them because there was wool in there, and Bunting came in and tripped over the cluster wires trailing about all over the deck and went right down into the lower hold. We were in the river, going up to Bowen, and the Old Man kept going. We had a doctor; he said we couldn't shift Bunting, somebody had to stay down with him to work the catheter. Well, at Bowen they got him ashore and we heard later that he'd died. Poisoned, actually, because nothing worked. He was all smashed up. He was a preacher's son...

Boat drill every week, even down south in those terrific swells. All boats had to be swung out. Radial davits. We could get a boat ready to go away in 17 seconds. Let go gripes, down chocks, swing out, the ship rolling all the time...

Always washing paintwork. When we were down between Cape Town and Fremantle, that's when the deckheads had to be done, and it was always cold down there. What we did was cut up inner tubes, then in each piece cut a small hole. Force your wrist through it and you've got a drip-tray. (*Nerbudda/Devon*, 1934-7.)[1]

Whether the rec fund paid for it or not (possibly the company contributed part or all of the cost), the cadets, with the instructors' assistance, produced a ship's magazine, first in the *Nerbudda* and then, when she was replaced, in the *Devon*. It was an impressive production, properly printed and bound by firms in England and Australia, a harvest of the literary talent over a voyage, including articles, stories, anecdotes, poetry, sports and games reports, details of social events, and illustrations:

---

[1] Contributors' private papers.

This, our first number, is a trial run. The response has been gratifying, for with one exception every article has been written by Nerbudda *people, although to most of us writing is "no end of a fag" and all our contributors have their regular duties, with little spare time...*

Our magazine calls for your literary and artistic efforts. Sailors are proverbially versatile; there are few things we can't make some sort of shape at, so to our accomplishments of navigating, painting, sail-making (and shall I include chipping?) etc let us add writing...
(Nerbudda Cadets' Magazine, *No.1, June, 1934.*)

Or even combine them:

GENERAL DECKWORK

They sent me to sea in a rusty old ship
They gave me a hammer and told me to chip.
We were hammering rust for the rest of the trip.
Sub admi chippin kia[1].

Day in and day out we were hammering rust,
Because the chief officer said that we must.
We chipped til we thought that the darned ship would bust.
Sub admi chippin kia.

We hammered at scuppers and bulkheads and decks,
At ladders and rails and derrick goose-necks,
We hammered until we got cricks in our necks.
Sub admi chippin kia.

We got into Liverpool. Supers galore
Came out in a tug. We got shifted o'er
To the Devon, *where we had to chip a lot more!*
Sub admi chippin kia.

Nerbudda *was rusty, the* Devon *was worse,*
The state of her bulkheads would make a saint curse,
And the Chief Engineer had his boilers to nurse.
Sub admi chippin kia.

We went round the coast in a blaze of red lead,
We dreamed about chipping when we were in bed.
And when Aussie was left we were all nearly dead.
Sub admi chippin kia.

We've got past Colombo, we're nearing Port Said,

---
[1] All hands are chipping – Hindi.

306

And now we are chipping the bridge's fore side.
But cadets will be chipping long after we've died.
Sub admi chippin kia.
(*ss Devon Cadets' Magazine*, No. 3. April, 1935.)

Apart from providing the literary bent with an outlet, ships' magazines were always a force for harmony, depending on the editor's (and his overlords') capacity for malice and satire, presented as palatably as possible in the form of innocuous *reportage*. They also had a beneficial effect on *esprit de corps*, highly valued by the owners in the battle against wastage. And to judge by comment, both *Nerbudda* and *Devon* were happy ships – for those who flourished on a daily portion of gregarious, not to say stifling, association. There was neither space for nor tolerance of the loner, the recluse, the misanthrope, or indeed the individualist: privacy could be snatched only in transient fragments, usually when on duty alone – in a hatch tallying cargo, for instance, amid the dust and clamour of the trade, the stevedores and their occupation existing at a remove, mentally and spiritually, from the cadet looking on; or on lookout on the focsle-head, where, even in daylight, an oddly unlikely solitude prevailed, uncomfortable to some, welcome to others:

We took the route through the Torres Strait. It wasn't often that one enjoyed focsle lookout but in that sublime climate it was an interlude of peace and tranquility. Our quarters were never quiet, but up there noise was absent; you were alone with the stars, and the sea murmuring soothingly at the bow. You could think, away from all the petty interests and worries of life. You could also sleep if you didn't beware and fend it off with a few turns of the focsle. (*Devon*, 1930-4.)[1]

Devon's first voyage as a BI cadet-ship covered some 30,513 miles and 20 ports, and was the scene of

...*tremendous activity: one has only to contrast the ship's appearance now with what it was in October 1934 to realise what pride of craftsmanship the cadets have shown.*
It is with profound regret that we record the death of Captain H.J. Rouse, Assistant Nautical Advisor to the Company, after 36 years of service from 4th officer upwards. He was keenly interested in this magazine, contributing an article to our first number and promising more about the Company's history [2].
We were sorry to leave behind cadets Hanlon and Crow in hospital. Hanlon has since joined the Nardana *and we hope soon to hear that Crow is performing his duties with his well-known cheerfulness and precision.*

---

[1] *Ahoy!*, p.67.
[2] It was, alas, dull stuff, pitched at a level noticeably aloof from the cadets, like much similar material anent other companies: a literal, unimaginative style tinged with admonition. Reading it evoked a sense of duty done in the face of adversity, and the implications of the worthy captain's passing would have been noted by at least some of the cadets with a feeling of release...

To our voyage 1 complement will always remain memories of much hard work and some discomfort but also of great happiness on the Australian coast and good fellowship on board. (Devon Cadets' Magazine No.3, April, 1935.)

...I've had quite a few adventures. The night before we crossed the line we went onto the for'ard of the bridge deck on the port side, as Neptune always arrives on the starboard side. Just as seven bells had gone, the look-out man in the nest rang his bell violently and shouted to the bridge "Two black lights on the starboard bow, Sir" – then soft weird music rising to a great blare from the fore peak. Neptune then shouts to the Bridge, demanding the name of the ship who[sic] dares to enter his domain, and if there are any greenhorns aboard. The Old Man replies with the name of the ship and the number of greenhorns..., at which Neptune replies that he will be aboard to judge them at two o'clock.

The next day at lunch time, we (that is the greenhorns) are allowed to go and hide anywhere above decks but not in cabins. I hid in the forepeak of one of the life boats I might as well tell you only three people have ever been known to get away with the ceremony not having been found.

I was found and rushed down to the afterdeck where I was affronted[sic] by cadets dressed in nearly everything under the sun, press men, natives, and some just daubed all over with grease paint. A hose was turned on me and while I waited my turn to go before King Neptune they made me sing "On Ilkley Moor".

Just before going before them I had my photograph taken by a camera which sent out a spray of black paint all over my face. I was then sent before the King and Queen and made to kiss their feet, which were smeared with strong mustard. Large shackle chains and shackles were hung round my neck, and I was accused and found guilty of being the smallest member of the crew without exception. I was then daubed with red lead. They asked where I hailed from and on replying "Darlington" they said "That's where the steam engines are made – Be a steam engine" so I had to be a steam engine. I was turned over to the Doctor, who took my temperature with a huge wooden thermometer smeared with a paste of hot spices, brasso and general filth. Having a high temperature I was given a pill the size of a fish patty and made to swallow it, washed down with mermaid's milk (Castor Oil). The Bishop anointed me with a can of winch oil and turned me over to the Barber who shaved me with cement and threw me into the bath where I was ducked ten times and the ceremony was at an end.

We do, as you know, a week at school and a week on deck, navigation in the morning and seamanship in the afternoon. Wheel practice twice a week and signalling twice a week. Our classes are under the third officer, a really brainy fellow, but hangish sarcastic. We have to write an official log which goes up to the commodore[1] every week to be marked. Now I'll give you a day out of the life of a rook boy.

3.0am	*Or some unearthly hour, a look-out in the nest for an hour.*
5.30am	*Turn out.*
6.0am	*Turn to – wash down all decks or Senior Cabin fatigue.*
6..0	*Breakfast.*
10.0	*Turn to:- On deck or school as the case may be.*
13.0	*Lunch.*
14.0	*Turn to – As in the morning.*

---

[1] First-voyager's misunderstanding: in BI the master was called the <u>Commander.</u>

16.0	*Tea.*
16.15	*Signals or steering practice on the Bridge.*
17.00	*Pipe down.*
18.00	*Dinner.*
18.30	*Cabin fatigue.*
19.00	*Toast for Senior Hands to be made in the galley by us (If it's late or not good, bang! bang!)*
20.15	*Dead beat but you can't turn in till 21.00 for there might be a Rook Call.*

You'll be glad to know that we have Service every Sunday morning after Divisions, which consists of the lining up of cadets in their No.1's while the old man gives us a word.

Oh! Another thing while I remember, don't expect any more cablegrams – they cost three shillings a time, and seeing that I was feeling pretty homesick I relieved my feelings and pleased you I hope by despatching it.

We've had the concert[1] now, and judging by the laughter of the Old Man and his fellow Officers it was a great success. It isn't settled that we are going to Melbourne yet but it's pretty certain, so you can write your letters to there and you might send Joyce's address, and I'll see if I can make time to see her.

Phoop! Phoop! That's boat stations on the siren – On with the old lifejacket and off to my boat. This is always followed by fire drill. I'm in the smoke helmet party – I rush to the Bridge for my smoke helmet, safety line and axe, shove them on and off to the hold where the fire has broken out.

To-day the Rooks had their Annual Semolina Pudding Derby. Each Rook is supplied with an extra large heaped porridge plate of Semolina pudding and two spoons. On the word Go you have to whack it back. I came second, time 30 seconds – the first only took 29 seconds.

Lots of love to you all

Ray.

PS Three of the new cadets had their fare paid to the ship, Hodges (that's the other one) and I didn't.

(Letter home, *Devon*, February 1937.)[2]

We weren't allowed to drink, and in Newcastle, NSW, the pubs closed at 6pm. I went ashore there with three of my pals to a pub where we knew we could get in through the back door. Whilst we were enjoying our first pint there was a knock at the door and the barmaid ushered us behind the bar and told us to sit on the floor. Then in came the Mate and the Second (whom we couldn't see but recognised them by their voices). They ordered their drinks and stood chatting at the other side of the bar, a situation that couldn't last as the Mate eventually realised that there were some bodies below his line of vision. We were ordered back to the ship and told to await his (the Mate's) return, which was not until about midnight. He then told us to change into working rig and go into No.2 hold and clean the bilges, which he would inspect at 0630. After the inspection we were split into two watches and for the rest of the time on the Australian coast did quartermaster duties on a four-on, four-off basis at sea and in port, with no

---

[1] The Rookies' Concert was the first of several each voyage (See appx. 10).

[2] Contributors' private papers.

shore leave. He was a man of dour nature who never smiled and had no sense of humour, the wrong type to be mate of a cadet-ship. (*Devon*, 1937-39)[1]

In August 1939 *Devon*'s cadets were transferred to the company's *Waroonga*, acquired only in May from the NZS Co., for which, as the *Hororata*, she had already been serving as a cadet-ship. A year older than *Devon*, she had space for 43 cadets, but her career with BI ended on her first voyage as a training-ship when war broke out and her cadets were dispersed round the fleet: presumably the company had learned to respect the U-boat after the experiences of WW1, for *Nardana*'s were similarly disbanded and the cadet-ship scheme suspended for the duration.

We left the *Devon* in Falmouth in August 1939 and joined the *Waroonga*. She was no more comfortable and far more ugly; however, she was an oil-burner which reduced work after bunkering. We left Falmouth in late August and were at sea in mid-Atlantic when war broke out. By the time we reached New York we had painted the ship grey with the exception of the hull: the paint just happened to be on board in 40-gallon drums! After loading in New York we bunkered in Newport News then went through the Panama Canal to Australia. Life on board was a continuation of life on the *Devon*. We loaded a fridge cargo and sailed for home. However, we were diverted to Colombo where everyone was sent to various ships on the coast[2] to serve the rest of our time.[3]

The cadet-ships were kept in service throughout the interregnum, through the trade depression that saw tonnage laid up wholesale for lack of paying freights and officers beached for lack of berths. Those who sought arguments against the system accordingly brought in the evident dearth of prospects facing cadets on completion of their time, accusing the companies concerned of cynical exploitation of youth, for the ships were undoubtedly cheaper to run with enthusiastic, fit crews paid only a fraction of the going rate, factors which played a significant part in the ships' continuing to run at all, though in the late 20s the seamen's unions made history by persuading their members to accept an actual cut in wages, albeit acceptance moved as much by the stark facts of life as by any sense of loyalty to employers, whom the average seaman held in cordial contempt. Moreover, there was a persistent Micawberish belief, or hope, among owners that things would get better one day, when officers would again be needed in numbers, and the apprentice was a visible sign of investment in this ever-retreating blue-chip future.

The system's detractors were, however, being disingenuous. While the owners were certainly able to keep ships running in such unfavourable conditions by dint of low-paid cadet crews (and the strict enforcement of good housekeeping on board), the cadets gained more than mere training in return. The cadet-ships went some way

---

[1] Contributors' private papers.
[2] That is, the Indian coast, the colloquial term for the BI's services east of Suez. There, it was hoped, the cadets would be at a remove from the vortex of war...
[3] Contributors' private papers.

towards allaying the social problems normally arising from youthful idleness, giving sea-minded boys of good character a chance to realise at least something of ambition where the alternative was a mire of aimlessness. For four years at a crucial age the youth was kept fully-occupied – sometimes over-fully – while also being fed and, up to a point, sheltered, in the process learning the subtle social skills of living in harmony with his peers and authority. Ships demanded, and nurtured, consideration for others in their way of life; without it they would founder as viable places of work and social order. None of this could be evaluated in financial terms other than that of continuance of the commercial enterprise.

As a case in point, an *ad hoc* arrangement was made by the Federal S.N. Co when an opportunity offered to run a ship that would otherwise have lain idle. She wasn't a cadet-ship, but for a single voyage that took her round the world on a spot charter she awoke echoes of the *Ellerbank*, manned by a crew of apprentices under a bosun and standard officer complement. There was no question of a training programme; no organised study, no exams, no special arrangements in port for social diversion: the boys were housed in the focsle and employed as deckhands, perhaps the single factor that enabled the company to make a successful tender for the charter without accepting a loss – if that was the outcome. In return the apprentices kept their jobs and sense of purpose while helping to keep a ship in gainful employment, instead of standing idly by while she rotted at the buoys.

When depression set in after the fleeting post-war boom the branch line operated by Federal was, naturally enough, the first of its services to be mothballed. It comprised five ships distinguished by names with the initial P – *Pareora, Pakipaki, Pipiriki, Papanui* and *Puriri*, all lying idle in the Fal in the spring of 1931, each with four apprentices aboard resigned to passing the time with odd maintenance jobs while failing to accumulate sea-time (which, it will be remembered, had to be actually on foreign-going service for 4/5ths of the indentured time). When the charter came up *Pareora* was selected and all apprentices in the P's assigned to her for the voyage.

Most of the time in the Fal we spent in the holds chipping and red-leading, but not many evenings were spent aboard. There were 15 to 20 ships upriver of us and more than 50 downstream. When the ship was prepared for the voyage all 21 apprentices came over. The four seniors were appointed quartermasters, the rest as deck crew under the bosun, housed in the starboard focsle, with 24 Arab firemen, 3 greasers and 2 donkeymen in the port focsle. Food was ferried from the galley by the peggy in metal trays and dixies. Hygeine was kept to a reasonable standard, prompted by a couple of mate's inspections a week, one on Saturday. Washing was done in a tiled area in a bucket and the loo was a 3-seater over constant running water discharging through a non-return flap. It would stick in a heavy sea when the ship was pitching hard and the unfortunate in the middle would get a 15-foot head of water straight up the pipe. With seventeen enthusiastic lads chasing around most jobs were done in double-quick time, balanced by episodes like the one in New York: burlap was stowed in the lower forepeak by six hands with the usual verve, leaving time for a quiet smoke-o. About 3 the following morning smoke was seen pouring from the forepeak ventilator. The NYFD arrived with three engines and filled the space with water, so the six enthusiasts spent the next two days pumping it out with the hand-pump...

We loaded sulphur at Galveston and discharged it at Geraldton, a one-horse town in Western Australia with unmade streets, a roller-skating rink and not much else. Some residents may recall at least fifteen tiddly cadets whooping it up one night.

From there we went to Bunbury to load logs for the new Ocean Terminal at Southampton, with some wool and cane sugar, then at Rabaul a few thousand tons of copra, which produced an invasion of copra bugs. They disappeared as if by command as we crossed the equator.

We discharged at Marseilles, Antwerp, Hull and Southampton, then returned to lie up at Falmouth, off the old Admiralty pier at Mylor because the river was full up. There we spent months, chipping, but eventually I was transferred with two seniors to the *Somerset*.[1]

The voyage occupied the ship for some six months. The P liners – tramps in practice – were regarded in a rather disparaging light by the body of the Federal/NZS organisation, NZS with its long tradition of training apprentices in both sail and steam. At the end of WW1 the tradition was further developed by the introduction of cadet-ships, all converted from general service for varying periods until the launch of the purpose-built *Durham* in 1934, with accommodation for 40 cadets.

To begin with the ships were *Orari* (7,207gt), *Whakatane* (5,902gt), *Essex* (7,016gt) and *Somerset* (9,589gt). *Devon* was brought into service in 1925, joined at different times by *Northumberland* (12,138gt) and *Westmoreland* (9,496gt) and for a while in 1933 *Cornwall* (11,234gt). After being laid up in the Fal *Hororata* was fitted out to take 20 cadets in 1934 and continued until she followed *Devon* into BI service. *Devon*'s cadets were transferred to *Northumberland*, which passed them on to the *Durham* in 1935, the ship which carried on the tradition alone until 1939, when her cadets were, like the BI's, dispersed round the fleet.

The company carefully selects the commanders, officers and petty officers to be carried on its cadet training ships. A doctor and PT instructor are provided on each ship. The boys do all the practical work in the deck department; they have a regular course of instruction in navigation and written examinations are held during each voyage. The company sets a good standard of physique for its new entrants, [and] entry is generally between the ages of 16 and 17 except for Conway, Worcester *or* Pangbourne *boys, who should be between 17 and 18* [2].

We had two lighter type of lifeboats, always swung out when the ship was at sea ready for emergencies. Five boys were appointed as accident crew and on the sounding of six blasts on the ship's whistle they would get to stations at top speed on the lee side ready to drop the boat... Accident boat drill was carried out at least once a week... The Mate had acquired a rather more slim-lined lifeboat for which he made a portable steel keel. We had a special mast, also sails of lighter canvas, and she sailed very well in some of the ports of New Zealand and Australia... Each voyage two cadets were appointed to look after her... The Pilot would be

---

[1] Contributors' private papers.
[2] *Seamen in the Making*, p.171.

asked to slow down so we could drop the boat two or three miles from the berth and sail in. Yes, that was a very pleasant job.

On a long voyage, say from New York to Brisbane, we had to carry extra coal in No.3 hatch and in time it had to be transferred to the bunkers amidships, and naturally the work was carried out by the cadets... A derrick would be rigged and coal shovelled into baskets then winched to the upper deck and barrowed along to the bunker hatch – not a great distance, but labour-intensive.

Navigation instruction was rather hit and miss because we didn't have additional officers for the work, and it was up to the 2nd mate or 1st mate to give up some of their off-duty time, which was fairly well occupied. (*Devon*, 1925-9.)[1]

At which date she was commanded by G.D. Kinnell, a popular man, nicely balanced by E.A. J. Williams, the mate –

...sail-trained and had a windjammer philosophy: a change of work was as good as a rest. He had two notable sayings; one was "Williams but not Welsh", the other "When I give you an order I don't want you to walk, or run, but bloody-well *fly!*" He was strict, just, and a splendid seaman – he wanted every pound of flesh, feared a little but respected by all. There were no smoke-os (unless a rare official one), no morning tea, no supper... Last meal of the day was 5pm. He handled his cadet crew through the bosun and the PTI, a former Indian Army NCO... The day commenced at 5.30am. Bunks were made, white singlets, shorts and sandshoes put on. Then coffee in the messroom aft, followed by concentrated PT which not only involved press-ups and so on but often a run round the ship. In port this might also embrace a gallop ashore. (1929-32.)[2]

They trimmed coal, dumped ashes, and the juniors got all the menial tasks. Study time amounted to five mornings of navigation instruction on each passage, with seniors spending a week on the bridge as junior OOW. The round voyage lasted on average 5 months or so, the routes passing through both Suez and Panama canals, rounding the Cape and the Horn, running between Europe and the Antipodes with occasional diversions to New York and Halifax.

We were a very contented crew. Commanded by a fine seaman and adviser in Captain Clarke, officered by mates who had been through the mill themselves and were ever ready to help those anxious to learn, well-berthed and fed. Captain Clarke was always good about arranging dances and socials for us...

At the mouth of a muddy river stood a single jetty. The goods shed, a café and post-office stood nearby, three sun-bleached houses on the river bank, and a single-track railway to Rockhampton, fifty miles upstream. The only attraction was two girls, but since there were thirty-six cadets and one of the girls had the misfortune to be cross-eyed, conditions rather cramped our style. Nevertheless, when we sailed both girls waved their handkerchiefs until we were out of sight. (Port Alma.)

---

[1] Contributors' private papers.

[2] Contributors' private papers.

Ragging wasn't always done for amusement, but the best rags weren't concerned with discipline. Some might have accused seniors of bullying, but as long as tempers were kept ragging did a lot for harmony. It was no good being annoyed; a good-tempered scrapper escaped lightly. One of the amusements was "football". Ten or twelve juniors were captured and stripped, then painted to represent opposing teams, one with yellow bodies and blue legs, the other the reverse. The rules were simple. A line was drawn on the deck and on the word the teams charged each other and endeavoured to push their opponents over the "goal" line, the incentive to win generated by the simple expedient of rope-ending the losers...

The ceremony of crossing the line was crude, and it didn't matter if you'd already been initiated. I'd done so four times, but it didn't signify. Neptune's messenger came aboard, insisted on being called "Sir" and knocked us about a bit before handing us a Marconigram commanding our presence next day, and a notice was posted in the messroom listing those who were to be towed astern. A rope was placed aft for the purpose and the notice warned each candidate that he'd have to tie his own bowline, for the Court would not be held responsible for lost cadets. First-trippers of the more gullible type immediately started practising tying bowlines, and on the day one poor fellow actually tied the rope round himself and got outside the rail in his abject fright and anxiety. When the Doctor and his assistants got to work they pumped medicine into the victim with a syringe of the garden pest variety – a tincture of black draught, vinegar, rotten eggs and dishwater (used), followed by a pill of soft soap, mustard and solidified oil. The dose was repeated a few times then the patient's remains passed to the Barber and his mate, when a lather of soft soap, black paint, winch grease and glue with a dozen or twenty duckings to follow calmed the most excitable. When it was all over we cleaned ourselves up and had high tea, if we felt up to it...

At Liverpool the *Nardana* was astern of us and we knew that if we didn't do something the BI cadets would. Someone had an inspiration, such a risky business that all hands stood by for emergencies. During *Nardana*'s lunch-hour our man, in working gear, boarded her among the stevedores, coolly ambled forward, hauled down her jack, stuffed it into his shirt and strolled back. Two days passed, then *Nardana* sailed. That was our moment of triumph, and as she got under way we ran up her jack under our house-flag to an accompaniment of cheering. In response, across the widening gulf between the ships, came a howl of rage and threats, but "Hetty" Moira kept his trophy...

Jack Clevely was our best all-rounder, and at Gladstone, where we held our sports day, he excelled. Back at work, when a cargo runner got loose and ran to the derrick-head, he went up after it. Then, half-way down, without any sign, he fell to the deck, fracturing his skull. All who saw it happen were completely nonplussed. Captain Clarke had him rushed to hospital, but he died five hours later. Practically the whole ship's company went to his funeral, the honour of bearing our comrade to his last resting-place falling to us seniors while the rest formed a guard of honour. After the committal all hands filed past the grave, turned and saluted, and passed on. So we left him, beneath the red ensign, and we were all glad when that voyage ended.

Then the parting came. *Devon*'s career as a cadet-ship was over[1] and our happy family was to be drafted elsewhere. A dozen went to the *Northumberland* and the rest to ships on the coast. (*Devon*, 1930-34.)[2]

---

[1] Under the NZS Co's flag, that is.

[2] Reconstructed from *Ahoy!*, pp.36-92.

A regime of comparatively strict discipline graded from the captain down through the seniority structure among the cadets themselves kept the lid on what would otherwise have been a formidable excess of high spirits likely to pave the way to serious mischief; combined with a constant supply of hard work and well-stocked leisure time it served the purpose, but tokens of what lay beneath the surface occurred from time to time, particularly when a legitimate excuse offered. *Northumberland*'s chief officer at one stage was the famous – and formidable, to the wayward spirits and square pegs who set themselves against the system – P.B. Clarke, the fine seaman and adviser later in command of *Devon*. He exercised his authority through the chief cadet captain.

At noon the green hands were rounded up and locked in the oilskin locker where a hose was turned on them to cool them down. There was the usual procession, the court assembled and the initiates arraigned before it to be given the usual treatment. The officers were also lathered and ducked, including the captain. He was a chain smoker, so while in the water his cigarettes were thrown in after him.

At Avonmouth we loaded tobacco and noted its location, and I made particular note of some Quality Street toffee. We had learned which items were most worthwhile, for both our own pleasure and for barter…

The mate saw me and Jarvis going to the bridge wearing singlets and gave us extra work holystoning the deck. But what did it matter, we thought, out in the middle of the Atlantic?

We had a boat race at Napier, and we won. The prize was a bottle of lemonade each, and collecting mine from the steward I lifted a tin of Cadbury's cocoa, for the third time. Pinching from the chief steward was a legitimate{*sic*] activity and a good joke. Cargo was also fair game…

At Glasgow I made a mental note of the ports' names marked on the cargo being loaded, while others took more of an interest in the stowage of whisky and tobacco[1]…

We shifted berth on Christmas Eve and afterwards there was a rag, when my cabin mate had far too much to drink and was dumped in the bathroom where he was doused with water and Lux as he lay on the deck. After a while he got to his feet and, covered in his own filth and Lux suds, fell into my bunk, so I spent the night in another cabin. Meanwhile two of the seniors were fighting in the mess, so when Christmas Day dawned I went on gangway duty feeling depressed and homesick…

We didn't think any company could be as bad as ours for apprentices. Even in the less glamorous[*sic*] tramp lines[*sic*] they usually got fairly good rations and were paid a little, in some companies were trained as officers, had good accommodation with a steward, lived in the saloon [*sic*] and were paid. So when we were in port with a BI, P&O, Commonwealth & Dominion[2] or Clan ship we made sure of invitations to dine. In Clan liners the black crews and white officers worked well together and the cadets had servants and everywhere was spotless.

---

[1] Which led, shortly afterwards, to several being brought before the magistrates.

[2] Later the Port Line.

If I had chosen a different company things would have worked out differently for me. (NZS, 1927-9.)[1]

Possibly, but the predilection for complaint and the resentful mood of these observations would have worked against it, as would the reality of life in the other companies' ships, each making its demands on the apprentice's strength of character in its own distinctive way. And the old question arises again: what makes an officer, after all? In the average merchant ship the least part consisted of what was implied here, decorating the scene in blue (or white) and gold – which, incidentally, seems to have taken second place to singlets in this particular cadet's inventory of criteria, though to give him the benefit of the doubt there was certainly a deficiency of tutoring in an officer's theoretical knowledge and an excessive emphasis on "practical seamanship", interpreted by the P.B. Clarkes of the system as semi-skilled toil coming under the general heading of "maintenance" – of which ships like *Northumberland* were in constant and voracious need. However...

[It was] a great relief to be away from the ship. I wrote in my log *Fed up with it all* after a sprained ankle and clashes with Nobby...
Father and I had to report to the London office, where it was decided it would be to everyone's advantage if I were sent to another ship, the *Otaki*. (*Northumberland*, 1927)[2]

I missed news of the other *Northumberland* chaps, but received a letter from Jack shrouded in secrecy. He and Philip Tutt finally decided they'd had enough and jumped ship somewhere in South Island. They were wanted men and had to be extremely careful, a terrible position to be in, for them and their parents. As for myself, I too had had enough and was determined to quit the sea. (*Otaki*, 1929)[3]

Square pegs were in the minority, if a substantial one, and it was better that they were weeded out early on, which was, after all, part of the training's purpose; but it wasn't all despondency and resentment, and the other side of the argument held the high ground:

And so farewell to my cadet days. To my officers I say "Thank you", not only for continual help but also for those most encouraging words, "Good luck. We are sorry you are leaving us." (*Northumberland*, 1934)[4]

Which is as much as any training system could hope – or wish – for, a fitting valedictory for the cadet-ship organisation as a whole when it was dissolved in 1939. Of the two archetypes of the fleet, *Devon* and *Durham*, only the latter survived the

---

[1] Reconstructed from *Green Seas, Green Fields*, pp.38-61.
[2] Reconstructed. ibid. pp.55-64.
[3] Reconstructed. ibid.
[4] *Ahoy!*, p.110.

war, to become the link between the old world and the new, resuming her duties in 1946 amid echoes of times past, summed up by another ex-*Northumberland*:

She was only two years old when I joined her as 4th officer, a beautiful cargo vessel of 10,893gt[1] making about 16½ knots with her two Sulzer diesels. My duties included taking a hand in the cadets' affairs. Captain Upton was a fitness buff, so it was my task, with the PTI and the school officer, to see it acted upon.

Life on board was, by comparison with what had gone before, comfortable and encouraging. Cadets' accommodation, below decks aft, was a great advance[2] and their welfare a major concern. School – about 3½ hrs daily – was compulsory at sea, run by the supernumerary 2nd officer, who held an extra master's ticket: four years of it fitted any normally industrious cadet for the 2nd mate's exam without the need to attend a nautical school. No cadet was granted shore leave in Australia or New Zealand unless he knew by heart four of the Articles[3]. The old tradition of ragging had died, and the most timorous lad could face Neptune's court without a qualm; no mother need have lost sleep on account of her darling away at sea. (1936)[4]

A somewhat equivocal conclusion.

Within the pale of the P&O caravanserai the NZS/Federal alliance lost no time in reviving the training regime thrown out of gear by the war, and while *Durham* soldiered on, as it were, others of her kind put in an appearance to pick up threads vital to the intake of new blood in the reviving fleet. In fact she retained her role as something of a grand old lady, the doyenne of cadet-ships, until honourable discharge and sale to a foreign buyer in 1965. Having already distinguished herself in wartime she maintained the tradition of sound seamanship exemplified by an incident in 1962, when she went to the assistance of a Norwegian ship in which an engine-room explosion had severely injured some crew members. In a bulletin the US Coastguard remarked

Despite the tragic outcome for two patients this rescue was an admirable coordinated action...We are very much impressed with the seamanship shown by the Durham *connected with her very efficient boatwork. Indeed, the highest praise is due to Captain Hollingdale and the men(sic) on his ship for outstanding efficiency and human spirit under pressing conditions.*[5]

She was remembered by her cadets for, among other things, the motto, open to interpretation, *The ship is mightier than the crew*, a point of possible debate with a school of thought favouring the proposition that the ship is only as strong as her men...

---

[1] 13,053gt quoted by Lloyd's Register, 1940-41.

[2] Advance it might have been, but all the same lacking in more than one respect, being placed directly above the twin 3-bladed propellers and prone to ingress of seas in heavy weather.

[3] Regulations for preventing collisions at sea.

[4] Reconstructed from *Ahoy!*, pp.206-210.

[5] US Coastguard *Bulletin*, Feb. 1962.

Launched in 1944 as *Empire Abercorn* for the MOWT, *Rakaia* entered service with NZS in 1946, converted in 1950 to carry some 39 cadets:

The doctor was a widower in his late 50s, reputed to be the result of a union between an Englishwoman and a Portuguese/Egyptian. He could speak Arabic, French and Spanish as well as his accented English. On the only occasion on which I had to consult him, over tonsilitis, he put me in the sick-bay for a couple of days to be sure of his diagnosis, dismissing friends who came [bringing] cans of beer. "No beer," he declared, but to celebrate the new year produced brandy instead, well diluted with water from the carafe. As it happened my friends had filled it with gin, and the cocktail's potency mystified Doc. (1952)[1]

When we reached deep water I was among the last to succumb, finally defeated when someone ditched his breakfast in the alleyway I was scrubbing – morsels of dried apricot in the grey waters of my bucket. Domestic routine was a novelty. Breakfast was a social ritual with the first-trippers forming the pantry staff – two washers-up overseen by a second-tripper on toast duty. The food was actually served by a pantryman but distributed by first-trippers: trays of fried eggs, twenty-eight in one solid slab with one separate for the senior apprentice. Afterwards we (first-trippers) sat down to share breakfast with Mr Bartholomew, the chief steward, and his saga of sexual adventure in the Orient Line. Then it was chores under the eye of the PTI, ready for the mate's daily inspection: Pete, an ex-RAF instructor, was Trinidadian, with a barrel chest, bandy legs and a depressingly sunny nature. Brass was cleaned with colza oil and bath-brick (Brasso was for wimpish stewards, rumoured to buy their own Duraglit) while bogs and other ceramic surfaces were attacked with what Pete called "Thoft thoap and thand"...

My first voyage coincided with the first appearance of table-linen, a controversial move because although it was only crew-mess green gingham *sans* napkins it meant we had to change for meals. The compromise was battle-dress, but it was still a mad rush to change between knock-off and the start of the meal. We could sometimes eat lunch on deck in working rig, but only if the job had been particularly dirty. Attempts to grab food on the hoof at the galley door were rigorously discouraged...

We learned to live together, combining tolerance with neatness and tidiness; peer pressure ensured that we cleaned out teeth regularly and changed socks and underwear daily. Dai had a habit of leaving the drawers under his bunk open, until a senior came marching in and trampled straight over the exposed white shirts in his tackity boots...

Getting ashore meant submitting to the whim of junior officers' or senior cadets' "inspection" and reciting the first sixteen Articles. First-trippers had to wear uniform along with those not yet possessed of an EDH ticket, though escape could be made by Jacob's ladder into the painting punt. We had to be back on board by midnight, the rest whenever they felt like it so long as they were on hand for the 0600 run that took the place of PT while in port...

On the NZ coast shipboard slang for the kind people who appeared with generous offers of hospitality was "bums", but we were the bums: there was little or no opportunity to repay the favours we received except by holding a ship's dance, the highlight of the voyage, when the boat-deck was fitted up in a passable representation of a society marquee. Carefully-vetted young ladies attended with a heavy escort of chaperones: mates and engineers headed for the

---

[1] Contributors' private papers.

escorts, seasoned cadets for the girls, and we first-trippers for the booze. I passed out quite peacefully to be regaled next day with the seniors' post-mortems, which decided me to give the bar a miss next time...

We crossed the date-line on Christmas Day and should have had another as our "Antipodes Day", but the mate, a fellow Scouser, called it our Boxing Day and turned us to on the 26th, to his undying disgrace...

Westerly gales accompanied us across the Atlantic while we enjoyed an easy regime of interior cleaning and painting, with extra school time. Radio Luxembourg came through with increasing strength and we new hands began to experience the unfamiliar symptoms of the channels. The last ritual was to receive a digest of our voyage reports from the mate, which were sent to our parents. Mine caused great frostiness at home, my father anticipating some part of his £50 surety being withheld. However, it was home for three weeks, a seasoned and knowledgeable seaman. (*Rakaia*, 1958)[1]

Never entirely at ease in the role, *Rakaia* was relieved of her training service in 1967 and sold for breaking in 1971, but by the time her cadets took their leave of her another ship had taken up the standard in the full panoply of purpose-design, the splendid *Otaio*. She was arguably the epitome of the genre, marking the apogee of cadet-training in the traditional manner, on the brink, as is the way of things, of abrupt extinction.

There was a builder's model of her in a glass case in the seamanship room, and we contemplated it with mixed feelings. "That's what you'll end up on if you join *that* outfit," said the pundits. "Bullshit to the Nth degree." (*Conway*, 1960)[2]

Everything went into her: generations of experience, the requirements of the day, a shrewd forecast of things to come, though not as shrewd as it might have been. Not that blame can be attached to thinking as progressive as any in the industry, none of it having reason to suspect the approach of cataclysmic change which, owing more to passing fashion and populist politics than to sound practice, rendered the methods of *Otaio* and her contemporaries as redundant as the Ark's before she was half-way through what would otherwise have been her useful life.

Delivered by John Brown of Clydebank in 1958, she measured 13,308gt, carried her cargo, including reefer, in six hatches, and accommodated 70 cadets in 3-berth cabins on the upper deck amidships; 30 were engineer cadets on the ATS. The spacious mess-room enjoyed direct access to the galley, with an ante-room adjoining, and sited at the after end of the accommodation was a writing-room with its SES library. Classrooms, science lab and machine-shop comprised the formal instruction space while recreation was catered for in a variety of directions including a swimming-pool of the collapsible type, deck space for the usual games, and two whalers with an assortment of dinghies. The teaching staff comprised two officers, two petty officers

---

[1] Contributors' private papers.
[2] ibid.

and a PTI, and the otherwise normal complement included a nominal crew of 6 deckhands and 10 engine-room ratings. Following standard practice and statutory ruling a doctor was also on the strength.

She took boys straight from school as well as from pre-sea courses, and time in training earned 6 months' remission on 3½- & 4-year indentures in the deck department; engineer cadets signed 4½-year indentures, and instead of spending Phase 1 in college passed it in the ship. Everybody profited (not always willingly) by the resulting improvement in understanding between the two traditionally reluctant professional departmental associates, and she was reputedly a happy ship, confirmed by a wake strewn with social events and admiring acquaintance. Her perverse capacity for disagreement with her element was, by comparison, an aspect of life acknowledged but discounted in the balance: she rolled at the slightest provocation, but there were plenty of poor sea-boats about possessed of none of *Otaio*'s indisputable advantages.

I spent most of my apprenticeship on the *Otaio*, altogether four voyages over a couple of years starting at the end of February, 1964. As was the usual procedure with NZS the last voyage before 2nd mate's was on another vessel, in my case the *Cornwall*, a voyage of 8 months 28 days[1]

– which meant a pro-rata reduction of sea-time remission.

After P&O changed its policy towards its partners-in-trade during the 1960s, embarking on a campaign of absorption and elimination which finally erased the distinctions between the constituent companies of the group, *Otaio* passed from the NZS/Federal operation to P&O's general cargo division in 1971, into P&O ownership in 1973, and in 1976 was sold to foreign interests as a training-ship, renamed *Eastern Academy*. After a subsequent period in other ownership she sailed into the glare of the breaker's torch in 1982, taking with her much of the optimism that had seen her down the ways 24 years before. Her decline and end were something of a metaphor for British-flag seafaring.

Having looked on with interest as the various cadet-ship schemes crossed the stage between the wars, and resisted Lawrence Holt's attempts to persuade it into sail, the board of directors of Blue Funnel took the plunge after the war with *Calchas*, delivered by Harland & Wolff, Belfast, in 1946 to enter service the following year as the company's first cadet-ship.

Not only is Calchas *a new ship, but she [also] inaugurates a new experiment in training. Unlike other seagoing training-ships her deck crew, except for the bosun and carpenter, consists entirely of midshipmen. There are 18 in the forecastle – no more than the normal deck complement. One holds the rank[sic] of Leading Seaman and he with ten others have obtained*

---

[1] Contributors' private papers.

their EDH certificate[sic]: the other seven have not yet had time to qualify and take the place of Ordinary Seamen and Deck Boys. In addition, as in other ships of the fleet, four midshipmen, supernumerary to the crew, occupy the midshipmen's quarters. The accommodation is exactly the same as the crew's quarters in all our new ships.

The whole of the deck crew's work is done by the midshipmen, but a rota is worked by which each boy in turn gets some bridge watchkeeping experience and in turn messes in the saloon with the officers. Their theoretical work is as usual controlled by the Midshipmen's Department.

The experiment is designed to make our future officers into first-class craftsmen[sic] and sailors[sic] – the technique of "learning by doing". It is hoped to give every midshipman at least one voyage in Calchas *during apprenticeship, most of them two – one as Deck Boy or OS and one later as EDH or Leading Seaman.* (Blue Funnel & Glen Lines Bulletin, 1947.)

However this struck the reader on paper, one thing became clear as time passed: training boys as deckhands produced, logically enough, deckhands. The *Calchas* experiment, to use the company's term for it, proved to be an ironic reflection on the system as it had evolved since the inception of compulsory examination and certification, a system that had rested almost entirely on the apprentice's self-motivation and aspirations, aided only minimally or not at all by "training" which consistently failed, or refused, to acknowledge the apprentice's accepted status as a trainee officer while nevertheless expecting him to become one in due course. Moreover, the term *midshipman* was, as already noted by one of its bearers, a nice conceit on the part of Blue Funnel, whose indenture was quite clear about his identity as an apprentice *seaman*, i.e. deckhand. The outcome of the *Calchas* style of training exposed the duplicity of the system, and the resulting embarrassment was, to onlookers, amusing as well as instructive: a substantial proportion of *Calchas* trainees departed for the focsles of other ships and other trades, never to enter the dusty confines of the BOT's exam rooms. Consequently, the "technique of learning by doing" (but doing *what* was the rub...) lasted no longer than two apprenticeships before drastic amendment. It came about through the efforts of Richard Hutson who, taking the venerable Brian Heathcote's place on his retirement in 1953, viewed the "experiment" not with amusement but through a glass darkly, and took steps to improve matters by getting rid of the focsle-orientated principle. Not surprisingly, he met with resistance from management, a stance rooted in the financial advantages of running a ship with a cheap, first-class crew, but as it happened it was this very point that gave Hutson the lever he needed. He discovered yet another embarrassment in an irregularity, albeit an uncharacteristic one, in the ship's administration that possessed every potential for serious unrest among the company's regular crews, and brought it to bear with signal effect.

A fund had been set up by agreement between the company and the seamen's union into which would be paid the difference between the respective wage-bills of the crew of midshipmen and the crew of regular hands they had, hypothetically, dispossessed. It was a neat little example of union guile matched only by the company's absentmindedness (to be kind to it), based on a fallacy. No regular seamen had been displaced because the ship had been designed and built for its crew of trainee officers (to concede the point for the sake of argument) and would not otherwise have appeared in that capacity, and further, because of the irony that, while they were expected to become officers in due course the midshipmen were actually apprentice seamen by contract: by definition, therefore, no seamen had been displaced.

But none of this entered the argument, apparently, and besides, British industry was moving into a position of vulnerability to union pressure best covered, to the corporate mind, by a policy of conditional appeasement rather than firm confrontation. The *Calchas* fund, as an example of amicable industrial relations (as the sparring was termed), was intended to assist ratings with the cost of attempting the 2nd mate's exam and to provide benefits of one kind and another for the ship's crew, but in fact it had never existed: nothing had been contributed to it. Unable to explain such an odd state of affairs the managers, somewhat shamefacedly, agreed by way of expiation, as it seems, to commission a new ship designed to accommodate and train potential officers rather than deckhands. They also agreed to make an annual grant of £2,000 towards recreational facilities including a new magazine, *The Half-Deck*, various prizes, and library. In the new ship the boys would do the work of the crew but live and conduct themselves as officers-in-waiting, so to speak.

Calchas's initial route had lain between the USA and the Far East, but was soon changed to join the company's established services linking the Far East and the UK, on which she remained until relinquishing her duties to the newcomer, *Diomed*, which, as events turned out, ushered in the concluding era of the cadet-ship.

Purpose-designed for her role and built by Robb Caledon, she was launched in 1956 to enter service carrying 26 midshipmen as crew and six in the half-deck, but with a training "technique" that paid due regard to the midshipman's ostensible status, housing the mass in suitable accommodation and providing it with classrooms and recreational facilities that lent substance to the revised training policy. Also a new departure, selected office staff, one or two at a time, were signed on as supernumeraries for a voyage of familiarisation seen as a desirable element in the relationship between sea and shore staff, as indeed it was. It was generally hailed as a success, though in later years a few sceptics voiced their doubts as they witnessed the Ocean Group's precipitate abandonment of its shipping interests and dispersal of its sea staff to the four winds.

However, *Diomed* gave satisfactory service until 1970, when she was transferred to the Glen Line as *Glenbeg*, the training ethos having by this date shifted its emphasis from ship to shore under the ONC/D system, and for this reason as well as the operators' changing policy on manning and training, no other ship took her place.

After the collapse of Kylsant's empire Elder Dempster had passed into the hands of Alfred Holt while retaining its old-established trade with West Africa, where it had built up an intricate servicing infra-structure, evidence of its experience and expertise. The war, however, left the fleet sorely depleted and looking towards a future in need of extensive reinvestment, and so, given financial and moral assistance by Holt, ED's resurgence was in full swing by the end of the 40s, at which point attention was given to the supply of officers and the matter of training. In 1950 some 50 midshipmen were on the books, a figure which, in view of pending developments, was inadequate; accordingly, steps were taken to increase it to 120, and in 1951 a midshipmen's department was set up followed in 1953 by modification of *Obuasi* for cadet training. In August that year she set off on her second voyage with a deck crew of 14 midshipmen and four in the half-deck after the example of *Calchas* but with, apparently, rather more fitting results. Launched in 1952 by Harland & Wolff, Belfast, she was a conventional break-bulk cargo liner with accommodation for 12 passengers.

For seven years "Bosun George" guided midshipmen in the ship's routine and passed on to them his knowledge of the art of true seamanship. They had their own cine projector, dinghies to sail, ample time to study, sextants with which to take sights and educational tours when in port. There is no doubt that the nine to twelve months spent in the ship did good morally and physically, instilled seamanlike qualities into future officers, and built an esprit de corps. (*Sea*, ED house magazine, 1962)[1]

She was accompanied from 1959 to 1961 by *Sulima*, training African cadets on a modified pattern, after which the purpose-designed *Fourah Bay* stepped into their shoes.

The foundation of our training is service in the Cadet Ship and attendance at the MAR course and there is no doubt that this arrangement provides an ideal balance between the practical and theoretical training for a career at sea...second to none in the Merchant Navy. Midshipmen will find their progression through apprenticeship indicated in clearly-defined stages. Every endeavour is made to avoid dull repetitive chores voyage after voyage... (*Sea*, 1964)

Appointed to manage the midshipmen's training, Captain John Smallwood, RN, was largely responsible for the selection of *Fourah Bay* for the purpose while still on the drawing-board:

No longer does the long ocean passage provide the best opportunity to learn practical seamanship. It is the preparation for entering harbour and coasting which provide the intensive experience necessary for training embryo officers. Our Cadet Ship is on an admirable schedule for training of this kind – in a two months' voyage the Fourah Bay *visits approximately twenty ports...* (*Sea*, 1964)

Which, whatever it did for training, kept the officers on the go. Fully air-conditioned, the midshipmen's accommodation included a duty mess which – a sure sign of decline in the opinion of some – enabled cadets to take meals in working rig. A

---

[1] Quoted in *Elder Dempster Fleet History*, p.491.

large room was equipped as a study, and leisure time catered for by, among other things, a smoke-room where officers and cadets could mingle informally, and a swimming-pool, while a feature of the usual five-day stay at Lagos was the active interest of a staunch supporter of the ship, HRH Prince William of Gloucester, a member of the British High Commission. The regular schedule permitted better organisation of the ship/shore training programme, including reliefs and appointments, and the ship continued her work until 1973, when expansion of the container service together with changes in the training system dictated a transfer to general service before sale to foreign interests in 1978.

The 1950s and 60s were the heyday of the cadet-ship. For various periods British & Commonwealth used Clans *Menzies*, *Matheson* and *Malcolm* for the purpose, their 12-passenger accommodation made over to the officers, whose quarters were in turn adapted for occupation by the cadets and a training officer. Study was by correspondence with King Edward VII school, conforming to the MNTB syllabus, supplemented by lectures, debates, discussions and organised shore excursions of an educational flavour, including ship-visits, balanced by a programme of social events and pastimes. Likewise the *Kilpurnie Castle* for a while from 1954. Others that made a brief appearance included the Clarkson training-ship *Clarkforth*, launched in 1962 and provided with "special facilities" for a number of apprentices, Denholm's *Wellpark* (1958) and *Ga Chow* (1977), and an ore-carrier under the colours of Scottish Ore Carriers Ltd., the *Crinan*.

She was something of an off-beat choice for a cadet-training ship, limited in her trading pattern and confined in her rather lacklustre special cargo, features which would have lent the proposed career a less than attractive aspect for those not irrevocably committed from the outset. As in tankers, the cadet brought up in this trade continued in not entirely blissful ignorance of better things, while on the other hand such a bleak introduction to the life could lay claim to the perverse virtue of acting as a filter, drawing off those unsuited to the sea in one of its more sombre guises, a clean cut that left them free of regrets.

Small at 14,000dwt, *Crinan* was built for charter to the British Iron & Steel Co., loading at ports in North Russia, the Baltic, the Mediterranean, West Africa and Canada, for discharge at Bristol Channel and some other UK ports, the round voyage lasting a month or so. Her cadets were quartered in 2-berth cabins in the after accommodation, where they were provided with a recreation/school room, mess and pantry, and the usual ablutions. They sailed in batches of up to 14 on a 6-month stint supervised by two or three senior cadets and a cadet-captain answerable to the chief-officer instructor. At the end of the training period a month's home leave preceded dispersal among the other ships of the fleet, while the six best of each batch could look forward to a return for the last 6 months of their time, when, as seniors, they were allowed a beer ration. Delivered in 1960, she served until sale to Norwegians in 1974.

Customs and practice in sea training never departed far from the classic pattern devised by Lord Brassey and D&M, with the exceptions of the Blue Funnel "experiment" and another, more outwardly conspicuous, venture. The Cardiff-based South American Saint Line, after taking on the combined might of Royal Mail, PSNC and Lamport & Holt before the war, survived it with heavy losses to continue progressive policies into the 50s with new tonnage a good twenty years ahead of its time in both appearance and function. The plan was to operate a regular line between Cardiff and the Plate with the new ships while employing older tonnage on tramp charters, but force of circumstance obliged the company to run liner services from near-continental ports and London, embarking passengers at Dover. In spite of setbacks it prospered, chiefly through the drive and ability of its founding partner and director, Dick Street, whose worth became ironically patent at his death in 1961. Deprived of his energy and vision the other directors threw in the sponge and the company ceased trading in 1965, passing its conference rights to Houlder Bros.

Street was one of those owners who placed high value on the sea staff's part in the company's overall strategy, understanding the function of sound training as not only an investment but also an incentive to recruitment and a promoter of company loyalty, the last particularly vital to a comparatively small enterprise. The level of service to customers depended in large measure on the quality and attitude of ships' officers, and a business of the modest proportions of the SASL needed every advantage it could get or contrive in a climate of mounting competition, which included the ever-present hazard of absorption by a larger operation. One such advantage was perceived in a training programme offering something more than shipboard activity, particularly where confined to a single route, and yet another unique experiment was tried taking the shape of a small vessel with big ideas, the ex-minesweeper *St Briavels*. Her duties were purely training while also part of a commercial operation, which qualified her as a cadet-ship in the way *St George* and lesser fry were not.

Bought in 1947 as HMM1009, she had been built in 1943 of oak on elm, measuring some 297grt on a length of 104ft, which provided space enough for 12 cadets as crew under training. The diesel main engine gave her a speed of about 12 knots ahead, augmented by movement in other directions that impressed itself on her company as much as did her chronic leaking and consequent frequent drydockings. Like all her kind, she was en expensive creature to keep.

Rolling, rolling, rolling, always steadily rolling,
Rolling, rolling, rolling, shall we ever stop?
Rolling when at anchor and always when at sea;
Away goes our breakfast, our dinner and our tea.
(SASL House Magazine, c.1947)

They've got the wrong name for her. She should be called the *St Vitus.* (1949)

The conversion replaced her warlike fittings and equipment with cabin accommodation, bathroom, lavatories and stores space, a cadets' lounge and a 16-seat saloon (there were four officers), and an extended bridge/wheelhouse. A 27ft sailing whaler and a 14ft naval sailing dinghy supplemented her 22ft lifeboat.

The training scheme of which she was a part began ideally at *Conway, Worcester*, the NCP or the Southampton School of Navigation, followed by several voyages in the ships before a first training cruise, by which time the cadet was expected to at least know his way round without posing a risk to himself and his shipmates. Then came another spell in the ships and selection for a second cruise (not everyone qualified) before going ashore to sit for 2nd mate. Potential second-cruisers had to demonstrate merit, for, as an introductory appreciation of the little ship put it,

> *It would obviously be a waste of time, effort and expense, and possibly detrimental to other Cadets, if a young officer who has shown himself to be unfitted for the senior ranks was included in the party undergoing the highest form of practical training to fit them for early promotion.*[1]

She was commanded by Captain A.A. Havers, OBE, DSC, RN(Rtd). He had a daunting record: term lieutenant at BRNC, then training officer at *Ganges*, he had commanded a number of ships during the war, been capped at rugby for the navy, and enjoyed a formidable reputation as a physical training and swimming expert. He was assisted (if such an all-rounder could be said to need assistance) by a deck officer from the company's fleet, with two engineers, two ABs, two stewards and a cook. All other responsible posts were filled by cadets – navigator, OOW, helmsman, cable officer (a distinctively naval slot), signalling and maintenance. The cadets were rotated through these duties during the 3-month cruise, usually taken in summer or autumn.

Starting in August from Cardiff, the 1949 cruise was a circumnavigation of Ireland, taking in Cork, Fishguard (to pick up three latecomers, completing a cadet complement of only seven), Dublin, Douglas, Bangor (near Belfast), Campbelltown, Portrush, Sheephaven, Killybegs, Galway, Valencia(*sic*), Bantry Bay, Cobh (Cork), Waterford and Milford Haven, thence to Cardiff.

> *We had grand weather all the time... A big swell on the west coast made us roll like a barrel, but it wasn't too unpleasant, just annoying and uncomfortable. Next year we hope to base ourselves at most of the southern and western Irish ports, using them as a base for water, mails, laundry and provisions, and for trips to neighbouring anchorages and places of interest. St Briavels has had 21 cadets under training this year and has motored just 4,108 miles, which would have been probably 1,000 miles more if we hadn't had to spend so much time in drydock.* (SASL house magazine, 1949)[2]

Her career of mixed fortunes ended with the company's.

---

[1] Article "The Training-ship *St Briavels*" in SASL Newsletter, May 1947.
[2] Article "*St Briavels* Autumn Cruise".

Having lost 51 ships in the war, then come to terms with the implications of Indian independence in 1947, the BISN Co nevertheless embarked on a programme of modernisation and consolidation which included a return to its cadet-ship operation with the building of two C-class vessels specially modified to carry a large complement of cadets – 31 apiece at first. *Chantala* and *Chindwara* took up their duties on the company's home line (UK-Australia) in 1950 as the sun began to set on its near-century of existence.

As the chairman, Sir William Currie, said, the method of cadet-ship training inculcated in the boys an *esprit de corps* and an atmosphere(*sic*) of tradition invaluable in later years. However, *esprit de corps* and tradition in this case turned out to be less valuable to the boys than to the company, which, like the others, shed its identity and seagoing staff with bewildering abruptness in later years, making a mockery of the "company loyalty" on which it had placed such emphasis.

Each ship was fitted out with a cadets' mess, lounge and classroom, where films were shown, and the port side of the upper tween-deck amidships was divided into two dormitories, with a 3-berth cabin for the cadet PO's. Instructor officers and petty officers supplemented the normal officer complement, but the usual lascar deck crew was absent, only the engine-room and catering ratings (respectively Muslim and Goanese by tradition) being present in customary strength. As their indentures stated, the cadets were apprentice seamen as well as officers, and outside school hours, which followed a rota, they worked as deckhands on the pre-war pattern. In 1959 the accommodation was extended by another dormitory with berths for 20, bringing the usual number carried to between 40 and 52. It was a tricky handful for the chief officer, but, firmly grasped in the pincers of the company's somewhat austere disciplinary code, performed with conspicuous efficiency and success, the rigours of labour and duty relieved by a liberal programme of social activities at sea and in port. The majority spent their entire apprenticeship on board, but a few were posted to general service to be replaced by either new entrants or, very occasionally, cadets from the fleet. It was the policy to appoint boys from the leading pre-sea schools to the general service ships and others to the cadet-ships, but there were exceptions according to variations in the proportionate intake.

I went over to the Chindwara *where Gordon met me and showed me round. Although she is a new ship with 38 cadets to look after her I don't think I'd like to sail on her. I met Donald, who has a large picture of Gordon's sister over his bunk in that hideous pink dress with a floppy red rose on it, and Gordon and Donald think it's marvellous!! After several games of Dirty Liz with these two and another cadet called Foxy (father is a P&O captain) I returned to the ship glad to get back to the privacy of a 2-berth cabin.* (Letter home, P&O ss *Bendigo*, 1955)[1]

---

[1] Contributors' private papers.

I joined direct from school, 6th form. She was at Avonmouth, coasting, and on the UK-East Africa run. It was a discouraging experience, and I wondered what I'd got myself into; if I'd had the courage I'd have got myself out again, but like most I just kept going in hopes that things would improve, which they did.

I joined with a few others, in uniform. What you'd find as you went aboard was a bunch of dirty louts in greasy jeans waiting for you, lounging around. You'd wonder who they were, no idea they were the cadets, the seniors, who threw their weight around, mainly amongst the first-trippers, who were fair game. The first thing they did was demand that I hand over my cap, which they kicked around a bit and jumped on before handing back the remains with a commentary on my general appearance. Life from then on was pretty miserable, forever plagued by sadistic harassment and indignities. You'd be turned out in the middle of the night in port when the seniors came back from ashore, well pissed, and ordered you to do something totally impossible, like rustle up some toast or other snack. There was none to be had, since the pantry and stores were securely locked after the last meal of the day, so you'd get a lot of aggravation until they finally tired and turned in.

Then there were the sports nights, and your heart would sink when you heard that there was going to be one. Match-box races were one of the worst events. You had to strip to your ball-bags, and a space was cleared all round the long table that occupied the centre of the dormitory to form the track. Then you had to shove a match-box along the deck with your nose, on your hands and knees, with the onlookers chasing you with lambs'-tails – company towels twisted into hard rope and doubled, then wetted. You'd be walloped on the backside as you crawled along, while others would hit you on the head with pillows so that your face was bashed down on the match-box and you'd split your nose; but you had to keep going, in a bloody froth.

Then there were punkah races. We'd have to scramble along on top of the punkah trunkings, beneath the deckhead, from one end of the dormitory to the other, helped along in the usual way, trying not to fall off, until you'd get to the end absolutely knackered and fall to the deck, about eight feet. Sports nights always began with the contestants being locked in the drying-room for a while to warm up, quite unnecessary in regions like the Red Sea, where the temperature was already something like 120° in the shade.

First-trippers were always told about the Gibraltar pilot, who was to board us for the transit of the straits. It was the alleged custom that he would take mail, and everyone was urged to write letters home in time. You'd see all these first-trippers frantically scribbling their homesick letters for a few days. They'd only twig as they saw the Rock go by without a sign of the pilot. The only thing that enabled you to put up with the worst of the terrors of the first trip was the knowledge that it wouldn't last and that soon others would arrive to take the heat off you, and after that you'd be a senior yourself, free to amuse yourself in the traditional way. You had to be philosophical about it. Of course it was all due to high spirits. There was a lot of excess energy crackling about that didn't all get worked off, or dissipated by recreational activities. Both cadet-ships were in port together once, and there was a virtual riot, battles between the cadets and a lot of damage done to the ships and the gear; afterwards the schedules kept them carefully apart, but other ships were never safe, and the officers were always shitting themselves wondering what we'd do next. Often the gangway would be hoisted to prevent us getting ashore, but that was just a hopeful gesture that didn't do anything of the sort. Of course in some ports there were better ways of entertaining ourselves – Mombasa was a fatal attraction, with the bars and girls, where we weren't interested in fighting with other cadets or painting ships alongside with us. When we did it was usually something pretty conspicuous, a slogan or something like that hidden by the jetty but visible to all as the ship drew away. There was an apocryphal story that an Ellerman liner pulled off the quay at Kilindini with six-foot-high lettering along her boot-topping reading *Ship and travel BI*.

When I joined there were 39 cadets in two watches, port and starboard. The cadet CPO and the two watch cadet POs lived in a 3-berth cabin, with six leading hands – three to a watch – in another cabin, and the rest in two dormitories in the tween-deck. Then on my second voyage the number went up to 52 and we were divided into 3 watches – port, starboard and midships. There was also a handful of kalassies, about half a dozen, and a couple of topasses. The engine-room was manned normally. On the UK coast half the cadets would go home on leave for half the coasting time, the other half for the remaining time. At sea we'd be in three watches, one studying, one doing practical seamanship and so on, one working round the decks as hands, and the duties would be rotated around the watches in turn. In port that routine was generally maintained, changed only if circumstances called for it. There were enough of us to get everything done without breaking watches, as a rule. (*Chindwara*, 1958-61)[1]

They appointed me to the *Chantala*, which came as a bit of a setback after two years at the *Conway*, but because I hadn't been home in that time I asked for a postponement, which was granted. In the event I was posted instead to the *Kampala*, escaping the fate I'd been warned about. *Chantala* was reputedly the tough one, *Chindwara* a more gentlemanly ship, but it was purely comparative and both were regarded as hard schools by cadets I met. As I found them when I visited *Chindwara* in Mombasa on one occasion, though, the cadets were an affable lot even though they considered that fellows like me led a life of undeserved ease. (1962)[2]

One learned that there was more to a toilet than merely sitting on it – it had to be cleaned; more to lino than walking on it – it had to be scrubbed; more to a porthole than looking out of it – it had to be polished. One was expected to run around after the other 48 cadets, all of whom were more senior and far more worldly-wise. (*Chantala*, 1962)[3]

Both remained on the UK-Australia run until displaced by the W- and N-class ships about 1959, when they were switched to the UK-East Africa and South Africa run via the Suez Canal. Then, following commencement of the P&O group's reorganisation in 1963, and also owing to the changes in the general system of training, *Chindwara*'s cadets were disbanded and posted round the fleet. In 1966 both became training ships for Indian ratings, also carrying 16 British cadets apiece in their capacity as what the company described, prosaically, as "Cadet Training Units".

From the *Dwarka* I went back to the *Chindwara*, but one no longer stuffed with cadets. This time there were seven of us, and the ship was training Pakistani seamen. Our function was to make up the numbers of boat tickets and EDH's. Something of an irony in the ship which had

---

[1] Contributors' private papers.
[2] ibid.
[3] ibid.

trained so many cadets over the years. My particular challenge was to complete the correspondence course, and two of us actually did so. (1965)[1]

Both ships were sold abroad in 1971, and the cadet-training scheme was overhauled, bringing into service for the purpose four new ships, *Manora*, *Merkara*, *Morvada* and *Mulbera*, the first delivered in 1970 and the others in 1971, each accommodating eight cadets. Two years later P&O ended their careers in the residual BI service, and with them the company's cadet-training scheme.

Irony was a frequent fellow-traveller at sea, and there was something of it about when the last cadet-ship to wear the red ensign began her duties in 1974. Half a century earlier the Anglo-Saxon Petroleum Company had come into possession of the *Medway*, last of the sail-training ships, and now it adapted one of its fleet for training some 28 deck cadets, a task she fulfilled until disbandment in 1980. Built by Cammell Laird in 1963, *Opalia* was a 53,660dwt crude carrier whose builders did the conversion work needed to accommodate cadets instead of the usual crew.

The deciding factor for such a radical move – more so as it was made when other companies were abandoning the intensive training of cadets – was the poor performance of Shell's cadets in the 2nd mate's exam. Its results vindicated the scheme's supporters and silenced all bar a bigoted minority among its detractors, the pass-rate jumping from shamefully poor to around 75% at the first attempt. In fact *Opalia* wasn't alone, but she was the largest: several other ships of the Shell fleet were fitted to carry a dozen cadets apiece following the same training regime – mini cadet-ships, as they were called.

Opalia adopted a high profile, taking part in the 1977 Spithead Review (in which, to the Shell people's delight, a BP tanker received a reprimand for laxity), impressing the DTI (the BOT by any other name...) to such an extent that it urged others to follow Shell's lead, and gaining, through weight of novelty as much as anything, the unions' approval: training emphasised good tanker practice as a priority, academic instruction deferring to it, against a carefully-gauged disciplinary base that fostered a spirit of competition. The ship was manned normally in the engineering and catering departments, the usual complement of deck officers supplemented by an instructor of chief officer rank, and the bosun was assisted by two or three instructor POs.

It has always been recognised that the efficient operation of our vessels depends greatly upon high professional standards among the officers. The importance of maintaining such standards has been reflected over many years in our commitment to extensive programmes of cadet recruitment and training. The introduction of the ss Opalia *as a training-ship for Navigating Cadets marks an important step forward in the training of future Deck Officers...* (Opalia *training manual.*)

---

[1] Contributors' private papers.

The training programme was designed to implement the MNTB scheme of ONC/D courses including A-level entry, augmented by specialist tanker work. Formal instruction was combined with practical work in maintenance and cargo-handling, balanced by bridge-work and engine-room familiarisation. All officers were involved, and the intense regime was relieved by comprehensive recreational arrangements on board, including a cadets' bar, and shore excursions at every opportunity. The cadets were grouped in divisions (not watches – terminology was losing some of its natural tenor) under the charge of seniors answerable to the chief officer, and cadet committees dealt with such matters as welfare and general administrative liaison.

We went through the Suez Canal to a place in the Gulf of Suez to load. A sea mooring, an awkward business with a green crew. Some were straight out of school, but we had to make it a viable operation. It was a tremendously difficult task to operate the ship under commercial conditions like that. There were inter-departmental jealousies about her, and both deck and engineer supers were down on her, out to give us a hard time. So we had to be really good. It was tough, but very rewarding. There was enormous prejudice against her throughout the fleet, mostly conservative views in support of the old way. We used to have uniformed cadets on the gangway and that sort of thing, unheard-of in tankers, and looked upon as pure bullshit by outsiders.

Unions? They approved. Couldn't do otherwise if they looked at it objectively. The idea was to produce a professional tanker officer, and nobody could quibble with that. And we had an excellent social structure. The cadets had their own bar, ran it themselves. Of course you had to have eyes like a hawk because there were three bars on the ship – crew's, officers' and cadets'. They were limited in the amount of stuff they were allowed in one night, but the little beggars used to get someone to invite them to another bar, and in one night you'd find someone getting through more than enough. You had to watch their bar accounts, examine them minutely. I mean, we had a highly-intelligent crew on our hands, and the officers were hand-picked. The corporate intelligence of the ship was formidable, which called for very fine tolerances.   She carried black oil – fuels and crudes – worldwide but mostly on the American coast in my time. Her schedule was varied, maintained interest. Some cadets were enthusiastic about her; she provided them with the sort of life they'd expected – the organised training, the social life. We used to hire buses to take them to places of interest, and there were boats – two Enterprise dinghies – used whenever possible. It was an interesting life and they loved it, but there were the ones who didn't; resented it from the word go. Reluctant Opalians! But on balance she was a very happy ship. (1975-77)[1]

And what price a happy ship? *Opalia*'s training career came to an end at a time when all the high-flown phrases, the lofty sentiments, the philanthropic bent, the declarations of faith in the future of a seafaring nation, the value of a system and the inherent worth of British youth properly disciplined and guided were brought to nothing by political trends, social sentimentality and degeneracy, and considerations of commercial ascendancy allowed to outweigh all others – others less easily defined and impossible to evaluate in terms of monetary gain that thinly veiled the spreading

---

[1] Contributors' private papers.

disease of sophisticated greed. In common with other UK-based shipping interests, Shell placed expedient before prudence and set about flagging out its fleet while shedding its commitment to a future composed of anything other than raw commerce. Training returned to the obscurity from which it had emerged barely ninety years before in an industry which would have to come face to face with the inevitable consequences before grudgingly giving credence to the need to re-invent the wheel...

EPILOGUE

A Bygone Era[1]

*

ALTHOUGH alluding to and hinting at the reasons for the apprentice's extinction, none of the foregoing has been – or, indeed, has attempted to be – explicit about why he disappeared; nor about what, if anything, his disappearance deprived us as a society, and it might be apposite to end his story by making just such an attempt.

Let me begin by considering the second point first and identifying the thing lost, for lost something certainly has been: society's leanings towards the trivial, the short-term, and material gratification have by their nature excluded it. What has been lost is a principle, one which was characteristic of a social order that placed seemingly (to the latter-day eye) arbitrary limits on personal freedoms now regarded as "rights". Part of the grand illusion of progress, these so-called freedoms, in their expression of sentimentality and selfishness, amount to a disregard of the obligations towards one another that should form part of the fabric of any society with pretensions to civilisation. The principle is the rather severely-visaged (by today's perceptions) one of disciplined service, the value of which, although quantifiable in monetary terms through its contribution to efficiency, is more importantly gauged in terms of social morale, in turn resolvable into philosophical values reflected in the standards of private and public behaviour considered acceptable. One of the causes of their inexorable deterioration is the loss of the principle of disciplined service, and a measure, in the negative sense, of its value.

The clauses of the apprentice's indenture amounted to as concise a summing-up of social morality as has ever been set out in black and white outside the pages of the Bible. They were a peculiarly candid declaration of an ideal to which both apprentice and master were to aspire, against which they could measure their value to each other and so to society at large, and from which, as their conduct fell short of expectations, they shrank until finally finding it easier on the conscience, or morally expedient, to abandon altogether. The standards demanded became inconvenient – "old-fashioned" – and therefore to be despised and ultimately rejected in favour of a more flexible, less onerous, and hence less valuable, canon.

Consider the comparison between an indenture issued during the system's closing years and an example of an earlier form which has already been outlined, though it will do no harm to look at it again, and more closely:

In Willoughby's indenture of 1845 the apprentice was first of all bound of his own free will to Samuel Cole; accordingly, he had no cause to complain of any treatment

---

[1] "…the bygone era of maritime adventure." *Joseph Conrad* (biographical study).

333

which complied with the contract's conditions. Under them he was to serve Cole exclusively for six years, "remaining and dwelling" with him "after the manner of an Apprentice" – that is, one whose duty was to learn his master's trade, craft or profession and carry it on with all its traditions, standards and aims including its further development.

He was to serve faithfully. That is, he was to exercise loyalty towards his master, which included keeping his (trade) secrets, to which, of course, he would become privy and which, disclosed to others, might bring about Cole's ruin.

He was to obey Cole's lawful commands, without quibble or question, cheerfully, and as efficiently as he could, commands not confined to the work but also embracing whatever domestic arrangements had been made, in this case aboard ship, which included his affairs when ashore either on business or on Cole's behalf or at leisure.

He was to do all in his power (including risking life and limb) to prevent anyone from doing Cole and his interests hurt or damage, including warning him of the threat. This meant, for example, that if Cole and his officers experienced problems with the hands, or if Cole alone experienced them with any of his officers, from disgruntlement over the victuals to mutiny, the apprentice was to declare himself on the side of authority in the interests of his master, the ship and its safe operation. Normally, if the master was the owner but not the ship's master, the apprentice gave service to the latter as his master's assign, but would be in an invidious position in the event of the ship's master working against the interests of the owner, as could happen, and did. In such circumstances he was bound to make the situation known to the owner if he could, but more often than not, being remote from him, found it healthier to remain ignorant of matters. On the other hand, he might decide to make what he could of them to whatever extent was tolerated or encouraged by the malefactors. Discovery would mean, of course, cancellation of the indenture together with whatever penalties were entailed, typically the loss of the agreed penal sum or surety, but to which would be added whatever punishment the law prescribed for any criminal offence involved, together with the implications of social outrage that would ensue in their various manifestations: being a betrayal of a particular trust the enormity of the crime would be proportionately magnified.

When required by Cole he was to make a true declaration of whatever of his master's possessions, including moneys, had been placed in his charge, also to give a "true account" of any wages or disbursements including prize money granted him should he enter Her Majesty's service, either navy or army, either voluntarily or by force, the press still being a legitimate, if by this date only theoretical, phenomenon. What was more, he was to hand it over to Cole and accept instead the wage agreed under the terms of the indenture. The fortunes, as distinct from the misfortunes, of war were thus cancelled as far as the apprentice was concerned; the binding agreement continued in force, though the practical aspects of the arrangement seem somewhat over-sanguine from the master's point of view, for this charge on the apprentice's honesty was for the most part proof against investigation. The master's wisest course of action was usually to write off the contract as a bad bargain, unless doing so relieved him of what had already turned out to be a miscalculation on his part.

Bedding, clothing and other necessaries were provided by the apprentice, the cost of anything of that nature provided by the master being deductible from the boy's wage, the purchasing power of which was miniscule and likely to be stretched to breaking-point by an unscrupulous master. It behoved the apprentice to attend to carefully to the small print, and to look ahead.

So much for what Willoughby was required to do. The remainder of his obligations came under the heading of "thou shalt not":

do hurt or damage to his master;

see or consent to its being done by others;

frequent taverns or alehouses unless on his master's business;

play at dice, cards, tables, bowls or other unlawful games;

embezzle, waste, lend or give away his master's goods without his consent;

absent himself from his master's service at any time without his consent.

Some, certainly not all, earlier indentures also forbade marriage (as in the case of the engineering indenture of James Robb, for example, but sea indentures were similarly phrased) and some fornication, though the famous "house of ill repute" was, as mentioned, a popular myth. Presumably one could enter it, whatever it was – a brothel is the assumption – provided the planned encounter was to be exclusively platonic.

Soberly considered, none of the apprentice's obligations were particularly onerous except in the sense that they were uncompromising and binding for the whole of the stated term, a condition that was nevertheless revocable: cancellation by mutual agreement was always an understood, where it wasn't an explicit, proviso.

The terms of Willoughby's indenture were in substance little different from those of the 15th century and earlier, while 117 years later they had altered only in detail, vestigial evidence of social change that was gathering pace with revolutionary speed, threatening to leave the indenture amid the detritus cluttering its wake. An indentured cadet, as the phrase ran, in the British India Steam Navigation Company' service in the early 1960s, had voluntarily bound himself to the company for three years, which, with twelve months' remission in respect of – in this case – two years at *Conway*, would qualify him to attempt the 2nd mate's exam. It was a prospect Willoughby wouldn't necessarily have had in view unless by choice, and one towards which he would, in practice, have received next to no instruction or preparation unless Cole deemed it to be in his own interests.

The cadet was to serve the company faithfully, and keep its secrets. This included restrictions on what he entered in the journal he was required to keep, its entries limited to observations about his daily work, the weather and other natural phenomena, his leisure pursuits and so on, religiously excluding reference to the company's commercial policy and practice, an indicator of paranoia that was largely groundless, for it was as much as the cadet was prepared to do to enter a daily resume that in its stilted brevity amounted to little more than token evidence of the fact of his existence.

He was to hold himself subject and obedient to the company's orders as received through its agents, ships' masters and officers as well as the advice contained in the Cadets' Manual. This applied at all times during the agreed term, whether at sea or ashore, at work or leisure, and when on leave he was to be ready for re-appointment at the company's convenience.

He was to prevent, if possible, damage being done to the company, its agents, ships' masters and officers, and was to warn them of any such threat.

He was to give a true account of goods or moneys entrusted to him by the company or its assigns. By this time the press was, of course, a historical curiosity, and likewise there were no strictures about handing over wages received for service in the forces, the cadet still being, in theory, free to transfer. Though impracticable for a variety of reasons, this was the only legitimate way of breaking the binding nature of the indenture short of mutual agreement.

At all times, day or night, whenever required, he was to be diligent in his duty and do everything in his power to "promote the company's interests". And he was to live in whatever part of the ship was assigned to him (by this date a two-berth cabin in the officers' accommodation, attended by a Goanese steward and usually enjoying all mod cons either *en suite* or close by), providing himself with suitable clothing, uniform and other necessaries.

Then, as with Willoughby, the rest of his obligations were prescriptive. He was not to

do any damage to the company or its assigns;

see or consent to its being done by others;

frequent taverns or alehouses (the company's business evidently excluding proceedings in or with them);

play at unlawful games (not specified);

embezzle or waste the company's goods, nor lend or give them away without consent;

absent himself from service without leave.

On the whole there was nothing much to choose between Willoughby's and the BI cadet's indentures as far as the boy's duties were concerned: the principle in each case was a tradition of disciplined service, integral to it a spirit of loyalty towards the master, who in turn was bound by certain obligations. In 1845, following long-established precedent, they were

to cause the apprentice to be taught "the Art, trade or business of a Mariner or Seaman". The manner in which this was to be done was open to free interpretation and implementation, with what results we have seen in some typical respects. There was no system of training in force, nor, except voluntarily from that year, any goal by which the instruction could be formulated or evaluated;

to provide the apprentice with "sufficient" meat, drink, washing, lodging and medical attention;

to pay him £35 over the 6-year term;

to deduct from that sum whatever was disbursed to cover the cost of clothing or bedding supplied.

And in 1962 the company undertook to

teach the cadet the business of a seaman and the duties of a navigating officer in its steamers;

provide him with sufficient board, but not wines or spirits, beers or liquors, all of which, as they were not in Willoughby's day, were available on board to others of the ship's company. The ruling was partly to protect the cadet from himself in a dangerous environment, and partly to prevent him squandering his small wage in a social atmosphere that encouraged it. In the event he seemed to be able to circumvent the rule, either at the captain's discretion (very rarely) or clandestinely, and free of charge, through the generosity of his better-paid shipmates, among them often enough a junior radio officer of his own age, a point of peevish mourning that fell on deaf ears;

provide all necessary medical attention including hospital costs, the latter only if arising from causes to do with his duties and not when following his off-duty bents, which could result in anything from mild sunstroke to syphilis;

pay him wages under NMB agreements or their equivalent in rupees[1] subject to satisfactory conduct and proper observance of his covenants (i.e. £12, £18 & £21 a month for the three years, the normal first at £6 discounted for remission);

provide sufficient bedding and table linen, a marked improvement on its total absence in Willoughby's case;

deduct from the cadet's pay the cost of any clothing or other necessaries supplied while in service, though buttons and uniform "facings" were supplied free.

Both Willoughby and his BI descendant agreed to bind themselves in a penal sum, £30 in the former case, £50 in the latter, against breaking the indenture, likewise Cole and the BISN Co respectively. In addition, BI required surety of £50 payable by parent or guardian against the cadet's failing to meet his obligations.

As with their duties, there was very little to distinguish the contractual aspects of the conditions under which Willoughby served from those of the BI and its

---

[1] After WW1 officers in the BI had threatened to strike if the company persisted in paying wages in rupees not equated to a stated figure in sterling, then on the gold standard. Based on the price of silver, the rupee's value fluctuated in sterling terms, and although it could mean a gain the officers were adamant and the company conceded the issue.

contemporaries; but the form and standards of instruction, as we have seen, changed vastly without accounting for the change from sail- to power-driven ships. Outside the indenture's milieu, however, literally earth-shaking changes had occurred in the state of society, of which the BI cadet was aware while remaining at something of a remove, more easily maintained at sea than ashore. While mods and rockers caroused and battled on the Brighton sea-front and university students exhibited a new aimlessness in their ventures into petty anarchy, symptoms of a decay the roots of which lay in the effects of two world wars, the apprentice, or indentured cadet, or cadet on articles, continued to inhabit a world in which order and responsibility, embodying a proper respect for authority, were the norm; but it was under threat, and one that very quickly crystallised to reduce order to *concordia discors*.

Whatever else suffered during the conflict, authority was a major casualty of the 1914-18 war, chiefly by dint of its being seen as allied to the gross ineptitude which wrought the slaughter of the trenches. It was a slaughter accepted at first as a patriotic sacrifice (at least by those at home) but soon perceived for what it was, a futile exercise in military and political incompetence. Not only that, but also the cynicism to which this gave birth, in penetrating the outer armour of appearances, saw what authority had come to represent – not truth, right and honour in the chivalric tradition as reflected in the sentimental mirror of popular history, but the world of profiteering and material gain that thrived on conflict: the war that killed so much of the best of the nation's youth to no advantage also killed respect and provided the fodder on which the armourers flourished. For the first time in the nation's history of warfare the soldier, and to a lesser but significant extent the sailor and the airman, realised that he was fighting not for the patriotic ideals with which he had been regaled by the propaganda machine, and in which he had believed, but for the defence of a way of life dominated by the industrialists, landowners and, worst of all, the speculators, to whom the war was a gilt-edged (perhaps better described as a guilt-edged) investment.

They were fighting for a bad smell which propagandists called the odour of sanctity; and the more people that were killed, the greater and more beautiful the sacrifice, and the more holy and fishy the odour. And if the Dover Patrol was costly in life, were not shipping magnates lousy with shekels? And when the war had been over a few years who would be the better man, rich Lord Neptune the well-known shipowner, or poor Jack Tar the unknown survivor and ex-hero? [1]

At the end of the cataclysm the ex-heroes found themselves disinherited into the bargain, objects not of admiration and gratitude but of embarrassment to a people which by the armistice was already going about its peacetime affairs in a fever of commercial opportunism that quickly deteriorated into the suppuration of trade depression. In the war itself, then in the fraught peace that followed, the old order of authority and loyal service was perceived as a sham, a superfluous and hypocritical

---

[1] *Winged Victory*, p.151.

luxury when set against the harsh reality of the struggle for a living. It became fashionable, particularly among the articulate intellectual classes, to deride the tenets of conventional society, while among the lower orders the union moguls discovered fertile ground in the understandable resentment that prevailed.

Then, twenty years later, the resumed war completed the work of moral destruction, if not in quite such a concentrated and spectacular way, a process obscured to some extent by the general sense of righteous struggle against evil personified in a way never before encountered – itself a consequence of the earlier upheaval. In its aftermath, at first not recognised for what they were, the first shoots of a bitter growth emerged in a variety of locations, the maturing growth not connected with its beginnings except in the perceptions of a minority element of scepticism whose attempts to rectify matters were thwarted by the general compliance with trends that, seen as freedoms, were becoming uncontrollable licence. At first merely derided and challenged, social order began to crumble under attack the underlying forces of which, when not misunderstood, were disavowed. The effort to recover what was seen (through a glass darkened by political expedient and dishonesty reminiscent of the corrupt authority of the wars) as some sort of golden age of innocence – which, again comparatively speaking, it had been – was beyond the moral power of a society which found it easier and more convenient to pursue its materialistic and hedonistic goals with dedicated, obtuse fervour. Authority, loyalty, faithful service, duty, mutual obligation – all had been expended in the cause of gain, returning not due reward and a better world but an exposure of the bitter truths they had been used to cloak. The loyal servant had been paid not in gold but in gall, and his disillusion was infectious and corrosive. Now, instead of duties and obligations properly recognised and observed, he felt he was due certain "rights" as an individual, even at the expense of the wider community; even at the expense of his fellow servant.

One of the bitter growths appeared in the education system, though at first it seemed an unlikely nursery, representing, as it had done hitherto, establishment values. Confirming and substantiating the tripartite secondary system that carried British education towards the top of the world league in the 1950s, the 1944 Education Act came into question from a political establishment that was itself partly affected by, and partly the result of, the accumulated disillusion of war. The system of authority was perceived by it as stemming largely from a selective process that sought to promote excellence, and excellence was seen, or portrayed, as tantamount to authoritarianism, since the successful were assumed to aspire to positions of authority, academically, commercially, professionally. And it wasn't difficult to portray authoritarianism as the manifestation of ineptitude and corruption. Accordingly, the political left set about promoting a (flawed) conception of "equality" at the expense of quality, doing its utmost to discredit the tripartite system while infiltrating the academic establishment and using its power therein to further its political doctrine of anti-authoritarianism. The prime vehicle was the comprehensive secondary school, "progressive" teaching methods the weapon. One of these, begun at the elementary stage where its effect was profound, was "child-centred" (i.e.self-centred) learning, a *non-sequitur* since learning must centre on the teacher as its possessor, not on the child, whose first lesson should be to pay attention if it is to learn anything more useful to society than self-gratification. The so-called achievements of this subversive method were – and are – reminiscent of the dame school's, though not as valuable.

Rote learning and whole-class teaching (the entire point of the classroom) were vociferously denounced as "repressive" and displaced by quasi-individual tutoring which allegedly allowed the individual freedom of expression, though it quickly became apparent that the means of expression weren't being communicated. The result was frustration on the pupil's part and decline in the standards of elementary learning which in turn affected its higher levels – a diminishing facility in the three R's without which all else must remain beyond reach. What was more, the disciplinary value of whole-class teaching, a subtle one from which the community benefits rather than the individual at its expense, was destroyed. The combination of frustration and indiscipline inevitably produced a rebellious attitude in the pupil which found in the establishment not resistance and correction but tacit accommodation by way of "understanding" (i.e. condoning), demonstrated in the abolition of the principle of punishment for wrongdoing – disobedience, for example – which was then in turn condoned in the sense that its definition was at first obfuscated and then lost. The new order's effectiveness was cemented when its initial promoters were succeeded in the system by those whom they had indoctrinated, and the cancer of subversion spread. By the late 60s it was well-entrenched, masquerading as liberalism, producing a character whose chief feature was the gratification of self through the exercise of rights to which the system averred he was entitled. Yet for all his gratification the means of articulate expression of self was notably absent, and the deficiency emerged at its worst in the form of a kind of brutishness that encountered no assertive censure in a society that was, as are all societies, the product of its own education system. At its best it tolerated low standards of conduct, at its worst promoted them.

Voices raised against the trend of events were few and feeble, lacking conviction and decision, and were, deservedly on those counts, drowned by the clamour from the liberal – that is, the subversive – establishment as it had become. It was an establishment which, characteristically, refused to admit to its failings (which, from its own point of view, were triumphs), resenting and rejecting all criticism from without while signally suppressing it from within, where it dared to exist.

So much for the educational scene. In the surrounding community matters were following a parallel path. The law gradually succumbed to "liberal" thought and principle, step by step moving away from a position of rigorous defence of right towards one of ambivalence – of sympathy for the transgressor coyly described as even-handedness or even justice, the latter a conception with which British law has traditionally confused itself, notably without justification in recent times. In this the principle of punishment was displaced by one of "rehabilitation", interpreted as in the education system (from which it had hatched) as a patent condoning of wrongdoing:

340

instead of being made to pay for his hurtful actions the criminal was encouraged to see himself as a victim of circumstance, not responsible for his actions and therefore to be given every facility to redeem himself, even at the expense of the community whose tenets he had outraged. Society, itself by this time largely compliant, was held to blame for his anti-social ways, and stood accused of tempting him into a regrettable predicament. The only forms of punishment he faced were either monetary penalties which reduced all values to cash terms or a period of squalid and idle detention, during which in most cases he accumulated a greater stock of resentment towards his fellow man, and learned further means of expressing it.

At sea, new regulations in the spirit of this liberalism deprived the shipmaster (and the apprentice's master) of his authority while at the same time bureaucratic edict, one of liberalism's natural parasites, piled responsibility on his shoulders, rendering the occupation less than attractive to the kind of youth who might otherwise have taken to it and made a success of it: statutory accountability without authority was rightly seen as the goal of fools.

Attacked and misrepresented in both educational and legal systems, authority was likewise beleaguered in (shore-based) industry, where the scene became a messy one of increasingly-inept management (suffering from the moral feebleness and indecision that was becoming endemic) and increasingly-anarchic union activity: the unions were essentially anti-authoritarian in outward policy, though they were themselves examples of draconian intolerance and autocracy bordering on tyranny, evidenced in restrictive practices (which helped to wreck the shipbuilding industry) and the excesses of the closed shop, a form of nepotism taken to destructive extremes. Freedom for unions didn't mean freedom for their members as individuals; indeed, the two were in polar opposition, and individuality of thought, let alone action, was rigorously, and sometimes brutally, suppressed.

Maritime unions – both seamen's and officers' – were by comparison moderate, but their aims and methods were nevertheless characteristic in principle, and where the law moved towards reduction of the master's (and employer's) authority, either directly or by means of restrictive regulation, the unions sought to further the process along various avenues of influence, through their presence on the boards of official bodies and by means of pressure brought to bear on the employer under the guise of "negotiation" or "free collective bargaining", euphemisms for blackmail. In all this, however, it remained axiomatic that that they were excluded from any part in the execution of the terms agreed between apprentice and master, and it rankled. Accordingly, they lost no opportunity to rail against alleged abuses of obligations by the master, allegations which savoured more of sentimental retrospection in the Dickensian mood than of contemporary observation.

The situation that evolved from this great transmogrification of society was one of contrast: whereas in Willoughby's day the ship, in its way of life, had been representative – a microcosm – of life ashore, for all that certain aspects of the nautical scene were peculiar to it, chiefly in the field of man's direct confrontation with the elements, by the last days of the BISN Co it had begun, because of what might be called social inertia, to represent an order at odds with the liberal-subversive trend of affairs ashore, though it was, as remarked, under pressure. One of the facets of this contrast was the authoritarian organisation of the owning company and the shipboard system, which, to Willoughby merely an extension of his shore experience, was to the BI cadet something to which he had to adjust as the 60s advanced, a process aided by his personal aspirations and pre-sea training. Not only that, but also the element of adventure, as perceived and once upon a time taken for granted, had visibly diminished, replaced by a drab patina of bureaucratic conformity through which was dimly visible the ever-receding age of risk and hardship, with its attendant rewards and disappointments, that had had its peculiar appeal. Where it appealed at all, the new age attracted a different kind of spirit altogether.

This was the climate in which the indenture found itself after a journey of some six centuries, and it was anything but congenial. Here was a problem, for in the 60s Britain's merchant fleet was still substantial, and in need of a supply of potential officers as much as it had ever been, if not more so. Wastage was a continuing bugbear and recruitment becoming a greater one. One way of changing the direction of the train of events seemed to be to make changes in the training system, changes which had in mind two basic aims: to improve the job's professional status by means of technological emphasis, the other, paradoxically, to render it less restrictive by presenting, through the training pattern and content, a field of qualification that would, in theory, be more equitable with career opportunities ashore. At one and the same time the system sought to make the sea both more attractive and more easily escapable, from which resulted not improved recruitment but, as might have been expected, confusion and a loss of direction characteristic of the liberal order in general. It was, of course, inimical to the tenets of apprenticeship, not only in this sense but also in the way in which the new ideas were put into practice. In the event the notion of a 4-year (or, for the engineer apprentice, 4½-year) apprenticeship was made redundant.

The new ideas were an extension of the long-established change wrought by the pre-sea training-ship, which had introduced the principle of equivalent sea-time, reducing time spent at sea aboard ship (for which, in fact, there was no viable substitute), and the outcome, not surprisingly, wasn't only a less intimate relationship with the sea itself but also a development that set the indenture at a discount: spending less time under the eye of the master (or his proxies) than under that of academic interests the apprentice began to stand remote from the essence of his agreement, which took on the rusty appearance of anachronism, relict of an authoritarian past that had not only been discredited by the system but was also looked upon by the potential apprentice – the emancipated product of a subverted education, or schooling – as an unwarranted imposition opposed to all the notions of individual assertion, or self-interest, with which he had been inculcated. Naturally, he wasn't disposed to sign away his "rights" in exchange for what looked like onerous duties, and he placed the sea, if not low on his list of career options, outside it altogether. The very term "apprentice" had become distasteful, though it was in the nature of things that those who had grown used to the title of "cadet" developed a perverse predilection for the old label with its connotations of hardship and manliness under trying conditions, a posture in which there was an amusing element of romantic fraud.

Formed as it was of elements which amounted to a concerted attack on the indenture's terms of reference, the climate of subversive liberalism finally brought about its extinction, and the apprentice tumbled, willy-nilly, off the gimcrack vessel of progress into the tide of history, taking with him something of value the price of which is being counted in widespread failure of social order and a decline of professional accomplishment. Much of what has been lost is masked by the developments of technology, visible only to those with enough perception to see through superficial appearances and the dazzle of science's amoral advances into a brave new world in which human values receive ever-lessening credit and labour against ever-diminishing currency. Whether or not what has been lost is of any concern to an island nation preoccupied with political rather than practical matters (where they are given any attention at all in preference to materialistic trivia) is debatable, and whether or not it will need to, or indeed can, be replaced with something of equal value and practical worth remains to be seen: it has not been as yet.

But the question at present seems to embrace a somewhat more fundamental area, the need for a home-flag merchant fleet, itself in danger of extinction. If and when that happens – and momentary recoveries of a minor extent offer no real prospect of a reversal of the trend – the debate on the subject of apprenticeship and what has succeeded it (inadequately) will become not merely academic but superfluous. It seems that, in competition with the welfare state, the sea has become too much for the spirit of today's equivalent of "wastrels and farmers, lazy clerks and penniless journeymen fond of the bottle, strong rogues and masterless men", and as for the "authentic adventurers for whom the native island was grown too small", while foreign-flag operators continue to open their arms to British officers, and even offer places in their ships for cadets, the confines of a modern container-ship or tanker and their humdrum trades – or, indeed, even of a cruise-liner on her apparently-exotic round crammed with the pleasure-seeking idle – are hardly likely to appeal, further confined as they are by the oppressive regime of regulation in league with unlimited (quite literally) responsibility and liability. The life of a lawyer or professional footballer seems to offer better prospects on all counts.

***

Finis

***

APPENDICES

Appendix 1.

The RNR.

TODAY's Royal Naval Reserve is formed from the merged RNVR and the reserve of merchant navy officers, the original RNR, now distinguished as List 1, the old VR of shore-based volunteers being List 3. They combined on 1st November, 1958, a reflection on the reduced size and perceived requirements of the Royal Navy, influenced as they were by political views.

The first instance of the formation of a reserve of trained men for the navy was in 1696, when an Act of Parliament (Will.III, c.788) provided for

> ...the furnishing and supplying of able mariners and seamen which may be in readiness at all times for that service.

Merchant seamen were offered inducement to volunteer for a naval reserve, including an annual retainer of £2 and further emoluments for service in the fleet. The outcome was a reserve of only some 17,000 men, whose willingness to come forward when called was much in doubt in view of the current pay crisis in the navy: seamen were in open revolt against the service in protest at the arrears of pay that were reducing them to beggary. In the end the reserve was dissolved while recruitment continued with the aid of the press when needed.

The next manifestation of a volunteer reserve took the shape of the Sea Fencibles, a coastal defence force raised by Pitt during the French revolutionary wars of 1792-1800, when invasion seemed likely. Liable to service in the fleet, the Fencibles were disbanded after the Treaty of Paris brought war with France to an end.

Then, in 1853, the Naval Volunteer Act (16 & 17, Vict. c.73) provided for the recall of naval pensioners within a certain time from the date of retirement, and a Royal Naval Coast Volunteer Force. Concern at its inadequate size and poor quality – W.S. Lindsay described Admiral Napier's crews as "a squalid lot of aquatics" – led to the RNR (Volunteers) Act of 1859, which provided for a reserve of 30,000, to include trained merchant seamen. In 1864, after an Act of 1862 had introduced recruitment of merchant service officers, the merchant seamen's section of the reserve became the RNR and in 1873 the RNCVR became the RNVR, whose members were liable for service in the fleet at any time.

In 1903, when it had become clear that Germany was harbouring territorial and commercial ambitions that would impinge upon British interests, an officers' volunteer force was formed from landsmen with appropriate backgrounds, and both RNR and RNVR continued recruiting as war descended on the scene. The RNR was closed to further entry at the end of WW1, and resumed in 1926 with an age limit of

26 on application, while in 1933 the RNSVR – the supplementary list – was formed of people ashore with professional seagoing experience, eligible for commissioned rank.

Recruitment to the RNR ceased in 1939 for the duration of the war to be resumed in 1950, aiming at a strength of 3,400 officers and men on the General List, as distinct from the Naval Patrol Service. Then, in 1957, recruitment of ratings from the merchant navy was discontinued, the men considered to be of greater usefulness serving in their merchant ships than in the increasingly-sophisticated warships of a smaller and more technologically-advanced navy.

When merchant service officers were recruited to form the RNR the rank of midshipman in the seaman (executive) branch was included, and at the turn of the 20th century the conditions of entry were that

1. he had passed the BOT eyesight test as established by the 1894 MSA;
2. he was a British subject;
3. he was aged 16 to 18, with exceptions to 19;
4. he had completed a 2-year pre-sea course in one of the recognised Mercantile Marine training-ships, and been nominated by its committee of management;
5. if at sea as an apprentice or cadet, he must have served satisfactorily for 1 year in a British ship or ships,

and after entry would be on probation pending completion of 2 years' satisfactory sea service in British merchant ships and 28 days' training in a ship of the Home Fleet ending with recommendation from the commanding officer. Further promotion (to sub-lieutenant, a rank introduced in 1861) depended on seniority, ability and attainment of the requisite paper qualifications upon examination.

After 1926 the training requirement with the fleet was increased to 6 months, with up to 12 in wartime, but post-WW2 was reduced as the fleet suffered cuts in strength. By the end of the 1970s conditions of entry were to the effect that the applicant must

1. be aged 17 to 21;
2. have completed 9 months' satisfactory service in a British ship or ships as cadet, apprentice or midshipman(*sic*);
3. certify that he intends to make the sea his profession;
4. have obtained passes at GCE "O" level in physics, mathematics, English or English language and one other subject.

No training commitment was specified, but a Short Introductory Course (14 days) at BRNC could be attended before promotion to Probationary Acting Sub-Lt.

Engineers were originally of warrant rank, with no entry at midshipman level for commissioned rank. This changed after 1926, and after WW2 entrants were accepted as probationary midshipmen (E). By the end of the 1970s the applicant had to be

1. aged 17 to 21;
2. under training in the Alternative Training Scheme, or have a background as a workshop apprentice, or as a student at a technical college, or have served satisfactorily for 9 months as an apprentice or cadet in a British merchant ship;

3.   intending to make the sea his career;
4.   in possession of GCE "O" level passes as for the seaman midshipman,
and the training requirement was similar, with promotion in due course to P/A/Sub-Lt(E).

*

Principal references:
How to Go to Sea in the Merchant Service (summary, RN entry regulations, c.1912);
List 1 RNR Officers' Directory & Summary of Regulations, October 1979;
Seamen in the Making;
The Nautical College, Pangbourne. Prospectus, 1936;
The Royal Navy Day by Day;
The Royal Navy Since 1945;
The Sea Our Heritage.

Appendix 2.

Dietary & health.

UNTIL the early 19th century the preservation of foodstuffs was effected chiefly with salt, and to a lesser extent with vinegar and aromatic spirits. Where they lent themselves to it some foods were preserved by drying – peas, for example.

Preservation apart, the nutritional value of ships' provisions fell short of the need, and long voyages produced diseases which killed more men than did the ordinary hazards of the sea and the attentions of various enemies. The difficulties were complicated and compounded by ignorance, administrative incompetence and corruption as well as the seaman's innate and usually irrational conservatism, by which he resisted innovation whether for his benefit or not. Cook, for example, had to flog two men for persistently refusing to eat the fresh meat he provided, while earlier in that century a privateer captain, William Hutchinson, had complained, in a more general sense, that too many men were so devoted to the methods to which they had become accustomed that they could not be prevailed upon to try others that were better.

Victualling, or dietary, scales were a matter of preference and agreement of a cursory nature between master and crew until, as such things will, the serious deficiencies and associated corruption provoked mandatory control under the 1906 MSA.

A victualling scale for ships in the West African slave trade was ratified in 1789 but lapsed with abolition (in the British Empire) in 1807. There was no further official intervention until the 1844 MSA required the ship's master to state the scale he had devised in the articles of agreement. The variety and quantity had to be declared, the only official proviso being "sufficient without waste". Bread (biscuit, or hard tack) was to be allowed up to 1lb per man per day, and the staples at the time were salt beef (or salt junk or salt horse, as it was called, junk horse-meat having been provided in some instances when beef had been scarce and too expensive to waste on common seamen) and pork, biscuit and water. Apprentices usually got what the hands were given.

The 1850 MSA (implemented 1851) introduced a recommended scale as a guide, the 1854 Act adding the requirement of weighing scales to enable the crew to satisfy themselves that they were getting their due. This list came to be known as the "Liverpool Scale", its basic elements being

per day	3 qts water
	1lb biscuit
	1½lb salt beef or pork
per week	1½lb flour
	1½ pts dried peas, and small quantities of tea, coffee and sugar.

Anything over and above this was at the master's discretion – biscuit *ad lib*, for example, and fresh produce when available, as well as items such as dried fruits, jams and marmalade. By the 1880s tinned meat was familiar, mostly mutton ("Harriet Lane"), and towards the 1890s a scale might offer

per day	3 qts water
	¾ lb salt beef (3 days per week)
	½ lb salt pork -do-
	1lb biscuit
per week	tinned mutton (1 day)
	stockfish
	¾ lb tinned butter
	1lb sugar
	few oz. beans, peas, rice, dried fruit
	soft bread (2 days)
	fresh onions & potatoes while edible
	condensed milk (from slops at master's price)

In 1894 the Shipping Federation set out a recommended scale which formed the basis of the one contained in the 1906 MSA, brought in by the BOT when under the direction of David Lloyd-George (and hence called the "Lloyd-George Scale"), and which required the ship to carry a qualified cook. Its chief features were a reduction in the quantities of salt meat, provision of fresh potatoes for the first 8 weeks of the voyage out of a home port between September and May, and an increase of the solid staples, providing also certain "substitutes" to allow for unavoidable shortages; this meant that the diet occasionally reverted to the salt meat, biscuit and peas of old, with 4d a day paid "in compensation" – but not to apprentices. The scale was mandatory, and replaced the niggardly "sufficient without waste" with a faintly reckless "generous surplus":

daily	4 qts water	
weekly	1lb soft bread on each of 3 days (3lb)	
	1lb biscuit on each of 4 days (4lb)	
	1lb salt beef on each of 3 days (3lb)	
	1lb salt pork on each of 2 days (2lb)	
	2¼ lb preserved meat	
	¾ lb fish (Friday)	½lb dried or compressed vegetables
	6lb potatoes	2/3rds pt split peas
	1/3rd pt green peas	1/3rd pt calavances or haricot beans
	2lb flour	½ lb rice
	½ lb oatmeal	1¾ oz tea
	4 oz coffee	1¼ lb sugar
	1/3rd lb condensed milk	½ lb butter

1lb marmalade or jam	½ lb syrup or molasses
¼ lb suet	½ lb pickles
5 oz dried fruits	2 oz fine salt
¼ oz mustard	¼ oz pepper
¼ oz curry powder	3 oz onions (on 1 day)
also ½ lb barley & ¼ lb cocoa, not mandatory	

The fish was dried, fresh or tinned, and could be substituted for preserved meat in equal quantity up to ¾ lb per week. In the tropics 2lb salt pork could be replaced with 3lb fresh or 1½ lb preserved meat. Fresh potatoes were to be issued "when procurable", otherwise an equal weight of yams or tinned vegetables (or dried/compressed potatoes or vegetables at the rate of 1lb to 6lb of fresh produce). Fresh/tinned could be substituted for dried/compressed vegetables in the ratio of ½ lb to 1oz. Coffee & chicory mixture could replace coffee in the ratio 5oz:4oz. A table of substitutes and equivalents permitted interchange of similar substances – meats, beverages, flour/biscuit/rice, butter & preserves, mustard & curry powder, and a miscellany of split peas/flour/calavances/beans/rice, "not to be used without Reasonable Cause".

The scale was subject to alteration by Order in Council, and remained in force with minor amendments until 1940, when it was increased substantially by the addition of items, fresh fruit in particular, which could now be preserved by refrigeration, though the ice-box had come into use in the late 20s providing limited cool storage. There was a greater variety of substitutes and equivalents, while bacon, eggs and cheese appeared for the first time, lagging behind some companies' victualling allowances. Moreover, by this date the apprentice was in process of shifting his messing-place from the half-deck with its statutory fare to the officers' saloon and its superior menu.

Bill of fare, c.1949. (The Hain Line)
Breakfast   Corn Flakes or porridge
                    bacon & egg or kippers or dry hash & egg
                    bread, butter, marmalade
Lunch   light cooked meal
Dinner   soup
                    stew or hot-pot
                    pudding
Other regular items: sausages, tinned tomatoes, salt fish, curry & rice, salads, corned beef, Spam, prunes & rice, semolina/sago pudding, steamed puddings, ice-cream.

Frozen and pre-cooked foods appeared in 1950 and in 1957 biscuit and salt provisions disappeared. By this time the BOT scales were virtually redundant, shipping companies having realised that a high standard of messing was expected as the norm and consequently providing far more than was required by law, though the quality of both the provisions and their preparation varied – God sent the food, and the devil the cook, as the old saying ran, assisted or frustrated, as the individual case might have been, by the training made compulsory under the 1906 Act. Nevertheless the apprentice, eating with the officers (though the (white) crew now had the same menu), usually fared at least as well, if not markedly better, than he did at home, particularly during the austerity of the immediate post-WW2 years with their rationing.

mv *Cyclops*
22nd Nov. 1955
(Farewell to Capt. H. Morley)

DINNER

Potage Americaine
Steamed Dee Salmon, Riche
Asparagus Melba
Roast Spring Chicken, Bread Sauce
Baked Cumberland Ham Madere
Potatoes: Garfield, Natural
Princess Beans Garden Peas
Swiss Apple Tart
Vanilla Ices
Biscuits Cheese Mixed Nuts
Dessert Coffee

mv *Landaura*
Christmas Day, 1963
(At Anchor, Kuwait)

DINNER

Hors D'Oeuvre
Cold Consomme   Cream of Mushroom
Fillet of Lemon Sole, Tartare Sauce
Lamb Cutlets Reform
Braised Ham Madeira
Roast Norfolk Turkey, Stuffing & Chippolata
Potatoes: Roast, Boiled, Saratoga
Vegetable: Brussel Sprouts Garden Peas
COLD BUFFET
Roast Beef Corned Ox Tongue
Garlic Sausage
Salad in Season
Peach Melba
Plum Pudding, Camperdown Sauce

Asparagus Vinaigrette
Savoury: Liver & Ham Toast
Dessert: Chow-Chow   Cashew Nuts
Mince Pie   Christmas Cake
Fresh Fruit
Coffee

mv *Somali*
23rd August, 1969

DINNER

Cream of Tomato Soup
Fillet of Turbot Meuniere
Cold: Boiled Ham   Fresh Salad
Fried Chicken Hawaii
Broad Beans   Roast Potatoes
Dundee Pudding, Citrus Sauce
Fruit
Coffee

It would be a somewhat diversionary exercise to discuss health to an exhaustive degree, beyond what has been touched upon in the main text, but further mention should be made not only of the several casual diseases to which the apprentice and his shipmates were prone as a result of contact in foreign parts and ashore at home but also of one in particular caused by shipboard conditions that prevailed until the demise of sail: sea scurvy was the abiding curse of the mariner on long voyages before efficient methods of preserving certain fresh foods had evolved, and its prevention and cure were the subject of a prolonged and mismanaged process that provides a classic illustration of the kind of obdurate conservatism for which the sea service has been and still is renowned and, in enlightened circles, patronisingly derided. In fairness, however, most of the confusion and resistance to developments emanated from the Admiralty rather than the much-maligned BOT, exacerbated by the stance of another service almost equally and obdurately resistant to unorthodox innovation, the medical one, though it is a mistake to judge long-defunct and discredited methods from the vantage-point of hindsight and its current self-satisfaction. Human nature is all too easily criticised, though it is an equal mistake to seek to protect it from reasoned and analytical judgment.

However, the other diseases played their part in the defeats and frustrations experienced by explorers and seamen from the beginning, and examples abound, latterly well-documented. In 1726, at the beginning of war with Spain, Admiral Hosier set up a blockade against Spanish commerce in the Caribbean, and out of an original fleet complement of 4,750 some 4,000 died of "scorbutic and other distempers", among which yellow fever was probably the most prominent, and the most feared, after scurvy. Of home-grown diseases, typhus was frequently brought aboard from the jails and other human cess-pits that furnished a variable proportion of naval crews while the press was the favoured wartime recruiting method. Merchant crews, being volunteers and enjoying, if that is the word, less cramped living conditions, were less prone to this than to impressment themselves.

Malaria, often referred to as "the ague", was widespread in all tropical coastal waters, and contracted by the seaman as inevitably as the common cold. In the East Indies amoebic dysentery could decimate a ship's company at short notice, while catarrhal jaundice (infectious hepatitis) added to life's miseries at random. Smallpox was frequently contracted during epidemics ashore, as was cholera, which could be brought aboard in the fresh water, and there were no effective remedies or preventives available until the last epoch of commercial sail. Worm infestation was another affliction borne by the seaman with more or less resignation, as were the variously effective remedies from purging to drawing out. Various infections were also common, arising from the generally poor hygiene and the occurrence of wounds and injuries both in battle and by shipboard accident, not to mention the "social diseases" to which the seaman was prone by temperament and inclination, regardless of whatever the indentures might contain by way of admonition.

Naval ships often carried a medical man; the merchant ship, however, was never under a statutory obligation to do so unless, latterly, carrying 100 persons or more, and treatment of sickness and injury was consequently a matter of self-help in many cases, rough and ready treatment that relied as much on the patient's robust constitution as on science. *The Ship Captain's Medical Guide* was first published in 1867 and retained its position as the definitive practical reference into the age of instant voice communication between ship and medical facilities ashore, aided by helicopter airlift. The ship's medical stores reflected the state of medical knowledge of the day.

Scurvy falls, or fell, into two classes: simple, which is a deficiency of vitamin C (ascorbic acid), and the sea variety, in which the sufferer lacks not only sufficient vitamin C but also a number of other water-soluble vitamins of the B-complex group, found in fresh fruit and vegetables and their products. Sea scurvy appears first as red blotches on the skin and gums which extend, harden and ulcerate to become festering sores impervious to treatment. Then the gums become putrid, and the teeth loosen and fall out. The legs swell, and the victim is gripped by extreme lassitude, prone to sudden death at the least exertion. Associated symptoms include fever, pleurisy, jaundice and chronic constipation with the belly distended, and difficulty in breathing. Old healed wounds break open and extend, and sight is affected. The disease has been described as the most loathsome and feared of all at sea, but has not manifested itself in fully-developed form for some 200 years. In partly-developed form it persisted into the Edwardian age, most notoriously contributing to the disastrous failure of R.F.

Scott's Antarctic expedition of 1911, in which the food supply was entirely lacking in the necessary vitamin content.

The curious thing about scurvy is that cures and preventives were discovered from time to time, only to be either forgotten or ignored, while the elements that effected the cure or prevented occurrence (the vitamins aforementioned, C the most significant) remained a mystery until 1932. Thus Scott's unnecessary demise while, as far back as Elizabethan times, the remedy was clearly known and documented: Sir Richard Hawkins (John Hawkins's son) noted that sea scurvy could be cured and therefore prevented by a regular intake of fresh fruit and vegetables, and carried a supply of citrus fruit aboard ship for the purpose. John Woodall, sometime surgeon-general to the HEIC, published *The Surgeon's Mate* in 1639. In it he dealt intelligently and perceptively with matters of diet at sea, and declared unequivocally that a daily dose of lemon-juice was a certain preventive and cure for scurvy – "let it have the chief place". There was always a vague and erratic understanding that fresh produce was in some way a preventive or cure, but except where individuals like Woodall made their findings public, it was more a matter of folk-lore and individual perception than a recognised scientific fact. While merchant ships were able to avail themselves of fresh victuals either in the normal course of trading or by diverting to known sources of supply, as did whalers in search of wild brassicas and scurvy-grass, warships were often stricken with the disease, and effectively disarmed, in the course of blockading and other prolonged station-keeping activities. It was not until the middle of the 18th century that a purposely-devised, fully-documented experiment, the first of its kind, was carried out, proving beyond all doubt that scurvy could be cured and prevented by the simple practical measure of including lemons or oranges, or their juices, in the diet. And yet it was ignored by Admiralty in what was described by the philosopher Herbert Spencer as "an example of the most outrageous, pig-headed bureaucratic indolence" – wonderfully hard-hitting words, though the bureaucratic establishment is well-armoured against such missiles by a practised, complacent indifference, which it demonstrates in other spheres as well.

In 1747 a naval surgeon, James Lind, carried out a controlled investigation into the cure for scurvy aboard HMS *Salisbury*. Taking twelve sailors afflicted with the disease he divided them into pairs and provided each with the same diet varied only by supplements which were to be evaluated as anti-scorbutics. They were cider, oranges & lemons, elixir of vitriol, vinegar, sea water and a mixture containing nutmeg, garlic and mustard as chief ingredients. Cider effected an improvement, but the others failed to prevent the sufferers growing worse (or might have exacerbated the complaint) except for the oranges & lemons, which brought about a complete recovery in a matter of a few days. The evidence was conclusive, even if the nature of the curative element remained unknown.

But conclusive evidence isn't always enough, and although Lind published them in his *Treatise of the Scurvy* of 1753, a year later, after due cogitation, the Admiralty Sick & Hurt Board rejected his findings, so subjecting generations of seamen and mariners to needless suffering, and indeed aggravating the dangers to the country from hostile powers faced with, on occasions, a weakened naval defence. Lemon juice was not prescribed for general issue in the fleet until 1795, a year after the death of the man who had observed, with characteristic self-effacement, in his *Essay on the most effectual means of preserving the health of Seamen in the Royal Navy* (1757), "The province has been mine to deliver precepts; the power is in others to execute."

The subsequent story of the muddle-headed battle with the disease involves prominent figures of the day, variously supportive of and opposed to the Lind thesis where they weren't in ignorance of it. No small part of the opposition came from those who followed Cook's view that citrus fruit or their juices were of no great value as anti-scorbutics, rating sauerkraut, portable soup and malt wort more highly. The freedom of his crews from terminal scurvy (outbreaks occurred which were countered by the periodic provision of fresh foodstuffs including, willy-nilly, oranges and other vitamin-rich items) earned him an undeserved reputation for having discovered the cure. Poor Lind, meanwhile, had lost his greatest supporter with the death of Anson[1] in 1762, and, with his hands full running the naval hospital at Haslar added to his naturally modest nature, took no steps to reassert his findings.

Sir Gilbert Blane was a firm supporter of Lind's methods. While on the West Indies station as Rodney's personal physician he experienced outbreaks of scurvy among the crews, and later returning to the station with the surgeon Thomas Trotter successfully treated outbreaks of scurvy with the juices of fresh lemons, oranges – and limes, the last proving to be, over time, the false trail that added to the general confusion. Trotter eventually published his *Observations on Scurvy* (1792) in which he strongly supported Lind, while Blane went on to become a Commissioner of the Sick & Hurt Board from 1794 to 1801. In this post he was able to introduce the issue of lemons to the fleet, but even at this the Admiralty demurred and did not make a general order, instead allowing the fruit or its juice to be issued to commanders on demand only. Subsequent obvious evidence made the demand general throughout the navy, while Trotter made it his business to encourage supply and consumption. Admiralty looked on with a somewhat sour ambivalence, and found reasons to prevent issue of the fruit to ships on certain stations in home waters, though they kept the sea for prolonged periods with inevitable consequences.

Then came confusion. In the 1860s the Admiralty transferred the contracts for supplying lemons from Mediterranean growers to British growers of limes in the West Indies and, to cut a long and involved story short, limes took over as the preferred anti-scorbutic by default. What was more, the difference between the lime and lemon – all too apparent to anyone taking the trouble to use his eyes if nothing more elaborate – seemed not to be noticed, and the words *lime* and *lemon* were used

---

[1] Who, of course, had survived his disastrous circumnavigation of 1740-44 during which he had lost 1,300 men through disease, chiefly scurvy, out of a total complement of 1,995. It was this incident that aroused Lind's interest and gained him Anson's influential support.

indiscriminately by people who should have known better, including medical men. Their appearance apart, the vitamin C content of the lemon and lime differed to a significant extent, the lime about half that of the lemon, rendering it a poor remedy for scurvy. On top of this a problem existed in the methods of preserving the juice without destroying the essential ingredient: vitamin C is destroyed by heat. Thus an increase in the incidence of the disease which led certain prominent figures to voice the conclusion that the *lemon* was the deficient fruit, and to promote the use of largely useless nostrums instead.

Into this scene of muddle, ignorance and prejudice stepped a somewhat ingenuous BOT to prescribe lemon-juice in the 1844 Mercantile Marine Act, its issue to begin ten days after the first meal of salt provisions. Whatever its value as an anti-scorbutic, it was often compromised by corrupt practices which led to its adulteration. The 1850 Act allowed the substitution of citric acid crystals (produced by heating, and hence useless) and changed the fruit from lemon to *lime*, in the accepted indiscriminate fashion. The indifferent results led to further regulation in the 1854 Act, which, in the usual heavy-handed way of bureaucracy, increased the penalties for adulteration and specified the daily issue of ½oz of juice per man in foreign-going ships. Yet the incidence of scurvy remained stubbornly unmoved, and after a report by the Society for Improving the Condition of Merchant Seamen the 1867 MSA specified fresh lime-juice fortified with 15% proof spirit as a preservative (lemons and limes still being indistinguishable in the eyes of officialdom, except for their respective prices...). The fortified juice was now to be issued 10 days into the voyage regardless of the menu, and was stored under bond as a protection against adulteration, at least until it got aboard ship.

Yet the disease persisted, as a threat to the ship's safe operation and a debilitating nuisance, with occasional more serious outbreaks, and in 1880 the BOT, noting a measurable increase in the incidence of cases throughout the 70s, was moved to announce its somewhat uncertain conclusions, to the effect that

lime-juice was ineffective;
its effect might improve in conjunction with the consumption of fresh meat and vegetables;
the diet should include fresh and preserved meats in place of or supplementary to salt;
more fresh vegetables should be supplied, particularly "raw potatoes";
while a statutory dietary scale was not yet desirable, it might become necessary if shipowners failed to act.

Not only was lime-juice ineffective, but, unable to meddle with it as easily as hitherto, unscrupulous masters took to issuing it *instead* of fresh provisions, a practice corrected to some extent by further regulatory measures (a classic example of the kind of conditions under which bureaucracy thrives and multiplies) including a fine of 3d for each refusal by crew-members to take the daily dose. This was the last measure taken against the disease before the 1906 Act and its compulsory dietary scale, after which, and partly owing to the demise of the square-rigger, scurvy became a quaint feature of history.

As for the anti-scorbutic elements themselves, while, in 1911, a Booth Line medical officer declared the cause of scurvy to be the presence of parasites on cockroaches, an original theory if wildly imaginative, more scientific investigation by the Lister Institute in 1918 first revealed the differences between the lemon and the lime and then confirmed the former's value, 165 years after Lind had published his treatise. In 1932 vitamin C was isolated and identified.

But custom dies hard, and in the 1960s the indentured cadet serving his time east of Suez in ships of the BI was served each morning with a large and very welcome glass of iced, sweetened, fresh-squeezed – lime-juice!

The orange, however, has the highest vitamin-C content of all...

*

Principal references:
A New History of British Shipping.
How to Go to Sea in the Merchant Service.
Life at Sea in the Age of Sail.
Limeys.
Poor Jack.
Ships and Ways of Other Days.
The British Navy, Vol.V.
The British Seaman.
"The Changing Character of the Sailor's Diet etc." in *Problems of Medicine at Sea.*
The Sea Our Heritage.
The Shipping Federation, 1890-1950.
The Way of a Ship.

Appendix 3.

Alfred Holt & Co. Ltd.
Letter to masters re midshipmen, c.1916.

India Buildings,
Water Street,
Liverpool.

Captain.......................
ss.............................

Dear Sir,

MIDSHIPMEN

The managers, having decided that the time has come when they can rely no longer on recruiting a substantial number of their ships' officers from men trained upon sailing ships, propose to train a certain number of boys upon the Company's steamers. These boys will be styled midshipmen.

It is with some reluctance that the managers have thus departed from the long established practice of the Company, for they feel some anxiety as to adequacy of the training which it may be possible to give upon the Company's steamers, but they are encouraged by the assurance that they may confide fully in the loyal and whole-hearted co-operation of the masters and officers of the fleet. The managers look upon the training of these boys as a grave responsibility and they will ever consider their own honour and reputation and that of the officers of their fleet to require that the training given upon the Company's ships shall be of the highest efficiency and repute. It is, therefore, of importance that at the initiation of the scheme a sound method should be adopted, and that the right spirit should be infused into its operation, and to this end the managers have drawn up some suggestions for the guidance of masters in training the boys placed under their charge. They are well aware, however, that the chief educative force is personality, and that no written advice can possibly take the place of the resourcefulness and example of yourself and your officers.

The midshipmen are to be deemed of equal social position with your officers. If they do not behave as gentlemen, and are not amenable to your correction, they will be asked to leave the service. The success of the enterprise depends upon the extent to which everyone concerned will co-operate in regarding it from the strictly professional point of view of turning out a thorough sailor and officer. The managers are prepared to give the personal trouble and to sanction the necessary pecuniary sacrifices for this purpose and they are confident that officers, in all grades, of the Company's fleet will be no less ungrudging in the sacrifice of purely personal considerations. They would pressingly remind their masters and officers, the majority of whom still possess square rigged certificates, that these boys will miss much of the toughness of nerve, the resourcefulness of improvisation, the habit of self-reliance, and the general elasticity, which is the unconscious inheritance of the hard but uniquely effective training, unless a real effort is made to supply these qualities in some other way. The training hitherto given to boys on steamers seems to them to be deficient in these respects. Something more than a mere full day of work about deck or in the holds and on the bridge is required to take the place of four years' daily duty up aloft on a windjammer in all weathers and frequently under conditions of great personal hardship and peril. It is with the object of supplying this deficiency that emphasis has been laid upon encouraging to the utmost the most varied athletic and mental activity of the boys. They must often be required to do as a discipline what circumstances compel should be done on a sailing ship as a duty and very often as self-preservation. That the boys should have a thorough and complete drilling in all the hardest and most monotonous work on board a steamer is of the first importance: they should indeed know their ship inside out from stem to stern; but it is no less important that by boating, swimming, boxing, and all other forms of athletic activity, together with considerable opportunity for scientific study, both generally and in regard to the structure and equipment of modern ships, they should keep alive and develop the qualities of personal courage, self reliance and sound knowledge which must continue to be the possession of every good shipmaster. The managers confide in the professional pride of their staff to work out a system that will attain these ends and nourish in the boys lasting interest and pride in their life's career.

The following suggestions are made as to training:-

A lad from his first year should keep regular watch, being employed during the day in the various duties of his profession, splicing, making knots and bends, cleaning paint, and mixing and applying same, overhauling of cargo blocks and the cleaning of them, rigging work, and (if used) sails, scraping of spars, chipping of iron, the cleaning out of holds and ballast tanks, shifting coal, etc. He should be given a thorough training by the carpenter and bosun of all work within their sphere. Whilst cargo is being handled he should be in the holds watching the breaking out and stowage, dunnaging, matting, slinging, and general stevedoring; he should understand thoroughly the position and use of limbers, sounding pipes, sounding rods, bilge pumps and bilges, the steering rods and steering gear, including the hand gear, and of the cable in the chain locker, and how to keep all these clean and in good order. His nautical duties should consist of learning the compass and how to steer, and plenty of practice with the leads, especially the hand lead and log line. The commercial code of signalling, and the other modes of signalling, especially the Morse code, hand flags, the semaphore, and by flash light, should also be taught. Every encouragement is to be given to the lads to learn how to operate the wireless installation and to obtain an elementary understanding of the work of the engineroom department. Your chief engineer has been requested to encourage the interest of the lads in the knowledge of machinery, and you should see that they regard this as amongst their serious duties. They should also be required at times to assist the chief steward in laying in stores, especially meat in the ice-house.

When sufficiently versed in the work a midshipman should be allowed to begin to handle men where Chinese crews are carried. This is a most essential part of his education; any mistakes he may make are to be at once corrected, but never in the sight or hearing of the men. He should assist the mates in watch keeping, but never must the presence of a midshipman on the bridge be allowed to relieve the officer of the watch of his duties, or to take the place of an additional officer when double watch is being kept. His cargo duties should be greatly amplified, and he should take part in all operations involving the slinging and lifting of heavy weights, and the rigging and working of heavy derricks and heavy weight spars. Whilst in the holds every opportunity should be allowed him to examine the construction of the vessel, and any tendency that may be displayed towards a study of naval architecture should be encouraged. He will, of course, be schooled in tallying cargo, and should be given charge of a boat during boat drill, and employed in these if there is any boating to be done. Provide as much rowing exercise as you possibly can. On suitable occasions make the boat drill at sea as complete as the circumstances permit, and in port make a special point of providing the lads with as much pulling and sailing as possible. The dinghy is provided for this purpose; let them use it freely and be entirely responsible for its upkeep. Where a motor boat is carried they should be required to become thoroughly competent in its management.

During his third year a boy should be given increased opportunity of learning navigation; the dirty work that he has had to do during the former years might now to some extent be curtailed, and more attention given to the scientific side of the profession. Whilst the vessel is entering or leaving port he should have experience given him of duties fore and aft, on the bridge, and in the engine room.

During his fourth year, he may be placed in the chief officer's watch, and where a fourth officer is not carried may take the place of one. He should now be required regularly to work sights, and given plenty of star work; being in the chief officer's watch will give him ample opportunities for this. He should take the azimuths in his watch, not only by the sun, but also the more important lunar and stellar ones. He should be given a good knowledge of chart work, and be invited with the officers to check off the courses you order to be laid down, and should always be present when the ship is swung to determine compass errors, or when the compass is being adjusted by the adjuster. The master must use his discretion as to the watch into which each midshipman is put, being careful to see that a fair experience of all work falls to the lot of each boy during his service as midshipman. It is important that he should be present at all sounding operations made with the sounding machine during his watch. He should at all times be employed in checking ship's distance from the land, and must receive a thorough drilling in the use of Lecky's danger angle.

The entry of offences in the official log must only take place in the case of midshipmen after the most thorough enquiry, and you will use great consideration in the matter. This is of the utmost importance as "logging" carries with it a black mark against a boy for the whole of his professional career, and what may be very serious in a man, might occur from want of thought in a boy. Punishment should be thorough but always free from ill-feeling.

The managers particularly hope that you will do your best to insist upon the physical development of the boys. Encourage them to go aloft, to practice work upon the spars, to climb ropes, to swim, to box, to race, and generally to exercise themselves to the utmost of their bent. Risks must be taken if nerve is to be obtained. A canvas swimming bath has been provided which the midshipmen should be allowed to use freely and be required to rig up and care for themselves. You may give at your discretion small prizes to encourage these activities, charging them in your account.

The managers have placed in the midshipmen's room a small library of books of scientific and general literature. They hope you will encourage the boys to read these books and to form a taste for scientific knowledge of the sea, and of its fauna, of meteorology and astronomy, and of good literature generally, rather than to allow them to waste their time, uncorrected, in reading trash. The boys will be expected to pass their Board of Trade examinations at the end of their training without cramming.

The midshipmen have been instructed to keep a daily log of natural phenomena observed during the voyage. This is for educational purposes, and it is important that each boy should record his own observations only, though general guidance may appropriately be given to him. Do not let these logs become in any way a record of the ship's doings, such as is forbidden in the Company's standing orders. The managers hope that both you and the boys will use originality to develop this valuable form of training.

Uniforms must be worn on shore and on bridge duty and all other proper occasions. Generally speaking, however, the managers hope the midshipmen will spend most of their time in working clothes. Do not let them neglect to keep their clothes washed and tidy and themselves clean.

The midshipmen are not to be allowed to mess alone, but with a certificated officer, presumably the third, the food served to them being the same as supplied to the officers and engineers of the vessel. It would be a good plan to invite them at times, singly or together, to your own table.

The midshipmen are to attend to their own room, and adequate time should be allowed them every morning for this purpose. Do not fail to inspect their quarters regularly and to insist upon the utmost cleanliness and neatness. The midshipman senior in service (unless good reason to the contrary exists) should be held responsible for the good order of the half-deck and for the good behaviour of its inmates. You should take an early opportunity each voyage of impressing upon him his responsibility to you in this respect and see that he fulfils his duty faithfully and in the right spirit. On arrival at a home port they must not leave the ship on holiday without obtaining from the officer in charge a certificate that their room is clean and shipshape. Holidays at home will be arranged through the Marine Superintendents.

If you have any reason to suspect that a midshipman is suffering in health, do not hesitate to have him properly overhauled by a doctor of good standing. Discourage them from doctoring themselves. When a doctor is carried, encourage him to train the boys in first aid.

Bullying or the use of foul language towards these lads, by any officer, or engineer, or other person, is to be reported to us. Similar misconduct on their part should be smartly punished.

In granting leave, please regard relaxation ashore as the reward of hard and enthusiastic work aboard ship. A ready and uncomplaining disposition to help the officers in their work should be expected of every boy. The Company's principal agencies have been asked to co-operate with the masters in providing suitable places and opportunities of training and recreation for the boys, and the managers will listen with sympathy to any proposals in this direction which may contribute to the boys' welfare. Remember that the midshipmen are over and above your ship's usual complement, and that it is the managers' purpose by providing a generous training to make them thorough sailors and to fit them as officers suitable for and attached to the Company's service rather than to extract from them the utmost amount of routine work during their indentures.

The managers expect you to do your utmost to protect the lads from the temptations inseparable from a seafaring life. They wish you to exercise a wise discretion in the giving out of money and not to hesitate to insist on paying the accounts for clothes, etc., yourself, if you deem it desirable.

Please make a confidential report in writing at the end of each voyage on each boy as to his abilities, general conduct, health, and aptitude for his profession. To the boys best reported on by you for all round ability and character, the managers are ready to give from time to time valuable prizes, such as sextant or binoculars.

Please let your chief officer have access to this letter. The managers invite from you and him the freest expression of advice and criticism. We hope you will both insist on the boys playing the game to the utmost and you may rest assured that we will loyally uphold your authority over them.

Finally, the managers remind you that these suggestions must not be allowed to interfere with the proper fulfilment of the instructions contained in the Company's standing orders to masters, mates and engineers.

Yours faithfully,

*

Appendix 4.

Amendment of Examination Regulations in wartime.

Extract: Ministry of Shipping Notice No. M.197. April, 1941.

Examinations of Masters, Mates and Engineers.
Wartime modifications of the Ministry of Shipping regulations.
Notice to candidates.
This notice cancels Notices Nos. M.185 & M.192.

Part 4:
Temporary Certificates as Second Mate (foreign-going) and Mate (Home Trade).
(a) The Ministry have decided as a war-time measure, to grant Temporary Certificates of Competency as Second Mate (foreign-going) and Mate (Home Trade).
(b) A candidate for a Temporary Certificate as Second Mate will be required to have performed three years' service at sea in foreign-going ships (or the equivalent, four years and six months in home trade ships) and a candidate for a Certificate as Mate (Home Trade) must have served three years at sea either in foreign-going or home trade ships. These periods of service will be calculated in accordance with the provisions of paragraphs 100 to 109 inclusive of the Examination Regulations, but no candidate will be admitted to the examination for a Temporary Certificate unless he has performed at least two years' sea service, as defined in paragraph 92 of the Regulations.
(c) When the holder of a Temporary Certificate of Competency as Second Mate (foreign-going) or Mate (Home Trade) has performed the sea service ordinarily required by the Examination Regulations, he may exchange this Certificate for an ordinary Certificate without further examination.
(d) Sea Service performed by the holder of a Temporary Certificate will not count as qualifying service for a higher Certificate until after the expiration of the time when he would normally have been eligible to sit for the examination for the ordinary certificate.

Part 5:
Age Limit for Examinations for Certificates as Second Mate (foreign-going) and Mate (Home-Trade).
During the war, candidates will be permitted to sit for the Second Mate's (foreign-going) and Mate's (Home Trade) examinations at the age of 19 instead of 20, if they have completed their qualifying service.

(Reproduced by kind permission of the Maritime & Coastguard Agency as the earlier Marine Safety Agency.)

NOTE.

Ministry of Transport Notice No. M.303.

From 1st January, 1948, the conditions set out in M.197 were revoked. Sea-time requirements and the minimum age of eligibility for the 2nd mate's examination reverted to pre-war regulations, i.e. 4 years (less any remission) and age 20.

Appendix 5.

National Service.

CONSCRIPTION dates from the Napoleonic wars, the French armies latterly composed of large numbers of conscripts. The belligerents of the Franco-German war of 1870 used conscripts, as also those of the following two world wars. Conscription was favoured by continental governments in a way generally avoided by successive British administrations unless and until it became necessary for the country's defence, but of course the navy had had its own peculiar system of conscription from early times, in the form of the press. Interestingly, this method of persuasion was peculiar to Great Britain, something of a perverse distinction for a self-professed maritime nation.

First World War.
    At first the army's strength was maintained by volunteers, but casualties made conscription necessary and it was introduced in January, 1916. For obvious reasons it was stopped immediately the armistice was declared. Men in some civilian occupations, e.g. mining, were exempt.

Second World War.
    In view of the increased level of technology and the training and skills it required the process of conscription was a much more selective business than hitherto, added to which was an acute awareness of the need to retain minimum numbers of skilled people in the country's key industries and civilian services. Nevertheless, while machinery reduced the numbers of men needed in battle, large numbers were required to operate the support and maintenance services that buttressed defence and followed advance. For the first time women were liable to call-up, between December, 1941 and January, 1947.

1939   May. Military Training Act. All men aged 20-21 liable to 6 months' service.
        3rd September. National Service (Armed Forces) Act. All men aged 20-41 liable to conscription.
1941   18th December. National Service (No.2) Act. Call-up into the army extended to men aged 18-51. Period of service extended to 18 months.
1946   National Service reduced to 12 months, then in
1945   increased to 2 years.
1947   National Service Act, amended 1948, 1950, 1955. Service reduced in
1949   to 18 months until

1950   Service extended to 2 years (Korean War, to 1953). Service from 1947 to 1955 included a requirement to serve for a further 3½ years in the TA or services reserves.

1956   Lower age increased to 19; part-time (TA & reserves) service reduced to 12 months.

1957   Defence white paper announced a proposed return to all-regular forces by the end of 1962. Age of call-up increased to 20, then 21.

1962   December. National Service ended. Last draft demobbed.

In both world wars the only ones exempt by statute (as distinct from special cases) were miners and merchant seamen, further exempt from peacetime national service together with agricultural workers. Under the 1947 Act men registering for call-up could state their preferences, and in 1955 (for example) 120,286 opted for the army, 82,449 for the air force, and 26,263 for the navy. Others expressed no preference or their conscientious objection, and the final allocation, reduced on health and other grounds, was: army 108,656; air force 42,072; navy 6,105.

It was a successful peacetime system, contrary to the prognostications of individuals and groups opposed to it.

*

Principal references.
Encyclopaedia Britannica, Vol.6, Vol.10.
Hansard, Vol.475, 1950.
Oxford Illustrated History of the British Army.
The Royal Navy Since 1945.

Appendix 6.

Captain's letter, t.s. *Mercury*.

CDR. R.F. Hoyle, RNR, *Mercury*'s last Captain-Superintendent, wrote the following letter to cadets and staff when the training-ship ceased its work in 1968:

There is no point in dwelling on sadness in this last magazine, for though the school is closing in its present form, *Mercury* will go on living. Indeed, she will live so long as any of you are left to say "I was at *Mercury*."

For all of us these last two terms have been worrying times, but thanks to the loyalty and hard work of the staff and the calm way they have overcome the many difficulties, the Ship has run as smoothly as ever. The great majority of cadets have faced the problem sensibly and by now have made arrangements for their immediate future.

Many of you are moving to other nautical schools, *HMS Conway*, the Nautical College, Pangbourne, the New Nautical School (*HMS Worcester*), the London Nautical School, and the Reardon-Smith Nautical College, Cardiff. You will find them different from *Mercury*, but at the same time you will find much that is familiar. To you and to the cadets moving to ordinary schools I say "remember *Mercury*."

Remember what *Mercury* has encouraged in you: discipline which starts with self-discipline; responsibility; reliability and hard work, whether in studies or in a boat's crew, playing for your Division or doing some rather dull territory [*sic*]; the ability to make decisions whether as cox'n of a cutter on a dirty night or sailing a dinghy on a Sunday afternoon; and most important of all your duty to your shipmates. Today these qualities are not easily acquired, and indeed there are many in this country who laugh at them and consider them unnecessary and square. You will find that "couldn't care less" is a poor shipmate in a Force 10 gale.

To all of you, staff and cadets, my wife and I send our grateful thanks for eight happy years, and wish you well for the future. We shall be staying at *Mercury* at least until Christmas, and if there is anything we can do, you only have to write. Good luck and good fortune to you all, and if life sometimes appears difficult and dull, just say "I was at *Mercury*" and be proud.

*

(Reproduced by kind permission of the TS *Mercury* Old Boys' Association.)

Appendix 7.

Sir Thomas Brassey: biographical note.

ELDEST of three sons of the wealthy railway contractor and civil engineer of the same name, Thomas Brassey was born at Stafford in 1836, educated at Rugby and Oxford, graduating with honours in law and modern history in 1859. While at school, holidays at Portsmouth and in France, and on yachting cruises, produced in him a love of the sea as well as a sound knowledge of French. He was elected to the Royal Yacht Squadron after coming down from Oxford.

Although called to the Parliamentary bar in 1866, he turned from law to a career in politics and was elected Liberal candidate for Devonport in June, 1865, only to be defeated in the following general election. Later, he gained the seat for Hastings, 1868-86, and pursued an interest in wages and the condition of the working classes as well as naval affairs including the formation of the RN Voluntary Artillery in 1873. He was made a civil Lord of Admiralty, 1880-83, then became its parliamentary secretary until 1885. From 1893-95 he was President of the Institution of Naval Architects, and from 1895-1900 a popular governor of Victoria, during which time he played a prominent part in the preparations for Australian federation, implemented by the Commonwealth Act of 1900. In 1908 he was made Warden of the Cinque Ports (to 1913). He was created baron in 1886, and earl in 1911.

He was a prolific author, publishing numerous articles, writing letters to *The Times*, issuing pamphlets, and giving lectures and presenting papers at meetings of various public institutions, mostly dealing with matters of labour and naval and maritime affairs. He was founder of the *Naval Annual* (1886) and wrote *British Seamen* (1877) and the five-volume *The British Navy* (1883).

The first private yachtsman to pass the examination for Master Mariner (a conditional distinction that did not entitle him to command of a commercial ship), yachting was a lifelong interest, and he completed a circumnavigation in *Sunbeam* 1876-77, the yacht he later (1916) donated to the government of India for service as a hospital-ship. Gladstone chose him for his second government, but he was a poor debater and was not selected to serve on Gladstone's next administration (1885).

Although his tireless industry made a weighty contribution to reform as the sailing navy gave way to the new steam-driven armoured force, his instinct was to maintain and make do rather than venture into new territory and utilise new material: he favoured the idea of AMC's and upgrading the armament of old warships over expenditure on new construction, and proposed making fishermen reservists instead of running a proper naval reserve, failing to realise the disadvantage to which such ideas put the country in the face of foreign technological advance. However, his kindly, genial outlook and sympathetic views, combined with a great capacity for personal industry, carried him through the problems he variously uncovered and tackled, and he spared neither himself nor his considerable resources in his support of the patriotic causes he espoused. Among the several organisations that were greatly indebted to him was, of course, the Devitt & Moore Ocean Training Scheme, which could not have managed without his financial, moral and political support.

He died in London in February, 1918.

*

Principal references.
Encyclopaedia Britannica, Vol.4.
The Oxford Companion to Ships & the Sea.

Appendix 8.

A father's letter to his son.

THIS letter was written by Mr George Galloway, Chief Inspector of Works at Enugu, Nigeria, to his son, aged 17, about to join his first ship in 1957.

Enugu.
26.3.57.

Dear Tom,

I've had so many letters from you without replying. This one is a "must" especially as it will probably be the last one before you are off.

I know it is soon now as I remember you saying "Early April" which could be next week!

You must look quite an Admiral in your new uniform & as I've already told Mum remember and get a snap taken before you go off.

You speak of "repayment some day", but the only repayment Mum and I want is to see you getting on, and when you do progress, it won't be just your chest that sticks out.

I hope it is one of the bigger ships you get, to start, as apart from the comfort there are more people so more chance of making friends and a lot will depend on your officers whether it is a happy ship or not, but for your own sake I hope they keep your nose to the grindstone, as sea life can be very monotonous and tends to make one lazy.

You won't have to think of a hobby to pass the time at the beginning, as you will have your lessons to keep you busy for some years. Stick into them, especially the harder ones – trig etc as these are the ones most important in navigation; the seamanship comes by experience. Never gloss over them – be very particular, and if you are not sure of anything, ask the officer in charge of you for assistance.

You will be sure to meet some queer characters, both on shipboard and in port but you will soon learn to distinguish the good from the bad.

You always get the odd bloke trying to borrow a quid, and a good idea is to play "broke" to your best friends.

In ports there are always the "sharks" trying to sell things and "do" you, so rather than learn the hard way, take the advice from some of the old hands. In foreign ports, either go ashore with an old hand, or take advice from one before going.

You will meet a queer lot of religions in your travels and you must be tolerant and respectful of them and never be drawn into arguments on religious subjects.

I can't give any advice on smoking and drinking as it's every man for himself as far as that goes – the main thing is no excesses.

Along with wine and song, you know what the other great danger is and you will find plenty of them in every port – real smashers too, but with such rottenness and wickedness as you never knew existed. I don't have to tell you to steer clear of that sort of thing as your head is screwed on right. I think somebody in Shell told you to stop thinking, even of girl-friends and it's good advice to start. Once you are "made" you will meet up with some nice lassie, and shape your future then.

Very often you will be lonely and fed up – everyone does who is away from home, but you must fight against it and remember it's your duty to a chosen job.

Look ahead to leaves.

Write regularly to Mum and drop me an occasional one letting me know how you are getting on.

Don't ever be stuck for anything. Let Mum or I know and we'll see what can be done. I know there will be instruments and some items of kit you will require later so don't stint yourself for the want of letting us know.

As you will probably visit ports all over the world a good thing is to keep an address book of people you could possibly look up, such as Uncle Jack near Durban and so on. Make my name the first and if ever you are going to be in Lagos or Port Harcourt, give me 3 days notice by cable of your ETA and I'll be there to see you!

Failing that we will just have to try to make our leaves meet up.

My first one starts in October but that will be a bit quick for you though you never know.

The big thing now is for you to stick in and do your best and above all look after yourself.

Never, even if the opportunity arises, try to be a hero but always think of No.1 – yourself.

I'm putting in a few P.O's to give you a start with your pocket money when you are on your way and as I've already said, sing out if you need anything.

Good luck on your big adventure lad and God Bless.

Love, Dad.

X.

*

(Reproduced by kind permission of Captain Tom Galloway.)

Appendix 9.

Mate's standing orders, mv *Katha*, c.1954.
(The British & Burmese Steam Navigation Co. Ltd.)

<u>Standing orders for cadets.</u>

The senior cadet is responsible to the chief officer for the cadets' work and the cleaning of their quarters. He has authority to keep order in the half-deck and to make certain that each cadet works to the best of his ability.

Cadets' cabins must be kept clean and tidy; beds to be made by 0900. The way your quarters are kept, also your general behaviour, will reflect on your home life and upbringing.

The bathroom must be maintained in a clean and sanitary condition.

No items of ship's gear to be kept in cabins or bathroom.

Care must be taken with ship's property.

There must be no fraternising with the native crew. Do not be impertinent to the serang or tindal if dealing with them in the course of the ship's work.

When you have occasion to enter the officers' accommodation do not cause a breach of the peace by whistling or making raucous sounds.

When on bridge watch, wear uniform. Do not show slovenly tendencies such as leaning, lounging or putting hands in trousers pockets.

Go to the saloon for meals clean and properly dressed. Remember your table manners. The use of bad language at any time is to be deplored; this is particularly so at table. Remember that a lapse into habitual bad language may result in a distressing slip of the tongue when at home.

Drinking of beer and spirits by cadets on board ship is forbidden by the company. A serious view will be taken of cadets who come on board intoxicated.

There are bad habits, indicated in the previous paragraphs, which when seen in others should not, <u>for your own good</u>, be imitated.

Any reasonable request or complaint should be brought to the notice of the chief officer, preferably by the senior cadet. If necessary, or if requested, the matter may be taken up by the chief officer with the captain. It is forbidden to deal directly with the company in the above and the Marine Superintendent stated in June 1954 that he will not tolerate any requests or complaints unless they have been passed through the proper channels, as outlined above.

APPENDIX 9: MATE'S STANDING ORDERS

Be respectful and obedient to your officers. It is expected you will become officers yourselves but remember that you must learn to obey before you can learn to command.

The use of the traditional, seamanlike reply to a command "Aye aye, sir" is not outmoded and is to be preferred to such disrespectful slang as "Right-oh", "OK", etc.

Time for study will be given at weekends when at sea and you may ask assistance from the officers. An interest will be taken in your training if you show keenness and aptitude.

Be conscientious and take a pride in your work, no matter what it is. Do not disparage your ship. She is your home when on a voyage, so take a pride in her appearance and efficiency and do your best to keep a good standard on board.

*

(Reproduced from the handwritten text in his cadet's work-book by kind permission of the late Mr Iain Baldock.)

Appendix 10.

The *Nerbudda* Concert.

NOTICE
————

PRIOR TO THEIR COMMAND PERFORMANCE BEFORE HIS OCEANIC MAJESTY
KING NEPTUNE
"THE NERBUDDA TROUPERS"
ANNOUNCE THAT THEY WILL GIVE ONE (THE ONLY) PUBLIC PERFORMANCE
OF THEIR
1934 TROPICAL REVELS
ON SATURDAY, AUGUST 18th at 7.30 p.m.
TENSE DRAMATIC MOMENTS!!
HILARIOUS COMEDY!!
HAUNTING MELODY!!
PATHOS!!
WIT!!
FOR THE SPECIAL BENEFIT OF THE LADIES WE ARE FEATURING
SERGEANT BILL!!
AND OTHER WELL-KNOWN SHEIKS!!
ALSO LOVELY LADIES!!
SINGING, DANCING AND OTHER ATTRACTIONS!!
100% ENJOYMENT!!

***

FORGET THE B.O.T. FOR ONE NIGHT OF MUSIC, MIRTH AND MELODY!!

————

PROGRAMME

1. **SEA PIE**   The Old Salts

2. Selected   Chamberlain

   3. Sketch – **FALSE LOVE**
   Mrs Ogsbody - Adcock
   Author   -   Bunn
   Miss Harwood - Sach

4. Selected   Dr Heming

   5. Sketch – **AH!**
   Wife   -   Oliver
   Husband   -   Suter
   1st lover - Chamberlain

2nd lover	-	Adcock
Policeman	-	Bailey

6. AROUND THE WORLD IN TEN MINUTES

7. Selected   A.B. Allen

8. CLARENCE COLLECTS IT

Duke of Clarence	-	Clarke
1st Murderer	-	Mr Turner
2nd Murderer	-	Dr Heming

Interval

9. THE HARMONY KINKS
Bell, Chamberlain, Keene

10. Sketch – THE MISTAKEN SINGER

Father	-	Adcock
Suitor	-	Clarke
Daughter	-	Oliver

11. SAM AND HIS MUSKET
Crow

12. Sketch – THE PREVIOUS REPORTER
Editor - Palmer
Reporters - Braidwood, Oliver, Suter, Crow

13. Selected   A.B. Charlton

14. COCK ROBIN
Walton, Crow, Blackett, Rendall

15. Extracts from Shakespeare   Cooper

16. THE VILLAGE BAND

Mr Snodgrass, Conductor	-	Taylor
Mr Blatherskite, Drummer	-	Braidwood
Mrs Winterbottom	-	Griffiths
Mrs Higgs	-	Blackett
Rev. Pickles, Flautist	-	Harris
Joe Bloggs, Banjoist	-	Crow
Joe Bunwort, Pianist	-	Bailey

———

The King

———

The second concert presented by the Nerbudda Concert Party was, considering the deplorable lack of stage props, lighting, and the shortness of notice for preparations, a definite success, and the ready acclamation of the audience thoroughly backs up this statement.

The show commenced with a skit on Sea Shanties and pully hauly, all went well but the act was abruptly ended by some dirty work behind the scenes. Some son of a sea cook let go the hauling rope, and our Shanteymen finished in a heap.

Chamberlain, a member of our now famous Harmony Kinks, sang two songs, accompanying himself on a banjolele. We all thoroughly enjoyed this and look forward to more.

"False Love" was a sketch by the junior element, in which Adcock as Mrs Ogsbody, the char-woman, excelled. The story concerns an author who engaged a lady secretary, whose charms he used as an inspiration for his writing, but Mrs Ogsbody did not give them the seclusion their inspirations merited. Mrs Ogsbody's "Oxford Brown" is "Oxford Brawn" a la Goanese.

Dr Heming, the ship's Surgeon, sang three songs from his repertoire, all of which we thoroughly enjoyed.

Next was a sketch entitled "Ah," being a play on the different meanings of "Ah" when exclaimed in various ways. An unfaithful wife and lover – enter husband Ah! (Triumph) bang!! enter policeman Ah! (retribution), then the wife's cry Ah! (fear), the awakening of another lover, and the lazy Ah! of a tired and sleepy man.

"Round the world in Ten Minutes" was a tour of the universe successfully conducted by Cadet Clarke. In the short time allotted, we visited London with its Eros bright and shining, Seville with its onion sellers, Port Said with its box-wallahs (Palmer needed no talent to take this part). Delhi with its babbling multitudes, Australia – Brisbane with its sports and spade work, a ship in mid-ocean (but we all know what happens on board, so nuff said!). Chicago of yesterday and to-day, still the same just one killing after another, then Dakar which we all love so much, that flower of West Africa whose inhabitants are so particular about their boats. Thence once more to London with a bedraggled

Eros as one of those periodical showers which always greets us on arrival home, is once more on the spot.

"Sparks", our dear old Oirish Bhoy, sang us two songs about "Taties" and "Divils", and though the brogue made them hard to understand, we all appreciated the effort, and enjoyed that twinkle in those smiling Oirish Oiyes.

Chamberlain sang again once more for us, on this occasion "Dear Old Fashioned Town."

Allen (AB), our Cornish canary, sang "Paddy McGinty's Goat" and "Glorious Devon" in that pleasant voice of his.

After this we had an exerpt from Shakespeare acted as he meant it to be; it was from Richard III, and concerned the murder of the Duke of Clarence in the Tower of London. Afterwards the scene was acted as interpreted by Hiram C. Boloney – Film Magnate from the Pacific coast. Clarence gets it in the neck, he is bumped off by two bums with a pineapple, and all for a thousand grand [sic!].

Then came the interval with refreshments and the babble of pent up speech, discussing the various turns.

The show continued after the interval with a sketch entitled "The Mistaken Singer." The daughter, a singer, asks the boy friend to call and see Pa, who is anxious to sell his car, a "Singer." When the two meet, one talks about his car, and the other about his "sweetie." Various complications arise, and the poor girlie loses her dearly beloved.

Bloggs at it again – our Yorkshire lad told us about Sam and a dropped musket at the Battle of Waterloo.

"Previous Reporters" – an editor, in keeping with the modern thirst for speed, desires news of the moment, but an energetic reporter gets ahead of him.

Charlton (AB) entertained us once more, with two of his monologues, "Shooting of Dan McGrew" and "Mad Carew"; we could not help but listen spellbound to both of these.

"Cock Robin" – all the artists in this were would-be singers and fighters, but the little fellow proved to be top dog in both.

Cooper as Marcus K. Antony, entertained us with Mark Antony's famous speech Americanised, and Oh! boy he sure did put it over.

Our last sketch was the "Village Band" which was a mixed gathering of artists who played various instruments. I am still trying to guess what band they represented, but I have a suspicion that it was the Band of Hope. They made enough noise – but the cat which was found in the piano can be blamed for that.

Without our accomplished pianist, C.H. Bailey, the concert could not have been the success it was. Our whole-hearted thanks are due to him for his delightful accompaniments, particularly in Charlton's monologues. We appreciate his talent and his generosity in contributing so much to our enjoyment.

So ended a pleasant evening, and we look forward to many more of this category.

[Cadet] F.D.G. Challis.

*

(Reproduced from the ss *Nerbudda* Cadets' Magazine No.2, October 1934, by kind permission of the Peninsular & Oriental Steam Navigation Co. Ltd.)

Appendix 11.

An apprentice.

*F*OUR *of the Seven Ages of Man* appeared first(?) in the British & Commonwealth Group's house magazine of April, 1959, the work of A.C. Linsley, 3rd Officer of the *Scottish Lion*. Since then different versions have appeared, adapted or adulterated to fit particular settings and changing times, none as good as the original and none acknowledging Linsley. The four ages were those of the apprentice, the third officer, the second officer and the chief officer, archetypes rather than caricatures, all answering the question "What is - ?"

What is an Apprentice?

CLOSELY following those carefree days of childhood comes the blissful state of Apprenticeship. Having done two years' solitary at some training ship or other, our little hero joins his first ship as a junior deck officer*. An apprentice is a deck officer with spots on his face. He is Nelson with holes in his socks; Raleigh with a rip in his pants; Professor Picard with an ullage tape in his hands.

Apprentices come in assorted shapes and sizes: big and burly, thin and wiry, fat and sleepy. All are hungry. All have a hidden ambition to eat more than the store-room will carry. No-one else can get so much into such a small locker: three weeks' dirty dhobi; a broken gramophone; a loudspeaker; half a coil of point-line; a dozen cigarette-tins of assorted paints; three hundredweight of brass; the hydrometer everyone has been looking for; last night's cheese sandwiches; fifteen pounds of cotton waste, and a tin of pineapple chunks.

The Apprentice likes girls, cooks, dances, rock'n'roll, a beer when no-one is looking, the last ship, time off, double helpings, pin-ups and a dirty face. He hates dhobying, the Mate, overtime, topping-off, draining, measuring-up, polishing brass, Chief Stewards, cargo clusters, *Nicholls's Concise Guide*, correspondence courses, MOT examiners, the Liverpool School, Sunday inspection and washing his hands. He can be found eating, dodging, sleeping, lying, in the galley, in the shower, in the soup, out of cigarettes, out of money, out of sea-time and out of reach.

To his mother he is her brave little boy; to his girl he is Prince Charming in a naval uniform; to the officers the lowest form of animal life. When the tank overflows, who is it that says, "Sir, I thought you knew there was two feet off that ullage tape"? Or who says whilst loading tea, "Sir, they've been loading the wrong mark for over three hours now"? None other than that underpaid, over-worked little hero, the apprentice.

*Not strictly correct, but no matter.

(With acknowledgments to the British & Commonwealth Group and Third Officer Linsley.)

Appendix 12.

Certificates.

A few examples of certificates accumulated by the apprentice, including the first qualifying him as a ship's officer.

1.   School ship *Conway* Extra [leaving] Certificate, 1933.

2.   Hull Trinity House Navigation School [leaving] Certificate of Remission, 1964.

3.   MNTB Certificate of Merit, 1941.

4.   Ordinary [square-rig] Certificate of Competency as Second Mate, 1867.

5.   Certificate of Competency as Second Mate (Foreign-Going), 1944.

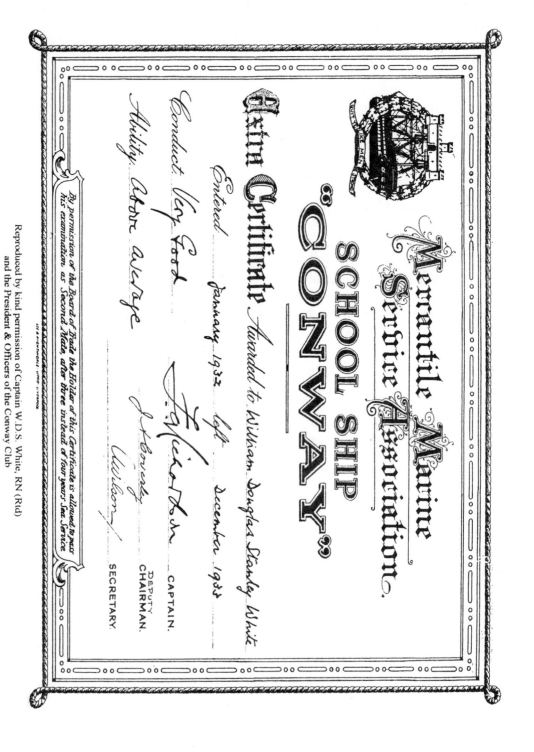

Mercantile Marine Service Association.

SCHOOL SHIP "CONWAY"

Extra Certificate Awarded to William Douglas Stanley White

Entered — January 1932 left — December 1933

Conduct Very Good

Ability Above Average

— CAPTAIN.

DEPUTY
CHAIRMAN.

SECRETARY.

By permission of the Board of Trade the Holder of this Certificate is allowed to pass his examination as Second Mate, after three instead of four years' Sea Service

Reproduced by kind permission of Captain W.D.S. White, RN (Rtd) and the President & Officers of the Conway Club

HULL TRINITY HOUSE   NAVIGATION SCHOOL

CADET   DEPARTMENT

This Certificate entitles

David Malcolm Shaw

to six months remission of sea service under Paragraph 109 (II) of the Ministry of Transport Regulations relating to the Examination of Masters and Mates.

He completed the

(a) Full Three Years Cadet Training Course

(b) ~~Twelve Months Cadet Training Course~~

on 25th Mar., 1964, and reached a satisfactory standard of proficiency. His conduct was good.

Dated this 25th day of March 19 64

.... Master Warden, Trinity House.

.... Chairman of School Committee.

.... Headmaster.

THE MERCHANT NAVY TRAINING BOARD

presents this

Certificate of Merit

To Mr. *R. Montgomery* in recognition of his careful attention to instruction and application to study as displayed by the high standard of work submitted by him in his 1st year Examination 19 41

Chairman of the Board.

Vice Chairman of the Board.

Secretary.

Reproduced by kind permission of Mr R. Montgomery, with acknowledgements to the late Merchant Navy Training Board

To The Lords of the Committee of Privy Council for Trade.

Certificate of Competency,

as

SECOND MATE,

To Thomas Horace Rawlins.

Whereas it has been reported to us that you have been found duly qualified to fulfil the duties of Second Mate in the Merchant Service we do hereby in pursuance of the Merchant Shipping Act 1854 grant you this Certificate of Competency.

Given under the Seal of The Board of Trade, this Twenty fourth day of September 1867.

By order of the Board

Registered

Officers of
the Marine
Department.

Entered at the General Register and Record Office of Seamen on the 25th day of September 1867.

Reproduced by kind permission of the estate of the late T.H. Rawlins
and the Maritime & Coastguard Agency

CERTIFICATE OF COMPETENCY

AS

SECOND MATE

OF A FOREIGN-GOING STEAMSHIP

No. 49460

To George Henry Harrison

WHEREAS you have been found duly qualified to fulfil the duties of Second Mate of a Foreign-going Steamship in the Merchant Service, the Minister of War Transport, in pursuance of the Merchant Shipping Acts, the Minister of Shipping (Transfer of Functions) Order, 1939, and the Ministers of the Crown (Minister of War Transport) Order, 1941, hereby grants you this Certificate of Competency.

SIGNED BY AUTHORITY OF THE MINISTER OF WAR TRANSPORT and dated this .... 25th .... day

of .... May 19 44

Countersigned

Registrar General

Deputy Director General,
Ministry of War Transport.

REGISTERED AT THE OFFICE OF THE REGISTRAR GENERAL OF SHIPPING AND SEAMEN.

GLOSSARY
of abbreviations & selected terms

<u>A</u>
AB	able seaman (<u>a</u>ble-<u>b</u>odied, but also possibly short for <u>ab</u>le)
ACF	Army Cadet Force, see also OTC.
AMC	armed merchant cruiser (converted merchant ship)
ATC	Air Training Corps (Air Cadets)
ATS	Alternative Training Scheme (marine engineering)

<u>B</u>
BA	Buenos Aires.
BAC	British Apprentice Club
bhandary	cook (Hindi)
BI	British India (Steam Navigation Co. Ltd.)
BISN Co.	-do-
BOT	Board of Trade (usually referring to its Marine Dept. and including that department of the Privy Council before the BOT assumed authority)
BP	British Petroleum
BR	British Railways
BRNC	Britannia Royal Naval College.
BTC	British Tanker Co. (later the BP Tanker Co.)
burra	big, large, senior (Hindi)

<u>C</u>
CC	(i)cadet captain (ii) correspondence course.
Cdr.	commander.
CO	(i) chief officer (ii) commanding officer.
cog (C.14th.)	single-mast, single-sail square-rigged, fully-decked vessel equipped with sweeps, c.90ft long.
compactum	cabin fitting consisting of bulkhead mirror & shelf above a washbasin & cabinet containing a slop-bucket; the washbasin is filled from an outside supply by bucket and emptied by tipping it back on its mounting hinges, and the slop-bucket's contents thrown overboard.
CPO	chief petty officer/cadet captain
crowd	(colloq.) deck crew (hands)
CSE	Certificate of Secondary Education.
c.t.l.	constructive total loss

D

d.	penny (old)
Decca 45	make & model of marine radar set.
DEMS	defensively-equipped merchant ship/s.
dhobi/dhoby	(n. or v.) soiled/clean laundry or to wash clothes (Hindi)
double	to pass or navigate round a cape from a point on one side to a corresponding point on the other.
DR	(i) dead reckoning (ii) Decline to Report (on seaman's conduct)
DTI	Dept. of Trade & Industry (its Marine Dept., successor to the BOT/MOT etc)
DOT	Dept of Transport
dw	deadweight.
dwt	deadweight tons/tonnes or tonnage.

E

(E)	engineer (RN)
EA	East African (money)
ED	Elder Dempster (Lines)
EDH	Efficient Deckhand (certificate & rating)
EIC	(The Honourable) East India Co. See also HEIC.
EK	Engineering Knowledge (in BOT/DTI etc. examinations)
ETR	Evan Thomas, Radcliffe & Co.

F

FG/f.g.	Foreign-Going (voyage, agreement or certificate of competency). See also HT.
FOC/foc	flag of convenience.
focsle	forecastle.

G

G	good (of seaman's conduct)
GCE	General Certificate of Education.
GCSE	General Certificate of Secondary Education.
GPO	General Post Office
GSK	General Ship Knowledge (in BOT/DTI etc. examinations, covering naval architecture, structures & deck fittings)
gt	gross tons/tonnes or tonnage.

H

HEIC	Honourable East India Company.
HMG	His/Her Majesty's Government / heavy machine-gun.
HMS	His/Her Majesty's Ship.

HND	Higher National Diploma.
hoveller	Deal boatman (the hovel was a local design of oared boat, used for any convenient profitable purpose)
hp	horsepower
HT/h.t.	Home Trade (voyage, agreement or certificate of competency). Confined to European waters between the Elbe and Brest, including the coastal waters of the British Isles, Ireland and the Channel Is.

I
ICI	Imperial Chemical Industries.
ICS	(i) Indian Civil Service (ii) International Correspondence School.
ID	identity/identification (card or book)
IOM	Isle of Man.

J
JLC	Junior Leading Cadet.

K
kalassie	Indian or Pakistani deckhand or rating (Hindi)
knot	sea mile per hour: a unit of speed, originally measured by the number of knots, or intervals marked by knots, in the log-line as they ran off the reel, counted by the officer overseeing the operation of heaving the log, and timed by a 28-second sand-glass. The interval was about 47ft (it varied very slightly), representing the sea mile of 6080ft. Thus, 5 knots running off the reel while the sand-glass emptied indicated a speed of 5 sea miles per hour, or simply 5 knots. *Knots per hour* is a misnomer – strictly speaking a unit of acceleration, and certainly not the number of knots counted in an hour! Often quoted (or misquoted) in books about the sea, and often by seamen, who should know better.

L
lancha	launch or lighter (Sp.)
lascar	general term for an Indian or Pakistani seaman of any rating or function, including engine-room crew.
LEA	Local Education Authority.
LCC	London County Council.
Lt./lt.	lieutenant

M
MAC	merchant aircraft carrier (converted)

malim sahib	deck officer (literally, the one who knows, or the knowledgeable one) (Hindi)
Marconi Mk.IV	make & model of marine radar set.
MAR	Mid-Apprenticeship Release (course)
MCA	Maritime & Coastguard Agency (successor to the MSA)
MCR	Mid-Cadetship Release (course)
MET	Marine Engineering Technician.
MM	(British) Mercantile Marine.
MMO	Mercantile Marine (Port) Office.
MMSA	Mercantile Marine Services Association.
MN	(British) Merchant Navy.
MNTB	Merchant Navy Training Board.
MNWB	Merchant Navy Welfare Board.
MOT	Ministry of Transport (successor to the BOT)
MOWT	Ministry of War Transport.
MSA	(i)Merchant Seaman/Shipping Act (ii) Marine Safety Agency (successor to the Marine Dept of the BOT/DTI etc)
mv	motor vessel.

N

NATO	North Atlantic Treaty Organisation.
nef (C.14th.)	single-mast, single-sail square-rigged vessel, partly-decked, 80-90ft long.
NCP	The Nautical College, Pangbourne.
new chum	first-term cadet (*Conway*); sometimes first-voyager.
NMB	National Maritime Board.
nrt	net register tons/tonnes or tonnage.
NYFD	New York Fire Dept.
NZSCo	New Zealand Shipping Co.

O

"O" level	Ordinary (grade of GCE)
OBO	oil/bulk ore (carrier)
ONC	Ordinary National Certificate.
OND	Ordinary National Diploma (above ONC)
OOW	officer of the watch.
OPEC	Organisation of Petroleum Exporting Countries
OS	ordinary seaman (MN)
OTC	Officers' Training Corps (schools'). See also ACF.
OTS	Devitt & Moore's (i) Ocean Training Scheme & (ii) Ocean Training Ships Ltd.

P

P/A	probationary/acting (RN rank)
pani	water (or fruit juice, as *lime pani*) (Hindi)
PD	Port Dinorwic (on Menai Straits)
PO	petty officer.
POW	prisoner of war.
ps	paddle steamer
psi	pounds per square inch (pressure).
PSNC	Pacific Steam Navigation Co.
punkah-louvre	ducted fan-driven fresh-air ventilation system for ship's accommodation; strictly, the manufacturer's trade-name, derived from the Hindi *punkah* – fan.

Q

QB	Quarter-boy (*Conway*): a cadet in his last term, implying (depending on conduct and ability) 12 months' remission of the required service of 4 years as an apprentice. Hence a boy with a quarter of his time completed.
Q-ship	merchant vessel fitted with disguised offensive armament used as a lure for U-boats, a WW1 ploy that met with variable success.

R

RAE	Royal Aircraft (earlier, Aeronautical) Establishment.
RAS	replenishment at sea.
RE	Royal Engineers.
RM	Royal Mail (referring to either RML or RMSP)
RML	Royal Mail Lines.
RMSP	Royal Mail Steam Packet Co., forerunner of RML.
RN	Royal Navy.
RNCVR	Royal Naval Coast Volunteer Reserve
RNR	Royal Naval Reserve
RNSVR	Royal Naval Supplementary Volunteer Reserve (see RNVR(S))
RNVR	Royal Naval Volunteer Reserve
RNVR(S)	Royal Naval Volunteer Reserve (Supplementary branch)
ro-ro	roll-on, roll-off (vehicle carrier, usually a ferry type)
R/T	radio-telephony

S

s.	shilling
SATS	South African Training Ship
SASL	S. American Saint Line
Scawegian	Scandinavian (usually Norwegian) seaman.

SCC	Sea Cadet Corps
SCOTEC	Scottish Technical Education Council.
serang	lascar bosun/head man/overseer (Hindi)
SES	Seafarers' Education Service.
SF	Shipping Federation.
ship (sail)	3 or more masts, square-rigged on all.
SLC	Senior Leading Cadet.
S.N.	steam navigation (as in Co.)
S.S./ss	steam-ship.

T

TA	Territorial Army.
tab-nab/s	cake or small cakes served with tea/coffee; sometimes biscuits.
TEC	Technical Education Council.
TH	Trinity House.
tindal	serang's assistant; lascar bosun's mate (Hindi)
topass	lascar cleaner/sweeper (Hindi)
TS/t.s.	training-ship
T2	wartime-built (WW2) tanker of about 16,000 dwt.

U

USSR	Union of Soviet Socialist Republics

V

VG	very good (of seaman's conduct)

W

wallah	man, person, functionary, as *dhobi-wallah* – laundryman (Hindi)
WCSA	west (Pacific) coast of South America.
W/T	wireless telegraphy.
WW1/2	World War, First/Second.

X

Y

Z

SELECT BIBLIOGRAPHY & REFERENCES

1. QUOTED/MENTIONED IN TEXT

1.1 Books.

Adams, Bill. *Ships & Memories*. Brighton, Sussex. Teredo, 1975.

Armitage, A. *Cadet to Commodore*. London. Cassell, 1925.

Ayre-Walker, B. *Ahoy!* London. Cassell, 1938.

Baber, A.E. *Voyages & Fragments*. Bristol. Cathedral, 1985.

Baillie, D.G.O. *A Sea Affair*. London. Hutchinson, 1957.

Barnes, W.M. *Rolling Home*. London. Cassell, 1931.

Bestic, A.A. *Kicking Canvas*. London. Evans Bros., 1959.

Birch, H. Clarkson. *An Old Sailor's Yarn*. Ipswich, 1914. (No publisher attributed: quoted in *The China Bird*. See MacGregor, D.R.)

Bisset, J. *Sail Ho!* London. Angus & Robertson, 1958.

Bisset, J. *Tramps & Ladies* (reprint). Wellingborough, Northants. Patrick Stevens, 1988.

Bone, D.W. *The Brassbounder*. London. Duckworth, 1913.

Boothby, H.B. *Spunyarn*. London. G.T. Foulis, 1938.

Boughton, G.P. *Seafaring*. London. Faber & Gwyer, 1926.

Brassey, T. *The British Navy, Vol. V. Part V: British Seamen*. London. Longmans, Green, 1883.

Bullen, F.T. *A Son of the Sea*. London. James Nisbet, 1908.

Chatterton, E. Keble. *Seamen All*. London. Heinemann, 1924.

Chatterton, E. Keble. *The Old East Indiamen*. London. T. Werner Laurie, c.1920.

Clements, R. *A Gypsy of the Horn*. London. Heath Cranton, 1925.

Compton, H. (Ed.) *A Master Mariner*. London. T. Fisher Unwin, 1908.

Course, A.G. *Painted Ports*. London. Hollis & Carter, 1961.

Course, A.G. *The Merchant Navy*. London. Frederick Muller, 1963.

Cowden, J.E. *Elder Dempster Fleet History, 1852-1986*. (Fragment: no publisher attributed.)

Cunningham, W. *Growth of English Industry & Commerce, Early & Middle Ages*. CUP, 1915.

Darwin, C. *Origin of Species etc.* (Fragment: no publisher attributed), 1859.

Dickens, C. *The Adventures of Oliver Twist*. London. Macmillan, 1897.

Downie, W.I. *Reminiscences of a Blackwall Midshipman*. London. W.J. Ham-Smith, 1912.

Eames, A. (Ed.) *Ship Master*. Gwynedd Archives Service, 1980.

Gee, M. *Captain Fraser's Voyages*. London. Stanford Maritime, 1979.

Gollock, G.A. *At the Sign of the Flying Angel*. London. Longmans, Green, 1930.

Green, S.R. *Whither, O Ship?* London. Peter Owen, 1989.

Hayes, B. *Hull Down*. London. Cassell, 1925.

Horn, T. *Way for a Sailor*. Bristol. Scan, 1979.

Jeffreys, D.E. *Maritime Memories of Cardiff*. Risca, Gwent. Starling, 1978.

King, G.A.B. *A Love of Ships*. Emsworth, Hants. Kenneth Mason, 1991.

Kinghorn, A.W. *Before the Box-Boats*. Emsworth, Hants. Kenneth Mason, 1983.

Lamb, J. *Backward Thinking*. London. John Lamb, 1954.

Large, V. *Windjammer 'Prentice.* London. Jarrolds, 1971.

Lindsay, J.M. *Sailor in Steam.* London. Angus & Robertson, 1966.

Lindsay, W.S. *History of Merchant Shipping & Ancient Commerce.* London,1874. (No publisher attributed: quoted in *A New History of British Shipping.* See Hope, R.)

Lubbock, B. (Ed.) *Barlow's Journal.* London, 1934. (No publisher attributed: quoted in *The Merchant Navy.* See Hope, R.)

Lubbock, B. *The China Clippers.* (2nd Edn.) Glasgow. Brown, Son & Ferguson, 1973.

Lubbock, B. *The Last of the Windjammers, Vol.2.* (1st Edn. reprint) Glasgow. B, S & F, 1970.

Making, V.L. *In Sail & Steam.* London. Sidgwick & Jackson, 1937.

Masefield, J. (1)*The* Conway. (Revised Edn.) London. Heinemann, 1953.
(2) *Collected Poems.* London. Heinemann, 1935.

McFee, W. *Sir Martin Frobisher.* London. John Lane/ Bodley Head, 1928.

Melville, H. *Moby Dick.* London. Collins, 1953.

Meyerstein, E.H.W. (Ed.) *Adventures by Sea of Edward Coxere.* OUP, 1945.

Millet, J.L.V. *Yarns of an Old Shellback.* London. Methuen, 1925.

Millington, E.C. *Seamen in the Making.* London. J.D. Potter, 1935.

Moffat, H.Y. *From Ship's Boy to Skipper.* Paisley. Alexander Gardner, 1910.

Morton, L. *The Long Wake.* London. Routledge & Kegan Paul, 1968.

Morris, R. *The Captain's Lady.* London. Chatto & Windus, 1985.

Moss, H.J. *Windjammer to Westminster.* London. Methuen, 1941.

Munro, D.J. *Roaring Forties.* London. Sampson Low, Marston, 1929.

Murray, M. *Union-Castle Chronicle.* London. Longmans, Green, 1953.

Owen, H. *Journey from Obscurity.* (Abridged) OUP, 1988.

Powell, L.H. *The Shipping Federation, 1890-1950.* London. The Shipping Federation, 1950.

Radford J. *Pilot Aboard.* London. Blackwood, 1966.

Rawson, G. *Sea Prelude.* London. Blackwood, 1958.

Riddell, W.G. *Adventures of an Obscure Victorian.* Greenock. James McKelvie, 1964.

Roberts, A.J. *Let Go Fore 'n' Aft.* London. Minerva, 1996.

Runciman, W. *Before the Mast – And After.* London. T. Fisher Unwin, 1924.

Runciman, W. *Collier Brigs & Their Sailors.* London. Conway Maritime, 1926.

Runciman, W. *Windjammers & Sea Tramps.* London. The Unicorn, 1902.

"Shalimar" (F.C. Hendry). *A Windjammer's Half-deck.* Penguin, 1940.

Shankland, P. & Hunter, A. *Malta Convoy.* London. Collins, 1961.

"Sinbad" (A.E. Dingle). *A Modern Sinbad.* London. Harrap, 1933.

Smith, C. Fox. *Ship Alley.* (2nd Edn.) London. Methuen, 1925.

Stafford, F.H. *How to Go to Sea in the Merchant Service.* Glasgow. James Brown & Son, 1912.

Stenhouse, J.R. *Cracker Hash.* London. Percival Marshall, 1955.

Stephens, L. & Lee, S. (Eds.) Dictionary of National Biography, Vols. V, VI. OUP, 1960.

Thomas, D. *The Fatal Flaw.* Ystradowen, Carmarthenshire. Phaiacia, 2001.

Thompson, D. *History of Hull Trinity House School.* Hull. T.H. School, 1988.

Villiers, A.J. *The Way of a Ship.* London. Hodder & Stoughton, 1954.

Watts, C. *Joseph Conrad* (biographical study). Plymouth. Northcote House, 1994.

Whitfield, G.V. *Fifty Thrilling Years at Sea.* London. Hutchinson, c.1937.

Whitwell, N.R. *Green Seas, Green Fields.* Edinburgh. Pentland, 1993.

Worsley, F. *First Voyage in a Square-rigged Ship.* London. Geoffrey Bles, 1938.

Yeates, V.M. *Winged Victory.* (Reprint). St Alban's, Herts. Grenada/Mayflower, 1974.

1.2 Booklets.

Ainsley, T.L. *Ainsley's Extra Master's Guide.* London. Ainsley, 1896.
Beetham, A. & Frampton, R. *Full Ahead. A Guide for Prospective Officers in the Merchant Navy.* London. The Marine Society, c.1982.
No author attributed:
A Challenge from the Sea. London. Seafarers' Education Service, 1935.
Blue Funnel & Glen Lines Bulletin, 1947. Liverpool. Alfred Holt & Co. Ltd.
Cadet's Manual. London. BISN Co Ltd. 1950s-60s (no date given).
List 1 RNR Officers' Directory & Summary of Regulations. Portsmouth. CinCNavHome, 1979.
ss *Opalia* Training Manual (Amended). London. Shell Tankers (UK) Ltd., 1978.

1.3 Articles, letters, features, papers, etc.

Chapman, W.E. "The *Verena* Broadcasting Corporation". *Marconi Mariner*, Nov/Dec., 1958.
Cotter, C.H. "Navigators in the Minories & Its Environs". *Nautical Magazine*, No.214, 1975. (Fragment)
English, D.A.S. *Problems of Manning in Tankers.* London. Tanker Operation Gp., 1960.
Francis, H.H. "Recollections of Captain Bellwinch". *Nautical Magazine*, Vol. 247, No.5. May. 1992.
Garthwaite, W. Letter to the editor. *The Times.* 12th Dec., 1929.
Hoyle, R.F. Captain's Notes. *Mercury Magazine*, 1968. Hamble. ts *Mercury.*
Hutson, R.E. "Blue Funnel Training" (Series). *The Nestorian.* (Fragments. No dates).
Jones, A.H. "The Story of a Scottish Engineer. Part 1. The Apprentice". *Sea Breezes*, Vol.54, No.409, June 1980.
Lindsay, A.C. "What is an Apprentice?" British & Commonwealth Gp. house magazine. April, 1959.
Twemlow. Liverpool Town Books. Vol.2, Appx. VI. (Abstract).
Villiers, A.J. "The Joseph Conrad". *The Trident*, Vol.9, No.97. May, 1947.
No author attributed:
"Alas, Poor Ghosts". ss *Devon* Cadets' Magazine No.3, April, 1935. London. BISN Co. Ltd.
"A Long Voyage". *The Argus.* Melbourne. 1st Jan. 1902.
"Gateway to the Sea". *Sea* 1962 (Fragment). Liverpool. Elder Dempster Lines Ltd.
"The *Armadale*". *The Argus.* Melbourne. 10th Nov., 1899.
Untitled. *The BAC Review*, 1922. (Fragment).
Untitled. *The BAC Review.* Vol.1, No.4. (no date: c.1924).
Untitled. *The BAC Review*, 1952. (Fragment).

1.4 Unpublished mss.

A *Conway* Diary, 1960-61.
Gibb, Ian. Diary, 1955-57.
Mackay, Alexander Stuart. Diary, 1899-1902.
Powles, William. Diary, 1879-80.

2. GENERAL REFERENCE

2.1 Books.

Adams, Bill. *Fenceless Meadows*. New York. Frederick A. Stokes, 1923.
Armstrong, R. *Sea Change*. London. Dent, 1962.
Arnott, R.H. *Captain of the Queen*. London. Quadrant, 1984.
Baines, F. *In Deep*. London. Eyre & Spottiswoode, 1959.
Barnard, H.C. *A History of English Education from 1760*. (4th Edn.) London. ULP, 1969.
Bergen, W.C. *The Practice of Navigation & Nautical Astronomy*. (7th Edn.) London. 1872.
                                                                (Abstract)
Bisset, J. *Commodore*. London. Angus & Robertson, 1961.
Blake, G. *BI Centenary, 1856-1956*. London. Collins, 1956.
Bone, D.W. *Landfall at Sunset*. London. Duckworth, 1956.
Bonwick, G.J. & Steer, E.C. *Ships' Business*. (5th Edn.) London. Maritime Press, 1963.
Cable, B. *A Hundred-Year History of the P&O, 1837-1937*. London. Nicholson & Watson,
                                                                1937.
Callender, G. *The Naval Side of British History. Part 1. 1485-1919*. London. Christophers,
                                                                1952.
Carr,W.G. *Hell's Angels of the Deep*. London. Hutchinson, 1932.
Chandler, D. (Ed.) *Oxford Illustrated History of the British Army*.
Chatterton, E. Keble. *Valiant Sailormen*. London. Hurst & Blackett, 1936.
Clarke, W.V.J. *Cole's Merchant Shipping Acts*. (8th Edn.) Glasgow. Brown, Son & Ferguson
                                                                Ltd., 1960.
Cole, S.D. *Shipmaster's Handbook to the Merchant Shipping Acts*. Glasgow. James Brown &
                                                                Son, 1913.
Course, A.G. *The Deep-Sea Tramp*. London. Hollis & Carter, 1960.
Course, A.G. *The Merchant Navy Today*. OUP, 1956.
Course, A.G. *The Wheel's Kick & the Wind's Song*. (2nd Edn.) London. Percival Marshall,
                                                                1951.
Cressy, E. *An Outline of Industrial History*. London. Macmillan, 1920.
Cunyngham-Brown, S. *Crowded Hour*. London. John Murray, 1975.
Curtis, S.J. & Boultwood, M.E.A. *An Introductory History of English Education Since 1800*.
                                                (4th Edn.) London. U. Tutorial
                                                Press, 1967.
Davies, J.I. *Growing Up Among Sailors*. Gwynedd Archives Service, 1983.
Davis, H.W.C. & Weaver, J.R.H. (Eds.) *Dictionary of National Biography, 1912-21*.
                                                (Supplement) OUP.

Edwards, B. *Donitz & the Wolf-Packs*. London. Arms & Armour Press, 1996.

Falkus, H. *Master of Cape Horn*. London. Gollancz, 1982.

Falkus, M. *The Blue Funnel Legend*. Basingstoke. Macmillan, 1990.

Fayle, C.E. *A Short History of the World's Shipping Industry*. London. Allen & Unwin, 1934.

Fife, C.W. Domville. *Square-Rigger Days*. London. Seeley Service, 1938.

Grant, G.H. *The Half-Deck*. London. Hurst & Blackett, 1935.

Grattidge, H. & Collier, R. *Captain of the Queens*. London. Oldbourne, 1956.

Hampshire, A.C. *The Royal Navy Since 1945*. London. Kimber, 1975.

Hannay, D. *The Sea Trader. His Friends & Enemies*. London. Harper, 1912.

Harvie, D.I. *Limeys*. Stroud, Glos. Sutton, 2002.

Hook, F.A. *Merchant Adventurers, 1914-18*. London. A&C Black, 1920.

Hope, R. *A New History of British Shipping*. London. John Murray, 1990.

Hope, R. *Introduction to the Merchant Navy*. (4th Edn.) London. Seafarers' Education Service, 1973.

Hope, R. *Poor Jack*. London. Chatham, 2001.

Hope, R. *The Merchant Navy*. London. Stanford Maritime, 1980.

Hurd, A. *The Triumph of the Tramp Ship*. London. Cassell, 1922.

Hutson, R. *The Nine Lives of Ding Dong Bell*. Beaumaris, Anglesey. Hutson, 1995.

Hyde, F.E. *Shipping Enterprise & Management, 1830-1939*. Liverpool UP, 1967.

Jones, W.H.S. *All Hands Aloft*. London. Jarrolds, 1969.

Jones, W.H.S. *The Cape Horn Breed*. London. Andrew Melrose, 1956.

Kemp, P. (Ed.) *Oxford Companion to Ships & the Sea*. OUP, 1988.

Knight, F. *The Sea Story*. London. Macmillan, 1958.

Laxton, W.A. & Perry, F.W. *BI. The British India Steam Navigation Co. Ltd*. Kendal, Cumberland. World Ship Society, 1994.

Lloyd, C. *The British Seaman*. London. Collins, 1968.

Lloyd, C. *William Dampier*. London. Faber & Faber, 1966.

Lubbock, B. *The Blackwall Frigates*. Glasgow. Brown, Son & Ferguson, 1962.

Lubbock, B. *The Colonial Clippers*. Glasgow. BS&F, 1975.

Lubbock, B. *The Last of the Windjammers, Vol.1*. Glasgow. BS&F, 1969.

Lubbock, B. *The Log of the* Cutty Sark. Glasgow. BS&F, 1974.

Lubbock, B. *The Nitrate Clippers*. Glasgow. BS&F, 1966.

Masefield, J. *The* Conway. London. Heinemann, 1933.

McCulloch, J.H. *A Million Miles in Sail*. London. Paternoster, c.1935.

McFee, W. *Letters from an Ocean Tramp*. London. Cassell, 1928.

Mitchell, P. *Deep Water*. London. Hurst & Blackett, 1934.

Mostert, N. *Supership*. London. Book Club Associates, 1974.

Oakeshott, W. *Founded Upon the Seas*. CUP, 1942.

Palmer, S. *Politics, Shipping & the Repeal of the Navigation Laws*. Manchester UP, 1990.

Rostron A. *Home from the Sea*. London. Cassell, 1931.

Sainsbury, V.R.D. *The Royal Navy Day by Day*. London. Ian Allen, 1979.

Saunders, H. St G. *Valiant Voyaging*. London. Faber & Faber, 1948.

Shaw, F.H. *Flag of the Seven Seas*. London. Cleaver-Hume, 1953.

Shaw, F.H. *Seas of Memory*. London. Oldbourne, 1958.

Shaw, F.H. *White Sails & Spindrift*. London. Stanley Paul, c.1946.

Sheridan, R.B. *Heavenly Hell.* London. Putnam, 1935.

Showell, J.P.Malmann. *U-boat Command & the Battle of the Atlantic.* London. Conway Maritime, 1989.

Steele, G. *The Story of the* Worcester. London. Harrap, 1962.

Stephens, L.C. *Pangbourne College.* Pangbourne C., 1991.

Stewart, J.C. *The Sea Our Heritage.* Banffshire. Rowan, 1993.

Thornton, R.H. *British Shipping.* CUP, 1939.

Thrower, W.R. *Life at Sea in the Age of Sail.* London. Phillimore, 1972.

Trevelyan, O.M. *Illustrated English Social History, Vols 1-4.* London. Longmans, Green, 1949-52.

Underhill, H.A. *Sail Training & Cadet Ships.* Glasgow. Brown, Son & Ferguson, 1973.

Villiers, A.J. *The Cruise of the* Conrad. (Reprint) London. Hodder & Stoughton, 1952.

Villiers, A.J. *'The Navigators' & the Merchant Navy.* Glasgow. Brown, Son & Ferguson, 1957.

Warner, G.T. *Landmarks in English Industrial History.* Glasgow. Blackie, 1921.

Waters, S.D. *Clipper Ship to Motor Liner.* London. The New Zealand Shipping Co., 1939.

Watson, D.P.H. *The Captains Watson & the Empire Line.* Ridgefield, Conn., USA. Deepwater, 1989.

Watts, A.J. *Axis Submarines.* London. Macdonald & Janes, 1977.

Whall, W.B. *The Romance of Navigation.* London. Sampson Low, Marston, c.1930s.

Woodman, R. *Voyage East.* London. John Murray, 1988.

No author attributed:

Encyclopaedia Britannica (1961) Vol.6., pp.284-5. *Conscription.*

Encyclopaedia Britannica (1961) Vol.10., pp. 698-9. *Great Britain: the Army after WW2.*

Hansard. Vol.475. H.C. DEB 5s. 14 Geo VI. London. HMSO, 1950.

2.2 Booklets.

Andrews, K.R. *The Elizabethan Seaman.* Greenwich. NMM, 1982.

No author attributed:

Blue Funnel & Glen Lines Bulletin, Centenary Edn. Liverpool. Alfred Holt & Co., 1965.

Expedition Notes. Aberdovey. Outward Bound Sea School, c.1945.

How to Become a Deck or Engineer Officer in the NZS. London. New Zealand Shipping Co., 1959.

Pocket Manual for the Sea Cadet Corps. London. The Sea Cadet Corps, 1971.

Regulations re Examination of Masters & Mates. BOT, 1913.

Regulations re Examination of Masters & Mates. BOT, 1918.

Schoolboy's Diary & Note Book. London. Charles Letts, 1930.

Standing Orders for Cadets. Southampton. Dept of Navigation, U. College, 1941.

Training to be an Officer. Apprentice's Handbook. London. MN Officers' Training Board, c.1939.

Training to be an Officer. Apprentice's Handbook. (Revised Edn) London. MN Training Board, 1952.

Training to be an Officer. Apprentice's Handbook. (Revised Edn) London. MNTB, 1960.

BIBLIOGRAPHY & REFERENCES

What Company Shall I Join? (5th Edn) Plas Newydd, Anglesey. *HMS Conway* MN Cadet
School, 1966.

2.3 Author's collection of indentures (originals & copies).
     (E) denotes engineering indenture.

J. Willoughby. To Samuel Cole. Hull, 1845. 6 yrs.
T. Mason. To Thomas Carruthers. Sunderland, 1852. 4 yrs.
W. Powles. To Wm Pellier. London, 1879. 4 yrs.
R. Squires. To S&W Brice (Sailmakers). Rochester, 1903. 7 yrs.
E. Osgood. To Blue Star Line. London, 1919. 3 yrs.
A. Cabot. To Alfred Holt & Co. Liverpool, 1924. 4 yrs.
S. Squirrell. To W.J. Tatem Ltd. Cardiff, 1927. 4 yrs.
E.J. White. To Federal S.N. Co. Ltd. London, 1928. 4 yrs.
P. Brailsford. To British Tanker Co. Ltd. London, 1932. 3½ yrs.
J.D.E. Lewis. To Royal Mail Lines Ltd. London, 1933. 3 yrs.
M. Peyton-Bruhl. To Anne Thomas S.S. Co. Ltd. Cardiff, 1934. 4 yrs.
W.D.S. White. To Alfred Holt & Co. Liverpool, 1934. 3½ yrs.
C. Burgess. To W. Guy Ropner. Hartlepool, 1935. 4 yrs.
W. Close. To Alfred Holt & Co. Liverpool, 1936. 4 yrs.
J. E. Robson. To Royal Mail Lines Ltd. London, 1936. 4 yrs.
J. Montgomery. To Hall Line. London, 1940. 4 yrs.
G. Griffiths. To Anglo-Saxon Petroleum Co. Ltd. 1942. 4 yrs.
A. Lester. To Prince Line Ltd. London, 1942. 4 yrs.
I. Jackson. To Alfred Holt & Co. Birkenhead, 1943. 3 yrs.
G.A.J. Balfour. To Alfred Holt & Co. Liverpool, 1944. 3 yrs.
A. Baines. To Hain S.S. Co. Ltd. London, 1945. 4 yrs.
C.B. Thompson. To Port Line Ltd. London, 1945. 3 yrs.
R.J. Williams. To Anglo-Saxon Petroleum Co. Ltd. London, 1945. 4 yrs.
M. Athoe. To Athel Line Ltd. Falmouth, 1946. 4 yrs.
A.G. Corbet. To Sir Wm Reardon-Smith & Sons. Cardiff, 1947. 4 yrs.
J. Cayzer. To Hain S.S. Co Ltd. London, 1949. 4 yrs.
T. Johnson (E). To New Zealand Shipping Co Ltd. (Agreement). London, 1953. 4½ yrs.
T. Galloway. To Shell Petroleum Co Ltd. London, 1957. 4 yrs.
J. Lightfoot (E). To Shell Petroleum Co Ltd. London, 1959. 4½ yrs.
D. Thomas. To British India S.N. Co Ltd. Salisbury, S. Rhodesia, 1962. 3 yrs.
D.M. Shaw. To BP Tanker Co Ltd. London, 1964. 3½ yrs.
I. Squires (E). To Peninsular & Oriental S.N. Co Ltd. Cardiff, 1967. 4½ yrs.
K. O'Neill. To Stag Line Ltd. (Agreement). N. Shields, 1968. 4 yrs.

Plus an extensive, comprehensive collection of published and unpublished material including
mss, brochures, pamphlets, leaflets, official notices, certificates and documents, private papers
and records relating to the schooling, recruitment, training, work, discipline and welfare of the
apprentice in the British merchant fleet, too numerous to list in detail.

CONTRIBUTORS

THE following people have kindly provided information of all kinds, variously from their own experience and from family and official records. The result is a vast collection of written and printed matter ranging through correspondence with the author, family letters, official documents, diaries and journals, mss, taped interviews, fragments, books, booklets, magazines and photographs. Regrettably, only a very small portion of this material has been directly transferred to the text, for obvious reasons. Nevertheless, all concerned may rest assured that without the material they provided this work would not have been possible, based as it is on extensive background reading. For the time and trouble they have taken in the interests of the work my thanks are due to

Alston, K.	E	A	Dymock, Capt J.	D	A
Athoe, M.*	D	A	English, Capt D.A.S.*	D	A
Bain, J.M.*	D	A	Epps, N.*	D	A
Baines, A.	D	A	Evans, Dr F.*	D	A
Baldock, I.*	D	A	Evans, Mrs F.	D	
Balfour, The Earl of *	D	A	Farragher, R.	D	
Baskerville, Capt G.	D	A	Fellingham, Capt H.*	D	A
Bechley, Capt. M.L.*	D	A	Frost, G.L.*	D	A
Bell, A.M.B	D		Galloway, Capt T.*	D	A
Bernthal, A.	D	A	Gates, Capt P.T.C.*	D	A
Brailsford, Capt P.*	D	A	Gibb, Cdre I.*	D	A
Brown, D.	E	A	Gibson, W.B.*	D	A
Burgess, Capt C.H.*	D	A	Giles, D.*	D	A
Burt, J.*	E	A	Glass, P.F.*	D	A
Cabot, A.N.*	D	A	Goble, J.C.*	D	A
Campbell, C.*	E	A	Grace, S. (MSA)	D/E	
Corbet, Dr A.G.*	D	A	Griffiths, Capt G.*	D	A
Cayzer, J.*	D	A	Gunn, Capt G.	D	A
Clarke, B.C.	D	A	Gunn, J.A.	D	A
Close, W.*	D	A	Hall, G.	E	A
Cooper, I.R.*	D	A	Hamilton, S. (MSA)	D/E	
Corkill, Capt C.	D	A	Harding, R.M.*	D	A
Cowden, J.E.*	D/E		Harrison, G.	D	A
Crone, Mrs G.	E		Hignett, H.M.	D	
Curry, J.W.	D	A	Hill, G.*	D	A
Dawson, Mrs H.G.	D		Hollingworth, J.L.*	D	A
Dunning, A.*	D	A	Hood, Capt. R.	D	A
Dunsford, Capt G.W.*	D	A	Hunter, Capt R.L.*	D	A
Durham, P.	E	A	Hutson, R.*	D	A

Irvin, M.W.	D	A	Robb, Capt. E.W.C.	D	A
Jenkinson, J.*	D	A	Roberts, Capt A.J.*	D	A
Jackson, I.*	D	A	Robson, F.*	E	A
Jewitt, J.R.*	D	A	Robson, J.E.*	D	A
John, Capt M.T.*	D		Shard, Capt A.*	D	A
Johnson, T.A.	E	A	Shaw, Capt D.M.*	D	A
Jones, D.M.*	E	A	Spinks, M.*	E	A
Jones, K.*	E	A	Squires, I.*	E	A
King, Capt G.A.B.*	D	A	Squirrell, S.*	D	A
Kinghorn, Capt A.W.*	D	A	Stammer, M.J.	D	A
Lester, A.S.*	D	A	Stanley, D.G.*	D	A
Lewis, J.D.E.*	D	A	Stephens, L.C.	D	
Lewis, Capt R.B.	D		Taylor, P.*	D	A
Lightfoot, J.H.*	E	A	Terry, F.W.	E	A
Llewelyn, H.S.*	E	A	Thomas, Capt I.E.*	D	A
Lloyd, A.	E		Thomas, Capt W.B.*	D	A
Lochhead, D.*	D	A	Thompson, Capt C.B.*	D	A
Lovegrove, J.W.	D	A	Thompson, Capt D.C.S. (MSA)	D/E	
MacMahon, D.A.	D	A	Towner, Capt R. (MSA)	D/E	
Mawer, J.	E	A	Traill, R.C.	D	A
Moffat, Capt J.C.*	D	A	Walker, D.H.	D	A
Morgan-Kirby, Mrs C.*	D		Ward, Capt A.L.	D	A
Mortimer, Capt W.W.*	D	A	Watson, D.P.H.	D	
Newton, C.	D/E		Webster, Capt R.S.*	D	A
Niblock, A.*	D	A	White, A.L.	D	
Noden, Capt J.D.*	D	A	White, E.J.*	D	A
O'Neill, K.	D	A	White, R.H.	D	A
Osgood, Capt A.H.*	D	A	White, Capt W.D.S. RN *	D	A
Owen, Capt J. Tudor	D	A	Williams, D.G.A.	D	A
Oxley, C.	D	A	Williams, Capt R.J.*	D	A
Parker, Capt J.*	D		Williams, Mrs R.J.	D	
Pattinson, Mrs L.	D		Willis, C.J.*	D	A
Pereira, Capt. D. (MCA)	D		Wills, Miss R. MVO	D	
Peyton-Bruhl, Capt M.J.*	D	A	Wright, T.	D	A
Rawlins, Capt A.A.	D	A	Wyatt, Mrs S.	D	

* Material quoted in text.
A apprenticeship served and material pertaining thereto contributed.
D information re deck department.
E information re engineering department.
(MCA) Staff, Maritime & CG Agency

(MSA) Staff, Marine Safety Agency.

NOTE.
Rank/title is quoted where known, but only MN rank where also RNR/RNVR or other.
I apologise to any whom I've overlooked or failed to cite in this respect.

***

INDEX